A GUIDE TO THE STUDY AND ENJOYMENT OF ANNUAL EDITIONS: PSYCHOLOGY 83/84

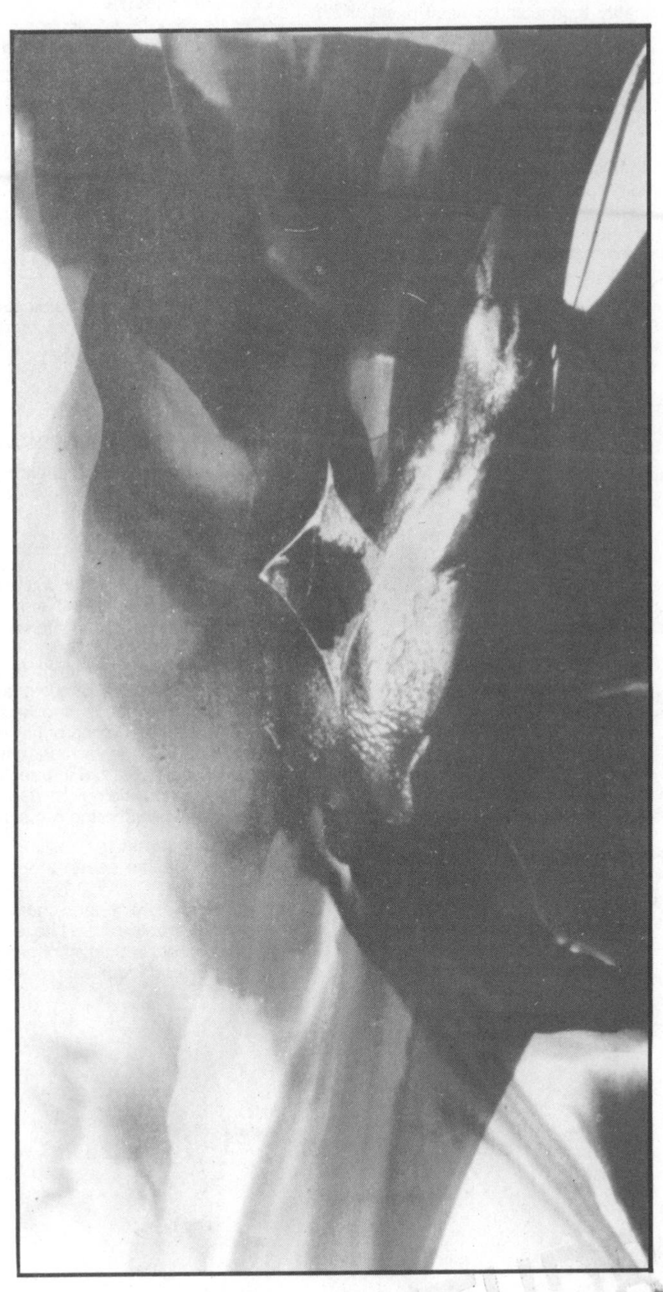

The Dushkin Publishing Group, Inc.
Sluice Dock, Guilford, Connecticut 06437
Toll Free 800-243-6532
In Connecticut, call collect:
453-4351

52. FINDING THE HIDDEN FREUD AE p. 254

Sigmund Freud is one of the most influential thinkers of the twentieth century. He formulated a sweeping theory of personality, which he viewed as the product of interactions among three sets of forces—the id (basic and primitive drives and desires), the ego (which has come to be called the self), and the superego (social strictures that are learned and come to serve as a conscience). Freud argued that much of this interaction takes place outside of awareness, in the unconscious that is dominated by suppressed id and unresolved conflicts. New studies of Freud's life suggest that his theory was a very personal one, derived in large part from insights into his own frailties. Was Freud envious, malicious, a pilferer of colleagues' ideas, a seducing playboy? This article looks at studies of Freud, and also describes the nature of the Freudian influence on current personality theory and clinical psychology.

Learning Objectives

After reading the article, you should be able to:

1. Summarize current views on what Freud was like and how his personal characteristics might or might not have influenced his theory.
2. Summarize differences between the way that psychoanalysis is carried out now and the way it was carried out by Freud and his students.
3. List at least three possible changes that might occur in the near future that would move therapy even further away from the techniques of classical psychoanalysis.

Essay Questions

1. Science is often described as an objective, empirical search for truth. How is *your* view of science changed (if at all) by the news that Freud's personal life may have played a large part in his scientific theorizing?
2. What aspects of Freud's theory and his therapeutic technique are still followed? What aspects are changing and why?

53. THE HEALING BRAIN AE p. 260

The brain may exhibit far greater control over our physical well-being than previously thought possible. The effects of cancer, diabetes, and other diseases may be made better or worse by our psychological reaction to them. Scientists in a variety of fields are beginning to study why.

Learning Objectives

After reading the article, you should be able to:

1. Describe the Precursors Study and what it has found.
2. Define endorphins and enkephalins.
3. Define hypothalamus, pituitary hormones, and T lymphocyte.
4. Define biofeedback.
5. Define vasopressin.

Essay Questions

1. Describe the evidence suggesting that cancer can be controlled through psychological means.
2. Describe the evidence suggesting that diseases can be made worse by a poor psychological attitude.

54. ROOTS OF MADNESS AE p. 263

Despite the promise of recent developments in biochemical treatment of mental illness, schizophrenia and other mental disturbances are still *psychological* problems—they drastically change the thoughts, emotions, motivations, and social competencies of the people they afflict. What is reality like for a schizophrenic? How do schizophrenics perceive the world, act toward other people, and react to the actions of others? How can you *get along* with a schizophrenic? Dr. Sam Keith of the National Institute of Mental Health says "You can relate to schizophrenics if you agree to meet them wherever they happen to be. They are very interesting people if you are willing to change your idea of what a relationship is."

Learning Objectives

After reading the article, you should be able to:

1. Describe the psychological characteristics of schizophrenia.
2. Describe what a conversation with a schizophrenic might be like.
3. List at least three possible causes of schizophrenia.
4. List at least three possible treatments of schizophrenia.

Essay Questions

1. What makes a schizophrenic different from other people? In your opinion, which of these characteristics is most "abnormal" and why?
2. How do modernized technological societies and more primitive agricultural societies differ in their treatment of schizophrenics? Which would be a better society for a schizophrenic to live in and why?
3. Should drugs and chemicals be given to schizophrenics as a form of treatment? Why or why not?

55. FIGHT FAT WITH BEHAVIOR CONTROL AE p. 268

Behavior modification techniques are applied to obesity. The problem with fad diets is that they focus on food rather than eating. The Mahoney's describe seven steps which, if followed, may lead to sustained weight loss.

Learning Objectives

After reading the article, you should be able to:

1. Describe perceptual, learning, and cognitive theories of obesity and the therapeutic interventions that have been developed from these theories.
2. Explain what is meant by behavior modification and indicate advantages and disadvantages of this approach to therapy.
3. Describe what is known about biorhythms and explain their influence on human behavior.
4. Describe Witkin's research on field dependence and link it to personality factors in obesity.
5. Discuss physiological, neurohumeral, and neurological mechanisms involved in the regulation of eating behavior.

Essay Questions

1. Describe the seven steps of the *Science* approach to weight control.
2. Describe the general characteristics of dieters and indicate some of the problems they have managing weight loss.
3. Describe a weight management program that would compete with the *Science* approach described in the article.

47. STRESS CAN BE GOOD FOR YOU — AE p. 223

Prevailing wisdom holds that stress hurts mental health, causes psychosomatic disease and shortens the lifespan. New research suggests that this may be true, but only when stress is accompanied by feelings that one cannot control one's situation, that decisions are largely predetermined or useless, or that one is an easily-replaceable pawn in the operation of some stress-producing system. When a person has the opposite view—that he or she exercises control, that decisions are influential, that actions lead to success—stress can be channeled in healthy and creative ways. As an example of the effects of this good stress, or "eustress," Metropolitan Life Insurance Company recently examined men who occupy one of the top three executive positions in the Fortune 500 list of top corporations, and found that the mortality rate of these men was 37% lower than that of other white males of similar age.

Learning Objectives

After reading the article, you should be able to:

1. Define and describe stress, bad or chronic stress, and good or eustress.
2. Describe the conditions under which stress will be bad for you and what is likely to happen physically and psychologically as well as the conditions under which stress can be good for you.
3. List at least three symptoms of stress and at least three strategies for turning bad stress into good stress.

Essay Questions

1. Describe the organization of an ideal society in which everyone would experience a maximum of eustress and a minimum of distress. How would such a society differ from your own?
2. Explain the stress cycle and how it is changed by the steps for converting bad stress into good stress.
3. Identify three situations in your own life experience that you find stressful; determine whether each is eustress or distress; and describe what you could do to alleviate each distress situation.

48. THE FOUNDATIONS OF THE PERSON-CENTERED APPROACH — AE p. 227

The tendency to develop into an independent, constructive, and complete person is but one aspect of a formative process that operates throughout the universe. The founder of the humanistic, person-centered approach to personality discusses his theory and its implications.

Learning Objectives

After reading the article, you should be able to:

1. Discuss the influence of humanistic psychology on the development of self-concept.
2. Describe role theory and indicate how roles may vary depending on social-cultural context.
3. Contrast Freudian, Rogerian, and Jungian theories of personality and approaches to therapy.
4. Explain how meditation and relaxation are used in counseling and psychotherapy.
5. Describe how psychology has treated the topic of consciousness throughout the 20th century and summarize current research on altered states of consciousness.

Essay Questions

1. Compare Rogers' person-centered theory with Skinner's theory as expounded in "Beyond Freedom and Dignity."
2. Critically evaluate the assumptions underlying Rogers' person-centered approach.
3. Describe what is meant by self-actualization. Give three examples of people who may have achieved this state.

49. THE FRIENDSHIP BOND — AE p. 234

Who is your best friend? How long has it been since you were together? Readers of *Psychology Today* indicate that close friendships endure geographic distance and time. Three important ingredients of friendship are: keeping confidences, being loyal, and showing affection.

Learning Objectives

After reading the article, you should be able to:

1. Describe the development of peer relations and friendships drawing attention to Selman's stage theory of friendship development.
2. Discuss survey research pointing out methodological problems associated with sampling, scale construction, and social desirability influences on responses.
3. Describe research on attitude formation and give examples of the relationship between attitudes and behavior.
4. Describe sex differences in friendship patterns during childhood and adolescence.
5. Explain attribution theory and describe how attractiveness attributions influence friendship choices and interpersonal relations.

Essay Questions

1. Summarize factors that are important for maintaining friendships and those that are relatively unimportant.
2. Discuss problems associated with survey research conducted by magazines among the readership of the magazine.
3. Describe factors that regulate friendships between opposite sex friends and same sex friends.

50. ALONE — AE p. 242

Alexis de Tocqueville first described the great premium that Americans place on independence and individualism. Many of our most heroic images portray the glory of solitude and self-sufficiency: Thoreau of Walden Pond, the "self-made man," the "lonesome cowboy." However, lack of companionship, social support, and interpersonal intimacy can take its toll—more and more Americans complain of a host of life dissatisfactions that all relate to loneliness. According to sociologist Robert Bellah, people no longer have communities of other people to which they are tied, and psychologist Philip Zimbardo says, "We must do something about any circumstances in which a person can say 'No one knows who I am or cares to know.' Anyone in such a predicament can turn into a vandal, an assassin, or a terrorist."

Learning Objectives

After reading the article, you should be able to:

1. List the positive and negative effects of loneliness.
2. Describe at least three ways in which modern American society causes or fosters loneliness.
3. Describe at least three things that people are currently doing to combat and decrease loneliness in America. Be concrete and specific.

Essay Questions

1. Explain the good and bad effects that emulating heroic images such as Thoreau at Walden Pond or the lonesome cowboy can have on a person.
2. Describe at least one major source of loneliness in each of the following groups and how members of that group have tried to cope with and overcome loneliness: (a) large business corporations, (b) the elderly, (c) homosexuals, (d) single adults.
3. Compare and contrast the effects of lack of companionship and lack of community as causes of loneliness.

51. SELF-FULFILLING STEREOTYPES — AE p. 248

Stereotypes are general ideas or beliefs about the characteristics of a group of people—the English are reserved, the Irish are heavy drinkers, athletes are big, dumb, and conceited. The author of this article offers an analysis that may at first sound strange: If you think that Their Kind (whatever group that may be) is lazy (or pushy, shrewd, dumb, weepy), then They will probably prove you right. That is because your stereotypes influence the way you act toward members of the group, which in turn influences the way they act toward you. Styles of interaction become established that tend to emphasize and bring out the very characteristics that you *expected* to be there, regardless of how often those characteristics are present in other circumstances and in other interactions. This is the rather sobering power of the *self-fulfilling* stereotype.

Learning Objectives

After reading the article, you should be able to:

1. Define "stereotype."
2. Describe the process by which stereotypes fulfill themselves.
3. Describe the empirical evidence for the existence of this process.
4. List at least two examples of the operation of self-fulfilling stereotypes from your own experience.

Essay Questions

1. To some extent, we *are* what we do. If someone behaves toward you in a way that seems to be attractive, lazy, or ambitious, how far can you legitimately go in concluding that the person *is* attractive, lazy, or ambitious? Defend your position.
2. Compare and contrast the arguments and theories in this article to those in "The Many Me's of the Self-Monitor."
3. What can (a) the person holding a stereotype, and (b) the person who belongs to a stereotyped group do to break the vicious circle of self-fulfillment that seems to occur in social interactions?

3. Why do you think that people count negative behaviors more heavily than positive behaviors in judging another person's intelligence? Defend your answer as best you can.

41. THE REMEDIAL THINKER — AE p. 195

In contrast with the view that intelligence is unchangeable, many researchers believe that appropriate training can improve the intellectual performance of people with subnormal IQs. This approach requires testing learning capacity, rather than current functioning, and applying appropriate remedies for cognitive deficiencies. This article describes a program of this type, some of the thinking problems that it has uncovered, and the results of research designed to assess its success in teaching children to overcome these problems.

Learning Objectives

After reading the article, you should be able to:

1. Describe the differences between Feuerstein's view of intelligence and the view of intelligence on which traditional IQ tests are based.
2. List the important features of Feuerstein's method of assessing learning potential.
3. Describe some common thinking problems of retarded performers, and Feuerstein's explanation for the problems.
4. Describe how the Intellectual Enrichment program remedies certain thinking problems.
5. Describe the results of research assessing the success of the Intellectual Enrichment program.

Essay Questions

1. Describe the difference between intelligence as measured by an IQ test, and intelligence as measured by the Learning Potential Assessment Device.
2. What is the difference between direct and mediated experience? Why aren't they equally valuable?
3. Discuss alternative explanations of the finding that even good students improved after training in the Instrumental Enrichment program.

42. MALES AND FEMALES AND WHAT YOU MAY NOT KNOW ABOUT THEM — AE p. 201

Opportunity, behavior, and achievement differences between males and females exist in many domains of life activity: education, child rearing, sports, the military, the market place, the workplace. This situation triggers some of the hottest social controversies of our day, centering around the causes of the differences. Are they biological (due to their nature), or experiential (due to nurture, learning and social organization)? The answer is more complex than that. In many areas, there appears to be some basic biological tendencies toward differences that can be exaggerated, diminished, or modified by experience. In other areas, however, differences appear to be minimal or nonexistent, despite persistent myths to the contrary.

Learning Objectives

After reading the article, you should be able to:

1. Summarize current findings on sex differences in physique, rate of maturation, physical health and life expectancy, mental health, social behavior, intellectual achievement, and brain processes.
2. Identify which differences seem to be largely biological, which seem to be largely experiential, and which seem to depend on both factors.
3. Compare and contrast the picture of sex differences painted in this article with the picture painted in "Girls vs. Boys—How Different Are They?"

Essay Questions

1. In what domains or areas do sex differences appear to be the greatest, and in what domains do they appear to be smallest? What implications does this pattern of differences and similarities carry for social policy concerning employment and promotion?
2. A well-known psychologist once said that "biology is destiny." What do you think he meant and do you think he was right? Defend your answer.

43. GIRLS VS. BOYS—HOW DIFFERENT ARE THEY? — AE p. 205

It is fashionable nowadays to erase the differences between the sexes, but, explains the author, differences do exist. She lists some of them.

Learning Objectives

After reading the article, you should be able to:

1. Describe Martin's findings on sex differences between boys and girls.
2. Explain why social conditioning does not determine the femininity and masculinity of girls and boys.
3. Explain the biological differences between the sexes.
4. Discuss the physiological differences between the sexes.
5. Explain left/right brain specialization and its relation to both verbal and spatial performance in boys and girls.

Essay Questions

1. How is the sex of a child determined?
2. What are some major physiological differences between boys and girls?
3. What is left/right brain specialization? Does it develop differently in boys than in girls? Explain.

44. PRISONERS OF MANLINESS — AE p. 208

Many of the old assumptions about what it means to be masculine or feminine don't hold up when one studies the evidence on which they are based. A new approach to understanding masculinity and femininity emphasizes avoiding the strain inherent in traditional sex roles.

Learning Objectives

After reading the article, you should be able to:

1. Define sex-role identity.
2. Describe the historical foundations of male-identity theory.
3. Define misogyny, homophobia, and hypermasculinity.
4. Describe the black emasculation hypothesis.

Essay Questions

1. Review the evidence for and against the assertion, "Boys need a father figure when they are growing up in order to become secure men."
2. Review the evidence for and against the assertion, "Male homosexuality reflects a man's confusion over his masculine role."

45. THE MANY ME'S OF THE SELF-MONITOR — AE p. 216

Is there a "true self" that underlies the various roles we play, or are we all "impression managers" who change personalities like chameleons change color?

Learning Objectives

After reading the article, you should be able to:

1. Describe the development of self-concept and indicate why some psychologists believe self-concept emerges from interpersonal relationships.
2. Describe research on body language and indicate how it fits into the human communication system.
3. Describe problems with measurement scales, especially with reference to reliability and validity.
4. Describe the development of prejudice and indicate how it may affect self-concept development.
5. Discuss how "impression management" could be used to explain the behavior of people who belong to cults.

Essay Questions

1. Discuss how impression management can be applied to explain the behavior of people who join cults.
2. Compare behavioral differences between high and low self-monitors.
3. Describe how nonverbal behaviors can reveal meaningful information about attitudes and feelings.

46. PSYCHO-IMMUNITY — AE p. 221

Disease, stress, and attitude interact in complex ways. This paper examines the relationship between bodily health and emotion, and suggests that our state of mind may influence how long we live.

Learning Objectives

After reading the article, you should be able to:

1. Define fight-or-flight response and withdrawal-conservation response.
2. How do these two responses contribute to sudden death, according to this article?
3. Describe the experiments done on wild rats that are cited as evidence for psycho-immunity.
4. Define distress and eustress.
5. Describe the human evidence that suggests a link between attitude and health.

Essay Questions

1. What emotional or attitudinal factors seem to make us more susceptible to sudden death? What can we do about them?
2. Almost everyone undergoes stressful changes everyday, yet many of us don't exhibit the psychological ailments described in the article. Evaluate the argument that emotional health influences physical health in light of this observation.

3. Describe how child-rearing styles may affect emotional development, and indicate how child characteristics may affect child-rearing styles.

35. YOUR CHILD'S SELF-ESTEEM — AE p. 167

Experiences that ultimately lead to competence in solving life's problems begin to have their effects during the first two or three years of life. Several factors reliably increase the probability that a child will grow up to be self-confident, comfortable, and able to make the most of his or her intellectual and social skills. Those factors include secure attachment, environmental stimulation, social interaction, and environmental responsivity. The result is a feeling of control that has many positive consequences.

Learning Objectives
After reading the article, you should be able to:
1. Define and give examples of "competence."
2. Define, give examples of, and describe the effects of secure attachment, environmental stimulation, social interaction, and environmental responsivity.
3. Describe an "ideal environment" for the early development of competence and control.

Essay Questions
1. What is "competence" and what evidence do we have that early life experience affects it?
2. Argue either for or against the proposition that it is best to be an only child if you grow up to be competent. Give the best evidence that you can for your position.

36. LEARNING RIGHT FROM WRONG — AE p. 171

Doing the right thing and knowing what the right thing is—two critical human abilities that change markedly with development. Many people believe that these changes result simply from teaching. Research on cognitive development, however, shows that children progress through distinct stages in moral behavior and knowledge. These stages differ in the kinds of reasons for right and wrong that children are capable of understanding. Research on moral development has produced great changes in moral education, and the changes have produced great controversy among parents and educators.

Learning Objectives
After reading the article, you should be able to:
1. Define cognitive moral development.
2. Define values clarification.
3. Describe educational practices that are based on theories of cognitive moral development.
4. List the advantages and the disadvantages that parents and educators see in these educational practices.

Essay Questions
1. How well does the old adage "Spare the rod and spoil the child" fit the views of the cognitive moral developmentalists?
2. Describe at least two different ways in which a curriculum based on cognitive moral development could accommodate the wishes and demands of parents concerning their children's moral behavior.

37. COPING WITH THE SEASONS OF LIFE — AE p. 174

Very often psychologists construct views of human existence that may not reflect everyday behavior. In this article the results of interviews with six hundred children and adults are reported. The interviews were designed to generate a subjective description of the human life cycle. Two major conclusions are suggested: First, there is little evidence to support the notion that life is divided into a sequence of age-related crises. Second, age does not seem to be particularly important as a determinant of self-perceptions or of perceptions of life events.

Learning Objectives
After reading the article, you should be able to:
1. State the main feature of each age period as described by participants in the survey.
2. Describe some of the positive and negative features of young adults.
3. State evidence suggesting that most people do not view middle age as a life crisis.
4. Describe several prominant concerns among the aged.

Essay Questions
1. To what extent can public opinion surveys be trusted to provide accurate information about attitudes, opinions, and beliefs? Are such surveys to be trusted as more accurate than are theories constructed by psychologists based on research and/or clinical experience?
2. Do the answers described in the survey match your perception of your own life situation? Might one expect to find different answers to this survey in different parts of the country? In different cultures?

38. IN SEARCH OF YOUTH — AE p. 176

New research shows that several factors of a biological and metabolic nature contribute to aging. Some of these factors can be controlled, and doing so promises to extend the lifespan and increase the health, activity, and satisfaction of older people by huge amounts. A complex process, the rate of aging seems to be regulated by hormonal factors under brain control, by genetic factors under the control of genes in each individual cell, and by metabolic changes that depend on nutrition and body biochemistry.

Learning Objectives
After reading the article, you should be able to:
1. List at least six factors that affect the rate of aging.
2. Classify each factor as hormonal, genetic, nutritional, or experiential.
3. For each factor, describe a way of reducing its effect on aging.

Essay Questions
1. Explain what a biological clock is and describe the evidence for a hormonal aging clock controlled by the brain and a genetic aging clock controlled by each individual cell.
2. What benefits and costs do you think would follow from gaining the ability to stop the aging process?
3. If your goal is to extend the useful lifespan, which of the mechanisms of aging would it be most important to control? Which would be easiest to control? Defend your answers as best you can.

39. ATTITUDES, INTERESTS, AND IQ — AE p. 182

Two educational psychologists review the evidence for the environmental and hereditary determination of intelligence and conclude that both are important. Their finding was confirmed in the authors' study of intelligence among adopted children. There is evidence that the verbal components of intelligence are the most heavily determined by environmental factors and additional research suggests that social attitudes and vocational interests are influenced by genetic factors. The article describes the political and social implications of recent controversies on the relative impact of heredity and environment on human behavior.

Learning Objectives
After reading the article, you should be able to:
1. Describe the extent to which the different components of intelligence are influenced by heredity and environment.
2. Explain how authoritarian attitudes and vocational interests are partly determined by genetics.
3. Describe the relationship between verbal intelligence and authoritarianism.
4. Describe the effects of genetic variability within reasonably good environments.
5. Describe the relationship between hereditarianism versus environmentalism and conservative versus liberal social policies.

Essay Questions
1. Why has environmentalism dominated the Western philosophy of child-rearing and social policy for many years?
2. On the basis of your reading, what are the specific individual differences most and least likely to be affected by environmental variables?

40. WHO'S INTELLIGENT? — AE p. 189

According to the author, "One could argue that the bulk of intelligence testing is not the kind that takes place in psychologists' consulting rooms, but the kind that goes on in face-to-face encounters between people: in job and admission interviews, in classrooms, in meetings, at cocktail parties, during coffee breaks, and in initial encounters with strangers." He then summarizes the standards that people apply in those face-to-face "intelligence tests" and compares the everyday-life conception of intelligence to the theories proposed by psychologists.

Learning Objectives
After reading the article, you should be able to:
1. List the major components of the layperson's concept of intelligence, list the major components of the psychological expert's concept of intelligence, and identify the major differences between the lay view and the expert view.
2. Discuss the relationship between laypeople's *theories* of intelligence and their *judgments* about whether an individual is smart or dumb.
3. Discuss the advantages and disadvantages of using behavioral checklists rather than IQ tests to measure intelligence.

Essay Questions
1. What is intelligence? Defend your answer, drawing on the views described in "Who's Intelligent" and comparing those views to your own.
2. Discuss the implications of replacing IQ tests with behavioral checklists. How would replacement by direct behavioral observation compare and contrast with replacement by checklists?

Learning Objectives

After reading the article, you should be able to:

1. Describe why it is so difficult to compare the intellectual capacity of the elderly with that of younger people.
2. Describe the "Mini-Mental State" test.
3. Describe the results of Sprott's research on environmental influences on mouse intelligence.
4. Define senile dementia.
5. Define mnemonics.

Essay Questions

1. Describe the differences between functional loss and mental loss. How can a researcher discriminate between the two?
2. Devise a test for comparing the mental abilities of old and young age groups.

30. THE MIND OF THE PUZZLER — AE p. 141

Do you like to solve puzzles? Are you good at it? New studies linking problem-solving ability with IQ suggest that problem-solving ability requiring inductive reasoning correlates highly with scores on IQ tests. Problems containing both relevant and irrelevant information were related to IQ, but "trick" problems were poor indicators of IQ. Three basic cognitive skills are described and linked to the role of insight in problem-solving ability. In addition, four complementary abilities influencing problem-solving are noted.

Learning Objectives

After reading the article, you should be able to:

1. Cite three types of intellectual processes that seem to be required in solving insight problems.
2. Indicate how inductive reasoning and deductive reasoning are related to IQ.
3. Cite four factors important to problem-solving other than those involving insight.
4. State Raaheim's view of the relationship between problem-solving and intelligence.

Essay Questions

1. The ability to solve problems ranks high among laymen's definitions of intelligence. Yet problem-solving ability is not exactly the same as intelligence measured by IQ tests. Which do you believe is the better measure of intelligence?
2. Problems such as those described in the article seem to require some degree of verbal sophistication. To what extent are the results described in the article constrained by the fact that the average IQ in the sample was 12 points above the national average?

31. LEARNING THE MOTHER TONGUE — AE p. 145

While traditional theories of language acquisition have focused on specific learning processes or universal grammars, the study of basic mother-infant interaction provides a functional typology of speech development. The Watts professor of psychology at Oxford University proposes that the early stages of language development involve indicating, requesting, and agency. Later the child passes through stages in which language acquisition is focused on the goals of sharing, taking turns, and interpersonal negotiation. Social affiliation and problem solving are facilitated by continued language development in the older child. The author proposes that language is acquired through a transaction between an active language learner and an equally active language teacher.

Learning Objectives

After reading the article, you should be able to:

1. Compare the learning theory and Chomskyan theory of language acquisition.
2. Describe Bruner's functional theory of language acquisition.
3. Describe the different stages of Bruner's functional theory of language acquisition.
4. Describe the role of the primary care-giver in the child's language acquisition.
5. Explain how language acquisition facilitates the processes of social affiliation and problem solving.

Essay Questions

1. Describe the inadequacies of learning theory and Chomskyan theory for understanding language acquisition.
2. How does Bruner's theory of language acquisition explain the difficulties of learning a second language?

32. THE LOSS OF LANGUAGE — AE p. 151

People who can speak and listen find it hard to imagine what tremendous problems would be created by losing those abilities. Gardner describes the causes, characteristics, and consequences of various language disorders associated with brain injury.

Learning Objectives

After reading the article, you should be able to:

1. Describe the neurological mechanisms involved with speech production and comprehension.
2. Describe the literature on hemispheric specialization including Sperry's work with epileptics.
3. Explain the difference between Piaget and Vygotsky with respect to the relationship between thought and language.
4. Describe the development of language including aspects of phonology, semantics, syntax, and pragmatics.
5. Review therapeutic techniques used in the treatment of aphasia, stuttering, and other types of speech pathology.

Essay Questions

1. Describe the differences between Broca's and Wernicke's aphasia.
2. Describe Melodic Intonation Therapy and indicate why it is useful in treating Broca's aphasia.
3. Describe five types of aphasia and indicate how they are related to localization of brain function.

33. NEWBORN KNOWLEDGE — AE p. 160

Infants enter the world as "sensible" people—that is, newborns are aware of their surroundings, attend to them and to the people in them, and begin almost immediately to interact with the world, to learn about it, and to form preferences for particular people and things. An especially lively and controversial topic in the study of newborn sensibility involves the importance for attachment of very early contact between infant and mother.

Learning Objectives

After reading the article, you should be able to:

1. Describe the perceptual and social abilities of the newborn.
2. Describe the different styles of interaction that infants engage in with parents, strangers, and toys, or other physical objects.
3. Discuss the pros and cons of mother-infant interaction in the first few hours after birth.

Essay Questions

1. Compare the picture of the newborn that is painted in "Newborn Knowledge" to the picture that you had before reading the article. What similarities and differences can you identify? Which ones surprise you and why?
2. Given the evidence on newborn sensibility and social responsiveness provided in the article, describe the ideal conditions under which a baby should be born and live the first few weeks of life. Why do you choose the conditions that you do?

solutions of personal problems as well as to creativity and self-redefinition.

1. Describe the various stages of sleep and indicate how studies

1. Discuss the potential costs and benefits involved in recombinant

34. CHILDHOOD — AE p. 163

Just about every psychologically important human characteristic changes across the life span. Developmental psychologists study these changing characteristics, including physical and motor skills, language, thought, emotion, and social competence. In an *Annual Editions* exclusive, Best and Harris provide an overview of what is known about these areas of development.

Learning Objectives

After reading the article, you should be able to:

1. Describe research on language development with special emphasis on pragmatics.
2. Describe Piagetian theory of cognitive development and contrast it with the IQ approach to the study of intelligence.
3. Summarize what is known about the development of play and peer relations.
4. Describe Erik Erikson's theory of psychosocial development and contrast it with Freud's theory of psychosexual development.
5. Describe research on styles of parenting using Baumrind's research as the focal point.

Essay Questions

1. Describe the development of perceptual and attentional skills from infancy through childhood.
2. Contrast social and emotional behavior of school-age children with that of toddlers.

Learning Objectives
After reading the article, you should be able to:
1. Review Garcia's research on conditioned taste aversions.
2. Describe the relationship between classical and operant conditioning.
3. Explain the various reinforcement schedules used in operant conditioning.
4. Describe the historical origins of conditioning procedures.
5. Discuss problems associated with generalizing from one animal species to another.

Essay Questions
1. Describe four problems that Gustavson and Garcia had to solve before they were able to apply their research techniques to condition coyotes to avoid sheep.
2. Describe several ways in which a program of conditioning can backfire.
3. Describe various techniques used to keep coyotes away from sheep and indicate why Gustavson and Garcia's technique seems to work.

25. CAUGHT BY CHOICE — AE p. 119

The freedom to choose entitles us to both the successes and the failures that choices entail. We have to learn to live with the paths not taken as well as those that are. This very freedom to choose often leads to entrapment, simply because individuals do not have to choose alternatives to the very comfortable status quo they are accustomed to.

Learning Objectives
After reading the article, you should be able to:
1. State the implications of freedom of choice.
2. Define the concept of entrapment as it applies to freedom of choice.
3. Understand the positive aspects of choice as a way out of entrapment.

Essay Questions
1. How does choice or the freedom to choose complicate our lives? How can one control the entrapment one experiences as an outcome of choice?
2. How would you react to the experiments outlined by the author of this article?

26. CONVERSION, BRAINWASHING AND DEPROGRAMMING — AE p. 123

Dr. Richardson takes apart our traditional notions about religious conversion and replaces them with a modern sociobiological view that emphasizes individual volition and internal, as opposed to external, control. According to Dr. Richardson, the typical "cult" (or "new religion") convert is best understood as a basically rational person striving to achieve a more fulfilling personal life-style, rather than as a hapless, passive victim of powerful yet mysterious brainwashing techniques utilized by religious groups whose primary purpose is to usurp the money and freedom of its members. While participation in the new religious groups does tend to require some attitudinal and behavioral conformity, efforts to deprogram group members may be more coercive than the activities of the groups themselves.

Learning Objectives
After reading the article, you should be able to:
1. Compare and contrast the old "invasion of the body snatchers" theory of religious conversion with the author's new theory.
2. Describe the typical or predominant pattern of individuals' involvement with new religious groups, including people's motives for becoming involved, the duration of their involvement, and the circumstances under which their involvement ends.
3. Explain why the subject sampling technique used in typical psychological research has produced results that conflict with those of the author.
4. Describe the origin of the term "brainwashing" and explain why it has become such a buzzword.
5. Relate the author's definition of brainwashing to the activities of the new religious groups and to the process of deprogramming.

Essay Questions
1. (a) Describe the theoretical approach to religious conversion that Richardson describes as the "invasion of the body snatchers" model. (b) Review the research findings described by Richardson that fail to support this view.
2. (a) Describe the origin of the term "brainwashing" and explain why it is so loaded with implications when used to describe the activities of a new religious group. (b) Given the research findings described by Richardson, do the actual facts of people's involvement with new religious groups support the "brainwashing" point of view? If so, why? If not, why?
3. Describe some of the techniques used in deprogramming. Distinguish between what Richardson calls coercive and non-coercive techniques. Which of these techniques depends more on the assumption that people are passive beings whose attitudes are best changed by external forces?

27. MY MEMORY/MYSELF — AE p. 130

The workings of memory fascinate and perplex both people who try to remember things and psychologists who study how they do it. This article outlines several of the most important general factors that determine the success—and the failure—of human memory. Adults have trouble remembering the events of childhood because the minds of adults are quite different from the minds of children. What one does remember depends on emotional arousal, on attention, and on personal meaning. Many memories, even those produced under hypnosis, are *constructions* rather than simple rote reproductions. All of these factors fit together to make memory a complex act of thinking that provides a window into personality as well as a reservoir of past experiences.

Learning Objectives
After reading the article, you should be able to:
1. Describe Freud's theory of memory.
2. Describe the roles of attention, emotion, and meaning in remembering.
3. Explain what it means to say that memories are benevolent.
4. Discuss the role of "targeting" in memory.

Essay Questions
1. Based on the factors discussed in this article, describe an event that would be very easy to remember and an event that would be very hard to remember.
2. What is an autobiographical memory and what factors influence it?
3. How are memories retrieved?

28. MOOD AND MEMORY — AE p. 133

How you feel may determine what you remember. Bower describes his research on state-dependent memory, which refers to problems remembering information learned in one psychological state when in a different psychological state. In other words, if you learn something when you feel good you may have difficulty remembering that information when you feel lousy. Bower's work demonstrates an emotional component to perception, learning, memory, judgment, thought and imagination. Homo sapiens are emotional beings indeed.

Learning Objectives
After reading the article, you should be able to:
1. Define state-dependent memory.
2. State the relationship between happy and sad moods and recall.
3. State at least two theoretical explanations for state-dependent memory.
4. State at least two explanations for the mood-congruity effect.

Essay Questions
1. If emotional state is such a powerful determinant of memory, should our educational system be revised to better match mood and memory?
2. Why, do you suppose, has it taken so long for psychologists to demonstrate a relationship between mood and memory? Have you noticed that your test performance differs depending upon your mood?

29. OUR INSATIABLE BRAIN — AE p. 138

Recent research suggests that our ability to learn does not necessarily diminish with age. Previous beliefs to the contrary were due to social stereotypes and changing definitions of intelligence. Given the proper intellectual and social stimulation, we can continue to learn until we die.

Learning Objectives

After reading the article, you should be able to:

1. Describe the basic workings of d'Acquili's model.
2. Characterize the parts of the brain that play a role in d'Acquili's model, including the left hemisphere, the right hemisphere, the limbic system, and the corpus callosum.
3. Understand how d'Acquili tries to distinguish between the phenomena he studies (*Weltschmerz* and transcendent elation) and "ordinary" mental irregularities (depression and schizophrenia).
4. Review criticisms of d'Acquili's theory.

Essay Questions

1. According to d'Acquili, what happens in the brain when we experience profound transcendent feelings of elation or despair? How is this chain of events different from ordinary thinking?
2. (a) How does d'Acquili distinguish between the phenomena he studies and the more "typical" mental states of depression and schizophrenia? (b) Given the information contained in the article, do you think that d'Acquili's distinction is valid? Why?
3. What criticisms have been raised against d'Acquili's model of transcendent experiences? If you had to take a position on d'Acquili's model—either for or against or somewhere in between—what would it be? Explain your reasoning.

20. THE WAY OF THE JOURNAL — AE p. 94

This article describes Dr. Ira Progoff's journal-keeping technique of self-revelation designed to heighten individuals' awareness of their own inner truths and personal goals. In today's modern society, characterized by a lack of spiritual intimacy and self-knowledge, the journal-keeping workshops conducted by Dr. Progoff and associates have helped people from many walks of life to make contact with more fundamental levels of being within themselves. Such increased contact with one's inner self is seen as an important source for clues to the solutions of personal problems as well as to creativity and self-redefinition.

Learning Objectives

After reading the article, you should be able to:

1. Describe the journal-keeping techniques used, including the "period log," the "life history log," and the "stepping stones" exercises.
2. Describe the goals of the journal-keeping activities and what type of benefit Dr. Progoff claims can be derived from them.
3. Understand Dr. Progoff's views on dream analysis.

Essay Questions

1. Describe some of the journal-keeping exercises used by Progoff in his journal workshops. Do you think these activities are likely to be useful to people from lower socioeconomic backgrounds? Why or why not?
2. According to Dr. Progoff, what benefits can be obtained from participating in his journal workshops? How does such a simple activity as keeping a journal contribute to attaining such benefits?

21. THE INSTINCT TO LEARN — AE p. 102

Ethologists are attempting to find a compromise between instinct theories of behavior and learning theories of behavior. They approach this compromise by positing that learning itself is a part of the species' biological heritage. To date, much of the evidence offered by ethologists to support their case comes from research with non-human species and is subject to question with respect to its generalizability to people.

Learning Objectives

After reading the article, you should be able to:

1. State at least three theoretical explanations or causes for behavior.
2. Give two examples of critical periods in behavioral organization.
3. Define releaser, imprinting, species-specific, feature detector, and mobbing.
4. Describe two constraints on a chick's ability to recognize its parents.

Essay Questions

1. Do explanations of animal behavior necessarily generalize to people? What factors determine whether they generalize or not?
2. If ethologists are arguing that learning is an adaptive process, are they adding anything new to what learning theorists have always contended? In other words, does the fact that the ability to learn may be genetic help to explain what actually gets learned during interactions between organisms and their environment?

22. SOCIOBIOLOGY STIRS A CONTROVERSY OVER LIMITS OF SCIENCE — AE p. 107

In his book, "On Human Nature" E.O. Wilson placed the origins of human nature solely in the genes. In this article, Rosenfeld reviews Wilson's thesis and provides counter arguments by biologists and other scientists.

Learning Objectives

After reading the article, you should be able to:

1. Explain Darwinian evolutionary theory, both historically and in its contemporary form.
2. Describe the sociobiologist's explanation of altruistic behavior and major criticisms of this interpretation.
3. Describe the problems associated with generalizing from animal behavior to human behavior.
4. Describe the mechanisms of genetics including sex-linked inheritance, genetic anomalies, Mendalian ratios, canalization, epigenesis.
5. Discuss the general problems of genotype-environment interaction.

Essay Questions

1. Define altruism and describe how some sociobiologists explain altruistic behavior.
2. Critically evaluate sociobiological theory and indicate how concepts such as "kin selection" and "inelusive fitness" are incorporated into the theory.
3. Cite at least three criticisms of sociobiological theory of behavior.

23. SOCIOBIOLOGY REDEFENDED — AE p. 112

In this rebuttal of criticisms against sociobiology, Dr. Richards advances a humanistic view of sociobiological inquiry in which the value of naturalistic or physicalistic explanations is stressed. Dr. Richards argues that sociobiology is not racist nor sexist, and attacks the foundations of such claims in cultural and conceptual relativism. While acknowledging the need to separate moral values from the process of scientific inquiry, Dr. Richards maintains that the construction of value systems based on scientific findings is both morally and pragmatically appropriate. Finally, the sociobiological perspective on causation and epigenesis is defended.

Learning Objectives

After reading the article, you should be able to:

1. Contrast humanism with animism and dualism as approaches toward explaining human behavior and personality.
2. Review Richards' account of pragmatism and explain why, in his view, pragmatic approaches to cultural anthropology are better than relativistic ones.
3. Describe some of the ways in which Richards feels that cultures can be "judged."
4. Describe Richards' position on the separation of value systems from scientific inquiry.
5. Review Richards' defense of sociobiological theory in the areas of gene-environment interaction, causation, and epigenesis.

Essay Questions

1. How is humanism different from animism and dualism? Explain Richards' reasons for concluding that sociobiology and humanism are so highly compatible.
2. (a) What is cultural relativism? (b) According to Richards, what are the limitations of cultural relativism in helping us to understand about cultural diversity and change?
3. How does Richards defend sociobiology from accusations that it contains sexist and racist sentiments? Do you agree with his defense? Why?
4. (a) What are Richards' views on the separation of scientific inquiry from moral and philosophical value systems? (b) Evaluate Richards' claim that "as a result of our scientific *knowledge* about population, contraception is essential and abortion is often justified. . . ." Do you agree with the implication that scientific knowledge can always determine the correct moral choice given that we are provided by science with enough information on the problem at hand?

24. PULLING A GAG ON THE WILY COYOTE — AE p. 116

In the modern world, the delicate balance between prey and predator often is affected by human needs. This article describes a program based on aversive conditioning that is intended to assist the coyote from becoming an endangered species.

14. SEARCHING FOR DEPRESSION GENES — AE p. 70

New discoveries on the genetic and biochemical foundations of severe depression have raised some scientists' expectations that we may soon be able to understand and control it. They have also raised considerable controversy. While evidence from some studies has shown that severe depression may run along family lines, efforts to isolate the responsible genes have produced mixed results with debatable interpretations. Biochemical research has indicated that the supply of substances in the brain called neurotransmitters may play a role, but more research is needed to determine the causes of the different types of depression and how they should be treated.

Learning Objectives

After reading the article, you should be able to:

1. Recount the basic distinction between "clinical" or severe depression and normal sadness.
2. Review in general the research evidence that led Pardue and Weitkamp to believe that severe depression may have genetic causes.
3. Explain why Weitkamp's genetic findings are currently in doubt.
4. Explain the connection between the supply of neurotransmitters and the emergence of bipolar and unipolar depression.
5. Name at least one drug that has been used to treat depression and describe how it affects the supply of neurotransmitter chemicals.

Essay Questions

1. Do you think that genetic explanations of depression necessarily preclude psychological ones (like Freud's assertion that "depression is anger turned inward")? Is there a theoretically useful sense in which psychological explanations can still be true if the genetic speculations turn out to be correct?
2. Review the evidence that supports the view that there may be a genetic cause for some types of depression. Why is this evidence a current focus of controversy?
3. How is the supply of neurotransmitters in the brain related to symptoms of depression? Does this relationship hold true for unipolar depression, bipolar depression, or both? Explain.

15. CHEMICAL FEELINGS — AE p. 73

Research in brain peptides competes with neurological studies of brain activity. Brain peptides are chemical neurotransmitters, but they differ from other transmitters in several ways. Some investigators believe these substances hold the key to understanding all of brain-behavior relationships.

Learning Objectives

After reading the article, you should be able to:

1. Describe neural transmission.
2. Describe the endocrine system and indicate how hormones are linked to the autonomic nervous system.
3. Describe the relationship between gonadal hormones and the brain.
4. Explain homeostasis and describe how it is related to metabolic regulation.
5. Describe recent advances in neuropsychology especially with reference to the relationship between neurotransmitters substances and behavior.

Essay Questions

1. Describe nervous impulse transmission.
2. Identify four peptides and indicate the function of each.
3. Discuss research on brain peptides as applied to study of the causes of schizophrenia.

16. IMAGES OF THE NIGHT — AE p. 78

Edwin Kiester reviews current knowledge about dreaming, including the neurological mechanisms that have been linked to dream and non-dream sleep states. The newly formulated Hobson-McCarley hypothesis challenges traditional interpretations of the meaning of dream content.

Learning Objectives

After reading the article, you should be able to:

1. Describe research on biological rhythms and indicate how they may influence human behavior.
2. Discuss the various stages of sleep and indicate why Dement asserts that sleep is a "waste of time."
3. Discuss various theories of REM-NREM sleep as well as the effects of sleep deprivation on REM activity.
4. Evaluate theories of dreaming, especially those of Freud and Hall, with respect to the meaning of the latent content of dreams.
5. Describe the neurophysiological mechanisms involved with sleep and dreaming.

Essay Questions

1. Describe the various stages of sleep and indicate how studies of brain mechanisms have advanced our understanding of dream activity.
2. Compare dreams of men and women as to the content of their dreams.
3. Describe several criticisms of Freud's work on dreams.

17. GOING BEYOND PAIN — AE p. 83

Standard medical treatments fail to help many individuals who suffer from chronic pain. New techniques, based on behavioral theories from psychology, teach chronic pain sufferers to reduce pain or to live with it. The idea is to reinforce "well" behavior and to extinguish "pain" behavior.

Learning Objectives

After reading the article, you should be able to:

1. Describe the haptic sense, drawing attention to the mechanoreceptors involved in touch and pain.
2. Explain what is meant by the "medical model."
3. Explain the mechanisms underlying respondant and operant conditioning.
4. Distinguish among autogenic training, progressive relaxation, and autosuggestion.
5. Explain various theories of nerve transmissions as they have been linked to the sensation of pain.

Essay Questions

1. Compare gate control and specificity theories of the neurological transmission of pain sensations.
2. Compare the medical model and psychological or holistic model for the treatment of chronic pain.
3. Describe some of the chief factors that induce learned pain.

18. BIOFEEDBACK SEEKS NEW MEDICAL USES FOR CONCEPT OF YOGA — AE p. 87

Biofeedback is a new technique that applies to treatment of a variety of psychosomatic disorders. It teaches people to take command of their own bodily functions—a bit of mind over matter!

Learning Objectives

After reading the article, you should be able to:

1. Describe various techniques used in behavior modification.
2. Describe research on operant conditioning of autonomic activity in human and nonhuman organisms.
3. Discuss the relationship between motivation and biofeedback.
4. Review various types of meditation and indicate how each relates to biofeedback as a therapeutic technique.
5. Discuss the relative success of biofeedback for various mental health behavior problems.

Essay Questions

1. Identify one psychosomatic illness and describe a biofeedback program that could be used to treat it.
2. Compare biofeedback procedures to those used by yogis in their meditations.
3. Indicate how biofeedback techniques make use of operant conditioning procedures.

19. BRAIN FLASH: THE PHYSIOLOGY OF INSPIRATION — AE p. 91

What happens in the brain when we experience moments of profound ecstasy or depression? Author Meme Black reviews the theories of psychiatrist Augene d'Acquili, who has developed a neurophysiological model of profound experiences that emphasizes the interaction of the left and right cerebral hemispheres and the limbic system. According to d'Acquili, holistic experiential feelings that usually originate in the right hemisphere—and normally pass to the left hemisphere via the corpus callosum where they have minimal impact on our conscious feelings—are occasionally "detoured" through the limbic system, where they may acquire powerful emotional charges that give rise to feelings of transcendence when received by the left hemisphere. While d'Acquili's theory appeals to some scientists, others have maintained that it depends too much on simplistic assumptions about how the brain works.

9. THE THREE BRAINS OF PAUL MACLEAN — AE p. 53

Many theorists have proposed that the brain is organized hierarchically, in layers or levels. MacLean takes this argument further than anyone, claiming that we actually possess three "brains": a low-level layer like a reptile's that controls basic bodily functions and self-defense; an intermediate layer like a mammal's that controls emotions and parenting behaviors; and a high-level layer, sort of like a computer, that thinks, reasons, and solves problems. The division of labor appears to be generally true, but the comparisons to reptiles, mammals, and computers cause considerable controversy.

Learning Objectives

After reading the article, you should be able to:

1. Define the triune brain and describe the functions attributed to each of its layers.
2. Describe how MacLean's theory explains contradictions in human character, personality, and behavior.
3. List several criticisms of the theory that has been made by other scientists.

Essay Questions

1. Is the triune brain theory consistent or inconsistent with the idea of localization of function described in your textbook's chapter on the nervous system and its organization?
2. How large a part do reptilian characteristics play in everyday human behavior? Do we need MacLean's theory to explain these characteristics, or could other factors account for them, such as learning?

10. TWINS — AE p. 57

Studies of identical twins separated at birth and raised apart supply the most direct evidence on the inheritance of psychological characteristics in people. Thomas Bouchard at the University of Minnesota currently conducts the most intensive study of this type ever done. Each pair of twins comes to the Minnesota campus for a week of tests and interviews, covering life history, intellectual abilities, emotional attributes, attitudes, opinions, and neurophysiological makeup. Though data analysis is far from complete and much of the evidence is at this stage little more than anecdote, the similarities between twins in all of these areas are so unexpected that Bouchard has said, "More of human behavior is genetically determined or influenced than we ever supposed."

Learning Objectives

After reading the article, you should be able to:

1. Describe the research techniques used to study twins.
2. Distinguish between coincidental and biologically-determined similarities.
3. Identify the psychological characteristic that is most similar in twins and the characteristic that is least similar.

Essay Questions

1. Is research such as Bouchard's important or unimportant? Why?
2. What changes, if any, would you make in your own view of human nature if Bouchard's conclusion, quoted above, turns out to be correct?

11. TINKERING WITH LIFE — AE p. 60

Genetic engineering and recombinant DNA research attempt to alter the natural genetic makeup of organisms from bacteria to people by modifying genes or replacing one gene with another. This line of scientific research promises tremendous advances in therapy for inherited diseases and in development of new or improved agricultural crops and livestock. It also promises tremendous gains for commercial corporations that can use the theory and technology for profit-making ventures rather than basic research. Already genetic scientists are leaving academia for private industry and corporations are embroiled with universities in lawsuits over patent rights to new genes and artificial organisms. According to one spokesman, "Society is losing out if scientists have commercial ties that lead them to keep corporate interest uppermost."

Learning Objectives

After reading the article, you should be able to:

1. Define gene mixing and gene splicing.
2. Describe the uses of genetic engineering in medicine.
3. Describe the uses of genetic engineering in agriculture.
4. Identify some advantages and disadvantages of allowing private industry to engage in genetic engineering.

Essay Questions

1. Either attack or defend the proposition that "Genetic engineering, like any other technological advance, should be available to private industry to develop in accord with the principles of free enterprise."
2. Should genetic engineering be used to try to eliminate inherited diseases among people? Why or why not?

12. THE VIOLENT BRAIN — AE p. 64

What are the causes of aggressive behavior? Learning? Environment? Heredity? This broad review of current knowledge and speculation on the topics of aggression and violence indicates that all these factors may play a role. Learning is implicated by studies showing that youths from violent backgrounds may tend to respond more violently later in life. Research on frustration and noxious stimuli like heat and pain has shown that environmental factors are also important. Studies of sex-linked genetic characteristics and hormonal regulation suggest that there may be a role for heredity as well. Finally, neurological impairments resulting from brain damage, tumors, and biochemical imbalances have been shown to be contributing factors. The picture that emerges seems complex and multi-faceted, but author Dina Ingber points out that the control of aggressive behavior may soon become an ethical rather than a practical problem.

Learning Objectives

After reading the article, you should be able to:

1. Summarize the frustration-aggression hypothesis and explain what influence environmental factors may contribute to aggression.
2. List three factors that may help to explain aggressive and violent behavior.
3. Explain how hormonal factors influence aggressive behavior.
4. Name some mind altering drugs and explain how they may bring about aggressive behavior.

Essay Questions

1. We have seen that a number of factors can help to explain the occurrence of aggressive and violent behavior. Pick three factors that you consider to be the most important and defend your choices.
2. Review the evidence that hormonal factors may play a role in aggressive behavior. Does the hormonal evidence pertain only to men? Explain.
3. Name and describe some of the environmental factors relating to aggressive behavior.
4. How can the erroneous perception of events around us give rise to aggression? Explain how the ingestion of mind-altering drugs like alcohol or PCP might bring about aggressive behavior.

13. THE ORIGINS OF VIOLENCE — AE p. 67

Cross-cultural studies show that societies which provide infants with large amounts of physical affection and bodily contact also produce comparatively nonviolent adults. Research on monkeys and human infants confirms that movement and physical contact are required for normal development, and the author speculates that specific parts of the cerebellum comprise a pleasure system which is activated by physical affection. Child abusers and other violent people may suffer from deficient pleasure systems. Recently developed techniques of artificial cerebellar stimulation now raise the possibility of producing less violent adults and societies.

Learning Objectives

After reading the article, you should be able to:

1. Describe basic cross-cultural findings on the origins of violent societies.
2. Describe the implications of animal research for understanding individual differences in violence among human adults.
3. Explain why the cerebellum provides an explanatory model for the effects of social isolation.
4. Describe the results of Heath's research on electrical stimulation of the limbic system and cerebellum.
5. Describe the characteristics of adults with inadequately developed pleasure systems.

Essay Questions

1. To what extent is the Harlows' research on the social isolation of monkeys useful for understanding the development of normal humans?
2. Describe Prescott's techniques for providing artificial cerebellar stimulation.

Learning Objectives
After reading the article, you should be able to:
1. Define reinforcement; values; survival value.
2. Describe Skinner's idea of how to use behavioral science.
3. List the Chinese inventions that advanced civilization.

Essay Questions
1. Discuss the central idea of "confidence" in this article.
2. To what end does Skinner use the extended comparison of our society to those more primitive that go without modern agricultural techniques?

4. SHAPING BEHAVIOR CONTEST FOR MINDS — AE p. 26

Behavior modification is an effective and highly controversial type of therapy for controlling behavior by manipulating reward and punishment. Its use among the sick is not so hotly disputed as its use among populations that are well. Behaviorists argue that, properly applied, behavior modification will produce happy, productive, and peaceful societies. Critics, many of them "humanists," react with fear, stating that behavior modification reduces the free will that we need to make intelligent decisions about ourselves and our environment. The debate has taken on large proportions as followers of each camp have argued their views and founded many and varied types of psychotherapy.

Learning Objectives
After reading the article, you should be able to:
1. Define and describe behavior modification.
2. Identify the critics and their arguments against behavior modification.
3. Name several important behaviorists.
4. List the ways that scientists can mold human behavior.

Essay Questions
1. Explain the pros and cons in the argument over behavior modification. Which side do you agree with, and why?
2. Under what circumstances is behavior modification very effective? What disorders is it most successful in treating? Under what circumstances might it be dangerous?

5. TOWARD A PSYCHOLOGY OF NATURAL BEHAVIOR — AE p. 30

The author argues that psychology lags behind other fields in developing adequate field work methods. He also believes that psychology needs a better balance between field and laboratory. Many studies performed in laboratory situations do not have relevance to events in nature, and they may lack validity when psychologists try to generalize from laboratory results to "real life." We have "hedged on the issue of generalization," the author maintains, and we must now "look at how people actually behave in their homes, their schools and their work places."

Learning Objectives
After reading the article, you should be able to:
1. Contrast laboratory methods with field work methods.
2. Understand the relative advantages and disadvantages of laboratory research.
3. Know what skills the naturalist must possess.
4. Define "generalization" in the context of research results.

Essay Questions
1. What does the author mean by the statement, "Too often the means of our research have become the ends"?
2. Define and describe several differences in method and result between naturalistic and laboratory research.

6. GENETICS: THE EDGE OF CREATION — AE p. 36

Recent advances in genetic research have opened vast new horizons in medicine and industry. They have also led to concern about the ethics of recombinant DNA research in which new gene-slicing techniques have enabled scientists to genetically engineer new life forms. Author Albert Rosenfeld reviews the promise—and the problems—presented in these discoveries.

Learning Objectives
After reading the article, you should be able to:
1. Discuss the number of nucleotides and the role they play in the DNA molecule and in the diversity of human and animal life.
2. Review the steps that have been taken to insure the proper handling of recombinant DNA research. Explain why some of the initial fears turned out to be unfounded.
3. Briefly characterize the following terms: (a) gene splicing; (b) gene mapping; (c) transposons; (d) introns; (e) pseudogenes.
4. List and explain at least three current or potential applications of recombinant DNA technology.

Essay Questions
1. Discuss the potential costs and benefits involved in recombinant DNA technology. If you were in a position to decide, what type of regulatory policy would you advocate to provide balance between the costs and benefits? Explain.
2. What were some of the specific fears that accompanied the initial realization that gene-slicing techniques were feasible? Did *all* these fears prove to be unrealistic? Explain.

7. THE CLOCK WITHIN — AE p. 41

Basic processes of the body and the nervous system vary rhythmically in their speed and efficiency. Depending on the time of day, a person's resting heart rate may be at its normal low of 60 beats a minute, at its normal high of 80 beats a minute, or somewhere in between, on its way up or on its way back down. Similar cyclical variation occurs in blood pressure, breathing rate, body temperature, mood, alertness, vigor, eye-hand coordination, memory, and susceptibility to drugs, among other things. Failing to account for these rhythms can have profound consequences for human performance, medical diagnosis, medical treatment, and basic research on physiological and psychological functions. This article summarizes some of the findings in the new field of chronobiology that studies such rhythms.

Learning Objectives
After reading the article, you should be able to:
1. Define circadian rhythm.
2. Describe current theories of how "the clock within" works.
3. List at least 6 physiological or psychological functions and describe their circadian variation.
4. Describe the problems that circadian rhythms can cause in (a) research on drug toxicity, and (b) planning schedules for people who work hazardous jobs.

Essay Questions
1. How could the human errors at Three Mile Island have been lessened given what is currently known about circadian rhythms?
2. Design an effective testing schedule for determining the lethal dosage of a new poison intended for rodent control.
3. Discuss at least two applications of chronobiology in therapy for psychological and medical disorders, such as insomnia, cancer, or high blood pressure.

8. DO DIETS REALLY WORK? — AE p. 46

Common misconceptions about the causes of obesity and the effectiveness of dieting have combined forces with the popular cultural value that "thin is beautiful" to produce generations of frustrated dieters. Available evidence indicates that the body sets its own optimal level of body weight and then enforces it through a variety of appetitive and metabolic controls. Efforts to change body weight without changing the body's preferred weight setting are likely to produce relatively small and temporary shifts, which become progressively harder to increase or maintain. Just how to change the body's weight setting is not well understood, but exercise seems to help.

Learning Objectives
After reading the article, you should be able to:
1. Identify three common misconceptions about obesity and dieting.
2. Evaluate and discuss the effectiveness of dieting in view of the setpoint theory presented in the article.
3. Discuss the basic method and results of the following four experiments: (a) Ancel Key's study of starvation in the 1940s; (b) Ethan Sim's study of overeating; (c) O.G. Edholm's study of unregulated food intake.
4. Define *luxoskonsumption* and trace the time course and nature of metabolic changes that occur as body weight moves away from its setpoint.

Essay Questions
1. Evaluate the claim that dieting is effective provided that a person has enough will power to control his/her food intake.
2. What metabolic changes come into play as a person's body weight moves away from its setpoint? Do these changes help or hinder the attempt to change body weight by calorie counting and regulating food intake? Explain.
3. Describe the results of experiments that have looked at people's efforts to gain weight. Is gaining weight easier than losing weight? Is weight, once gained, easy to lose? Explain.

A GUIDE TO THE STUDY AND ENJOYMENT OF ANNUAL EDITIONS: PSYCHOLOGY 83/84

This guide has been prepared to help the reader get the most from the 55 articles contained in *Psychology 83/84.* For each article the guide contains (1) a brief introduction providing background on the topic of the article and the author(s) and occasionally showing the relationship of one article to another, (2) Learning Objectives directing the reader to some of the important terms, concepts, and issues treated in the article, and (3) Essay Questions for stimulating the reader to go beyond the article in thinking about the issue(s) involved.

There are a number of ways this guide can be useful. One suggestion is that it be reviewed prior to reading the article, that the article then be read through for enjoyment, that the article then be reread to answer the learning objectives and finally that the article be reviewed in the context of the essay questions.

We hope you find this guide useful. We would appreciate any comments you have on how it can be improved in next year's *Annual Edition.*

Prepared by Tracy L. Brown,
Thomas H. Carr and
Hiram E. Fitzgerald,
Michigan State University

1. UNDERSTANDING PSYCHOLOGICAL MAN: A STATE OF THE SCIENCE REPORT — AE p. 4

What have psychologists learned about how people think, behave, and believe that they didn't know 15 years ago? This question is addressed by 11 prominent psychologists whose interests—and answers—range across the entire spectrum of psychological inquiry. Some authors emphasize advances in particular areas of knowledge including brain functions, the relationship between mental and physical health, and the power of social motivation. Other contributors cite theoretical advances—a shift in the types of questions being asked (and hopefully answered), an increased emphasis on mental processes like memory and problem solving, and a focus on human development, which includes the entire human life-span. The answers are as diverse as the problems facing modern society, but virtually all the contributors agree that increased applicability to such real life problems is an immediate and urgent goal.

Learning Objectives

After reading the article, you should be able to:

1. Characterize and discuss: (a) the decline of behavioral approaches and the increasing popularity of cognitive ones; (b) recent advances in the understanding of the brain; (c) increased awareness of the relationship between mental and physical health; (d) advances in the area of social motivation and leadership, and (e) the emergence of a life-span perspective in human development.

Essay Questions

1. Different psychologists have different views on the advances made in psychology and the challenges it faces in the future. Based on your reading, describe what *you* think to be the most important advances.
2. Summarize the relationships between leadership motives, "Type-A behavior," and physical health.
3. Why is the shift to a life-span perspective in human development considered to be a major advance? According to Neugarten, what factors have precipitated this shift in orientation?

2. FREEDOM TO CHANGE — AE p. 17

Sigmund Freud, with his ideas about the origins of adult personality in the experiences of childhood, has exerted a greater influence on Western psychology than any other single thinker except Skinner. Just how important are the experiences of childhood? Just how firmly set is adult personality—can adults change, can they overcome adverse early conditions, do they respond primarily to the momentum of life history or to the exigencies of current situations and events? Tavris argues that flaws can be found in many of the fundamental assumptions of the individual case study method favored by Freudians, that longitudinal data show much less consistency across the lifespan than Freud's theory predicts, and that adults appear to be much more flexible and sensitive to current pressures than Freud would allow. These findings cast a new light on the origins of personality that enables us to progress beyond the valuable beginnings that were Freud's contribution.

Learning Objectives

After reading the article, you should be able to:

1. Describe the basic concepts underlying Freud's theory of personality development.
2. Identify at least three problems with using case studies of a person's past experiences to explain that person's current problems.
3. Describe the results of longitudinal studies of the effects of early experience on adult characteristics.

Essay Questions

1. What difference would it make in your reaction to a serious personal problem if (a) Freud were right about the relation between early experience and current characteristics, or (b) Brim and Kagen were right?
2. If people's memories and understanding of causality are so deceptive, how much should you believe anyone's explanation of why they are feeling, thinking, or behaving in a particular way?

3. WHY AREN'T WE USING SCIENCE TO CHANGE BEHAVIOR? — AE p. 23

B.F. Skinner, one of the founders of the behaviorist school of psychology, argues in this article that we are so devoted to our habit of interpreting our actions through emotions that we fail to take advantage of what social science can do to help solve problems. We are just as blind in this way, he argues, as the people we scorn for rejecting advanced agricultural technologies.

PSYCHOLOGY 83/84

Thomas H. Carr, Ph.D., *Editor*
Michigan State University

Hiram E. Fitzgerald, Ph.D., *Editor*
Michigan State University

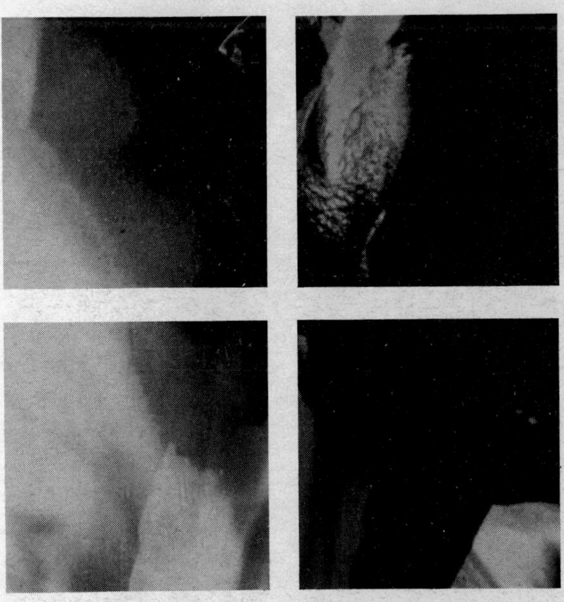

Cover Credit: Jenkins, Paul, "Phenomena Day of Zagorsk"; Courtesy, Corcoran Gallery of Art.

ANNUAL EDITIONS
The Dushkin Publishing Group, Inc. Sluice Dock, Guilford, Ct. 06437

Volumes in the Annual Editions Series

- Abnormal Psychology
- ● Aging
- ● American Government
- ● American History, Pre-Civil War
- ● American History, Post-Civil War
- ● Anthropology
- Astronomy
- ● Biology
- ● Business
- ● Comparative Politics
- ● Criminal Justice
- Death and Dying
- ● Deviance
- ● Early Childhood Education
- Earth Science
- ● Economics
- ● Educating Exceptional Children
- ● Education
- ● Educational Psychology
- Energy
- ● Environment
- Ethnic Studies
- Foreign Policy
- Geography
- Geology
- ● Health
- ● Human Development
- ● Human Sexuality
- ● Macroeconomics
- ● Management
- ● Marketing
- ● Marriage and Family
- ● Microeconomics
- ● Personal Growth and Behavior
- Philosophy
- Political Science
- ● Psychology
- Religion
- ● Social Problems
- ● Social Psychology
- ● Sociology
- Twentieth Century American History
- ● Urban Society
- ● Western Civilization, Pre-Reformation
- ● Western Civilization, Post-Reformation
- Women's Studies
- World History
- ● World Politics

● Indicates currently available

Thirteenth Edition

Manufactured by George Banta Company, Menasha, Wisconsin, 54952

Library of Congress Cataloging in Publication Data
Main entry under title: Annual editions: Psychology.
1. Psychology—Addresses, essays, lectures—Periodicals. I. Title: Psychology.
BF 149.A58 150.5 79-180263
ISBN 0-87967-448-2

ADVISORY BOARD

Members of the Advisory Board are instrumental in the final selection of articles for each year's edition of *Annual Editions.* Their review of articles for content, level, and appropriateness provides critical direction to the editor and staff. We think you'll find their careful consideration well reflected in this volume.

AND STAFF

CONTENTS

1 The Science of Psychology

2 Biological Bases of Behavior

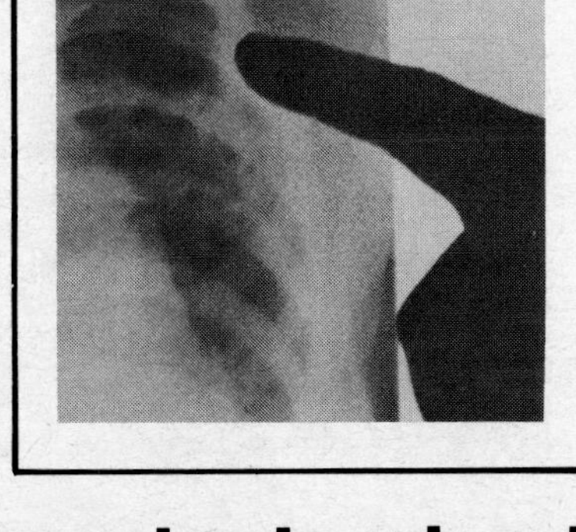

3 Psychological Bases of Behavior

B. *MEMORY AND COGNITION*

C. *LANGUAGE*

4

Development

5

Individual Differences

6 Personality and Social Processes

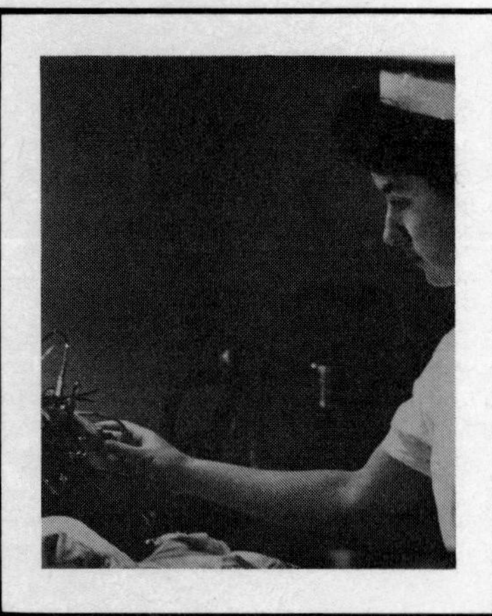

7 Disorders and Therapeutic Processes

TOPIC GUIDE

This topic guide can be used to correlate the readings in *Psychology 83/84* with the topics that are usually covered in psychology textbooks. This guide is intended for use as a general aid to identifying topical coverage, and does not necessarily define the total content of any given article.

TOPIC AREA	TREATED AS A PRIMARY ISSUE IN:	TREATED AS A SECONDARY ISSUE IN:
Adulthood and Aging	29. Our Insatiable Brain 37. Coping With the Seasons of Life 38. In Search of Youth	2. The Freedom to Change
Behavior	3. Why Aren't We Using Science 21. The Instinct to Learn 55. Fight Fat With Behavior Control	2. The Freedom to Change 4. Shaping Behavior Contest for Minds
Behavior Modification	4. Shaping Behavior Contest for Minds 24. Pulling a Gag on the Wily Coyote 55. Fight Fat With Behavior Control	8. Do Diets Really Work? 17. Going Beyond Pain 26. Conversion, Brainwashing, and Deprogramming 45. The Many Me's of the Self Monitor
Biofeedback	18. Biofeedback Seeks New Uses for Concept of Yoga	
Body Rhythms (Biorhythms)	7. The Clock Within	8. Do Diets Really Work?
Brain Chemistry	14. Searching for Depression Genes 15. Chemical Feelings 29. Our Insatiable Brain 38. In Search of Youth 53. The Healing Brain	6. Genetics: The Edge of Creation 12. The Violent Brain
Brain Damage	32. The Loss of Language	
Cognition	27. My Memory/Myself 30. The Mind of the Puzzler 36. Learning Right From Wrong 41. The Remedial Thinker	19. Brain Flash 31. Learning the Mother Tongue 32. The Loss of Language 34. Childhood 33. Newborn Knowledge 34. Childhood
Dreams	16. Images of the Night	
Friendship	17. The Friendship Bond	
Genetics/Heredity	6. Genetics: The Edge of Creation 10. Twins 11. Tinkering With Life 22. Sociobiology Stirs New Controversy 23. Sociobiology Redefended	12. The Violent Brain 21. The Instinct to Learn 33. Newborn Knowledge 39. Attitudes, Interests, & IQ
Humanistic Psychology	48. The Foundations of the Person-Centered Approach	20. The Way of the Journal 23. Sociobiology Redefended 26. Conversion, Brainwashing, and Deprogramming
Intelligence and IQ	30. The Mind of the Puzzler 39. Attitudes, Interests, & IQ 40. Who's Intelligent? 41. The Remedial Thinker	19. Brain Flash 29. Our Insatiable Brain
Language	31. Learning the Mother Tongue 32. The Loss of Language	34. Childhood
Memory	27. My Memory/Myself 28. Mood and Memory 29. Our Insatiable Brain	34. Childhood
Mental Illness	46. Psycho-Immunity 47. Stress Can Be Good for You 52. Finding the Hidden Freud 54. Roots of Madness	15. Chemical Feelings 18. Biofeedback Seeks New Uses for Concept of Yoga 48. Foundations of the Person-Centered Approach 53. The Healing Brain
Obesity	8. Do Diets Really Work? 55. Fight Fat With Behavior Control	
Parenting	31. Learning the Mother Tongue 35. Your Child's Self-Esteem 36. Learning Right from Wrong	
Personality	45. The Many Me's of the Self-Monitor 48. Foundations of the Person-Centered Approach 52. Finding the Hidden Freud	14. Searching for Depression Genes

TOPIC AREA	TREATED AS A PRIMARY ISSUE IN:	TREATED AS A SECONDARY ISSUE IN:
Person Perception	51. Self-Fulfilling Stereotypes	
Psychotherapy	52. Finding the Hidden Freud 53. The Healing Brain	2. The Freedom to Change 4. Shaping Behavior Contest for Minds 24. Pulling a Gag on the Wily Coyote 55. Fight Fat With Behavior Control
Self-concept	35. Your Child's Self-Esteem 44. Prisoners of Manliness 45. The Many Me's of the Self-Monitor 48. Foundations of the Person-Centered Approach	20. The Way of the Journal 46. Psycho-Immunity 47. Stress Can Be Good for You
Sensation/ Perception	17. Going Beyond Pain	16. Images in the Night 34. Childhood 33. Newborn Knowledge 34. Childhood

TOPIC AREA	TREATED AS A PRIMARY ISSUE IN:	TREATED AS A SECONDARY ISSUE IN:
Sex Differences	42. Males and Females and What You May Not Know About Them 43. Girls *vs* Boys 44. Prisoners of Manliness	23. Sociobiology Redefended 34. Childhood 51. Self-Fulfilling Stereotypes
Stress	13. The Origins of Violence 46. Psycho-Immunity 47. Stress Can Be Good for You	18. Biofeedback Seeks New Uses for Concept of Yoga
Violence/ Aggression	12. The Violent Brain 13. The Origins of Violence	

PREFACE

Psychology focuses on people: how we perceive, learn, think, feel, behave, and get along with others. Its historical roots trace back to philosophy and theology. Its currently-growing branches extend to the scientific laboratory, to the arenas of everyday living, to the psychological clinic and hospital, even to the mysteries of psychic phenomena. Psychologists take many different approaches and employ many different methodologies in their studies, but share a common goal. All want to contribute new discoveries to our rapidly expanding knowledge about the human being.

If these discoveries are not communicated, they are useless. Professional journals disseminate information to specialists in the field, but what of the nonspecialist? The popular media have taken up this challenge to provide communication links between psychologists and the public. Radio, television, newspapers, and magazines regularly carry reports of significant and intriguing psychological research. It is not surprising that this coverage frequently informs the professional as well as the layperson about the most recent developments in the field.

Unfortunately, tracking down and sorting through this wealth of material requires a great deal of time. Reports appear in hundreds of different sources. Many are accurate, well-written, and informative; many others are inaccurate and misleading. *Annual Editions: Psychology 83/84* is designed to simplify the task of finding those accounts that do the most to inform in accurate, timely, and readable ways. This *thirteenth edition* includes a broad cross section of articles from a variety of sources. Some of these articles have earned awards for distinguished scientific writing. Others are the work of experienced science writers who regularly scan the professional literature for reports of interest to the public. Some of the articles are first-hand accounts by the scientific researchers themselves, providing rich detail for all of us who are interested in what is happening in the laboratory and in field work.

Some of the selections are theoretical, some are empirical, and others are both. Some contain intriguing, even frightening, implications. Many are concerned with the ethical issues inherent in the science. This broad range of attitudes and outlooks reflects the field of psychology itself, as a profession and a science.

We hope that you will find *Annual Editions: Psychology 83/84* to be an up-to-date and useful book. Please take a minute to fill out the article rating form on the last page of this book, and let us know your opinion. Any anthology can be revised and improved. With your help, this one will be—annually.

Thomas H. Carr, Ph.D.
Hiram E. Fitzgerald, Ph.D.
Editors

The Science of Psychology

1

Psychology can be defined as the science that studies the nature, mental life, and behavior of humans and other animals. Philosophers have long been involved in this study, but the emergence of psychology as an empirical science is comparatively recent, usually marked by the opening of the first psychological laboratory in Germany in 1879. Since then several schools of thought have developed to comprise the science of psychology, including among others, structuralism, functionalism, behaviorism, psychoanalysis, Gestalt theory, biological psychology, and cognitive theory.

This section includes articles that survey some of the major issues and areas of theoretical controversy in the field of psychology today. "Understanding Psychological Man: A State of the Science Report," asks 11 leading psychologists to describe their views on where psychology stands at present. In "The Freedom to Change," Freud's contribution to current psychological thinking is examined, and some of the shortcomings of his theory are identified. B.F. Skinner's "Why Aren't We Using Science to Change Behavior" presents the eminent behaviorist's evaluation of the problems supposedly caused by wrong-headed beliefs about subjectivity and his imperative call to use behavioral science to "help solve the problems of the world now." "Shaping Behavior Contest for Minds" analyzes the conflict between behavioral and humanistic approaches to human nature and human problems, cataloguing the ways in which behavior modification has gained acceptance and cautioning against the creation of "Skinner's engineered society." "Toward a Psychology of Natural Behavior" examines the role of empirical laboratory investigation in the field of psychology and calls for more studies of people in the natural settings of their everyday lives.

A review of this section will show how scientific psychologists attempt to reconcile our capability for understanding and controlling behavior with the need to account for mental life and acknowledge the requirements of personal freedom.

Looking Ahead: Challenge Questions

What are the major areas of psychological study and some of the main recent achievements in each area?

Should students of psychology be more concerned with collecting data or with interpreting it?

Need the study of behavior automatically translate into behavior control? In what ways is behavior control the legitimate concern of parents, school administrators, prison officials, and psychologists? What is "the mind" and why do psychologists need to think about it?

Is psychology a culture-bound science? Do the prevailing opinions of society become the scientific principles of psychology, or do psychologists formulate theories objectively without nonscientific influences?

Understanding Psychological Man: A State of the Science Report

Contributions by:
Jerome Bruner
Richard S. Lazarus
Ulric Neisser
B.F. Skinner
Stanley Milgram
Neal Miller
Donald O. Hebb
Bernice Neugarten
David McClelland
Rollo May
Philip G. Zimbardo

What have we started to learn about human psychology—the processes behind our behavior, perceptions, and beliefs—that we didn't know 15 years ago?

This is what is known in the survey game as an open-ended question, designed to give free rein to respondents' thinking about the subject at hand. Here, the subject at hand is, broadly speaking, "Psychology Today: The State of the Science." The "respondents" are as distinguished and creative a group of independent thinkers as we've ever assembled in a single issue.

Fifteen years ago, this magazine began as "a forum for the exchange of new ideas in the various disciplines of psychology." That's still the way we read our mandate, but it's a good thing to call time out every once in a while, as we're doing in this anniversary section, and take a perspective break. Accordingly, we asked 11 of the best minds in the field to tell us what they think has been the most significant work in psychology over the last decade and a half.

It's a temptation, even for people who ought to know better, to get carried away by the sheer esthetics of an elegant study, or the cosmetic appeal of a fresh theory that slicks down a cowlick of heretofore unruly findings. Yet progress in the so-called "human" sciences, as in any other field of scientific inquiry, is usually measured in tiny steps, forward and sometimes backward in the right direction. Satisfactory answers to deceptively simple questions about how and why we do what we do usually turn out to be as elusive as your elbow when you try to kiss it.

A few months ago, *U.S. News and World Report* proclaimed psychology "the 'in' profession of the '80s," a proposition as demeaning as it is flattering in that it implies that psychology is something that bobs with the tide of fashion. The fact is that most people still do not have a very clear notion of what psychology is and what psychologists do, at least when it comes to research. Taken together, the reports that follow provide, among other things, a pretty good picture of the wide-ranging concerns of psychologists today. They help us see past the headlines to the through-lines of psychology's ongoing work.

—*Jack Nessel*

JEROME BRUNER

I don't think we've had Big Bangs in psychology in the last 15 years, but I do see two related signs of growth. The first is the continued movement of psychology away from the restrictive shackles of behaviorism toward a more flexible emphasis on cognitive processes. The second is the increase in intellectual commerce between psychology and neighboring fields that also study man.

The Skinnerians were impressed with how easily they could manipulate animal behavior through different sets of rewards and punishments. They assumed that all human actions—even thoughts, language, and supposed motives or personality traits—could be explained by similar, if somewhat more complex, patterns of conditioning. The new breed of cognitive psychologists rejected such a mechanistic view, arguing that there are structures and processes of mind that are not reducible to combinations of reinforced responses.

Some like to date the beginning of the Cognitive Revolution back to 1956, when a first freshet of new work appeared. Something earth-shattering did happen in the mid-1950s, I'm sure. Before then, studies of mental processes were considered eccentric, if interesting; definitely not in the mainstream of psychology. Afterward, the "metaphor" of human thought became crucial. In the new dispensation, perception, memory, and the like, rather than being reduced to a type of learning, were conceived of as instances of problem-solving.

The change was not limited to American psychology. It ranged from Russia (first inspired by Vygotsky and then by Luria), through Switzerland (with the impetus of Piaget), through Britain (where Bartlett and Craik planted the seeds later harvested by Broadbent and Gregory), to America.

In time, the metaphor was extended to perception and memory, and eventually to human development, social psychology, and personality. It emphasized how performance in particular tasks was derived from stored knowledge or "representations" of the world through the principled application of operating or processing principles: strategies, "filters," and so on.

As a result of this new willingness to entertain the idea that human beings think and have a mental life, psychologists now make common cause with those intellectual neighbors who were before considered off-limits as too "mentalist." Linguists are one such group. The crew of psychologists and computer scientists sailing under the flag of Artificial Intelligence is another. We even enjoy a new kinship with anthropology, which has had its own cognitive revolution. And after a half-century of estrangement, we have rejoined the philosophers, who, it turns out, are no slouches in the formal study of mind, language, values, even perception; Hilary Putnam, John Searle, and Robert Nozick are among them.

What gave psychology the courage and impetus to move ahead in this way? There are some who will say that the computer cleared the way by making *thought* and then *mind* metaphorically respectable. In this view, we cleansed our ancient concepts by converting them to computer terms—much, say, as the Mafia launders its money by depositing it in respectable but unregistered Swiss bank accounts.

At the risk of being an overly speculative historian, I suggest that psychology is responding to the so-called Post-Industrial Revolution. In the Industrial Revolution, the emphasis was on energy and its transformations—the forces that make not only the world but its man-made machinery run. Now, with the growth of science and technology, the mechanics of energy have been displaced from the center of our attention by the problems of information and control: how you manage the thing once you have it running. Even conventional Marxist theory, so wedded to its materialist base, has undergone a cognitive revolution that a generation ago would have been labeled bourgeois idealism. Once you have enough trucks running, you begin to wonder why so many empty ones are passing each other on the motorway from Moscow to Leningrad.

These changes started before the computer came on the scene to run interference for us. Indeed, the development of the computing sciences is as much a reflection of the deep trend as is the cognitive revolution.

Brood on it. Orwell's *1984* will not arrive; neither will Huxley's *Brave New World*, nor the Pavlovian fantasies of Čapek's play *R.U.R.* or E. M. Forster's short story "The Machine Stops." Extremist behavior modification is still with us as an omnipotence fantasy, to be sure, and so is the new powerhouse "instinctualism" of sociobiology. But the new fantasies—and the new facts—are about intelligence, autonomy, and about *controlling* technology with thoughtful planning rather than smashing it, as the 19th-century Luddites did to their looms. I think that the concept of mind is here to stay.

Jerome Bruner is George Herbert Mead University Professor on the Graduate Faculty of the New School for Social Research in New York. He has done influential research in the fields of memory, perception, language, and intellectual development, and is also a respected voice in American education.

RICHARD S. LAZARUS

When I was a graduate student in the late 1940s, emotion was hardly a respectable concept in academic psychology. Because emotion was not easy to define, behaviorists took little interest in it. One of the most widely read articles in *The Psychological Bulletin* of 1951 was a paper by Judson Brown and I. E. Farber, which stated the commonly held view that emotions had no distinct, knowable existence, but were simply to be regarded as an "intervening variable" that connected a stimulus with a response.

Indeed, for the next 20 years psychologists for the most part investigated only one emotion—anxiety—which they thought could help to explain pathological states. They regarded anxiety as a learned drive, accompanied by physical arousal, which could motivate the organism to learn ways of reducing tension. Other emotions, such as fear, guilt, envy, joy, or happiness, were not considered important enough to study.

Nor were the behaviorists very interested in cognition—that is, thinking processes. No one took seriously the possibility that the way people construed or thought about things that threatened their well-being was important to emotion and to coping with the threat.

The roots of the drive-centered idea were firmly embedded in a distrust of speculation about what was going on in the mind. Only laboratory experimentation could lead to dependable knowledge, went this line of reasoning, and a corollary was that psychological processes should be reduced to the lowest common denominator of animal life. B. F. Skinner wrote of the behavior of "organisms" in outrageous hyperbole, suggesting that his behavioral principles could apply to all animal life and perhaps to all living creatures, though I do not suppose he had protozoa and plant life in mind.

The dramatic change that became evident in the early 1960s was a gradual abandonment, or at least weakening, of this restrictive outlook. The "cognitive revolution" that took place renewed interest in people's thoughts and knowledge as causal factors in feeling and action, and in the different ways in which they appraised events.

When I wrote *Psychological Stress and the Coping Process* in 1966, it was still necessary to argue against theories of emotion and thought that were based on drive-centered conditioning and to make a strong empirical case that individualized cognitive appraisal affects emotional response and the ways an organism copes with stress. I tried to do that with subjects by showing them films of distressing events. Some of these films were accompanied by narration that enabled the subjects to intellectualize the disaster and thus distance themselves from it. Others were accompanied by narration that encouraged denial of the threat. Those who heard these narrations—during the film or even before it—exhibited less stress than those who did not.

We can now unabashedly argue, as I did somewhat defensively against the mainstream in 1966, that the intensity and quality of an emotion result from the ways in which people construe or appraise what is happening to them on the basis of its effect on their well-being. Each kind of emotion and its intensity reflects a person's distinctive way of interpreting his or her plight. That view now permeates the social sciences, although, as might be expected, by no means all psychologists accept it. Some, like Neal Miller, continue to hold on to the earlier model of emotion as learned drive. People like Robert Zajonc and Silvan Tomkins disagree in other fundamental ways, suggesting that emotion can arise before cognition, and that each is served by a separate neural system.

Though one might wax enthusiastic about the changes since the early 1960s, there are some real dangers, too. If we regard the behaviorist constraints of the past half-century as an unproductive, temporary aberration, then the advocates of the newer approach must move smartly beyond where we are now, lest we vanish, too.

The older dogmas about dependable knowledge and how to obtain it were formulated with a well-intentioned concern about preserving scientific dependability, though, sad to say, they were modeled on a conception of the physical sciences that was already out of date. The weakening of our old standards of scientific evidence could be a double-edged sword. Along with creating new flexibility of thought and expanded strategies of research, it could also encourage acceptance of ideas that lack empirical support or practical value, resulting in a kind of chaos of knowledge in which everything is taken seriously and one cannot tell what is valid or important. I would like to believe that we are actually on the way to substantial progress and that the new emphasis on cognitive factors in emotion and adaptation will lead to theoretically valuable and practical insight and understanding.

Richard S. Lazarus, professor of psychology at the University of California, Berkeley, has made major contributions to an understanding of stress, health, and the coping process.

ULRIC NEISSER

The enterprise that I identified as *Cognitive Psychology* in a 1967 book was a rather modest affair, but it has come a long way in the last 15 years. Beginning with the study of perception, memory, and thinking, it now covers a spectrum from "cognitive science" on one side to "cognitive therapy" on the other. It has become a rival to psychoanalytically based psychology and to behaviorism—a third way of looking at human nature. Indeed, the fact that it takes ideas and information at face value gives it a certain advantage over its competitors, which often emerge as self-contradictory. If all ideas are wish-fulfillment, then psychoanalytic ideas just express the wishes of the psychoanalyst. If every belief just results from conditioning and reinforcement, so does the behaviorist's belief that this is the case.

Cognitive psychology, in contrast, conceives of men and women as seekers after information, who can discover truth, though they are not immune to error. It tries to understand how knowledge is possible: how we obtain information, order it, and use it; what we perceive and how we conceive of it. To the extent that it succeeds, cognitive psychology may at least establish a conception of human nature that is not self-contradictory. It can maintain that theories of cognition come into existence in much the same way as other beliefs do, more or less justified by evidence. Ideas need not be either rationalizations or conditioned responses; rather, they can be rationally responsive to existing facts.

Moreover, all versions of cognitive psychology agree, at least implicitly, that people *choose* much of what they know: The choices are made in many ways: through selective attention, the application of cognitive strategies, the acquisition of cognitive skills. But human beings are not just the playthings of blind instinct or the slaves of repeated reinforcement. They can see, learn, and understand. We have always known this about ourselves, but no other approach to psychology has legitimized that knowledge and tried to deepen it.

There are several approaches to cognitive psychology. My own begins with cognition as it occurs naturally. The psychologist James J. Gibson was the first to insist on an ecological approach, beginning with a description of the information on which perception depends. That description is most complete for the act of seeing.

In almost every environment—in every illuminated room, for example—there is a structured pattern of light. Gibson called this immediately available structure the *optic array*. It is determined by the layout of objects in the room and the events that take place there. The array may have a sequential as well as a spatial structure; a perceiver who moves through it can pick up additional information from the resulting optical transformations.

I want to stress the central roles that movement and exploration play in making the information in the optic array available. Emphasis on the perceiver's own activity is one of the characteristics of the ecological approach, distinguishing it from other cognitive theories as well as from noncognitive forms of psychology. In the ecological approach, it is not necessary to think of people as if they were looking through peepholes, confined to boxes, responding to stimuli, or blinded by their instincts. A more accurate image of humanity is that of the active organism, learning more about its environment and itself as it explores.

People are born with the ability to pick up information this way. Psychologist Eleanor Gibson and her associates have recently shown that a 3-month-old can tell whether an object is rigid or flexible by how it looks when it moves. In another important experiment, psychologist Elizabeth Spelke has demonstrated that when two films are shown side by side, babies will look at one rather than the other if they hear its soundtrack. For example, an infant who sees a film of blocks being banged together and hears the corresponding sounds will detect some kind of sameness in what he hears and what he sees. That common structure, both visible and audible, specifies some real characteristic of the perceived event and guides his further visual explorations. In ordinary life, picking up this kind of information allows all of us to know our environments in increasing accuracy and detail.

Perception involves more than the pickup of currently available information. There is always an element of anticipation, of readiness for what will appear next. Infants' skills of perceiving develop smoothly into skills of expecting and imagining. Imagining, thinking, and remembering free us from the immediate environment. We pay for that freedom with the possibility of error—we may imagine things that are not true and remember things that never happened—but we gain the ability to explore remote possibilities and consider novel alternatives.

Perceiving and imagining, like all other activities, involve choice. There is generally more to see than we can look at and more to hear than we can listen to. Perceptual choice has been much studied by cognitive psychologists, who call it "selective attention." While we are looking at one event, we see very little of others, even if they are equally present to the eye. We are largely responsible for what we come to know.

Perceiving and imagining are not the only cognitive skills. *Language* is especially important for our conception of human nature because language is uniquely our own. This point has sometimes been disputed, but recent research has put it beyond doubt. There have been several concerted attempts to bestow sign language on apes, for example, and they have essentially failed. Full records are not available, but the published reports of these studies present no convincing demonstration of anything beyond what other animals can be trained to do: make isolated responses to isolated stimuli, or produce repetitive behavior in the hope of a food reward.

The failure of these intensive efforts is even more impressive when it is contrasted with the naturalness and spontaneity of human language. Children all over the world learn an amazing variety of languages, all at about the same age and all without formal instruction. People everywhere use language for artistic as well as utilitarian purposes, in both social and nonsocial ways. We tell each other the truth, or lies, or nothing; there is as much choice in speaking as in perceiving. We cannot avoid those choices any more than we can avoid language itself—because we are human.

Not all cognitive psychologists would agree with the account of human nature I have presented. Many reject the ecological approach, preferring to begin with the metaphor of a computational device: They take their task to be the study of human information-processing procedures, much as one might study a program that happened to be running on a particularly complicated computer. It is an important approach, and one that has made substantial advances in the last few years. Whether those advances will continue remains to be seen; the notion of information-processing may be reaching the limits of its usefulness. In any case it is easy to see one major disadvantage of the computer metaphor: It leads to a particularly unattractive conception of human nature. Machines have no passions and make no commitments. They are not even well suited to empirical explorations; no one has adequately simulated ordinary visual perception on a digital computer. Machines do not grow. We all act like machines on occasion, but it is nothing to be proud of.

Cognitive psychology is still far from complete. So far it has said too little about humanly significant issues, and dealt too much in positives. It has more to say about truth than error and more about reason than delusion, but error and delusion are not in short supply. Many theorists complain that cognitive psychology has too little to say about affect, and they are right. An adequate conception of human nature will have to go beyond what cognitive psychology can offer, at least today. But whatever the next step may be, we must continue to think of ourselves as psychologically equipped to discover the truth. Otherwise, we are not likely to find it.

Ulric Neisser is Susan Linn Sage Professor of Psychology at Cornell. He is highly respected for his books *Cognitive Psychology* (1967) and *Cognition and Reality* (1976), as well as for his experimental studies of visual search and selective attention.

B.F. SKINNER

I am not particularly well informed about recent progress in psychology as a whole and can speak only about my own field with any degree of confidence. In that field I am inclined to rank the progress in basic laboratory analysis first. With the aid of miniaturized controlling equipment and computers, behavior is now observed and measured with increasing precision in operant laboratories throughout the world. Repertories of behavior are being studied that have a much greater breadth and complexity. It is still a hallmark of the operant-conditioning method, which illuminates the ways that behavior is shaped by contingencies and reinforcements in the environment, that the results may be formulated in centimeters, grams, and seconds rather than in the nonphysical dimensions of mental life.

These advances have greatly increased the extent to which the terms and principles drawn from an experimental analysis can be used in interpreting behavior in the world at large. This use of interpretation has not been well analyzed by scientific methodologists, and it has been widely misunderstood by critics of the operant field. Astronomy offers an example. Astronomers can rarely predict and can never control the events they talk about, yet they have made extraordinary progress in describing the history and current state of the universe. They have done so because they can use principles discovered in the modern physics laboratory. Behavior in the world at large is certainly complex and hence confusing, but it is far more accessible to scientists and scholars than is the world of the astronomer, and it is being better understood because of the increasing precision of principles drawn from an experimental analysis.

Among the processes that have been submitted to more careful analysis and interpretation are many that have been attributed to higher mental processes—such as concept formation, creativity, and decision-making. A number of these are being clarified as an operant analysis of verbal behavior is better understood. Some behavior is contingency-shaped, that is, it has been selected by reinforcing consequences in the past. That can scarcely be true of behavior that occurs for the first time, but an operant analysis also covers imitating the behavior of, or following the advice of, another person whose behavior has been selected by its consequences. This distinction between rule-directed and contingency-shaped behavior is only one example of a new approach to the analysis of so-called cognitive processes.

One advantage in relating behavior directly to environmental conditions is that one can then move directly to technological control. An experimental analysis points to the conditions that must be changed to bring about changes in behavior for practical purposes. The public is aware of this as behavior modification, a term that has been widely misunderstood because it has been associated with brain surgery, brain stimulation, or Pavlovian conditioning using shock or vomit-inducing drugs. These rather dramatic measures have tended to attract attention, but the proper application of a behavioral analysis using positive reinforcement has been well demonstrated. Achievements in the classroom, work space, personal and family counseling, institutions for the psychotic and retarded, ethical and intellectual self-management, and many other fields are only preliminary to greater achievements ahead.

Interest in the experimental analysis of behavior and its use in interpretation and practical control has spread rapidly throughout the world during the last 15 years. Associations have been organized and annual conferences held in the United States, Latin America, Europe, Israel, Japan, and elsewhere. The Association for Behavior Analysis, an international organization, attracts new members each year and its programs show an increasing scope.

Philosophers, political scientists, economists, and others who once dismissed behaviorism as rat psychology are now seriously considering its implications. The journal *Behaviorism*, with its large international board of editors, now in its 10th year, has become an important forum.

I myself am most concerned with the possible relevance of a behavioral analysis to the problems of the world today. We are threatened by the unrestrained growth of the population, the exhaustion of resources, the pollution of the environment, and the specter of a nuclear holocaust. We have the physical and biological technology needed to solve most of those problems, but we do not seem to be able to put it to use. That is a problem in human behavior, and it is one to which an experimental analysis may offer a solution. Structuralism in the behavioral sciences has always been weak on the side of motivation. It does not explain why knowledge is acquired or put to use; hence it has little to tell us about the conditions under which the human species will make the changes needed for its survival. If there is a solution to that problem, I believe that it will be found in the kind of understanding to which an experimental analysis of human behavior points.

B. F. Skinner, the dean of American behaviorists, is professor emeritus of psychology at Harvard. He is currently at work on the third volume of his autobiography.

STANLEY MILGRAM

The appearance of *Psychology Today* in 1967 was itself part of an important trend: the spread of psychology beyond purely academic and professional boundaries into the wider culture. Of course, this was not entirely a new phenomenon. Techniques like hypnosis and psychoanalysis had enjoyed a vogue in previous years. But a magazine devoted to the popular dissemination of psychological thought and research had never previously taken hold in American life.

I was, incidentally, an intrepid contributor to the charter issue, reporting my work on the so-called small-world problem: In those studies, I would pick two people at random out of the American population and examine how many links were needed to forge a chain of acquaintances between them. Nowadays we might refer to such a chain as a "network," which, in addition to its scientific interest, is supposed to help people get jobs and otherwise propel them upward in the social world.

Among the more enduring achievements in psychology since that time are some of the recent developments in brain research, and specifically the discovery in the mid-70s of endorphins, the morphinelike substances manufactured in the brain that act as painkillers. Their discovery helped to explain some previously mysterious aspects of human experience—for example, why certain people inflicted with serious bodily injury have been able to carry on, apparently oblivious to pain. How clever of the body to dispense its own anodynes, and how clever of researchers to decipher their chemistry, note their kinship with addicting narcotics, and probe deeply into the means by which such substances lock onto specific receptor sites in the brain.

Why do I, a social psychologist, celebrate a biochemical discovery? It is in recognition of the essential unity within psychology—the understanding that all psychological events rest on a biological substrate, and that frequently our most durable solutions to psychological problems occur at this level. Every advance in our understanding of how the two hemispheres of the brain work, every new insight into how the nervous system propagates its spiky signals, and every new technique for mapping brain metabolism during thought processes—and we've learned a lot about all of these things in recent years—can be counted as an achievement for psychology as a whole.

Not that the biological side of psychology is the only area that has moved ahead. Behavior therapies are now widely available to relieve phobias, inhibitions, and destructive habits. Operant-conditioning techniques, first developed by Skinner with rats and pigeons, have recently been used with great success in teaching retarded children skills that were formerly beyond their reach. If biology regulates behavior, the reverse has also been shown to be true, as psychologists teach people to relax and to adopt less stressful ways of life, which would reduce the risk of heart disease.

In experimental social psychology, various forms of cognitive exploration have dominated the field, but I prefer those experiments that illuminate dilemmas of the human condition. For example, Bibb Latané and John Darley's 1970 book, *The Unresponsive Bystander*, deals with a fundamental question: "Should I involve myself in other peoples' troubles or remain aloof?" The investigators showed that it is not just a general "morality" that determines whether a person will help someone in trouble, but that the exact details of the situation significantly shape their responses.

Philip Zimbardo's 1973 report on his simulated prison was another eye-opener, demonstrating that when ordinary people are arbitrarily assigned the role of "prisoner" or "guard," they quickly fall into the patterns that those roles imply, displaying some of the harshness and cunning we sometimes ascribe to personality rather than to social roles. And my 1974 book, *Obedience to Authority*, reported on how readily people will succumb to authority, even when they are instructed to act harshly against an innocent victim. Each of these studies demonstrated how powerfully we are affected by social forces even while believing in our independence of them.

Finally, psychologists have learned to do something that has eluded human beings since prehistory—namely, communicate better with animals. By teaching primates elements of sign language, thus bypassing their inadequate vocal apparatus, we've equipped animals with a larger vocabulary than they have ever possessed, and gained new insights into animal cognition. Not bad, after all these years of mutual incomprehension.

We have been looking back. Now let us briefly

change direction and speculate about the future. Two achievements of modern science, though they lie outside psychology, have made their presence felt in psychology in recent years, and are likely to exert even greater influence in the next 10 years. The first of these is the computer. So powerful, pervasive, and compelling is this tool that psychology will be hard put to avoid its seductive, metaphorical impact. Theory and experiment will be increasingly colored by the information-processing idea, and indeed, recent broad shifts toward cognitive psychology and cognitive social psychology already reflect this ensnaring influence.

A second major achievement of 20th-century science, the decoding of DNA (and the growth of molecular biology), has also begun to create an intellectual field of force from which psychology will not easily escape. We have already seen a reinvigorated genetic viewpoint in the emerging field of sociobiology. Its attempt to elucidate the genetic basis of altruistic behavior is but one salvo in a theoretical battle that lies ahead.

Stanley Milgram is Distinguished Professor of Psychology at the Graduate Center of the City University of New York. Best known for his research on obedience to authority, he is currently studying the psychology of urban life.

NEAL MILLER

Two of the most significant developments with which I am familiar have occurred at psychology's expanding frontiers, where it merges with other disciplines. One of these is an enormous increase in our knowledge of the complexity and functions of the brain. The other is the development of behavioral medicine, which is the study of the role of behavioral factors in physical illness and the use of behavioral methods in preserving health and treating disease.

Studying how the brain functions greatly increases our respect for what is involved in different kinds of behavior that we all take for granted; for example, the ability to recognize a friend's face at different distances and in different positions from the exact center of our visual field. Such recognition occurs in spite of the fact that each change in position means the stimulation of a different array of rods and cones on our retinas. It would be impossible to program even the most powerful computers to recognize such changes.

In the last decade and a half, brain researchers have discovered many entirely new kinds of connections between nerve cells, many new types of neurotransmitters (the chemical messengers that cross the minute gaps between nerve-cell endings), and many other new phenomena. On the one hand, this complexity is dismaying; on the other, it enables the brain to perform the incredible functions that we know it must perform in order to account for behavior.

There is space to mention only a few fragments of the entire brain story. The examples are selected from a much larger number of discoveries that are especially relevant to behavioral medicine.

Psychologists and other students of behavior have discovered that there are certain pathways in the brain that, when stimulated, inhibit an animal's responses to conditions that otherwise would be painful. Pharmacologists and neurochemists have found that these are the regions of the brain in which painkilling drugs such as morphine bind to receptors that control the activity of certain nerve cells there. These findings have led to the discovery of endorphins, substances naturally found in the brain that bind to these same receptors. We are beginning to learn how the brain controls pain.

We are also continuing to learn about the many specific ways in which the brain, via the nerves and the hormones that it controls, can affect the health of the body. For example, researchers have found that cells in the immune system have receptors for a variety of hormones that are controlled by the brain. Some of these hormones—cortisone, for example—are released under emotional stress and are known to depress functions of the immune system and to increase susceptibility to infections and implanted tumors. But these medically important effects are complex; they merit much further investigation.

There has been a concurrent surge of development in behavioral medicine. One reason is the discovery of brain mechanisms, like the cortisone effect, through which psychological factors may influence health. Work on other such mechanisms—on how strong fear can cause a patient with a damaged heart to die suddenly, for example—is also making rapid strides.

Another notable development is the growth of evidence showing the dangerous effects of certain conditions that might loosely be described as stressful—social disorganization, membership in groups with conflicting mores, or sudden changes in the conditions of life produced by migration or by the loss of a job or a spouse.

For example, more than 20 studies have shown that people in certain primitive tribes, who live under simple, stable conditions with many social supports, have low blood pressure, which does not increase with age. When some of these same people move to the cities, they have much higher blood pressure, which, as in the average person in Western industrial society, does increase with age.

Similarly, lab experiments have shown that when mice that have not previously lived together are placed in a colony designed so that they have constant confrontations with one another while seeking food, this exposure to chronic stress causes them to develop progressively higher blood pressure; they die early deaths from heart attacks, kidney trouble, or strokes.

Such lab research provides a scientific foundation for a variety of behavioral treatments—psychotherapy, assertiveness training, meditation, and relaxation training with or without biofeedback, which uses measuring instruments to guide the therapist and help the patient know how well he is succeeding in relaxing various muscles.

Behavior therapists have found that a significant number of patients who continue to have physical complaints for which no organic basis can be found are actually being rewarded for the types of behavior that cause them to be considered sick. Discovering the conditions that are rewarding the symptoms and changing the environment so that healthier, independent behavior is rewarded has produced dramatic cures. Biofeedback has also proved useful in helping patients suffering from neuromuscular disorders, such as those produced by accidents or strokes, to learn better control of their hands and feet.

The Surgeon General's 1979 report on *Health Promotion and Disease Prevention* points out that with the conquest of infectious diseases, many of the remaining health problems in this country have strong behavioral components. To quote: "Perhaps as much as half of U.S. mortality in 1976 was due to unhealthy behavior or life styles; 20 percent to environmental factors; 20 percent to human biological factors; and only 10 percent to inadequacies in health care." This report concludes that some of the greatest opportunities for future improvements in health lie in the area of health-promoting and disease-preventing behavior. Already, various psychological approaches—such as "immunizing" youths against peer pressure to start smoking, and community projects to reduce the risk of cardiovascular disease—are making modest but cost-effective progress. The problems are difficult, but I expect further research in these areas to continue to produce significant improvement.

Neal E. Miller, whose research led to the development of biofeedback techniques, is professor emeritus and head of a laboratory of physiological psychology at Rockefeller University in New York City.

DONALD O. HEBB

Our view of the unconscious, and the special creative powers it is supposed to possess, may be profoundly changed by Ernest Hilgard's discovery of what he calls a hidden observer in hypnotized subjects. At the very least, that eminent psychologist's finding is important to us because it brings hypnosis closer to everyday experience.

Hypnosis has persistently lacked satisfactory explanation, even in comparison with other psychological processes, like learning, that are not yet fully accounted for. I think that because of this, it has remained very much a special topic, separate from the rest of psychology and regarded with suspicion and distrust. Why, for example, has so little use been made of its anesthetic possibilities in medicine and dentistry?

Hilgard's work in the 1970s showing that part of the hypnotized person's mind is fully aware of what is happening to him—but remains a passive observer unless called upon to comment—brings hypnosis close to those common situations in which one attends to two things and engages in two activities at once. An obvious example is driving a car and arguing politics at the same time, but there are others: listening to oneself while telling a story to see that one is being clear, or scanning the faces of the audience as one tells a joke, to make out whether it is going over well. There are experienced secretaries who can carry on a conversation while continuing to produce accurate typewritten copy at normal speed, and Ulric Neisser and his colleagues at Cornell have shown (in experiments with subjects who learn to write from dictation while reading other material at a normal rate) that this sort of double activity can be developed with practice.

The circumstances of Hilgard's discovery of a doubled train of thought in hypnosis were suitably dramatic. He was giving a classroom demonstration of hypnosis using an experienced subject who, as it happened, was blind. Hilgard induced deafness, telling him that he would be able to hear when a hand was put on his shoulder. Cut off from what was going on around him, he became bored and began to think of other things. Hilgard showed the class how unresponsive he was to noise or speech, but then the question arose as to whether he was as unresponsive as he seemed. In a quiet voice Hilgard asked the subject whether, though he was hypnotically deaf, there might be "some part of him" that could hear; if so, would he raise a forefinger? To the surprise of everyone—including the hypnotized subject—the finger rose.

At this, the subject wanted to know what was going on. Hilgard put a hand on his shoulder so he could hear, promised to explain later, but in the meantime asked the subject what he remembered. What he remembered was that everything had become still, that he was bored and had begun thinking about a problem in statistics. Then he felt his forefinger rise, and he wanted to know why.

Hilgard then asked for a report from "that part of you that listened to me before and made your finger rise," while instructing the hypnotized subject that he would not be able to hear what he himself said. It turned out that this second part of the subject's awareness had heard all that went on and was able to report it. Hilgard found a suitable metaphor to describe this detached witness—the hidden observer. Further investigation found that about half of a group of highly hypnotizable and experienced subjects had hidden observers when hypnotized, though none had been aware of the fact until then.

If the subject had no access to the hidden observer and did not know of his (or her, or its) activity, was this an unconscious or part of an unconscious? No, for Hilgard tells us that it was fully conscious. This fact may be related to the current notion that what is creative about art or science originates in the unconscious. The idea apparently began with a lecture by the eminent French mathematician Henri Poincaré, who described how on several occasions his unconscious mind had come up with an important discovery. Having struggled with a problem for days and gotten nowhere with it, he had set it aside. Later, when he was thinking of something else, he suddenly found that he was conscious of the answer. A bit of a surprise! Jacques Hadamard, also a French mathematician, takes the matter further. Good mathematical ideas are beautiful, Hadamard says, so the unconscious, to be creative, must have an eye for beauty, more so than the conscious mind. Similar notions about creativity are widespread, especially in literary circles.

But this particular case for an esthetically gifted unconscious rests on a very flimsy foundation. All that Poincaré really knew, all he could have sworn to in a court of law, is that he had no recollection of consciously working out a solution to his problem. As we have seen, the double stream of thought is not foreign to ordinary experience, and in the richly creative mind of a Poincaré there may be a greater than ordinary separation of a second stream, nondominant like Hilgard's hidden observer and unrecallable until the right questions cue the answer.

The first importance of Hilgard's research, in my mind, is the link that it makes between hypnosis and the rest of experimental psychology, but fundamentally the fact is that he has cast a new light on the functioning of the human mind.

Donald O. Hebb, widely known for contributions to the fields of learning, perception, and neuropsychology, retired from the faculty of McGill University in Montreal a few years ago and now lives in Nova Scotia.

BERNICE NEUGARTEN

The last several years have been a period of extraordinary growth and vitality for developmental psychology. One of the major achievements has been a transformation of perspective. We have come to understand that our domain is the entire life span, from conception to death.

This extended view has come about for various reasons. One is the so-called demographic imperative. The changing age distribution of the population, with its increasing proportions of middle-aged and older people, has forced psychologists, just as it is now forcing investigators in other disciplines, to rethink our theories and models. One example with important implications is the new debate among biomedical investigators: As more people live into their 80s and 90s, will there inevitably be a longer period of decline? Or will most people stay healthy until about 85, and then, like the one-hoss shay, suddenly begin to break down and not live much beyond that age?

Another reason for the new perspective is that gerontologists have moved from studying old age itself to studying the processes of aging. Because it is clear enough that aging does not begin at 60, they have begun looking into middle age. A few have gone back much further than that. On the logical grounds that aging begins at the moment of conception, they are suggesting that development and aging should be thought of as similar, perhaps synonymous, terms.

Still another reason is that the psychologists who have been following the development of children have found their research moving up into adulthood. As they do so, they are re-examining the question: Is it really true that the child is father to the man? The problem is that as the segments of time under observation are lengthened, we find that we can make fewer predictions about people's lives. As a result, the question becomes: Are the differences between childhood and adulthood so great that discontinuity should become the more compelling interpretation? In either case, there has been a great new interest in adult development, seized upon eagerly by the textbook writers and by the public.

Developmental psychologists are already committed to the view that change is continuous throughout life. Changes are multiple, and they are multidirectional. Some are incremental over the span of life, like the ability to generalize from experience; others are decremental, like the physical endurance that waxes and wanes. Development occurs in infancy; it occurs also in old age.

Human behavior is malleable. Infants learn; old people learn. We all learn best what we are motivated to learn. We all seek ways of exercising our competencies as long as we live.

Aging (or development) is social as well as biological destiny. From our earliest days of life, we are active, exploring creatures who influence our social environments. As we move from childhood through adulthood, we select and interpret our experiences. Our own decisions and commitments become major determinants of change. Chance events and luck are important, but to a significant degree, we create our lives.

Because all this is so, we become more different from one another as we grow older. Especially in the second half of life, age becomes a poor indication of a person's condition or behavior.

As teachers and advocates, we developmental psychologists need to push our views of the life span as vigorously as possible—in the school system, in the mass media, and at our own dinner tables. We will be doing the right thing for older people, but especially for children, if we help everybody see the complexities, the challenges, and the opportunities that come with long life.

Bernice L. Neugarten is one of the country's leading authorities on adult development and aging. She is now a professor of education and sociology at Northwestern University.

DAVID McCLELLAND

We've learned a great deal from studying people's need for power. The improved method of measuring the power motive developed by David Winter in the early 1970s turned out to explain many interesting things about behavior, from why some men make successful managers to why others are susceptible to various illnesses.

Winter's method assesses power motivation from the stories that subjects make up to describe a series of ambiguous pictures. The stories can be scored to assess qualities associated with more or less need for power, with more or less inhibition or self-control, and with more or less need for affiliation. The power motives of both men and women can be measured with Winter's technique, but since few female executives have been studied so far, the findings on leadership are valid only for men (and I will therefore use the male pronoun throughout).

Men who score high in the need for power, low in the need for affiliation, and high in inhibition and self-control fall into a motivational profile that we have called the Leadership Motive Syndrome. Navy officers with this profile were judged more often than their peers to be outstanding leaders. Young managers who displayed it when they entered AT&T were more likely to have been promoted to higher levels of management in the company after 16 years.

Men with the Leadership Motive Syndrome also proved more apt to get sick, particularly if they were under stress. They acted in many ways like the men with Type-A behavior as described by Murray Friedman and Ray Rosenman in their influential book *Type-A Behavior and Your Heart*. They were hard-driving, impatient, always sitting on the edge of their chairs, so to speak, and constantly ready to erupt into anger if blocked, although normally such outbursts were kept under control. Friedman and Rosenman collected evidence suggesting that Type-A men were in a state of chronic sympathetic nervous-system arousal, in which the production of emergency-related hormones like adrenaline and cortisol is increased, with potentially damaging effects in the long run on the cardiovascular system. So if the Leadership Motive Syndrome produced Type-A behavior, it could be associated with chronic sympathetic activation and thus with illness.

That turned out to be the case. In a study that followed college graduates for some years, the investigators found that men who had high scores on the Leadership Motive profile at about age 31 were much more likely to have high blood pressure 20 years later than men who did not have high scores on the profile. The explanation seemed to be the same as that which Friedman and Rosenman had given: The inhibited Power Motive profile, if combined with the stress of a high-level occupation, can lead to chronic sympathetic activation, which in the long run damages the mechanisms controlling blood pressure.

These studies further suggested that the stress hormones released by chronic sympathetic activation might damage the immune system and make people more susceptible to disease. To date, seven different studies have investigated this possibility, and all support, in one aspect or another, the following chain of events: Men with the Leadership Motive Syndrome show signs of increased sympathetic activation, as indicated particularly by increased adrenaline in their urine; the adrenaline released into the blood is associated with lowered immune function, as indicated by weaker concentrations of immunoglobulin A in saliva, which, in turn, is associated with more reports of severe illness in the prior year, particularly from upper respiratory infections against which immunoglobulin A in saliva is the body's first line of defense.

This chain of events is even more likely to occur if the man reports being under power stress—for example, from losing his job, failing an examination, or fighting with his parents. (Again, most of the research has been done on men, and preliminary evidence suggests that the relationship may not be the same for women, perhaps because of differences in the pattern of hormone release.) This line of research opens up the new field of psychoimmunology, which deals with psychological factors that may influence the immune system and threaten health.

People who are higher in the need for affiliation than in the need for power, and who are low in inhibition, resist the effects of stress and remain healthier. That conclusion links this line of research to two other important developments in psychology in the last 10 to 15 years—namely, research on maturity and meditation.

The way the power motive expresses itself depends on a person's level of ego development or maturity, which can be assessed with a coding system worked out by Abigail Stewart to measure the stages of development first proposed by Freud and expanded by Erik Erikson. Thus, people high in power drive who are also very competitive have reached the third of four stages in Erikson's terms; if this tendency is inhibited, they are more likely to get sick when under stress. But there is a higher level of maturity (Stage Four), characterized by mutuality or generativity, in which the person loses his primary focus on self and turns to serving others, as when parents put their child's interest above their own. This suggests that one way to avoid the stress and illness associated with a strong power drive is to grow up, to turn the power drive into helping others.

It also suggests that the results of meditation research should be relevant here. Early research, summarized in Herbert Benson's *The Relaxation Response*, suggested that meditation reduces anxiety; more important in terms of the theory just outlined, it quiets the symptoms of the fight-or-flight response from activation of the sympathetic nervous system.

Furthermore, other studies have shown that when male prisoners are trained in meditation, they not only become more motivated to achieve intimacy (a variety of affiliation, measured by a somewhat different scoring method) but also score higher on maturity. So now the bits and pieces of evidence begin to make a very interesting picture. Meditation may increase maturity, encouraging a concern for others and lessening the need for self-assertion. Maturity, love, and detachment reduce sympathetic activation and its potentially bad effects on one's health.

The path of progress is often as erratic in psychology as in other fields. Certainly psychologists who have been working for many years on measures of maturity and on the need for power had no idea that their work would link up with independent research on the effects of meditation. Yet today, these different lines of investigation have come together to give us a much better understanding of the underlying processes governing disease and health.

David C. McClelland, professor of psychology at Harvard, is a leading investigator of psychological motives, maturity, and occupational competence.

ROLLO MAY

One of the most remarkable phenomena in our culture in the last few decades has been the tremendous growth of both the profession of psychology and the public's interest in it. This can be explained, I think, by the absence of guideposts; by what people seem to perceive as the loss of rules for living their lives.

The symbols and myths that our culture was based upon and that gave it a structure of meaning, which in turn yielded values by which people could live, have disintegrated. (I use "myth" not at all to mean falsehood, but to refer to a lasting truth rather than the changing truths of empirical science.) One of the main symbolic myths that had guided Western culture and served as a guidepost for individuals was rationalism, the belief that we could arrive at a satisfactory way of life simply by thinking enough about it and by acting on our conclusions. But by the time of Freud it was clear that our decisions were more the result of our feelings and our unconscious urges than our reason. Hence tremendous numbers of people, floundering without direction, flocked to psychologists on legitimate and illegitimate quests for guidance in how to live, or, failing that, at least some help in existing while bereft of the spiritual aids that had once sustained them.

The outstanding development in the last 15 years seems to me to come directly out of this changed view of how we operate. It is what I call the populist trend in psychology. The signs of that trend are everywhere. Today, many people can at a moment's notice name a dozen different forms of psychotherapy, from orthodox Freudianism to the more radical Primal Scream. On radio stations across the country, psychologists purporting to have answers for every kind of personal problem attract large followings. Even at cocktail parties, one may hear talk of how the right hemisphere of the brain functions differently from the left hemisphere, a discovery that won a Nobel Prize last year for Roger Sperry of the California Institute of Technology.

The profession itself has grown apace. In 1918 there were 367 members of the American Psychological Association. In 1981, there were more than 52,000.

On the other hand, the more familiar that psychology has become, the more its magical aura has faded. A case in point is the growing criticism of IQ testing. A related example was Ralph Nader's attack on the college entrance exams at the national convention of the American Psychological Association four years ago. Nader charged that the psychologists who direct the Educational Testing Service had arrogated to themselves life-and-death decisions affecting the future of multitudes of young people, that the ETS tests were inaccurate, and that many who took them developed inferiority complexes as a result. The president of ETS denied the charges, but his arguments could not change the fact that the authority of the examinations had been undermined.

Another aspect of this populism is the new awareness of psychological influences on disease. John Thompson, director of psychological services and professor of psychology at Oberlin College, recently summed up this change of perspective: "Over the past 20 years we have gone from a place of seeing very few physical disorders as having psychological components as causative factors in their development, to the point where perhaps the majority of what we have seen as physical disorders [now] may have important psychological 'causations.' "

Psychology has even moved into matters that used to be left to poetry. Psychologist James Lynch, in a 1977 book entitled *The Broken Heart*, cites statistics showing that unmarried, widowed, and divorced men are two or three times as likely as married men to suffer from cardiovascular disease. Hearts really can be broken! Along the same lines, Harry Harlow's famous studies with monkeys at the University of Wisconsin powerfully suggest that without tenderness—a central element in love—humans may be susceptible to neurosis, too.

As I said, I believe that the underlying reason for the vast popularity of psychology is that it is all we have left for coping; from the myth of an afterlife to the more modern beliefs in the virtues of family and state, the myths and symbols that once drained off anxiety, assuaged guilt feelings, comforted people, and gave them strength to face the problems of life have lost their vitality. It follows that the only real cure for the psychological problems that ail us is to develop new forms of our historic symbols and myths.

Whether psychology can do more in the interim than patch people up, I do not know. It seems clear, though, that only from art, literature, the humanities, and religion, all of which presumably embody the wisdom of the culture, can we expect a rebirth of cultural myths and symbols. It also seems clear to me that the great ages in history—such as the sixth and fifth centuries B.C. in Greece, the 12th century in the Middle Ages, and the beginnings of the modern period, the 16th and 17th centuries—were not periods in which psychological concerns were dominant, but rather were ages of philosophy and religion.

The development of new myths and symbols would make psychotherapy in all its forms less necessary. People would then seek and experience education rather than re-education, learning rather than therapy.

Rollo May, the father of existential psychotherapy in the United States, edited the major work in the field, *Existence: A New Dimension in Psychiatry and Psychology*. The author of *The Meaning of Anxiety, Love and Will,* and the recent *Freedom and Destiny* now lives in California, where he teaches, writes, and continues to practice psychotherapy.

PHILIP G. ZIMBARDO

I want to suggest some things that psychologists ought to be doing over the *next* 15 years. The most important thing they can do, it seems to me, is to keep in mind that psychology is a study of people by people, and that it should be *for* people. As researchers get caught up in the excitement of discovering new truths about human nature, "people problems" become less compelling than do abstract paradigms and processes.

Years ago a teacher of mine at Yale, A. R. (Bob) Cohen, conveyed to me the shortsightedness of this attitude. One day, while I was analyzing data for an article that had just been accepted by *Science*, Bob inquired about the reason for my high spirits. When I started to tell him about the effects of caffeine and chlorpromazine on the sexual behavior of the adult male rat, he suddenly interrupted me. He asked me to tell him what was going on across the street, outside the medical-school dorm. "Nothing," I said. "Just some people standing around talking." He pressed me to speculate on what they might be talking about. I ventured that the woman was upset by something the man had told her and that she was being comforted by the other woman. Bob asked me about possible reasons for her distress, about how she was being consoled, and so forth. Then he hit below the belt: "Suppose *you* knew how to comfort her. Then you could help her, and, while figuring out how people hurt and help each other, you might discover that ordinary people are more fascinating than your well-bred white rats."

Before I could defend the value to science of studying basic processes in simple creatures, Bob had a parting shot: "Think it over. See if you can't find a little time to study people and accept the challenge of finding new solutions for the everyday problems of the human condition." I did, and I am still trying to. (I learned later that Bob was suffering from a terminal case of Hodgkin's disease, which ended his career and life all too soon.)

To be more responsive to the needs of people, psychology does not have to give up its efforts to understand basic human phenomena. Kurt Lewin reminded us that there is nothing so practical as a good theory. So, too, there is nothing so relevant to the solution of human problems as a basic understanding of human nature.

But psychologists must be willing to translate that abstract knowledge into a concrete, mundane form that the average consumer of psychology can understand. Moreover, some researchers will have to adopt the role of advocate for social and personal change. They will have to go beyond the data to recommend plans of action. Like all interventions that may alter the ways people behave, those plans will have to be subject to formal evaluations of their effectiveness.

In addition to mining existing knowledge, psychologists will also have to address new, emerging areas of concern. What follows is a shopping list for the 80s—some of my thoughts on what psychologists need to study more fully and on what they now know enough about to be able to prescribe action:

1. The electronics revolution will transform our work and our schools, our patterns of leisure and home life, and our sense of self-efficacy more than any technological innovations in history. We need to anticipate some of these changes, monitor them, alter structures to accommodate positive influences, and discover ways to minimize their dangers. For example, the video games that are proving so addictive to young people may not only be socially isolating but may actually encourage violence between people. The games could be easily reprogrammed to promote cooperative play among several players, to focus on rescue operations, say, instead of destruction. The instant feedback for fine motor movements that such electronic games provide is a powerful reinforcer that is transforming youngsters whom teachers describe as unmotivated or distractable into highly motivated, totally focused game players. It should be possible to use this game structure to enhance a student's skill at creative problem-solving, productive decision-making, and the ability to analyze complex patterns of information. (I worry, however, that middle-class youngsters will increase their educational lead over lower-class children when affluent parents begin to raise their children with microcomputers in the nursery.)

2. Cognitive psychologists know enough already to make a substantial contribution to educational curricula. On the basis of much solid research, children could be taught strategies for more effective studying, for improving memory, for avoiding pitfalls in problem-solving, for making less biased inferences and more accurate predictions. School texts could be better designed to improve story comprehension and the ability to generalize across domains of knowledge and different settings.

3. In moving away from the limited, cost-ineffective, one-on-one model of traditional psychotherapy, many clinicians and health psychologists have been advocating community mental-health programs that emphasize preventive treatment and health maintenance. I foresee greater use of cable television in the next 10 years to give large numbers of people access to expert therapists, social-skills trainers, and other professionals willing to undertake the responsibility of "therapy for the masses."

4. Social psychologists have discovered some important truths about human vulnerability to social pressures. These truths need to be translated into a form usable by the public. First, we have learned that people underestimate the subtle yet pervasive power of situational and social forces operating on them (such as social roles and rules, and pressures to conform, to be a "team player"). Second, they overestimate their power to resist external pressures, to take "one little step" without being drawn into taking the final big step that may be alien to their natures or best interests.

Third, bright and good people have been casually seduced into voluntarily agreeing to suffer, to harm others, or to engage in foolish acts. They do so initially because they are coerced by a legitimate authority that they were not prepared to challenge, or because they are insensitive to other situational forces that are operating. Once converted, however, they come to believe that they have freely chosen their foolish or evil cause, and they are ready to proselytize for it. To offset the power of such decisions requires training not only in awareness of subtle authority control tactics but, more profoundly, training in the willingness to admit our mistakes and reverse our decisions.

Fourth, when people feel anonymous, depersonalized, or dehumanized, they can turn into monsters. We must do something about any circumstances in which a person can say, "No one knows who I am or cares to know," for anyone in such a predicament can turn into a vandal, an assassin, or a terrorist.

5. Developmental psychologists have made us aware of the importance of early attachments to infants and young children. But somehow, scant attention has been paid to how we may encourage meaningful attachments in adults. Surveys tell us that we are a nation of lonely people, unable to make lasting commitments to one another and no longer loyal to our employers or their products. Cult recruiters tell us that thousands of our children and neighbors would rather spend their lives as beggars for an alien cause than as aliens in a society of beggars. The time is now for beginning to learn what kind of candy the strangers are using to lure our young people away. It might turn out to be an old-fashioned variety filled with love, pride in work, and a sense of place and spiritual purpose.

Now that cognitive psychology has taken the head once lopped off by radical behaviorism and returned it to the body of psychology, we might in the next 10 years consider implanting a heart or a little soul in the same body. When that takes place, it may be easier to know what psychologists can offer to people and how they can do so, because then *they* will be *us*.

Philip G. Zimbardo is best known for developing methods of treating shyness and for his laboratory and field research on the influence of social situations on behavior. He is a professor of psychology at Stanford University.

THE FREEDOM TO CHANGE

CAROL TAVRIS

Carol Tavris, Ph.D., is a social psychologist who writes frequently on adult development and social change. She is co-author of The Longest War—Sex Differences in Perspective.

Some years ago a friend of mine, a confirmed believer in astrology, offered to draw up my horoscope. A life chart, no less. I gave him my date of birth, down to the hour and minute: 9:15 a.m. He went away and called me two days later. "Something's wrong here," he said. "Are you sure it was 9:15? Please check it out." Amused but determined to do this thing right, I asked my mother to look at my birth certificate. Sure enough, I was born at 9:45 a.m. I told my friend, who said, "Aha" and went back to work.

The next day he showed up with my horoscope, explaining that it would apply retroactively as well as predictively. "For example," he said, "I see that a close family member died when you were three and a half. You have my sympathy." "Actually," I said, "three was a very good year. In fact, I *acquired* a close family member, a half-brother who came to live with us." He fussed with his chart. "Oh, I see the mistake. You were eight years old when the death occurred, yes?" "No," I said, "but my father died when I was eleven." "Of course, of course," he said without missing a beat. "It's as clear as day, right here."

My friend's every effort to be precise about events in my life was way off the mark. He did not conclude that astrology was wrong. He concluded that my birth certificate was wrong.

Now the irony is that many people who are not fooled by astrology for one minute subject themselves to therapy for years, where the same errors of logic and interpretation often occur. Psychoanalysis, like many other kinds of therapy, begins with the belief that every present problem has its origins in the early conflicts of life and that the bedrock of one's personality is set by the age of 5. The only way to solve a problem, therefore, is to dig back to bedrock. The cause of your neurosis may be conscious—a family story you remember—or it may be buried in the unconscious, where it must be rooted out, like crabgrass, with free-association techniques, hypnosis, or other devices for emotional catharsis. Astrologists think we are determined at birth (or even conception) by our stars; psychoanalysts think we are determined within a few years of birth by our parents (and our anatomy).

But when an analyst cannot find the childhood cause of your troubles—or, more likely, when knowledge of that supposed cause doesn't do much to fix up your life now—chances are that neither of you will conclude that the premises of the therapy are faulty. The fault, you will probably decide, lies in you. You must be blocking or hostile or neurotically defensive.

It took sixty years for the Freudian revolution to filter down into everyday language and practice, and just when everybody got the hang of it, it turns out to be as old-fashioned as a Model T. This is the impish nature of scientific discovery, of course. Today, many of the psychological assumptions held by professionals and laymen are coming unraveled. An onslaught of new research challenges the belief that personality is formed forever in the first years of life and that those years are crucial to a person's later development, mental health, and happiness. Not even belief: *conviction* is more like it. And on that conviction we have built schools of therapy, philosophies of child-rearing, and notions about the (im)possibility of adult change. Now the post-Freudian revolution is upon us, and what we thought was bedrock has turned into shifting sands.

Everyone likes to play the childhood game, whether for

ktail-party chitchat or therapeutic enlightenment. It s fun and, we believe, useful to try to pinpoint the critical ages and specific events that caused us to become what we think we are. No matter that another person who undergoes the same events turns out differently. No matter that memory is as unreliable as a politician's promise. No matter that most of us comfortably ignore or forget the episodes that do not suit our self-images. The belief prevails that the road from infancy to adulthood is a straight line, and we all have cherished landmarks. The latest studies show, however, that the line is neither straight nor continuous—a dotted curve is more like it.

The links between childhood and adulthood have been forged by two methods: retrospective accounts and longitudinal studies. Both approaches, on closer inspection, have serious flaws. In fact, it seems to me that the belief in the persistence of personality has survived in spite of the evidence, not because of it. The child, it turns out, is but distant cousin to the man.

LOOKING BACKWARD

There you are, talking to your favorite therapist, astrologer, or next-door neighbor, trying to find a reason for your recent bout with the blahs. You are unhappy about your work and your family, and you feel disoriented. So you and your confessor rummage around in your history until you find a plausible explanation for your gloom. Memories of your childhood well up: bits of conversation, dozy afternoons, embarrassing gaffes that you quickly consign back to oblivion, family scenes, patterns of your past come into focus, only to resettle, like a kaleidoscope, as other remembrances come to mind. But you are still unhappy.

"It's because you're a Virgo," says the astrologer, "and Virgos can't handle chaos."

"It's because you're an obsessive-compulsive," says the therapist, "and you can't handle change."

"It's because you married Sidney," says the neighbor, "and Sidney is an old boot."

Any of these efforts to reconstruct the cause of one's present circumstances by recourse to past events is subject to three barriers. Let's call them the mirages of memory, the cause-and-effect fallacy, and the egocentrism of case studies.

1. *The mirages of memory.* You think you're the only one who has dwindling savings in your memory bank? You worry that you can't remember the name of the movie you saw last night, much less the name of your high school sweetheart in 1946? Well, memory researchers now confirm the worst for all of us: Memory is, in a word, lousy. It is a traitor at worst, a mischief-maker at best. It gives us vivid recollections of events that could never have happened, and it obscures critical details of events that did.

Psychologists Elizabeth and Geoffrey Loftus have been studying memory for years, showing how erratic and unreliable even eyewitness testimony can be. They started with the popular assumption, held by most psychologists and laymen alike, that memory works like a video recorder, that is, that everything we learn is stored permanently somewhere in the brain. Oh, we may misfile some items (this view runs), forget some details, repress some sensational stuff, but eventually it can all be retrieved with judicious digging. "Lost" memories can certainly be recovered with the help of hypnosis, or brain stimulation, or the clever sleuthing of psychotherapy.

The Loftuses carefully sifted through all the evidence for these assertions, including published anecdotes of miraculous recall through hypnosis and clinical accounts of horrifying childhood events dredged up in free association. Such revelations are fodder for newspapers, movies, and pulp paperbacks ("Hypnotized mother of four remembers face of children's assailant!"). But these reports, the Loftuses concluded, usually are not memories of actual past events at all. Most of them turn out to be "constructions created at the time of report," they say, "that bear little or no resemblance to past experience."

Under hypnosis, people do babble on about their fourth birthday party, naming all the participants and the flavor of the cake, but the simple fact is that most of these "recollections" are made up. They are part family history (all those stories your mother told you about that party), part inference (if Susie was there, her brother Jimmy must have been there too), and part pure imagination. Hypnotized people do not remember any more or any more accurately than people in a normal waking state do, although the trance makes them more willing to report information—that is, to play the part of a good hypnotized subject.

"People can flat-out lie under hypnosis," according to a report in the *American Bar Association Journal*, "and the examiner is no better equipped to detect the hypnotic lie than any other kind. Even more serious, a willing hypnotic subject is more pliable than he normally would be, more anxious to please his questioner. Knowing even a few details of an event, often supplied in early contacts with police, may provide the subject with enough basis to create a highly detailed 'memory' of what transpired, whether he was there or not." I read newspaper accounts of criminal mysteries more carefully now, and in addition to sensational newsbreaks about successful hypnosis, I notice the many times hypnosis fails to discover the killer.

As with hypnosis, so with therapy. Perhaps more so, because the individual is motivated not only to please the therapist with the "proper" dreams and memories, but also to find the supposed childhood cause of his problems. Unfortunately, efforts to retrieve "repressed" memories aren't much more accurate than hypnosis. The Loftuses find that people who think they are remembering an event from childhood may be making up plausible scenarios—not actual experiences, they say, but "fanciful guesses, fantasies, or plain confabulations." One psychologist, Ulric Neisser, who reviewed the available studies that have tried to verify the accuracy of patients' memories, concluded flatly that most of their recollections were inaccurate.

We ought to know this, of course. Three friends who go to a party will have three different interpretations of what happened there and who said what to whom; why should we think that three family members would be any more likely to agree on a version of an event that happened 25 years ago? And whose memory would be "right"? The impermanence of memory, the Loftuses believe, should give pause to all who hope to find the truth about a past event. *What questionnaires and therapies measure is not your real past but your present beliefs about your past.*

Now, no psychologist, not even the Loftuses, would argue that *all* memory is illusion. Many memories are vivid and accurate, and they are the table of contents of our lives. But even these can cause us to fall victim to the second barrier to accurate retrospection:

2. *The cause-and-effect fallacy* is the mistaken logic that confuses sequence with causality. Any of us, looking backward over our lives, can array the events of our pasts to make them seem causal and continuous. If I went to graduate school and did not get married, then it feels to me that I did not get married *because* I went to graduate school. Just because B comes after A, however, does not mean that A caused B. Both A and B may have been caused by Q. A and B may be unrelated events. What if I had not gone to graduate school? Can I be so sure I would have married?

But everyone is inclined to string past events together, like beads, to make a pattern. Freud himself recognized the logical dangers in this tendency:

"So long as we trace the development from its final stage backwards," he wrote in "The Psychogenesis of a Case of Homosexuality in a Woman," "the connection appears continuous, and we feel we have gained an insight which is completely satisfactory or even exhaustive. But if we proceed the reverse way, if we start from the premises inferred from the analysis and try to follow these up to the final result, then we no longer get the impression of an inevitable sequence of events . . . . We notice at once that there might have been another result, and that we might have been just as well able to understand and explain the latter."

In other words, psychoanalysis cannot *predict* how a child will turn out, said Freud, because some qualities would prove "so weak as to become suppressed by others . . . . we never know beforehand which of the determining factors will prove the weaker or the stronger. We only say at the end that those which succeeded must have been the stronger." Indeed! But this cannot be a scientific explanation, because there is no way to disprove an *ex post facto* analysis.

As a result, any six therapists who rely on childhood experiences to explain your current problems are apt to come up with six different versions. Depending on their school of thought, they will arrange the beads on your life string differently. Some will choose only the bright red beads (say, your sexual history) and others only the yellow ones (say, your feelings about your parents). Finally, you mutually agree on a design. But it is not the only design possible.

3. *The egocentric case study method* is, for many people, the highest court of judgment: If it happened to *me* (or to my patient) this way, that's how it must be for everyone else. If I feel my life has been consistent from childhood to adulthood, if I feel that my childhood traumas made me what I am—and am not—today, well, who can argue with me? No one. But neither may I conclude that my childhood traumas would affect anyone else the same way. Nor can I ever know whether I would have turned out the same had my childhood been different. The case study cannot answer questions about consistency because none of us can be our own control group.

Many therapists commit the egocentric fallacy by generalizing from the experiences of one client to all individuals. They rarely draw on the appropriate comparisons: people who are not in therapy and who may or may not have the same histories and complaints as patients have.

For example, consider a man who comes to a psychoanalyst, complaining about impotence. The analyst may conclude, after numerous sessions, that the man's mother was overprotective and smothering, and that his impotence is "really" a sign of anger towards his mother, if not towards women in general. (Usually the analyst decides this without ever having seen or spoken to the mother, so he doesn't know her actual behavior, only the son's perception of it. Based on his memories.)

What's the analyst's error? Before he can deduce that overprotective mothers produce impotent sons, he must know the answers to three other questions: How many men who are impotent do *not* have overprotective mothers? How many men who are not impotent have overprotective mothers? And how many men who are not impotent do not have overprotective mothers? (To these, I would add another: What the hell is "overprotective"?)

To get around some of the problems in the case-study and clinical approach, large-scale surveys gather data on many people. I've looked at a batch of these surveys by now and have conducted a few of my own. The subjects they cover are highly disparate—for example, marriage, masculinity and femininity, money, sex, work, happiness—and yet their efforts to find the childhood experiences that are reliably related to adult attitudes and experiences typically have failed.

For instance, Susan Sadd and I prepared a questionnaire on money for *Ms.* magazine. We put in a stack of items to see what influences a woman's financial knowledge, spending habits, and economic values. Naturally, we thought that what the women learned as children would be important. So we asked what, if anything, their parents had taught them about money; whether they had had to work for money as children; whether the Depression had influenced them, or their parents; whether their parents were sexist, teaching their sons but not their daughters about money; and many more.

None of them made any difference. We got zilch. This means that for every two women who now spend money like water, for example, one had frugal parents and one's were spendthrifts. For every two women who now manage money carefully, one learned about high finance on daddy's knee, and one never gave money a moment's thought until she was divorced at age 53.

Now the interesting thing was that the women themselves believed that their childhood training accounted for their adult habits. One woman wrote, "In my puritanical home, there were two large taboos—sex and *money*! I now know why, even though I was a math major at Harvard, I have such difficulty understanding money and financial matters." In fact, though, it might not have made much difference if her parents *had* taught her about wills, bills, and budgets. You know what influences the spending habits of adult women today? Current income, feeling of control over money, level of education, extent of debts, and how they get on with their husbands.

Well, you may say, that makes sense with something like money. But what about psychological qualities, such as happiness? Surely a good childhood makes for happy adults? Surely a miserable childhood makes for miserable adults? On this premise, basic to so many kinds of therapy practiced today, clients cheerfully try to dredge up excuses for their misery (often on the line of "my mother did this" or "my father didn't do that"). But in survey after survey, researchers so far have found very few childhood factors that predict whether or not a person will be a happy adult.

In one such questionnaire, Jonathan Freedman and Phillip Shaver found that the only thing that childhood unhappiness was related to was other childhood problems, such as illness or frequent moves from city to city. What makes adults happy? Being in love, having a good income, enjoying their work—and not being in therapy.

Adult personality, in short, is overwhelmingly the result of adult experience. Change is as much the rule as consistency. I am not saying that people are like jellyfish, soft and squishy under the foot of life's adventures, or that parents make no difference at all. A few dimensions of personality do seem to be characteristic of a person throughout life—such as level of energy, sociability, mannerisms, habits, creativity. But many aspects of a child's personality—behavior, interests, values, self-esteem, temperament—can be mitigated and even completely overturned in adolescence and adulthood. Sometimes by choice, and sometimes by happenstance.

LOOKING AHEAD

It looks as if the only way to prove that personality persists into adulthood is to nab some kids when they are little, wait around as long as your patience and your grant last, and then try to catch them all again when they have grown up. Nowadays, this is not easy. People have acquired a disconcerting habit of changing their names, jobs, houses, and spouses. That, of course, is precisely the point. When people used to sit tight in the same place for 45 years, you could come around every decade or so and draw conclusions about the consistency of personality. Now you come around and find that Grandma Ida has opened a boutique in Poughkeepsie, Cousin Charlie has resigned the vice-presidency and repaired to a dairy farm, Sister Millie ran off with her secretary, and the only one minding the fort is Uncle Manny, who left home at the age of 8 and finally wants to settle down.

Most researchers have not concluded from these events that there is something wrong with their belief in the permanance of personality. They have concluded that there is something wrong with their questionnaires.

One psychologist who *has* changed his mind about the possibility of adult change is Orville G. Brim, Jr., of the Foundation for Child Development in New York. Most of Brim's career has been devoted to charting the course of child development and its relation to adult personality; recently he has become increasingly convinced that, far from being programmed permanently by the age of 5, people are virtually reprogrammable throughout life. "Hundreds and hundreds of studies now document the fact of personality change in adulthood," he says. "People change their looks, their attitudes, their pleasures, their reactions, their relationships, their feelings about themselves. We have more evidence of these changes than we know what to do with. We've got self-reports, objective observations, longitudinal studies, clinical protocols. Social scientists are unable to predict adult personality from childhood or even from adolescence in any important way. We can't blame the methods anymore, and we can't say that people who don't fit the predictions are deviant, unhealthy, or strange. They are the norm."

Across the country, other social scientists are coming to the same conclusion. Like Brim, Jerome Kagan of Harvard has made a 180-degree turn in his ideas of child development. For most of his academic career, he shared the conventional wisdom about the importance of the first few years of life to adult development and intellect. Why not? His own classic book in the field, *Birth to Maturity: A Study in Psychological Development* (written in 1962 with Howard Moss), was one of the few longitudinal studies that managed to track the actual courses of people's lives. And those lives seemed perfectly consistent. Rowdy little boys grew into aggressive teenagers and thence into competitive executives. Passive little girls grew into dependent little wives.

But that was in 1962, before competitive executives were going to Esalen to liberate their "humanity," and before dependent little wives were joining the work force in unprecedented droves. And it was before Kagan set off for San Marcos La Laguna, an isolated, painfully poor farming village in Guatemala, where he expected to demonstrate the persistent effects of deprived childhoods.

Infants in San Marcos are treated badly enough to send the average American parent into Spock shock. Babies spend their first year confined to a small dark hut. They have no mobiles over their cribs. No one babbles to them or cuddles them. They have no teddy bears. They get little food and less love. They suffer from respiratory and intestinal problems much of the year.

Compared to American babies, the Guatemalan infants are retarded at the end of this dreadful twelve months—in speech, in memory, in symbolic play. By the age of 2, San Marcos children leave the hut and wander freely; at 5, they are playing with other children; at 8 or 9, they have adult responsibilities of working in the fields, cooking, or watching over their siblings. By the age of 10, they are still inferior to American middle-class children in memory, reasoning and perception, but by adolescence the gap has nearly closed.

Kagan discovered, to his amazement, that the majority of San Marcos teenagers, although severely deprived as infants, could solve difficult intellectual problems, approaching the level of children who had grown up in enriched environments. The gap in scores, he felt, was as likely to come from the Guatemalans' cultural isolation and poor schooling as from their early years of deprivation and illness.

Curious about the dramatic and unexpected results of this research, Kagan took a second look at *Birth to Maturity.* He and Moss, he recalls, "could find little relation between psychological qualities during the first three years of life—fearfulness, irritability, or activity—*and any aspect of behavior in adulthood*" (italics mine). Kagan now believes that few of a baby's attributes last indefinitely, unless the environment perpetuates them. "The fears and joys of the first year seem to be part of nature's script for development," he concludes, "not harbingers of adolescent anxiety or prophetic signs of childhood happiness."

This was a remarkable and courageous statement for a man who had spent so many years trying to demonstrate precisely the opposite view. The San Marcos study and Kagan's intellectual about-face are matters of enormous controversy among child psychologists, as you might imagine, especially since child psychologists, make their livings and reputations on the fundamental belief that the child is the father to the man (and, nowadays, mother to the woman). But most of their research is based on a snapshot of children's behavior, taken at one specific point in time, and then perhaps compared with another snapshot taken six months or a year later. Few academics have been able to check up on their infant objects of study when the infants grew up to adulthood.

Researchers, like most parents, have concentrated so much on what they assume to be the normal pattern—roughly, that healthy kids come from good homes and disturbed kids from bad homes—that they have overlooked the other possibilities: the disturbed kids that come from good homes and the terrific kids that survive bad ones. "We think, here's this awful home; here are these awful parents; here's this awful upbringing, and, we expect, here is the awful result," psychiatrist E. James Anthony told Maya Pines in *Psychology Today.* "But, instead, here's a really remarkable child—contrary to one's predictions, to everything one might think possible."

Anthony and other researchers are now tracking the progress of children who somehow manage to survive, indeed transcend, poverty, racism, illness, bad schools, and parents who are schizophrenic, alcoholic, cruel, or abusive. Across the diagonal from these success stories are their unhappy counterparts: children of kind, loving, affluent parents who turn out to be hostile, depressed (some, tragically, suicidal), apathetic, or rejecting. As many parents have learned from experience, the connection between what they do and how the kids end up is all too often unpredictable.

One thing that creates this unpredictability is the mysterious aura of one's generation—its economics, opportunities, outlook. A scientist who can gloomily testify to the power of the generation is Jack Block, whose book *Lives Through Time* reports the results of a massive longitudinal study. The research followed several hundred children in Berkeley and Oakland, California, from 1929-1931 to their junior and high school days in the 1940s, to adulthood in the 1960s. Block pummeled his data every which way he could to show a continuity from childhood to adulthood, and finally squeezed out a few weak, half-hearted patterns. He aimed for an elephant and captured a mouse.

Even the mouse nearly escaped. Block bravely acknowledged at the end of his hard work that the generation he and his colleagues had followed so industriously might be one of a kind, and that the few consistencies they turned up might be peculiar to that cohort. Observing that this generation seemed to differ so remarkably from their children—especially, he thought, in matters of morality, impulse, and conscience—Block speculated that longitudinal studies may be valid only for the people interviewed, that they describe "a time or circumstance that will never recur."

Children growing up today will face the same complicated events that have made you as complicated as you are, that have made you change over the years, and that have made you different from your parents: such as the person you married (or didn't), the job you took, the place you live, the friends you have, and the shared experience of your generation. The teenagers who came of age in the 1930s or 1950s are different in outlook from those who came of age in the late 1960s, just as people who are now 50 are different from those who were 50 twenty years ago. Cohort effects can supersede the "best" parental efforts.

The thing is, people often love generational differences when they compare themselves to their parents. ("Hah! I escaped the tentacles of that stingy old coot!") and worry about them when they think of their children ("What did I do wrong?"). Whenever I tell a friend about the studies that fail to find a connection between the child's and the adult's personality, the first reaction typically is: "You mean I was good to that brat for nothing? You mean I could really have let her have it?" and the second is: "You mean it's not *my* fault that he became a dope-smoking hairball and lives in a tent in Tucson, Arizona?" The answers seem to be no, it's still not a good idea to bludgeon your child, and yes, it probably isn't your fault that Freddy is following someone else's footsteps.

"I think people ought to be nice to children," says Brim, "because you get nice kids as a result and because it is morally right to give kids as good a childhood as you can. But it's not worth knocking yourself out to try to make them perfect little adults—say, replicas of you. For better or worse, you can't take full responsibility for the adult your child becomes, for the same reason your parents can't take all the credit or blame for you."

The once-predictable lives of many adults have lately sprouted tangents, reversals, and, in Laurence Peter's felicitous phrase, lateral arabesques. The only problems occur when the self-concept of consistency clashes with the self-evident fact of change: when a person *wants* to change, but feels he or she cannot; or when a person does *not* want to change, but is required to by circumstances. Continuity reassures; complete metamorphosis, whether in fact or fable, is frightening, as Dr. Jekyll would testify.

Each of us, write Brim and Kagan in a new book on life-span development, has "a powerful drive to maintain the sense of one's identity, a sense of continuity that allays fears of changing too fast or of being changed against one's will by outside forces." At the same time, each of us strives to be something more than we are now: "From making simple new year's resolutions to undergoing transsexual operations," they note wryly, "everyone is trying to become something that he or she is not but hopes to be."

How, then, are these hopes achieved? Many of us know people who have been in intensive psychotherapy for years, with no apparent change in their neuroses and relationships. Insight, clearly, is not enough. Many therapeutic explanations fail because they are frozen at a level of blame—"I'm timid because my father roared at me every time I spoke up." "I hate myself because my mother was so critical and picky." "I'm aloof because I was never allowed to express my feelings." But blame, unless it is attached to a program of action, tends to rigidify the behavior in question, not alter it.

In order to change, a person has to abandon most of this who-struck-John, who's-to-blame, woe-to-my-childhood business and get on with it. The major benefit of the post-Freudian revolution, I suspect, will be to help people do just that. Adult growth is not in the genes, causing eruptions at ten-year intervals, nor in some fuzzy-headed 1960s notions of liberation of the self, but in the intricate circumstances of our lives. Timidity, aloofness, and self-esteem are a result of what we do, not of what we were.

Of course, not everyone welcomes change. Once the anchor of childhood is hoisted, one may float listlessly in the breeze, or set sail for new directions.

Why Aren't We Using Science to Change Behavior?

B. F. Skinner

B.F. Skinner is a professor emeritus of psychology at Harvard University and author of "Beyond Freedom and Dignity."

Things are happening today that seem completely senseless, irrational, insane. The population of many countries has been allowed to reach a point at which two or three bad harvests will mean death by starvation for tens or even hundreds of millions of people. The United States and Russia spend a staggering part of their incomes on military systems that everyone hopes will never be used and will therefore prove to be a total waste. Our supplies of energy and many critical materials are running out, but we have done little to curtail current or future use. The environment grows steadily less habitable.

With the technologies of physics and biology, the species has solved problems of fantastic difficulty. Yet with respect to its own behavior, something always seems to go wrong. It is easy to understand why people ask: "When shall we have the behavioral science and technology we need to solve our problems?"

I believe that that is the wrong question and that we should be asking: "Why do we not use the behavioral science we already have?"

Consider the position of an agricultural specialist visiting a developing country. He sees farmers planting varieties of grain that are not best suited to the soil, rainfall or climate or the most resistant to disease. He sees them using too little fertilizer, fertilizer of the wrong kind. They are cultivating and harvesting with primitive equipment and processing and storing food in wasteful ways. If they then ask him, "When shall we have the agricultural science we need to make better use of our land?" must he not reply, "Why are you not using the science which already exists?"

There could be many answers. Special seed, fertilizer, machinery and storage space are costly. If money is available, those who have it must be convinced that spending it will bring results. New methods often throw people out of work and take control out of the hands of those who have profited from the old.

But there is a special kind of explanation that is more important. We have all heard stories of Third World farmers who change to new methods while they are being demonstrated, only to change back as soon as the reformer leaves. The stories may be apocryphal but they are easy to believe, because people do persist in doing things as they have always done them. The entrenched ways often postpone or block any advance toward something better.

We have no reason to feel superior to those who reject improved methods of agriculture, for we are doing much the same thing with respect to behavioral science. The parallel with agriculture breaks down because I cannot point to any part of the world today in which a behavioral technology flourishes, but recent advances in a science of behavior have led to substantial achievements in the management of human behavior in such special fields as government, industry, schools and colleges, institutions for the care of psychotic and retarded people, and personal and family counseling. I shall not review this work, or try to indicate how extensive it is. I simply want to ask why it is not more widely accepted in the solution of our problems.

The main obstacle is the entrenchment of old practices—in this case, old ways of thinking about human behavior. It is not so much the complexity of human behavior that causes trouble as the traditional practice of looking for explanations inside the behaving person. People are said to act as they do because of their feelings, their states of mind, their intentions, purposes and plans. They act because they will to act.

Let us look at some examples in which this abiding concern for an inner explanation has diverted attention from environmental measures that might have brought us closer to solving our problems. A feeling or state of mind familiar to everyone is confidence. The term is useful in daily communication. As a behaviorist I do not blush to say that I am at this moment possessed of a number of different feelings of confidence, and I shall list a few in order of degree. I have complete confidence that this chair and desk will hold me as I write. I have a fair degree of confidence that the words I am writing will eventually reach readers. I have some confidence that a number of those who start reading will finish the paper, and just a touch of confidence that some of them will come to behave in a slightly different way because of what they read. I thus report certain conditions of my own body.

But I hasten to point out that the degree of my

From *Newsday,* April 16, 1978. Excerpted from BEYOND FREEDOM AND DIGNITY.

confidence is related to the extent of my past successes and failures. Similar desks and chairs have always held me. Similar writing has usually been published. But I am writing because of the consequences, not because of the feelings. My feelings and my behavior are collateral products of my personal history.

The point is important when the word is used in discussing practical affairs. The Journal of the Royal Society of Arts in London recently reported the remarks of a speaker who had discussed the appearance of the British countryside. He had told his audience that "the key to the survival of our present landscape lay in the word 'confidence'—without which people would not plant trees." In the past year or two, he said, "confidence had been completely destroyed."

But the important fact was simply that people no longer planted trees. Why did they not do so? It is not difficult to point to relevant facts. People move about a great deal these days, and when they do so they never watch a tree they have planted grow to maturity. As new roads are built and land is broken up for housing developments, trees are likely to be wantonly destroyed. More people now live in cities where the government plants the trees. Changes of this sort make it less likely that people will plant trees, and are, therefore, the real key to the survival of a landscape. There is no reason to say that they first destroy confidence in tree-planting; "confidence" is not a key to anything.

Several years ago, in a weekly news magazine, David E. Lilienthal discussed "the prevailing American mood," which he said "has become negative and fearful." It is "a mood of self-doubt and fear which paralyzes the very will to act," and, he added, it is the will to act that alone can "remove the causes of fear and lack of confidence." What America needed was more confidence, and Lilienthal offered the Tennessee Valley Authority as an example.

In the early 1930s the soil in the valley of the Tennessee River had lost its fertility, the forests had been almost destroyed, the land was eroding and nothing much could be done. People were idle and poor.

After the TVA dams were built, electric power and fertilizer were available and the people turned to new methods of agriculture and restored the land. Their incomes rose and the valley became green. Lilienthal attributed this highly desirable change to "restored self-confidence." But surely it was the dams and their products that made the difference. People began to do things they could not do before, and being successful, they no doubt felt confident.

When we speak of a nation's confidence in itself, the behavior at issue is much more complex than planting trees, and we are therefore much more likely to give confidence a power of its own. But if we are content to say that all America needs today is a new spirit of confidence, we shall neglect the things that can be done to bring about the changes we desire.

Feelings play a different and possibly more destructive role when they are seen not as causes that precede behavior but as values that follow it. Nutritious food is essential to the survival of the individual; is it not therefore extremely important that it taste good? Sexual behavior is essential to the survival of the species; is it not extremely important that sexual contact feel good?

But the important thing for the individual and for the species is not how things taste or feel but whether they are reinforcing—that is, whether they strengthen the behavior upon which they are contingent. Susceptibilities to reinforcement have presumably evolved because of their survival value. When, through a mutation, an organism's behavior is more strongly reinforced by nutritious food or sexual contact, the organism is more likely to get the food that it needs and to have offspring. The increased susceptibility to reinforcement is then contributed to the species. The important thing is that the susceptibility should survive. The feelings involved are incidental.

The same thing is true of social reinforcers, which are more likely to be called values. People are said to treat each other in ways that express compassion and love and which inspire gratitude, but the important thing is the contribution of this treatment to the way the culture functions. The kind of behavior we describe as ethical makes a group function more effectively. The feelings or states of mind associated with such behavior are collateral products.

Happiness is a feeling often taken as a value. We often feel happy when we behave in ways that lead to the possession of goods, and we then mistakenly take the possession to be the cause of the feeling.

Whole philosophies of government have been based on the theory that if goods are distributed "to each according to his need," people will be happy. But happiness is the accompaniment of successful action, rather than of whatever goods the action brings. It is characteristic of getting, rather than of possessing. Possession leads to happiness only when it makes further action possible. Whether people are happy is of great political significance, but a subjective measure of the quality of life will do little more than tell us whether most people are in situations that allow them to act successfully.

And so, in general, we enjoy life and call the world beautiful and ourselves free and happy when our behavior leads to an abundance of good things. No structural account of the things themselves or any analysis of the feelings that arise when these things strengthen behavior will make life more enjoyable and ourselves freer and happier. Only discovering the contingent relations between specific behavior and its consequences will help us move toward those goals.

Such a program does not rob people of their feelings. It simply puts feelings in their proper place, and by doing so allows us to move more rapidly toward the kind of environment in which they can be enjoyed. In refusing to accept feelings and states of mind as causes, we do not make the behavior that is said to follow from them any less important; instead we make it possible to deal with behavior more successfully.

There must be some reason why we have failed to make the same kinds of technological advances in the management of human behavior that are so obvious in other fields; the reason could be our lingering commitment to the individual as an initiating agent. When it comes to human behavior, seemingly trivial causes have profound effects, and there is a historical example which illustrates the point. I am not a historian, nor do I usually trust arguments based upon history, but in this instance the evidence is, I think, persuasive.

From the Fifth Century BC to about 1400 AD, China was as advanced in physical technology as any culture in the world. The recent exhibition of early Chinese pottery and ceramic and bronze sculptures sent around the world by the Chinese government displays an art and a technology fully equal to those of the Greeks of the same period. The two cultures maintained a comparable position for nearly 2,000 years. Then three great Chinese inventions—the compass, gunpowder and moveable type—brought about extraordinary changes. But not in China. Gunpowder was of little practical use in China because military activities there were ceremonial and largely under the control of astrologers. Long sea voyages were forbidden and the compass did little to increase the efficiency of coastal shipping. The Chinese system of notation, with its thousands of characters, could not take advantage of moveable type.

But the West seized upon these three great Chinese inventions and exploited them with extraordinary results. With the compass the West explored the world, and with gunpowder conquered it. Moveabe type and the printing press brought the revival of learning and the spread of western thought. As William McNeill points out in "The Rise of the West," while Chinese inventions were changing western culture, China remained a medieval society. Certain inoffensive cultural practices had deprived it of the benefit of its own discoveries.

Something of that same sort may be happening again. This time western culture may suffer from essentially ceremonial, astrological and geomantic practices. China, fortunately untouched by the Greek "discovery of the mind," could take over the behavioral equivalents of compass, gunpowder and moveable type and dominate a new era. But perhaps it is not too late to profit from our discovery of behavioral science and use it to help solve the problems facing the world now.

Shaping Behavior Contest for Minds

Joel Greenberg

At the center of the conflict is the very nature of man.

It's 1984, or sometime thereafter, and you're getting ready for work. You smile into the bathroom mirror and soothing strains of Brahms' "Eternal Love" fill the air. When the smiling stops, so does the music.

You greet your fellow workers with a cheerful "good morning," and they respond with warm handshakes and grins. Any other greeting, and they would ignore you.

Those are the rules.

The rest of the day, and month, and year, are governed by similar "rewards" and "non-rewards." Your behavior becomes nearly automatic. You are "happy."

That this type of society—or worse—will become a reality in America is a growing fear among a significant number of psychologists.

They are concerned about "behavior modification"—a form of therapy that has been highly successful in the 1970s in treating certain emotional illnesses and mental retardation.

Particularly in cases of severe retardation, autism, learning disabilities and toilet training, few argue with the effectiveness of the technique.

Rather, it is the use of behavior modification to control "healthy" populations in schools, businesses, towns and perhaps entire societies that is spurring nightmarish predictions.

Behaviorists who advance such far-reaching uses of control say the fears are unfounded. Applied properly, they say, behavioral techniques will mold a happier, more productive culture free of war and major conflict.

They note that industry and education have already begun to use behavior modification, and with encouraging results.

Their critics—mainly of the "humanistic," individualized school of psychology—remain far from convinced. Some predict nothing less than a "Clockwork Orange" society of automatons with no free will to act as they please.

At the center of the conflict is nothing less than the very nature of human beings.

Free will is not a factor, some behaviorists say, because people have practically none to begin with. Like an animal's search for food and shelter, man's search for happiness is almost totally dictated by the outside environment and events over which he has no control, they say.

Humanists counter that free will is the major factor that separates man from lesser forms of life. Behavior control is dangerous, they say, because it works, and could effectively stamp out man's humanness by robbing him of his free will.

"Behavior control does not involve a change in attitude or motivation—it's not much different from the way we train dogs and horses," says one critic.

The debate has become so heated and widespread that the entire question of behavior control and personal freedom was the theme of the recent annual meeting of the *American Psychological Association* in Washington, D.C.

Behavior modification is basically a system where rewards are administered to a person who behaves in a desired way. Undesired behavior results in no reward or some form of punishment.

Rewards can range from candy to money to subtle actions, such as friendship and certain privileges. Punishments may be simply the withholding of those things or in some cases, the administration of "aversive" techniques, such as electric shock.

Though behaviorism was founded by John B. Watson in 1912, it was not until the early 1970's that it became widely popularized by Harvard University psychologist B.F. Skinner.

Skinner, a spry, skinny 72-year-old man, astounded the psychological community with his book, "Beyond Freedom and Dignity." He proposed boldly that man has no free will and would be infinitely better off in a controlled society governed by a complex system of rewards and punishments for almost all aspects of behavior.

Since then, the therapeutic use of behavior modification has spread rapidly throughout the country. Along with it—though not necessarily a product of behavior modification—has been a boom in the use of psychoactive (behavior changing) drugs; and a partial resurgence of psycho surgery, an updated form of lobotomy.

Behavior modification is threatening to traditional psychotherapists because it ignores such long-held

From *The Miami Herald*, October 3, 1976. Reprinted by permission.

Freudian concepts as the subconscious and intellect. Instead, it focuses on comparatively mechanical means of changing a person's current actions to what the therapist thinks they should be.

Says Skinner, simply: "I don't believe feelings or states of mind are important."

Personally, Skinner—"Fred" to close acquaintances—projects an image far less threatening than the "Big Brother" portrait some have assigned him. He speaks softly, is quick to smile, and listens attentively to opposing arguments.

He talks soothingly of "designing a social environment in which people treat each other well, keep the population size within reasonable bounds, learn to work productively, preserve and enhance the beauty of the world and limit the use of energy and other resources."

Even Carl Rogers, Skinner's counterpart in the humanistic psychology movement, concedes that the two men "want the same things."

But their proposed means of achieving such long-sought human goals are so diametrically opposed that some humanists have called Skinner "the next Hitler."

Humanists believe that man has an infinite capacity to make choices and judgements on his own. Only by developing that capacity "within" the person—rather than by outside control—can man improve himself and create a better world, they say.

In contrast to behaviorism, humanism is practiced in relatively unstructured "encounter" sessions—sometimes painful meetings where people try to help uncover one another's inner feelings; or in various forms of introspection, where the individual confronts himself in isolation.

That philosophy has spawned a counter-behaviorism avalanche of "human potential" groups in this country over the past decade. Since the Esalen Institute in California kicked off the large-scale group encounter movement in the 1960s, hundreds of thousands of Americans have flocked to numerous personal growth programs in search of the road to nirvana.

There are now an estimated 8,000 ways to raise your consciousness in America. The methods have names like bioenergetics, est (Erhard Seminars Training), psychosynthesis, Silva Mind Control, Arica, and rolfing, along with meditation, yoga and many variations on the standard encounter technique.

All focus in one way or another on the individual's inner strength and power to develop it.

Rogers first began promoting personal growth methods in 1946 by organizing encounter groups where returning servicemen were encouraged to share their gut emotions.

"The human being is a trustworthy organism, and has vast abilities to improve himself if exposed to the right attitudinal climate," Rogers says. "The individual modifies his own behavior, rather than having someone else in control."

Therein lies the key to the controversy surrounding behavior modification: who will be chosen to manipulate the lives of others and decide what is "desirable" behavior, opponents ask. And what guarantee is there the controllers will not abuse such massive powers?

"I question whether an ordered, regulated life is the kind of life I want to live," says Carmi Harari, professor of psychology at Goddard College in Vermont and director of the Humanistic Psychology Center of New York. "No system of one person doing something to another leads to a very good end."

Skinner says that argument is academic, since we are already living in a highly controlled society, and one that is becoming more so every day.

Nearly everything we say and do, he suggests, results from a network of laws and controls imposed by government, businesses, school and social interaction with groups and individuals. Stopping at a red light, buying a certain brand of hot dogs, doing a homework assignment, showing up for work and even kissing your spouse or petting the dog are largely dictated by the conscious and unconscious rewards and punishments offered by each, according to Skinner. Such actions are not products of a person's free will, he says, because people are not free to choose.

National governments have historically chosen to direct societies through the use of legal punishments, or "aversive control," he says. Behaviorists should use their sophisticated techniques, Skinner says, to wrest such powers from the government and "return (to) the control of people by people."

Such a system would be based on positive rewards, rather than punishments such as imprisonment and monetary fines, he says. People would behave in order to gain something, rather than to avoid punishment for breaking a rule or law.

"I do not mean modification of behavior through the use of implanted electrodes or psychotropic drugs," assures Skinner. "I do not mean respondent conditioning with vomit-inducing drugs or electric shock."

Former APA President Kenneth B. Clark of the City University of New York created a national furor five years ago when he suggested using "peace pills" to control the destructive behavior of national leaders.

Clark, like Skinner, believes that the tools of power and control are much safer in the hands of behavioral scientists than in those of politicians.

"We must control the moral behavior and ethical perceptions of our national leaders," he said at this year's meeting, defending his previous stance.

"We need to control the human power drive, and we can control human abuses of power through science," Clark says. "The issue of behavior modification abuse is a danger we face now. The power and control of the human species is (already) in the hands of a very few people—for freedom to be meaningful, (that) species must survive."

How Psychology Can Shape the Behavior of People

Behavior modification is widely used in the treatment of emotionally disturbed, retarded or disruptive individuals. More recently, the technique has spread to "healthy" groups, such as industrial workers and school children, in an effort to increase productivity and learning.

The concept's roots were planted more than 70 years ago when Pavlov learned how to make dogs salivate on command. Several years later John B. Watson adopted the theory for human psychology.

Harvard psychologist B.F. Skinner created modern behaviorism when he learned that he could get almost any kind of behavior from a pigeon by rewarding and punishing properly.

Human application of behavior control has grown rapidly in the 1970s. Some of the ways that scientists mold human behavior include:

- Positive reinforcement—rewarding someone with kind actions or words or material goods if they act in the desired way. The technique is the basis for teaching retarded or chronically mentally ill persons to be more self-sufficient.
- Extinction—ignoring disruptive conduct, such as a student's annoying actions in class. At the same time, the teacher rewards another well-behaved student with a compliment.
- Contracting—negotiating an actual, written contract for behavior between husband and wife, employer and employe, patient and therapist or parent and child. Living up to the contract brings certain rewards, primarily an improved relationship between the parties concerned. Breaking the agreement may carry specific punishments.
- Token economy—reinforcing a person's desired behavior with tokens that entitle the person to certain privileges or monetary purchases. This is frequently used in mental hospital settings.
- Behavior rehearsal—enacting a scene of conflict between two people before it actually takes place. Rehearsing a "healthy" response can lead to a more healthy relationship, some scientists say.
- Desensitization—simulating a situation that may be frightening to an individual. This method is used primarily in treating persons suffering from fears and phobias, and may help them realize much of their distress is unfounded.
- Aversion therapy—punishing undesired behavior with electric shock, discomfort-inducing drugs or other means. The technique, severely criticized by many scientists, is used mainly in treating sex offenders, chronic drug addicts, and other persons with extreme personality problems.

Skinner says he too is against the method, but concedes there are some instances in which "nothing else works."

Along with the behavior modification boom has come the widespread use of psychoactive drugs to help people cope with the pressures of modern society; and, in some cases, the continued use of psychosurgery to alter the behavior of persons with "incurable" emotional handicaps.

Even those who might agree idealistically with Skinner and Clark say there is one fatal flaw in their vision of a utopian society: ultimately, some person or group must decide what is "desirable" for everyone else.

And that, they say, smacks of totalitarianism.

"The question is not what can we do, but what ought we do?" says Harari. "You either view people as innately good, or wild, antisocial beings that need control. The aim of control is to suppress the human spirit. Nazi Germany used the very techniques we are talking about."

He and others argue that no one, no matter how good his intentions, has the capacity or the right to decide what is best for other people.

Responds Skinner: "The implication is that a technology of behavior will naturally fall into the hands of despots. It will no doubt do so if no action is taken by those who are not despots. Behavioral scientists are no more likely to use their principles to control people than atomic scientists are to build and use atomic weapons."

The humanists advocate systems of far less control than exists now, where people have a wide range of choices based on what they want, not on a contrived reward.

In education, for example, Rogers advances a "person-centered approach" where students share more in deciding what is to be taught, and the teacher does "not hide behind the instructor's mask."

Harari agrees. "A kid who is ordered around all the time never makes intelligent choices."

Rogers says the experiments with this approach in the classroom and industry, as well as encounter groups, have yielded not only more humanistic relationships, but increased efficiency as well.

Behaviorists such as Nathan H. Azrin of Anna State Hospital in Illinois would disagree.

One of behavior modification's staunchest proponents, Azrin states flatly that the technique has "no competition" for effectiveness in areas such as classroom management, retardation, child discipline at home, obesity, fears and phobias and some marital problems.

Skinner is reluctant to talk about the exact mechanics of molding a happier society. But when pressed, he speculates like Rogers that at least initially the process could begin—and already has to an extent—in schools, offices and controlled communities such as he described in his book, "Walden II."

Some observers believe much of the behaviorism/humanism controversy is premature because neither side has found an effective technique to substantially alter the course of the human race.

"We're a long way from 1984, even though the years are getting pretty close," says Nicholas Hobbs, a Vanderbilt University psychology professor.

Hobbs, not opposed to behaviorism on ethical grounds, says he favors it, "everywhere it would work. But what upsets me are the extravagant statements that (behavior control) can engineer all kinds of happiness and social contentment."

Controlling the behavior of individuals is far more complex than many, including Skinner, would admit, Hobbs says. "In some cases, it's probably more effective to simply ask a youngster to do something than spend days trying to coax him with sugar cubes," he suggests.

He believes Skinner has admirable motives, but may be unrealistic when he talks of applying his techniques to 200 million people.

But even Hobbs says Skinner's visions of totally engineered societies "eventually may come to be possible."

And that possibility even now is frighteningly real to humanists and other critics of behavior control.

"Skinner has made a lot of contributions," says Harari. "And I'm not saying there is only one right way to do things—it simply doesn't exist. But if Skinner's engineered society ever came about, it would indeed be a Clockwork Orange situation. Make no mistake, we *can* train human beings to do almost anything. Behavior control can work, and with devastating effects.

Toward a Psychology of Natural Behavior

Robert Sommer

Social psychologist Robert Sommer is professor of psychology and environmental studies at the University of California at Davis.

Psychology entered the laboratory almost a century ago and has not yet recovered from the experience. Since the centenial of the first psychological laboratory founded by Wilhelm Wundt in 1879 is rapidly approaching, this seems a fitting time to examine the role played by this important and ubiquitous institution in the development of psychological research.

It has been only recently that the effects of laboratory settings have been made the subject of social psychological investigation. Researchers had operated in much the same way as the experimental psychologists who tested rats, mice and monkeys without ever knowing the effects of the cage environment upon the animals. The trend to the laboratory peaked some time in the 1960s. Although things seem to have improved, traces of the preoccupation with control and contrived encounters still remain.

Too many researchers look upon field research as laboratory studies done outdoors. Rather than leave the laboratory, these psychologists have either snail-like carried their laboratories with them or tried to turn the world into an experimental chamber with separable dependent and independent variables. No doubt those researchers who are dark-adapted and sallow from years spent in dim closets gazing through one-way mirrors will benefit from the fresh air and exercise, but there is more to field work than this. What is omitted or neglected is sensitivity to the setting. The credo of the naturalist is to study nature while disturbing it as little as possible since any deviation from natural conditions will lower the validity and generalizability of the results.

The term field can be applied to any setting which has not been deliberately created by the psychologist. Appropriate research techniques include observation, archival research using trace measures, surveys and experiments. These differ in their degree of reactivity, i.e., in the extent to which they affect on-going behavior. There are frequently good reasons for introducing a variable into a field setting on a systematic basis. The crucial question is whether the changes and the means of introduction are appropriate to the setting. If they are, generalization to life will be easier. Instead of spending weeks on the street corner waiting for an event to occur, such as a person stopping to ask for assistance, it is terribly tempting to stage it artificially. I will not deny the value of shortcuts when the terrain is well known. Common sense tells us that when an area is *terra incognita,* one should be wary of shortcuts. It is important to know not only people's reactions to someone asking for help, but how often this actually occurs, the sorts of people they approach and so on. Such information is indispensible in designing a field experiment and in generalizing from it. Ideally the sequence should *always* be non-reactive observation before interviews or experimentation.

If field research is not the same as doing laboratory studies outdoors, what is it? The answer can be seen in the work of those psychologists who have studied ongoing behavior in an environmental context, people such as Evelyn Hooker, who has been studying the gay community in Los Angeles for several decades; the Sherifs in their studies of teen-age gangs; and Stanley Milgram who has been doing research on sensory overload and alienation in the city. Milgram does not study overload in some abstract sense, but as it occurs in a particular neighborhood among a particular group of residents. When the process under study cannot be observed directly, questionnaires and interviews are indispensible.

Roger Barker and his associates have pioneered a strictly naturalistic approach to child psychology at their field station in Oskaloosa, Kansas. Barker's students subsequently applied his methods to churches, schools, public housing projects and most recently, Dew Line stations. When I reviewed a book of Barker's, I was struck by how few of his studies and those of his students had appeared in APA journals. This situation is not atypical of other field researchers. The ingenuity that is required for doing naturalistic research is also helpful in locating sympathetic outlets for publication.

Some years ago, I was interested in testing the social facilitation hypothesis that people in groups would drink faster and more than people alone. The method I used was straightforward and appropriate both to the hypothesis and the beer parlor. My students and I visited each of the pubs in a middle-sized city, ordered a beer, and then sat down and recorded on napkins or pieces of newspaper the consumption of lone and group drinkers. We found that group drinkers consumed more, not because they drank faster, but because they remained longer in the pub. The longer people remained, the more they drank.

It can be noted that time-in-the-setting is usually excluded from social facilitation studies done in the laboratory. People are tested alone and in groups for specified periods of time and their performance compared. The notion that people in groups would remain longer did not enter experiments on social facilitation because time-in-the-setting is not a typical laboratory variable. Under natural conditions, however, we vote with our feet in expressing our likes and our dislikes. The reviewer of my paper expressed concern that I had not controlled the two populations, and there might have been other differences (unspecified) between lone and group drinkers to influence these results.

Perhaps there were, I don't know. We sampled all 32 beer parlors in town and there were no obvious differences between the lone and group drinkers in age or dress. There was no way that we could control whether people who entered the premises sat alone or in groups. Maybe we could have undertaken random assignment in the basement of the psychology department if we had gotten everyone's permission and authority to do this from the state liquor commission and money to buy the beer, but I am not sure that the results would have been valid or generalizable to any other place. My colleague Rudy Kalin sponsored beer busts for fraternity students and found that their responses in their own living rooms were very different from those in the laboratory.

The important questions in assessing a naturalistic study are whether the researcher learns what went on and whether this knowledge is important to a psychological audience. The notion of control has little or no meaning in a naturalistic study. It can be imposed in some metaphorical sense while analyzing the data by breaking down observations into categories, but this bears so little resemblance to the behaviorist's use of control that it is better to dispense with the term.

One cannot learn how to do field research simply by reading about it. We must develop the means to provide supervised experiences in field observation and recording. This may involve the establishment of research stations in the community. If field stations can operate in Oskaloosa and the Gombe Reserve, why not in St. Louis and Cleveland?

Barker and his associates operated in a completely open relationship with the residents of Oskaloosa. They knew he was there to study them and they accepted it. In settings with transient populations, such as street corners or playgrounds, this may not be possible. Researchers must rely either on non-reactive observation such as sitting on a park bench and watching children play or participant observation where one has a role in the action. Psychologists may opt for participation observation since it provides the opportunity to be in a service capacity as well. It is a method ideally suited for the clinical student who must serve an internship at a mental health clinic. Field research will make much more sense to such students than the umpteenth correlation of the MMPI with the Rorschach.

At present, there are not many dissertation committees that would allow a purely observational study. Observation has been equated with anecdote, and is considered less rigorous and reliable than experimentation. This is partly true because psychologists receive no training and encouragement in observation and therefore most don't do it very well. In theory it shouldn't require training to become a naturalist, since it amounts to doing what comes naturally. However, following decades of formal schooling and discipline in classification and conceptual learning, a student's abilities to observe have largely atrophied. Students look at things and try to figure out what they are supposed to remember. Training in observation requires some bracketing of categorical thinking.

The ability to "read" environments is the basis of the naturalist's craft. One is able to examine a living room, classroom or street corner in terms of constraints this puts upon behavior, the kind of actions it facilitates, encourages, demands. There are lessons in the kind of furniture in a person's living room, how it is arranged, how it is cared for, the decorations, the location of the television set or stereo, and so on. One can also "read" a city park, prison or restaurant interior, in each case attending to somewhat different items. Experience in making observations and comparing different settings provides clues as to what is important. Frequently the omission of something (the absence of books in a living room, or the absence of wall decorations in a college classroom), is as significant as what is there.

Although one begins with seemingly mundane behaviors, rather quickly the questions become more complex and far reaching. Why aren't there green plants in a classroom? Should there be plants there? What is the role of decorations or amenities in motivation, interest or learning? Do people have a need at some level for plants? Is there likely to be vandalism and if so, how can it be minimized? How can living plants be maintained with a transient population?

It doesn't matter where one starts, the inquiring mind soon reaches questions of considerable relevance and depth. Not all of these may be regarded as psychological questions—some may be more adequately handled by sociologists, anthropologists, horticulturists or police. However, the relationship between people and living plants is of considerable ethological and psychological importance and it has hardly been touched as a research area. There are profound design implications in giving apartment dwellers, workers in high-rise office buildings or college students in dormitories, prisoners, and old people in convalescent homes access to garden plots or at least a window location for growing plants.

We will have to give students specific skills for handling the richness, complexity and flow of ongoing behavior—courses in content analysis, behavioral mapping, observational methods, archival measurement and photography. The camera is an indispensable tool for gathering naturalistic data and conveying it to others. The specialty within psychology that has had the most experience using photography is animal behavior which also has a strong field orientation. I have occasionally found it helpful to ask my students to sketch a place to sensitize them to what is going on. There are methods for using the camera or the sketch pad in a minimally reactive way without playing "super spy." Often the best approach is to be very open and obvious as a tourist might act.

Very few psychology departments offer courses in field work and indeed there are very few psychologists who are capable of teaching it. The situation is better in anthropology where studies *in situ* of both humans and non-humans are emphasized, and somewhat better in those sociology departments where the traditions of the Chicago school are still felt. Of all the behavioral sciences, psychology lags furthest behind in the development of field methods. Serendipity is the rule in field research and flexibility of mind and quick reflexes are necessary to capitalize upon it. Because there has been very little money available for naturalistic studies, field researchers are skilled at borrowing, improvising and scrounging. This is not a bad model for graduate students and researchers in an era of tight budgets. No-budget research often involves the use of local people as data collectors and analysts.

Too often the means of our research have become the ends. Animal behavior which was once seen as a way of learning about people became a subject of study in its own right. The same occurred with statistics, methodology and test construction. This is not necessarily undesirable since specialists in techniques are needed as well. However, we have to make sure that the original goals are not forgotten in the search for better tools and theories. We also should try to learn the extent to which this means-centeredness is produced by institutional and professional pressures. And we are going to have to be sure that at least some of our graduates have a problem-solving orientation because we can't go on indefinitely identifying group differences and computing correlation coefficients.

When it comes to making decisions on campus, issues such as enrollment predictions, curriculum planning, traffic flow, attitudes towards intramural sports, or the effectiveness of counseling services, psychology faculty operate as blindly as faculty from other departments. Training in evaluation and generating useful data could be complementary to using the campus as a research station. For this to happen, we will have to change student and faculty conceptions about the nature of appropriate research. Somehow we have gotten to the point where studying monkeys in cages or rats in mazes is real psychology while studying undergraduates in dormitories or libraries is not.

I do not advocate abandoning the laboratory as a workplace or training tool. There are some topics for which it is the best approach available. But even here it should be supplemented by field methods. When the response is made that no analogues to the behavior exist in nature, then one must raise questions about the importance of the topic. Not exclude the research automatically on this basis, but at least face the question my grandmother raised—Why is a grown person like you spending your time doing something like this? A better balance between field and laboratory would benefit all areas of psychology.

The tremendous leap of faith needed to go from laboratory to life is particularly evident to the increasing number of psychologists who are being asked to testify before government committees, courts and administrative bodies. Whether the issue is abortion, busing, prison reform, visual pollution or occupational health, it is a good bet that there will be a psychologist testifying.

For those of us who have done this, the chasm between what is known and what information is needed is enormous. Reviewing the research literature as a potential witness on the effects of solitary confinement, I was appalled by the absence of relevant data. Although countless inmates have served time, sometimes years, in solitary confinement, there is little or no research documenting its effects. Judges are not terribly interested in stories about crowded rats or Sika deer. Nor is it clear that the predicament of inmates in smelly, filthy and noisy steel cages eating prison slop and facing occasional brutality resembles the antiseptic circumstances of the paid volunteer in the sensory isolation experiment.

For ethical reasons and for face validity, the only fully convincing data on solitary confinement or long-term imprisonment will have to come from studies of actual prisoners or long-term mental patients or others who have been subjected to involuntary confinement for long periods. I do not question the value of studying crowded rats. This work has been very important in shaping our thinking about crowding. But if we want to generalize from lab to life, we are going to have to learn more about life too.

We know that misperceptions of reality occur in the laboratory, but not how often and under what circumstances in the outside world. We know more about how students learn nonsense syllables than we do about how elementary pupils learn geography or college students cram for exams—and most do cram despite our exhortations that spaced practice is superior to massed practice. We also know much more about laboratory rats in mazes than about wild rats in their own habitats. The list could be continued indefinitely.

We have developed a science of psychology based largely on behavior in the laboratory and have hedged on the issue of generalization. Some say we are not ready yet to generalize. Give us 10 years, 20 years, 50 years, then we may be ready. If I had confidence that we would have answers on issues like solitary confinement or visual pollution in 20 years, I would be willing to wait. But what I have seen is a *decreasing* generalizability as the problems and methods chosen by experimenters become more esoteric and hermetic.

Researchers such as Montrose Wolf and Teodoro Ayllon who have applied behavior modification in schools and mental hospitals have found that their work is *dis*continuous with the previous animal studies. They had to develop new techniques, reinforcements and contracts appropriate to the setting. The plea for "more time" makes good sense if the researchers are actually working on problems important to society. It seems disingenuous if they are not.

We have come far down the road to developing a laboratory model of human behavior based on studies of people on our turf and our terms. Now it seems time to look at how people actually behave in their homes, their schools and their work places.

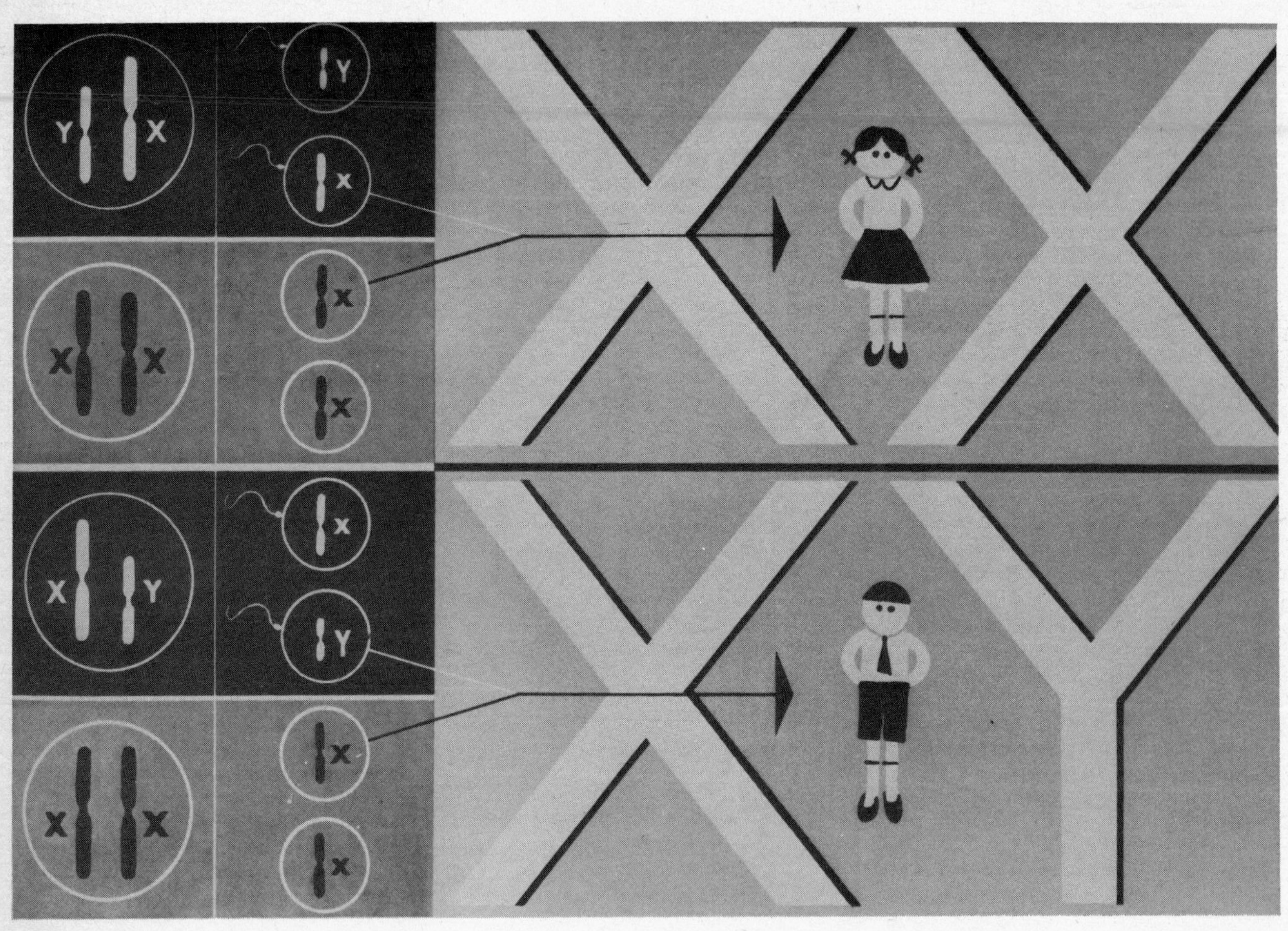

Y
Y X
X
X
X X
X
X
X Y
Y
X
X X
X

Biological Bases of Behavior

Psychologists have long sought to define and describe the biological correlates of behavior. They have explored and tried to comprehend the brain and nervous system in order to understand the mind as well as to treat disorders and change behaviors. Contributions from laboratory scientists have vastly improved our knowledge of the biological bases of behavior. And as our knowledge increases, our ability to influence and sometimes even to control that behavior raises some profound ethical and social questions.

This section incorporates three subtopics concerning the biological bases of behavior. The first is *Biology, the Nervous System, and Behavior.* "Genetics: The Edge of Creation" introduces us to the most basic of the biological bases of behavior, the genetic code transmitted by DNA. "The Clock Within" discusses regular and sometimes not so regular cycles of biochemical activity in the nervous system that seem to produce cycles in our thoughts and actions as well. "Do Diets Really Work?" takes up another set of processes that run in cycles, the mechanisms of hunger and weight regulation. In "The Three Brains of Paul MacLean," a controversial theory of brain organization is examined. Could each of us possess a three-layered brain that is part reptile, part mammal, and part computer? "Twins" takes up the role of our genetic heritage in shaping our psychological as well as physiological makeup, and "Tinkering with Life" takes what is known about that role one step further, discussing the possibility (and the profitability) of genetic engineering.

The second topic is the *Emotions.* "The Violent Brain" is concerned with the causes and control of anger and aggression, and "The Origins of Violence" argues that aggression ultimately results from an inability to properly and fully experience pleasure. How genes contribute to negative and debilitating responses such as depression is considered in "Searching for Depression Genes." "Chemical Feelings" rounds out this topic by considering the brain chemicals called peptides, looking carefully at their apparently very critical role in all of the emotions.

The third topic is *Consciousness.* "Images of the Night" takes up one of our "altered states of consciousness"—dreaming. New theories clash with old as researchers try to understand this very common but very perplexing experience. Yet another manifestation of conscious experience is the perception of pain. In "Going Beyond Pain" you will discover that when medical efforts at pain control fail, behavioral techniques can sometimes make mind over matter (or at least, mind over body) a reality. "Biofeedback Seeks New Medical Uses for Concept of Yoga" takes you further into the issue of mind-body relationships, exploring the extent to which people can gain conscious control over their own bodily functions. "Brain Flash: The Physiology of Inspiration" tries to explain the characteristics of different states of consciousness as well as the "Aha! experience" of insight in terms of interactions between different parts of the brain. And to complete the section with a shifting of gears, "The Way of the Journal" discusses spirituality and its relation to the process of turning unconscious images and memories into conscious ones.

A review of this section will acquaint you with the range of current investigation into the biochemistry and neurophysiology of being human, and shows you some of the ways in which the findings of biological biopsychology can help to solve some age-old problems.

Looking Ahead: Challenge Questions

What capabilities do we now have to improve human psychological welfare through application of existing knowledge about physiology?

What ethical questions arise regarding the physiological manipulation of behavior?

Some people might say that biopsychology is combining the idea of "Better Living Through Chemistry" with a newer idea of "Better Living Through Behaviorism." What indications do you see that biochemistry and behavioral science together could lead to better living? To worse living?

GENETICS THE EDGE OF CREATION

Albert Rosenfeld

With its golden-yellow color and its slight froth of silent bubbles, the liquid in the flask seems to generate an eerie glow. The young man holding the flask has about him the air of a latter-day alchemist. Perhaps it is only the way the lab lights illuminate the scene, or merely my own boggled mind conjuring up a medieval atmosphere based on my knowledge of what the flask contains: a thick soup of *pure genetic material,* the raw chemical information that dictates what all living organisms, including people, are and do. As I reach to touch the liquid's surface, I am surprised to discover that it is in fact not liquid at all: it is crisp to the touch, readily scraped into a powder. The bubbles are tiny empty pockets left over from the chloroform used in the purification process. I remember reading a book in the late 1950s in which the great French biologist Jean Rostand calculated that the amount of DNA (deoxyribonucleic acid) required to transform the heredity of the entire human population would fit into a cube measuring only one twenty-fifth of an inch on each side—something like a thimbleful. And here I am in Rockville, Maryland, scarcely two decades later, standing in the laboratory of the Genex Corporation next to a biochemist named Stephen Lombardi, who calmly holds in his hands not a thimbleful but a *10-liter flaskful* of the very stuff of life!

What the flask contains is not yet the same fully constituted, working DNA that resides in the cells of your body and mine, spelling out our hereditary traits as well as the detailed instructions for the minute-by-minute functioning of our cellular processes. This solid broth does, however—in concert with the contents of three similar flasks—hold the makings of every possible variety of DNA molecule. The genetic alphabet consists of only four chemical "letters," called bases or nucleotides, and each of the flasks holds 220 grams of one of these nucleotides in pure, raw form with one of its ends chemically "open," ready to join with the others in whatever combinations might please the new breed of genetic engineer exemplified by Lombardi and his colleagues at Genex.

It is basically these four genetic letters, in the diversity of their arrangement, that determine whether a given creature turns out to be a rattlesnake or a grizzly bear, a mollusk or a Michelangelo. The same four-letter genetic code specifies the characteristics of every organism that now lives, or has ever lived, on earth—and could specify those of creatures that have never before existed anywhere in the universe. Until now, genetic change or mutation came about only through the forces of nature—blind or purposeful, evolutionary or divine, but in any case outside the control of mere women and men. But now that we have learned how to manipulate genes, we have suddenly become the trustees of our own further evolution, if any—as well as the mediators of all future life on our planet.

I am not suggesting that the Genex scientists, or that any scientists anywhere, are yet capable of creating living creatures out of their new chemistry sets. But so breathtakingly rapid has progress been in this field that geneticists find themselves matter-of-factly doing things that 10 years ago they would have deemed close to impossible. Though it was theoretically plausible to think about recombining genes, for example—that is, snipping genes out of one organism and transplanting them into the cells of another organism, even of another species—no one had the foggiest idea of how this might actually be done. Yet today not only has the feat been attained in the laboratory but it has been attained so readily and so easily that recombinant DNA, or "gene splicing," has become the basis of a rapidly growing new industry. Genex, with operations already spreading to Europe and the Far East, is only one of more than a hundred new bioengineering firms that have sprung up in the United States alone over the past few years. So far the companies are based more on promise than on product—but what promise! The ability to splice genes and to implant them with exquisite precision into the genetic apparatus of bacteria means that the host organisms are endowed with the capacity to turn out whatever protein product is dictated by a given gene. The bacterium thus implanted can then be cloned—that is, pure strains can be grown from the original, each one inheriting the new gene. In

From Cell . . . to Nucleus . . . to Chromosome . . . to DNA

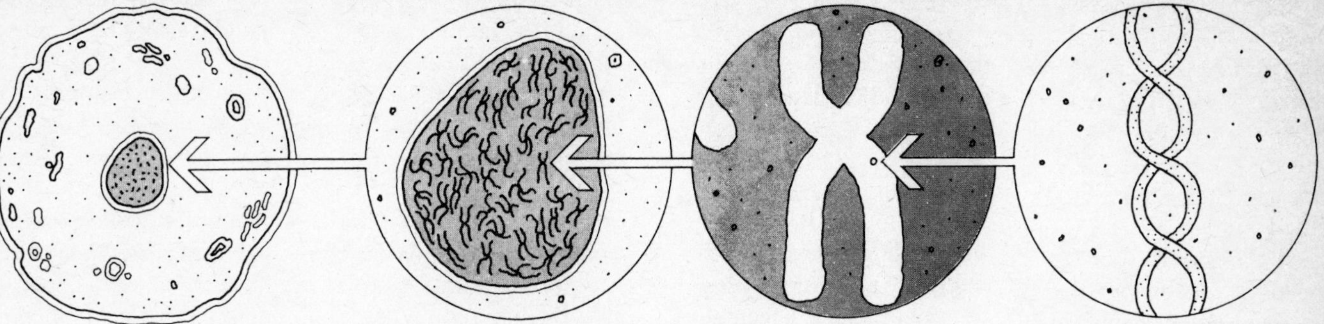

All life is based on the cell—a nucleus surrounded by cytoplasm. The human body is comprised of 60 trillion of these living units in a variety of shapes and sizes.

The nucleus is the director of all activity in the cell. The genetic instructions that determine what each cell's particular function will be are sent from the nucleus.

Every living thing has a specific number of threadlike chromosomes in its nucleus. The chromosomes always exist in pairs: human beings have 23 pairs, or 46 chromosomes.

The DNA coiled within each chromosome contains our hereditary plan. It consists of four chemical bases—thymine, adenine, guanine and cytosine—wound in a double helix.

fact, multiple copies of the gene can be spliced into the same microbe. Suppose it takes a bacterium 20 minutes to divide; when you consider that in 24 hours you will have billions of bacteria manufacturing your product, this offers an inkling of the vast new possibilities that have opened up, virtually overnight, for industry, agriculture and medicine.

There have been extensive debates about the ethics of conducting some of this research. It is to the scientists' credit that they were the first to bring the issue to public attention. With the first successful experiments in gene transfer and gene splicing in 1973 and 1974, it was clear to everyone that we had suddenly entered a vast, unknown territory. Might we endow infectious microbes with the power to resist antibiotics? Or inadvertently insert genes into organisms that could get into our bodies and increase our cancer risks?

Small groups of molecular biologists began to meet under the auspices of the National Academy of Sciences, and in July 1974, an unprecedented event took place: a letter signed by Stanford University's Paul Berg and nine other scientists appeared simultaneously in *Science, Nature* and *Proceedings of the National Academy of Sciences,* perhaps the three most prestigious scientific journals in the English-speaking world. The letter asked scientists everywhere to institute a voluntary moratorium on certain kinds of genetic experiments until an international conference could be held to discuss possible dangers and necessary safeguards. To ensure that the public would know what was going on, a news conference was arranged to coincide with the letter's publication.

In February 1975, a group of 139 researchers from 17 nations, along with a smattering of lay people and a large corps of journalists, assembled at Asilomar, a conference center in Pacific Grove, California, to spend several long and frenetic days hammering out guidelines and recommendations for conducting research in recombinant DNA.

Even before the conference, a storm of controversy far beyond the scientists' expectations erupted—and it was destined to accelerate in the months following Asilomar. Scare scenarios were freely composed in which bizarre new microbes escaped from the lab to decimate the earth's population like nothing since the black plague. In many communities around the United States, people worried about research being conducted at their local universities, and in some cases they demanded that the work be monitored if not altogether halted.

The scientists' task at Asilomar was made somewhat easier by new reports assuring them that bacteria could be specifically bred and "disarmed" so that they could not survive outside the laboratory environment. Experiments were classified according to their estimated degree of hazard, and strict safety and containment measures were recommended for each level. Thus, only properly equipped labs would be permitted to carry out the riskier experiments. The irony was that by the time the National Institutes of Health had appointed its Recombinant DNA Advisory Committee, held meetings and issued its own stringent guidelines, many of the Asilomar scientists had come to believe that much of their earlier concern had been unwarranted. Apart from the disarming of the bacteria employed, it became clear that recombinant DNA had been going on in nature over the millennia—transferred by viruses, for example. Moreover, it is no easy matter for a microbe to learn to become infectious: it requires long periods of evolving with the organism that eventually becomes susceptible to infection. So a brand-new organism would have a hard time finding a hospitable host—unlike the celebrated "Andromeda strain" of science fiction. These were some of the considerations that led to a gradual relaxation of gene-splicing regulations and even to some sentiment in favor of dropping them altogether.

But the implications for humans are even broader than these debates imply in what we must begin to recognize as a new Age of Genetics. To transfer naturally occurring genes is impressive enough, but scientists are now learning how to fabricate genes out of the basic building blocks—as the Genex people were preparing to do with their flasks. In fact, there already exist "gene machines" so automated that almost anyone can, with minimal training, learn to turn out gene fragments in a few hours, a task that formerly would have taken a skilled chemist several months of assiduous effort. Scientists have also begun to "map" genes—that is, to pinpoint the locations of specific genes on specific chromosomes; and the first attempts have been made to replace missing or faulty genes with the intent of curing, or at least of treating, human genetic disease. It is becoming increasingly evident, too, that genes contribute substantially not only to our physiological makeup but to our personalities and behavior as well.

In studying and manipulating genes, scientists naturally turned to the simpler organisms first. When Paul Berg of Stanford inserted the first foreign gene into an organism, he chose the SV 40 virus, which has only five genes. (Berg and his associates were later able to transfer a bacterial gene to a human cell in tissue culture, where it was able to produce the missing enzyme that caused a human genetic disease.) The genome, or full set of genetic instructions, of the common intestinal bacterium *Escherichia coli*, or *E. coli* for short, with its single chromosome and ready accessibility, has been investigated diligently; and *E. coli* remains the favorite vehicle for both research and production in gene splicing. But the human genome has barely begun to be explored, and its exploration is of course incomparably more complex and difficult than that of *E. coli*. At one time, locating the insulin gene was beyond anyone's capacity. Fortunately, the protein chemists did know how to take apart the insulin molecule itself. With that information, it became possible to reconstruct the gene. Genentech, Inc., the best-known and so far the most successful of the new bioengineering companies, farmed out the task to scientists at Cal Tech and City of Hope National Medical Center in Duarte, California. As a result, Eli Lilly and Company, under an agreement with Genentech, is already able to produce human insulin in experimental quantities. In fact, the first trials undertaken by Lilly with British and American volunteers indicate that the product is both safe and effective.

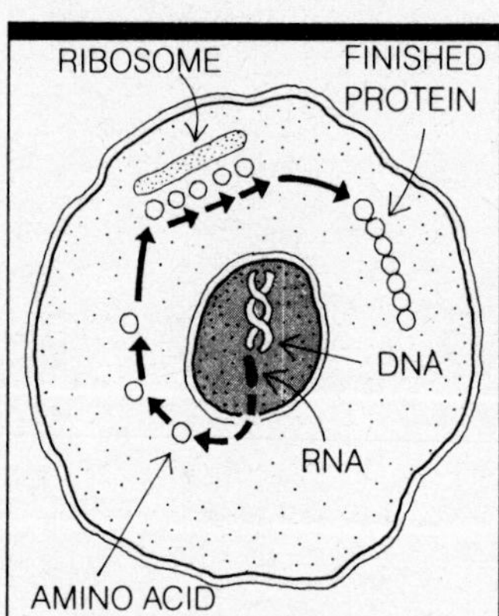

What Happens

The code for the protein that determines a cell's particular form and function originates with the DNA. This code is copied in the nucleus by the RNA, which then goes out into the cell body and collects the necessary amino acids. At the ribosome, the amino acids are assembled in the order that was originally dictated by the genetic information contained within the DNA. The amino acids are then linked in a protein chain and are ready to work.

Gene splicing must surely be rated as one of the seminal biotechnological breakthroughs of this century—and therefore of all time. It suddenly became feasible in the early 1970s with two discoveries. One was that a class of bacterial proteins called restriction enzymes had the capacity to sever DNA molecules at predictable sites (other enzymes had already been found that could "suture" genes back in place). The other was that loose, circular pieces of DNA called plasmids could pass genetic information along from one generation of *E. coli* to the next. The plasmid that has now become historic is the one called pSC101; the *p* is for "plasmid," and *SC* are the initials of Stanley Cohen, who is one of Berg's colleagues at Stanford.

Cohen's pioneering feat was achieved in collaboration with biochemist Herbert W. Boyer of the University of California at San Francisco and two associates. They first transferred genes to *E. coli* from another *E. coli;* then from another bacterium, *Staphylococcus aureus*—the first gene transfer between species; and finally, working with other scientists, from an animal—the frog *Xenopus laevis*. These experiments represented the practical beginning of genetic engineering.

As I sat with Cohen recently in his lab at Stanford, he was willing enough to reminisce a bit about these exciting events out of a past that already seems remote. But he was more interested in talking about the scientific questions now engaging his attention—and that is what I was more interested in hearing about, too.

The irony is that in the period just before the gene-splicing breakthroughs occurred, many molecular geneticists were feeling glum because they thought there was really not much more to discover about DNA. Oh, yes, more details to be sure, but the basics were all in place. They could not have been more mistaken. The current paradox is that while we can manipulate genes with an ease and a dexterity not even contemplated a decade ago, we have at the same time discovered how much less we know about genes than we thought we did. New mysteries arise, it seems, with each new set of experiments. Such a state of affairs would produce despair in most other spheres of human endeavor, but scientists find it exhilarating. It is nevertheless also disquieting to learn that a stable, reliable, orderly molecule such as DNA is really full of quirks and caprices.

One of the aberrations of

Entering the New Age of Genetics

The implications of genetic engineering for agriculture and industry are impressive enough, but the potential applications in medicine border on the awesome.

Genetic diseases can be identified and possibly corrected at their inception. To date, more than 3,000 such diseases have been classified; fortunately most of them are very rare.

Genetic-counseling centers around the country now routinely service couples who are worried about passing familial ailments to their offspring. Prenatal tests to determine genetic disorders are regularly performed throughout the country. For groups of people particularly susceptible to a genetic disease, mass

Scientists can now create unlimited quantities of almost any antibody—which has far-ranging implications for diagnostic tests, better vaccines, new treatments for cancer and infectious diseases.

Soon gene therapy—the transferring of genes into people to correct deficiencies—may become commonplace. In fact, some controversial attempts have already been made.

Many diseases never before thought to be specifically genetic—cancer, heart disease, hypertension, arthritis, diabetes, mental illness—and even the aging process have turned out to have genetic and familial components. More than 70 "genetic markers" have been discovered that can foretell a person's vulnerability to a variety of diseases, allergies and even environmental pollutants.

DNA that has particularly preoccupied Stanley Cohen's lab involves a class of "transposable elements," or transposons—segments of DNA that can combine and recombine in various ways, switching around whole groups of genes among plasmids and viruses as well as within the genomes of living organisms. Earlier in the 1970s, in West Germany, Peter Starlinger and his associates at the University of Cologne had come upon curious DNA fragments they called "insertion sequences," which, though they had no discernible function of their own, were mobile units that readily intruded on other genes. Meanwhile, experiments by Cohen and other investigators in England offered clues about how movable elements were able to transfer antibiotic resistance from one bacterium to another. Transposons appear to be important in causing some types of disease to occur—and they also help to set up bacterial defenses against man-made remedies designed to combat those diseases.

Apart from the obvious health implications, another reason for Cohen's fascination with transposons and their ability to bring about what he calls "illegitimate recombination" is that they "offer insights into how evolution may be able to occur in quantum leaps" as well as by slow accretion. Moreover, "transposable elements may explain how whole blocks of genes can be turned on or off during the development of an organism."

Earlier that day, one of Cohen's Stanford colleagues, biochemist David Hogness, had explained how this can occur in fruit flies, which have a much higher number of transposons than most species. The transposons can cause very striking spontaneous mutations. Because a single mutation may control a significant block of genes, entire segments of the body can be drastically affected: part of an eye will turn into genitalia; an abdominal segment that normally has no appendages could be transformed into a thoracic segment and develop legs.

Genes and gene fragments, then, "jump" in totally unexpected ways, moving about from one part of the genome to another. In fact, chromosomes are known to exchange large packets of DNA. Genes have even been observed to undergo complete flip-flops, executing 180-degree reversals on the DNA chain so that their genetic messages read backward. A group of scientists at Cal Tech has been especially intrigued by this jumping-gene phenomenon. The head of this aggregation is Leroy Hood. Hood and his colleagues have been able to explain how jumping genes serve a vital developmental purpose by making it possible for the body's immune system to turn out an extraordinary diversity of antibodies—a capacity that has always been a source of mystery.

Another surprise that recent genetic research has turned up is the fact that genes are not necessarily, as formerly believed, continuous stretches of DNA that spell out precise instructions for making, say, proteins. Genes have in many cases (some geneticists believe in most cases) turned out to be split up in the most bizarre fashion. Such genes have their intelligible stretches of nucleotides constantly interrupted by what appear to be nonsense sequences—at least they are not part of the gene's instructions for making the given protein. These "intervening sequences" (labeled introns by noted Harvard gene splicer Walter Gilbert, as distinct from exons, the sequences that express the needed instructions) are as long as and frequently longer and more numerous than the "real" genetic sequences. It would be as if we were to take a word such as *inspiration* and spell it *i-n-s-x-q-l-x-x-p-i-s-q-w-a-m-g-r-a-t-i-z-z-q-p-t-x-o-n* and expect the reader's eye to pick out the meaningful letters and ignore the rest.

Apart from introns, there are other perplexing reiterative sequences of apparently unused DNA, including many nonoperating "pseudogenes." Are they really meaningless? If not, what could they possibly mean? Guesses have ranged all over the lot: the untranslated sequences could have something to do with gene regulation and control, or with species differences, or with differentiation during fetal development, or with evolutionary mechanisms. It has even been suggested that a lot of genetic material may be purely self-serving, just taking advantage of the free ride in order to perpetuate itself; as long as it doesn't particularly interfere with other functions, it just replicates along with the rest of the genome during procreation. Clearly, no one has yet begun to solve the puzzle.

Another new wrinkle: DNA, instead of being strung out smoothly, is folded in upon itself in unexpected ways, coiling and "supercoiling" into intricate configurations that still remain undivined. It turns out, too, that mutations and mistakes occur all the time, but DNA fortunately possesses the capacity to repair itself—most of the time, anyway.

With the rise of recombinant-DNA technology, it has become fashionable to say that genetics will dominate the 1980s just as, say, computers dominated the previous decades. But it seems to me that this is understating the case. Rather, we are entering a much more sweeping Age of Genetics, an age that perhaps has no more recent parallel than the revolution that occurred during the Neolithic era, when our ancestors discovered how to domesticate animals and raise crops. We will now be able to create some plants that will photosynthesize more efficiently and others that will fertilize themselves, perhaps via the insertion of nitrogen-fixing genes, thus saving the billions of dollars and the millions of barrels of oil that are now spent every year on synthetic fertilizers. We will create bacterial strains capable of converting wastes into useful products, even into foods and fuels. With our genetic know-how only in the infancy of its development, we can hardly imagine how far-reaching the impact of genetics on every branch of industry and agriculture will be.

But more than any of that, we will become the masters of the molecules we are made of—and therefore of our bodies and psyches and of all living things that creep or swim or run or fly. Hardly any facet of our personal lives will be unaffected, and the political questions raised will often require solutions on a global scale. Every genetic benefit carries with it a concomitant worry. Will attempts to cure genetic diseases, for instance, lead to gene tampering to "improve the race"?

The picture comes back to me of Stephen Lombardi at Genex, holding up his flaskful of pure nucleotides. I had compared him to an alchemist. But I now realize what a pale comparison this is. The alchemists' dreams seemed grandiose and arrogant for their time, but their cravings were really fairly modest. They dealt with gross elements and mixtures of elements, whereas the Stephen Lombardis of contemporary science deal with the tiniest components of the living genetic code—which they know how to read and with which they are learning to write. Whereas the alchemists merely wanted to find the "philosopher's stone" that would transmute base metals into gold, we may soon be able to transmute almost anything into almost anything else. Ethical and moral dilemmas abound at every step of the genetic path along which we are now traveling so rapidly. And our inner voice keeps asking: Are we ready for this?

We have always treasured the advice, "Know thyself," inscribed on the temple of Delphi. To know our genetic selves is to seek an ever more profound self-knowledge—and in no way is that incompatible with the more traditional, spiritual paths to self-knowledge. The control of our genes surely entails risks, but is it really less risky to continue to let our genes control *us*—assuming we have the choice? Do we want to keep arguing about whether or not our genes *are* in control—or would we rather find out? In this time of troubles, it seems we were never more in need of knowledge we do not now possess.

The way we should enter the Age of Genetics is with exhilaration tempered by caution.

THE CLOCK WITHIN

Philip Hilts

Philip Hilts is a staff writer for The Washington Post.

There is a drawer called "the catastrophe file" in the office of biologist Charles Ehret at the Argonne National Laboratory. It holds reports of various disasters: an air crash that killed hundreds, a ship collision in which crew members drowned, a hospital accident that will bring members of the staff to trial, embarrassing errors in the Pioneer space probes, blunders in Middle East diplomacy.

All the items have one element in common. In each case, human biology was a factor, if not the primary cause of the accident. Or to be more precise, the cause was failure to account for human biology .

Among the catastrophes on Ehret's list is the nuclear accident at Three Mile Island. It was on the night shift, at 4:01 A.M. on a chilly March morning, that three young men sat in the control area at the nuclear power station. The three worked on a shift system called slow rotation—days for a week, evenings for a week, then late nights for a week. If a biologist like Ehret, who is versed in a relatively new discipline called chronobiology, were to design a shift to guarantee the worst possible human performance, slow rotation might well be it.

During the first 100 minutes of the nuclear accident, the control room workers made a surprising series of mistakes. Fourteen seconds into the accident, one controller failed to see two warning lights. A few seconds later, a valve that should have closed did not, but operators did not realize it. As the president's investigating commission later said, "Throughout the first two hours of the accident, the operators ignored or failed to recognize the significance of several things that should have warned them that they had an open valve and a loss-of-coolant accident. . . ." The president's commission concluded that ". . . except for human failures, the major accident at Three Mile Island would have been a minor incident."

One of the relationships discovered by chronobiology is that the many rhythms within the human body normally move in a set synchrony with one another. For example, body temperature, pulse, and sleep-wake cycles follow roughly the same beat, while other processes vary with a quite different beat—and the relations among them may change, slightly but predictably, day after day. Each gland, each organ, each chemical has its own beat, and together they are orchestrated as harmoniously as the players in a symphony.

They are harmonious until some internal change or catastrophe occurs. Illness can throw the body's rhythms out of phase or frequency. Drugs can do it. Jet travel over many time zones can do it. Putting workers suddenly onto the night shift can do it.

Over the past three decades biologists have found that in practically every function of living systems, time is of the essence. The rhythmic frequency of many biological functions operates approximately on a 24-hour cycle, which led Franz Halberg at the University of Minnesota to coin the term "circadian rhythm." In Latin *circa* means "about," *dies* means "a day."

We think of our heartbeat as a constant, but it is not. It will vary by as much as 20 or 30 beats per minute in 24 hours. At one time of day it may beat 60 times per minute, and at the opposite time of the circadian cycle, it may beat 80 or more times per minute. Blood pressure may measure 120 over 80 in the morning, but in the evening it is likely to be higher, possibly as much as 140 over 100, an unusually high reading. Body temperature does not hover around 98.6 degrees, as most of us believe, but varies by one and a half to two degrees over a day—from as low as 97 degrees to more than 99 degrees. The scores of other functions which have been shown to swing up and down widely during the day include more than three dozen separate chemicals in the blood and urine, as well as mood, vigor, eye-hand coordination, counting, time estimation, addition, and memory. Cell division rate in the body has been found to vary by 1,200 percent over a day; one chemical in the rat's pineal gland varies by 900 percent over a day.

After the TMI nuclear accident, several utilities, including the General Public Utilities Corporation which runs the plant, turned to biologists for help in lessening the dangers of erratic human performance.

"We may be able to improve the situation by several orders of magnitude," says Ehret, who has consulted with the nuclear utilities and drawn up alternate night work plans, all according to biologically based rules that have emerged from research in chronobiology.

But there is another, equally critical area where a failure to take into account the circadian fluctuations of the body's natural rhythms will lead to trouble: medicine and medical research.

In medicine, the prevailing biological idea has been that the body seeks equilibrium, a steady state. When it is ill, say with a fever, it tries to return to wellness by sweating and other means of cooling itself. This is the homeostatic view. It states that in each bodily function there is an ideal mean, and that a healthy person's functions will flutter randomly about that middle number. For example, in temperature, 98.6 degrees is the accepted mean. In blood pressure, 120 over 80 is the rough center.

Now it is clear that this approach is faulty, or at least incomplete. Bodily functions do fluctuate, but not randomly. They move up and down quite regularly. They keep in order among themselves, and the varying numbers they produce may result in all sorts of different interpretations by doctors who are unaware of this wide, normal variation.

Since so much of the chemistry and biology of the body changes each day, and changes by as much as tenfold, biologists have gradually come to realize that an animal—whether human or guinea pig—is virtually a different creature, physically and chemically, at different times of day.

This means that we may be more susceptible not only to accidents but also to disease at certain predictable times. It means that a drug taken at one time acts differently than the same drug, in the same dose, taken a few hours later or earlier.

Chronobiology has already begun to transform the way biological research is conducted, and it is expected to have a major effect on all of medicine as well. It can alter results at every stage of practice, from preventing time-linked illnesses, to improving diagnoses, to improving treatment. Some of the conventional medical rules of thumb may have to be abandoned; for example, drugs are now given three times a day or four times a day, completely without regard for the differing effects they produce at different hours.

The evidence from the laboratory is clear: When rats are given a nearly lethal dose of amphetamine, their survival depends chiefly on what time the agent is given. At one time in the animal's circadian cycle, six percent of them die. At another time, 78 percent die.

Certain insects have now been found to be far more vulnerable to some commonly used insecticides in the afternoon than at any other times. Rats given a sleep-causing drug will nap for about 50 minutes when the drug is given at one time, but will sleep twice as long when the drug is given later.

High levels of noise usually cause convulsions in animals. But the probability that an animal will be thus afflicted varies according to its body's clock. At the worst time, the probability is 100 percent higher than the daily mean. At the best time, it is 80 percent lower than the daily mean.

In yet another study, rats were given enough phenobarbital to kill at least half of them. But during the most favorable time, none of the animals died. At the least favorable time, the same dose killed all of them. The list could go on. There are already many drugs and active chemicals whose ability to kill or to cure has been shown to swing widely with the rhythms of an animal's body. There are, in short, "windows" of daily drug resistance and effectiveness.

Because of this, chronobiologists say, the results of some previous drug and cancer research studies are now dubious. Chronobiologists suggest that studies of toxicity, especially of the behavioral effects of toxic agents, must now be completely redone. At the very least, the conduct of scientific research must be changed for all future studies. Time must now be included as a major factor in medical and biological equations.

Colin Pittendrigh, among the most respected of the biological researchers in the field, says that this kind of biological research has begun to have an important impact on medicine. "There are some very important findings, principally from Franz Halberg and his people, on the time-of-day dependence of drug action. That is a first-rate result . . . but I have talked to good pharmacologists, and most of them don't yet know the facts. That is worth reporting: The pharmacological fraternity is not informed on what's been found."

One thing that Pittendrigh suggests should be done immediately is change the federal guidelines that govern research. The time of an animal's cycle must be taken into account in the research that determines the safety and effectiveness of drugs, he says.

Federal agencies provide most of the money for basic research and they also set the guidelines. Thus far, the government has not recognized chronobiology as a major variable in setting guideline policy, and it now appears that a significant factor is being left out of most of the testing.

Despite the evidence that has built up, the common practice in laboratory testing includes such hazardous actions as testing nocturnal animals in the daytime; testing animals that have not had time to adjust to a new laboratory environment; testing animals that are kept in crowded cages, a condition which has been shown to cause altered internal rhythms among animals; testing animals in light and dark cycles that are unregulated; testing animals in conditions subject to frequent disturbances, such as turning on lights during a dark phase; and testing animals whose feeding schedules are not fixed and recorded. All of these can cause altered rhythms in animals, but none are mentioned in federal research guidelines. Meanwhile,

Chronology of chronobiology

The curiosity about rhythmical events in nature is ancient, but probably the first experimental test of the idea occurred in 1729. The French astronomer Jean de Mairan had become curious about a heliotrope plant that opened its leaves to the morning light and closed them at dusk. He discovered that the opening and closing was apparently not controlled by the light in the plant's environment.

Observations like de Mairan's were recorded again and again over the next two centuries by scientists in many fields. At the beginning of this century a major question was whether the cycles in plant behavior were being regulated by a clock within the plant, or by some outside rhythm such as night and day or changing temperature. Experiments that attempted to disrupt the 24-hour rhythms of plants, and later insects and animals, failed. The cycles persisted despite environmental changes.

It was Colin Pittendrigh of Stanford who, in the middle 1950s, finally put into clear terms all the evidence collected up to that time. He and others had proved that clocks exist in life forms as simple as single-celled animals and as complex as man. Internal clocks, he said, are a fundamental property of life.

While clocks are definitely internal, they may follow external rhythms, be reset by external rhythms, or be disrupted by them. It is, he said, as if two oscillators were operating—one inside the body and one outside.

Most recent research in the field has centered on one main question: Where within the body is the clockwork? Is it an organ or one function of an organ? Is it within the cells, and if so, where within the cells?

The sophisticated clocks found operating in single-celled animals settled at least part of the question by proving that one need not look to higher life forms for a fully operating biological timer. Two competing lines of recent research have tried to locate the clock mechanism either in the membrane of the cell, or in the process of protein manufacture.

The first approach holds that the membranes of a cell function by opening and closing channels through which chemicals pass. The process is thought to be electrical: When a certain number of ions build up on one side of a membrane, the flow across it is shut off until the ionic concentration drops again, triggering a feedback mechanism which starts the flow of material through membrane channels again. This theoretical model for an open-and-close rhythm within the cell may be the oscillator, the heart of the ticking clock.

The other approach puts the rate of protein-making at the center of the clockwork. Research has shown again and again that when cells are flooded with substances that foul up the manufacture of proteins, the cells' clocks are reset to a new time. But until recently, it was not certain that the clock was reset only because the protein-making process was disturbed.

Now, in research just completed, Jerry Feldman a former student of Pittendrigh, has demonstrated that one particular chemical that slows the clock does so specifically because it damages protein-making. Cycloheximide injected into the ordinary strain of *Neurospora* fungus normally will foul up the cell's internal clock. But Feldman used a mutant strain of *Neurospora*, one in which cycloheximide does not damage the protein-making machinery. He wanted to see how the cell's clocks would react to doses of cycloheximide.

Since the protein machinery is unaffected by the chemical, the cell clock should run normally despite the addition of cycloheximide. If the clock changed, however, it would mean that something besides the protein machinery functioned as the clock.

The clocks of the fungus ran normally. "We proved that protein synthesis is necessary for the clock to run," he said. "Of course," he added, "since proteins are also important to the function of cell membranes, it is probable that both approaches are correct, differing only in emphasis. The one may depend on the other, and thus the two approaches merge."

many far less important factors are mentioned.

Lawrence D. Scheving at the University of Arkansas Medical Center, whose work has established chronobiological effects for a number of drugs, says that time is a variable important enough to affect the validity of some experiments and the accuracy of many.

"We are very careful about controlling the sex, weight, age, and other things. Time is equally important if not more important than the other variables that we rigorously control for," Scheving says.

One kind of study commonly carried out in toxicology laboratories is the "LD50" study. Animals are injected with a poisonous agent to determine what dose is lethal to 50 percent of the animals. Commonly, rats for testing may be flown in from halfway across the country, hurriedly brought to the lab, and given the lethal compound. There is no quarantine, no adjustment to environment, no regular feeding regimen, and no attention to the light-dark cycle. Similar tests for the same drug often provide results that vary as much as 100 percent. Paying no attention to an animal's cycle, says Morris Cranmer, the former director of the National Center for Toxicological Research, results in studies that are consistently inaccurate. "This means the variation in experiments is increased—and as you increase the variation, you decrease the resolving power of the experiments. That is my concern," says Cranmer.

He added another reason to take biological time into account, a reason that may be even more important than inaccurate results. If a strong effect of biological time is ignored by federal regulations, food and drug manufacturers could use to their own advantage an animal's resistance to toxic effects. Toxicity tests could be designed around an animal's highest tolerance period so that resulting effects would be the most negligible.

The attitude of federal officials varies greatly. William D'Aguanno, the Food and Drug Administration's officer on the toxicology of new drugs, says the FDA has no policy on chronobiology. But the attitude of Cranmer's successor at the National Center for Toxicological Research may be seen as a bellwether. Thomas Cairns came into the NCTR when that agency was about to conduct a series of experiments that would have tested the importance of biological time in toxicology. That study got scrapped in the transition from Cranmer's to Cairns' administration. The matter was left there, untouched, for two years. A reporter recently asked Cairns about the importance of chronobiology. He was not up on the literature, he said, and felt that it was probably not very important. But he requested a few days to look into the matter.

Cairns has now begun to worry about the effects chronobiology may have on scientific research funded by the government and on industrial research as well. "My problem is . . . that this could easily be used in reverse to a manufacturer's benefit."

A good example of the way in which chronobiology might possibly change medical practice is in the treatment of high blood pressure. Howard Levine, chief of medicine at New Britain General Hospital in Connecticut, and long interested in chronobiology, suffers from high blood pressure. But, he says, "diagnosis of my condition was delayed a couple of years because I used to go to the doctor in the morning. That is when my blood pressure was at its circadian low, and so it seemed normal when actually it wasn't."

Levine also found that late at night the percentage of red blood cells in his blood normally dropped by about four and a half percent, and the total volume of red blood cells in his blood changed by almost ten percent. A five-percent drop in red blood cells often prompts a transfusion in a hospital setting.

Frederic Bartter, an eminent endocrinologist at the University of Texas who has done numerous studies of drugs, blood pressure, and their rhythms, points out that "every drug that has ever been explored for the rhythmicity of its action has been found to have such rhythms." In normal practice, it is quite likely that physicians are prescribing drug doses that are anywhere from half to twice as much as a patient needs.

Body Cycles
BODY TEMPERATURE—Regulated by the hypothalamus, body temperature follows a 24-hour cycle regardless of external factors. The slight change of a degree or two that usually occurs within that cycle has a profound effect on performance and physiological activity. High and low points vary for each individual.
SLEEP/WAKE CYCLE—The enforcement of regular hours of sleep keeps us in tune with the 24-hour unit by which our society clocks time. During sleep, brain wave activity changes according to dream stages, which tend to follow a regular nightly schedule. During the day and into the evening, alternating periods of drowsiness and alertness also follow a schedule.
PULSE RATE—The heartbeat, which begins to quicken its pace in the last moments of sleep, rises and falls throughout the day in tandem with the rate of respiration. The pulse beats 60 to 80 times a minute, its rate peaking several times during the day and falling to its low in the last hours of sleep.
BLOOD PRESSURE—People with problems of elevated blood pressure may have normal pressure levels in the morning, which rise to a dangerous high by the afternoon. Though less is known about normal blood pressure, it is believed that the circadian rise and fall is actually tied to the sleep/wake cycle; the pressure begins to rise when the body is upright and falls when it lies prone.
CELL DIVISION—The circadian nature of cell division is most pronounced in surface tissues subjected to stress. Skin cells divide most frequently during the sleeping hours between midnight and 4 A.M.

Once a patient's 24-hour rhythm is established, blood pressure need not be measured repeatedly because the pattern is predictable. "Then you can *know* to what extent a given medication will take away those peaks," says Bartter. "To

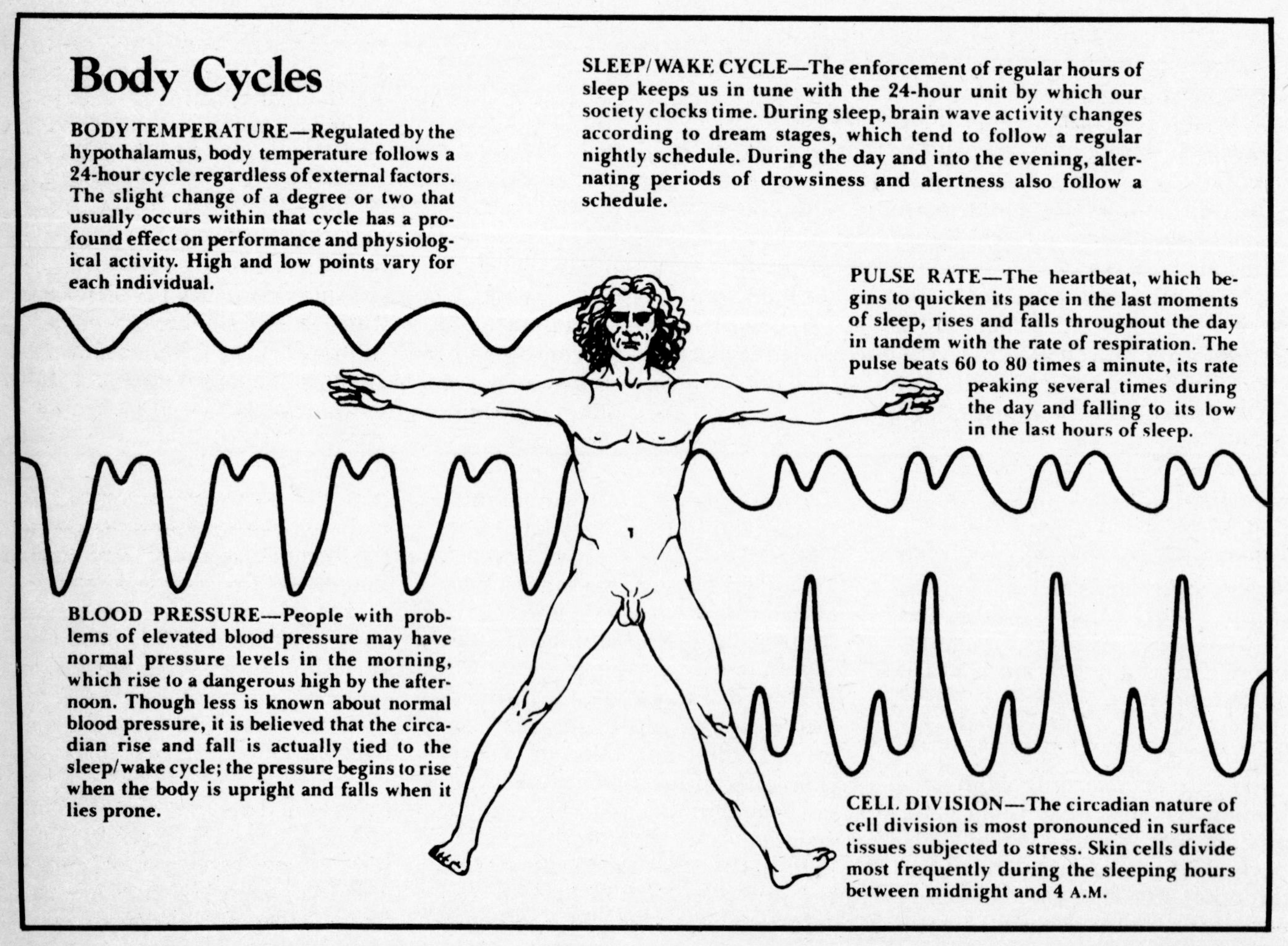

know how bad it is, you *must* have some estimate of a patient's peaks, and not just his morning pressure."

Probably the most studied of all human rhythms are those in sleep, and one of the interesting findings of researchers Elliot D. Weitzman and Charles Czeisler in New York is that the label "insomnia" covers at least two quite different ailments. Insomnia has been presumed to be a disruption of the normal sleep pattern, but the Montefiore Hospital and Medical Center researchers have found that 10 to 15 percent of "insomniacs" have no trouble at all sleeping a full eight hours. Their trouble is that their bodies insist that they sleep their full night between about 4 A.M. and 11 A.M.

These night owls are unaware of this natural rhythm and spend their lives being analyzed by psychiatrists and drugged by doctors because their natural sleep cycle wreaks havoc with their jobs and social lives. Weitzman calls the malady "delayed sleep-phase syndrome." He corrects the problem by getting patients to go to bed three hours later every day until they have wrapped all the way around and end up awakening early in the morning.

Weitzman's patients, once they have been shifted, have been able to adjust easily and have continued to sleep normally for the several years since the treatment began. After an average of more than a year, none of his patients has relapsed. "This may apply to 10 to 15 percent of all insomniacs. There are 25 million insomniacs, so we are talking about two to three million people . . . ."

One of the most important medical applications of chronobiology may be in cancer treatment. Franz Halberg of the University of Minnesota is perhaps the foremost advocate of "chronotherapy," and he has led a group in studying the possible application of chronobiology to cancer therapy. The group has proved that an animal's resistance to cancer drugs is high at one time and low at another. It has also proved that if this changing resistance is exploited by changing the drug dosage according to time of resistance, it is possible to improve treatment effects by giving animals much higher total doses of cancer drugs than was possible before. Or, it is possible to give the same dose far more safely.

"We do know that some death occurs in cancer treatment not due to the disease, but due to the drug," says Erhard Haus of Minnesota. The number of deaths caused by the treatment rather than the disease may be as high as ten percent. If drugs were used at different times in different doses, Haus believes, lives would be saved.

It is also hoped that the cycles of cancer cells themselves may be shifted so that their resistance to drugs will be low when the body's resistance to drugs is high. Then the maximum possible dose could be given for maximal therapeutic and minimal toxic effect. These hopes have been realized in practical cancer therapy being conducted by Francis Levi of France, Salvador Sanchez de la Pena of Mexico, and William Hrushesky of the Masonic Cancer Center of the University of Minnesota, in cooperation with Halberg and Haus. "Even now, even with all the money spent by the National Cancer Institute and others to compare treatment effects with different drugs and different combinations of drugs," says Hrushesky, "there has not yet been a single study anywhere in America that has taken time into account. Not one. We will try to do that next."

Other potential applications of chronobiology include treatments ranging from an improved drug therapy for asthmatics and rheumatics to a cure for jet lag. Chronobiology has shed new light on the cause of manic depression with the work of Thomas Wehr and Frederick Goodwin at the National Institutes of Health. They have achieved temporary cures in bringing depressive patients' wobbling body rhythms back into step.

Though there is resistance to chronobiology from doctors because they will have to make more measurements to diagnose and treat patients, though there is resistance from federal bureaucracy, including such agencies as the FDA, the Federal Aviation Administration, and Environmental Protection Agency, still the advances in the biology of time go on. Chronobiology's advocates maintain that the emerging discipline will gradually take its place alongside others that cut across conventional boundaries of study, such as genetics, evolution, and developmental biology. Each of these is a synthesizing discipline, one that brings together many ideas and fields of work, and knits them into a single pattern of knowledge. Each deals in a different scale of time: Evolution counts in millions of years, developmental biology counts in tens of years, and, says Charles Ehret, chronobiology "deals with the phenomenology of minutes and days, and contains more hardcore rules of general and predictive consequence than any of the others with the exception of genetics."

Slowly the question turns from whether biological time will be accounted for in science and health, to when. It is a matter of time.

Do Diets Really Work?

William Bennett and Joel Gurin

William Bennett is director of the writing program at M.I.T. Joel Gurin is the managing editor of American Health *magazine.*

If the millions of pounds lost on diets stayed lost, Americans wouldn't be spending billions of dollars each year on diet books, low-calorie foods, and weight loss drugs. Even those dedicated dieters who turn to weight loss clinics for help find their fat hard to part with. For example, studies show that only about five percent can expect to lose 20 pounds and keep them off.

Diets may not work, but people want to believe they do. Like any ritual, dieting has found a myth to give it meaning. The central tenet of the diet mythology is that thin people are *better* than fat ones—more beautiful, healthier, stronger of will. The only way to make this invidious attitude palatable has been to argue that virtually anybody can, with a reasonable amount of conscious effort, control how fat he or she becomes. But with rare exceptions, dieters lose weight temporarily and then gradually regain it.

Common ideas about weight control are based on three assumptions. First, that overeating is the key behavior; fat people must eat more than normal. Second, that the body doesn't really "care" how much fat it has; it merely stores the energy leftovers from each meal. Third, that the conscious mind can be used to balance intake and expenditure of energy and thus achieve any desired weight.

These familiar and apparently obvious assumptions are now proving false. It is not true, for example, that a fat body must belong to a big eater. To find out just how much people of different sizes eat, psychiatrist Albert Stunkard and his colleagues observed patrons of fast-food restaurants, snack bars, and ice-cream parlors, places where portions are so standardized that it is relatively easy to calculate the number of calories on any tray that is served. The observers were, to be sure, watching people eat only one of their day's meals and that one in public, where obviously piggy behavior might be embarrassing. But the anonymity of the setting should have been sufficient protection for anyone who wanted two or three hamburgers instead of one. When the observers' sheets were tallied, Stunkard found that the fat customers (those judged to be 30 percent overweight) had eaten no more than the thinner ones. Stunkard's finding is the rule rather than the exception; other studies have also shown that fat people eat normal quantities of food and, in some cases, even slightly less.

Other common notions of fatness are that laziness or a sluggish metabolism is responsible. Such popular theories of weight control have one crucial feature in common: They asssume that getting fat is an accident. If appetite, physical activity, and metabolic needs are all "normal" (whatever that is), then by a stroke of divine good fortune, the person is spared from obesity. But if one of these variables is slightly out of line, the difference accumulates in fat. As an explanation of fatness, any one of these theories leaves much to be desired. Saying of someone, "He's fat because his metabolic rate is low," doesn't answer the question, "Why isn't he eating less to compensate?" And saying, "He's fat because he eats too much," merely restates the problem.

An alternative theory holds that fatnesss is not an accident, that the body does "care" about its fat stores. According to this view, now popular among psychologists, there is a control system built into every person dictating how much

From *Science 82*, March 1982. Adapted from THE DIETER'S DILEMMA ©1982 by William Bennett and Joel Gurin. Reprinted by permission of Basic Books, Publishers.

fat he or she should carry—a kind of thermostat for body fat. And like a thermostat set to maintain a certain temperature, the body's control system has its own *setpoint* for fat. Some individuals have a high setting; others have a low one. The difference is not between the weak and the strong, or between the impulsive and the abstemious. According to this theory, it is a matter of internal controls that are set differently in different people.

Going on a weight loss diet is thus an attempt to overpower the setpoint. The skinny person who attempts to overeat and gain weight is fighting a similar battle. But the setpoint is a tireless opponent. The dieter's only allies are willpower and whatever incentives make chronic physical discomfort worthwhile. But willpower is subject to fatigue, and incentives often lose their value after a time.

The ideal approach to weight control would be a safe method that lowers or raises the setting rather than simply resists it. So far, no one knows how to change the setpoint, but some leads exist. Of these, exercise is the most promising: A sustained increase in physical activity seems to lower the setting. Most people fatten with age, probably because they exercise less and their metabolism decreases.

To date, there is no easy way to measure what your setpoint might be. It is simply the weight that you normally maintain, give or take a few pounds, when you don't think about it. Of course, many people go through a spontaneous change of weight at one time or another—a gain or loss of five to 10 pounds that occurs within a few months and often after a change in lifestyle that affects daily activity levels. But some variation is to be expected from the setpoint; its tolerance, for example, can be seen in people who repeatedly gain and lose the same 10 pounds.

A few very unhappy individuals seem not to have a functioning setpoint at all. One such person was Robert Earl Hughes of Monticello, Missouri, who died in July 1958 at the age of 32. According to the *Guinness Book of World Records,* Hughes weighed 1,041 pounds when he was buried.

If we all depended on conscious management of our food intake instead of an internal control system, it would be incredibly easy to suffer Hughes's fate. Innumerable diet manuals have presented weight control as simply a matter of measuring calories in against calories out. Fat has been described as the bottom line on a caloric balance sheet. *Credit*: breakfast, lunch, dinner, snacks. *Debit*: the energy used in breathing, running up and down the back steps, having sex, playing tennis. *Net*: an ounce of adipose tissue, one way or the other. It looks easy enough on paper, but consider what it takes, theoretically, to gain 10 pounds in one year. This gain requires no more than a hundred "extra" calories a day. This excess amounts to one tablespoon of butter or a plain muffin without butter or a pear or a cup of minestrone or a biscuit of shredded wheat. And the caloric mistake need not be made at a single meal. It can be spread out over an entire day in which 2,000 to 3,000 calories are being eaten and burned away. Just a few extra flakes of cereal at breakfast, three more bites of cheese at lunch, a couple of Life Savers in the afternoon, a chicken breast instead of a drumstick at dinner, and the jig is up.

Even Hughes, according to the standard charts, needed to make only a small daily error to become the "heaviest medically weighed human" on record: 265 calories, about the equivalent of an apple, a tablespoon of butter, and a small glass of orange juice. At this rate he could, theoretically, gain the 523 pounds that he added in the 19 years before his death.

Measuring caloric intake is only half the task. You also have to know how much energy you are expending in the course of a day. For example, a 170-pound man scrubbing the floor for approximately 12 minutes will use up a biscuit of shredded wheat. As he will by spending 30 minutes cooking dinner, or swimming a fast crawl for about eight minutes. But these estimates are even less accurate than the assessment of intake. When you add it all up, the chance of coming out within 500 calories of the real balance between what you have eaten and what you have burned off is ridiculously small.

The alternative is to let your body do the subtraction, and measure the difference on your bathroom scale. But someone who gains 10 pounds a year does so at the rate of three ounces a week, an amount that defies the precision of even the best scales in common use. Hughes himself needed to gain little more than an ounce a day.

According to the setpoint theory, the setpoint itself keeps weight fairly constant, presumably because it has more accurate information about the body's fat stores than the conscious mind can obtain. Critics of the setpoint concept have joked that we would all have to have scales in the soles of our feet to make it work. More likely, at least one chemical substance is released by the cells that store fat. The blood level of this material, which is proportional to the amount of fat being stored, is monitored by the brain. If it falls too low, a complex control system within the brain somehow begins to compensate. This setpoint mechanism may slow the metabolic rate through hormonal and neural signals, so that energy is used more sparingly. At the same time, it pressures the conscious mind—at first almost imperceptibly—to change behavior. This pressure may be experienced as a kind of agitation—a "noshy" feeling, a restless inclination to eat between meals and to eat a little more at each meal. Later, the feeling may harden into voracious hunger, and restlessness gives way to energy-conserving lethargy. This succession of events was vividly observed during an artificial famine staged nearly 40 years ago.

In the rainy November of 1944, 36 conscientious objectors to military service took up residence in dormitories at the University of Minnesota. They came with the intention of dieting very strictly for 24 weeks. The investigation was led by epidemiologist Ancel Keys, who hoped that information from this experimental starvation would be useful in rehabilitating the starved populations in World War II war zones.

The volunteers were in their mid-20s, of normal height (5′5″ to 6′3″) and weight (136 to 184 pounds) for their age. In the first three months of their stay at the university, the volunteers ate normally—about 3,500 calories a day. They were required to walk about three miles a day, engage in other physical activity several times a week, and carry out various maintenance jobs around their living quarters.

On February 12, 1945, the experiment began. The men were put on half their usual caloric intake while they continued to work and exercise as before. The new diet was principally whole wheat bread, potatoes, grains, turnips, and cabbage—foods intended to resemble those available in European famine areas. Adequate amounts of vitamins and minerals and token amounts of meat and dairy products supplemented their rations.

In the early phases of their diet, the men were cheerful, if uncomfortable, and they sometimes even experienced euphoria. But hunger never went away, and their highs were always followed by depression. They began losing weight rapidly, most of it from their fat stores and a much smaller proportion as protein. After a couple of months, they had lost about half their total body fat. Virtually all of the fat stored under their skin and in their abdomens was gone.

By now the men were irritable and quarrelsome. They also began to conserve energy. Though they continued their required walks and exercise, lethargy led them to avoid as much work, study, or play as they could. Small chores around the dormitory were neglected; their hair went uncombed, their teeth unbrushed. By the end of their sixth month of semistarvation, virtually all the men were deeply apathetic. They were indifferent to their visitors. Mealtimes, which came at half past eight in the morning and five in the evening, became the focus of their lives. The men were impatient to receive each meal but then would toy with it for as long as two hours. They were far from indifferent to flavor, however, and many of them experimented with unorthodox combinations or covered their food with salt and spices to intensify its taste.

At the end of the starvation period, three months of gradual refeeding began. The men had all lost a quarter of their starting weight, and on their new, but still restricted, diets they all began to gain. Even so, they remained miserable. This suggests that daily energy balance was not the secret to the men's discontent since they were now eating more calories than they were burning each day.

At a farewell banquet marking the end of dietary restriction in October 1945, the men were still ravenous; many of them became ill from overeating. Thereafter the 12 who stayed on ate steadily, consuming a daily average of 5,000 calories. Still they reported that they were hungry, even at the end of a very large meal. The overriding sense of hunger that these men felt was not appeased even by a large daily excess of food.

By the time they sat down for the Thanksgiving meal, a year after they had convened for their experiment, about half the men felt that their interest in food had returned to normal. At the same time, something else had returned to normal: their weights. Other measurements made at that time revealed that the men were just recovering all their original amount of fat, though muscle tissue was still significantly depleted. This observation suggests that the missing fat was what made them feel deprived, that their bodies had some means of recognizing the deficiency and strove to restore it as fast as possible. Once that occurred, they no longer felt a caloric monkey on their backs.

People who diet successfully and lose weight only to succumb guiltily to a binge of eating may recognize their experience in this story. They will recall the ceaseless hunger that is not relieved by a single indulgence and the internal pressure to go on eating until all the pounds so triumphantly shed have returned. Keys' experiment provides some of the clearest evidence that the human body itself demands a certain amount of adipose tissue. Severe disruption can alter this balance, but it is restored with adequate time and food.

If everyone's body really decides on its own how fat to be—if there is a setpoint—then gaining appreciable amounts of weight should be as difficult as losing. Such a project was initiated two decades later by a wiry, soft-spoken New Englander named Ethan Allen Sims. Sims was interested in the metabolic factors connecting obesity and diabetes. In the mid-1960s, after experimenting with hamsters, he realized that nobody really knew whether the metabolic differences between fat and thin people resulted from their different quantities of fat or were instead the cause. So he resolved to find a group of thin people he could make temporarily fat.

In 1964 Sims began an experiment in overeating at Vermont State Prison. A small research area, including a recreation room, dining room, and kitchen, was set aside in the prison's hospital area. Prisoner-volunteers entered the project committed to gaining up to 25 percent of their weight. For 200 days they ate heroically. In the early weeks of the experiment they continued with their usual prison regimen, but near the end they also cultivated sloth as part of the attempt to gain even more weight. To reach their goals, the prisoners virtually doubled the amount of food they normally ate. Only two of the men (later discovered to have a family history of obesity or diabetes) found it easy to gain; the others had to struggle. And once they had successfully added 25 percent to their starting weights, the prisoners could keep it on only by overeating an average of 2,000 extra calories a day, not just the couple of hundred that might seem theoretically necessary. One of the prisoners who gained relatively easily went from 110 pounds to 143, but he had to consume 7,000 calories a day during the last two months of the experiment to acquire and keep his adipose baggage.

The prisoners evidently did not suffer from their experience in quite the same way that Keys' con-

What sets the setpoint?

According to setpoint theory, when fat stores fall below a certain level, the body reacts by "desiring" more fat. This yearning for body fat is orchestrated by an unconscious portion of the brain, which coordinates behavior and biochemistry to keep the stores relatively constant. The amount of fat that is called for depends, in part, on the number of fat cells in the body.

The cells that store fat are located mostly under the skin, where they are arranged in clusters, like microscopic soap bubbles. Once acquired, the number of fat-storing cells appears not to diminish during a lifetime, and each cell resists shrinking below a minimum fat content. A few years ago, the notion was popular that overfed infants would sprout extra cells, which then would cry "feed me" for the rest of their lives. It now seems unlikely that eating patterns in early childhood have much to do with the way fat cells are acquired. Rather, heredity exerts the major influence.

The brain learns about the state of the body's fat stores through chemical messages, some of them presumably sent by the fat cells. Glycerol may be one of the most important of these molecular signals. When fatty acids (the circulating form of fat) are stored in the fat cell, they are bound to glycerol. Fat cells continually bind and release an amount of glycerol proportional to the fat content of the cell.

By itself, the blood level of glycerol cannot be interpreted, but in conjunction with other information—for example, the blood level of insulin—glycerol may accurately inform the brain about the body's fat reserves. This role of glycerol as a signal for fat control has been highlighted by experiments performed at the University of Illinois. Glycerol injected into a rat's brain suppresses the animal's appetite, presumably by lowering its setpoint.

Fat cells do not, however, run the whole show. An elaborate brain mechanism, which includes regions of the hypothalamus, synthesizes information about the state of the body and the environment and then "decides" what the setpoint should be. External influences, such as the taste and smell of especially rich food, appear to raise the setpoint—probably as a way of allowing the body to take advantage of scarce resources. For example, rats fed on cookies, peanut butter, salami, and other sweet or fatty foods seem to raise their setpoints in response to their new diet and eat more to maintain a higher level of fat.

Certain drugs have the opposite effect; they act in the brain to lower the setpoint. When these drugs, such as amphetamines and other diet pills, are discontinued, the setpoint returns to normal, and weight rebounds. Nicotine often acts in the same way. Physical conditioning also appears to lower the setpoint—most dramatically in fat people—and inactivity causes otherwise normal individuals to get fatter. How exercise works to lower the setpoint is not known, but for now it seems to be a healthier and more effective approach to weight loss than pills or cigarettes.

scientious objectors did. But they all found it trying, and everyone considered dropping out at one time or another. At the peak of their obesity, the men were lethargic, disinclined to take initiative, and neglectful of their prison tasks—an observation suggesting that the weight at setpoint is optimal for activity and mood. Much above or below, apathy sets in.

When the experiment was over, weight loss came readily to all the men, except for the two who had gained most easily. The prisoner who gained 33 pounds by eating 7,000 calories a day began to lose weight the day he stopped force-feeding himself. In this phase of the study he was required to exercise vigorously but allowed to eat whatever he felt like. Of his own accord, he consumed about half his normal daily diet and in 75 days was almost back to his starting weight, though he remained about four pounds heavier.

Sims' experiments demonstrated a remarkable tenacity in human physiology. Even in the face of extreme overload, the prisoners fattened very slowly. Exactly how their bodies kept from getting fat remains unclear, although it seems probable that they had some biochemical means for burning off their surfeit of food.

Most of the time no such sleight of hand is needed. From week to week, though not day to day, appetite spontaneously balances the amount we eat against the amount of energy we burn in activity. In 1953, a dozen British military cadets were followed by physiologist O. G. Edholm at the National Institute for Medical Research. Edholm and his colleagues attempted to record everything the cadets ate and everything they did, compare the two, and see how the books balanced. All of what the cadets ate was weighed when it was served to them, as were leavings on their plates, and careful estimates were made of the calorie content in anything else they ate, such as "chocolate and biscuits" and other foods purchased at the canteen. The energy expended by the cadets in various activities—resting, standing, sitting, drilling—was measured in a series of brief tests. The cadets then kept a record of everything they did all day. The upshot of the study was that, although these normal-weight (137 to 184 pounds), 19-year-old men gave no conscious thought to balancing their energy budgets and were not restricted in how much they ate, during the whole fortnight they managed to eat just what they needed to account for the energy they used.

Edholm's group was curious to

see whether it could find a pattern in the cadets' eating habits: Did they eat a lot on the days when they were most active? They did not; rather it appeared they were consistently eating to compensate for energy they had used two days earlier. A lag between exertion and intake would be expected if increased appetite is a response to depleted fat stores. Although Edholm could not confirm his first finding, the same two-day lag has appeared in other experiments.

At the University of Pennsylvania, another group proved that they could do their caloric arithmetic without referring to a calorie chart, without seeing what they were eating, and without weighing themselves. These men and women agreed to subsist entirely on Metrecal, a milkshake-like diet drink, dispensed to them from a contraption belonging to Henry Jordan, a psychiatrist at the university. A volunteer would enter Jordan's laboratory and sit down at a desk from which a wooden arm jutted up to mouth level. Emerging from this support was a stainless steel nipple connected with tubing to reservoirs of Dutch chocolate, vanilla, strawberry, or coffee flavored liquid in a nearby refrigerator. The volunteer would attach himself to the metal spout and, by pushing a button, start a pump to deliver his meal. He stopped drinking when he felt full.

From a series of experiments with this device, Jordan concluded that people who came in to take a single meal from it were not much influenced by the number of calories in the liquid. Feeling full was mainly a reaction to tasting the fluid and perceiving its volume in their stomachs. Theresa Spiegel, a psychologist working with Jordan, then set out to learn whether the same would hold true if the subjects were to spend several weeks depending on the machine for all their nourishment.

Spiegel's volunteers were instructed to consume nothing but black coffee, tea, or water outside the laboratory and not to weigh themselves. They would come to the laboratory at any time to take as much or as little Metrecal as they wanted. Their only cue to start eating was hunger, their only cue to stop was feeling full.

Most of her nine subjects took a few days to adapt to their new way of life. At first they ate too little, but two to four days later they were back up to their normal intake (about 3,000 calories a day). A week after the experiment began, without telling the volunteers, Spiegel cut the concentration of calories in the Metrecal in half. The fluid was doctored to keep about the same taste and texture, and few of the subjects guessed that it had changed. Again, for a couple of days they took in too little but then, by roughly doubling the amount of fluid they swallowed, brought themselves back up to the number of calories they needed to hold a reasonably steady weight.

What happened to the Metrecal volunteers and the people in the three other experiments tells us a lot about everyday experience, about such things as appetite, hunger and satiety, and the substance—fat—that seems to bind these states of mind together in a working system. One group was starved. One was stuffed. One lived a more-or-less normal life but kept meticulous records. And one was reduced to eating everything from a metal teat. But though these groups were widely separated in time and place, they all showed that certain kinds of behavior—the quest for food, the choice of how much to eat, and so forth—are directed by forces outside of conscious awareness. These forces are not the familiar denizens of a Freudian unconscious—repressed conflict, displaced anger, infantile deprivation. They are, instead, real physiological pressures that are always working to keep a foreordained amount of fat on the body. In this case, anatomy is indeed destiny.

The setpoint, it would appear, is very good at what it does best: supervising fat storage. On the other hand, it has some serious blind spots. It cannot tell the difference between a reducing diet and starvation. The dieter who enters the battle with a high setpoint experiences constant hunger, presumably as part of his body's attempt to restore the status quo.

Hunger does accumulate. Dieters demonstrate it; Keys' volunteers demonstrated it. Any laboratory rat will demonstrate it: Take away its rations until the animal loses an ounce or so, then give it free access to food, and it will eat very earnestly until it has restored the missing fat. Satiety also accumulates. Force feed a rat with rich eggnog through a stomach tube, and if you give it more calories than it needs, it will fatten. When you stop, the rat will eat less than normal until the excess is lost. Sims' overfed volunteers showed the same effect.

Rare individuals manage to diet and stay relatively thin, despite permanent hunger. But even dedicated dieters may find, to their dismay, that they cannot lose as much weight as they would like. After an initial, relatively quick loss of 10 or 20 pounds, for example, dieters often become stuck at a plateau and begin losing weight at a much slower rate, though they remain as hungry as ever.

As this experience demonstrates, the body has more than one way to defend its fat stores. Long-term caloric deprivation acts, in ways that are not clear, as a signal to turn down the metabolic rate. Calories are burned more slowly, so that even a paltry diet almost suffices to maintain weight. The metabolic rate, in short, can evidently adjust up or down to correct for deviations from the setpoint. This phenomenon was identified at the turn of the century by a German nutritionist, R. O. Neumann.

Neumann's idea that the body adjusts its metabolic rate in response to under- and overfeeding has been debated, in one form or another, for decades. Accumulating evidence shows that some excess calories can be burned simply to prevent them from being stored. This type of metabolic heat production is critical to the body's energy equation. It now appears that Neumann's *Luxuskonsumption*, which translates roughly as "extra burning," begins after about two weeks of overfeeding, and a cumulative excess of about 20,000 calo-

Thin may be in, but fashion isn't health.

Go into a typical doctor's office, and you will find posted on the wall, near the scales, the venerable "height-weight chart." It says that, for example, a six-foot man with a light frame should weigh between 152 and 162 pounds. Anything above that "desirable weight" is *overweight,* and, as generations of people have been led to believe, overweight is bad for you.

The truth is, there is nothing terribly scientific about the charts. They are not based on any real medical evidence, and there is no good reason to believe that most people who are heavier than the charts' "desirable" range are any less healthy for it. The key phrase here is "most people."

This does not include truly obese people, a category comprising those who are more than 25 percent over their chart weight. Such people *are* at greater risk of developing high blood pressure, diabetes, and heart disease. Also at greater risk are those who have a family history of these diseases. Medical research shows that such people, as well as those who already have these diseases, can and should improve their health by losing excess weight. However, many of the millions of Americans trying to lose weight do not fall in any of these categories and, therefore, have no medical reason to slim down. These people may not look as trim as a fashion model, but that's fashion, not health.

The height-weight charts grew out of the life insurance industry's desire to find a convenient way of identifying high risk customers. It began in 1901 when Oscar H. Rogers of the New York Life Insurance Company refined the practice of looking for risk factors that would predict a higher death rate in applicants. He found that fat policyholders died younger than those of average weight. The insurance industry didn't care whether fatness *caused* disease and death. It was enough for them to see an association.

It was not long, however, before insurance companies began to think of this marker as a cause of early death. They reasoned that if they could get overweight people to reduce, customers might live longer (and pay more premiums). A pioneer in this effort was Louis I. Dublin, a young biologist who went to work in 1909 for the Metropolitan Life Insurance Company. For the next 43 years Dublin, who was passionately committed to public health education, served Metropolitan not only as chief statistician but as house intellectual and publicist. Dublin coined the phrase "America's No. 1 Health Problem" and applied it to obesity in a campaign to get so-called overweight people to slim down.

In the 1940s, Dublin produced his table of "Ideal Weights," as it was first called. In addition to actuarial figures, it used three somewhat faulty premises. One was Dublin's belief that people should not gain weight after the age of 25. The second assumption was that people could be assigned to one of three "frame" sizes. To this day there is no objective way to measure frames. The third and most critical assumption was that buyers of life insurance were representative of the population at large. It is known now that they are not.

While Dublin's tables were gaining acceptance, medical researchers were beginning one of the most far-reaching studies of health ever undertaken, a study that would prove Dublin wrong.

In 1948 about half the population of Framingham, Massachusetts, between the ages of 30 and 62, some 5,200 men and women, were enrolled in a study that continues to this day. They were examined every two years, and when they died, the cause of death was carefully determined. Although the sample was smaller than Dublin's, it was more representative of Americans at large.

In 1980 the Framingham doctors concluded that, among men, life expectancy was worst for the lightest weight group. Above this lowest level, weight did not have much effect on life expectancy unless it was more than 25 percent above average. Among women, death rates were highest for the lightest and the heaviest, but between the extremes, weight had little correlation with mortality. If the data hint at a "best" weight, it is at or somewhat above the national average for men and women.

Carol Schwartz

ries is required to trigger it.

Ethan Sims' work with overfed prisoners provided some of the first modern confirmation of the phenomenon. "I remember" he says, "we used to be really embarrassed to say anything about *Luxuskonsumption*. Dieticians have assumed that people simply burn with an even flame; stoke it a little and they'll gain weight. But we now know that it's a very dynamic situation."

The *Luxuskonsumption* hypothesis, by itself, begs a crucial question. People may burn excess calories when they eat too much—but how much is "too much"? How does the body "know" when it has been overfed? *Luxuskonsumption* does not seem to be triggered by a single eating bout—say a Thanksgiving dinner—but by some cumulative change in the body. The simplest explanation, though it is by no means proven, is that the body only increases metabolism when it begins to move significantly above the setpoint. Deviations in the other direction have the opposite effect: The metabolic rate drops to conserve calories and maintain a stable amount of fat.

The body reacts to stringent dieting as though famine had set in. Within a day or two after semistarvation begins, the metabolic machinery shifts to a cautious regimen designed to conserve the calories it already has on board. The willing spirit is opposed by flesh that is not at all weak; it is perfectly determined to hoard the remaining supply of energy pending nutritional relief. Because of this innate biological response, dieting becomes progressively less effective and, as generations of dieters have observed, a plateau is reached at which further weight loss seems all but impossible.

If it turns out to be true, the setpoint theory may be disappointing news to people who want to get thinner by eating less. But it may help to counteract the mania for thinness that has become so pervasive, especially among women. In 1979, Bloomingdale's department store advertised its summer line of women's clothing: "bean lean, slender as the night, narrow as an arrow, pencil thin, get the point?" The fashions, and the bodies they enclosed, were illustrated with sketches, perhaps because not even a model could achieve the designer's ectoplasmic ideal.

The vogue for thinness which began around World War I was initially a sign of emancipation. The slender, almost tubular, form came to symbolize athleticism, nonreproductive sexuality, and a kind of androgynous independence. But in a culture that decrees everyone should be thin, the fashion for leanness has become more oppressive than liberating.

Of course, there will always be those select few who can starve themselves by an act of will to overcome their setpoints. But such examples have little to teach the majority of people, who have other things to do with their lives.

The Three Brains of Paul MacLean

Ruth Daniloff

Ruth Daniloff has written about scientific subjects for the *Washington Post Magazine, Harvard Magazine*, and *Working Woman*.

Imagine yourself driving a carriage pulled by a crocodile, a horse, and a computer. The crocodile tries to slither into the nearest swamp while the horse bolts for the stable and the computer spits printouts on road conditions. You cling desperately to the reins, trying to hold the trio in harness. According to Paul MacLean, chief of the National Institute of Mental Health's Laboratory of Brain Evolution and Behavior, that is what goes on inside your head.

MacLean's research has taken him 250 million years into the past to postulate that our skulls contain three brains, layered one over another, each with its own unique mentality. While people still have trouble believing our descent from the apes, MacLean is suggesting we go one step down the evolutionary tree and accept our heritage from reptiles as well. Survival, he believes, may depend on our understanding of our three cerebral heritages.

"The brain evolved and expanded along the lines of three basic patterns characterized as reptilian, paleomammalian, and neomammalian," says MacLean, a courtly man whose career is drawing to a close after forty years of mining the neural landscape. These three brains are interconnected, but each has a special intelligence, method of communication, memory, motor, and sense of time, he maintains.

MacLean has the rounded shoulders of a researcher who has spent too long hunched over a microscope. What little time he has for relaxation is spent on what he calls his "farm"—a twenty-acre woodland sanctuary adjoining his house in Potomac, where he keeps ducks, geese, bantams, dogs, cats, horses, and a goat. "Animals and I have no trouble communicating," he laughs.

As he talks, two male lizards in the aquarium at his laboratory confront each other with threatening push-ups. Suddenly, one of the small beige creatures flashes a bright-orange crest under his chin. The other lizard backs off.

In the nineteenth century, anatomists recognized that some parts of the brain were older than others in terms of evolution. In the early 1970s MacLean came up with the idea of the "triune brain," made up of three distinct layers. By tracing different kinds of behavior, like the struggle to be top lizard, to specific areas of the brain, he has identified neural formations that could explain the conflicting personalities in each of us.

MacLean says our oldest cerebral inheritance is the reptilian brain, which he dubs the "R-complex" or, when he wants to convey its primitive nature, the "dragon." When a stain is injected into tissue sections of the brain, the older formations at the base of the skull show up as copper colored under a microscope—different from other sections—and conform chemically to the brain of a lizard, he says.

"Lizards and other reptiles provide illustrations of complex behavior commonly seen in mammals, including man," says MacLean. "Besides being deceptive, predatory, and intolerant, the reptilian brain appears to be hidebound. It operates compulsively according to routines, rituals, and schedules."

According to MacLean this structure deep in the brain is the neural storehouse for behavior necessary to preserve both the individual and the species. Put another way, the dragon holds the key to our life force and personalities.

The next step up the evolutionary tree, according to MacLean, is the paleomammalian brain, or limbic lobe, which dates back 150 million years to the time when warm-blooded animals entered the world.

"The big evolutionary news for animals at that time was that the young became important," says MacLean. "Most reptiles have no regard for their offspring. Mammals, on the other hand, must nurture their young if their species is to prosper. There must be appropriate feelings somehow built into the brain."

In the early 1950s MacLean won acclaim in medical circles for demonstrating that the paleomammalian brain, which surrounds the dragon, is the seat of emotions. His subsequent research suggests that these emotions also guide behavior necessary to preservation of the species. Before MacLean's work, the limbic lobe was thought to be primarily involved in the sense of smell.

The limbic system, as textbooks identify it following MacLean's work, is, in turn, subdivided into three sections. The two older formations govern smell and

Reprinted from *The Washingtonian* magazine, Washington, D.C.

control appetite and sexual drive. The third subdivision, which relates to sight, acquires its greatest development in humans.

At the top of the evolutionary scale is the youngest brain—the neomammalian brain, or neocortex, which fits over the two older structures like a thinking cap. MacLean describes the neocortex as a computer that nature introduced some 250,000 years ago to counteract the organism's domination by emotions and gut reactions. The neocortex processed information largely from the outside—from the eyes, ears, and body walls—and survival came to depend on the ability to reason. MacLean regards this most recent brain as "the mother of invention and the father of abstract thought." As the brain responsible for mankind's greatest scientific achievements, it must also take responsibility for its mistakes, he maintains. It is the brain of concentration camps and Hiroshima.

MacLean's evolutionary view of how the brain functions is iconoclastic. The conventional approach is to study the brain in terms of systems—such as sensory or motor—as they operate now.

The implications of MacLean's work are considerable. By examining certain behavior common to reptiles, animals, and humans, and by identifying the neural formations that cause each type of behavior, he challenges the behaviorist school that has dominated social science for most of this century.

"Until now we have accepted the view that the human mind and human society are essentially unorganized masses that get structure mainly from the environment," says Edward O. Wilson, a Harvard biologist who says MacLean's research reinforces his own findings on the biological basis of behavior such as altruism and hostility in animals.

Though Paul MacLean's work has been largely devoted to unlearned behavior, he refuses to be drawn into nature (heredity) versus nurture (environment) arguments. The environment does play a vital role in behavior, he says, referring to the fact that outside stimuli can trigger genetically programmed behavior. He cites the way a hawk-shaped shadow in a lab can cause a newborn chick to run for cover.

The triune brain has gained some recognition outside the neurosciences. MacLean's research formed the neurological underpinning of *The Dragons of Eden,* Carl Sagan's best-selling account of the evolution of human intelligence. Dr. Murray Bowen, who heads the Georgetown University Family Center, depends on MacLean's lab work to bolster his theory that nature more often than nurture is responsible for emotional problems. A few educators are starting to consider curriculum for the three brains.

But in the hard brain sciences the triune brain gets plenty of criticism. Colleagues admire MacLean's lab work, but his theory gives scientists in comparative evolutionary neurobiology "apoplexy and is virtually ignored," says Dr. C.B.G. Campbell, a prominent research neurologist at Walter Reed Army Institute of Research.

A professor of neuroanatomy at a midwestern university who did not want his name used calls the triune brain "a naive and fanciful notion appealing to the lunatic fringes of neuroscience."

Critics claim MacLean's theory is so broad it fails to reflect the complexity of the brain and leads to misinterpretation by people outside his field. "MacLean gives the impression, for example, that the so-called reptilian parts of our brain are unchanged from reptiles," says Campbell. "That's not true. They are similar. The general organization is the same, but that doesn't mean there are no differences between those parts of our brain and a reptile's brain."

Another scientist who questions the theory says MacLean "is more your old-time scientist than the Young Turk who spends all his time worrying about little squiggles. The man thinks broadly, reads widely in many areas, and is contemplative and philosophical."

Others view MacLean as one of the brain's great pioneers. Dr. Henry Lederer, a neuropsychiatrist and associate dean of Georgetown University Medical School, says, "In America we produce first-class researchers, but not many original thinkers. MacLean is a great scientist as well as one who has the guts to speculate."

"No hypothesis is ever introduced without exaggeration," says Dr. Walle Nauta, a prominent neuroanatomist at the Massachusetts Institute of Technology. Nauta admires MacLean's work and is not alarmed that all the pieces don't fit. "What we know of any one subject at any moment is only twenty percent of what will survive," he notes.

Academic infighting is inevitable, especially when most of the brain is still uncharted territory.

We do know that during the later stages of evolution, as humans changed from their ape-like ancestors, the size of the brain trebled, reaching its present size of around three pounds some 250,000 years ago in the most dramatic transformation in the history of anatomy. We know that five sixths of the brain's physical growth takes place after birth, reaching maturity around age sixteen. We know also that among humans intelligence appears to be unrelated to brain size: The fact that the Russian writer Ivan Turgenev's brain weighed four pounds and Anatole France's just over two pounds is no reflection on French literature.

Thanks to spectacular advances in molecular biology and to the development of extraordinarily sophisticated research tools, we have come in recent years to know a great deal about the brain's electrical and chemical makeup.

We now know, for example, that the brain is like a switchboard beyond the wildest imaginings of Ma Bell's most sophisticated engineers. It contains more than 100 billion cells. Ninety percent of the cells are glial cells, from the Greek word for glue, and comprise the white matter. The remaining 10 billion are nerve cells, or neurons, which make up the gray matter. Consider that each nerve cell contains about 20 million molecules of ribonucleic acid (RNA); that each molecule of RNA is capable of converting genetic instructions from deoxyribonucleic acid (DNA), also present in the cells, into any of 100,000 proteins and you begin to understand the task confronting brain researchers. In addition, each cell is capable of linking across special pathways with up to 300,000 other cells. The links are made possible because each cell has hundreds of branches. In turn, each branch has hundreds of terminals along its membrane. In fact, if you hooked up all the world's telephones simultaneously, the brain would still make more than a million times the number of connections.

Making our understanding of the brain more difficult, researchers have concluded that one side of the brain operates differently from the other: The dominant left lobe thinks in words and analyzes all sorts of data, and the right lobe registers images and reasons intuitively. Yet the split-brain theory does not contradict MacLean's three-in-one brain model. When the brain is cut down the middle, each half resembles a three-layer sponge.

The trouble is that the more we learn of this organ—which looks so uninspiring that for centuries men insisted our mental abilities lay in the heart or the liver—the more elusive it appears. In the academic community, where researchers communicate in complex footnotes, MacLean has also come under criticism for using simple anatomical terms. "He commits the unforgivable offense of trying to make the brain understandable," says Richard Restak, a Georgetown University neurologist. "Anyone who does that is in trouble. A lot of people think these things should not be discussed unless in a forum of boring journals."

If MacLean is right, the battle for cerebral control in our skulls that results from the three competing layers could explain contradictions of human character. How, for example, could Hitler have exterminated 6 million people and yet been squeamish about fox hunting?

MacLean believes that a psychiatrist may have problems understanding patients because their reptilian and paleomammalian brains cannot speak, at least not in words. Their "say" in our behavior, however, is vital. "When a psychiatrist asks a patient to lie down on the couch, he is asking him to stretch alongside a horse and a crocodile. The crocodile may shed a tear, the horse neigh and whinny, but when they are encouraged to express their troubles in words, they cannot," says MacLean. "No wonder the patient who must serve as their mouthpiece is sometimes accused of being full of resistance."

MacLean has traced twenty types of behavior related to the reptilian part of the brain.

For instance, a person may place belongings on the next bus seat and feel an irrational stab of hostility toward the stranger who wants to sit down. This reaction could be triggered by the old reptilian brain's establishment-of-territory instinct. Like the dog who defines his neighborhood by cocking his leg against trees and lamp posts, we spot our borders with flags, fences, guards, patrols, customs officers, ornaments, and personal belongings. At the beach we stake out a place on the sand with blankets, towels, and baskets, our hackles rising—especially if the beach is crowded—at the approach of another group of sunbathers. Atavistic neural reactions might also explain protracted border disputes between nations, often involving relatively useless pieces of land.

Establishing status through little rituals is also inborn reptilian behavior, MacLean says. The government executive with two telephones in his chauffeured limousine may be responding to ancient neurological programming related to the social pecking order rather than to a need to call the office on the way home.

Another reptilian legacy, deception, is required for stalking prey and avoiding predators. "If culture teaches us that honesty is the best policy, why are so many people willing to take such enormous risk to practice deception?" MacLean asks. "Why do the games we teach our youngsters place such a premium on deceptive tactics?"

Our reptilian habits also surface in compulsive, repetitive behavior, according to MacLean. We feel comfortable—that is, we can survive—by doing the familiar. Reptilian logic says that if it worked once, it will work forever.

Trivial behavior can be nature's reptilian way of preserving individual and group identity. A son, for example, often takes on his father's walk, while a daughter may copy the way her mother crosses her legs. Imitation is a reptilian survival habit that can lead to trouble, says MacLean: Watching TV violence may trigger real violence.

But for all the problems they create, Paul MacLean says our animal habits are innate protective devices, and people should learn to live with them. He compares a lizard's selection of a special basking spot to a scientist's habit of returning to the same seat throughout a three-day conference. "More often than not, we are victims of our constitutional beings." Freud, he notes, "concentrated on the major drives like food and sex, but ignored all the other built-in dispositions we share with animals."

Paul MacLean started life in Phelps, New York, 67 years ago as a minister's son believing in angels. The first thing he learned in school was that angels didn't have wings: a most disillusioning experience, he recalls. But a career in brain research, he says, has helped him put the angel wings back.

In 1936 MacLean graduated in English from Yale University and left for Edinburgh to study philosophy. Instead, he studied medicine. "Every hard fact undergoes subjective transformation of the brain," he jokes. Back at Yale to continue medical studies, he lost his original enthusiasm for the brain. At that time scholars focused on reflexes and viewed the brain mostly as a push-button organ. So he turned to pathology and specialized in cardiovascular disorders. His interest in the brain was rekindled during World War II, when as an Army doctor he became frustrated by his inability to treat or understand severe psychiatric problems in combat casualties. In 1957 the US government persuaded him to give up his appointment at the Yale Medical School and come to the National Institute of Mental Health here to head a research team and continue his work on how emotions are affected by the paliomammalian, or limbic system, which governs sight, smell, appetite, and sexual drive.

In 1973 MacLean moved his researchers to a 130-acre tract outside Poolesville, Maryland, and established his laboratory on brain evolution and behavior. The 25 or so researchers under his direction include neuroscientists as well as experts from other fields. On a recent day one researcher was reading the fossilized impressions of reptile skulls to learn how these prehistoric beasts regulated their body temperatures. Another researcher listened to the blip-blip-blip of isolated groups of neurons in the brain. Someone else, a "hamster psychologist," watched fluffy rodents hide snacks within nibbling distance of their sleeping quarters.

Seeking the origin of parental care, MacLean and an associate, Michael Murphy, deprived female hamsters of their limbic tissues. The hamsters then ignored their newborn youngsters. Embedded in the paleomammalian brain, MacLean believes, lie the evolutionary roots that bind family, clan, and society.

In an earlier experiment, a researcher destroyed the pathways between the reptilian and limbic formations in vigorous male monkeys. They turned into doddering old primates in less than two months. When other major pathways were destroyed, the monkeys lost all simian characteristics.

At times, certain parts of MacLean's own triune brain are in conflict. In the name of science, his neocortex, the cold computer, allows him to make a hole in a monkey's head. Yet his paleomammalian brain, capable of compassion, gives him pause. Having to hurt animals obviously pains him. Later, as he makes the rounds of his lab, he stops to chatter with the monkey and passes nuts through the bars.

If we are endowed with three not-well-coordinated brains, what prospects do we have for survival? After all, about 99 percent of all recorded species have ended in extinction. Some experts estimate that every hour a form of life becomes extinct. Why are our prospects any better than those of the animals and reptiles whose fossilized bones clutter MacLean's laboratory?

MacLean ponders these questions in the office where he has been working on the final chapters of a book about the triune brain. Survival is something he feels strongly about; it's one reason he speaks to audiences outside his field, risking the accusations of "neurophilosophizing."

MacLean is confident humans can survive. He points to the neural circuitry that he believes throws light on an issue that has plagued philosophers, theologians, and social engineers for centuries—the perfectability of mankind. MacLean refers to the neocortex—the thinking cap that ballooned so late in evolutionary history.

Nature must have concluded that a genie had been let out of the bottle and could have become a Frankenstein, he contends. At first the neocortex developed as a "cold, reasoning computer," but then a change started. "Slowly, but progressively, nature added something to the neocortex that for the first time brought heart and a sense of compassion into the world," says MacLean, pointing to a diagram of the brain's frontal cortex. "Note how its circuits tie in with the limbic system. Clinically, there is evidence that this frontal cortex—by looking inward, so to speak—obtains insights required for one individual to identify with another."

This component of compassion evolving in the human brain over 250,000 years argues against the theory of the German philosopher Friedrich Nietzsche that there is no inherent goodness in humans, MacLean believes. Why nature took this altruistic evolutionary fork is a mystery. If nature had not forced some neural circuitry to connect with our emotions, could we have become extinct? The Neanderthal brain, MacLean notes, was larger than ours, but he suspects it did not have such circuitry.

Our concern for suffering extends beyond human beings to animals and even plants—there are people who wince when they nip leaves off their potted plants. "Altruism! Empathy! Why, these are new words!" MacLean says with passion. "As human beings, we seem to be acquiring the soft stuff of which angels are made. Perhaps it is time to take a fresh look and behave a little more like angels."

MacLean suggests that in education especially, we should not focus solely on the neocortex but should consider the two older brains as well. "With an imagination that exceeds the speed of light, the neocortex may be able to keep up with the accelerated tempo of life through speed reading, computers, and other contrivances, but our other animal brains, which are our constant companions, move at their own slow pace. They have their own biological clocks and their own sequential ways of doing things."

Educators should realize that introspection is very important, MacLean insists. Survival, he says, depends on linking the cold light with which we see to the warm emotions with which we feel.

As MacLean approaches the end of his career, one senses in him an urgency, a desire to pass on insights, to explain his work in hopes of shedding light on the complexities of human behavior. "The more you know, the more ignorant you feel," he says, obviously frustrated. "I cannot think of any worse position to be in at the end of a life—to have worked and struggled so hard to learn something, and to end up in this terrible, terrible ignorance." He shrugs and falls silent.

TWINS R·E·U·N·I·T·E·D

Constance Holden

Constance Holden is a staff writer for Science.

Anyone who knows identical twins has undoubtedly experienced profound paradoxical reactions: astonishment at their similarities and amazement at their differences. Twins have always been regarded as special; in some aboriginal societies they are venerated, in some they are slain. Identical twins also have figured as protagonists in one of the oldest and bitterest disputes among scientists—the nature/nurture controversy.

It has been almost a century since Sir Francis Galton, the founder of the science of eugenics, first proposed studying identical twins to determine the relative influences of heredity and environment on human development. Now a group of researchers at the University of Minnesota are involved in the most comprehensive investigation ever undertaken of twins raised apart. Initiated by psychologist Thomas Bouchard, the study consists of exhaustive physical, psychological, and biographical inventories of every twin. So far, 15 pairs, each of whom spent a week at the university, have been tested. Bouchard has located 18 additional pairs with the help of the publicity the project is getting.

It will take at least five or six years to analyze definitively the masses of data accumulated so far. But after a year and a half of examining twin pairs, the 17 members of the research team, which includes six psychologists, two psychiatrists, and nine other medical experts, have been overwhelmed with the similarities of the participating pairs. Some similarities, of course, are clearly coincidental, such as the twins who are both named Jim. Others may only seem to be: Twin sisters who had never met before each wore seven rings on their fingers. They may not have inherited their fondness for rings; perhaps only the same pretty hands prompted the fondness. And still other similarities, like phobias, which were long thought to be learned, may turn out after all to be hereditary.

"I frankly expected far more differences than we have found so far," says Bouchard. "I'm a psychologist, not a geneticist. I want to find out how the environment works to shape psychological traits." Bouchard has encountered some hostility on the Minneapolis campus because he remains aloof from the ideological fashion, which holds that behavior is largely shaped by environmental influences. Student hostility is ironic in view of Bouchard's political activism at the University of California in the radical 1960s.

Actually Bouchard's quest is considerably more sophisticated than critics perceive. To discover how the environment shapes behavior, one first must have an idea of how innate tendencies work to select a particular environment. The same surroundings can be interpreted very differently by two individuals. One person may find a library a good place to read, for example, while another may regard it as an excellent hunting ground for members of the opposite sex.

In the hope of making some of these distinctions, Bouchard has drawn upon his extensive experience in personality testing to develop the battery of tests for each twin pair. In addition, the scientists take detailed medical histories that include diet, smoking and exercise habits, electrocardiograms, chest X rays, heart stress tests, and pulmonary exams. They inject the twins with a variety of substances to determine allergies. They wire them to EEG machines to measure their brain wave responses to various stimuli.

During the six days they devote to each twin pair, the team intersperses the physiological probes with several dozen written tests, which ask some 15,000 questions. These cover family and childhood environment, fears and phobias, personal interests, vocational aptitudes, values, reading and television viewing habits, musical tastes, and aesthetic judgments. Each pair of twins undergoes three comprehensive psychological inventories. In addition each takes ability tests: the Wechsler Adult Intelligence Scale, the main adult IQ test, and numerous others that reveal skills in information processing, vocabulary, spatial abilities, numerical processing, mechanical ability, and memory. Throughout the week there is a good deal of overlap in an attempt to "measure the same underlying factor at different times," says Bouchard.

No scientific conclusions can yet be drawn from the masses of data collected, but the team has made a number of provocative observations.

The "Jim twins," as they have come to be known, have histories that are riddled with bizarre coincidences. Jim Springer and Jim Lewis were adopted as four-week-old infants into working-class Ohio families. They never met each other until they were 39 years old. Both had law enforcement training and worked part time as deputy sheriffs. Both vacationed in Florida; both drove Chevrolets. Much has been made of the fact that their lives are marked by a trail of similar names. Both had dogs named Toy. They married and divorced women named Linda and remarried women named Betty. They named their sons James Allan and James Alan. While the laws of chance dictate against such an unlikely string of coincidences, Bouchard has noted that twins seem to be highly subject to such strange similarities.

Other similarities, however, are probably more than coincidental. In school both twins liked math but not spelling. They currently enjoy mechanical drawing and carpentry. They have almost identical drinking and smoking patterns, and they chew their fingernails down to the nubs. Investigators thought their similar medical histories were astounding. In addition to having hemorrhoids and identical pulse, blood pressure, and sleep patterns, both had inexplicably put on ten pounds at the same time in life. Each suffers from "mixed headache syndrome," a combination tension and migraine headache. Both first suffered headaches at the age of 18. They have these late-afternoon headaches with the same frequency and same degree of disability, and the two used the same terms to describe the pain they experienced.

The twins also have their differences. One wears his hair over his forehead; the other has it slicked back with sideburns. One expresses himself better orally, the others in writing. Even though the emotional environments in which they were brought up were different, still the profiles on their psychological inventories were much alike.

Another much publicized pair is 47-year-old Oskar Stöhr and Jack Yufe. These two have the most dramatically different backgrounds of all the twins studied. Born in Trinidad of a Jewish father and a German mother, they were separated shortly after birth. The mother took Oskar back to Germany where he was raised as a Catholic and a Nazi by his grandmother. Jack was raised in the Caribbean as a Jew by his father and spent part of his youth on an Israeli kibbutz. As might be expected, the men now lead markedly different lives: Oskar, an industrial supervisor in Germany, is married, a devoted union man, and a skier. Jack runs a retail clothing store in San Diego, is separated from his wife, describes himself as a workaholic, and enjoys sailing as a hobby.

Their families had never corresponded, yet similarities were evident when they first met at the airport. Both sported mustaches and two-pocket shirts with epaulets. Each had his wire-rimmed glasses with him. They share abundant idiosyncracies: The twins like spicy foods and sweet liqueurs, are absentminded, fall asleep in front of the television, think it is funny to sneeze in a crowd of strangers, flush the toilet before using it, store rubber bands on their wrists, read magazines from back to front, dip buttered toast in their coffee. Oskar did not take all the tests because he speaks only German, but the two had similar profiles on the Minnesota Multiphasic Personality Inventory. Oskar yells at his wife, which Jack did before he was separated. Although the two were raised in different cultures, investigator Bouchard professed himself impressed by the similarities in their mannerisms, the questions they asked, their "temperament, tempo, the way they do things." He also thinks the pair supply "devastating" evidence against the feminist contention that children's personalities are shaped differently according to the sex of those who rear them, since Oskar was raised by women and Jack by men.

The Bouchard team has enjoyed a run on female British twins in their late 30s, all separated during World War II, and all raised by people who did not know each other. Although Bridget and Dorothy, the

The Coffman Gallery area of the Coffman Union Program Council is responsabile, for the visual arts programs and exhibitions which are presented in it's three formal gallery spaces and other facilities

The Coffman Gallery area of the Coffman Union Program Council is responsible for the visual arts programs and exhibitions which are presented in its three formal gallery spaces and other facilities.

Though Barbara and Daphne were raised separately, their handwriting is remarkably similar.

housewives sporting the seven rings each, were reared in different socioeconomic settings, the class difference was evident only in that the twin raised in modest circumstances had bad teeth. Otherwise, the investigators conclude, the twins share "striking similarities in all areas."

Another pair, Daphne and Barbara, are fondly remembered as the "giggle sisters," because they were always setting each other off. There are evidently no gigglers in their adoptive families. The sisters both handle stress by ignoring it. Both avoid conflict and controversy; neither has any interest in politics. This similarity is particularly provocative since avoidance of conflict is "classically regarded as learned behavior," says Bouchard.

Irene and Jeanette, 35, who were brought up respectively in England and Scotland, turn out to have the same phobias. Both are claustrophobic, and balked when invited to go into a cubicle for their electroencephalograms. They independently agreed to enter the cubicle if the door were left open. Both are timid about ocean bathing; they resolve the problem by backing in slowly. Neither likes escalators. Both are compulsive counters, of everything they see, such as the wheels of trucks. Both count themselves to sleep.

Other similarities turned up in a number of twin pairs. Tests of vision, for example, showed that even in cases in which one twin wears glasses and the other does not, both require the same type of correction.

Bouchard says it is commonplace for identical twins to engage in coincidental behavior: Both will buy the same gift for their mother, or even select the same birthday card. But he is finding that such coincidences often crop up with twins raised apart. A favorite episode involves two middle-aged women in his study. Once, as children, they were brought together briefly to meet each other. Both turned up wearing the same dress.

As for IQ, a hotly controversial area of psychological testing, the Minnesota study confirms what other researchers repeatedly have shown: that of all psychological traits measured in identical twins, this one shows the highest degree of similarity. Bouchard, mindful of charges of investigator bias that are often leveled at IQ testers, arranges for outside contractors to come in to administer and score the Wechsler intelligence test. He wants to avoid imputations of fraud such as those leveled recently at the eminent British educational psychologist, the late Sir Cyril Burt, who some accuse of "cooking" his IQ data in order to buttress his belief in the heritability of intelligence. In the case of the Minnesota study, most of the scores do not differ any more than those of two tests taken by the same person at different times. In the few that vary considerably, the variance appears to reflect large differences in education.

Psychological histories also correspond well to studies of twins reared together. Psychiatrist Leonard Heston, the father of identical twin girls, is particularly well suited to studying these histories. Scientists have known for some time that there is a genetic component, often involving chemical imbalance, in many mental illnesses. For example, if one twin suffers from depression or schizophrenia the other stands a 45 percent chance of succumbing as well. Heston was surprised by the extent to which twins raised separately tend to share emotional problems—"things such as mild depressions and phobias that I would never have thought of as being particularly genetically mediated," Heston remarks. "Now at least, there are grounds for a very live hypothesis."

Psychologist David Lykken finds that the brain waves of the twin pairs in the Minnesota study resemble each other in the same way as those of twins who have been raised together. Moreover, Lykken finds that tracings from each twin of a pair differ no more than tracings from the same person taken at different times.

To be sure, identical twins differ in myriad ways. One of the most common is in tendencies toward introversion and extroversion. Another common difference, according to the English researcher James Shields, is dominance and submissiveness. Bouchard and his colleagues note that one twin is likely to be more aggressive, outgoing, and confident.

But they find twins reared together usually differ the most in that respect. In other words, dominance and submission seem to be traits that twins use to assert their individuality. Because twins brought up together often feel compelled to exaggerate their differences, David Lykken thinks it is possible that twins reared separately may actually have more in common with each other than those raised together.

Because of the comparatively small numbers of twins they have studied, the investigators face difficulties in proving that their results are more than a random collection of case histories. What they would like to do, according to Tellegen, is "invent methods for analyzing traits in an objective manner, so we can get statistically cogent conclusions from a single case." This will require first establishing what is to be expected on the basis of chance alone. For example, how likely are two randomly selected IQ scores to be as similar as those of two identicial twins? This method of analysis will be crucial in weeding out similarities between twins that may be no more common than coincidences that occur between randomly paired people.

Of all the members of the Bouchard team, Lykken is the most willing to entertain ideas that so far are only supported by subjective impressions. He says, "Looking at these 15 pairs of identical twins, I have an enhanced sense of the importance of the genes in determining all aspects of behavior." But he acknowledges the importance of the environment as well. "What is emerging in my mind," Lykken concludes, "is that the most important thing to come out of this study is a strong sense that vastly more of human behavior is genetically determined or influenced than we ever supposed."

TINKERING WITH LIFE

Boyce Rensberger

Boyce Rensberger is a senior editor of Science 81.

As the relentless revolution in genetics continues year after year, it becomes clear that we are learning enough about life's molecular dance to begin to become its choreographers. Some new geneticists now talk not just of engineering the genes of bacteria; they want to redesign the genetic core of higher organisms including those of human beings.

Indeed, the first attempt at human gene therapy has already been made. Two victims of beta-thalassemia, an often fatal disease akin to sickle-cell anemia, had bone marrow cells removed and incubated with quantities of the normal hemoglobin gene they lacked. It was hoped the cells would take up the genes and function normally when injected back into the patients.

The experimental results were inconclusive, and the scientist who tried it, Martin Cline of the University of California at Los Angeles, has been found guilty by the National Institutes of Health of violating its regulations concerning the use of recombinant molecules. An NIH panel recommended severe penalties against Cline and advised a detailed review of his existing federal grants.

Nonetheless, some molecular biologists feel it is only a matter of time before people with hereditary diseases are given engineered genes to cure them. Others discourage such expectations, arguing that many basic problems remain. For example, natural genes have regulatory mechanisms that are only beginning to be studied. There is also the formidable problem of installing helpful genes in all the appropriate cells of the body.

Success in this direction, so far, has been confined to inserting new genes into embryo cells. For example, Frank Ruddle and his colleagues at Yale have put a gene for an enzyme called thymidine kinase (TK) into fertilized mouse eggs. The genes were injected into the eggs' nuclei using a micropipette with an opening small enough to enter a nucleus without damaging it too much. The eggs were then implanted in the uteri of female mice. Of the first 180 mice that developed from injected eggs, three incorporated the TK gene.

Ruddle then put a human interferon gene in mouse embryos, which matured and passed the gene to their offspring. By creating mice with an antiviral gene no mouse ever had, Ruddle has launched a new method of controlling evolution. Animal breeders, of course, have been controlling evolution for millennia by breeding only selected animals. But putting novel genes into animals is a radically new form of control that may eventually lead to much faster rates of altering domestic animals.

But before this can happen, geneticists must show that they can get the genes into animals and make them function normally. Stanford's Paul Berg, one of the pioneers in the field, has put foreign genes into cell cultures and gotten them to manufacture the enzyme missing in victims of Lesch-Nyhan disease. It is an often fatal childhood disease that has many effects, including mental retardation.

Berg waves off any suggestion that he is close to a cure for the disease. Getting the gene into a few cells growing in a bottle is one thing; getting it into every cell of a human body is quite another. Berg notes that too little is known about how to regulate introduced genes.

Nonetheless, the promise of gene therapy has become so widely appreciated that leading journals of clinical medicine are already discussing the weighty, ethical implications of deliberate, fundamental alterations in the human genome. "Gene therapy for some genetic disorders will be possible in the foreseeable future," according to W. French Anderson and John C. Fletcher, scientists at the National Institutes of Health writing recently in *The New England Journal of Medicine*. But, they say, before it is tried in human beings, standards of medical ethics require an advance determination that the probable benefits outweigh the probable risks.

In adapting these ethical principles to the question of gene therapy, the two scientists say three conditions must be met: First, in animal experiments the gene must be put into the target cells and remain there. Second, the gene should be properly regulated so that it makes the correct quantities of its product, neither too much nor too little. And third, it must be shown that the gene will not harm the cells or the animal.

Gene therapy "offers the strong possibility of enormous good by reducing the suffering and death caused by genetic diseases," the two scientists wrote. "We hope that this laudable goal will not be jeopardized by premature experiments."

On a more popular level, some people have raised the question of whether it is somehow wrong to mix the genes of different species no matter how "successful" an experiment may be in purely scientific terms. Although the issue was raised by a few observers in the early days of gene splicing five or six years ago, it is seldom raised nowadays within science or among professional ethicists. Even the World Council of Churches, which has held meetings and published books with discussions on the ethics of genetic engineering, did not consider it a consequential issue.

It may be that the visceral reaction some people feel when told about gene mixing is simply a new version of the reaction voiced years ago when the first heart transplants were done. We no longer believe that the heart contains the soul or essence of the person, but we may still feel that the genes *do*.

Less ethically complex perhaps but probably of more worldwide significance is a long list of proposals for putting foreign genes into food crops and livestock. The insertion of new genes could enhance the nutritive value of certain crops or enable them to get their own fertilizer by taking nitrogen from the air. Most such efforts involve taking the desired genes from existing plants or nitrogen-fixing bacteria and installing copies in the target species.

Some scientists are even talking about replacing cows with vats of blue-green algae that would be given a gene for the synthesis of casein, milk's protein. The stuff would not be milk, but as a high quality protein it could prove an excellent nutritional supplement for a hungry world.

So great is the potential for the new genetics in agriculture that one study has forecast a staggering \$50 billion to \$100 billion world market developing in 10 to 20 years. Independently financed by two private consulting firms, the study suggests that although the potential market is greater in agriculture than in pharmaceuticals, applications in agriculture will be slower to develop. The reason is that the privately financed drug industry, in contrast to agricultural research, has a strong tradition of investing heavily in basic science and has already absorbed most of the small pool of people trained in the field.

There are also many proposals for putting engineered genes in bacteria to carry out industrial processes such as scavenging metals from low grade ores, breaking down pollutants in contaminated water, and even extracting residual oil from otherwise depleted wells. In fact, so many applications for the new genetics are now under consideration that the Office of Technology Assessment, a sober-eyed analytic arm of the Congress, recently described the new genetics as encompassing "the most rapidly progressing areas of human knowledge in the world today."

As if it were not progressing fast enough, the genetic revolution is now shifting into an even higher gear with the advent of "the gene machine." It is a comparatively cheap, desk-top device that will automatically synthesize fragments of any gene whose genetic code a technician can type onto its keyboard. Until gene machines went on the market earlier this year, it took scientists months or years to synthesize a whole gene. Now the machine will do in one day what used to take four to eight months "by hand."

The machine can be used to make a synthetic version of a natural gene that can be spliced into the DNA of a living cell. It could enable a scientist to invent his own gene, one that is unknown in nature, and synthesize it in the machine. He could then insert the gene into a bacterium just to see what happens. The gene machine works so fast that lots of marginal ideas for genes could be tried out.

One idea is to [illegible] make modified vers[illegible] genes in the hope o[illegible] them. Interferon, for ex[illegible] toxic when given to cancer p[illegible]ts in large doses. Geneticists could create slightly different versions of the gene, which would yield minor variants of the interferon molecule, and hope to eliminate some part of the molecule that might be toxic. Theoretically, scientists could make genes that have never before existed and insert them into the genomes of animals. If the genes were passed on from parent to offspring, this method could create new animal and plant species. Thanks to the gene machine, the questions that genetic engineering might not have posed for decades must now be answered in years or perhaps even months.

It has been only six years since newspapers headlined the great public controversy over the "doomsday bugs" that many people, including some geneticists, feared might escape from gene splicing labs. So vehement was the public opposition to recombinant DNA experiments then that some cities tried to ban them. Subsequent findings have shown that the early fears were unfounded, and most of the tighter restrictions imposed by the National Institutes of Health have been relaxed. Gene splicing researchers now use crippled bacterial strains that die when removed from artificial laboratory conditions.

Not only have the fears largely evaporated, they have been replaced by one of the most vigorous endorsements of a new technology that American society can confer—the rush of venture capitalists to cash in on what many see as the most promising and profitable new technology since computers.

In the eight years since a commercially useful gene splicing method was developed by Stanley Cohen of Stanford and Herbert Boyer of the University of California at San Francisco, some 200 American companies have taken up the method with the hope of producing some marketable substance. Many are long-established firms such as the major pharmaceutical houses, but the field is also crowded with small, new companies, including such heavily promoted names as Genentech, Cetus, and Biogen.

Although engineered genes are being used to make small amounts of insulin, human growth hormone, and interferon for research, no therapeutic product of the new genetics is yet on the market. The first is expected next spring—a vaccine against scours, a cattle disease that kills about 10 percent of the U.S. herd each year.

Other products are said to be likely to reach the marketplace in the next few years, though some observers caution that the scramble for investment dollars has led to inflated claims and hyped business forecasts. Often overlooked in the optimistic predictions is the fact that a great deal of development work is required to turn small-scale laboratory production of some gene product into a large, industrial operation. Also, new drugs must always pass a grueling process of government-required testing that can continue many years.

Even so, capitalists are competing so fiercely to capture what is called the biotechnology market that they have already signed nearly every one of the country's top, university-based geneticists to lucrative contracts as consultants or board members. Some geneticists have even formed their own companies and become, at least on paper, overnight millionaires.

Since most of the experts in this field are at the major universities, and nearly all have accepted corporate ties that require them to keep proprietary information secret, some observers fear the traditional openness of academic science may be in jeopardy. Currently there is not a single top-ranking molecular biologist at an American university who has not signed up with one of the new genetics companies. The development dismays some biology watchers. One of science's brighter points as a human endeavor has been the traditional willingness of scientists to share time, information, and even specimens and equipment. That scientific knowledge should be considered private property is a concept repugnant to many scientists.

The conflict between scientific freedom and corporate profits strikes some observers such as Stanford University president Donald Kennedy as "possibly more serious" an issue than the safety questions raised six years ago. Kennedy, a former head of the Food and Drug Administration, describes the situation as "the present helter-skelter pattern of affiliation" between the academic geneticists and industry. "There is the prospect," he recently told a congressional hearing, "of significant contamination of the university's basic research enterprise by the introduction of strong commercial motivations and potential conflicts of interest."

Already legal battles have erupted. There is one case in which a new cell was developed at UCLA and specimens routinely shared with a scientist at the National Cancer Institute in Washington, D.C. According to David Golde at UCLA, a cell line capable of producing interferon was sent without his permission from NCI to a scientist at the Roche Institute of Molecular Biology, a nonprofit center supported by Hoffmann-La Roche, the drug company. Roche says that in collaboration with Genentech, the genetics company, it used genetic engineering techniques on the cell line to develop a means of making large quantities of interferon. Envisioning commercial production, Roche applied for a patent. The university threatened to sue the drug company for unauthorized exploitation of its research. The drug company filed first, however, claiming the university was interfering with *its* research. The university went ahead with its suit, and now the two are locked in a titanic legal battle over the ownership of a cell line originally developed in part with federal tax dollars.

Harvard recently faced the conflict-of-interest question head-on when it considered the possibility of becoming a shareholder of a private genetic engineering company. "We appear to be poised on the edge of some vast biomedical revolution," Harvard president Derek C. Bok says. "Indeed, the prospects seemed all but irresistible to us when we initiated discussions last year to explore the possibility of helping to create a new commercial venture. As we thought more about the matter, however, we came to realize that the path of success would be marked by every kind of snare and pitfall."

Harvard opted out but, in the face of declining federal support for science, didn't rule out research funding by a private company, and okayed a grant of at least $50 million from the West German drug company Hoechst to go to its affiliate, Massachusetts General Hospital. Hoechst wants the money to go for biotechnology but, aside from that, says it will not try to influence the research. What Hoechst is buying for $50 million, apparently, is an exclusive right to look over the shoulders of the scientists using the money. Though the hospital will get patent rights, Hoechst will have license to further develop and manufacture products developed exclusively with its money. Some are hailing the deal as a new way for financially strapped universities to get money and preserve academic freedom. Others suspect there will be conflicts of interest.

Concern about commercialization of the new genetics, however, runs deeper. Who, asks Sheldon Krimsky, a philosopher of science at Tufts University, speaks for the public? "Society," he says, "needs to have neutral scientists who can address problems of whether the research is proceeding in the best interests of humanity. It would be unfortunate if no one is left to take the long view. Society is losing out if the scientists placing priorities on the research have commercial ties that lead them to keep corporate interests uppermost."

Krimsky, a member of the National Institutes of Health Recombinant DNA Advisory Committee for two and a half years, cites an example. One of the new products offered as a potential benefit of gene splicing is human growth hormone, a substance that could be given to children suffering pituitary deficiencies who would otherwise become dwarfs. But, Krimsky points out, the market for human growth hormone is comparatively small. Much larger is the market for bovine growth hormone that would stimulate the growth of normal cattle. Since the research and development costs for the two would probably be the same, a decision based on corporate interests might well bring to market a growth hormone for the beef industry before one for people.

Krimsky also points to what he considers a related problem. The Recombinant DNA Advisory Committee is the government's regulatory body for the field. It is supposed to look out for the welfare of the country as a whole. Yet some of its members are scientists with ties to the new genetic engineering firms. "At the very least," Krimsky suggests, "Congress should require the people who serve on the committee to make their commercial ties public. With all the various kinds of associations that scientists have with the business world, it's not always easy to learn which committee members may have conflicts of interest."

Stanford's Kennedy believes the commercialization of genetics poses enough problems to warrant a special conference to hammer out new policies. It would be similar to the historic 1975 conference at Asilomar, California, when, at the birth of recombinant DNA research, there was worry that dangerous organisms might be created. The conference led to a voluntary moratorium on many experiments until government-enforced guidelines could be worked out.

Kennedy has called for a new Asilomar-type conference to produce guidelines under which universities can continue to get the funding they need without compromising the advantages of scientific freedom and openness.

Although the original post-Asilomar guidelines have been relaxed, not all biology watchers are satisfied with the field's safety. One worried observer is Clifford Grobstein, a professor of biology and public policy at the University of California, San Diego. Recombinant DNA research has been responsibly pursued for seven years. In that time not one unfortunate incident has occurred. But, Grobstein wonders, what if the techniques were used by a terrorist group or some unscrupulous person deliberately to make dangerous microorganisms? He believes the possibility has not been properly addressed.

Grobstein favors a continuing inquiry into the field by an independent body. It is not a prospect favored by many of the new geneticists. Most feel burned by the Asilomar experience during which they were responsible enough to discuss potential problems but found themselves attacked by a frightened citizenry that saw the scientists in the role of Dr. Frankenstein, bent on a mad vision of controlling life or creating monsters.

Most of the new geneticists, now satisfied that they are proceeding safely, would rather be left alone to continue their study of the molecular machinery of life. The financial rewards of commercialization are hard to resist, and perhaps they are necessary to pay for the research. But what really drives the best of scientists is simply a powerful desire to understand how life works.

What is becoming increasingly clear, however, is that as their understanding deepens, the new geneticists are likely to confer upon society unprecedented power over the ultimate character of life.

THE VIOLENT BRAIN

DINA INGBER

Dina Ingber, science writer, recently covered an international conference about aggression.

A large crowd is waiting to board the bus. Most people hang back, shuffling along slowly with the group, but one woman shoves her way forward. Swinging her satchels, elbowing her way through, cursing at those who won't move, she makes her way in before the rest of us and grabs the last seat. She's aggressive, and for the duration of that uncomfortable ride, all the crowded standees wonder why they couldn't have been as aggressive as she had been.

Then there's the other scenario. Another long line, this time at the gas pumps during the gasoline shortage. There's pushing and shoving and honking of horns. But now someone pulls a gun and shoots.

That's aggression, too. What went wrong?

Our society has a mixed view of aggression. We all fear the mounting crime rate. Each year thousands of people are murdered in this country. And yet, we want our own lawyers to be aggressive on our behalf; we admire executives who claw their way to the top. Winners are called aggressive competitors, and employment ads seek aggressive salespeople.

As one who never gets that seat on the bus, and whose only violent confrontations are with paper and ink, I've always wondered what aggression really is. What is it that makes some people behave more forcefully? And will I ever be like them? Is it something in my blood, my upbringing, my brain, my genes that makes me hang back? Or are we all capable of aggression, of violence, even murder?

According to ethologists such as Konrad Lorenz and Robert Ardrey aggression is an instinct inherited from our prehuman ancestors. It survived evolutionary changes, they say, because it helped us survive.

Other researchers contend that people are not naturally aggressive. Rather, they say, society teaches us to be aggressive. People who grow up in a more violent—or more frustrating—environment learn to respond with violence.

Yale neurologist Jonathan Pincus is not satisfied with that explanation, however. "We usually blame adverse socioeconomic factors for violence—poverty, broken families, etc.," he says. "But very few poor people or those from broken homes are violent. Why?"

So today, scientists interested in aggression and violence think that something within each of our bodies—in our genes, our brains, our blood—may sow the seeds for violence. In their attempts to find out why one individual is more aggressive than another, they spend their days watching rats fight, shocking mice into action, dissecting brains, scrutinizing human wrestlers and hanging out with convicted killers.

SEX-HORMONE LINK

One of the earliest known links between physiology and aggression had to do with sex hormones. Centuries ago, farmers learned that they could calm an obstreperous male animal by castrating it, thus eliminating its supply of the hormone testosterone.

Testosterone levels also seem to be related to victory and defeat. In a recent study, Michael Elias, formerly of Harvard, studied hormone levels in university wrestlers and found that winners had higher levels of this hormone than the losers. "All the wrestlers showed increases in their testosterone levels after the match, which was expected, because testosterone should increase after exercise," Elias explains. "But winners had a greater percentage of increase than the losers, even if they started with the same level before the fight."

Elias believes his preliminary findings indicate that the changes in hormone levels must have had some adaptive value for our species. "I think there is a reason for having a lower testosterone level in defeat. It means that the losers—the less aggressive and less dominant of the species—have a lower sex-hormone level and therefore wouldn't have as many offspring as the victors," he says.

Are victory and dominance facets of aggression? Aggressors are the more dominant. And in most societies, males (who always have higher testosterone levels than females) are the more aggressive and therefore the more dominant sex.

Does that mean males have evolved as the more aggressive of the species? That's an old issue. Am I off the hook as a killer just because I'm female? No such luck. Other sex hormones are also involved. Experiments show that both boys *and* girls born to women who had taken synthetic progestins (a hormone normally associated with females) during pregnancy were more aggressive than their nonexposed siblings.

Some women may be particularly inclined to violent behavior during about eight days each month, the days before and during menstruation, as a result of hormonal changes. In England, as a result of studies by British scientists, premenstrual syndrome (PMS) is now legally argued in the courts as a defense in criminal cases.

Can it be that aggression is defined in the individual at birth? Is it in the genes? Several studies both here and abroad have indicated that children of violent parents are more likely to be violent themselves, even if they are raised by nonviolent foster parents.

One study of violent patients by neurologist Frank Elliott, professor emeritus at the University of Pennsylvania Medical School, found that 94 of them out of 132 had a family history of violence. In some, violence could be traced back as far as four generations. And 12 adoptees who were children of violence-prone families were violence-prone themselves, even though their adoptive parents were not.

Geneticist Benson Ginsburg, of the University of Connecticut, and endocrinologist Michael Selmanoff, of the University of Maryland College of Medicine, contend that certain genes on the Y chromosome (the Y chromosome is the one that distinguishes males from females; males have the Y chromosome and females do not) are related to prepuberty surges of testosterone, and thereby of aggression, in certain genetic stocks of male mice.

"There are genes on the Y chromosome that are linked to aggression. But they don't cause aggressive behavior in

"The Violent Brain," by Dina Ingber, from *Science Digest,* April 1982. Reprinted by permission.

every case, and they are not the only mechanism involved," Ginsburg hastens to add.

So if it's not just hormones or just heredity, what other mechanisms are involved? The most obvious place to start looking, a place through which all behavior seems to filter, is the brain.

Dr. Pincus of Yale divided juvenile offenders in a Connecticut reform school into two groups: more violent (that is, those who committed rapes, murders and personal assaults) and less violent (those arrested for break-ins, thefts or just the threat of assault).

NEUROLOGICAL ROOTS

He found that 46 percent of the more violent group had one or more major neurological problems, as compared with only 7 percent of the less violent group.

Other researchers have been able to pinpoint the problem area more specifically—narrowing it down to the brain's limbic system.

As brain researcher Dr. Paul MacLean, of the National Institutes of Health, emphasized several years ago, our brain is divided into three parts: the R-complex, or reptilian brain, inherited from the reptiles; the limbic brain, inherited from the early mammals; and the neocortex, which is prominent in the brains of higher mammals.

The neocortex is supposed to act as a control on the animal impulses generated by our more primitive brains. But damage to the limbic system can short-circuit that control.

"Cortical disease rarely produces aggression. But limbic damage does cause violent outbursts," says Elliott. So perhaps violence really is the animalistic part of our nature.

Specifically, the frontal and temporal lobes are most vulnerable. And located within those are the regions called the amygdala and the hypothalamus, both of which have been closely linked to aggressive behavior.

"If you stimulate the hypothalamus in an animal, you will get an immediate violent reaction," says Elliott. He calls this explosive rage "very primitive reptilian behavior."

To illustrate this, Harvard neurosurgeon Vernon Mark and colleagues have inserted electrodes into target areas of the brain in epileptic patients with violent behavior and then passed weak electric currents. When the currents reached the nucleus of the amygdala, the patients bared their teeth, grimaced and then lashed out like enraged animals.

Case histories showing the effects of brain damage on behavior are not lacking. Perhaps the most famous is the case of Charles Whitman, who in the 1960s climbed to the top of a tower in Austin, Texas, and began shooting at passersby. He killed 17 people.

"Whitman had displayed a striking behavior change for the few months prior to the incident. He even went to see a psychiatrist. But in those days, nobody thought in terms of physiological causes," Mark explains. "A postmortem later showed that he had a brain tumor. But people were still reluctant to make the connection between the tumor and his violent behavior! Today, we know better than that."

Mark has handled a number of patients with abnormal aggression related to brain disease and has seen how treatment of the brain abnormality can usually clear up the problem.

"I once had a patient who tried to decapitate his wife and daughter with a meat cleaver. He was so violent, the police had to bring him in wrapped in a fishnet. His family explained that his personality had started undergoing a change about six months earlier. And he had been complaining of headache and blurred vision. A neurological exam showed that he had a tumor underneath the right frontal lobe, pressing directly on the limbic system. We removed the tumor and the patient had a dramatic reversal in behavior."

Tumors are not the only factors that can cause the brain to malfunction and lead to violence. Alcohol or mind-altering drugs can result in violence because of what Mark calls brain poisoning. The TV show *Quincy* recently dramatized a famous California case in which a policeman shot and killed a young man who, the officer claimed, had come at him in an unprovoked attack of rage. After an autopsy showed that the victim had been on angel dust (PCP) when killed, doctors testified that PCP can indeed cause violent behavior, and all charges against the policeman were dropped.

In an effort to find out just what is happening in the brain to cause these behavioral changes, biochemists are now studying the brain's chemistry to see what changes occur during aggressive behavior. It has been found that a group of chemicals known as amines are at a low level just before the onset of aggression and that they increase as the aggression is acted out. Some doctors have therefore taken to using the drug propranolol to treat violent patients because it seems to block the action of some amines and so prevent rage.

To get an even closer look at what's happening in the brain during aggressive behavior, neurochemist Bruce Morton, of the department of biochemistry at the University of Hawaii, has utilized a unique system for zeroing in on the different parts of the brain responsible for different behaviors.

"The brain is very se… it uses for energy in doin… plains Morton. "It likes to … cose." So Morton injects m… small dose of a radioactive glu… a-logue, which is absorbed by the ce…s—including the brain cells—in a very short period of time. He then induces aggressive behavior in the colony male by introducing an intruder male. After 30 minutes of aggressive behavior by the mice, he removes the brain of the resident male, sections it and places these sections against X-ray film. Three weeks later the film is developed to reveal an activity map of the brain during aggression. This map points out the areas of the brain that have been activated or inhibited to produce the aggressive behavior.

Drs. Caroline and Robert Blanchard of the University of Hawaii, as well as other researchers, are finding that animals appear to have different kinds of aggressive patterns. They have very generally grouped the patterns into offensive and defensive behavior. And in the case of rodents, these behaviors can be identified by very specific sets of actions. If a rat is placed in another rat's cage, the home rat sees the new one as an intruder and attacks offensively. The hair on his back stands up. He chases the other rat, smells his genitals, jumps him from the side and bites his back. The intruder rat reacts defensively. He tries to flee, and when he finds this is not possible, he emits a high-pitched scream and freezes. Then he gives up and gives in to defeat. The two animals roll around the floor of the cage, with the attacking rat ending up on top and the intruder badly bruised or bitten.

GENETICALLY BASED

Preliminary evidence from another researcher shows that each of these two kinds of aggression is associated with activity in a different part of the brain. And biochemists think that different chemical reactions may also be at work. Moreover, genetic researchers think they may have come up with differing chromosomal patterns for each reaction. Dr. Stephen Maxson, of the department of biobehavioral sciences at the University of Connecticut, believes that offensive attack behavior may be coded on the Y chromosome. A strain of mice bred with specific genes on the Y chromosome exhibited certain aspects of the offensive behavior more than other mice. They charged, attacked and wrestled the intruder and inflicted more bites per minute on the enemy.

The Blanchards believe this offensive-defensive breakdown can be applied to humans. In humans, most aggression includes a combination of both offensive behavior (which results from anger) and defensive behavior (which results from fear). "When we're fearful, we emit a high-pitched scream, like a cornered rat," they say. "When we're angry, we yell. Biting and clawing are defensive."

Pain causes a defensive reaction, the Blanchards continue. Thus the violent lashing out of patients whose brains were given electric shocks is defensive. That would account, perhaps, for their animal-like reactions.

Certainly there are many discomforting stimuli that can cause violence in humans. Heat is one; more riots occur during heat waves than at any other time. Overcrowding, loud noises, noxious fumes—all have links with aggression.

The Blanchards theorize that defensive violence cannot be treated with punishment, because punishment merely serves as yet another painful stimulation and increases the violence.

But offensive attacks are something different again. An offensive attack, they think, occurs when the person perceives that his rights are being violated. Like the rat who attacks an intruder, people attack when they think their own rights are being intruded upon. It may be that a perceived breach of the right to a job or a decent place to live would account for the anger and violence among the unemployed and the poor.

But the key word here is *perceived.* The aggressive person reacts to what he perceives as a threat, and sometimes his perception is impaired. And that brings us full-cycle back to the physiological causes of aggression. If a person's physiology is unbalanced because of brain damage, hormonal irregularities or genetic abnormalities, then his ability to judge a threat is also off balance. What may seem to the normal person to be a minor intrusion becomes a major threat to the person with a low aggression threshold.

"I've had cases of a man attacking his wife because she burned the toast or a boy shooting a grocer because he didn't say 'thank you,' " says psychiatrist Frank Ervin, of McGill University in Montreal. "These are often misinterpreted as cases of unprovoked violence. But there is no such thing as violence without a cause. What happens is that the brain misperceives some incoming stimulus—a harmless gesture or a joking remark—as extremely threatening or enraging."

Is all violent behavior physiologically controlled? Well, yes . . . and no.

In that study done by Pincus of juvenile offenders, the more violent youths did tend to come from more violent environments. Seventy-five percent of the violent youngsters had been physically abused by their parents, and 70 percent had seen extreme violence in the home.

But studies have shown that experience does affect the brain. "Experience can create aggressive neural pathways in the brain," says Ervin.

Learning, environment, limbic brain, genes, hormones, chemicals . . . I am still not sure I can explain the lady who got the seat on the bus or understand the shoot-out on the gas line. But what seems obvious is that scientists are making headway in understanding and treating aggression. Relieve the painful stimuli in our society, give kids nonaggressive role models, treat limbic disorders with medication and surgery—and we may have a nonaggressive society. That's a fantastic thought. But what are the implications of such control? Consider what psychologist Bryan Robinson, formerly of Florida State University, said at a symposium several years ago:

BEHAVIOR MOD

"Aggression is not inherently bad. What is bad is too much of it, or too little, or misdirected aggressivity. It is conceivable that experiments such as we have heard about will lead to techniques or drugs that will selectively modify, or perhaps manipulate is a more honest word, human aggression. A very real problem then arises of who will do that manipulating and of exactly *what* will be modified . . . can certain individuals, classes of peoples or nations be made more or less aggressive? . . . The problem is a real problem and, before too many more years have passed, will be an *immediate* real problem."

The Origins of VIOLENCE

Richard Restak

IN RECENT YEARS psychobiologists have started assembling the pieces in a vast jigsaw puzzle whose solution may finally result in an understanding and reduction of violence in different cultures. Anthropologists are fond of pointing out that not every culture is violent. Some, in fact, are nonviolent. The key question is, of course, What accounts for the differences?

One intriguing association that emerges from cross-cultural studies relates early infant-care practices to the later development of violence. With few exceptions, societies which provide infants with a great deal of physical affection and bodily contact produce relatively nonviolent adults. In societies where infants are touched, held, and carried, the incidence of violence is much less than in societies where infant care is restricted to merely feeding and changing. Left at this, such findings tell us little about the mechanisms involved. A superficial interpretation might be that touching and carrying are two aspects of good mothering. Or put differently, infant stimulation and interaction with a mothering (or fathering) figure are important for normal development.

In the late 1950s and early '60s, Harry and Margaret Kuenne Harlow, at the Primate Laboratory of the University of Wisconsin, began a series of experimental observations on rhesus monkeys that provided the first experimental evidence to suggest that abnormal early brain development, brought on by poor mothering, might be the key to understanding some forms of violence. Rhesus monkeys make excellent experimental subjects for investigating such a relationship. Along with humans, rhesus monkeys undergo a long period of physical and emotional development which is heavily dependent on early physical contact and attachment between infant monkeys and their mothers. The Harlows first studied the effects of isolating the infant rhesus monkeys soon after birth. Alone in a cage, the isolated monkeys were able to view other monkeys in similar cages across the laboratory, but weren't able to make physical contact with them.

When later studied as adults, the isolated monkeys were withdrawn, often sitting for long periods of time staring blankly into space. In addition, they exhibited self-mutilating behavior, often pinching a patch of skin between their fingers hundreds of times a day. On occasion, the animals bit parts of their own bodies, often in response to the approach of their human caretakers. At still a later point, self-aggression changed into aggression toward others, a "cringing fearfulness" merging into "prominent displays of hostility."

But the most intriguing observation of the isolated monkeys concerns their later behavior toward their young. Isolated females become brutal, indifferent mothers who, as a group, show less warmth and affection and, on occasion, kill their offspring. This was the first indication that the mother-infant interaction was a reciprocal one. Isolated, unstimulated monkeys grew up to become unstable, brutal parents. Deprivation of some aspect of the physical closeness usually bestowed on an infant resulted in a later inability to be a good parent. But what aspect of the mother-infant interaction is most important?

In an attempt to understand the mothering process, the Harlows placed a group of newborn monkeys in cages with two types of surrogate mothers—one made of cloth, the other made entirely of wires. In almost all instances the infant monkeys spent more time clinging to their cloth-covered mothers than to their wire mothers, even when the monkeys obtained milk from a bottle attached to the wire mothers! The Harlows interpreted these findings as showing the overwhelming importance of bodily contact and the immediate comfort it supplies in forming the infant's attachment for its mother.

If the wire surrogate was replaced with a cloth mother, one capable of rocking, the monkeys, in most cases, preferred the rocking to the motionless cloth mother. When the two groups were later compared, their behavior contrasted dramatically. Those monkeys raised with motionless cloth mothers now showed repetitive rocking motions, while the monkeys provided earlier with moving cloth surrogates failed to show abnormal movement patterns. From here, psychobiologists speculate that sensory stimulation might be an absolute requirement for normal brain development. If this is true, however, what kinds of stimulation are most important?

Infants and children immobilized in bed for the treatment of bone fractures often develop emotional disturbances marked by hyperactivity and outbursts of rage and violence. Since only movement, and not sight or hearing, is restricted, a relationship is suggested between early diminished movement and later abnormal, often violent, behavior.

A similar correlation can be demonstrated in adults. When a group of adult faculty members at a university took part in an experiment testing the effects of immobilizing their heads in a halter, 85 percent reported the experience as "stressful." Vision and hearing were not interfered with and the subjects were free to converse with each other and engage in any activity they wished as long as their heads remained in the halter. Restriction of movement alone resulted in "intellectual inefficiency, bizarre thoughts, exaggerated emotional reactions, and unusual bodily sensations." In adults, as well as infants, immobility alone, despite intact vision or hearing, can result in abnormal mental experiences, disturbed behavior and, in many cases, violence.

Observations of mother-infant interactions in the laboratory yield similar results. Physical holding and carrying of the infant turns out to be the most important factor responsible for the infant's normal mental and social development. Dr. Frank Pedersen, chief of the Section on Parent-Child Interaction of the National Institute of Child Health and Human Development, compared the effects of visual, auditory, and movement stimulation on the infant's mental and psychomotor development. Out of six variables ranging from social responsiveness to object permanence, movement correlated positively with all six areas, whereas vision and hearing were important in only one.

So far, the results I've been describing are a matter of hard scientific fact. From here we move into issues that are more speculative. Not all psychobiologists are in agreement here, but the general trend is toward a revolution in our concept of the role of the environment in normal brain development and the subsequent tendency toward violence.

Any type of body movement, even something as passive as being held or rocked, results in a train of impulses directed toward a specific part of the brain, the cerebellum. Traditionally, the cerebellum, a small three-lobed structure behind the occipital lobe at the posterior part of the brain, is considered an important coordinator for movement. When you reach for a cup of coffee, for instance, the cerebellum is responsible for the smooth coordination necessary to bring the liquid to your lips. Patients with diseases of the cerebellum cannot lift a cup of coffee without spilling it. They also frequently sway when walking and, in some cases, cannot even sit without tilting to one side or the other. In a phrase, the cerebellum is responsible for smoothly coordinated muscular efforts. A ballet dancer represents perfect cerebellar functioning in which thousands of muscles are controlled with exquisite precision.

Without physical closeness, the infant's pleasure system is stunted. His difficulty in feeling pleasure may later tip him toward violence.

When an infant is rocked or cuddled, impulses are directed to the cerebellum that stimulate its development, a process that goes on until at least age two. In fact, the cerebellum is unique, since it is the only part of the brain where brain-cell multiplication continues long after birth.

"The cerebellum provides an explanatory model for the effects of social isolation," says Dr. James Prescott, a developmental neuropsychologist at the National Institute of Child Health and Human Development. "The rocking behavior of isolation-reared monkeys and institutionalized children may result from insufficient body contact and movement. Consequently, both touch and movement receptors and their projections to other brain structures don't receive sufficient sensory stimulation for normal development and function."

Prescott's unorthodox theory emphasized the role of a brain structure, the cerebellum, which, according to traditional psychobiological thinking, has nothing to do with behavior. Not surprisingly, it was originally greeted with a good deal of disbelief and skepticism. For one thing, how could such a radical proposal be proven? What data exist to prove that emotional reactions, such as violence, are related to activities in the cerebellum?

"The first requirement was to demonstrate that the cerebellum is connected with the emotional control centers of the limbic system," says Prescott. "There was really no reason to think that there were such connections other than the observation that lack of cerebellar stimulation, such as with isolation-reared monkeys or institutionalized children, leads to emotional disorders. The obvious place to look, it seemed, was in the brains of Harlow's isolation-reared monkeys."

In 1975, Prescott sent five isolation-reared monkeys from Harlow's laboratory to Robert G. Heath at Tulane University in New Orleans. Heath, a 64-year-old neuropsychiatrist, is a fiercely controversial figure who, over the past 25 years, has implanted stimulating and recording electrodes deep within the brains of a wide variety of people. In the process Heath, a flamboyant but indefatigable researcher, has created for himself an international reputation for work which has ranged from studies measuring the brain's electrical changes accompanying normal orgasm to the detection, by electron microscope, of the subtle alteration in the brains of monkeys trained to smoke marijuana. Heath's principal research interest, however, has always remained the psychobiology of psychosis and violence.

Psychosis, particularly schizophrenia, is marked by dramatic alterations in the patient's ability to experience pleasure. Anhedonia—literally the loss of the pleasure sense—is often accompanied by excessively painful emotional behaviors such as fear or rage. Although seemingly incapable of deriving pleasure, schizophrenics have heightened appreciations of pain, anguish, and loneliness. In 1954, Heath began a lifetime study looking for the brain mechanisms responsible for this pleasure-displeasure disturbance.

What emerged from Heath's rather unorthodox experiments (one patient retained an electric stimulator in his head for over three years) was a "map" of the brain's pleasure and displeasure centers. Patients implanted with electrodes in their septum, for instance, would selectively self-stimulate repeatedly. At other times during pleasure, such as an orgasm, activation could be detected in the septal region. With more intense sexual orgasm, faster-frequency activity occurred which appeared similar to the brain waves seen during some forms of epileptic seizures. In some cases, even talking about sexual matters was enough to elicit similar septal activations.

Heath's experimental findings on pleasure-displeasure complemented Prescott's observations on the important role of early movement stimulation and violence. Certainly, according to traditional ideas about the cerebellum and the limbic system, there seemed to be no way to correlate them.

At the base of Prescott's hunch that emotion and movement are interrelated were some common observations. Children like to be picked up, rocked, and taken on merry-go-rounds and roller coasters, as well as being whirled through the air. Most of us enjoy warm baths and soothing massages as calmers of tension and anxiety. Physical exertion such as sports or hard physical work can be exhilarating, even on occasion providing a "natural high." In all these instances, body movement seems to induce pleasurable emotions.

If these behavioral correlations exist, then, Prescott reasoned, there *must* be connections between the brain areas responsible for emotion (the limbic system) and those controlling movement (cerebellum). To look for these connections, Dr. Heath employed the method of evoked potentials. After implanting electrodes into several brain sites, a brief electrical stimulus was delivered to one of them while simultaneous recordings were made from the other sites. If activity could be detected, it provided an indication that the two sites were interconnected.

Heath's initial results with the Harlow monkeys showed, not surprisingly, that the limbic areas responsible for emotion (hippocampus, amygdala, and septal areas) were directly linked. What was more surprising, however, was the discovery of connections between these emotional centers and the cerebellum. In addition, two-way communication could be shown between the centers in the cerebellum and the emotional areas of the brain for pleasure and displeasure.

These results, Prescott believes, provide a preliminary basis for a psychobiological theory of the origin of human violence, which may result from a permanent defect in the pleasure centers secondary to inadequate early mothering experiences. The infant who is deprived of movement and physical closeness will fail to develop the brain pathways that mediate pleasure. In essence, such people may be suffering at the neuronal level from stunted growth of their pleasure system.

In this model the expression of pleasure cannot be transmitted through the appropriate parts of the brain, because there are fewer cell connections. Since the infant is deprived of movement and touch stimuli, fewer impulses are relayed to the immature cerebellum; as a result, it develops abnormally.

Fewer connections are then made between the cerebellum and the pleasure centers. Later, the person may have problems experiencing pleasure and, as a result, develop an insatiable need for it. In the absence of pleasure, the balance tips toward dysfunctional states such as violence.

"Think of these people as similar to diabetics," suggests Prescott. "As long as the diabetic gets his regular supply of insulin, everything is fine. Deprive him of insulin, and all kinds of physical and emotional disturbances may result. In a similar way, a child deprived of physical closeness will develop an extraordinary need for affection later in life which is unlikely to be fulfilled in the real adult world. This person often lapses into periodic violence."

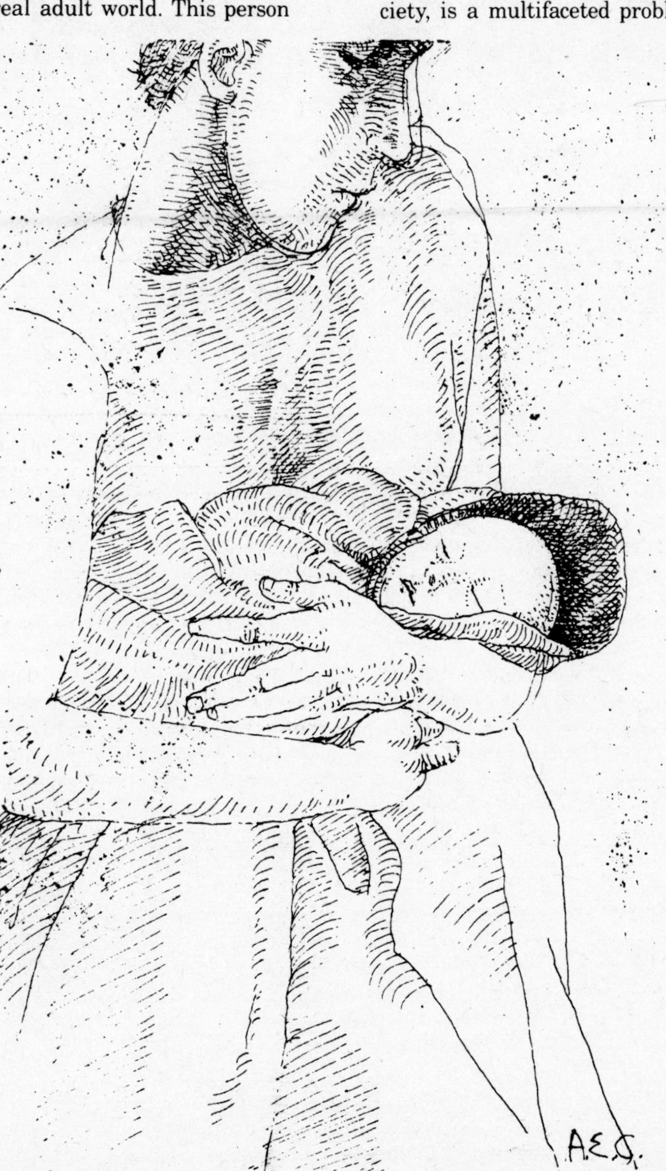

Obviously, the relationship of environmental stimulation, brain development, and subsequent violence is complex. So far, the theory that early physical contact and movement may play a later role in a tendency toward violence remains an intriguing but unproven possibility which can only be settled by further psychobiological research. In the meantime, however, increasing violence on our streets and in our homes underscores the importance of carrying out whatever research will enable us to decide one way or another.

Child abuse is one promising area worthy of further research. Pediatricians have known for years that violent parents are often themselves the victims of child abuse. Psychiatric interviews with child abusers reveal a pattern of reduced pleasure in daily living. In addition, they typically report little enjoyment of sexuality, with only a few of the mothers reporting that they have ever experienced orgasm. Most appear so involved in catering to their own insatiable emotional needs that they have little time to respond to the basic needs of their children.

Open discussion with such parents often reveals an isolated, alienated person with a quick temper, low frustration tolerance, and a sense of personal deprivation. Since they cannot receive pleasure, they are also poor providers of pleasure to their infants. Child-abusing mothers rarely report having "fun" with their babies, and in a physician's office demonstrate little positive interaction, often spending the examination time concentrating on how to satisfy their own emotional needs. The abusive parent's behavior is, in essence, reminiscent of the mothering patterns of Harlow's isolated monkeys, who, in many cases, had to be physically restrained from abusing their infants. The most pernicious aspect of the child-abuse syndrome, of course, is its tendency to repeat itself from generation to generation.

Thanks to a greater awareness of child abuse on the part of physicians and the general public, child abusers are now coming to public attention sooner. In addition, major hospitals are setting up child-abuse clinics with established protocols designed to improve the quality of interaction between parent and child. Increased infant-care instruction, a lengthened period of maternal "lying in" arrangements, instructions on feeding patterns which emphasize physical closeness—these are only a few of the newer methods being tried, all of which tend to increase cerebellar stimulation through early and sustained physical contact between parent and child.

Child abuse, along with other forms of violence in our society, is a multifaceted problem. To explain violence as entirely the result of a brain dysfunction is unrealistic and socially disastrous. Still, I consider the current attempts to relate pleasure-displeasure states, mental illness, and the early patterns of parenting as exciting and promising. If the technique of cerebellar stimulation works as well as early reports are suggesting, psychobiologists may soon be able to improve the lives of thousands of "hopeless" patients. Despite the success of medication in the control of mental illness, there remains a small core of untreated, frequently violent patients who are doomed to spend the rest of their lives in institutions. It is with these patients that the cerebellar-stimulation techniques seem to work best.

Along with basic brain research, however, we need parallel studies on the social aspects of violence and child abuse. Warm, demonstrative parents...should...be less likely than their cold, aloof counterparts to produce violently disturbed children. Is this true? At this point, no one can be certain. In fact, research couldn't begin to investigate the question until the recent suggestion that movement might be important for healthy brain and behavioral development. The acceptance of such a view, however, requires a paradigm change in our attitude toward the effects of the environment on brain development. It isn't intuitively obvious that the cerebellum, a regulator of movement, might also be involved in the modulation of pleasure or the later propensity to violence. Although we are still not sure a new and exciting approach is now available which may reward the collaboration of psychobiologists and social scientists. Who would have even imagined 10 years ago that studies on early brain development and infant stimulation might someday suggest a provisional theory about the origin and treatment of human violence?

Richard Restak is a neurologist and author of Premeditated Man: Bioethics and the Control of Future Human Life.

Searching for Depression Genes

LOIS WINGERSON

For years, psychiatrist Larry Pardue thought he had a character flaw. When he lost interest in life during college and his grades fell, he wrote himself off as "just a morning-glory," doomed to fail. He made it through college, but later, during his psychiatry training, he was plagued by insomnia, thoughts of suicide, and a sense of inadequacy. The very doctors who were training him to recognize clinical depression never saw that Larry Pardue had it himself.

Other members of his family also suffered from depression—although Larry Pardue did not know it then. His father had been so severely affected by something called "melancholia" that in 1952 he underwent a prefrontal lobotomy, a brain operation that left him incapable of ever again holding a job. When his niece began showing symptoms of depression in 1973, Pardue began to wonder. Then, when his great-uncle recalled that *his* uncle had killed himself, Pardue began to suspect that more than coincidence was involved. He decided to search his family tree for the "character flaw." What he now regards as the illness of depression turned up with depressing regularity: at least 19 Pardues had clear signs of it.

Pardue published his startling discovery (concealing the identity of his family) in 1975 in the *American Journal of Psychiatry*. His report became the starting point for a new research effort to determine if depression—or the tendency toward depression—can be inherited as well as caused by environmental influences. That notion, which not long ago would have been considered heretical by most psychiatrists, was strengthened in November by a report in the *New England Journal of Medicine* that a gene apparently linked to depression had been located in human chromosomes.

The discovery, quickly challenged by some experts, was made by Lowell Weitkamp, a geneticist at the University of Rochester, in New York. Studying the anonymous family tree in Pardue's report, Weitkamp noticed that it seemed to fit a genetic pattern. He telephoned Pardue, now on the staff of Tulane University in New Orleans, and asked for blood samples from "his patient's family." Pardue eagerly agreed.

Weitkamp's analyses of the blood samples did reveal a genetic pattern, but not the one he had expected to find. This encouraged him to undertake a broader study; he began looking for that particular unexpected pattern in 20 different families with histories of depression, found it, and eventually zeroed in on the depression gene.

The Weitkamp study is one of the latest developments in a promising new approach to depression research. While Freud and his followers regarded depression as a result of anger turned inward, there is growing evidence that the illness may stem as much from body chemistry (controlled by genes) as it does from psychological pressures. The facts are not all in, but researchers like Weitkamp believe that important discoveries lie just beyond the horizon.

In the spirit of this fresh assault on an ancient human misery, Larry Pardue decided, after Weitkamp's November report, to reveal that the family referred to as "kindred M001" is actually his own—something that even Weitkamp was unaware of until a few months ago. "It is time to de-stigmatize depression, now that we're picking up its biological framework," says Pardue. "We're not alone. Many, many studies indicate there are other families like us."

Characteristics and conditions other than depression seem to run in families—poverty, religion, even cake recipes. That does not necessarily mean they are inherited. But recent studies of depression in twins and in adopted children strongly suggest that susceptibility to depression *is* passed on in the genes. But how? One reason the answer has proved so elusive is that a baffling variety of emotional troubles go by the name of depression.

"The word depression represents everything from normal sadness to a full-blown mental and physical illness," Dr. Frederick Goodwin, chief of clinical psychobiology at the National Institute of Mental Health, told DISCOVER's Sana Siwolop. By "clinical depression," psychiatrists do not mean the unhappy phases that give rhythm and depth to life. What they do mean by it is harder to define, but it is much more serious, affecting about 2 per cent of the U.S. population. At its worst, depression leads to suicide, which claims about 75,000 American lives each year.

In describing the spectrum of depression, Goodwin draws a horizontal line; at one end is a normal (and transient) bad mood, at the other the emotional roller-coaster of alternating despair and euphoria known as manic, or bipolar, depression. Goodwin thinks the daily pressures of normal life can account for the milder forms of depression; but at the other extreme, while daily experience may still play a role, genes and chemistry may be the main culprits.

Between the mildest and the most severe forms of depression is an ill defined problem called unipolar depression, which probably results from a mixture of causes. People who have it report "low" episodes that last for weeks or months, loss of interest in food and sex, insomnia, and suicidal thoughts. There seem to be many varieties of unipolar depression; some doctors believe alcoholism is one of them.

Most studies show that the inheritance of depression is much too complex to be explained by a single, isolated gene. That was the intriguing thing about the Pardue family tree: it did seem to fit a one-gene pattern.

The best way to find a gene is to show that it is near another gene already known to cause a certain trait, and to demonstrate that the two traits are passed along together. But until now, every suggested link between depression and another trait had been disproved by later studies. The Pardues provided a chance to try again. Weitkamp tested them for 35 such traits—and failed. Once again, no single gene could be linked to depression.

But Weitkamp did find a pattern in the Pardues, one he later discovered for juvenile diabetes. The pattern was in a class of substances called human leukocyte antigens (HLA), which are essential to the immune system. The production of these proteins by the body's cells is controlled by a specific group of genes on chromosome six in the human genome (all the chromosomes in a cell). Some fifty diseases have been linked with particular HLA types.

Weitkamp found that not everyone with depression in the Pardue family had the same HLA type, but that close relatives often did. The pattern seemed suggestive enough for Weitkamp to test for it in 20 other families that had been diagnosed by psychiatrist Harvey Stancer of the University of Toronto as having many depressed members.

The resulting paper by Weitkamp and Stancer (the one that caused all the fuss) conceded that, in general, the depression patients they had studied did not share HLA types more often than expected. Nevertheless, Weitkamp claimed that his statistical interpretation of the results (in which families with one or two depressed children were considered separately from families with three or more) did point to a genetic pattern. Only if they had *all* had the same HLA type would the results support a single-gene theory, but Weitkamp claimed that the pattern he found would be consistent with a secondary gene, near the HLA genes, contributing to depression—working with a yet-undiscovered primary gene somewhere else. The *New England Journal of Medicine* evidently agreed. Its editorial said the report represented "major progress in understanding the genetics of depressive disorders."

Other geneticists are skeptical. One of them, Dr. Elliot Gershon, chief of the psychogenetics section at the National Institute of Mental Health, says Weitkamp's method "doesn't make sense." Gershon says that his own studies have failed—even when he analyzed his own data by Weitkamp's methods—to show a link between depression and 24 selected genetic traits, including HLA. Weitkamp is not persuaded: he thinks Gershon's data do support his theory. "Weitkamp and I are both gentlemen and scholars," says Gershon, "but we don't agree about depression."

Robert Cloninger, of the Washington University School of Medicine in St. Louis, who is studying the genetics of alcoholism, thinks Weitkamp's sample may have been too small, and suggests that a new study, using larger families, might produce different results.

The answer only awaits the next spring thaw in Pennsylvania. When the snows melt and travel is easier, Janice Egeland, a University of Miami medical sociologist, will begin collecting blood samples for HLA typing from depressed people among the Amish, a religious sect who, among other things, travel by horse and buggy and refuse to use machines or electricity—and who have huge families. After decades of study, Egeland knows everyone with clinical depression among the 12,500 Amish people living near Lancaster. Although the depression rate among the Amish is only about half the national average, they are good subjects for medical studies, and not only because of their family size (each depressed person in Egeland's sample has about 13 immediate family members). They are also inbred and have lived in the same area for generations (Egeland has traced their family trees carefully). Alcoholism and drug addiction are almost nonexistent among them, so depression seldom masquerades as something else.

Weitkamp also plans to do genetic studies of larger families, and he hopes that, in addition to supporting his earlier findings, the results will stimulate new kinds of brain research. One question he would like to see answered is why the brains of people who commit suicide often contain an abnormal protein also found in the brains of people with multiple sclerosis. When David Comings, a geneticist at the City of Hope Medical Center in Duarte, California, discovered the protein in suicide victims, multiple sclerosis had already been linked with particular HLA types. Comings speculated that the "depression protein" mig[...] by a gene in the HL[...]

Could this be Wei[...] gene? Weitkamp an[...] in fact, that they may [...] ent manifestations of t[...] chemical abnormality, and that further research may establish the connection.

The chemical secrets behind depression lie hidden deep within the brain, in a primitive region called the limbic system, which controls such emotions as fear, hunger, and rage. The limbic system lies at a crossroad, receiving signals from both the cortex, where decisions are made and memory is stored, and the thalamus, the receiving center for sensory messages. The central location of the limbic system may explain how any chemical variation there could bring on the many mental and physical symptoms of depression. Such chemical cross-linking turns up in unexpected ways. For instance, a chemical test used since the 1960s to diagnose a hormonal disorder called Cushing's syndrome turns out to be useful in identifying certain depressed people who can be helped by drugs.

Scientists have barely begun to explore the role of chemistry in moods and feelings, but some general principles are becoming evident. Messages travel along the brain's billions of nerve cells electrically, but to get from one cell to the next across the synapse, or gap, between, the electrical impulses must be translated into chemical reactions. Messages are passed across the gaps by some twenty chemicals called neurotransmitters, three of which, norepinephrine, dopamine, and serotonin, seem to be implicated in moods. Knowledge of this fact has already opened avenues for exploring and treating psychiatric illnesses.

Harvard psychiatrist Joseph Schildkraut and others discovered two decades ago that the supply of certain neurotransmitters in the brain, especially norepinephrine, is associated with mood swings in manic-depressives. They found deficiencies of such chemicals during periods of depression and overabundances of them during euphoria. Demonstrating this variation in supply was no easy task; neurotransmitters never leave the brain, and therefore cannot be measured directly in living people. But when norepinephrine breaks down, one of the resulting products, called MHPG, does escape into the blood stream, and can be measured.

Unfortunately, the relationship between the supply of neurotransmitters and mood is not so simple in people with the unipolar form of depression. For this reason, Schildkraut

…ves that unipolar depression may …tually be a catch-all term for several different diseases with similar symptoms but different chemical causes. There is support for this idea in the wide variety of responses to antidepressant drugs. For example, everyone with depression in the Pardue family has been treated successfully with the same class of antidepressant drugs (tricyclics), which work by preventing nerve cells from reabsorbing neurotransmitters after they are released. But these drugs do not work for everyone. Some people respond to monoamine oxidase inhibitors, for example, which prevent a brain enzyme from destroying neurotransmitters like norepinephrine.

Antidepressant drugs might be expected to relieve the depressive phase of manic-depression, but for some unknown reason they do not. Manic-depressives have been greatly helped, however, by a drug called lithium carbonate.

None of these drugs is ideal. They can have side effects that range from dryness of the mouth to heart trouble. Furthermore, overdoses can be lethal, and some depression victims have used their medicine to commit suicide. For these reasons, drug companies are seeking antidepressants that are both safer and more specific.

In the latest efforts to understand and treat depression, Schildkraut sees parallels with the early clinical battles against pneumonia. Pneumonia was once diagnosed purely on the basis of symptoms, but today a doctor can tell from laboratory tests the specific type of pneumonia he is confronting and which drugs will be most effective against it. Ten years hence, Schildkraut says, present methods of treating depression will seem as crude as former pneumonia treatments seem now.

Geneticists will need more time to make sense of the causes of depression. But many believe that within the next 20 years, using new genetic engineering techniques, they will have mapped the locations on the chromosomes of most of the human genes. By then, any genes that contribute to depression should be much easier to spot than they are today.

Egeland, the scientist studying Amish families, is looking far into the future. She plans to freeze some samples of Amish blood so that they can be analyzed years from now to test new genetic theories. "We're closing in," she says, "and that's the exciting thing for everyone."

CHEMICAL FEELINGS

The search is on for drugs that would mimic the brain's own pharmacy—to make you passionate, free you from pain, lull you to sleep, and stop your craving for food.

Joel Gurin

In the Middle Ages, Europeans used mandrake root yanked from the ground by a black dog in moonlight. Asian folklore prescribed ground rhino horns. Greenlanders ate the bills of water birds; Central Africans the bark of the yohimbé tree. In virtually every culture and every age, people have sought an effective aphrodisiac.

Now science may have found one, and it is no bizarre blend of herbs and incantations, but a chemical that occurs naturally in the brain. The chemical, called luteinizing hormone releasing factor, or LRF, has already helped impotent men regain lost sexual powers. A well-placed shot of it can drive rats to mating. In short, LRF—or a substance very much like it—may be the chemical "turn on" that has been sought for centuries.

The implications of LRF go well beyond its libidinous potential, because it is only one of a score of recently discovered brain chemicals that may profoundly influence feelings and behavior. Already identified in this new chemical family are substances that may help regulate pain, mental disorders, the desire to eat, drink, and sleep, and perhaps even the facility for learning and memory. The study of these chemicals and their mode of action is forcing a revolution in our understanding of the brain and how it functions. And this may only be the beginning. Referring to the "statistics of serendipity," one scientist says "I would guess that if 20 have been discovered, there must be 200 we have missed."

The pharmaceutical potential of these discoveries has not been overlooked by the nation's drug companies, which are rushing to synthesize and test hundreds of new substances. Speculation is rampant, with press accounts forecasting a "choose-your-mood" society and hailing the advent of mind-control drugs powerful enough to make even Timothy Leary blanch. In a pill-conscious and drug-dependent age, the unlocking of the brain's medicine chest may unleash an enormous potential for abuse. It is not only a matter of being sold medicines we may not need. There is the poetry of life to consider as well—do we really want the chemistry of sexual attraction to come from the pharmacist's shelf?

Fortunately, perhaps, the ultimate aphrodisiac is still far from appearing in the corner drugstore. Despite the undoubted promise of the brain's chemical repertory, the record to date provides a warning against expecting too much from these substances too soon. Not only is it difficult to artificially raise the levels of these chemicals in the brain, but experience has shown that the human brain will not be so easily manipulated. Indeed, the most immediate impact may be to revise our ideas of the brain and how it works.

The putative aphrodisiac LRF is one of a family of intriguing brain substances that take the chemical form of small proteins known as peptides. To biologists it makes sense that peptides should help run the brain, since proteins are ubiquitous in biological systems. Most of the newly important peptides were in fact originally found in places humbler than the brain, such as the human gut and the skin of frogs. But it has taken years to locate and study peptides in the brain itself.

The first experiments in the field, performed in the 1960s, were painstaking, slow, even heroic. Researchers had to grind up millions of sheep and pig brains just to identify a few peptides. But today research on the brain peptides proceeds at a rapid, accelerating pace, thanks largely to new techniques and to the excitement generated by a special group of peptides called the endorphins.

The name endorphin means "the morphine within." In the early 1970s, work on the chemistry of drug addiction suggested that the brain might actually contain natural substances chemically similar to opiate drugs. A global hunt by researchers at Stanford, Johns Hopkins, New York University, the Universities of Uppsala, Sweden, and Aberdeen, Scotland, tracked down the brain's morphine-like chemicals. They discovered a small family of these endorphins with three prominent members: beta-endorphin and two smaller peptides, called the enkephalins. Beta-endorphin can relieve pain even more effectively than morphine when injected into the brains of laboratory animals, and there is some evidence that the endorphins, like morphine, may also affect emotions and mood.

The search for nonaddictive pain-killers and for possible new treatments for mental illness catalyzed a surge of interest in the endorphins. Despite this flurry of activity, however, the early predictions of addiction-free pain relief and miracle mental cures now seem to have been premature. Many scientists proposed, for example, that an enkephalin should be an effective analgesic—and nonaddictive because it is a natural substance. After all, how could the body become addicted to a substance that resides in the brain all the time with no ill effects?

This reasoning proved faulty. Natural enkephalin is broken down very rapidly in the brain, which may account for its lack of addictive effects. To build usable drugs, scientists had to begin by making related substances—chemical variants, or analogues, of the natural opiate—that have long-lasting effects. Many of the new enkephalin analogues do relieve pain in animals, but at a price; pharmaceutical researchers have found that they also produce tolerance and dependence, the hallmarks of an addictive drug. "We did tell them in the first place that that was likely to happen," says Stanford pharmacologist Avram Goldstein, whose work on addiction began the search for the brain's natural opiates.

Enkephalin-analogue drugs also turn out to produce unpleasant side effects, such as severe abdominal cramps. And an epic patent fight is raging among drug companies and the government's National Institutes of Health over rights to the most effective technique for making analogues. The real irony of the enkephalin story, though, is that the drugs now being tested are products of such careful chemical design and synthesis that they are actually no more natural than morphine itself.

Although they have not yet resulted in a pharmacological bonanza, endorphin discoveries ignited an explosion of work on other brain peptides. More than 20 peptides have been identified and the first clues about their roles in the brain are now beginning to emerge. These chemicals appear to be involved in everything from promoting sleep to stimulating thirst, from regulating appetite to the body's temperature. Some are known to assist in transmitting pain signals from body to brain—the opposite effect of the endorphins. So prevalent are the effects of the peptides in the nervous system, says Emery Zimmerman of UCLA, that they may represent "a fundamental new language"—a chemical

False hope for schizophrenics

Two years ago, Nathan Kline announced that a 34-year-old schizophrenic felt so much better after receiving a dose of beta-endorphin that he cried for happiness. Depressed patients were given the substance, the New York psychiatrist said, and their spirits miraculously lifted. A shot of the brain chemical dispelled an agoraphobic woman's fears for an entire week. Kline was the first to give beta-endorphin to psychiatric patients, and, he later boasted to a medical writer, "We've probably set psychiatry back 100 years if the same substance works in all these disorders."

Kline's experiment did set psychiatric research back, in the opinion of many researchers, but not for the reasons he thought. The promise that the endorphins would prove the key to treating mental illness has simply not panned out. "I feel badly when false hopes and distortion are projected to the scientific and lay public," says Solomon Snyder, a psychiatrist and endorphin researcher at Johns Hopkins. Because of news reports connecting the endorphins with schizophrenia, Snyder and other researchers get letters daily from the families of schizophrenics asking them for help they cannot give.

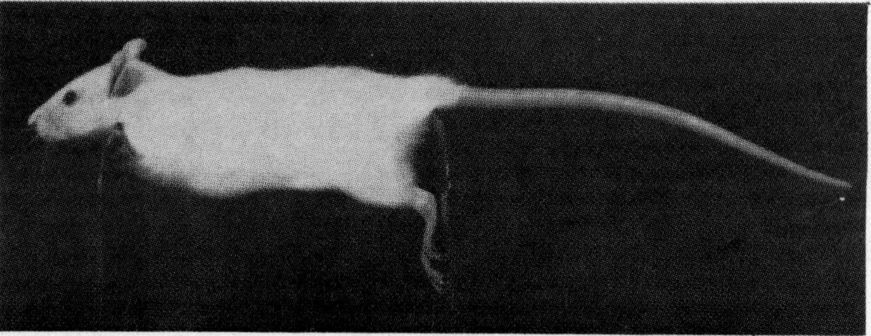

Is this drugged rat experiencing catatonic paralysis or therapeutic tranquillity?

One hint suggesting a link between the endorphins and schizophrenia was the discovery that rats behave very strangely indeed when beta-endorphin is injected into their brains. The rats become so rigid they can be suspended between two bookends by their necks and tails for hours at a time.

The phenomenon attracted differing interpretations. To New York researcher Yasuko Jacquet, it seemed that the rats were responding as they would to tranquilizers used to treat schizophrenics; perhaps endorphins, too, could be used to treat the disease. At the Salk Institute, Floyd Bloom and Roger Guillemin looked at the same unhappy rats and saw not tranquillity, but the immobility of catatonic schizophrenia. They suggested the endorphins were related to the causes rather than the treatment of mental illness.

In retrospect, both of these

language—that the brain uses to communicate with itself.

Like the endorphins, most of the other brain peptides are unlikely to prove useful in their natural forms. The brain is a well-protected organ, as it must be; cerebral chaos would result if all the chemicals in the blood could reach the brain. Peptides injected into the bloodstream often cannot penetrate the blood-brain barrier without extensive chemical modifications that may alter their properties as well. In addition, large peptides have been notoriously difficult and expensive to produce. Rather than work with the peptides themselves, drug companies are now developing and testing hundreds of simpler analogues.

Designing drugs that have specific effects will not be easy in part because of the staggering versatility of the peptides, most of which play multiple roles within the brain. "I don't think there's any logical basis for assuming that a single substance controls a single behavior in the brain," says one researcher. "That's just absurd."

Just what effects a particular drug will have is also hard to predict. A team at the Salk Institute has designed variants of LRF, the possible aphrodisiac, that are many times more powerful than the natural peptide. Now being tested, the compounds can act either as a fertility pill or as a contraceptive, depending on the dose taken.

The obstacles to creating a peptide-based pharmacopoeia will not be solved overnight, or probably for years to come. In the meantime, faced with such a plethora of peptides, scientists are beginning to revise their most basic notions of how the brain works. The immediate theoretical question is, why does the brain need all those peptides in the first place?

ideas were probably far from the mark. Snyder, for example, now believes the rats were merely suffering from a form of muscle paralysis. "Catatonia, schmatatonia," he says. "That has nothing to do with emotion, it has to do with not being able to move." Today, says Bloom, "I don't think there is any viable endorphin hypothesis for the causation of schizophrenia." But, for good or ill, those first ideas about beta-endorphin quickly led to experiments with mental patients around the world.

Kline's work with 15 patients was disputed almost immediately as his research procedures were scrutinized. Many researchers also questioned Kline's judgment for giving endorphin to his patients without FDA approval. Three U.S. laboratories and others in Taiwan and Europe are now giving beta-endorphin to schizophrenics in more carefully controlled experiments. So far, none of them has found anything comparable to the dramatic results Kline reported. In fact many researchers now believe that beta-endorphin should not be expected to help schizophrenics for a very basic reason: There is no direct evidence that the chemical can cross the blood-brain barrier to reach the brain after it is injected.

Still, hope dies hard. A group of Dutch researchers led by David de Wied has reported success in treating schizophrenics with a chemical related to beta-endorphin, and several laboratories are planning to repeat the experiments. Some investigators are pursuing promising but as yet inconclusive work with schizophrenics using a chemical that actually blocks the action of opiate drugs and endorphins in the brain. This same chemical and beta-endorphin itself are also being tried on manic and depressive patients.

Other researchers are planning to check the blood and spinal fluid of schizophrenics for abnormal levels of other brain peptides to see if something unusual turns up. Schizophrenia is such a puzzling disease, and finding a cure would be such a scientific prize, that researchers are anxious to follow up every possible lead.

—*J.G.*

For years neuroscientists looked to the brain's electrical circuitry to explain how we think and feel. The discovery of the brain peptides shows that the chemistry of the brain may be far more complex and sophisticated than scientists had imagined.

Each of the brain's nerve cells has thousands of inputs from, and outputs to, other cells in the brain and throughout the body. When a cell is stimulated by a sensation or a thought, it carries that information to other nerve cells through electrical impulses. Two nerve cells meet in the junction called a synapse, where electrical signals are converted into chemical signals and back again. An electric current comes to the end of the first nerve fiber where it triggers the release of chemicals called neurotransmitters.

These chemical messengers diffuse across a tiny gap to a second nerve cell where they react to spark a second electric current. Their job finished, the transmitter molecules are inactivated and broken down within a millisecond.

Until recently only a dozen or so transmitters were known. Scientists thought that was enough. Each transmitter seemed to be a simple conduit for the brain's electricity, although different transmitters were prevalent in different parts of the nervous system, and some transmitters actually inhibited nerve cells from firing, rather than stimulating them.

But the peptides are unlike any transmitters previously known. Chemically, these small proteins are much larger and more complicated than conventional transmitters. The peptides may also act differently than other chemical messengers on nerve cells. While conventional transmitters act quick as a flash, disappearing within a millisecond, new evidence suggests that some peptides may remain active at the cell membrane for minutes, even hours.

The peptides may be a whole new class of chemical messengers in the brain. The well-known transmitters, present in much larger concentrations than the peptides, may be the workhorses that do the

The peptide hit parade

LRF has become the object of intensely competitive research because of its potential aphrodisiac effects. One prominent researcher claims that a company hired to analyze blood samples of impotent men given LRF, stole the data for its own use.

Beta-endorphin seems to help the body turn off its response to pain much as morphine does. There is some evidence that acupuncture anesthesia and pain-relief placebos may work by bringing beta-endorphin or a similar chemical into action.

Enkephalins, the smallest endorphins, take their name from the Greek words for "in the head." What they are doing there no one knows for sure, but they seem to share some of the pain-relieving potential of beta-endorphin.

Factor S, which has been studied by Harvard researcher John Pappenheimer and his colleagues, may be a sleep-promoting peptide. Isolated from the brain fluid of goats and sheep that were forced to stay awake, this substance increases sleeping time when given to rabbits.

Bombesin, first discovered in the skin of the frog *Bombina bombina,* can turn rats from warm-blooded to cold-blooded animals when injected into their brains. The chemical also seems to turn on the sympathetic nervous system, which regulates basic functions like the stress response and blood pressure, and may help determine whether calories in food are used to produce heat or stored as fat. Thus, speculates Marvin Brown at the Salk Institute, bombesin could form the basis of an anti-obesity drug.

Somatostatin seems to have the opposite effect from bombesin in the brain; it generally turns off the sympathetic nervous system. Drugs based on this peptide may therefore be useful in lowering blood pressure.

Substance P is involved in transmitting pain signals from the body to the brain. If various technical problems can be overcome, "an antagonist to Substance P could be the ideal anesthetic," according to physiologist Roger Nicoll at the University of California, San Francisco.

Bradykinin may play a similar role in pain transmission. Very low doses of this peptide cause intense pain when injected. It may be the most painful substance known.

Angiotensin, a peptide that regulates fluid excretion in the kidneys, makes experimental animals drink copiously when injected into their brains. It may also be used to develop new anti-hypertensive drugs.

Cholecystokinin, originally discovered in the intestine, appears highly concentrated in the brain's most evolved region, the cerebral cortex. Some researchers have suggested that cholecystokinin normally carries the brain signal to stop eating, and that a deficiency of the peptide may lead to obesity. Rosalyn Yalow, at Veterans Administration Medical Center, Bronx, has found that the peptide is much less prevalent in the brain of a strain of genetically obese mice than in normal mice.

Neurotensin shows a powerful analgesic effect in animal experiments, and a drug company is now testing a number of drugs based on this peptide to see if they are also effective pain-killers.

ACTH, a peptide manufactured by the pituitary gland, is also found in nerve cells in the brain. Over the past decade several studies have shown that people can learn and remember better when they are given a small fragment of an ACTH molecule by injection. Dutch researcher David de Wied has found that the peptides vasopressin and oxytocin can also aid learning and memory. The results are intriguing, but since most chemical models of learning and memory have proved false, many researchers view these experiments with caution.

basic job of transmitting nerve impulses. The peptides, in contrast, may act at the membrane for a longer time, making a nerve cell more or less responsive to the signals of other transmitters. If one imagines the brain as a radio receiving a constant flow of information through the neurotransmitters, the peptides may be important in its fine-tuning.

Why are so many chemicals necessary? On one level, the brain may use a variety of distinct peptides to help keep its signals straight, much as the telephone company uses different colored wires in its cables. Candace Pert of the National Institute of Mental Health notes that many different peptides are found in the amygdala, a key center of emotional arousal in the brain. "It's almost like a master switchboard," she says, "and when a lot of nerve cells converge on it they rely on their chemical coding to keep them insulated from each other." The emotional complexity of human beings may even demand a wide range of peptide transmitters. "We may need a lot of them," says Pert, "because we're complicated."

Given the complexity of the body's emotional and behavioral pathways, many brain scientists have turned their attention back to the single nerve cell. But even research at this level can raise more questions than it answers. Scientists are baffled by a controversial new finding that two different peptides may serve as neurotransmitters in a single cell at the same time.

Previously, a cell with two transmitters would have been considered rarer than a two-headed cow. Now the peptide Substance P has been found in nerve cells containing a conventional transmitter, and Stanley Watson and Huda Akil at the University of Michigan have evidence that beta-endorphin and another peptide may also share the same cell. If these findings are borne out, Watson says, "It means that the brain not only has the complex network of billions of cells talking across thousands of connections, but each cell can get two or more messages at a single synapse."

The final puzzle of the peptides—which no one has really solved—is that these brain substances are identical to hormones found throughout the body. Several peptides that were regarded for a long time as obscure substances in the gastrointestinal tract have suddenly become super stars in the fast-moving field of neuroscience. The Horatio Alger story of these newly prominent brain peptides carries the lesson, perhaps, that the mind and the body are more intimately connected than we have thought.

IMAGES OF THE NIGHT

The physiological roots of dreaming.

Edwin Kiester jr.

She walked down the steps of the public library, wearing her nightgown and cradling a bowl of raspberry Jell-O in her arms. At the foot of the long staircase she could distinguish the dim figure of her high school algebra teacher. His right arm was upraised and he seemed to be shouting at her, but she could not make out the words. She hurried toward him, straining to hear . . .

Suddenly the scene shifted. Now she found herself traveling through a dense forest. The sun was setting ahead of her and the forest deepened in darkness. She felt afraid. An unseen menace seemed to be following her, dodging from tree to tree, but when she glanced back in fear she saw no one. She tried to run faster, but her legs would not respond. The pursuer drew nearer, gaining on her, but she was powerless to escape and . . .

Most of us will recognize this intriguing combination of strange behavior, outlandish dress, abrupt scene shift, and inability to run away as the stuff of which dreams are made. We all dream, every night of our lives, and the feelings of flying or falling, the kaleidoscope of colors, and the jumbled memories and prophecies are a source of endless fascination and discussion. What importance we place on dreams, and how we interpret them, of course, is a strictly individual matter. An orthodox Freudian, for example, might see the above dream as supercharged with sexual symbolism. The rhythmic descent of the staircase represents the sex act, the container the female sex organ, the scene shift an avoidance of unpleasant material, the inability to run a suppressed desire to be chased and caught.

But, is it possible that dreams have been overinterpreted? That these mini-dramas of the night do *not* represent the unconscious mind trying to smuggle a message to the conscious one? That dreams are nothing more than the thinking brain's valiant efforts to weave a coherent plot out of disparate and contradictory signals from the lower brain centers during sleep?

That is the new—and controversial—view of this most universal experience. In a number of centers around the world, researchers have put together a neurophysiological picture of dreaming sleep that two Harvard scientists think may change many of our notions about the meaning and origin of the images of the night. J. Allan Hobson and Robert W. McCarley, professors of psychiatry at Harvard and co-directors of the Neurophysiology Laboratory at the Massachusetts Mental Health Center, are careful not to say that dreams are meaningless and state specifically that everyone's dreams reveal elements of personal experience. Nevertheless, Hobson and McCarley think of dreaming as the psychological concomitant of an essentially biological process. In other words, dreams are the sideshow, not the main event.

The "activation-synthesis" theory of dreaming advanced by Hobson and McCarley is simplicity itself. Based on new knowledge of brain anatomy and chemistry, it states that certain cells of the brain's "sleep center" become activated during Rapid Eye Movement, or dreaming sleep. Like a husband jostling his wife when they share a bed, the cells transmit their activation to nearby cells that control other body functions. These cells in turn signal the higher brain centers that they have been activated. Drawing on previous experience and memory, the brain areas concerned with processing and interpreting information try to assemble these uncoordinated and often contradictory messages into a sensible pattern. The result is the bizarre, disconnected playlet we call a dream.

The world was not exactly lacking for a theory of dreams when the neurophysiological one came along. As the Bible, Shakespeare, and Abraham Lincoln tell us, man always has struggled to understand and explain his dreams but has been handicapped by having little more to guide him than introspection. Freud was one of the first to try to put dreaming on a scientific footing. After his training in the then new science of neurology, he wrote in *The Interpretation of Dreams* that the nighttime images represented repressed taboo wishes pushed out of the conscious mind during the day. They bubbled up in the night in disguised form to be assimilated into the dreamer's psyche.

Freud's theory of dreams held sway for half a century and still influences psychoanalysts' thinking. But in 1953 an important discovery sent researchers off in a new direction. Eugene Aserinsky and Nathaniel Kleitman found in their sleep laboratory at the University of Chicago that there are actually two kinds of mammalian sleep—REM (for Rapid Eye Movement) and non-REM, or NREM, when eye movement is lacking. Most REM coincided with vivid dreaming and produced a distinct set of physical phenomena. The eyes darted rapidly back and forth behind the closed eyelids; brain waves changed in amplitude and frequency; the body lost muscle tone; heartbeat and respiration increased; males had erections and females vaginal engorgement. NREM, on the other hand, was the deepest kind of sleep, divided into four progressively deeper stages, and its mental activity was strictly humdrum. If you waked a sleeper during NREM and asked what she was dreaming about, she was likely to say, "I was dreaming about what I had to do at the office tomorrow."

Further investigation showed that REM and NREM alternated through the night with approximately 90-minute intervals between REM periods. The REM periods started out lasting five to ten minutes and gradually lengthened until the final one lasted about 50 minutes. In a normal night's sleep, REM totaled 90 to 120 minutes, so that total dreaming time equaled the length of a feature movie. The researchers also found that REM was somehow essential to the body process. Deprived of REM, it becomes increasingly difficult to keep a person from launching into that phase of sleep.

Once they learned to identify the onset of REM sleep, researchers relentlessly began waking sleep lab subjects to inquire what they were dreaming about. They quickly discovered that dreams fell into a pattern. After listening to hundreds of dream reports, Milton Kramer of the Veterans Administration Hospital in Cincinnati, who was confirming and extending the work of Calvin Hall in California, described a typical dream. It features two characters in addition to the dreamer, takes place indoors, is more passive than active, more hostile than friendly, and is more likely to be unpleasant than pleasant. More strange males than females appear, and most of the hostility centers on these male strangers.

Like fingerprints, Kramer found, dreams are individual and identifiable. But men and women dream differently. Men's dreams are more active and friendly—but also more likely to include fighting. Men also dream more often of appearing naked in public places. Men are the most common characters in the dreams of both men and women—but in men's dreams, they are more likely to be antagonists. In recalling their dreams, men are more likely to use words like "vehicle," "travel," "automobile," "hit"; women use words of feeling and emotion. Women are more often pursued or endangered; men are more likely to find money.

Rosalind Dymond Cartwright of Rush-Presbyterian-St. Luke's Medical Center in Chicago, found that dreams often follow a ritualized format, like a sonnet or an opera. The first "scene" states the night's theme—usually a quick review of a concern left over from the day. The next two review scenes of the past in which a similar problem was confronted and dealt with. Scene Four is a future, wish-fulfillment dream: "What would life be like if I did not have this problem?" The final dream wraps all these elements into one stirring present tense extravaganza. Unfortunately, since most of us only remember the final dream, we are just a[illegible] waking as if we had wa[illegible] finale of *Don Giovanni* [illegible] nessing the previous act[illegible]

The research also casts [illegible] on Freud's theories about dream symbolism and repressed wishes. Far from avoiding delicate material, many dreams are frankly sexual and some are direct representations. "A dream about a banana may quite literally be a dream about a banana," Cartwright once said, suggesting an alternative to the view that any long, cylindrical object represents a disguised penis. In fact, Cartwright said, many dreams are transparent in meaning and often funny. "I often wonder that people don't wake themselves up laughing," she says.

But like the details of dreams themselves, certain elements of dreaming continued to elude the most zealous research. They revolved around two central questions: What do dreams mean? And what function do they serve? The problem was compounded by the fact that dream language was highly individual. "Suppose people go to sleep very thirsty," said Cartwright. "Some may dream of the ocean; some may dream of the desert; some may dream of drinking; some may dream with an emotional quality associated with thirst neither they nor we can understand; and some may have dreams that may not be related to thirst at all. We need a more refined measure of dream content before we can understand meanings."

When Allan Hobson began his research, these questions were still unanswered, and he decided that they were not likely to yield to a direct approach. A Harvard Medical School graduate, the lean, blond, intense psychiatrist had studied sleep phenomena with Michel Jouvet in France. Jouvet is a noted neurophysiologist who has deduced that REM sleep is regulated in that area of the brain known as the brainstem. This rudimentary cluster of neurons, or nerve cells, just above the spinal cord controls many of the body's automatic functions, not only sleep and waking but respiration and heartbeat. It is so central to REM, Jouvet found, that when the higher brain centers were destroyed in a laboratory cat, the animal went into regular REM sleep despite the deprivation.

Hobson decided to apply Jouvet's observations to dream research. "Previously," Hobson says, "most investigators had been following what I call a 'top-down' approach to dream theory. They took the dream reports and tried to relate it to the physiology. But because the human head is hard to gain access to, it was very difficult to learn precisely what was occurring at the cellular level. We decided that this psychophysiological approach had been very valuable, but that it had reached its limit and that it was time to move on to Stage Two, what we call the 'bottoms-up' approach. We wanted to find out what was actually happening in the brain during REM sleep and compare that with formal aspects of dreaming. In other words, we didn't ask, 'Why does the dreamer see his mother?' but 'How does he see anything? Why are dreams predominantly visual? Why is there no sensation of smell and very little of the auditory?'"

In collaboration with McCarley, Hobson began the investigation of the neuronal mechanisms of sleep. The cat was chosen as the model for REM sleep study. It had long been established that the REM process is similar in all mammals, differing in intensity and length of cycle. The differences seem to be related to body size: the cat's REM-NREM cycle is 30 minutes, the rat's 12, compared to the human's 90. Cats, of course, could not report what they dreamed about, if they dreamed at all. But presumably, a neurophysiological understanding of cat REM could illuminate human REM and its associated dreaming.

The researchers also benefited from advances in technology. By using a microelectrode, a tiny probe that could be directly inserted into the cat's head, they could tap the activity of a single neuron and even influence it. By injecting microscopic quantities of pharmacological agents resembling the brain's own neurotransmitters, they could actually alter the neuron's normal activity.

For the past 12 years, Hobson and McCarley have been pursuing this line of investigation in their laboratory in the Massachusetts Mental Health Center. The lab, housed in the basement of a fortress-like red brick building in Boston's Back Bay, provides a fascinating glimpse into how modern science approaches an age-old question. A tiger-striped cat lies restrained in a glass box. Leads from its head extend to a polygraph where brain waves, heartbeat, muscle tone, and eye muscle movement are recorded. An audio output snaps and pops—the sound of the neuronal discharge. From time to time, the beat changes as the cat moves from NREM to REM sleep.

"Our cats are kept awake at night so that they will sleep in the daytime," Hobson says, sweeping papers off a chair so a visitor can sit to watch the show. "It can sleep perfectly normally, except that its head is restrained. The small cylinder-like arrangement you see was implanted a month ago. The microelectrode, used to record from nerve cells, can be positioned inside it by remote control so that the cat's normal activities are unaffected."

The activation-synthesis hypothesis of dreaming is based on observations of the behavior of the giant cells of the pontine ("bridge") section of the brainstem during REM sleep. These cells, as their name implies, are unusually large neurons with lengthy fibers that extend into other parts of the brainstem, including those concerned with eye movement, balance, and such patterned repetitive body and limb actions as walking and running. During immobile waking and NREM sleep, the giant cells are relatively quiet, apparently inhibited by the activities of another group of cells in the nearby locus ceruleus (LC). Just prior to a REM episode, LC inhibition diminishes and the giant cells become excited. This continues at peak level throughout the REM period. Then the excitation gradually dies away, LC inhibition returns, and the giant cells remain quiet until the next REM interlude. Based on these studied observations, Hobson and McCarley developed the reciprocal interaction model of sleep-cycle control.

The mirror sequence of excitation and inhibition is based on the delicate interaction of brain chemistry. In order for a nerve impulse to be carried from one nerve cell to another, a chemical called a neurotransmitter is required to help bridge the gap, or synapse. In the case of the giant pontine cell, this substance appears to be the common transmitter, acetylcholine. At other synapses, an inhibitory transmitter prevents bridging the gap. In the LC neurons, that chemical appears to be norepinephrine.

"The on-off switch for dreaming sleep is quite simple," Hobson says of the apparent relationship between the giant cells and the LC neurons. The LC neurons are off when the giant cells are firing, and we have dreaming. When the LC neurons are on, the giant cells are off and we have waking. This model not only can explain REM sleep and waking, but NREM as well. NREM is an intermediate stage between waking and dreaming when the balance between excitation and inhibition is changing.

"Furthermore," he continues, "if the model is correct, it should be possible to turn the switch on and off chemically. First we tried activating the on switch for REM sleep by injecting the drug carbachol, which mimics the action of acetylcholine. We were able to produce a very dramatic enhancement of REM sleep. We activated the off switch for REM by using propranolol to block the norepinephrine."

The excitation, of course, extends beyond the giant cells. Among other cell groupings that may be affected are those governing eye movement, those related to the vestibular system which gauges balance and the position of the head and neck, and those of the "motor-pattern generator" that regulates walking, stepping, and running. As they do in waking, these cells "inform" the higher brain centers of the cerebral cortex of their activities; and the cortex interprets them in light of what similar messages have meant in the past. To the sleeper, it all adds up to a dream.

Hobson was intrigued by the pattern of eye movements during episodes of REM. The conventional explanation of the rapid eye movements, which are clearly visible to an observer, even though the lids are closed, is that the dreamer is busily scanning dream images as they pass before him. Hobson holds that the reverse is true. The dream represents the brain's efforts to explain why the eyes are "jiggling around." "Of course," he adds, "the mechanisms are not mutually exclusive and both could be operative. But it may be the non-voluntary movements of brainstem origin that give dreaming its unique visual characteristics.

"Suppose in a dream you are watching a man standing at an intersection," Hobson says. "Suddenly the man turns to the left and runs across the street. The explanation for this event in the dream would be that the REM-generating pontine cells activated nearby eye-movement neurons, specifically those that move the eyes to the left. The cerebral cortex registered this activity and attempted to make sense out of it in light of what had previously occurred in the dream. The logical solution, based on the speed and direction of the eye movements, was to move the man across the street.

"Look here," he says, going to the polygraph and pointing to a distinctive spike in one of the wavy lines. "This represents an abrupt shift of the animal's eyes during REM. Here (pointing to another line) we find that certain activities in the cerebral cortex followed the eye movements by many milliseconds. This may be the substrate of visual imagery and strongly favors the idea that at least some visual cortical events are determined by activities in the brainstem." In fact McCarley has found cells in the brainstem that transmit information about the direction of eye movement to the visual system in REM sleep.

Another intriguing aspect of dreaming is that, although the visual aspects of dreams are highly active, the dreamer is actually immobilized, prevented from moving during REM sleep. Sequential photos clearly show that he does not budge a muscle during REM. Yet motor commands are obviously being generated during REM sleep. Hobson explains this apparent discrepancy by declaring that the motor neurons are inhibited during REM sleep. The Italian physiologist Ottavio Pompeiano was the first to show that there is a blockade against motor output, just as there is a blockade against the reception of outside stimuli during REM sleep.

The explanation that motor commands are given but not obeyed during REM has also been confirmed in an oblique but convincing way. Following up an earlier observation by Jouvet, Adrian Morrison of the University of Pennsylvania has removed parts of the pontine area in cats, then allowed them to go into REM sleep. With the inhibitory areas destroyed, the cats literally act out their dreams. They run, walk, knead their claws, and toy with imaginary mice. Some arch their backs and assume the classic feline attack-and-defense posture. Watching them, one would suppose they were fully awake, but they are generally unresponsive to external stimuli.

"The inhibition of motor activity may help us explain the classic chase dream," Hobson says. "We do not need an elaborate theory about the wish to be pursued and caught. We feel that we are paralyzed or running in slow motion because the brain is being told we are running but is not receiving feedback from the periphery to confirm it. We are unable to move our feet and that fact is readily communicated."

The "top-down" dream investigators analyzed dreams and tried to fit them together with the physiological facts. But how does the "bottom-up" approach square neurophysiological data from cats with the detailed narratives of dreamers? Over the past two years McCarley, the more subdued member of the team, has been studying dream reports provided by Cincinnati's Kramer, and he finds that the fit is very good.

"If you analyze the dream reports in terms of verbs used in description," he says, "80 percent talk about motion. Thirty-eight percent describe movement of the lower extremities—running, walking, stepping, the kind of activities governed by the motor pattern generator.

"Eight percent of dream reports describe vestibular disturbances. The subject feels that he is floating, flying, or spinning—or that his environment is doing so. This is the kind of experience that almost never occurs in waking life. The frequency in dreams may be due to the fact that the world *does* seem to move when there are sudden, uncoordinated eye movements. Or it may be the influence of the pontine cells on the neurons regulating the position and balance of the head and neck.

"One of the most common expressions in dream reports is, 'And then the dream changed.' Thirty-eight percent of dream reports mention sudden scene shifts. The classic psychoanalytic explanation is that the dreamer is trying to avoid unpleasant material. Our explanation is that a shift occurs when different runs of neuronal activation complete their course and are followed by another sequence with other neuronal activity.

"When you look at dream reports, you also find some sense modalities missing. Visual sensations are heavily represented and sounds are often reported, but almost no one mentions sensations of taste or smell. Pain is seldom mentioned. We are still not sure of the brain mechanisms involving pain, but the absence of the others may result from the fact that they are not integrally connected to the generator cells of the brainstem.

"Seventy percent of dreams could be classified as bizarre. They violate the dreamer's normal behavior and disregard physical laws as well. One explanation may be that the brain must knit together a vast amount of contradictory information, and the only way to do so is by fantastic images like the woman walking down the steps with a bowl of Jell-O."

Perhaps the outstanding example of the interrelationship between the physical phenomena of REM and the psychological aspects of dreams may be the male erection, McCarley says. Erection occurs in every REM period regardless of dream content. When a sexually explicit dream does coincide with erection, it may represent the brain interpreting the information it receives in terms of previous experience, rather than the body reacting to the stimulating images of the brain.

When Hobson and McCarley first published their hypothesis in *The American Journal of Psychiatry* in 1977, a great hue and cry was raised. The initial article analyzed Freud's theories about dreaming as discussed in his unpublished (and disowned) *Project for a Scientific Psychology.* It concluded that Freud's ideas had been based on a misreading of the then fledgling neuron theory and that it had been perpetuated by his disciples even though it was clearly outdated by more recent neurophysiological knowledge. A second report outlined the activation-synthesis theory. The articles brought forth a blizzard of letters, most of them critical.

"Many of our critics said it was unfair to hold Freud responsible for unpublished material. Others read us as saying that dreams mean nothing, that they can tell us nothing about the dreamer," Hobson says, "even though we stated—and believe—the content of dreams is certainly influenced by the individual's motivational state, by his memories, drives, and personality. The memories and experiences on which the brain draws to interpret the messages it is receiving are unique to that individual. How the brain elaborates these details certainly tells us about the individual. We dream about what we're concerned about. Dreaming is a physiological Rorschach test if you will.

"But our hypothesis does raise important questions about accepted dream theory. Most importantly, this view damages the notion that psychological purposes are the primary explanation for dreaming. We reject the disguise-censorship notion of dreaming which ascribes the bizarre features to the mind's need to conceal meaning. Instead, we view bizarreness as the natural consequence of the operating properties of the brain in dreaming sleep. The brain is making the best of a bad job. A dream is a psychological concomitant of an essentially biological process. I certainly don't think a complex decoding system is any longer necessary or justified. Intuitively, I also consider it improbable that nature would invent an important self-communication system and then make it so inaccessible as to require interpretation. A corollary hypothesis is how dreaming sleep serves a fundamental purpose: brain development and maintenance. Dreams may be the signals made by the system as it steps through a built-in test pattern—a kind of brain tune-up crucial to prepare the organism for behavioral competence."

Because dream theory is the cornerstone of the whole psychoanalytic edifice, shock waves continue to ripple through the psychiatric community. Psychiatrists, like the rest of us, cherish the notion that dreams are especially meaningful and can tell us something about ourselves in a way that nothing else can. According to Cincinnati's Kramer, the Hobson-McCarley hypothesis is "not central to the functional problems of dreaming. When it comes to dreams, two things are important—meaning and function. Do dreams enlighten us about ourselves? Will they make us smarter, change our personality, change our mood, solve our problems, have any application to our daily lives?

"I think the essence of dreams is psychological. It's all very well to find in dreams that a person is walking. The important questions are, 'Where is he walking? Why is he walking there?' Those are the continuing mysteries of dreams, and that is what we want to know."

To which Hobson, reached by telephone, gives an almost audible shrug. "The formal approach *is* relevant to content analysis because it helps us decide at what level to seek meaning in dreams," he says. "But the most important thing is that sleep research reminds us once again that mind and body are one. Even in sleep and dreaming, they cannot be divorced."

Going Beyond Pain

Constance Holden

The current national debate on health is ensnarled in a tangle of political, economic, scientific and philosophical issues. The inadequacies of the "medical model" are becoming increasingly apparent in the treatment of the diseases of modern America, the preponderance of which are not amenable to quick technological fixes.

The victims of chronic pain may be counted among the most desperate and overlooked failures of the health care system. A new movement is emerging though, that offers hope where none existed before—by offering a holistic and as yet unconventional approach to ameliorating pain.

For millions of sufferers, the human costs of pain are incalculable. In terms of medical bills, lost wages, and workers' compensation, the price tag is an estimated $50 billion a year. Chronic pain has a multitude of causes: amputations, arthritis, degenerative diseases, and, of course, cancer. Orthopedic injuries that lead to lower back trouble account for some 70 percent of recurrent pain problems. Sometimes, as with headache pain, no organic cause can be identified.

Whatever the source, pain is an elusive, highly subjective experience—a combination of physical sensation and the emotional response to it. When pain persists over time, its emotional components become increasingly dominant. Chronic pain then takes on a life of its own, sometimes only vaguely related to the physical events that triggered it.

Recently, in recognition of the impossibility of treating chronic pain by standard medical interventions such as analgesic drugs and surgery, a new movement has emerged which treats it as an inextricable combination of emotional and physical phenomena. Capitalizing on the theories and methods of psychology, behaviorism in particular, multidisciplinary pain clinics have been established which treat intractable pain as a problem in its own right, rather than as a symptom of some underlying physical disorder. There are now, by one estimate, some 85 pain clinics scattered across the United States.

Utilizing a wide array of techniques and therapies, ranging from operant conditioning to biofeedback to hypnosis, the clinics share a common purpose: to teach patients to assume control of their own lives, to learn to reduce their pain and, when it cannot be eliminated, to accept it and live as fully as possible within the limitations it imposes.

This novel assault on pain operates at the interface of prevailing notions of psychological and physical health. Indeed, it may demonstrate an alternate conceptual model for all medical care—one based on prevention, education and self-knowledge, in which the patient, not the healer, assumes ultimate responsibility for sustaining or regaining health.

Chronic pain patients present a formidable challenge to these goals. Typically, by the time they reach one of the new pain clinics, they have been thoroughly conditioned to a passive, patient role. Chronic pain is usually defined as that which has persisted for six months or more. Most patients, by the time they arrive at the clinics, have suffered for an average of six years, years filled with doctor-hopping, drug-taking, a succession of disappointing operations, staggering medical bills, unemployment, inactivity, and increasingly warped and troubled personal relationships.

People who must live with pain live on an emotional rollercoaster, hoping for relief from each new doctor or operation. Groggy and depressed from painkilling drugs, they are also irritable and guiltridden for not being able to take care of their families. They are angry at doctors for being unable to help them; doctors, in turn, begin to regard such patients as pests and to avoid them through referrals elsewhere.

Chronic pain is, in short, a monumental disrupter of lives. The problems it causes reinforce one another, bundling into a tight, unravellable ball. As a result, most pain patients are also enormously depressed.

As Gerald Aronoff, psychiatrist at Massachusetts Rehabilitation Hospital, says of chronic pain patients, "we are dealing with a group of people who have given up on life." He compares pain sufferers with alcoholics, in that many have made "careers" of their lifestyles and hang onto them despite diminishing returns. Just as alcoholism becomes the primary symptom for a host of other problems, pain can be a translation of emotional problems into physical manifestations, and is often found preferable to yet more painful emotional conflicts.

Up to now, dogged attempts to attack pain by purely medical means have impeded both innovative thinking and the development of effective treatments: since pain is traditionally viewed as a neurophysiological problem, it is initially presumed to have organic causes. If the diagnostic evidence in a given case fails to yield a clear physical basis for reports of pain, a doctor frequently assumes the pain is psychogenic or emotional and refers the patient to a psychiatrist. The psychiatrist, in turn, failing to find clearcut evidence of mental pathology, will simply refer the patient back to yet another specialist.

Pain clinics aim to break this hopeless and demoralizing cycle. All operate on the assumption that pain is pain; and whether it is organically or emotionally caused is irrelevant. Nonetheless, most pain therapists, or "dolorologists" as they are sometimes called, now believe there is such a thing as a chronic pain personality. Patients referred to the clinics are subjected to detailed psychological evaluations that rely strongly on the Minnesota Multiphasic Personality Inventory (MMPI). While a person who suffers persistent pain often undergoes a radical personality deterioration as a result, there is evidence that, in many cases, there are certain preexisting psychological factors that make some people susceptible to protracted suffering from an injury that might be quickly overcome by others. They tend to score high on the first three scales of the MMPI—hypochondriasis, depression

This article is reproduced with permission of the Executive Board of *Psychology: A Quarterly Journal of Human Behavior.*

Hypnosis and Pain: exploring the hidden powers of an old technique

Hypnosis is available to patients at some pain clinics; however, it is not widely believed to have much use in ameliorating chronic pain. Some clinicians have said that it is inappropriate as an adjunct to an operant conditioning program because it does not involve "learning" or because it confuses the message of self-responsibility by putting the patient under the apparent control of the hypnotist. Others say that patients resist the idea, or simply that the technique hasn't been considered.

Psychologists—who use hypnosis far more widely than do psychiatrists—cannot even agree on what it is. Theodore X. Barber of Medfield State Hospital in Massachusetts, one of the foremost researchers in the field, insists that hypnosis does not induce a "trance" or "state" associated with any unique kind of brain activity. Rather, he says, it is simply a means for focusing the imagination in such a way that one's consciousness can be disassociated from pain messages. Most practitioners, however, tend toward the view of Ernest R. Hilgard of Stanford University, who has probably done more than any other researcher to make hypnosis a legitimate tool in medicine. Hilgard believes that at the very least hypnosis, like any number of relaxation techniques, can help reduce pain by reducing anxiety. According to Hilgard, however, 10 to 20 percent of people are capable of a trance state so profound that they can achieve total analgesia, even to the point where they can undergo operations without anesthesia.

No one is sure just what qualities make for a hypnotically susceptible subject or how many people can learn susceptibility. Psychologist Harold Wain of the pain clinic at Walter Reed Army Medical center regularly does hypnotherapy with pain patients both for direct pain relief and to help patients uncover emotional events that may have been associated with the onset of pain. He believes that "hypnosis is a capacity, a gift that people have or don't have." His experience has been that intelligence, a strong will, and freedom from psychopathology are important factors in successful use of hypnosis. Psychologist Frederick Evans, who does research at the psychiatric institute at Pennsylvania Hospital, agrees that motivation is crucial—"I wouldn't use hypnosis on any pain that has important psychological worth," he says. Hilgard has not found that any particular personality type correlates with high hypnotic susceptibility; the one quality he has found to be most important is the capacity for imagination.

A significant population usually not found in pain clinics are people suffering from the persistent pain of terminal cancer. Many are of course bedridden, but even those whose condition is relatively stable are not considered good candidates because clinics feel the additional problems of death and dying are more than they can handle at this point. Hypnosis is particularly appropriate for these people, many of whom continue to suffer even when drugged to near-insensibility. For some, says Hilgard, "nothing is as comforting as hypnosis." Evans says the procedure has been so successful with some terminal cancer patients that their families got the impression the cancer was retreating.

The practice of hypnosis in medicine suffered a big setback when pain-killing drugs were discovered in the last century. Now it is struggling to overcome the hocus-pocus image created for it by stage hypnotists, and the reluctance of doctors to explore something they weren't taught in medical school. Yet what if a new drug were discovered that had dramatic, side-effect free results for 20 percent of a population of sufferers? Hypnosis is clearly a major treatment approach whose potentials have only begun to be realized in the context of modern medicine.—C.H.

and hysteria—known as the "neurotic triad." Their life histories show a greater-than-average prevalence of stress-related disorders and significant incidences of emotional problems in their families.

The emotional factors that may predispose a person to chronic suffering tend to be reinforced by the present health care system, which fosters addiction to analgesic drugs, for example, and breeds a sense of helplessness and fear on the part of a patient. Health insurance systems add to the problem by subsidizing inpatient care, but not the outpatient programs increasingly favored by some pain therapists, and by covering physical, but not psychological, treatment. Pain patients, in common with victims of all chronic illnesses, says anesthesiologist Stephen F. Brena, director of Emory University's three-year-old pain clinic in Atlanta, "are intensively trained to be sick for the rest of their lives." The medical model of care encourages patients to relinquish control over their illnesses to someone else, teaches them to avoid activity, and reduces them to dependency on doctors and drugs. Brena calls such people "the failures of the conventional health care system" and thinks it will be another generation at least before chronic pain and the clinics now springing up to treat it are widely understood by the medical profession.

That's because psychologically oriented pain clinics, by and large, assume an essentially non-medical orientation. They view chronic pain as basically learned behavior; their aim is to encourage patients to change their attitudes toward pain and to unlearn the behaviors that reinforce it. At the Emory clinic, says Brena, patients are told, "it's up to you to use your life well or to make it miserable."

The founder of the pain-treatment movement is University of Washington anesthesiologist John J. Bonica, who set up the first multidisciplinary pain clinic at the University of Washington in Seattle, in 1960. Psychologist Wilbert Fordyce joined the Seattle clinic in 1969, and devised a systematic behavioral approach to pain management that has been widely imitated elsewhere. The Fordyce program is one of pure operant conditioning that was initially developed for use in the rehabilitation of stroke victims. Fordyce rejects the simplistic distinction often drawn between "real" and "imagined" pain that leads some physicians to dismiss a patient's pain as being "all in the head." Instead, he classifies pain as "respondent" or "operant." Respondent pain is a direct response to a specific organic stimulus. Operant, or learned, pain may be a mask to cover old emotional hurts, and may develop as a result of reinforcement of a patient's "pain behaviors." For chronic pain patients, Fordyce believes, respondent pain is usually amplified by layers of operant pain inadvertently reinforced by both the health care system and the patient's social environment.

The chief factors that induce learned pain, according to Fordyce, are attention and sympathy from doctors and family; pain-relieving medication; an excuse to avoid activities—from work to sexual performance—that the patient finds distasteful or anxiety-producing; and money, typically in the form of disability compensation or the hope of winning pending (usually accident-related) litigation. Another powerful reinforcer for pain is guilt and the consequent need for self-punishment.

Fordyce's present-centered program is aimed not at eliminating pain itself, but t reducing a patient's "pain behaviors;" e., moaning, wincing, limping, complaining and inactivity. All aspects of the program are designed to reinforce "well behavior" and to discourage "pain behavior." During what is typically two months of intensive inpatient operant conditioning at a cost of around $5,000 (note that it's not unusual for a patient to arrive at a pain clinic having accumulated $70,000 or more in medical bills) patients learn that expressions of pain bring no demonstrable rewards. Nurses, for example, are instructed to ignore complaining and to lavish attention on patients when they're engaged in activities antithetical to pain behavior. This, says Fordyce, rapidly helps to extinguish such behaviors. Involvement of the patient's family is crucial to success, he believes, since it is they who must continue the positive reinforcement outside the hospital.

The key to the Fordyce program is that no treatment is administered on a "pain contingent" basis, a significant departure from standard medical practice. Analgesics, for example, are traditionally prescribed on a PRN (as needed) basis. If you hurt, you get a pill or an injection. From a behavioral standpoint, this becomes reinforcement for hurting. The Fordyce program is intended to sever such connections by administering medication at regular intervals, on a non-pain contingent basis. Drug intake is gradually reduced, a process that is masked by mixing the medication in a strongly flavored "pain cocktail." In some cases, it has been found that withdrawal of analgesics results in the actual elimination of pain, a testimonial to the powers of short-term reinforcers to perpetuate misery.

Fordyce is widely credited as being the first to demonstrate the viability of operant conditioning for pain management. Psychologist Richard Sternbach, who now directs an outpatient program for pain patients at the Scripps Clinic in California, calls him "the inspiration for all of us." Until Fordyce showed that it could be done, says Sternbach, "nobody thought that behavior modification could be applied to 'organic' pain problems." Psychologists, he observes, were "too busy trying to be junior psychiatrists. Then we realized there were other areas we could get involved in, and have carved out a separate domain in rehabilitation and neurophysiology."

In less than a decade, pain clinics have become a significant part of the health care landscape. The operant approach has been elaborated upon, added to, and in some cases abandoned altogether in favor of newer therapies. Sternbach himself, for example, adds a cognitive overlay to the operant program, drawing on the principles of transactional analysis to help patients understand why they cling to their pain, and how they manipulate other people into reinforcing their sick and dependent status.

One of the most enthusiastic and colorful innovators in the pain movement is neurosurgeon Norman Shealey, who operates the Pain and Health Rehabilitation Center in Lacrosse, Wisconsin. Discouraged by the ineffectiveness of most of the operations he was performing for the relief of pain, Shealey, in 1971, went to Seattle to see the program Fordyce had begun. Since then, Shealey has essentially abandoned neurosurgery in favor of noninvasive forms of treatment for chronic pain, and is currently working on a PhD in psychology. Starting with a strictly behavioral approach fashioned closely to the Fordyce model, Shealey's program quickly grew into a "comprehensive" one that included nearly everything but drugs and surgery—total body massage, ice rubdowns, acupuncture, whirlpool baths, external electrical stimulation, biking, walking and swimming. But still, says Shealey, "I wasn't happy."

He then added biofeedback and autogenic training, and has continued to broaden and intensify this aspect of his "holistic" program. Today, Shealey, who approaches his work with a touch of evangelical zeal, runs an intensive 12-day "psychological retraining" program for 12 patients, the main focus of which is a series of "mental programming" exercises. They combine elements of autogenic training, progressive relaxation and autosuggestion techniques aimed at achieving general "homeostasis of the autonomic system." Shealey's program even includes pastoral counseling, provided by the Rev. Henry Rucker of the Psychic Research Foundation in Chicago, a man whom Shealey calls "an extraordinarily effective faith healer." Shealey claims about a 60 percent success rate in terms of pain reduction and improvements in lifestyles, a rate he says would be much higher if all patients continued the rigorous homework prescribed after they leave the program.

While Shealey and others are experimenting with an expanding range of therapies, neurological research continues apace, in an attempt to shed further light on the mysteries of the pain response. Traditional explanations, still taught in medical schools, are based on the so-called specificity theory, which postulates that pain transmission works more or less like a telephone system, with special pain receptors in the peripheral nervous system sending pain messages directly to the brain. This rather simplistic explanation was debunked in 1965 with the publication, in *Science*, of the now-famous, controversial, and far more complex "gate control" theory postulated by Ronald Melzack, a psychophysiologist at McGill University and Patrick Wall, a neuroanatomist at University College in London.

Gate control theory holds that sensation is transmitted by two kinds of nerve fibers: fast-acting, large-diameter fibers and slower-acting, small-diameter fibers, which transmit the most intense feelings. Stimulation of the large fibers can bring about an overload, thereby closing a "gate," which results in inhibition of pain transmission by the small-diameter fibers. Proponents of the gate control theory say it offers an explanation for many phenomena not covered by specificity theory: phantom limb pain; pain not associated with any organic lesion; the sensation of pain on one side of the head when a tumor is on the other side; acupuncture anesthesia; and hypnosis-induced analgesia.

Neurosurgeon Benjamin Crue, director of the City of Hope National Medical Center in Duarte, California, believes that even the gate control theory puts too much emphasis on peripheral stimulation and the concept of "nociceptors" (special pain receptors). He's convinced that pain should be regarded as a "central nervous system percept," and not a primary sensory modality, the implication being that pain perception is controlled by higher centers in the brain. Phantom limb pain (which affects at least five percent of amputees) is one of the most dramatic examples of this—the pain is real, but the limb is no longer there. The likely conclusion is that the patient is responding to remembered pain that has been stored in the central nervous system.

In this burgeoning and as yet dimly explored field, the various clinical approaches must be regarded as experimental, the theories on which they're based up for challenge. And, there are broad issues awaiting resolution: can operant conditioning be of lasting value even where it merely removes a patient's pain behaviors without necessarily lessening the pain? How much self knowledge does a patient need to sustain newly learned "well" behavior? Aronoff of Boston says, "my experience tells me that if you allow people to get rid of certain symptoms without understanding why, then very often you get a return of the symptoms." What's more, the symptoms may recur in another form: it has been noted that some "graduates" of pain clinics have been rehospitalized not for pain, but for depression. In extreme cases, patients, once rid of the pain shrouding a multitude of other problems, have turned to suicide.

Nonetheless, the success of pain clinics has been striking, since they are dealing with a desperate and hitherto intractable population. In some cases, success means total pain relief; more often it means freedom from analgesics, a significant reduction in suffering and a new ability to carry on a life minimally influenced by pain.

Those working in the field hope to intersect the medical route much earlier, intervening in the treatment of patients before they have settled into "pain careers." Faced with choices of alternative treatments, including behavioral approaches as well as the standard fare of surgery and drugs, patients would be actively participating in what course to take, breaking the cycle of passive acceptance of pain and medical procedures. In some places, the amount of surgery performed has been radically reduced because of early intervention. In such cases, pain 'treatment' has served a unique preventive role by forestalling other, perhaps unnecessary or fruitless 'treatments.'

In fact, early intervention may be the key to the future of the pain movement, and, by implication, to the applicability of its approach to chronic illness in general. Clinics and therapies can remain the last resort for those whom the traditional medical enterprise has cast aside—an appendage tacked onto the tail end of the health care system. Or, they may begin to encroach on the very structure and operation of that system.

With health care costs spiralling further and further out of sight, it is clear that we have reached a state of diminishing returns. A great many people are beginning to realize that the pattern of available services no longer conforms very well with the major health problems. Pain clinics, therefore offer not only a treatment approach but a philosophy that attempts to put technology in its proper place and to put the whole person back into medicine. This philosophy recognizes the importance of a person's lifestyle and environment in maintaining health and, above all, the necessity for individual to take responsibility for their own lives.

For further information, see

Behavioral Methods for Chronic Pain and Illness, by Wilbert E. Fordyce, The C. V. Mosby Company, 1976.

Pain Patients—Traits and Treatments, by Richard A. Sternbach, Academic Press, 1974.

"Management of Chronic Pain: Medicine's New Growth Industry," by David N. Leff. *Medical World News,* vol. 17, no. 22, pp. 54-77, October 18, 1976.

Biofeedback seeks new medical uses for concept of yoga

Thomas W. Pew jr.

Keeping up with Dr. Kenneth Greenspan through the labyrinthine passages of the Columbia-Presbyterian Medical Center in New York City turned out to be an unexpected substitute for my morning jog. As I followed him down wide corridors, past stretcher-size double doors, up and down a disorienting array of elevators, I stuck my head inside a closet-size room for a brief meeting with intense researchers, listened to an inquiry about the comfort of a patient propped up in a hospital bed outfitted with some unusual looking exercise and monitoring devices, and took hasty notes in a computer room that looked more like the control center for operating a Minuteman missile silo than a medical facility.

This is how Dr. Greenspan usually begins his day at Columbia-Presbyterian, where he is assistant attending psychiatrist and director of the Laboratory and Center for Stress-Related Disorders. In his office, 30 floors above the Hudson River, overlooking the stress-related snarl of traffic trying to get on or off the George Washington Bridge, once again I found the inconspicuous little biological "listening" devices I'd been plugged into from San Francisco to Topeka in my quest for an understanding of biofeedback. Dr. Greenspan introduced me to his own research by flashing a series of slides on the office wall, including a color picture of himself, stripped to the waist, stretched out on a bed and attached to the exercise equipment and monitoring devices we'd just seen on our tour.

"I try everything on myself first," he explained. "How else can I feel what the patient is feeling?" The concept was a new one to me—a doctor trying his own treatment so that he could get closer to his patients.

Using slides of himself and one of his biofeedback trainers working with patients, Dr. Greenspan quickly laid out the ideas he believes underlie the success of biofeedback treatment at the Medical Center. "Patients come to us feeling like victims," he said, "sick and unsure of what to expect, and we try to help them develop an attitude of mastery. We share with them what we know, and we seek their active participation in their own treatment. The goal is self-responsibility for the maintenance of one's own health," he added, "and to assist the doctor within us."

Dr. Greenspan's description of patients as "victims" illustrates a concept that pioneer biofeedback researcher Dr. Barbara B. Brown calls the "second illness": a person may actually get a lot sicker from the stress of being sick and from the fear and anxiety that can accompany modern treatments—especially the trauma of hospitalization. Dr. Greenspan's practice of trying out on himself the equipment he uses on his patients, and his emphasis on the medical benefits of compassion on the part of the physician and his aides, could reduce the risks of "second illness."

While I was still chewing on these ideas, Dr. Greenspan showed me data on 22 patients whose treatment represents a provocative study of biofeedback's potential benefits. Most of the patients had been referred to Dr. Greenspan by Dr. Arthur B. Voorhees jr., chief of cardiovascular surgery at the medical center. When they first arrived, they could not walk from the hospital parking lot to the stress center—the equivalent of two city blocks—without pain. Their circulatory systems were choked with clots, their legs crippled from lack of proper circulation. In only three months of intense biofeedback training and behavioral therapy, in which these patients consciously learned to regulate the temperature in their legs, they were able to walk a mile on the laboratory treadmill without pain, and some changes in their cardiovascular systems were similar to those seen during athletic conditioning. Even a rudimentary understanding of the medical data before me showed changes that appeared to be beyond the explanations of the best modern treatments, especially in cases of this severity.

These patients were allowed to "see" or "hear" a problem in circulation and to find a natural method for solving the problem, aided in their "seeing" and "hearing" by a rigorous training program using muscle and temperature biofeedback devices on their hands and legs. While the patients relaxed in recliners, temperature information on their blood-starved limbs was monitored, amplified and relayed to them. By learning to raise the temperature of their limbs (which meant sending more blood to the affected areas), they

From *Smithsonian,* December 1979. Reprinted with the permission of the author and Smithsonian Magazine.

gradually accelerated the development of collateral blood vessels around the clots. In effect, they developed a natural bypass system to the areas that previously had been cut off by the clots, restoring needed circulation to their crippled limbs. They also achieved deep relaxation and lessened the cardiac stress that often accompanied their efforts at walking.

I have experienced this type of biofeedback training at both the Biofeedback Institute in San Francisco and the Biofeedback and Psychophysiology Center at the Menninger Foundation in Topeka. Watching a large dial thermometer on the biofeedback instrument or listening to electronic beeps indicating temperature changes, I was soon able to raise the temperature of the part of my body to which the sensor was attached. When I saw the temperature start to go up—usually after a few moments of relaxing—I just "went with" the feeling that accompanied it, and the temperature continued to rise. It was quite easy to achieve. Most of the other participants at a Menninger biofeedback workshop found it the same. Interestingly, for those who insist that no such thing will happen when they are attached to temperature trainers, the thermometer will often remain stationary or actually fall when they attempt the training. To biofeedback researchers this only underscores the importance of motivation, and further serves to show that the body tends to do what we visualize—negatively as well as positively.

Dr. Elmer E. Green, founder of the Biofeedback and Psychophysiology Center at Menninger's, who previously worked as a physicist analyzing the performance of self-controlled guided missiles at a naval ordnance test station in California, pointed out that biofeedback uses an approach to self-regulation in human beings similar to that employed by such missiles as the supersonic heat-seeking Sidewinder. The Sidewinder homes in on the target aircraft by detecting heat from the engine exhaust and transmitting that information to a computer which uses it to constantly adjust the missile's flight controls.

Biofeedback, Dr. Green said, means getting immediate, ongoing information about one's own biological processes or conditions—such as heart behavior, temperature, brain-wave activity, blood pressure or muscle tension—and using the information to change and control voluntarily the specific process or response being monitored.

Once the signals are heard or seen an individual is able to influence their direction by willpower. "We don't know how visualization and volition get converted into action," Dr. Green told a workshop of doctors and counselors at Menninger's, "but we don't need to know everything in order to use biofeedback."

Yogis and similar individuals in many societies learn or seem to possess naturally the same self-regulating abilities the average person can acquire relatively quickly through biofeedback training. In their 20-year study of the mechanisms of biofeedback, Dr. Green, with colleague and wife Alyce M. Green, studied yogis and others with unusual control over their minds and bodies, traveling from the Menninger laboratories in Kansas to the banks of the Ganges River. What they found and documented on a sophisticated array of electronic instruments was that there are people who are conversant with the most subtle workings of what we in the West call the autonomic or involuntary nervous system.

Some yogis can alter their heartbeats on command (starting and stopping fibrillation, for example). They can alter their respiration rates, apparently enabling them to enter a kind of hibernation for long periods of time, and they can produce a whole range of brain waves, changing them at will. In addition they can exercise control over the temperatures of their bodies, stand extremes of environmental temperatures, and they seem able to make themselves impervious to pain.

One of the most impressive people ever studied at Menninger's is a Netherlander, Jack Schwarz. Participants in the biofeedback workshops are shown a film made in the laboratory there in which Schwarz runs a large, rusty sailmaker's needle through his upper arm while his body's reactions are closely monitored by a bank of electronic instruments designed to detect the slightest response to this ordeal. Just watching the dull, unsterilized needle puncture the soft flesh and be forced through the biceps with heavy pressure, finally to pop out the opposite side of the arm preceded by a great pointed bulge in the skin, was enough to raise my own blood pressure, increase my heart rate and make the moisture content of my skin leap. From the uneasy squirms and fidgets in the auditorium around me it was obvious that others watching the demonstration were reacting as I was.

Meanwhile, there was Jack Schwarz on film calmly carrying on a conversation with a slightly incredulous-looking Elmer Green. After Dr. Green was satisfied that he had all the readings he wanted on the instruments, Schwarz began withdrawing the needle from his arm. The tissues inside the arm were clinging to the metal because as the needle was withdrawn the flesh was pulled far out like bread dough.

I had heard of this demonstration prior to seeing it at Menninger's but I had no idea of the size of the needle and had not realized it was run completely through the arm. At the final moment the camera zoomed in to concentrate on the point where the needle was slipping out of Schwarz's arm. As it emerged, the hole could be seen closing instantly, allowing no more than a drop of blood to run down the skin. Within a matter of hours the wound had completely healed and the flesh exhibited no bruises, needle marks or signs of internal bleeding. Furthermore, none of the instruments recording Schwarz's heart and respiration rates, galvanic skin response, hand temperature and brain-wave activity showed he had experienced pain.

Schwarz has repeated this demonstration of control over pain and healing many times in the presence of medical doctors. One witnessing physician attempted to repeat the Schwarz demonstration himself. He had to halt in the middle, overcome with pain, but Schwarz coached him through the rest of the way by telling him to close his eyes and "think about the jonquils" blooming outdoors. Unfortunately the doctor could not control the bleeding and was left with a heavily bruised and sore arm for several days.

In spite of this evidence—open to investigation by any serious researcher or physician—the documented abilities of people like Jack Schwarz (and even of average individuals to control and alter functions in their autonomic nervous systems through biofeedback training), many doctors who went through medical school more than a decade ago still find it a difficult concept to accept. Several doctors at the Menninger workshop admitted that the idea of the inviolability of this nervous system had been so thoroughly drummed into their heads in medical school that they felt a strong involuntary resistance to accepting what they were hearing and seeing (as well as experiencing).

Almost everyone has at some time in his or her life been hooked up to some of the more obvious biofeedback equipment. A simple blood-pressure cuff can be used for biofeedback training, as can an electrocardiograph, and even, as in Dr. Greenspan's work, a thermometer. In traditional medicine, the information produced by these biofeedback instruments is primarily for the physician's eyes and his use. In biofeedback training, the diagnostic or feedback instruments are primarily for the patient's information. It's up to the patient to use the information—whether it tells about heart rate, blood pressure, temperature, muscle contractions or brain waves—to help restore normal functions to the body. And how does anyone do this?

If you are doing your biofeedback training at Menninger's under the guidance of Dr. Green, he will tell you to "visualize what you want the body to do. Tell the body to do it. Then relax and let it do it." Then something changes in the body, and the biofeedback instruments show that change. And with a little practice, when the patient sees the change and realizes that he or she does have an observable physiology, then the patient is on the way to self-regulation.

The remarkable thing that follows the instruction is the rapidity with which many people "get it," learn to "play" their biofeedback instrument, and advance from being mere observers of the workings of their autonomic nervous systems to being able to exercise their will over it. Biofeedback itself, Alyce Green pointed out, "does nothing *to* the person." It is only "a tool for releasing potential."

No amount of conscious effort usually works in learning biofeedback. The trick is just to listen to the feedback signal and when the changes you want begin, "go" with that feeling. "There is another way to say it," advised Dr. Green: "the person visualizes and feels the desired change that will influence the meter, and allows the body to carry out the instruction. The feeling seems to be the instruction. This feeling has been reported by many successful performers to be, at least in the early stages of learning, a composite image, emotion and body sensation, but after a skill is thoroughly learned, the body sensation can be 'turned on' at will, often with no need for any particular mental image or emotion. Often feedback is not needed for more than a few weeks. Most important, biofeedback is not addictive because voluntary internal control is established, rather than dependence on an external agency.

"The point is we're used to having the voluntary muscles of our body do what we visualize. And you don't have to understand the body to make it work for you," Dr. Green said, "any more than you have to know the mechanism of a car to drive it. In teaching control of 'involuntary' body processes, we explain the neuromechanism to patients to get them over their sense of something outside themselves being in control. The rest is up to them."

Not all biofeedback practitioners are as sanguine about the medical miracles biofeedback can achieve. Dr. DeLee Lantz, a clinical psychologist and until recently acting director of the Biofeedback Institute in San Francisco, believes it may be possible for biofeedback trainers to "cure" migraine headaches, but there's not enough clinical evidence to know yet. Dr. Joseph D. Sargent, the chief of internal medicine at Menninger's and in charge of the clinic's biofeedback headache research and training project, says biofeedback is no cure for migraine, only a way of "managing" the headache. Alan J. Tyler, a counselor and biofeedback trainer with the Associates in Human Development in Tucson, believes it is quite possible for patients to become dependent on the biofeedback equipment. He finds it is common for the old symptoms to recur when patients who have successfully used the training no longer get their weekly dose of reassuring feedback from the machinery and fail to practice their daily image-altering exercises.

Dr. Sargent has confirmed this experience with his migraine patients at Menninger's. "As soon as they withdraw attention from the task—in this case, increasing the blood flow in their hands," he said, "they return to the base line. The headache comes back. They've got to keep repeating the task, repeating, repeating." When boredom with the training sets in, some of his patients rationalize: "Why bother with this when I can take medicine instead?" They aren't willing to stick with the program; they would just as soon take a pill, and they say they don't worry about what the drugs may be doing to them.

Biofeedback is for people who are highly motivated, or who suffer unbearable side effects from alternative medication. It is not a panacea. "We will need drugs plus biofeedback," said Dr. Sargent, and he sees self-regulation being applied most successfully in skeletal muscle control for stroke victims and in relaxation techniques for those on Valium, Librium and other minor tranquilizers. He also believes it will be effective in helping treat many psychosomatic diseases caused by or related to stress. Physicians believe that 75 percent or more of modern disease is related to stress, which makes biofeedback a potential tool for virtually all of the medical and psychological specialities.

A study made in a British factory threatened with a permanent closing illustrates the point. The study showed marked increases in workers' blood pressures, an increase which remained even among those employees who were never actually laid off. What had changed in the workers' environment was their sense of security, their image of themselves as valuable members of society. Even when they retained their jobs and the threat was past, their blood pressures did not return to the pre-threat, normal levels. What happens in cases such as this, according to Dr. Barbara Brown, is that "the problem-solving effort fills all the body's circuits, blocking off any other inputs. The natural, unconscious awareness of how the body is behaving is blocked off by the cortex when the person is under constant stress. Under normal circumstances the cortex would allow tension to relax, but in the context of the social system the cortex doesn't know how to relax. The tension is held and held, and pretty soon physical disease arises."

In the modern vernacular, such a person is "uptight" to the extent that something has to give. What reacts is blood pressure, lower back, head, stomach, legs, heart, any place in the body where the stress can be converted to disorder-creating tension.

Yoga, golfing, tai chi, running—all body-awareness techniques—are good for relieving stress, but when a person is ill (when there are actually blood clots in the legs, for example) there isn't time to learn yoga. This is where the accurate and sensitive biofeedback instruments come in. The individual can see that the hands are too cold, that circulation is being restricted, that muscles are too tight, that brain waves are racing, or that the stomach is too acid. These are typical stress-related symptoms known to almost everyone, and if allowed to continue without relief they can be precursors of serious disease. With the use of biofeedback training, many people can learn to alleviate them.

Even in instances of disorders that do not arise from stress, biofeedback has found the way to innovative cures. In a program at the University of Alabama Medical Center in Birmingham, deaf children have learned to speak more clearly by using a feedback device called a "palatometer." This visual biofeedback instrument shows the deaf child the position and shape of his or her tongue alongside that of a hearing person speaking the same sounds. Fifty to 100 sensors imbedded in a custom-designed plastic palate are activated whenever the tongue touches the palate. The positions of the tongue show up as white dots on a TV screen, showing the child an outline of where the tongue is located for a specific sound. He can match the position of his own tongue to that of the instructor. To the child who has never heard speech, it is another way of learning to talk.

Another impressive application of biofeedback has been found to help victims overcome "foot drop," a nerve injury which causes an impaired gait often requiring the use of leg braces. In still another application, some California schools have achieved dramatic improvements in children with problems of concentration, anxiety and hyperactive behavior. Often if a child—or an adult for that matter—can just learn to raise the temperature of his or her hands it affects all kinds of other problems. Once an individual sees that it is possible to control one thing, he realizes the potential to control other things—concentration or hyperactivity, for instance. In these cases biofeedback simply gives the individual a sense of self-control and mastery, something beyond the reach of "others."

The extent of self-influence can be impressive. Patients working with muscle biofeedback learned to reduce the electrical firing of nerves leading to the point where an electrode was attached to their skin, until only a single nerve cell was being triggered. Firing the one nerve at will, they could produce a drum roll or tap out a song on biofeedback audio equipment.

What biofeedback seems to be showing is that sometimes people have hidden abilities to deal with the kinds of stress they encounter in the modern world. The rapidity with which we can learn to use biofeedback makes this conjunction of Man and machine appear as a natural extension of our own nerves and muscles. Or perhaps biofeedback is just a reminder of something we've had all along but lost the ability to perceive and use. "In psychology," the Greens have written, "there has been a tendency to look on humans as 'king-size rats,' reflective only of genetics and conditioning. In medicine we have accepted the idea that the doctor must 'cure' us. In order to be made well we must undergo surgery, drug treatment, radiation treatment, or some other kind of manipulation by outside forces. We have not been informed that our bodies tend to do what they are told *if we know how to tell them*." If we can have psychosomatic illness, then why can't we have psychosomatic healing? asked Dr. Green. "You meet one of these guys who can do impossible things. It makes you think there is something to be learned about a person's ability *not* to be programmed solely by his genes and his conditioning. You *can* make a better life for yourself."

BRAIN FLASH

THE PHYSIOLOGY OF INSPIRATION

MEME BLACK

Meme Black, who has written and edited for several national magazines, is interested in the link between philosophy and neurobiology.

While on vacation with his wife in the English Lake District a prominent 48-year-old research biologist walked past a cave where spiders were spinning their webs over the cave opening. For a moment he just stared at them. Then in a flash he *knew* that the spiders' precise, artful labors reflected universal order and purposefulness in nature. "He couldn't express strongly enough," recalls psychiatrist Eugene d'Aquili, who has interviewed the biologist extensively, "that words were inadequate to convey the extent of his exhilaration and the fact that his whole life was transformed in that instant. That was four years ago. He still has those feelings today."

Another such incident ended in a religious conversion. "A thirty-seven-year-old physicist was visiting a friend in the country," d'Aquili recounts. "He arose early one morning to take a swim before breakfast. He dove in and had the sudden sensation of being one with the water that enveloped him, followed by extreme elation at the thought that the Universe was fundamentally beautiful and good. Although the intensity of that feeling waxed and waned over the next six years, it never left him. He became interested in religion and joined the Episcopal Church. His scientific research career continued unabated. In fact, this experience brought a whole new motivation and perspective to his life."

The neurological mechanisms behind these episodes, as well as the more common feeling of exhilaration that accompanies events such as solving a stubborn problem or viewing a particularly beautiful sunset, may explain how the brain intersects with the shimmering nether world of the spirit, according to d'Aquili, who is a professor of psychiatry at the University of Pennsylvania Medical School. Drawing on his unique background—brain research, medicine, psychiatry, anthropology and philosophy—d'Aquili has developed a theory that he believes will show the circuitry that underlies mental states from flashes of inspiration to altered states of consciousness. He feels it holds for episodes as varied as poet William Blake's hallucinatory epiphanies and Saint Paul's rendezvous with Christ on the road to Damascus. Our emotions, says d'Aquili, hold the key. Strong feelings activate a certain part of the right hemisphere of the brain, boosting our minds into what he considers a separate reality.

TRANSCENDENTAL BIOLOGY

How (or if) biology can explain religious belief has always preoccupied d'Aquili, in part, he thinks, because of his strict Roman Catholic upbringing. During medical school he did research at the Institute for Neurological Sciences at the University of Pennsylvania and studied the trance states of shamans in primitive cultures. But neither neurology nor anthropology provided the insights he desired. Then a fellow academic lured him to a Zen meditation group where, in spite of his doubts, he experienced a transcendent state. "It probably wasn't the real thing," he recalls, "but it was close enough to get rid of any personal doubt that these things exist."

D'Aquili has since become well known in the psychiatric profession for his interest in the neurobiology of transcendence. His psychiatric practice attracts people who have had positive spiritual experiences, as well as those who have had negative experiences of an equally profound nature. Rather than dismiss these people as mystics or madmen, d'Aquili uses what he has learned about where and how these baffling episodes occur in the brain to help reorient his patients and reassure them that they are not psychotic. This is no mean feat since, for most of his patients, reality simply slipped away one day, as if a veil had been lifted revealing alien mental terrain. "Since most psychiatrists and medical doctors really know very little about mystical states," he says, "they refer patients to me to get a judgment. They ask 'Is this guy crazy? He doesn't look crazy—doesn't seem to have a thought disorder. Let's send him over to d'Aquili and see what he thinks.'

"Typically a guy comes in and says, 'I think the world is good. I'm no longer afraid to die,'" d'Aquili reports. "Even if they're not religious, they say, 'Basically its okay—whatever *it* is.' They become good people, corny as it sounds, concerned about others. Sometimes it trans-

"Brain Flash: The Physiology of Inspiration," by Meme Black, *Science Digest,* August 1982. Reprinted by permission.

forms their lives. Now, they don't all go off to India like Mother Teresa, but they might."

On the other hand, d'Aquili has seen more than a dozen patients who have described a state he calls *Weltschmerz*—after the philosophical gloom cultivated by languishing heroes of eighteenth-century German novels. "The entire Universe is perceived as negative," he explains. "A person feels sadness, futility and a sense of man's incredible insignificance in the Universe, the pain of the world and the suffering of the human condition. In *Weltschmerz* the whole Universe is one vast pointless, purposeless machine."

The case of a 25-year-old chemistry graduate student is typical. While vacationing on the coast of Maine, he sat alone on a cliff watching a storm at sea. Suddenly he saw streaks of lightning through the clouds and was overwhelmed by an oppressive sense of futility. The world was heartless. His sadness was so deep he became nauseated. Although the intensity of his despondency varied, *Weltschmerz* persisted for two years.

In another case, a young bank teller awoke from a horrible nightmare. "The contents of the dream eluded her," d'Aquili says, "but she felt despair about the world in general. Not about herself, but that the very structure of the world was empty, meaningless and devoid of purpose." Even after months of treatment, d'Aquili unearthed no psychiatric cause for the woman's abrupt descent into profound gloom.

"These people come for treatment not because they're disturbed—this is *not* what we call clinical depression—but because they want relief," he points out. "They truly believe that the state they're in is ultimate reality. Their misery makes them wish to be taught to think it illusory so they can survive."

D'Aquili presents a neurological model to explain spontaneous altered states in terms of brain function, and, specifically, the growing significance attached to the right hemisphere. He draws heavily on ideas sparked by Caltech neurobiologist Roger Sperry's Nobel Prize-winning brain research, which demonstrated that each of the two hemispheres of the brain has its own range of preferred functions. Sperry's research has led some to speculate that the left hemisphere is primarily responsible for analytical and logical functions, while the right hemisphere controls artistic and musical abilities—instantaneously comprehending wholeness, or, as some psychologists have in modern times come to call it, the gestalt.

Ordinarily information passes from right brain to left across a thick band of nerve fibers called the corpus callosum. In the case of altered states, however, d'Aquili postulates a sort of spiritual detour through the inferior, or lower, parietal lobe of the right brain and the limbic system, our emotional "mission control," which spans both sides of the brain. "Most messages from the right are broken down by the left into its own verbal, analytical language," explains d'Aquili. "Don't forget, the right relies on the left for speech—thus the message received by the left is only an approximation of the original sent by the right. For example, a thought like 'Look at that gorgeous sunset. There must be a God' is far too vague and metaphysical for the left brain and would never make it to the conscious mind. Instead you would comment off-handedly on the sunset's colors. But when the limbic system gets involved, the thought travels from right to left brain uncensored, because emotions drive it home. In effect, gestalt perception and a simultaneous surge of emotion convince the left that the perception is true."

A brief word about the limbic system. Once thought simply to be important in smelling, the limbic system is now known to influence elation and rage, sexuality and hunger. Researchers have just begun to discover how extensively and subtly our emotions, all processed in the limbic system, influence every aspect of our behavior. D'Aquili attributes altered states of consciousness to a finely tuned interplay between the limbic system and the inferior parietal lobe of the right brain, which he finds to have unusually rich limbic connections.

POSITIVE PERCEPTIONS

D'Aquili thinks the exhilaration of confronting awesome metaphysical questions or profound aesthetic experiences could both trigger and perpetuate cosmic consciousness in the brain. "So powerful is the emotional arousal when the gestalt right brings these holistic truths to consciousness that the right hemisphere, spurred on by the emotions, convinces the left brain of its validity." Tying the emotions closely to neuroanatomy, d'Aquili explains, "The occipital parietal region on the right, which constructs our sense of the world or reality from sensory input, is flooded with positive feeling. Usually the connections between that area and the limbic system 'balance'—we feel neither elated nor sad. During cosmic consciousness, the balance is altered so perception becomes completely positive. The exact opposite occurs during *Weltschmerz,* when perception is totally negative."

D'Aquili has also studied individuals who report the far more spectacular altered state he calls Absolute Unitary Being. "Time stands still," he says. "A person sees only the totality of a given situation or psychological reality. There is a sense of absolute and complete unity—of self, of cosmos—caused by the occipital parietal region on the right practically obliterating the rest of the brain, perceptually. Those with a religious background think it's a direct experience of God." Of two scientists who experienced Absolute Unitary Being, one "got religion," the other remains agnostic. "But,"

WELTSCHMERZ

The profound cosmic depressions and feelings of futility that psychiatrist Eugene d'Aquili treats are similar to Weltschmerz, *the philosophical gloom evoked by eighteenth-century German writers. The following passage from the novel* The Sorrows of Young Werther *by Johann von Goethe captures the intangible—one man's sense of despair.*

My full, warm enjoyment of all living things that used to overwhelm me with so much delight and transform the world around me into a paradise has been turned into unbearable torment, a demon who pursues me wherever I go. . . . Something has been drawn away from my soul like a curtain and the panorama of eternal life has been transformed before my eyes into the abyss of an eternally open grave. Who can say, "That's how it is!" when all things are transient and roll away with the passing storm, and one's powers so rarely suffice for one's span of life but are carried off in the torrent to sink and be dashed against the rocks? There is not a moment in which one is not a destroyer and has to be a destroyer. A harmless walk kills a thousand poor crawling things, one footstep smashes a laboriously built anthill and stamps a whole little world into an ignominious grave. The rare disasters of this world, the floods that wash away our villages, the earthquakes that swallow up our cities—they do not move me. My heart is undermined by the consuming power that lies hidden in the Allness of nature, which has created nothing, formed nothing. . . . Surrounded by the heavens and the earth and the powerful web they weave between them, I reel with dread. I can see nothing but an eternally devouring, eternally regurgitating monster.

At the end of the story, Werther blows his brains out. Inspired by his example, a number of real young people of the day joined him in suicide.

adds d'Aquili, "everyone who goes through this is absolutely certain that the transcendent, absolute realm of things does exist."

EXOTIC PSYCHOSES

D'Aquili has become expert at distinguishing these mental enigmas from ordinary psychoses. "My subjects of study fit no formal criteria of psychosis," he says. "Hallucinations and delusions may be present but not as in a demonstrable thought disorder. None have hallucinations in the schizoid sense.

"These people cope very well with living," he goes on. "They do well at their jobs and thrive with their families. As a matter of fact, after experiencing cosmic consciousness some people cope better. For those who have experienced both realities—the reality of the daily world and objective science and the reality of transcendent unitary being—the problem is not reducing one to another. These people say they 'know' *both* are real. The problem is reconciling two drastically different perceptions of reality, something like developing a theory to explain why it's true that light has the properties of wave propagation while it's also true that light has the properties of a stream of particles." D'Aquili sees his role as a provider of support and guidance, both psychoanalytically and philosophically. "I don't take a closed, nineteenth-century mechanistic view—that biology answers all the fundamental, bottom-line questions," he adds. "Right now that's impossible, given all the unknowns about the brain."

D'Aquili's views do not always sit well with other scientists. Psychiatrist and pharmacologist Nathan Kline, research director of Rockland Research Institute in Orangeburg, New York, and one of the leading proponents of the use of lithium for manic-depressive illness, takes a pragmatic view. "Dr. d'Aquili makes the brain sound like Rubik's cube," says Kline. "It isn't a push-pull kind of thing with each part having a particular function. We know the brain as a much more vital, palpating series of events." As for altered states, Kline doubts that *Weltschmerz*, for instance, is anything but depression. "If a patient such as he describes came to me, I'd say 'atypical depression' and treat it as a clinical problem rather than becoming philosophically ecstatic because someone had achieved this marvelous state described by the German Romantics. *Weltschmerz* that interferes with productivity or causes excessive pain certainly constitutes a pathological state, no matter what you decide to label it."

Kline is equally leery of cosmic consciousness. He would be apt to diagnose hypomania if the condition altered perception of reality or healthy relationships and would prescribe lithium. While agreeing that the unconscious mind might provoke an altered state, Kline thinks d'Aquili is premature in naming the neurological mechanisms involved. "He makes it sound like he's got it all programmed. God knows, we don't even know what the hardware is," says Kline, "let alone the *software*."

But Richard Restak, a neurologist and neurobehaviorist at Georgetown Medical School in Washington, D.C., thinks there's room for bold ideas such as d'Aquili's. "We are now at a point where we have enough basic understanding of the brain to begin speculating in a controlled, meaningful way," states Restak. "This idea of the limbic system firing up certain parts of the brain suggests that we can change what we know and how we know it—perhaps even change behavior and life-style. We know that people get caught up in transcendental, preverbal behavior—look at Jonestown. When someone says a guru took them over, was that it? Or was the brain expressing a need?"

A comment by entomologist and sociobiologist Edward O. Wilson puts d'Aquili's theories in perspective: "Soon we may have to pick and choose among the emotional guides we have inherited and determine those that should be followed and those that should be sublimated or redirected, so that our behavioral patterns will both conform with biological principles and foster the growth of the human spirit."

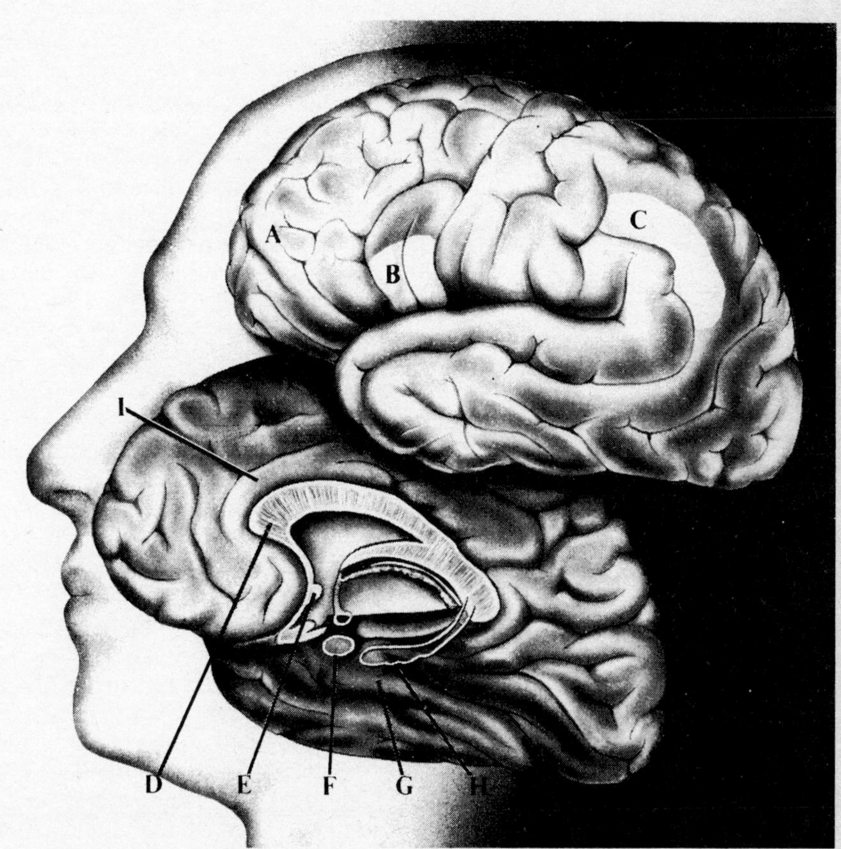

Dr. d'Aquili traces rational consciousness to a few areas of the left brain: anterior convexity of frontal lobes (A), Broca's area (B) and inferior parietal lobule (C). If intuitive messages traveling from the right brain to these areas go through the corpus callosum (D) and anterior commissure (E), the left brain censors them. If they go by way of the limbic system—uncus (F), hippocampal gyrus (G), hippocampus (H), gyrus cinguli (I), amygdala and hypothalamus (not shown)—they keep their emotional charge.

THE WAY OF THE JOURNAL

ROBERT BLAIR KAISER

Last year, thousands of Americans with no literary pretensions whatsoever started producing stories of surpassing interest that will probably never be published, or even read by their best friends. They were writing their own, often eye-popping, tear-evoking journals, under the direction of a tieless, tireless New York psychologist named Ira Progoff.

They wrote these journals in 392 workshops sponsored by colleges and universities across the land, by branches of the armed forces, by army hospitals and women's prisons, by groups of artists, priests, poets, business people, and engineers (and combinations of all of the above); they didn't enroll in them (for an average tuition of $70 each) because they felt they needed therapy, but because they wanted to put their lives in perspective and find in them some deeper meaning.

The Intensive Journal method comes from everywhere—and from nowhere, except the synthesizing mind of Ira Progoff. Because he is a psychologist who studied under Carl Gustav Jung and is one of the founders of the Association for Humanistic Psychology, people have a mistaken notion that he is either a therapist or the newest in a long line of gurus—like Abraham Maslow, Fritz Perls, and Werner Erhard—who helped people "actualize" themselves.

"Wrong," says Felix Morrow, the editor of Progoff's last two books, *At a Journal Workshop* and *The Practice of Process Meditation*. "It's hard to get a handle on Ira. He's an original. He's not a therapist and he's not in the human potential movement. But if you're looking to see what 'line' he's in, I think you'd have to say he follows Martin Buber and Paul Tillich."

By many accounts, Buber and Tillich, who both died in 1970, were the 20th century's greatest philosopher-theologians. They were great because they refused to be confined by the traditions they grew up in—Buber was Jewish and Tillich, Lutheran—and because they were open to the full horizon of possibilities reachable by men and women with dynamic religious faith. Furthermore, they were able to communicate their vision to a wide group of followers.

Ira Progoff has the same vision and the same thrust: he is now very much like a philosopher-theologian himself, interested not only in helping people find meaning in their lives but also in making the world a gentler place. Progoff may never write anything as deep as Buber's *I and Thou* or as broad as Tillich's *Systematic Theology*. But he may be doing something even more important: working out a method that will help people find ultimate meaning, both for themselves and for others. That method is the Intensive Journal system, which many believe is a unique tool that contemporary men and women can use to make tangible the most elusive, most subjective parts of themselves—those subtle "intimations of truth" that give direction to their lives.

At the beginning of his book on process meditation, Progoff tries to explain what he is up to by recalling a story. When he returned to civilian life after World War II, he had a recurrent daydream. He wondered what might have happened to civilization if the Nazi's ritual book burnings had continued until all the recorded wisdom of mankind had been destroyed—all the bibles of the world, the Old and the New Testaments, the Tao-te Ching, the Upanishads, the Koran, and all the others. "If that happened," he asked himself, "what would befall mankind?"

Finally the answer came to him, and in a very matter-of-fact tone: "We would simply draw new spiritual scriptures from the same great source out of which the old ones came." And soon another thought came: "If mankind has the power to draw additional spiritual scriptures out of the depth of itself, why do we have to wait for a Hitlerian tyrant to burn our bibles before we let ourselves create further expressions of the spirit? . . . Perhaps there are new bibles, many new bibles, to be created as the sign of spiritual unfoldment among many persons in the modern era. It may be . . . part of the further qualitative evolution of mankind."

There not only *may* be new expressions of the spirit, Progoff added, there *must* be. Why? Because we find that the old bibles of whatever tradition are being lost to moderns. Contemporary men and women live in a different way than Moses, David, Matthew, Mark, Luke, Paul, and all the rest; they have begun to think differently as well. Progoff's solution: mankind has to renew its old bibles, get in touch with the profounder meanings of life, which he claims are in everyone, "whatever their faith or lack of faith."

A member of the Teilhard Association for the Future of Man and a peripatetic scholar who is always on the move, always talking to people with ideas, Progoff sometimes sounds like an affable missionary of the mind who wants to enlist much of mankind, person by person, in the task of "extending the process of evolution." He believes that men and women who plumb the sources of meaning are automatically "building up the noosphere," that cloud of thought which, according to Pierre Teilhard de Chardin, the French Jesuit paleontologist, philosopher, and theologian, hovers over the earth and somehow provides the nurturing environment mankind needs in its march toward an omega point of fulfilling perfection.

For those who want to plumb the sources of meaning, Progoff likes to use a metaphor that many find helpful. He says that there's an underground stream of images and recollections within each of us. The stream is nothing more or less than our interior life. When we enter it, we ride it to a place where *it* wants to go. He says this is not a discursive method, not analytic: "There's no neat wrap-up; you don't end up with 'insight.' It's *an event*, and when it's happened, your life is different."

All of this may sound rather mystical. But then the mysticism gets terribly concrete, because everyone at a Journal workshop ends up with a workbook weighing several pounds, full of stories and recollections and often surprising new insights about the most fascinating mystery of all: themselves and their relation to the world around them. To produce a Journal, however, Progoff is quick to point out, "You don't need to be a mystic. All you need is a life. Almost anyone can do it."

A trip to Dialogue House, Progoff's cluttered third-floor headquarters in a Lower Manhattan office building, provides proof enough of that. Thomas Duffy, Progoff's director of advanced studies, opens his files to me and shows me reports from workshops across the land. In Morgantown, West Virginia, for instance, I see that Dr. Virgil Peterson conducted a Journal workshop for faculty members at the University of West Virginia. James Armstrong, a professor at Loyola University of Chicago, gave a Journal workshop at the annual convention of the American Holistic Medical Institute. For the past three years, Sister Maureen McCormack, a Sister of Loretto, has been giving Journal workshops to groups in Lakewood, Colorado, who are training for the lay ministry. An organization in Chicago called the Institute of Women Today has sponsored 16 Journal workshops in six different women's jails and prisons in the Midwest.

In one experimental program at a New York City facility for the elderly, some 300 recruits from the city's welfare and unemployment rolls were enrolled in a Journal workshop as part of their on-the-job training as nurse's aides, dietary workers, security guards, maintenance men, and housekeepers. Most of them were either unlettered blacks from the South or recent immigrants from the Caribbean, people likely to fail in the big city and end up on its bulging welfare rolls. Ninety percent of them kept their journals over a six-month period (they met once a week), finished their training, and stayed on to perform their low-status hospital jobs. After a year, 80 percent of them either were still on the job or had gone on to better jobs. One in three had moved on to better housing; one in four had started night school or community college. Program officials gave the Journal method much of the credit and agreed with Progoff: "Poverty is not simply the lack of money. Ultimately, it is a person's lack of feeling for the reality of his own inner being."

Perhaps this is one reason for the popularity of Progoff's Intensive Journal method today: people feel poor and alone and devoid of ultimate meaning in their lives. In the Journal workshops, they have found a way to remedy that.

But how? I didn't quite understand until I had gone to a Journal workshop myself. Last spring, I spent a weekend with a disparate group of artists, teachers, housewives, and some college students at the Terros Center in Warwick, New York. Father Lewis Cox, a tall, placid New York Jesuit who is one of 95 consultants trained by Progoff and authorized to give the workshops, got us started at 8:00 P.M. on a Friday by passing out loose-leaf notebooks filled with blank, lined paper and a series of 21 colored dividers. He invited us to enter the interior worlds of our own memories and imaginations, opening our "exploration" by helping create some preliminary moments of meditative silence. Then he invited us to answer the question for ourselves, "Where are you now in your life?"

Father Cox said the answer might not, probably would not, come in the form of a judgment or as an answer in a college quiz. We might have an image—see a picture of ourselves on a bumpy plane ride or hear the strains of a favorite symphony. Whatever it was, the point was not to merely *think* about it. We were to write it down in a section of the Journal called the "Period Log" and were to refrain from making any judgments about whether the images we recorded were good or bad. It was all right, Father Cox said, soothingly and assuringly. We would return to it later.

After perhaps half an hour of work on the Period Log, Father Cox asked us to turn to some red sections in the middle of our books, first to the "Life History Log," subtitled "Recapitulations and Rememberings." He invited us to submerge ourselves in our own underground stream of recollection, but not to begin writing anything like an autobiography—just quick, significant *scenes* in our lives. Again, no judgment. Just get into that underground stream.

Soon we were into the next section of the Journal workbook, called "Steppingstones." Here, Father Cox asked us to set down what could be chapter headings in an autobiography—not only an objective sequence of events, epitomized in a word or two or an image, but also a subjective perception of meaning and value. My Steppingstones turned out to be people; I wrote down a few dozen names—people I'd loved, people I had a hard time loving. Next, I wrote down the titles of the four books I'd published, the significant jobs I'd had.

And then it was time to retire until the next morning. So far, there had been hardly any conversation, hardly any noise. At one point, I had looked around the room and seen a few dozen heads bobbing over a few dozen notebooks, a few dozen ball-point pens gliding away. A lot of intensity and then, when the evening ended, a collective exhaling of breath and blinking of eyes. I thought I noticed tears streaming down the cheeks of an elderly man with a gray beard.

For some of the next day we amplified our Steppingstone section, going deeper into any period that seemed to draw our special interest. We made the same meditative trip in another section of the workbook, called "Intersections," subtitled "Roads Taken and Not Taken." I thought of my own spiritual intersections: I'd studied to be a priest for 10 years, then took another path. I thought of my emotional intersections: marriages, other loves. I thought of my career intersections: I'd worked for *Time*, then went free-lance and lived in a paradise in the High Sierra, then opted for a richer life of the mind by taking a job in New York with the *Times*.

And then Father Cox asked us to move to another section of the workbook, the "Twilight Imagery Log." "We turn our attention inward, and we wait in stillness," he said, "and let ourselves observe the various forms of imagery that present themselves. We let them come of themselves. As they take shape, we perceive them. We observe them as though they were dreams. We describe them in the same neutral, noninterpretive, nonjudgmental way that we record our dreams."

Unbidden, the image of a roller coaster came to my mind, and I recorded the roller coaster of my life. I didn't dwell much on it there and then, but later I realized that that was what Progoff meant when he wrote that, frequently enough, images deep inside us "enable our life to disclose to us what its goals and its meanings are." For me, the image of the roller coaster was fun—and depressing: how can I ever manage to get *off* the roller coaster without breaking up in little pieces?

For many of us, the most creative time was spent in the "Dialogue Dimension," part of an entire system of "Journal Feedback" where, after laying out our life, we could not only step back and look at it but also explore its meanings. We did this, in part, by engaging in imaginary conversations with some of the significant people we'd already listed in the Steppingstones section.

To help make sure that the conversation wasn't one-sided and that we didn't give ourselves all the good lines, Father Cox suggested that we go through a short Steppingstones exercise for "the other." (I recalled an old Indian proverb I'd heard in my Arizona boyhood: "Judge no man until you've walked a mile in his moccasins." Father Cox's suggestion made sense.)

I did the Steppingstones for my daughter Polly, in England, who has been visiting me only in the summers since she was a tot, except for last summer, when she didn't come to the United States at all. I got into her moccasins, and this dialogue ensued:

Polly: You going to ignore me again?
Me: Ignore you?
Polly: You did last time.
Me: I was in a different place last time. That was two years ago. I was broke, alone, insecure.
Polly: And now?
Me: I've got some money in my pocket, I've got friends, I'm secure. And I'm so happy you're coming this summer.
Polly: You'll spend some time with me?
Me: I'll have to—or lose you.
Polly: No. Not for that reason. Because you want to, because I am someone, too. I don't want you to love me because you have to. I want you to love me because you want to. I am a person, too, flesh of your flesh, but my own person, too. Look at me, listen to me, understand what I want.
Me: That's very hard. I get a lump in my throat.
Polly: You feel . . . ?
Me: I don't know. Guilty, maybe. Afraid that I won't come through for you?
Polly: I don't want anything from you. Just your undivided attention for a time.
Me: Polly, you have to let me be me, too. I enjoy the roller coaster. If you want to be with me, you've got to get on the roller coaster, too.
Polly: Okay. But don't forget I'm here, next to you.

At the end of this exercise, Father Cox suggested we might start to reread what we had written, then write down how we felt. I wrote: "Sense of shame: I knew this all the time, but I wasn't paying attention. Enlightening. Shocking."

There were other dialogues: with society, with events, with the body, with works. The most productive dialogue was with the book I'd been doing on and off, mostly off, for two years.

Book: Help!
Me: Hello.
Book: Don't you recognize me?
Me: Oh, yes, you're my memoir.
Book: You're not paying me enough attention.
Me: Strange, that's what the women in my life keep telling me.
Book: You can't do everything.
Me: I try.
Book: At what cost?
Me: Everything suffers. I suffer.
Book: So?
Me: So, I guess I'd better set some priorities.
Book: That sounds very old and very . . .Jesuitical. What do you really want?
Me: I want it all.
Book: You've got to conserve your energies for the most important things first.
Me: The old "necessary, useful, agreeable" rule, huh?
Book: That's too puritanical. Have you ever thought about going with your feelings?
Me: Sometimes it gets me in trouble.
Book: Some people call that living.
Me: Say, whose side are you on, anyway? I thought you were complaining that I wasn't giving you enough attention.
Book: I was, but if you're harried when you come to me, what good are you? You're only going to be writing down stuff you end up throwing away.
Me: So how do I arrange to come to you unharried?
Book: Don't be taking on so many things, so many people.
Me: Some call it living.
Book: Touché! But can't you strike a happy balance? Get a rhythm going?
Me: I got rhythm, I got music.
Book: Buffoon. You're avoiding something by being a buffoon. What is it?
Me: I don't know.
Book: You afraid of something?
Me: Maybe. Some of this stuff is pretty intimate.
Book: That's what makes a good memoir. I *love* that.
Me: But I just don't want to look like a fool.
Book: You want to write an honest memoir?
Me: Yes.
Book: Then maybe sometimes you have to risk looking like a fool—*if* you want to be honest.
Me: An honest fool, huh? Some people may laugh at me.
Book: Who?
Me: Stupid people.
Book: Good people?
Me: No. They'll applaud me for taking chances.
Book: Then why don't you?
Me: Loosen up, huh?
Book: You don't want me to sound

staid and stuffy and boring, do you?
Me: Nope.
Book: Then let go.
Me: Okay.

For the record, although I did not make any "resolutions" at the Journal workshop, that dialogue helped point a way for me: I started working on my memoir, something I had been postponing for 10 years, and finished it just before Christmas. The book took about nine months to "emerge." I must have a dialogue with it soon. Or, at least, Soon.

At the Journal weekend, there was hardly any interplay among the members of the workshop. We'd chat a bit at coffee breaks or at lunch, and that was it. There were none of the social pressures I'd experienced in any number of encounter groups, and therefore, no play acting was necessary. Furthermore, since I knew no one was going to see or hear what I was writing, I felt a sense of perfect freedom. Several times Father Cox drew a session to a close by issuing an open invitation to the group: would anyone care to read what he or she had just written? Some accepted his invitation, some didn't. It didn't seem to matter. Father Cox said that reading aloud was for the reader's benefit, not the group's. Even so, I couldn't help feeling good about the feelings, often of joy, that were evident in the notebooks of others.

One woman reported that she had kept a diary for 50 years and had "never listed a feeling or an awareness—just events as they happened." Now, under guidance, she said she had been able to write down her own feelings and felt exhilarated in the process. Moreover, she found new direction in her life: recently widowed, she simply didn't know what she'd do next. But in the Journal chapter called Intersections, she remembered a road she had very much wanted to take at one time—but had taken another that led to marriage and a family. Now, she realized, there was nothing stopping her from going back and taking the other road.

After my own Journal workshop, I was all too aware that I'd only just begun to scratch the surface of the Journal process. There were a good many sections of the Journal that Father Cox hadn't even told us about. I found that I was in the first of three stages: a Life Context Workshop. I could go on to a Depth Feedback Workshop and then, finally, to a Process Meditation Workshop; in these, I would get a chance to work with, among other things, my own dreams.

In brief, Progoff looks at dreams as most benevolent messengers, bringing things up from our own inner wisdom. "Dreams," he says, "reach back into the past and call our attention to those experiences that can give us a clue with which to solve our present problems and move into the future. Our dreams can give us these clues, however, in the only mode of functioning that is available to them—that is, on the unconscious level, by indirection, allusion, imagery, and symbolism." In one of Progoff's theoretical works, *Depth Psychology and Modern Man*, he says: "Image-making is not a conscious process. We cannot create our images. The very reverse is true." In a way, then, we don't make our dreams; our dreams make us. Sounds intriguing, I said to myself. I have to go on with this.

I thought I might attend further workshops. However, I also realized that I could work on alone and at my own pace, using Progoff's two major guides in the Journal method: *At a Journal Workshop* (now in its 12th printing), a basic introduction that would help me take my life in my own hands and draw it together, and *The Practice of Process Meditation* (just published), which would help me open up a whole new spiritual dimension. A warning: like the *Spiritual Exercises* of St. Ignatius Loyola, written more than 400 years ago, these Progoff works, though often original, are not so much books to read and understand as they are manuals of things to do. *Do* them, and then you understand better.

Anaïs Nin, a diarist who logged an estimated 150,000 pages before her death in 1977, reviewed *At a Journal Workshop* in 1975 and noted that Progoff had found a way to help people toward intimacy, intimacy with themselves, intimacy with others. She then remarked:

"The lack of intimacy with one's self, and consequently with others, is what created the loneliest and most alienated people in the world. Progoff ultimately proves that the process of growth in a human being, the process out of which a person emerges, is essentially an inward process."

And where does that lead? Progoff's answer is commonplace: it leads to meaning and to truth.

But when you ask "Whose meaning? Whose truth?" Progoff answers: "Your own . . . To the reality of your own inner being."

The reality of your inner being. If *that* is what Progoff is about, he is a braver man than his quiet, unassuming, professorial demeanor suggests. He tends to agree that he's not selling 1981's hottest product. "In Freud's Victorian age," he says, "the awful secret that nobody wanted to talk about was sex. Today, the awful secret is spirituality. People today will discuss anything but their inner life." The wonder is that Progoff has gotten thousands to start working on (if not actually talking about) precisely that—and, moreover, in the hard-driving hurly-burly of the United States today, where men and women are lucky simply to keep the body alive, never mind the soul. Some sociologists of religion claim that a majority of Americans have rejected the very notion of spirituality as something pious and impractical and all-too-dependent on unreal dogmas committed to memory long ago by their local priests, ministers, and rabbis and handed on to the faithful in the form of slogans that were sappy and of categories that did not contain.

Nevertheless, Progoff has gotten precisely those secularized Americans involved in a search for meaning. He's done it because, though he has a reverence and a respect for all the great thinkers and all the great religions, he has recognized that this is a time when autonomous men and women need to find their own meaning. "It is," says Progoff, "a difficult time, because the old answers don't respond to the new questions. It is also a time of opportunity, because now we have to work out new ways of dealing with ourselves, with others."

In brief, Progoff seems to have secularized spirituality. How has he done it? His immediate answer is: "*I* don't do it. The people who come into the workshops do it—for themselves." He quotes Karl Rahner, the German Jesuit theologian: "The theological problem today is the art of drawing religion out of a man, not pumping it into him. The art is to help men become what they really are."

Progoff, of course, quotes a good many men and women who come from traditions quite different from Rahner's. He is rather proud that his theory of human personality and human creativity has come from a long line of thinkers stretching back into history: Lao-tzu, Buddha, Augustine, St. Francis of Assisi, Feodor Dostoevsky, Jan Christiaan Smuts, Henri Bergson, Carl Gustav Jung, D. T. Suzuki, Martin Buber. The amazing thing is that this disparate bunch end up saying pretty much the same thing to Progoff. "I am not so original," he says. "I am a synthesizer."

The synthesizer began life on August 2, 1921, in the Williamsburg section of Brooklyn, the son of a man who dropped out of the rabbinate to sell furs. One of Progoff's earliest recollections: his grandfather, an Orthodox rabbi, prostrate before the ark, rising to tell him: "You are the one who will do great things."

He wondered for a good long time what the great things might be. "The 'right answers' that people gave me," he told me recently, "were usually superficial. I went to Brooklyn College in the late 1930s and early 1940s and found that the Marxism so popular there was superficial, too." But he had an economics professor, an Australian named Findlay MacKenzie, who "had a habit of putting mystical books in front of Jewish boys. He handed me a copy of Manly Palmer Hall's lectures on ancient philosophy, and that gave me the realization that history didn't start with the French Revolution. That the main things about history were not economic. And that they were mysteries."

Four years in the U.S. Army were, for him, a dark night of the soul. "The only good thing that happened to me," he says, "was that a chaplain gave me Israel Zangwill's *Dreamers of the Ghetto*. It brought together the tragedy and the pathos of Jews like Heine and Spinoza who were trying to enter the modern world. It introduced me to Ba'al Shem Tov, the founder of modern Jewish spirituality, Hasidism. And it brought me closer to my own Jewish roots."

After the war, although he got "a European education" from a whole mob of brilliant expatriate professors who had fled Germany and taken up residence at the New School in New York, Progoff floundered academically. He did a dissertation on Jung that was "too long for a master's and not long enough for a doctorate." He got a job working as a welfare investigator on the Bowery, "out of a sense of giving up."

But he spent his evenings reading the novels of Balzac and the spiritual journals of Emanuel Swedenborg, "the Buddha of the North." He read *Holism and Evolution* by Jan Christiaan Smuts, who claimed that "psychology shouldn't deal with sick people, but with great people," and he read Thorstein Veblen on "the unfoldings of history and whether anything can be done about it." He read the poems of Walt Whitman who said yes to life and yes to the spirit in the midst of a brutal America. He read Lao-tzu, the first philosopher of Chinese Taoism, whose meditations on the cyclic in all earthly affairs rang true to him, and he read the essays of Henri Bergson, whose insight into the creative evolution taking place in Everyman, the *élan vital*, rang even truer.

But it was also a period in Progoff's life in which he really didn't know where *his* vital force was leading him. He was tempted to cry out, almost in despair, "If God had wanted something great from me, He would have worked it out for me by now." Finally, he finished his thesis, *Jung's Psychology and Its Social Meaning*, and found on the strength of it, and to his surprise, that something called the Bollingen Foundation had given him a fellowship to go to Zurich and study under Carl Gustav Jung himself.

He was with Jung from 1953 to 1955, met D.T. Suzuki, the great Zen master, at Jung's table, then returned to direct the Institute for Research in Depth Psychology at the graduate school of Drew University in New Jersey, spending a good deal of research time with his students on the great creative lives of all history. "At the time," Progoff recalls, "I was making the grand sum of $300 a month. To save money, I started writing my books on half-sheets of typing paper. My manuscript looked like a stack of toilet paper."

The "toilet paper" was to become *The Death and Rebirth of Psychology* in 1956, and the first work in a trilogy of his own theoretical synthesis. *Depth Psychology and Modern Man* followed in 1959, and *The Symbolic and the Real* in 1963. At the same time, as a licensed psychologist, he started taking in patients.

"People came. I had a large practice. They paid me. But I should have paid them. I was learning from them; I was beginning to see in them how a life unfolds. In terms of any social interest, I didn't know what that meant. But the Quakers soon showed me. In 1957, I was invited to spend a weekend at Haverford College at 'The Friends' Conference on Psychology and Religion.' Robert Greenleaf, one of the participants, an executive with AT&T, turned his life around after that meeting. He went on early retirement and opened up the most creative time of his life."

Progoff was learning the impact of his holistic depth psychology on others. Soon he would start learning what impact it could have on himself. In the mid-1960s, he went through a profound emotional crisis: he and his wife separated, and it looked for a time as if he might lose his two children. What to do? He started noodling around in a notebook and discovered that he was able to get a fix on his life by writing things down, going over them, feeding them back into the computer of his mind, as it were, engaging in a dialogue with himself and with his wife and children.

"I could see that I was onto something, but I wondered how original the method was. At the Quaker Library at Pendle Hill, I found (and read) Quaker journals of the 17th and 18th century. As far as I could see, the Quakers used their journals as a way of keeping tabs on their consciences (after they'd thrown away ritualized confession). For them, it was only a means of self-measurement—against which they inevitably failed.

"I looked at other journals, notably those of Dostoevsky and Anaïs Nin, and I could see that, for them, the journal was a vehicle that led to greater creativity. But I found that a good many other journals were just diaries: without a project to be done, people's diaries just went around in circles."

Without a project—that was the key that opened the door for Progoff. He'd already seen in his own case that a journal could lead somewhere for him if he had a problem. It could also lead somewhere for a novelist or a writer with a project. But what about everyone else in the world? What projects do they have? The answer came to Progoff in a flash, the result of all his previous reading, from Lao-tzu to Smuts to Buber: everyone has a life and that life must be his or her great work of art. The synthesis had produced something new, the Intensive Journal system, aimed at helping almost anyone who wished to start thinking of life as a work of art, of becoming, in Rahner's words, "what they really are."

A Thomist philosopher would explain the process, in part, by citing the notions of Aristotle and Aquinas on potency and act, final and efficient causality. You plant an acorn and you get an oak. You plant a tomato seed and get a tomato plant. But what do you get when you plant a human seed? Nothing so identical as oaks to oaks or tomatoes to tomatoes. In what direction does a human life go? Says Progoff: "We're limited, in part, by our own culture. Gautama Buddha couldn't become a Francis of Assisi. But aside from that, we all have free will. We can become pretty much what we want to."

But why do some people go only so far, and others much further? Ah, that's Progoff's *next* book, the work he began years ago at Drew, the study of creative lives.

"I'm 59 years old," Progoff says, with a smile. "As a good Jewish boy, I have to believe I'm going to live to be about 120. So I figure I'm just about to the halfway point in my life, the point where Jung says we begin our most serious work. . . . Now, what I'd like to do is get the most creative men and women in the world and give them Journals. . ."

For further information, read:

Progoff, Ira. *The Practice of Process Meditation*, Dialogue House, 1980, $12.95; paper $7.95.

———. *At a Journal Workshop*, Dialogue House, 1975, $12.50; 1977, paper, $7.95.

———. *Jung's Psychology and Its Social Meaning*, Doubleday, 1973, paper, $3.50.

———. *The Symbolic and the Real*, McGraw-Hill, 1973, paper, $4.50.

———. *The Death and Rebirth of Psychology*, McGraw-Hill, 1973, paper, $4.50.

———. *Depth Psychology and Modern Man*, McGraw-Hill, 1973, paper, $3.95.

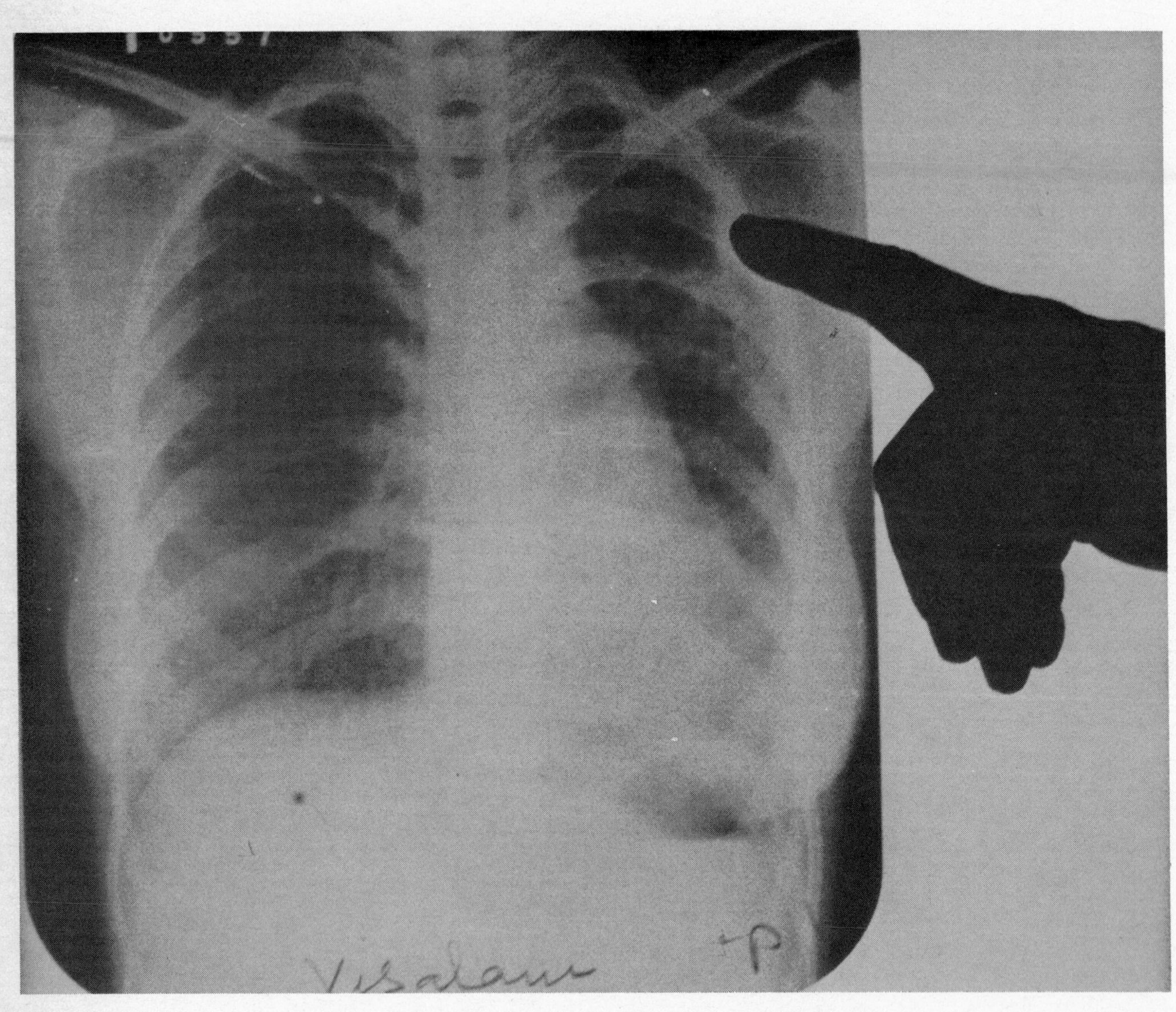

Psychological Bases of Behavior

3

Though the biology of the human being is important to psychologists, their higher goal is to understand mental life and behavior, not biology per se. This section considers three major topics concerned with the psychological rather than the biological bases of behavior: how people adapt to their environments through learning, how they think and remember, and how they use language. A principal issue will be how these three aspects of mental life relate to the observable actions that constitute behavior.

The first subsection is *Learning and Adaptive Behavior.* "The Instinct to Learn" argues that we come into the world with a genetically-provided curiosity, a biological urge to learn about our surroundings. "Sociobiology Stirs a Controversy Over the Limits of Science" and "Sociobiology Redefended" contrast more traditional views on learning with new and very controversial ideas coming from evolution-oriented thinkers who believe that some of our most cherished attitudes and behaviors—and some of our least cherished ones—are the result of our biological heritage rather than our intellectual and cultural sophistication. "Pulling a Gag on the Wily Coyote" looks at the effects of a kind of learning experience that plays a critical role in the survival of most organisms—getting sick from something you eat. Many animals learn from this experience with amazing proficiency, and that fact can be turned into a humane and effective method of controlling predators such as the coyote. Whether people are as good at this kind of learning as the coyote, however, is another matter. "Conversion, Brainwashing, and Deprogramming" considers some practical and ethical issues of learning and behavior change as they arise in a very personal and controversial arena of life, religious belief.

The second subsection is *Memory and Cognition*—the ways in which we remember, think, and make decisions. "My Memory/Myself" reviews principles of remembering to explain why we forget some things and recall others. "Mood and Memory" discusses the intimate relationship between how you feel about something and how well you can remember it. "Our Insatiable Brain" argues that the propensity to learn stays with us throughout our lives, despite some claims that elderly people lose their learning abilities. "The Mind of the Puzzler" goes beyond learning and memory, delving into the cognitive consequences of possessing an insightful mind.

The third subsection is *Language.* In "Learning the Mother Tongue" Jerome Bruner takes an historical journey through the many views on how children learn to speak, and reaches some up-to-date conclusions on the active role that children take in teaching themselves—with more than a little help from mom. The last article, "The Loss of Language," describes what brain damage has taught us about how the mind works when it is using language, and how much the ability to speak and listen means to our lives.

A review of this section will familiarize you with current approaches to mental life as a basis of behavior, highlighting the critical roles that learning, cognition, and language play in everyday activity.

Looking Ahead: Challenge Questions

Are we creatures of biology, pre-programmed to behave as we do or does learning determine what we are?

It is crucially important to do the right thing at the right time in our technological society (consider the Three Mile Island nuclear power plant accident, for example). What precautions might be taken to prevent memory failures and poor approaches to problem-solving from causing disaster?

What can parents do to increase the chances that their children will learn quickly and easily?

THE INSTINCT TO LEARN

James L. and Carol Grant Gould

James L. Gould, professor of biology at Princeton University, studies the navigation and communication of the honey bee. Carol Grant Gould is a writer and research associate in Princeton's biology department.

When a month-old human infant begins to smile, its world lights up. People reward these particular facial muscle movements with the things a baby prizes—kisses, hugs, eye contact, and more smiles. That first smile appears to be a powerful ingredient in the emotional glue that bonds parent to child. But scientists wonder whether that smile is merely a chance occurrence, which subsequently gets reinforced by tangible rewards, or an inexorable and predetermined process by which infants ingratiate themselves with their parents.

If this sounds like another chapter in the old nature/nurture controversy, it is—but a chapter with a difference. Ethologists, specialists in the mechanisms behind animal behavior, are taking a new look at old—and some new—evidence and are finding that even while skirmishing on a bloody battleground, the two camps of instinctive and learned behavior seem to be heading with stunning rapidity and inevitability toward an honorable truce.

Fortunately for the discord that keeps disciplines alive and fit, animal behavior may be approached from two vantage points. One of these sees instinct as the moving force behind behavior: Animals resemble automatons preordained by their genetic makeup to behave in prescribed ways. The other views animals as basically naive, passive creatures whose behavior is shaped, through the agency of punishment and reinforcement, by chance, experience, and environmental forces.

In the last few years, however, these two views have edged towards reconciliation and, perhaps, eventual union. Case after case has come to light of environmentally influenced learning which is nonetheless rigidly controlled by genetic programming. Many animals, ethologists are convinced, survive through learning—but learning that is an integral part of their programming, learning as immutable and as stereotyped as the most instinctive of behavioral responses. Furthermore, neurobiologists are beginning to discover the nerve circuits responsible for the effects.

Plenty of scientists are still opposed to this new synthesis. The most vociferous are those who view the idea of programmed learning as a threat to humanity's treasured ideas of free will. However, it now appears that much of what we learn is forced upon us by innate drives and that even much of our "culture" is deeply rooted in biology.

As though this were not enough of a shock to our ingrained ideas of man's place in the universe, it looks as though the reverse is true, too: Man is not the sole, lofty proprietor of culture; "lower" animals—notably monkeys and birds—also have evolved various complicated ways of transferring environmentally learned information to others of their own kind.

The honey bee provides entrancing insights into the lengths to which nature goes in its effort to program learning. These little animals must learn a great many things about their world: what flowers yield nectar at what specific times of day, what their home hives look like under the changes of season and circumstance, where water is to be found.

But new work reveals that all this learning, though marvelous in its variety and complexity, is at the same time curiously constrained and machinelike. Certain things that bees learn well and easily, they can learn only at certain specific "critical periods." For example, they must relearn the appearance and location of their hives on their first flight out every morning; at no other time will this information register in the bee's brain. Beekeepers have known for centuries that if they move a hive at night the bees come and go effortlessly the next day. But if they move the hive even a few meters at any time after the foraging bees' first flight of the day, the animals are disoriented and confused. Only at this one time is the home-learning program turned on: Evidently this is nature's way of compensating for changing seasons and circumstances in an animal whose vision is so poor that its only means of locating the hive is by identifying the landmarks around it.

Since bees generally harvest nectar from one species of flower at a time, it seems clear that they must learn to recognize flower species individually. Karl von Frisch, the noted Austrian zoologist, found that bees can distinguish any color, from yellow to green and blue and into the ultraviolet. However, they learn the color of a flower only in the two seconds before they land on it. Von Frisch also discovered that bees can discriminate a single odor out of several hundred. Experimentation reveals that this remarkable ability is similarly constrained: Bees can learn odor only while they are actually standing on the flower. And finally, only as they are flying away can they memorize any notable landmarks there might be around the flower.

Learning then, at least for bees, has thus become specialized to the extent that specific cues can be learned only at specific times, and then only in specific contexts.

The bees' learning programs turn out to be restricted even further. Once the bits of knowledge that make up a behavior have been acquired, such as the location, color, odor, shape, and surrounding landmarks of a food source, together with the time it is likely to yield the most nectar, they form a coherent, holistic set. If a single component of the set is changed, the bee must learn the whole set over again.

In a very real sense, then, honey bees are carefully tuned learning machines. They learn just what they are programmed to learn, exactly when and under exactly the circumstances they are programmed to learn it. Though this seems fundamentally different from the sort of learning we are used to seeing in higher animals such as birds and mammals—and, of course, ourselves—careful research is uncovering more and more humbling similarities. Programmed memorization in vertebrates, though deceptively subtle, is widespread. The process by which many species of birds learn their often complex and highly species-specific songs is a compelling case in point.

Long before the birds begin to vocalize, their species' song is being learned, meticulously "taped" and stored somewhere in their memory banks. As the bird grows, the lengthening days of spring trigger the release of specific hormones in the males which in turn spur them to reproduce first the individual elements of syllables and later the sequence of the stored song. By a trial and error process the birds slowly learn to manipulate their vocal musculature to produce a match between their output and the recording in their brains. Once learned, the sequence becomes a hardwired motor program, so fixed and independent of feedback that if the bird is deafened his song production remains unaffected.

This prodigious feat of learning, even down to the regional dialects which some species have developed, can be looked at as the gradual unfolding of automatic processes. Peter Marler of the Rockefeller University and his students, for instance, have determined that there are rigorous time constraints on the song learning. They have discovered that in the white-crowned sparrow the "taping" of the parental song can be done only between the chicks' 10th and 50th days. No amount of coaching either before or after this critical period will affect the young birds. If they hear the correct song during this time, they will be able to produce it themselves later (or, if females, to respond to it); if not, they will produce only crude, vaguely patterned vocalizations.

In addition, the white-crowned sparrow, though reared in nature in an auditory environment filled with the songs of other sparrows and songbirds with rich vocal repertoires, learns *only* the white-crowned sparrow song. Marler has recently been able to confirm that the parental song in another species—the swamp sparrow—contains key sounds that serve as auditory releasers, the cues that order the chicks' internal tape recorders to switch on. Ethologists refer to any simple signal from the outside world that triggers a complex series of actions in an animal as a releaser.

Here again, amazing feats of learning, particularly the sorts of learning that are crucial to the perpetuation of an animal's genes, are rigidly controlled by biology.

The kind of programmed learning that ethologists have studied most is imprinting, which calls to mind a picture of Konrad Lorenz leading a line of adoring goslings across a Bavarian meadow. Newborn animals that must be able to keep up with ever-moving parents —antelope and sheep, for example, as well as chicks and geese— must rapidly learn to recognize those parents if they are to survive. To achieve this noble aim evolution has built into these creatures an elegant learning routine. Young birds are driven to follow the parent out of the nest by an exodus call. Though the key element in the call varies from species to species—a particular repetition rate for one, a specific downward frequency sweep for another—it is always strikingly simple, and it invariably triggers the chicks' characteristic following response.

As the chicks follow the sound they begin memorizing the distinguishing characteristics of the parent, with two curious but powerful constraints. First, the physical act of following is essential: Chicks passively transported behind a calling model do not learn; in fact, barriers in a chick's path that force it to work harder speed and strengthen the imprinting. Second, the cues that the chick memorizes are also species-specific: One species will concentrate on the inflections and tone of the parent's voice but fail to recall physical appearance, while a closely related species memorizes minute details of physical appearance to the exclusion of sounds. In some species of mammals, the learning focuses almost entirely on individual odor. In each case, the critical period for imprinting lasts only a day or two. In this short but crucial period an ineradicable picture of the only individual who will feed and protect them is inscribed in the young animals' memories.

By contrast, when there is no advantage to the animal in learning specific details, the genes don't waste their efforts in programming them in. In that case, blindness to detail is equally curious and constrained. For instance, species of gulls that nest cheek by jowl are programmed to memorize the most minute details of their eggs' size and speckling and to spot at a glance any eggs which a careless neighbor might have added to their nest—eggs which to a human observer look identical in every respect. Herring gulls, on the other hand, nest far enough apart that they are unlikely ever to get their eggs confused with those of other pairs. As a result, they are unconscious of the appearance of their eggs. The parents will complacently continue to incubate even large black eggs that an experimenter substitutes for their small speckled ones. The herring gulls' insouciance, however, ends there: They recognize their chicks as individuals soon after hatching. By that time, their neighbors' youngsters are capable of wandering in. Rather than feed the genes of their neighbors, the parents recognize foreign chicks and often eat *them.*

The kittiwake gull, on the other hand, nests in narrow pockets on cliff faces, and so the possibility that a neighbor's chick will wander down the cliff into its nest is remote. As a result kittiwakes are not programmed to learn the appearance of either eggs or young, and even large black cormorant chicks may be substituted for the small, white, infant kittiwakes.

Simply from observing animals in action, ethologists have learned a great deal about the innate bases of behavior. Now, however, neurobiologists are even tracing the circuitry of many of the mechanisms that control some of these elements. The circuits responsible for simple motor programs, for example, have been located and mapped out on a cell-by-cell basis in some cases and isolated to a single ganglion in others.

A recent and crucial discovery is that the releasers imagined by ethologists are actually the so-called feature detectors that neurobiologists have been turning up in the auditory and visual systems. In recent years, neurobiologists have discovered that there are certain combinations of nerve cells, built into the eyes and brains of all creatures, that respond only to highly specific features: spots of a certain size, horizontal or vertical lines, and movement, for example. In case after case, the basic stimulus required to elicit an innate response in animals corresponds to one or a very simple combination of discrete features systematically sought out by these specialized cells in the visual system.

The parent herring gull, for instance, wears a single red spot near the tip of its lower bill, which it waves back and forth in front of its chicks when it has food for them. The baby gulls for their part peck at the waving spot which, in turn, causes the parent to release the food. First, Niko Tinbergen, the Dutch Nobel Prize winner and cofounder of the science of ethology with Lorenz and von Frisch, and later the American ethologist Jack Hailman have been able to show that the chicks are driven to peck not by the sight of their parent but at that swinging vertical bill with its red spot. The moving vertical line and the spot are the essential features that guide the chicks, which actually prefer a schematic, disembodied stimulus—a knitting needle with a spot, for example.

Though the use of two releasers to direct their pecking must greatly sharpen the specificity of the baby gulls' behavior, chicks do quickly learn to recognize their parents, and the mental pictures thus formed soon replace the crude releasers. Genes apparently build in releasers not only to trigger innate behavior but, more important, to direct the attention of animals to things they must learn flawlessly and immediately to survive.

Even some of what we know as culture has been shown to be partially rooted in programmed learning, or instinct. Many birds, for instance, mob or attack potential nest predators in force, and they do this generation after generation. But how could these birds innately know their enemies? In 1978 the German ethologist Eberhard Curio placed two cages of blackbirds on opposite sides of a hallway, so that they could see and hear each other. Between the two cages he installed a compartmented box, which allowed the occupants of one cage to see an object on their side but not the object on the other. Curio presented a stuffed owl, a familiar predator, on one side, and an innocuous foreign bird, the Australian honey guide, on the other. The birds that saw the owl went berserk with rage and tried to mob it through the bars of the cage. The birds on the other side, seeing only an unfamiliar animal and the enraged birds, began to mob the stuffed honey guide. Astonishingly, these birds then passed on this prejudice against honey guides through a chain of six blackbirds, all of which mobbed honey guides whenever they encountered one. Using the same technique, Curio has raised generations of birds whose great-great-grandparents were tricked into mobbing milk bottles and who consequently teach their young to do the same.

What instigates the birds—even birds raised in total isolation—to pay so much attention to one instance of mobbing that they pass the information on to their offspring as a sort of taboo, something so crucial to their survival that they never question if or why these predators must be attacked? The mobbing call, it turns out, serves as yet another releaser that switches on a learning routine.

Certain sounds in the mobbing calls are so similar among different species that they all profit from each other's experience. This is why we often see crows or other large birds being mobbed by many species of small birds at once. So deeply ingrained in the birds is this call that birds raised alone in the laboratory are able to recognize it, and the calls of one species serve to direct and release enemy-learning in others. Something as critical to an animal's survival as the recognition of enemies, then, even though its finer points must be learned and transmitted culturally, rests on a fail-safe basis of innately guided, programmed learning.

The striking food-avoidance phenomenon is also a good place to look for the kind of innately directed learning that is critical to survival. Many animals, including humans, will refuse to eat a novel substance which has previously made them ill. Once a blue jay has tasted one monarch butterfly, which as a caterpillar fills itself with milkweed's poisonous glycosides, it will sedulously avoid not only monarchs but also viceroys—monarch look-alikes that flaunt the monarchs' colors to cash in on their protective toxicity. This programmed avoidance is based on the sickness which must appear within a species-specific interval after an animal eats, and the subsequent food avoidance is equally strong even if the subject knows from experience that the effect has been artificially induced.

But what is the innate mechanism when one blue tit discovers how to pierce the foil caps of milk bottles left on doorsteps to reach the cream, and shortly afterwards blue tits all over England are doing the same thing? How are theories of genetic programming to be invoked when one young Japanese macaque monkey discovers that sweet potatoes and handfuls of grain gleaned from a sandy shore are tastier when washed off in the ocean, and the whole troop (except for an entrenched party of old dominant males) slowly follows suit? Surely these are examples pure and simple of the cultural transmission of knowledge that has been environmentally gained.

Perhaps not. What the blue tits and the monkeys pass on to their colleagues may have an innate basis as well. The reason for this precocious behavior—and we say this guardedly—may be in a strong instinctive drive on the part of all animals to copy mindlessly certain special aspects of what they see going on around them. Chicks, for instance, peck at seeds their mother has been trained to select, apparently by watching her choices and copying them. In the case of many mammals, this drive is probably combined with an innate urge to experiment. The proclivity of young animals, particularly human children, to play with food, along with their distressing eagerness to put virtually anything into their mouths, lends support to the experimentation theory. Perhaps it is the young, too naive to know any better, who are destined by nature to be the primary source of cultural innovation. The more mature become the equally indispensable de-

The cells that bring you the world

There was a time when the visual system was thought of as little more than a pair of cameras (the eyes), cables (the optic nerves), and television screens (the visual cortex of the brain). Nothing could be farther from the truth. We now know that the visual system is no mere passive network of wires but an elaborately organized and highly refined processing system that actively analyzes what we see, systematically exaggerating one aspect of the visual world, ignoring or discarding another.

The processing begins right in the retina. There the information from 130 million rods and cones is sifted, distorted, and combined to fit into the four or so million fibers that go to the brain. The retinas of higher vertebrates employ one layer of cells to sum up the outputs of the rod-and-cone receptors. The next layer of retinal cells compares the outputs of adjacent cells in the preceding tier. The result is what is known as a spot detector: One type of cell in the second layer signals the brain when its compare/contrast strategy discovers a bright field surrounded by darkness (corresponding to a bright spot in the world). Another class of cell in the same layer has the opposite preference and fires off when it encounters dark spots.

The next processing step takes this spot information and, operating on precisely the same comparison strategy, wires cells that are sensitive only to spots moving in particular directions at specific speeds. The output of these spot detector cells also provides the raw material from which an array of more sophisticated feature detectors sort for lines of each particular orientation. These feature detectors derive their name from their ability to register the presence or absence of one particular sort of stimulus in the environment. Building on these cells, the next layer of processing sorts for the speed and direction of moving lines, each cell with its own special preference. Other layers judge distance by comparing what the two eyes see.

The specific information that cells sort for in other retinal layers and visual areas of the brain is not yet understood. Research will probably reveal that these extremely complex feature detectors provide us with what we know as conscious visual experience. Our awareness of all this subconscious processing, along with the willful distortions and tricks it plays on us, comes from the phenomenon of optical illusions. When we experience an optical illusion, it is the result of a particular (and, in the world to which we evolved, useful) quirk in the visual mechanism.

Feature detectors are by no means restricted to the visual system. In birds and bats, for instance, specialized cells have been found that recognize many nuances in sound—locations, repetition rates, time intervals, and precise changes in pitch—that allow the creatures to form an auditory picture of the world.

There is every reason to suppose that our experience of the world is based on the results of this massive editing. Since neural circuits differ dramatically from species to species according to the needs of each, the world must look and sound different to bees, birds, cats, and people.

—J.L.G. and C.G.G.

fenders of the faith, the vehicles of cultural transmission.

Patterns, then, however subtle, are beginning to emerge that unify the previously unrelated studies of instinct and learning. Virtually every case of learning in animals that has been analyzed so far depends in at least some rudimentary way on releasers that turn on the learning routine. And that routine is generally crucial to the perpetuation of the animal's genes.

Even the malleable learning we as humans pride ourselves on, then, may have ineradicable roots in genetic programming, although we may have difficulty identifying the programs, blind as we are to our own blindness. For example, you cannot keep a normal, healthy child from learning to talk. Even a child born deaf goes through the same babbling practice phase the hearing child does. Chimpanzees, by contrast, can be inveigled into mastering some sort of linguistic communications skills, but they really could not care less about language: The drive just is not there.

This view of human insight and creativity may be unromantic, minimizing as it does the revered role of self-awareness in our everyday lives, but the pursuit of this line of thinking could yield rich rewards, providing us with invaluable insights into our own intellectual development. The times we are most susceptible to particular sorts of input, for instance, may be more constrained than we like to think. The discovery of the sorts of cues or releasers that might turn on a drive to learn specific things could open up new ways of teaching and better methods for helping those who are culturally deprived. Best of all, analyzing and understanding those cues could greatly enrich our understanding of ourselves and of our place in the natural order.

Sociobiology stirs a controversy over limits of science

Albert Rosenfeld

Research into biological basis of behavior has been applied to humans by some scientists, and it is triggering a vociferous response

Sociobiologist Edward Osborne Wilson paused in mid-sentence to allow a large black ant that was crawling across his desk to climb into the palm of his hand. He set the creature down on the floor and watched as it headed straight for the open door leading to his lab, where it would find plenty of company. Wilson is the world's leading authority on insect societies. Even his detractors readily admit as much; they just wish he would keep his interests focused right there. But Wilson has no intention of obliging them. "To deny that genes have an important role in human as well as in animal behavior," he said, picking up our conversation, "is simply to turn one's back on the copious evidence to the contrary."

His name is now synonymous with sociobiology, which he defines as the study of the biological basis of all social behavior. The underlying idea is that of the "selfish gene," genetic material manufacturing new organisms that will best perpetuate the same genes. It is a modern version of Samuel Butler's well-known aphorism that a chicken is only an egg's way of making another egg.

Since the publication in 1975 of his monumental (697 double-sized pages, half a million words) study, *Sociobiology: The New Synthesis,* Wilson has been the center of an ever-widening storm which his more recent book, *On Human Nature* (1978), has done nothing to dispel. In these books, Wilson has promulgated far-reaching theories regarding the evolution of such traits as altruism, aggressiveness, spite, xenophobia and homosexuality. Anyone who emphasizes the role of genes in human behavior, as Wilson does—not to mention their putative influence on everything from sex roles to religion—shouldn't be too surprised when the wrath descends.

Wilson was not so naive as to expect uncritical acceptance of his work—and he would probably include himself among those he describes as the adventurous ones who enjoy "a not unpleasant whiff of grapeshot, the crackle of thin ice." He was pleased to get as much acclaim as he did. But he certainly foresaw scientific critiques of his methodology, for instance, and arguments that his theories had been put forth with too little hard data to support them. He knew that anthropologists and sociologists would not take kindly to his brash invasion of their turf. What he was not ready for was the kind of emotional criticism that escalated to all-out personal attack.

But Wilson happened along with his sociobiological synthesis just in time to present an irresistible target. A process of ideological polarization had already been taking place among biologists, particularly in regard to the genetics of behavior. To the "anti-geneticists" (some of whom are also geneticists), the "new knowledge" was not only spurious but was much too easily latched onto by racists and eugenicists as scientific "proof" of racial superiorities and inferiorities.

A return to social Darwinism?

Moreover, any suggestion that our behavior is dictated by our genes, to whatever extent, implied to some that we were genetic robots acting without free will. If our traits are inscribed in our genes, then how can we change or improve ourselves—or our society? Sociobiology was seen by critics as a justification for maintaining the status quo—almost a return to the long-discredited social Darwinism of the past century.

Beyond all that, there was a prevailing concern about our new abilities to "tamper" with nature, ranging all the way from test-tube babies to cloning and genetic engineering. Wilson was destined to become the symbol of a growing polarization. He was appalled to find himself lumped, for instance, with the likes of William Shockley, who had postulated a permanent economic stratification between blacks and whites based on genetic differences (Wilson vigorously disavows such notions), and to hear himself depicted as the ultimate archreactionary.

If one had to select his opposite number, the ultimate archradical, on the same dubious scale, a likely candidate might well be molecular biologist Jonathan Beckwith, also of Harvard, with whom I had shared breakfast that morning, before calling on Wilson.

"To stress the genetic basis of behavior, as Wilson does with such conviction," Beckwith said, "is bound to lead to mischief—to political use and abuse—as it always has in the past." To underline his point, he handed me an article by a British neo-Fascist who was quoting Wilson to bolster his racist viewpoint.

"Sociobiology Stirs a Controversy Over Limits of Science," by Albert Rosenfeld, *Smithsonian*, September 1980. Reprinted by permission.

Back in 1969, Beckwith, as part of a group that succeeded in purifying the first gene, began to worry about potential abuses of the new knowledge. He bases his concern on "a long history of wrong, misguided, scientifically flawed studies in social policies." He is not, he emphasizes, opposed to all genetic research, but argues that studies and conclusions such as Wilson's are flawed because "they ignore the complex interaction between environment and genes, and they ignore basic principles of genetics in a misuse of the concept of heritability."

As I sat with Wilson, recalling Beckwith, I also recalled a Washington meeting of the American Association for the Advancement of Science (AAAS) in February of 1978. Wilson was part of a daylong panel discussion on sociobiology. Beckwith was in the audience (as was I) that filled the hotel ballroom to overflowing. Speaker after speaker had risen, more to criticize Wilson than to praise him, and finally it was Wilson's turn. Before he could utter a syllable, about a dozen young men and women materialized, shouting "Fascist!" "Nazi!" "Racist!" "Sexist!" They said he shouldn't be allowed to speak. They wanted equal time. Then one of them, saying "You're all wet, Wilson!" emptied a bucket of water on his head. Even Wilson's critics, including Beckwith, were indignant and apologetic.

And so the battle lines have been drawn. Biologists from all parts of the country are on both sides of the controversy, but Cambridge, Massachusetts, has been the hub of the action. There, at Harvard, reside not only Beckwith, but a pair of evolutionary biologists—Stephen Jay Gould and Richard C. Lewontin—who have been equally vehement in denouncing Wilson's sociobiological tenets. There is also biologist Ruth Hubbard, who chaired a symposium at the same AAAS meeting in which the participating scientists, all women, characterized Wilson as a sexist and male chauvinist pig. (In *Sociobiology,* Wilson argued for a genetic basis for certain sex differences.)

Also in residence at Harvard, on Wilson's side this time, are other sociobiologists such as Irven DeVore, a social anthropologist—and, until recently, Robert Trivers (now with the University of California, Santa Cruz), perhaps the boldest theorist in the field.

All a matter of degree

The specific debate over sociobiology is sometimes put, for simplicity's sake, into the antiquated framework of nature versus nurture, heredity versus environment. It would be hard to find a scientist of any repute these days who really believes that genetics alone, or environment alone, *determines* human behavior. Virtually everyone agrees that genetics and environment interact in complicated ways to influence the outcome, that an individual's genetic endowment represents his overall potential—what he might become, depending on the opportunities which the environment provides. It is a matter of degree. The sociobiologists certainly believe that the genes exert a much more profound influence than their opponents are willing to concede, but the real differences in their positions are not as great as one might think.

The argument, in fact, would be much lower-keyed if it were just a matter of deciding whether the data and the arguments were convincing or not, whether genes were more influential or less so. The real question (in my view—and that of many others), the question that gives the debate its emotional power, is: *do we really want to know?*

Over the past few decades, biologists have advanced with fairly astounding leaps in their efforts to understand the basic workings of life's processes—down to the cell, to the molecule, sometimes to the atom or the electron. Not content merely to pick apples off the tree of knowledge, they have been brazenly shaking the tree, causing the fruits to rain down faster than they can be harvested.

We have always been wary of such acquisitions. We know what happened to Adam and Eve, to Icarus, to Prometheus, to Faust. When our hubris leads us to attain godlike powers, the gods will punish us. We will be driven from the garden, have our wings singed and be cast to Earth, chained to rocks and have our vitals gnawed at, lose our souls. These are deep-rooted feelings and fears.

The ideological opponents might be characterized, in a word, as those who look upon the "new knowledge" mainly with dismay, considering it not knowledge at all but unsubstantiated guesses, and those who look upon it with exhilaration. Let me admit, right now, that, for me, the exhilaration prevails over the dismay. My feeling is that, in the absence of a compelling reason to desist in specific instances, it is usually better to know than not to know. I tell you this not to try to convert you to my view, but merely to warn you of my bias.

E. O. Wilson did not invent sociobiology, but he defined the field brilliantly, crystallized its concepts and made it eminently visible. Though most of the components of his work were borrowed, with careful attribution, the synthesis itself amounted to a large original contribution. Had he been content merely to write a book of 26 chapters, masterfully putting together the known studies of animal societies—with perhaps a modest epilogue speculating cautiously about the eventual implications for human social behavior—*Sociobiology* would probably have been universally acclaimed. It won high praise from most reviewers anyway, especially in the beginning.

Even Stephen Jay Gould, who openly calls himself a "detractor," has written: "Most of *Sociobiology* wins from me the same high praise. . . . For a lucid account of evolutionary principles and an indefatigably thorough discussion of social behavior among all groups of animals, *Sociobiology* will be the primary document for years to come." But Wilson did add Chapter 27, which he called "Man: From Sociobiology to Sociology," and that's the chapter that has received perhaps 90 percent of the attention. It begins:

"Let us now consider man in the free spirit of natural history, as though we were zoologists from another planet completing a catalog of social species on Earth. In this macroscopic view the humanities and social sciences shrink to specialized branches of biology; history, biography, and fiction are the research protocols of human ethology; and anthropology and sociology together constitute the sociobiology of a single primate species." An irresistible call to battle.

This is the chapter that leaves Gould "very unhappy indeed," for, in Gould's words, "Chapter 27 is not about the range of potential human behavior or even an argument for the restriction of that range from a much larger total domain among all animals. It is, primarily, an extended speculation on the existence of genes for specific and variable traits in human behavior—including spite, aggression, xenophobia, conformity, homosexuality, and the characteristic behavior differences between men and women in Western society."

In the earlier chapters, Wilson was trying to reconcile certain apparent paradoxes in Darwin's theory of natural selection, the principal quest perhaps being for a more comprehensive definition of genetic fitness.

Fitness, in Darwin's evolutionary scheme, was measured strictly in terms of procreative proficiency—the contribution of a given individual's genes to the gene pool of the next and following generations. Thus, oversimplified, the fittest individuals were the parents of the largest number of children who survived to their own reproductive years.

These competitive circumstances connoted a certain ruthlessness, hence Tennyson's "Nature, red in tooth and claw." But if, in this "survival of the fittest," the payoff lay in the maximum practice of selfish aggressiveness, how to explain the development of a quality like altruism? In insect societies, individual workers, eschewing procreative activities of their own, labor a lifetime so that others in the colony may reproduce. Certain birds give warning signals or engage in "distraction displays" at the approach of a predator, thus calling attention to themselves; the signaling bird may thereby sacrifice itself to save the others. How can this kind of defensive and sometimes suicidal behavior—observed in many variations in species as diverse as nighthawks, musk oxen and baboons—enhance one's own genetic fitness? How would any behavior traits that result in early death, and possibly the failure to procreate, be transmitted through the generations?

This dilemma had worried Darwin himself. He came up with an answer of sorts ("selection may be applied to the family, as well as to the individual"), as did others after him. But Wilson was dissatisfied with these formulations and, early in his big book, identified the question that was for him "the central theoretical question of sociobiology: how can altruism, which by definition reduces personal fitness, possibly evolve by natural selection?" A satisfying answer to this puzzle, Wilson felt, might provide insights to help explain other traits that persist over the generations without having any discernible survival value.

Kin selection the key

Without going into the details, two essential concepts—which Wilson borrowed from the British biologist William D. Hamilton—seemed to clarify the basic paradox. One of the concepts was "kin selection." If a bee or a bird or a baboon sacrifices itself, but in the process saves its close kin so they can reproduce successfully, then the altruistic behavior will have helped perpetuate the genes which they *share*. The closer the kin, the *more* genes they share. In Wilson's calculations, kin selection—rather than strictly individual selection—made excellent quantitative sense. If the requisite selfishness for selection is shifted to the collective gene pool, then its conservation through individual altruistic acts is not a contradiction after all. Hence the second concept—"inclusive fitness"—to encompass all related individuals in the kinship network, which thus becomes a multiple fitness pool. The sterile ants, without whose labor the ant society could not survive, pass on their shared genes via the relatives they support—a kind of procreation by proxy.

This kind of reasoning has led Wilson and other sociobiologists to tentative explanations of a variety of other traits. Robert Trivers, for instance, postulates the existence of a genetically based "reciprocal altruism" in human societies. This is altruism that goes beyond the kinship network. Again, oversimplified, the reasoning goes something like this: if I save you from drowning, you might some time save me from drowning—or, if you don't, someone else might. I do favors with the expectation that they will somehow be reciprocated. If we all do good things for one another, we will—within certain limits—all be better off. Over hundreds of generations, if primitive men and women behaved this way, reciprocal-altruistic genes could have been passed along.

Trivers has also put forth some controversial notions about parent-offspring relations. Any sociobiologist would, for instance, have to recognize that when a mother protects her children, she is protecting her own genes; the same, of course, is true of a father. Trivers argues that, while a parent's genetic investment in his child is spread among as many children as he has, the child's genetic investment in himself is 100 percent, and thus he competes for as close to 100 percent of the parents' time and attention as he can get.

This is the kind of speculation that Stephen Jay Gould ridicules as "just-so stories" (after Kipling). They *are* only stories, he says, and have no more scientific validity than Kipling's tale of how the camel got its hump. Gould is right, of course, because in many instances the extrapolations have been made with no scientific *proof* adduced. But this is not as much of a putdown as Gould believes, since, as Sir Peter Medawar said, in explaining how science is really done, "Scientists are building explanatory structures, *telling stories* which are scrupulously tested to see if they are stories about real life." The just-so stories of sociobiology are intriguing, and they are not necessarily useless—as long as the narrator makes clear that, so far at least, he is only telling stories.

Since Wilson wrote his big book, continuing sociobiological research has spawned at least three new scientific journals and a small library of books. The "just-so stories"—usually much more sophisticated than my oversimplified accounts would suggest—have not only stimulated new studies; they have provided the impetus to go back to older studies to see what new insights might be gleaned. The stories, in Irven DeVore's view, make up a set of testable hypotheses. He has been redoing and rethinking much of his own earlier work on primates and on human tribal societies—not merely observing behavior but doing extensive biochemical studies, looking for genetic "markers" and for signs of "inclusive-fitness behavior."

Wilson says that, as a result of all this activity, there has been "a substantial increase in sophistication of theory and method," particularly on the origins of aggression, territoriality, altruism, polygamy, infanticide, sex-role behavior and child-rearing. He does not expect anyone to find a specific gene for altruism, or aggression, or homosexuality. He rather expects such predispositions, if they exist, to result from the influence of many genes, operating in complex interaction with variable environmental factors—much like the "multifactorial" genetic predispositions presumed to exist in certain diseases. He is hard at work, in collaboration with a theoretical physicist, Charles Lumsden, on a new book that seeks to establish the linkage between cultural and genetic evolution.

Is sociobiology of any real use to anyone, then? I think it clearly is, especially as a set of approaches to social behavior, particularly in animals. Not that I regard it as useless in looking at human society; it's just that, as yet, there does not exist a true science of *human* sociobiology—and the just-so stories, as of the year 1980, do not seem to have any immediate practical applications. Sooner or later, however, we may have to take cognizance of our biological inheritance.

An intuitive leap?

Frequently in the history of science, the great creative leap forward has been made by someone who has first steeped himself in the data, absorbed the literature, let it all simmer—and then come up with concepts that feel intuitively right, that hold together logically, but for which there was then little evidence. (Consider Einstein's tall tale of relativity, beside which Kipling's story of how the camel got its hump is downright plausible.) This seems to me to describe what Wilson has been doing, so the lack of supporting evidence for his just-so stories doesn't worry me too much. I am prepared to see where they lead.

I cannot pretend to do justice in this space to Wilson's ideas, or to the spirited arguments marshaled against them. But it's not as if I were trying to decide here whether sociobiology is right or not, whether E. O. Wilson is correct or not. I am more interested, for now, in the larger question being raised: is this kind of research and theorizing pernicious in itself, because of its potential for misuse? Should it be done at all? Specifically: do we want to know whether our genes have any influence on our behavior—and if so how, and how much?

I personally would vote Yes.

If I am deluding myself in thinking that I am exercising free will when I really am not, I'd like to know that. If I am informed in what ways and to what extent my genes are in control, then merely by becoming aware of that, I can help subvert the influence of my "selfish" genes, and, by so doing, gain a greater measure of real freedom.

If someone had planted electrodes at strategic points in your brain and had, unbeknownst to you, been influencing your behavior by remote push button, wouldn't you want to know it? If you never permit yourself to find out—if you instead curse the messenger who brings you the news and drive him away—then you will have preserved your prized illusion of free will while cutting off the possibility of attaining it.

The potential for abuse

At the same time, of course, the potential for abuse of new knowledge is very real. Even without going back to the many cautionary examples in history, one only need look at the mass sterilizations performed legally in Virginia on persons presumed to be retarded or in some other way inferior. The law was based on "knowledge" that their problems were genetic in nature. The critics of sociobiology are incensed because they believe that once again we are dealing with "knowledge." And how is the public to discriminate between knowledge and knowledge in quotes, if the scientists who are propagating it are not careful to make the distinction themselves? And if they are not (or even if they are), is there not a high probability that their just-so stories will be taken as justification to support the continuation of discrimination—or even to invent new discrimination?

The position of people such as E. O. Wilson is clear. He, DeVore and Trivers all agree that any discrimination against any individual based on rough *average* genetic differences—even if proved valid—is ludicrous and unwarranted. (Differences between individuals in a group are greater than differences, if any, between groups.) Wilson emphasizes the overriding importance to our evolutionary future of a healthy human diversity. He is no advocate of eugenics, and says he can't conceive that there will be enough knowledge (without quotes) during our lifetimes for anyone to think about putting into effect eugenic policies. He doesn't say this will be true forever, however, and here he differs from his critics, who maintain that we can never possibly acquire reliable knowledge in these areas of genetics.

These critics serve a valuable function for which we should all be grateful. With their steady radar scan on genetic research, they keep us aware of the potential abuse of knowledge, and the need to examine it carefully for left-out quotation marks. They remind us, too, that even the most well-meaning scientists can be the transmitters of their own politics and cultures—or, for that matter, their genes; moreover, that some scientists, such as the late Sir Cyril Burt, the British psychologist whose work early in this century served as the foundation-stone for many current theories regarding genetic differences in intelligence, have been simply dishonest in presenting data on genetic differences that was known to be erroneous, if not downright fraudulent.

So it would be counterproductive to wish to silence the critical gadflies—who have been accused of "academic vigilantism"—even on those occasions when one feels that they have gone too far, that they have been unfair in their charges, or have distorted claims and impugned motivations.

In a society with problems as great as ours, when there is so much we need to know that we do not know —and we usually seek the knowledge most urgently for medical ends—it would be a pity to put a moratorium on the acquisition of knowledge out of fear that someone will misuse it, even if the fear is based on high probability. I would rather try to improve our democratic monitoring procedures—to ascertain that knowledge, so labeled, is really known (though it can never be known with an absolute absence of uncertainty or risk) before we apply it, to keep a sharp eye on those who would misuse it—so that we can simply do our human best to minimize the hazards. As Robert S. Morison has observed, "The basic thesis that certain aspects of nature simply should not be investigated because of the possibility of unfortunate social consequences has not been seen in Western Europe since Bruno was executed for his interest in the heliocentric theory."

Besides, it is really impossible to predict that any research, or any ideas, in science will be immune to abuse and misuse. This came home to me again sharply on the day in Cambridge when Wilson helped the wandering ant off his desk. Ironically, the reinforced insight came through none other than Beckwith. You will remember that Beckwith had expressed concern about the misuse of knowledge resulting from some genetic research. But over coffee that day he told me, somewhat sheepishly, that even his research into protein transport across cell membranes had turned out to have unforeseen consequences: his collaborator in Paris was using his techniques to turn bacteria into exactly the kind of hormone-manufacturing bugs, with strange genes incorporated into them, that so many had predicted and feared as the product of recombinant-DNA research!

I am going to give biologist Lewis Thomas (SMITHSONIAN, April 1980) the last word on the matter. At the same AAAS meeting at which water was poured on Ed Wilson's head, I appeared on a panel with Lewis Thomas. The question of recombinant-DNA research was much in the air at the time, and the panel had been discussing what limits should be placed on the quest for scientific knowledge. "There are probably no questions we can think up that can't be answered, sooner or later, including even the matter of consciousness," Lewis maintained, and continued, "Within our limits, we should be able to work our way through to all our answers, if we keep at it long enough, and pay attention.

"I am putting it this way, with all the presumption and confidence that I can summon, in order to raise another, last question: Is this hubris? Is there something fundamentally unnatural, or intrinsically wrong, or hazardous for the species, in the ambition that drives us all to reach a comprehensive understanding of nature, including ourselves? I cannot believe it. It would seem to me a more unnatural thing, and more of an offense against nature, for us to come on the same scene endowed as all human beings are with curiosity, filled to overbrimming as we are with questions, naturally talented as we are for the asking of clear questions, and then for us to do nothing about it, or, worse, to try to suppress the questions. . . . This, to my way of thinking," declared Thomas, "is the real hubris, and it carries danger for us all."

Sociobiology Redefended

Guy Richards

Guy Richards is an associate professor of sociology at the University of Saskatchewan and has taught medical sociology, demography, and sociobiology during the past ten years. A graduate of Cambridge, England, he has for the past twenty-five years practiced general medicine with his wife. Elizabeth, in Saskatoon. He served as an AHA board member from 1966-1969.

Humanism implies naturalism, the belief that the world can be explained in natural ways, as opposed to animistic (spiritual) or dualistic (spirit-body, God-universe) ways. Other words with almost the same meaning are physicalism, materialism, scientific monism; but, whatever word you prefer, our belief includes the idea of the oneness and continuity of the universe and of all forms of matter from the simplest to the most complex, from elements to living things such as ourselves. We do not need to believe that at a certain state of evolution suddenly some new vital influence emerges such as mind, culture, or "genetic independence." The beginnings of these properties can be seen in other species, even in some very simple organisms, as Professor John Tylor Bonner describes so charmingly and clearly in his *The Evolution of Culture in Animals* (Princeton University Press, 1980).

Professor E.O. Wilson in his letter (Readers Forum, *The Humanist,* July/August 1981) rightly expresses surprise that some humanists do not see sociobiology as an integral part of their world view. He and other naturalists will be equally puzzled by the two criticisms of him and sociobiology in the same issue—"Human Sociobiology: Wilson's Fallacy" by Dr. Nathaniel Lehrman and "Creationism and Popular Sociobiology as Myths" by Linda Wolfe and J. Patrick Gray. Why are these scientists so critical? Having lived long among both doctors and sociologists as a "participant observer" of these two cults, let me try my hand at answering.

We can understand some more traditional believers objecting to sociobiology, since it carries natural explanation a stage closer to human behavior. But humanist critics should welcome greater understanding of this kind. Why do they seem to fight the same battle as the traditionalists? They exclude the full implications of naturalism from certain areas of their thinking. Perhaps we all do that to some extent—until challenged.

I think, and Syracuse University Professor Alexander Rosenberg agrees (naturally) in his *Sociobiology and the Preemption of Social Science* (Johns Hopkins University Press, 1980), that sociobiology faces a serious difficulty: accepting it requires a more radical naturalism or physicalism (his preferred word) than most social scientists, with their frequent hostility to natural science, are willing to concede.

Anthropology vs. Pragmatism

Wolfe and Gray rightly point out that people nurture shared beliefs, regardless of their truth or falsity, because they serve a useful social function in their dealings with other members of their own society. We can agree that, if heretics are to be burned, then there are functional advantages in conforming to the local religion. But, if you wish to be effective with the subjects of your belief, you need a realistic view. They describe how the New Guinea Abelem people had strange views about the prevalence of femininity among all wild birds, but, as they admit, they had to be more practical-minded about the sex ratio of domestic birds from whom they wished to get eggs and chickens.

Like many functional social scientists, Wolfe and Gray feel that they have done their job if they discern a belief's social function. The degree to which it conforms with the environment—that is, its truth or falsity—does not concern them.

Applying the word *myth* to both creationism and sociobiology is only permissible if you are addressing professional anthropologists who will understand that you refer to traditional beliefs and stories which may or may not be true. To any other sort of audience, *myth* also implies falsity. Wolfe and Gray thus imply the latter meaning, while sheltering behind the professionalism of the former.

Proponents of this kind of functionalism and of the doctrine of cultural relativism, the view that the tests for moral value of acts and beliefs in all cultures are equally valid, recognize the importance of shared beliefs for intra-social relations—relations between members of the same society. However, these doctrines gloss over the fact that cultures are very unequal in the power that they bestow on their adherents, as individuals or groups, in their extrasocial dealings with the physical environment and with other societies—interactions in which truth, conformity with reality, and pragmatic knowledge matter. Better knowledge of environmental factors, including soil, weather, seasons—science, in other words—leads to better agriculture, among other consequences. Better knowledge of materials leads, among other things, to better tools and weapons.

This article first appeared in *THE HUMANIST,* January/February 1982 and is reprinted by permission.

The doctrine of cultural relativism implies that all cultures fit humans equally well. In fact, taken seriously to its logical conclusion, this doctrine denies there can be a bad "fit" between culture and humanity, since human nature is entirely shaped by culture. However, power, for example, is not something humans can view with indifference. Whatever the peculiar joys and ideals of my native culture, my human nature disposes me to want to live, preferably be on the winning side in a battle, and not be stuck supporting a dud culture. This means that we all have an interest in making our culture and its world view as true as possible—true to us and true to the world.

Wolfe and Gray and many others criticize sociobiologists as being sexist. This is grossly unfair. It is some *anthropologists* who imply that the cultural arrangements of all societies, including male dominance, must not be judged by any universal standards. Might not the degree of sexual equality be such a standard? Sarah Blaffer Hrdy, in her *The Women that Never Evolved* (Harvard, 1981), shows that power relations between the sexes are more subtly shaped by species and circumstance than social scientists have hitherto supposed. Sociobiologists would agree with anthropologist Marvin Harris, in his *Cows, Pigs, Wars, and Witches* (Vintage, 1974), that hitherto the importance of conflict with other groups has given us a world in which males have had priority. Partly because we have enough young warriors and more than enough weapons, male dominance is no longer adaptive. Of course, there are better reasons than this for sexual equality. It is not sexist to say that we have hitherto had a world to suit men; what we need now is a world to suit people, and that means considering the needs of both sexes. It is not sexist to seek what are the short-term and long-term needs of men and women. The extent of the difference is useful knowledge for shaping a more just society. If the difference turns out to be zero, then that would be useful knowledge. Assuming that it is zero will not make it so. Long-term aims of both sexes may be similar, but the greater investment by women in pregnancy and lactation make it almost impossible that the sexes' short-term aims can be the same.

We no longer need male sexism. We can do even better than feminism. We need humanism.

The Functions of Social Scientists' Beliefs

Functionalism is useful, to a certain extent. Let us try it on the "culture" of social science. Perhaps we might ask these questions: Are there professional advantages from certain ideological stances? Are some more fashionable, more chic, than others? Is there more psychological satisfaction in being pro-establishment, whatever that may currently involve, or in being able to make bold rhetorical attacks on it? Do some social scientists earn points with one another by attacking natural science and subjects like sociobiology, which encroach on "their" territory? Do social scientists denounce theories of territoriality? Do some sociologists enjoy, exploit, and create for themselves the role of "morally unassailable, oppressed minority?" Do these social functions of ideology and doctrine within the society of social scientists lead to a truer, more useful social science? Perhaps eventually, but it is sure taking a long time. The *function* of a belief and its *truth* are obviously different matters.

Conceptual Relativism

Evolutionary thinking was a prominent feature of sociology in the latter half of the nineteenth century, but in the early years of the twentieth century anthropologists turned away from it in reaction against its misuse. Functionalism and cultural relativism characterized the new anthropology. These are useful research devices. They encourage a respect for non-European-type culture.

But the shortcomings of various kinds of relativism are clearly revealed by a University of Warwick philosopher, Roger Trigg, in a short, very readable book, *Reason and Commitment* (Cambridge University Press, 1973). Relativistic thinking in general is a good way of getting people to reexamine their opinions. One says, in effect, "Your ideas and values are part of your group's upbringing. It is not therefore proper to judge other groups' behavior by your criteria." *Group* here may refer to society, religion, class, sex, ethnic culture, or generation. But conceptual relativism, to use Trigg's general term, is only a stage in rethinking opinions. One cannot leave it at that stage, because the very next statement becomes, "Say, some of my ideas, values, behaviors are not just part of my upbringing but are almost universal requirements of all successful human groups. If this is so, then there are some universal standards by which we can judge all cultures, our own and others."

As we have seen, we can also add two important ways in which cultures can be judged—namely, by the degree to which their world view conforms with the environment and by the power which this pragmatism bestows on the society. The twentieth century anthropologist would probably disagree with us, but we would add a third—namely, the extent to which a culture conforms with the desires, drives, values, and enjoyments of humans. The sociobiologist would claim that these are part of our innate human nature and are genetically based. Today's anthropologist is inclined to the view that these things are products of culture and therefore cannot be used as tests of culture.

Evolutionary thinking seems to have been discarded by most sociologists, except in a certain form by Marxists, because it could be and was misused to lend support to some of the more ruthless forms of capitalist power seeking. But with the advantage of our present knowledge, we can see that that was like discarding spades because they can be used as a weapon. Any good instrument—physical or mental—can be used well or poorly.

Science and Values

Many people, especially economists and sociologists, once said, "Science has nothing to do with values. We can tell you what will happen if you do certain things, but not whether or not you should." Priscilla Robertson, a former editor of *The Humanist,* as long ago as 1956, wrote an excellent refutation of this view ("On Getting Values Out of Science," *The Humanist,* 4, 1956).

Lehrman correctly recognizes that values enter into science as in any human activity. Scientists place a very negative value on deception for a start. Certainly values determine scientific strategy and its application, but scientists, as do the rest of us in ordinary life, do try to exclude their values from the actual experiment or collection data. If we nudge an experiment the way we think it ought to go, we end up with no new information.

However, Lehrman, Wolfe, and Gray would exclude science from moral values and ethics. This just won't do. These subjects are susceptible to examination, reason, and knowledge—that is, science—as is any other aspect of life. Knowledge about what is and has been—evolutionary knowledge—must influence our ethics and what we think ought to be. We have to bear in mind that all knowledge, not only evolutionary knowledge, is about the past. The future is extrapolation. Some behaviors are no longer adaptive. For instance, male dominance was adaptive in past days of group conflict, but weapons and other machines and the need for zero growth make it no longer so. For this same reason, and as a result of our scientific *knowledge* about population, contraception is essential and abortion is often justified; yet, in the past, these practices were accorded a negative value. Thus knowledge, including scientific knowledge, can change our values and our ethics.

The human ability to value is admittedly very mysterious. Those who would exclude science from values may be correctly sensing that the core process involved remains unchanged. What we value changes slowly. How we value is more stable. George E. Pugh, in his *Biological Bases of Human Values* (Basic, 1977), makes the useful distinction between primary inherited values and secondary learned values, the former being largely genetic. Primary values are things we enjoy from the start, from sweet foods to sex, love, friendship, and fame. Secondary values are the things we have learned that lead to primary values.

Some sociobiologists, such as David Barash in his *Sociobiology and Behavior* (Heinemann, 1977), maintain that, as with other species, our values are designed to maximize our genetic fitness—that is, our chances of being survived by progeny. I think he is nearly right, but I would suggest that humans can go one logical step higher. Parenting involves power. It is very enjoyable for some. They want to be "parents" to the world. Also, some men enjoy "parenting" machines, which are also our progeny. Robert Jastrow develops this theme in *Until the Sun Dies* (Norton, 1977).

Gene-Environment Interaction

Lehrman, in most of "Human Sociobiology: Wilson's Fallacy," is very ungenerous to Wilson. He accuses Wilson of not understanding the great difference in rate between genetic and cultural change. This is absurd. Wilson writes about this extensively. But Lehrman exaggerates the slowness of genetic change. Gene changes occur with every generation and gene frequencies can change in one generation with sufficient selection against certain alleles or gene combinations. Admittedly this happens rarely, but the 1918 influenza pandemic must have eliminated a large proportion of those whose immunity systems were genetically slow to make antibodies to the new virus.

Lehrman does not let himself agree with Wilson even where sociologists would. Most sociologists would agree with Wilson that culture often amplifies small genetic differences, such as those between the sexes or between races. These cultural "amplifications" seem to be lessening, but I do not see how this latter fact negates the former sentence. Incidentally, this phenomenon closely resembles the *multiplier* effect in which very small genetic differences between two variants of a species may produce marked differences in social organization. Wilson describes this in a baboon species in *Sociobiology* (Harvard, 1975). Many sociologists have expressed the same thought with almost the same words both before and since Wilson said it.

Furthermore, many sociologists would find the statement that "genes are the biological foundations of altruism" fairly innocuous, although some people, including Lehrman, infer from it the meaning that "genes are a *sufficient* explanation of altruism." But that is not Wilson's claim nor that of W.D. Hamilton, the British biologist who introduced the theory of kin selection and inclusive fitness in order to modify genetic theory to *allow* for altruism. All human behavior has a genetic *basis,* because our behavior is shaped by our body structure, including our brain structure. Just think how much of our culture depends on the shape of our hands and the way our limbs function, not to mention the more subtle genetic input into our brain design.

Multiple Causes

Biologists are used to the idea of multiple causation. If some function is very important, nature is apt to be redundant. A mechanism at one level will be reinforced at several other levels. Other people, such as social scientists, often do not think this way. If they identify one cause of a phenomenon, they think that settles the matter and there is no need to search for other causes. This either-or thinking is manifest in sociologists' favorite mode of classification: dichotomy. They like to classify things into two categories: inherited or acquired, genetic or cultural. Lehrman is mistaken, for instance, in assuming that there is no genetic component in our disinclination to incest. Brother-sister incest avoidance has a strong physiological component as part of the natural pressure toward exogamy in all primates. It is, of course, reinforced by a cultural taboo. Incidentally, one must distinguish between the genetic consequences of incest, the distal cause, and the *proximal cause* of incest avoidance, the physiological mechanism which renders children reared together uninterested in one another sexually. It applies to early adopted children, but is not thereby nongenetic. This itself is a good example of the interaction between a gene-based mechanism triggered by subsequent experience. Father-daughter incest, in view of its frequency, would seem to have a weaker physiological taboo. Perhaps the taboo is largely cultural, or possibly incest occurs in families in which the father has played a very distant part in rearing his daughter during her early years.

Epigenesis

Many of these criticisms of sociobiology would be mitigated if more people understood the long complex process which intervenes between the inheritance of a gene at conception and the final expression of it as a recognizable trait. The gene and its products enter into this long interaction with the immediate internal and external environment. Each stage of the process determines the next. The British biologist C.H. Waddington used the word *epigenesis,* and Gregory Bateson, in his most recent book, *Mind and Nature* (Bantam, 1980), used it in this sense, as do Charles J. Lumsden and Edward O. Wilson in their *Genes, Mind, and Culture* (Harvard University Press, 1981). The longer this epigenetic pathway, the greater is the probable impact of environment on the outcome. Genes to social trait is the longest, but even physical traits may be modified by environment. The acquisition of antibodies to bacteria and foreign substances is a prime example. Behavioral traits are subject to even more environmental influence—that is, learning. But our genes influence us through our simple primary values, the things we enjoy on first experience and strive for by direct or devious means.

People tend to speak separately of our spiritual nature and our biological nature; the latter being in some way not quite nice. I prefer to think of human nature as all biological, but it is convenient often to distinguish our conscious, calculating long-term nature from our subconscious, emotional short-term nature (Freud's id). Sex involves the id; love involves the whole. The id may sometimes be racist and sexist, but our long-term biological nature, ego if you wish, values a peaceful and just society—not racist nor sexist nor even feminist but humanist.

Pulling a Gag on the Wily Coyote

A bullet works wonders on a sheep-killing coyote, but the shoot-on-sight policy is hard on a useful species. Instead, two experts propose, let's use aversive conditioning to make coyotes sick of eating lamb. Seems to pay off with mountain lions, too.

Carl R. Gustavson
and John Garcia

Carl R. Gustavson took up his duties as adjunct professor of psychology at Eastern Washington State College, where he is pursuing his research on the application of psychological techniques to wildlife management. He was born and raised in Salt Lake City and received his Ph.D. from the University of Utah. In his coyote studies, Gustavson worked closely with his wife, Joan, an active conservationist. Gustavson's coauthor, John Garcia, is professor of psychology and psychiatry at the University of California, Los Angeles. Garcia received his B.A., M.A. and Ph.D. degrees from the University of California, Berkeley, and later became chairman of the psychology department at the State University of New York at Stony Brook. Garcia's past research includes work on the behavioral effects of x-rays, toxins and vitamins.

Americans have slaughtered wolves, bears, mountain lions, and coyotes—among other predators—for centuries. Recently, conservationists have become appalled at the killing, recognizing that many species might go the way of the timber wolf and disappear from the wilderness and the open range. The U.S. death record for 1972 includes 90,000 coyotes, 300 mountain lions, 21,000 bobcats, 2,800 red wolves and 800 bears. But how many deaths go uncounted? Probably more than are ever reported.

Sheepmen who graze their untended herds on the public lands of the western United States insist that coyotes are responsible for important losses, and that predators are raising the price of lamb and wool and threatening the economic viability of the whole industry. So they kill coyotes whenever they get the chance, although by law the Federal Government is supposed to take care of the problem. Guns, traps and lethal poisons are among the tools of this campaign.

Conservationists say the sheepmen have exaggerated the true statistics of predation, and growing numbers of ecologically minded activists defend the wisdom of letting coyotes run free in their natural habitat. In several ways, coyotes are allies of the stockmen. They consume huge quantities of mice, gophers, squirrels, rabbits and even grasshoppers. All these small animals eat grass and plants, literally taking food from the mouths of stock. Without the population control exerted by coyotes, rodents and rabbits could become serious pests. Their numbers explode. They ravage pastures and farms. What is worse, as the population density increases, the ticks, lice and other vermin they carry become a source of disease for both domestic animals and man. Some sheepmen, however, remain unconvinced.

Life-Saving Compromise. In the fall of 1972, we proposed a way out of this impasse. One of us (Garcia) had been researching conditioned responses to the taste of food for over 15 years, using laboratory animals as subjects. The other was interested in the foraging behavior of wild animals, particularly carnivorous hunters. The two of us compared our ideas on the control of sheep-killing coyotes. Common sense and experimental evidence told us that if an animal ate a meal that made it sick, it would avoid that kind of meal in the future. We decided, therefore, to feed tainted lamb to a number of coyotes in an attempt to make them sick without killing them. We would condition coyotes to hate the taste of lamb, and with any luck we would demonstrate the possibility of protecting our coyotes *and* our sheep.

Several difficulties plagued us. We had used rats in most of our previous research on taste aversion. But the rat cannot vomit to get rid of poison in the stomach, so nature seems to have designed the rat to be an expert at avoiding the taste of poisonous foods.

It also occurred to us that it might be very hard to turn coyotes away from meat since coyotes are normally meat-eaters. Moreover, our idea depended on teaching coyotes to avoid only the taste; we didn't know if the sight, sound or smell of sheep might still provoke the carnivores to attack and kill. Finally, we wanted to find out if a conditioned aversion to one valuable species of prey, such as lambs, would discourage the coyotes from eating fair game, such as rabbits and rodents.

Seven Healthy Carnivores. We collected seven coyotes to take part in our experiment. All were adults about two to four years old. Five of them had been taken from their den in the wild at the age of three weeks. These were relatively domesticated, although they attacked both lambs and rabbits when they got the chance. The coyote named Brujo, a male, and the females Luna and Coty had hunted rabbits out in the desert; the male Feisty and the female Dizzy had no hunting experience. The other two coyotes, Sam and Mary, were shy creatures. We had captured them as adults; each had lost a forepaw as a result of trapping. Sam, after several months in captivity, attacked and ate rabbits. He refused to attack lambs even when we put them in his pen for hours. Mary wouldn't attack either animal.

After several weeks of observing the coyotes' reactions to various foods and to various doses of lithium chloride, which causes nausea and vomiting, we conducted an experiment to see if lithium would put them off hamburger. Brujo, Coty, Luna and Mary lived normally on dog food. One day we gave these four coyotes fresh hamburger laced with six grams of lithium. Mary gulped down the whole meal; the others separated out some of the lithium capsules. But each animal ingested at least three grams of lithium, and they all became ill.

Two days later we offered them some hamburger without any of the emetic lithium in it. They turned it down dramatically. They tipped over their food dishes and acted the way many dogs do when they encounter some disgusting, putrid material. They sniffed the hamburger and retched; then they either rolled on the food, urinated on it, or buried it. And apparently, the aversion was specific to hamburger, for the coyotes all ate a full ration of dog food after the tests.

Lamb *à la* Lithium. Encouraged by these results, we decided to see if an aversion for meat would stop a coyote from attacking the animal that provides the meat. We experimented with live lambs and rabbits, which we placed in an enclosure where the coyotes could see them. First we used rabbits. We timed each coyote's reactions from the moment the door opened between its pen and the enclosure, and we filmed their behavior as they attacked and ate these healthy and nutritious rabbits. Two days later, we performed the same kind of test with a live lamb.

On the fifth day we gave them some minced lamb meat, tainted with lithium chloride and wrapped in a fresh lamb hide. Then about a week later we offered them a second live lamb to see what they had learned. Brujo and Coty attacked immediately—and fatally for their lambs—but it took them much longer to start eating, and they ate less heartily, although they hadn't been fed for the past 48 hours. In contrast, Luna sniffed at the lamb and then moved away. She vomited within a minute, then retreated to her pen. The lamb followed her. She growled and snapped at it, but soon she was retching again and broke off her attack.

After 15 minutes we took the lamb away and presented Luna with a rabbit. She attacked it right away and immediately ate it.

Two days later we gave Brujo and Coty a second lithium treatment, because the first treatment hadn't suppressed their attacks on the lambs. Apparently they hadn't eaten enough of the emetic. To be certain, therefore, we also gave them an injection of 2.5 grams of lithium chloride mixed with water.

This second treatment seemed to cure their taste for lamb. When we offered each of them a lamb four days later, not one of them attacked. They did, however, attack and eat rabbits after their second treatment.

We tested Dizzy, Feisty and Sam with tainted rabbits plus injections of lithium chloride and got comparable results. They refused rabbits but attacked lambs. These coyotes, in short, learned not to attack their normal prey.

The Interrupted Kill. We [illegible] weeks afterwards to see [illegible] would remember the lesso[illegible] for eight weeks without a sin[illegible], although every week we offered him a live lamb. Coty made a lunge at her lamb after the second lithium treatment; but then she stopped abruptly, turned her back on the lamb, and spent the rest of the test period eating grass. Brujo also ate grass on his last three trials. These coyotes not only nibbled grass the way a sick dog will, but sometimes they snapped at other plants as if frustrated by their inability to bite into the lambs.

The three coyotes we conditioned not to eat rabbits eventually learned to eat them again. Sam attacked and killed a rabbit after a week. Feisty attacked again after four weeks and Dizzy after two. Each waited several minutes before attacking, as though unsure of what to do. And interestingly enough, each coyote ate its rabbit in the same cautious way. First they chewed off and consumed the rabbit's ears. Then they waited for about half an hour. Next they ate the head, waited another half hour, and finally ate the body. Before lithium treatments, the coyotes had attacked the back of the rabbit's head and eaten the neck, head and ears without any long periods of waiting before devouring the body.

After the lithium treatments, apparently, the coyotes reacquired their taste for rabbit by eating slowly and discovering that the meat wouldn't cause nausea and vomiting.

Better Than Skunk Spray. Our work with coyotes points to the definite possibility of suppressing sheep predation by means of tainted—not lethally poisoned—bait. Presumably the coyotes would subject themselves to repeated trials until the flavor, the smell, and eventually the sight of sheep would become associated with nausea and vomiting. When foraging for a meal on the open range, conditioned coyotes could be expected to avoid even the tracks of sheep, so that they might not see their former prey. Our experimental coyotes lived artificially close to lambs, which may have presented them with an unusual temptation.

It's possible, in fact, that many coyotes wouldn't have to undergo conditioning. They might learn as pups to eat other prey than sheep, since their eating habits may be conditioned partly by the kinds of food their mothers bring home to the den, and also by the flavor of their mothers' milk. If

Predators Learn to Avoid Their Natural Prey

Coyotes	Attack Times	
	Before Treatment	**After Treatment**
Luna	1 second (lamb)	no attack
Brujo	1 second (lamb)	no attack
Coty	1 second (lamb)	no attack
Dizzy	1 second (rabbit)	no attack
Feisty	61 seconds (rabbit)	no attack
Sam	231 seconds (rabbit)	no attack

mother coyotes don't eat sheep, perhaps their young won't either.

Over the past several years, scientists have devised various plans to keep coyotes away from sheep without having to kill the predators. Perhaps the most famous technique is the use of noxious or dangerous smells such as skunk spray or the urine of mountain lions. It isn't clear, however, that such methods really scare away many coyotes. In fact, changing the odor of a lamb by spraying it with coyote repellent may cause the mother sheep to reject her own offspring, since smell is one way sheep identify each other.

Attempts have also been made to scare coyotes by using painful electric shocks. But this method isn't very effective, since animals that are conditioned to avoid such pain learn quickly to avoid the source of the shock, rather than the prey.

The Complexities of Nature. Our method of control takes advantage of Mother Nature. An animal avoids the kind of meal that once made it sick because its brain is wired that way. The coyote doesn't need to remember that lamb acted as a powerful emetic; rather, the taste of lamb simply disgusts it. Conversely, if an animal eats a nutritious meal that satisfies its hunger, then the same sort of food will taste better the next time.

Obviously the coyote needs to have an alternative food source. If it has rodents and rabbits around, it's not likely to return to sheep.

Several questions must still be answered before embarking on any large-scale conditioning campaigns. There are many ways in which a program of conditioning may backfire, especially when we're dealing with something as complex as an entire region. Our experiment, for instance, included injections of lithium chloride, but it's clear that we can't run around the open range chasing coyotes with syringes. Tainted bait would have to do the trick.

Then again, coyotes might learn the crucial difference between dead lambs and live ones and begin to eat only lambs which they have killed, while never touching carrion or bait. Coyotes are famously adaptive. The emetic bait will have to be designed to taste and smell like lamb on the hoof.

It is just as likely, though, that the aversion to lamb will drive the sheep-killers completely out of the sheep range. For five weeks after treatment, Brujo hid under his cage every time we presented him with a lamb. He wouldn't even eat a rabbit if a lamb was nearby. Coty didn't have such a strong aversion to lambs, although once she began attacking lambs again, she would break off her attack to chase a rabbit; and whenever the lamb approached, she'd pick up her rabbit and move to another corner of the enclosure. The coyotes wanted to put as much distance as they could between themselves and the disgusting sheep.

There is always the possibility that our lithium lessons might have to be repeated over and over again at some expense, but lithium chloride is cheap compared to the control methods used now. Our technique would be specifically aimed at the sheep-killers who live near the sheep ranges. This is a small part, incidentally, of the whole coyote population. As it is, bounty hunters, traps, and lethal poisons don't distinguish between sheep-killers and nonkillers.

Fred's Bad Deerburger. Recent studies have demonstrated that our general method of control can be applied to other animals besides coyotes. We tried it out, for example, on a cougar named Fred, a 20-year-old geriatric case living in Salt Lake City's Hogle Zoo. Normally he ate a seven-pound ration of beef and horse meat daily.

One day we gave him about four pounds of "deerburger" containing six grams of lithium chloride. He ate it all. Fred did not vomit afterwards. He appeared sluggish and unhappy, and he drank more water than usual, but otherwise he looked well enough. He ate all of his daily ration for the next two days. Then we gave him another deerburger, without lithium this time. Fred sniffed the food and then deliberately turned over his dish, dumping the deer meat on the floor. He spent a long time examining the food, sniffing and licking it as if in search of some good part to eat. In the end he walked away, shaking each paw in disgust, the way cats do when they step in water.

We suggest that this method of aversive conditioning will work with most wild predators. Our coyotes wouldn't kill what they didn't intend to eat. The coyotes that became sick after eating a rabbit examined subsequent rabbits thoroughly. Like the cougar, they seemed to be looking for edible parts. Large predators in general, in North America or on the African Veldt, reveal little if any wanton killing. A predator that wastes its food supply just won't survive.

Predators and Pets. Domesticated carnivores such as cats, dogs, and laboratory ferrets are another matter. Bred in captivity for generations, where their daily rations are provided by man, they may lose the biological wisdom of "waste not, want not." Some of our laboratory ferrets persisted, over and over again, in killing and eating mice that made them sick. And after they had finally learned not to take mice in their mouths, the ferrets would still murder them with their forepaws. Killing, for these ferrets, had become play and exercise, as it is for cats and dogs. Such animals have forgotten the grim economics of nature in the wild, where killing is a chore with but one purpose —survival.

These preliminary studies would not have been possible without the help and advice of the sheepmen of Utah. They considered the aversion technique worth investigating, and they provided the test lambs. These sheepmen feel that experiments in animal behavior, together with sound ecological judgments, can result in a design for predator control which will be both restrained and effective. It would save the lambs for our own tables and clothes, while allowing coyotes and other predators to roam the wild country as they have for the past million years.

Caught by Choice

JEFFREY Z. RUBIN

Jeffrey Z. Rubin is professor of psychology at Tufts University, where he directs the Center for the Study of Decision Making. Portions of this article will appear in his book, THE BOOK OF TRAPS.

AMONG THE LITTLE GADGETS that kids in New York City fancied during the 1940s and 50s, when I was growing up, was the "Chinese finger trap." A woven straw cylinder a few inches long, the opening at each end was just large enough for a child's finger to be inserted—and trapped. One tried to escape, of course, by tugging in opposite directions, but the harder one pulled, the tighter the fabric stretched around each finger. Only by pushing inward, by moving counter to the direction in which escape appeared to lie, could one get free.

The Chinese finger trap is wonderful in its elegant simplicity, but there are other traps that are far more terrible in their subtlety, unexpected power, and destructive consequences. These are the traps we spring upon ourselves, the psychological devices that ensnare us in our daily lives, at work, and in international affairs. Like reptiles, these psychological traps are cold-blooded, with no energy of their own. They can be sustained only by the continued infusion of energy from without—from us, their human contrivers. They are the passive machinery, the receptacles, that make it possible for us to pull and tear at ourselves.

We fall victim to these traps in countless ways: waiting—and waiting—for a bus to lumber up the avenue to justify the time already spent waiting; remaining in a destructive relationship with a spouse, lover, or friend because one has invested so much of oneself that it seems crazy to give up; refusing to enter psychotherapy because one has survived for so long without it; avoiding the end of one's psychotherapy because one has been in it for so long; continuing to pour money into the repair of an old car to justify the money already spent; continuing to fight in Vietnam, Afghanistan, El Salvador, the Falkland Islands, or Lebanon, to justify the loss of lives, money, matériel, and face already incurred. In such situations, in which the longer we remain the more difficult it becomes to get out, innocent involvement becomes entrapment.

Ironically, entrapment arises from freedom of choice, the right to take one road over another. For thousands of years we have gone to extraordinary lengths, fought countless wars, and lost countless lives, to win that privilege. But the freedom to choose entitles us to both the successes and the failures that choices entail. Choices have consequences that we must learn to live with—those of the paths not taken as well as those that are. Inherent in the privilege of choice, then, is an invitation to rationalize, justify, and otherwise explain our behavior. Without the presence, or at least the illusion, of choice, we cannot really know the Janus-faced ambivalence that often accompanies the process of choosing. And it is out of this ambivalence—the experience of each move, gesture, or choice as both pleasurable and painful, rewarding and costly—that there arises a need to simplify our world through the rationalization that is the hallmark of entrapment.

To understand entrapment by choice, journey to San Juan, Puerto Rico, on the sunny, breezy day of March 22, 1978. Karl Wallenda, the seventy-three-year-old patriarch of "The Great Wallendas," the famed family of circus aerialists, plans on that day to walk on a high wire from one building to the other of the Condado Holiday Inn.

You are Karl Wallenda. Step into his soft shoes, climb out onto the railing of the hotel balcony, and prepare to walk the high wire. It is shortly before noon, and a crowd has gathered eleven stories below to watch you walk two hundred feet along a tightrope. The wind is gusting, and you'll have to be especially careful today. Gripping the balance pole, you step out onto the wire and begin to inch your way along. Suddenly the wind blows up and you take a quick step or two backward. You don't really need to walk across that wire today. You're the world's premier high-wire aerialist, and this event is nothing more than a promotional appearance. You clearly have a choice.

But you're also a man of considerable pride. All your life you've faced the adversity and danger of the high wire. Your reputation is once again "on the line." Below are people watching in judgment—especially now that you've shown them a moment or two of hesitation in your retreating steps. And so, your decision is made. Back out you go, gripping the high wire through the bottoms of your shoes, every muscle taut with concentration. Slowly you begin to inch your way across the wire, sliding and stepping a bit at a time. Each step brings you closer to the other side, to the successful end of another journey. Soon you're out over the middle of the street below—almost halfway to your destination.

Then the wind picks up speed again, and you're in serious trouble. Each step that has moved you palpably closer to the other side has also inched you farther from the safety of the starting point. Even as you think about this, you continue to inch forward. Still it's not too late to turn back. You could reverse course and begin to retrace your steps over familiar terrain. To do so, of course, would mean sacrificing all the work you've already done and admitting defeat—both in your own eyes and in those of

The Sciences, October 1982, ©1982 by The New York Academy of Sciences.

the spectators below. Why not continue forward? In an emergency, you can always fall to the wire and grab it with both hands. So you go on ahead, the wind gusting, the cable swaying.

And then it is all over. A powerful gust suddenly lifts Wallenda into the air. He lands atop the wire, and for a moment seems to be safe—if only he could get rid of his pole and grab the wire with both hands. But only one hand manages to grip the wire, and Wallenda falls to his death.

THE HIGH WIRE that day was, for Wallenda, a most effective trap, and it reveals a number of underlying features that such traps share. First, an effective trap must lure or distract the victim into behaving in costly ways, perhaps even risking its life. This is often accomplished with some form of bait so enticing, so well suited to the victim's particular needs and inclinations, that the victim is induced to enter the trap, quite oblivious to its jaws. Wallenda could see the distant side of that high wire drawing closer with each step; he could feel the distracting gaze of the people below. For all his knowledge and experience, Wallenda's attention on that fateful day seems to have been focused too narrowly on the lure of his goal up ahead.

Second, an effective trap bears traffic in one direction only. How much easier for a lobster to push its way through the cone-shaped net into a trap than, once inside, to claw its way out. The bait that motivates the victim to enter the trap obscures the irreversibility of that move. Doors that yield easily, inviting the victim's entry, slam shut with a vengeance. Wallenda could have turned back, of course. But with each passing step, reversal became increasingly difficult.

Third, an effective trap is often designed so that the victim's very efforts to escape serve to entrap it all the more. A fly's tendency to wriggle free of the sticky paper that holds it merely gets it more stuck. An effective trap thus induces the victim to become the source of its own entrapment or possible destruction. Wallenda's inclination to respond to the danger of a gusting wind by pushing farther ahead served only to further entrap him. Indeed, even as he thought about what to do, he continued to take the forward steps that made escape more difficult.

Finally, an effective trap must suit the particular attributes of its intended victim. One cannot catch a guppy with a lobster trap or a flea with a butterfly net. Wallenda, on that windy day in Puerto Rico, seems to have entered a trap tailormade for him. Someone else might have refused to walk the wire, retreated when the wind came up, had less of a reputation to sacrifice to the crowd below, or even had younger, stronger hands with which to grab the wire.

All traps, whether physical or psychological, whether designed to capture oneself or others, share these four characteristics. Animal traps, for instance, have existed for thousands of years, ever since people realized that active pursuit of a quarry through hunting is often impractical. A trap permits the hunter to outwit stronger, faster quarry simply by bringing the quarry to the hunter rather than the other way around. The trap provides a way for the quarry to catch itself. Once set, the trap becomes a surrogate hunter that can wait tirelessly for the quarry to make an indiscreet choice. The hunter's limited resources can then be devoted to other pursuits—including the construction of more traps. Traps beget traps.

The record of human history is engraved not only with tales of cleverly devised animal traps, but also with horror stories of people's efforts to destroy one another. Consider the man-trap of the civilized British Isles of the nineteenth century, a trap devised to deal with poachers, its teeth of steel hidden in loose leaves in the fine English woods. Once caught, the victim was often maimed for life by the trap's great jaws, and could be counted on not to poach again. By comparison, a little game of three-card monte is nearly harmless, but confidence games, too, are devices for the capture of others.

Con artist and mark, trapper and quarry; in the realm of psychological entrapment, each of us simultaneously occupies both roles. As with physical and psychological devices for the capture of others, psychological traps for self-imprisonment work only when we are interested in, and distracted by, the lure of some goal. A big killing at the gambling table, the other side of the high wire, or simply the arrival of an uptown bus all may be viewed as worthy goals—or as bait that conceals a vicious hook. In entrapping situations we initially look in one direction only—forward—as we pursue a goal that lies just beyond our reach.

It is in this single-minded rush toward some objective that we fail to see that we might be sucked into a narrowing funnel from which escape may prove difficult. The first stage of entrapment, eager pursuit of a goal, is thus followed by attention to the costs that have been unwittingly incurred along the way. The gambler's drive for a killing is inevitably followed by attention to the mounting costs of staying in the game, costs that in turn need to be justified by greater commitment. And the more resources committed to attaining a goal, the greater the trap's bite.

In certain entrapping situations, those in which several of us are competing with one another, pursuit of a reward and justification of costs incurred are followed by a third stage—we try to ensure that our competitors end up losing even more than we do. Like two children in a breath-holding contest, or two nations in a dangerous encounter in the South Atlantic or the Middle East, many entrapping situations reach a point where each side focuses no longer on winning or minimizing losses, but on getting even.

Only by letting go at some point can the trap be escaped. This is the final stage of entrapment, the point where we quit because our resources are exhausted, because we have been "rescued" by another person, because we have set a limit to our involvement, or because we have learned that the world is not a just place where one invariably gets what one wants or deserves.

ALTHOUGH VERY LITTLE IS KNOWN at present about the kinds of people who are habitual candidates for entrapment, it is possible to engage in a bit of informed speculation and creative guesswork. People who are tempted to go for the bait, for instance, are likely to end up hooked. Those who are unusually greedy, or unusually self-assured about their ability to reach a goal, or excessively trusting of the world as a good, safe place where the living is easy, ought to beware. Those who believe that the world is just, with inputs and outcomes corresponding in some neat and orderly way, may also end up caught; their need for order and justice drives them to rationalize and justify the continued investments that tighten a trap all the more. Finally, those who believe that there is little worse than being made a fool of by someone else should watch out for the flypaper.

If entrapping situations are indeed ubiquitous, how do people ever avoid getting hooked? Over the last ten years or so, my co-worker Joel Brockner and I, along with Sinaia Nathanson, Robert Houser, Susan Small-Weil, and other students at Tufts University, have attempted to obtain some answers. In one of our experiments, people are given an opportunity to win a cash jackpot by solving a series of word puzzles, some of which are so difficult that the use of a crossword dictionary is required. To obtain this scarce resource, participants have to wait "in line" until it becomes available. The catch is that the longer they take, the smaller the prize, until they finally have to pay out of their own pockets when the time limit is reached. In another, more abstract experiment, people are invited to pay for the ticks of an incrementing numerical counter, in the hope and expectation that they will win a jackpot—either by reaching a number that has been generated randomly by a computer or by outlasting an adversary. A third experiment challenges people to solve a jigsaw puzzle correctly within a limited time. If they succeed, they win a cash jackpot, but if they fail to complete the puzzle, they expect to pay for the number of pieces they requested along the way. In yet another experiment, college students are given an opportunity to wait for someone to arrive at the laboratory—late, of course—so that an experiment can be completed and necessary research credit obtained.

In each of these situations, there is some rewarding goal toward which people are invited to move, an increasing cost in time or money, and the option to quit the experiment at any time. On the basis of this research and the earlier related work of psychologists Allan Teger, most recently of Boston University, Barry Staw, of the University of California at Berkeley, Roy Lewicki, of Duke University's Fuqua School of Business, and Max Bazerman. of Boston University's School of Management, we can advance several generalizations about how to avoid entrapment: First, it is important that people set limits in advance regarding the extent of their involvement and commitment. Our research indicates that people who are not asked to specify the limits of their participation become more entrapped than those who set a limit beforehand—especially when this is done publicly. A limit may provide an external structure within which people can roam and ramble, secure in the knowledge that they will go only so far and no farther.

Once people set a limit, they must be prepared to stick to it. We all play little games with ourselves, like flipping a coin to make some decision; if we don't like the result, we then decide to make the contest two out of three, or four out of seven—a regular World Series! Too often we set limits that are modified and shaded as we get close to the crunch; structures crumble, and new ones are erected in their place. Each new investment tends to be evaluated, not in relation to the total cost of the investment, but in relation to the current, already very high level of commitment.

Next, it is important to avoid looking to other people for guidance about what to do. Entrapping situations are typically fraught with uncertainty; indeed, that is one of the things that makes them entrapping in the first place. If we knew for sure how much it would cost to reach a goal, and how close that goal was to attainment, then we could calculate precisely the rewards and costs involved and make a rational decision. Given uncertainty, however, it is tempting to look to others for clues about the appropriateness of one's own behavior. Our research suggests that this may be a serious mistake. The presence and continued involvement of another person in an entrapping situation increases our participants' own degree of entrapment, and this effect occurs even when the fates of the people involved are completely independent. In other words, you are more likely to continue waiting for that uptown bus if other people are also waiting in line—even though they are complete strangers.

Furthermore, the need to impress other people may engender behavior that promotes entrapment. We all want to be liked, loved, and respected, particularly by those whom we happen to admire. Although such motives are perfectly healthy and appropriate, in entrapping situations they wreak considerable havoc. Our research indicates that people become entrapped when they believe that their effectiveness as decision makers is being judged. This effect is particularly powerful when evaluation by others occurs early in the game, and diminishes in importance when the judges are introduced later on. We also find that people who are unusually anxious about their appearance in the eyes of others, and who feel that they have something to prove, become more entrapped than those who are less anxious.

In addition, people must be reminded, or remind themselves, of the costs involved in their continued participation in entrapping situations. Our findings indicate that people are less likely to become entrapped when they are made aware of these costs early on. Even the availability of a simple chart depicting the costs of investment can reduce entrapment. Such information offsets the seductive lure of the goal up ahead—particularly when cost information is introduced close to the start. People who do not consider the costs of their involvement until late in the game may feel compelled to justify these costs by investing even more of their resources.

Finally, since traps seem to lurk everywhere, it is important to remain vigilant at all times. People who successfully understand and avoid one kind of trap still manage to fall into others with startling frequency and ease. Although you may be one of the world's reigning experts at avoiding the uptown-bus trap, you may still find yourself persisting too long in a destructive relationship, or edging too far out on thin ice or a high wire. In our research, people who are informed about entrapment and its dangers are less likely to become entrapped themselves, even when the description of entrapment has nothing directly to do with the situation at hand.

Despite such cautionary advice, people continue—and always will—to find themselves caught in the jaws of a variety of terrible traps. How, then, can we learn when and how to quit? Entrapment involves the coupling of short-term gains with long-term expenses, looking no further than the nose on our face in the pursuit of some coveted objective. A striking alternative to this pattern stems from a willingness to give up, at least temporarily, our ardent quest for the grail. Indeed, sometimes the sacrifice of short-term advancement may be the surest road to long-term success. Entrapment is a monstrosity born of choice, and choice may prove the key to the way out as well. Just as we have the right to become entrapped, so too do we have the right to quit—perhaps to come back another day. What today seems the only way through the woods may be but one small shard in a mosaic of pathways, all of which lead to the other side.

Conversion, Brainwashing, and Deprogramming

James T. Richardson

James Richardson is a Professor of Sociology at the University of Nevada at Reno. He has written a number of books and articles on recruitment and resocialization in the new religions, including an analysis of the People's Temple mass suicide in Guyana. A draft of this paper was prepared while he was a Fulbright Fellow at the Catholic University of Nijmegen, the Netherlands, in the Department of Psychology of Culture and Religion. An earlier version was presented to a faculty seminar at the Free University of Amsterdam.

In recent years considerable controversy has raged about the new religions. That controversy has centered on two major issues, both of which have engendered legal debate. One center of controversy involves how the new religions raise and spend money, and their tax status. The other major focus of conflict — the one which I would like to address — has been recruitment practices of the new religions. These have brought accusations of brainwashing which in turn have played a role in the development of the new quasi-profession of deprogramming, which furnishes services to parents who want their children removed from new religious groups. The level of societal concern and the degree of involvement of different groups in this controversy make a close examination of conversion and related issues an important undertaking in contemporary social analysis.

Conversion studies have, until recently, been dominated by an interpretation of one particular event: the conversion of Paul on the road to Damascus. Paul's conversion has usually been viewed as sudden, dramatic, and emotional. It was thought to have been irrational, and was explained in reference to an agent not under the control of Paul. Traditional views of his conversion attribute agency or cause to an omnipotent God. More recent views attribute agency to unconscious psychological forces, or to social-situational factors such as peer pressure, affective ties, social networks, or personal influence. Whatever the characterization of the agent, it was assumed that Paul did not act under his own volition, but was temporarily incapacitated by the actions of some outside force.

Paul's experience appeared to be a single event that thoroughly changed his life. The conversion has been viewed as a total negation of the old self and an affirmation of a new self. One conversion was expected to last a lifetime; only some serious problem could require another. Paul's conversion has usually been interpreted in cognitive terms. His vision caused him to change his beliefs, and then his behavior changed accordingly. Behavior follows belief in the traditional conversion paradigm. Thus, in this prototypical interpretation, Paul's experience was individualistic, deterministic, and passive, and has been viewed as predestinational (to use a theo-

Reprinted from *The Center Magazine,* March/April 1982, with permission of the author.

logical term), or predispositional (to use a psychological term), or situationally determined (to use a sociological term).

Early conversion research promoted by psychology and psychotherapy that used this approach has led to a psychologizing of conversion phenomena. Many have assumed that something was wrong with anyone who espoused religious beliefs, and that religious conversion is often a symptom, if not a cause, of psychological problems.

Although sound research on new religions is being done by a few members of the psychological and psychotherapeutic communities, most in these disciplines seem to accept unabashedly the traditional view of conversion that I have described. Some have updated the jargon and ideas, but the same basic assumptions remain. Thomas Robbins has called this view the "invasion of the body snatchers" or "Little Red Riding Hood" theory of conversion to new religions. Instead of an omnipotent God striking down and blinding Paul on the road to Damascus, we have omnipotent techniques and processes of brainwashing, hypnotism, mind control, and coercive persuasion leading to "snapping" that are used to strike down passive and innocent youngsters. That members of this most educated and privileged generation in American history would succumb to the entreaties of strange gurus is accepted *ipso facto* as proof that the gurus' techniques are omnipotent, and that drastic measures must be taken to rescue those who fall prey to the proselytizing of the new religions.

Recent work by sociologists and social psychologists, and a few psychologists and psychiatrists, however, has produced a new view of conversion to the new religions. The major findings can be summarized:

(1) Contemporary conversion is usually not a once-in-a-lifetime event. It is better characterized as a series of affiliations and disaffiliations in a *conversion career*. Many people, particularly younger people, are taking advantage of the many opportunities in our pluralistic society and are trying out serial alternatives in life-style, some of which are religious. Many people experience ideological and behavioral variety and mobility as they move through individual conversion careers.

Only a small proportion of people contacted by new groups actually join, and of those who do, only a relatively small proportion remain. A pattern of sampling and then moving on seems the predominant style of relating to the new religious groups. Just as the institutions of the larger society have a problem obtaining long-term commitment, voluntary attrition is also a major problem for the new religions. Perhaps the major difficulty of young converts is not becoming overcommitted to any one group, but a general lack of commitment to *any* stable social mooring. What Robert J. Lifton has referred to as the protean-man style of life has become a dominant theme of the age.

(2) Decisions to join or participate in new religious movements can be made suddenly, dramatically, or emotionally — as Paul's is usually viewed — but the most fruitful way to view conversion to new religions is as a series of experiments entered into somewhat gingerly. Many join with what Hans Toch calls latent reservations, and for many affiliations are temporary and the groups themselves are often "on trial." Leaving religious groups and movements is as important as joining, and about as frequent. It can also be as sudden and emotional in appearance as was the act of joining, because the same process is operating — people decide to stop occupying one role (member) and opt for another role (nonmember or member of a new group).

(3) Beliefs do not necessarily change prior to joining. Instead, a person decides to *behave* as a group member for a while, as he or she tries out a new life-style. This deciding to behave as a proper group member has been mistaken for instant conversion by some outsiders, who assume that some sinister force or technique must be at work. However, cognitive changes are actually much more gradual and much less complete in most converts than is commonly assumed. Participation in group activities does not necessarily indicate total commitment to the group's ideology. Even for those who do make a total commitment to a group, normal processes of maturation and changes of status such as marriage usually work to undermine that initial commitment. Research on nearly all new religious groups — from the Moonies to the Divine Light Mission to radical Jesus Movement groups — has demonstrated that marriage, having children, and economic problems can overwhelm ideological factors. These findings support the sociological truism that individuals usually act in ways dictated by their social situation, and that beliefs are modified to be consistent with behaviors.

(4) Contemporary conversion is a social phenemenon. People affiliate with groups because they want affection, they want friends and loved ones to care for them. Affiliation with social groups is a normal and essential process in which virtually all people are involved. When ties are weakened with groups and institutional structures in which people usually participate, other structures will be sought. When ties with society are especially problematic, as was the case for many in the late nineteen-sixties and early nineteen-seventies, many seek out communal groups as substitute communities. But those substitute communities are normalized quite rapidly by financial concerns and by development of the organizational bureaucracies, families, and other social institutions that pervade modern life.

A few new groups have recruited predominantly among those who have few ties with society. This was particularly prevalent in the late nineteen-sixties and early nineteen-seventies. But most now recruit along friendship network lines, again indicating the importance of social considerations.

(5) Thus, recruits to new religions are active individuals involved in seeking appropriate life-styles. The notion of a passive person absorbing anything he or she is told, driven by independent psychological and sociological forces, does not apply to most conversions to new religious groups. Rational decisions are being made by most educated converts, who are, after all, members of our most educated generation ever. Converts are usually seeking to affirm themselves rather than to negate themselves and run away. Certainly some of these decisions are difficult to understand from the perspective of the outsider, but this does not change the basic character of the decision from the point of view of the person making the decision. Most members of new religious groups talk of autonomy and volition when they describe what they are doing, and they stress change, not stasis. Some even admit that they are exploiting the groups (instead of the other way around), or that they are at least engaged in negotiations with the groups concerning what they have to do and believe in order to remain a member in good standing. Often members will even reveal plans to leave the group at some future time.

This summary gives a somewhat idealized view of contemporary conversion; not every individual case fits. But the new model I have described is closely approximated by most of the people who are associating with the new religious groups, based on a decade of my own research on groups in the United States and abroad, and on the work of others.

Why do these findings differ from the results of earlier conversion studies and from some other contemporary studies? The most straightforward and in some ways appealing explanation is that conversions have changed. But the assumption that conversion some decades ago was similar to Paul's experience while contemporary conversion is typified by the activist-seeker begs important questions. It is entirely possible and even probable that conversion phenomena have stayed the same while their *interpretation* has changed.

Because most earlier conversion studies were dominated by psychological approaches, and most researchers studying conversion to the new religious groups are sociologists, the methods used to study the phenomena of conversion have changed. Typically psychological research has relied on comparing standard personality assessments of individual cult members with assessments of so-called normal populations, and on the case-study method of psychotherapy. The case-study method has also been particularly important to a few contemporary psychotherapists who have furnished much of the material that has lent legitimacy to the anti-cult movement. Some therapists have used therapy not just for counseling but as a data-gathering opportunity for such case studies, and have risked compromising the integrity of both endeavors. Nearly all such research has focused on ex-members whose membership or withdrawal from the group was problematic.

For instance, Margaret Singer's well publicized 1979 *Psychology Today* paper on problems faced by ex-members of new religious groups contains a telling admission. She says that seventy-five per cent of those she has counseled and studied "left the cults not entirely on their own volition but through legal conservatorships." Most of her research group had apparently been deprogrammed. Thus, her study should be viewed mainly as research on problems encountered by those who have been deprogrammed, not as a definitive work on new religious group life-style and recruitment practices. The same comment apparently applies to the work of John Clark, a psychiatrist, who has been engaged in therapy on ex-members of newer religions. Also, the recent article by Flo Conway and Jim Siegelman (the authors of *Snapping*) in *Science Digest* shows the same problem. Their sample was selective; seventy-one per cent admitted having participated in some form of deprogramming.

Those who have dealt with a narrow segment of ex-members and who have done little if any on-site research in the new groups have, predictably, found little to counter their traditional view of conversion. They believe that conversion happens to passive objects, and that such occurrences are, almost by definition, bad. Coupled with a therapeutic focus on furnishing an interpretation of past events acceptable to the client and the client's family, this prejudice seriously jeopardizes the quality of the data obtained. Such studies do not offer reliable conclusions on group conversion/resocialization practices. They might give adequate information about deprogrammed ex-members or about ex-members with psychological problems, but even that remains to be seen.

The usual method of study for sociologists, on the other hand, has been participant observation coupled with lengthy interviews and/or conversations with group members and leaders. Thus, most sociologists doing such research have typically been dealing with members within the group setting. The sociologists could themselves be accused of some selectivity, since they have been studying members who are at least contented enough to remain in the group temporarily. However, their research has revealed a great deal about members' experiences, which is especially significant in light of the continuing charges that life inside the new groups is hellish and demeaning. Their work generally dispels any notion that such groups constitute prison camps, or that members are zombie-like automatons. Life in most new religious groups may be considerably different from that to which researchers and others are accustomed. But to accept without question that such a life-style is wrong or horrible is problematic.

One other reason for the historical differences in how conversion has been viewed is that there has been a discernible shift in the social classes of subjects and researchers involved in conversion studies. Much earlier conversion research involved middle-class researchers studying lower-class subjects who had converted to some form of Pentecostal religion or a snake-handling cult in Appalachia. Since the researcher and subject did not share similar subcultural cognitive worlds, this may have prevented researchers from fully understanding what was happening in conversion. Today, fairly young middle-class researchers are studying middle-class youths affiliating with new groups. The researcher and the subjects may share similar values, beliefs, and general cognitive worlds, and perhaps this has led to a more sympathetic treatment of the phenomena of conversion; what might be called a mirror effect. It is understandably difficult to conclude that people like oneself are pushed around by psychological and sociological forces over which they have little or no personal control, and it is understandably easy to say they are exercising their own volition and making rational decisions. But perhaps converts in the earlier days of such research were also exercising volition and making rational decisions from their perspective, while researchers were too culturally blind to recognize it.

One's perceptions will always be influenced by direct contact with those whom one studies, and usually for the better. Many therapists who are opposed to the new religions have not had direct contact with members of the groups in their everyday life setting. One key opponent of the new religions, psychiatrist John Clark, makes it a point not to go near the groups for "scientific, legal, and ethical reasons." He has demonstrated his position by stating in a professional paper, in all seriousness, that the urgent question motivating his work is "What kind of nutty people get into these crazy groups?" Such an obviously biased statement suggests that there may be significant perceptual limitations in his research.

Brainwashing is a popular term that has been applied to a supposedly mysterious process whereby Chinese and Russian Communists extracted confessions from prisoners and seemed to change, at least temporarily, their beliefs and even values. A number of studies and interpretations of this phenomenon have been offered by scholars, including especially Robert J. Lifton, Edgar Schein, and William Sargent. Nearly all such studies, with the exception of Edgar Schein's work, treat brainwashing as an extreme example of traditional conversion similar to Paul's experience.

Most interpretations of brainwashing assume a relatively passive subject under the control of all-powerful (and, in the case of new religions, evil) external agents who use omnipotent and evil techniques. The change associated with brainwashing involves a total negation of the old self and the substitution of a new one in its place. The change is viewed as relatively sudden, dramatic, and emotional. Physical and mental coercion are assumed to be crucial in bringing about significant cognitive changes.

Twenty years ago, A. D. Biderman offered an analysis of why the term brainwashing came to prominence in the nineteen-fifties and nineteen-sixties in the West. He noted that most of the researchers were caught up in the anti-Communist rhetoric of the cold war, which permeated their analysis. Biderman said that there seemed to be an assumption that Communist beliefs were "fundamentally alien to human nature and social reality. The acceptance of Communist beliefs is consequently regarded as *ipso facto* evidence of insanity or a warped, evil personality, or both." This anti-Communist sentiment was also antitotalitarian and anticollectivistic in orientation, with even an element of racism, and contributed to a misunderstanding of brainwashing phenomena in the nineteen-fifties that still persists.

As the era of new religious movements arrived, brainwashing provided a ready-made, simplistic term to apply to these new phenomena by those who disapproved or who sought a scapegoat. The use of the "brainwashing defense" in the trial of Patty Hearst brought the idea even more into common use, althought the term had been used to refer to recruitment to new religious groups even before her trial. The accusation of brainwashing thus became what Richard Anthony and Thomas Robbins call a social weapon to be used against groups and beliefs that were not acceptable to those who had vested interests in the society, including some families of recruits, representatives of certain religious groups who found themselves in open competition with the new groups for members, and some therapists. The charge of brainwashing is now also being used to discredit new religions in several other countries by representatives of the same groups and others.

The brainwashing view of why and how people join new religious groups does not mesh well with the facts. Several psychiatrists such as Marc Galanter and Tom Ungerlieder have been involved in well-conceived and -executed research on the effects of joining the new religions and on the process whereby affiliation is effected. Some of their major conclusions are noteworthy: those who are members of new religions studied are normal people in nearly every way, and their ability to care for themselves is not impaired; also those who join generally benefit from their participation by improved psychological health (a conclusion consonant with much of the sociological work already mentioned). Of special note is a 1980 paper by Marc Galanter in which he studies a cohort of people going through a three-week training session for the Unification Church. Galanter administered personality assessment instruments to over one hundred in the cohort, and compared those who joined with those who did not. He found that only about eight per cent of those who started the training actually joined, and that they were basically normal. Those who are members for some time improve their psychological health. Galanter's paper demonstrates the low retention and high drop-out rates of this group, a finding also of Eileen Barker, an English sociologist who has studied the Moonies in England extensively. American social psychologist Philip Zimbardo's study of youths and the new religions in the San Francisco Bay Area reveals that only a minute fraction of those contacted by members of new religions actually follow up on the contact. Such low success rates, coupled with low retention rates and high attrition, support the conversion career notion that converts are active seekers trying out many different groups and lifestyles over time. Galanter, in the 1980 study, found that ninety per cent of the cohort had been in other religious groups prior to attending the Unification Church training session.

Some researchers have found similarities between the tactics used by some new religious groups and those employed in brainwashing. But the key elements of guilt-inducement and physical coercion are muted or totally absent in the new religions. Even some outspoken critics of the Unification Church admit that coercion is not used, and that nearly all the participants are present voluntarily. Some of the new groups have developed amazingly sophisticated tactics to persuade potential recruits to join and remain members, but it is deceptive to refer to these as brainwashing. "Love bombing," a term sometimes used to refer to recruitment tactics of some new groups, is simply not equivalent to physical torture, although apparently some would have us believe that love bombing is totally sinister and actually worse (more effective) than the physically coercive tactics of the Chinese and Russian Communists. This logic seems ludicrous, and those who use it should go into some of the groups and experience for themselves first-hand the sense of community and love that is usually present. To call these elements methods in some sinister plot is cynical reductionism.

Thus it appears that brainwashing is a much-too-simple answer to complex questions. Brainwashing explanations of what happened in Russia and China blinded many Westerners and led to a less-than-complete understanding of the Communist revolution. Reliance on similar explanations to interpret the rise of the new religions also conceals more than it reveals, and should be abandoned.

Deprogramming involves the extraction, often by force, of a member from a new religious group, and incarceration of the member by quasi-professional people, usually hired by a blood relative, to change the beliefs and behaviors of the person. Efforts to change the person's beliefs include initimidation and the commission of acts held to be sacrilegious in the belief system of the deprogrammer. Sometimes an effort is made to get the subject to affirm a general version of traditional Christian beliefs. Deprogramming can be rapid, or it can last for days. The setting is usually a motel room, and the persons involved are usually marginal representatives of the ministerial or psychological professions, or cult ex-members who were themselves deprogrammed. The process is expensive — deprogrammings were going for twenty-five thousand dollars in the Netherlands last year — and it is usually illegal. Yet deprogramming has gained some tacit and even direct support from representatives of law. Policemen and district attorneys have sometimes looked the other way in America when deprogrammings are taking place, and the courts have sometimes granted temporary "conservatorships" of thirty or sixty days that have allowed the forcible removal of members from their groups by legal means.

However, such support is not the rule. Deprogrammers have spent time in jail for their efforts, and suits have been filed against some of those involved in deprogrammings. Deprogramming does not always succeed, and many of those deprogrammed return to their group of membership. The threat of deprogramming has often united the groups and given them a tangible "devil" to fight against. Deprogramming also apparently heightens negative feelings in individual members toward those who attempt such acts.

Trudy Solomon has observed that those who go through deprogramming are more prone to espouse afterward a brainwashing interpretation of what they experienced while in the group, a finding also apparently supported inadvertently by the work of Singer, of Clark, and in Conway and Siegelman's recent paper. Therefore, as a tactic deprogramming cannot be viewed as an unqualified success by opponents of the new religions, unless one believes that convincing someone he or she has been brainwashed is a worthy goal. Deprogrammings have had some obvious negative effects on the groups, though, since they have lost members, and since a sizeable proportion of deprogrammers have themselves been deprogrammed.

Anson Shupe and David Bromley have written in their recent book on the anti-cult movement about a "noncoercive" type of deprogramming that does not include kidnapping and forced incarceration. Instead, the emphasis is on getting the member away for lengthy conversations about his or her beliefs and practices. This has probably become the more often used tactic by those opposed to the new religions, if only because of the expense and legal problems associated with the more coercive deprogramming.

No one knows how many deprogrammings of both varieties have occurred, but estimates range into the thousands in America. Ted Patrick, one of the most prominent deprogrammers, who has spent time in jail for his efforts, claims to have been involved in over two thousand deprogrammings himself. Deprogramming has been exported; about a half-dozen citizens of the Netherlands were deprogrammed in the last year. Some deprogrammings have even involved people who were not members of a religious group, but were just engaged in a life-style with which their parents disagreed.

It is possible to characterize deprogramming within the traditional paradigms of conversion and even so-called brainwashing because of its assumptions of passivity of the subject and the idea of a sudden total change brought about by an external agent. These key assumptions of the traditional view pervade the approach taken by the deprogrammers toward the initial conversion of the member, and they also pervade assumptions about how to change the person's beliefs back to those held before conversion.

In the case of more coercive deprogramming, the deprogrammers assume that brainwashing has taken place and therefore drastic measures are required and justified to undo the alleged damage. Noncoercive deprogramming relies slightly more on a view of the person as an active agent because it requires that he or she voluntarily cooperate to a degree. But both see the act of affiliation as brainwashing, and every effort is made by the deprogrammers to take control of the situation and effect something akin to a dramatic reconversion in the traditional mode. There are, of course, important differences in classical brainwashing and deprogramming, but there seems no question that coercive deprogramming is more like brainwashing than are the recruitment and resocialization techniques used in the new religions.

Ironically, the deprogrammers have adopted what they perceive to be the tactics of their opponents. One is reminded of the famous quote from the comic-strip character Pogo: "We have met the enemy and it is us." Those who engage in or support deprogramming should bear the responsibility of demonstrating that their "solution" is not worse than the alleged problem of membership in new religious groups. Given the weight of evidence, proving that point will be difficult indeed.

My Memory/Myself

Our earliest memories help shape us in many ways. But these memories are not always objective. In fact, sometimes we vividly "remember" things that never happened.

Anne Bernstein

Anne Bernstein, Ph.D., is a California-based family therapist and the author of "The Flight of the Stork" (Dell), a book about how to discuss sex and birth with children.

The first years of life are packed with the most fascinating and absorbing experiences. An infant's discoveries of the sights and sounds, tastes, smells, and textures of the world around him rival those of Columbus and Marco Polo in their strangeness and novelty. Yet for all their richness, these early experiences are virtually inaccessible in later life. It is hard for most adults to remember, or even imagine, the experience of the young child, but the memories children carry of these early years shape their lives in many ways.

In fact, Sigmund Freud tells us—and most psychological thinkers agree—that our earliest experiences leave "ineradicable traces in the depths of our minds." But as influential to our behavior as these traces are, we are not necessarily conscious of them.

The popular explanation of why we don't remember so much of our early childhood is that we reject unacceptable memories. Freud theorized that to avoid pain we automatically block out the unpleasant or traumatic aspects of our early lives and prevent them from becoming conscious. This concept is called *repression,* and it is the basis of the worrisome question, "If I don't remember, does that mean something terrible happened?" The comforting answer to that question is no. Credible alternative explanations for lapses in memory abound.

The process of remembering.

To understand why we remember or fail to remember early-childhood experiences, it is important to look at the way we store and retrieve memories. To begin with, what we pay attention to and what we think important at any particular age influence what we select to be remembered. Moreover, the way in which we search for hidden memories may determine what we find.

Attention is a key factor. We do a great many things without paying attention—breathing, crawling, and running, for instance, and even many activities we've had to learn consciously, such as skating, cleaning, and driving. We don't always realize, however, that what we do without paying attention may not be stored in memory. Consciousness does not occur without need, and we don't need to become conscious of an action if it succeeds. This is why many children and adults, when asked to crawl and then questioned about the movements they have made, cannot describe their own actions accurately. Things we do automatically are hard to remember.

On the other hand, a dramatic change in routine or an unusual occurrence is likely to make an impression on the memory of a child—but it is not always possible for an adult to predict exactly what a child will find dramatic or unusual. Breaking a doll may matter more to him than the outbreak of a war. Hitting a catsup bottle against a table to get it unstuck and having the catsup hit the ceiling, being carried under Mother's fur coat on a cold day, and getting lost in a supermarket for a few minutes are all events that may find their way into a child's memory.

Emotional arousal intensifies attention—which is one reason so many of our early memories are of fear, shame, physical pain, deaths, fires, and the births of siblings.

One example of how this works is provided by the detail with which most of us who are old enough can recall where we were and what we were doing the day that President Kennedy was assassinated.

Meaning is in the eye of the beholder. Although we may feel our memory is objective, in fact we all remember our own comprehension of events, not just simple perceptions of what happened. And what is meaningful to us is more likely to be remembered.

Even more than adults, children remember their interpretation, rather than the full range of sensory data that gave rise to it. Children's drawings depict what they know to be there, rather than what they see. For example, a face drawn in profile will still show two eyes and two ears. So even at the point of entry into memory, what is stored is a reconstruction of the world based on interpretation, not a copy of the world as seen by a camera.

My own earliest memory, as distinguished from anecdotes told to me by my parents, is of a long train trip taken at age two. I remember thinking how funny it was that my daddy had to sleep in a crib (the upper berth with its guardrail), while I, who shared the lower with my mommy, did not. A complete reversal of the world as I knew it, this seemed very important at the time.

After I told this to a friend, she remembered her own experience on a long train trip she took with her mother and sister, from Chicago, Illinois, to Birmingham, Alabama. It was the late forties, and in southern Illinois her family, being black, was required to change to a segregated car. As a three-year-old she did not comprehend the full meaning of racial discrimination, but the disruption and her mother's emotional response to it marked this event as meaningful and, therefore, potentially memorable.

Confusion about meaning is another way in which attention is heightened. Knowing one's understanding is incomplete is an irritant that keeps the mind working to know more. A twelve-year-old recalling his earliest memory tells of the puzzling discrepancy between what he thought was happening and his mother's reaction. She was expecting a visitor and very much wanted her two-year-old son to go to sleep. Yet each time she put him to bed, he would crawl out, put his head through the beaded curtain that hung in the doorway of his room, and grin at her. The twelve-year-old recalls this as a delightful game and also remembers his bewilderment at her angry lack of appreciation of the fun. The intensity of his mother's response, which she recalls as the angriest she had ever gotten at him, may have made this an occasion for heightened attention.

Mental development influences how memories are shaped. Researchers have widely observed that children younger than six or seven have trouble remembering events from their lives as complete stories. Memories that originate earlier than that are brief and fragmentary—images, feelings, or incidents, rather than narratives that develop from a beginning through a middle to an end.

In fact, the child's idea of himself as a separate person who has the same identity throughout his life span develops only gradually. Memory of personal experience depends on this growing understanding of identity and on the understanding that events that happened in his lifetime can be located with respect to other events to form a personal history.

How memories are retrieved.

Retrieving memories occurs in two ways. The first is involuntary. The smell of bread baking, the sensation of going down a slide, the sight of a red plaid skirt, call forth memories of other times and places where these smells, sensations, and sights have occurred. Spontaneous rather than purposive, these recollections are generally not triggered by words. Most of our earliest memories are retrieved in this way.

The alternative route to remembrance is voluntary, involving an organized search, and is dependent on language and rational connections. These more adult ways of thinking are not suitable receptacles for childhood experience. Although a young child's clearest memory of President Kennedy's assassination might be that it caused his mother to cry, an older child might attach special significance to the words "sniper" and "Dallas."

Our personal histories are reconstructed piecemeal from past events, built on the fragmentary [...] arise unbidden and supplemented by a delibe[...] So much is lost (and found) in the process tha[...] more accurate to talk about memories "relating [...] hood, rather than memories "from" childhood. [...] we remember is actually created at the moment of its revival; it does not emerge fully formed from the recesses of memory, even if it seems to.

Why we remember what we remember.

Motives for selecting the raw material for our autobiographical memories and weaving the strands into a narrative thread need not include historical accuracy. While memory may depict the past, it occurs in the present and serves its current employer's needs. Faithful to current interests, it reconstructs the past to fit the stories we tell ourselves about who we are and how we got that way. Facts that do not fit prevailing theory are discarded; those that support our present notions are embellished, embroidered, and set in relief.

One way that early memories are created is through the anecdotes parents tell their children about what they were like and what happened to them when they were little. Jean Piaget, noted Swiss psychologist of mental development, told of an incident from his own life that made him skeptical of childhood memories.

"I was still in a baby carriage, taken out by a nurse, and she took me down the Champs-Elysées . . . . I was the object of an attempted kidnapping. Someone tried to grab me out of the buggy. The straps held me in, and the nurse scuffled with the man, who scratched her forehead; something worse might have happened if a policeman hadn't come by just then. I can see him now as if it were yesterday . . . and the man fled. That's the story. As a child I had the glorious memory of having been the object of an attempted kidnapping. Then—I must have been about fifteen—my parents received a letter from the nurse, saying that she had just been converted and wanted to confess all her sins and that she had invented the kidnapping story herself, that she had scratched her own forehead, and that she now offered to return the watch she'd been given in recognition of her courage. In other words, there wasn't an iota of truth in the memory. And I have a very vivid memory of the experience, even today. I can tell you just where it happened on the Champs-Elysées, and I can still see the whole thing."

Family folklore, told or overheard, had been the basis for Piaget's reconstructing a memory that felt real. As Piaget's story shows, visual images are no guarantee of accuracy; the pictures in our memories can be created like the pictures in our dreams.

Hypnosis and memory.

Hypnosis is popularly given credit for recovering completely forgotten memories. What hypnosis does do, according to experimental psychologists Elizabeth and Geoffrey Loftus, is to encourage people to relax, cooperate, and concentrate. A good hypnotic relationship leads the subject to try to please the hypnotist; rather than being more *able* to remember, he may be merely more willing to remember. This is also the case with the free association employed by psychoanalytic psychotherapy. In informal ɔnversations, therapists have observed that Freudian patients tend to have Freudian dreams, while Jungian patients dream in images that support Jung's psychological theories. These memory-retrieval techniques lead people to relax their standards for certainty. The resulting wealth of remembrances need be no more accurate or complete than ordinary waking recall. Indeed, according to Geoffrey Loftus, several experiments have shown that people under hypnosis "confidently recall events not only from the past but from the future as well."

Knowing that substitutions in memory can occur helps us to understand how our memories are constantly being updated. Like Piaget, we may substitute what we have been told about events for our own experience. Parents' accounts of their children's early years form a large part of the memories later available to their offspring. Photographs strengthen the recall of the scenes they record; do we then remember the snapshot or the time itself? Any memory that includes "seeing" yourself as a child playing with other children or sitting on your father's lap—or in any tableau seen from the point of view of an observer outside the situation—is proof that the memory has been pieced together from scraps of reality but is not itself a record of that time gone by.

Targeting memories.

Another influence on early memory is that we are *taught* to remember, to target for later recall the events that people agree are memorable. Most families pull out the camera at birthdays, weddings, graduations, demonstrating to all concerned that this is "an affair to remember." Psychoanalyst Ernest Schachtel discusses how memory leans toward the conventional: more than ordinary thinking, memory can be dictated by social pressure because there is no immediate evidence of the senses to counterbalance the stereotypes. In other words, since our memories are based on experiences that are distant in time, we tend to organize them in conventional categories. According to Schachtel, "The memories of the majority of people increasingly come to resemble the stereotyped answers to a questionnaire, in which life consists of time and place of birth, religious denomination, residence, educational degrees, job, marriage, number and birthdates of children, income, sickness, and death."

However, not all the selection that goes into memory is dictated by social convention or other people. Memory, like other mental activity, tends to look for patterns and to cut the cloth of the past to piece together a costume that suits the characters we have become.

Reconstructing our own dramas.

For example, the daughter of an alcoholic father who frightened her with his rages and a mother who was the family mainstay may remember only good of her mother and ill of her father. Her images of her parents may have been oversimplified, but they helped her feel she could predict how each would behave, giving her some feeling of security in an often scary and chaotic home. Her initial impressions of each parent made her more alert to times when each ran true to form. Behavior that did not conform to her images of her parents failed to register; so in later life she may have no recall of her mother's self-righteous blaming and her father's helpless eagerness to please. She will explain her own fears, needs, and interests in terms of her father's alcoholism and her mother's courage, not relating her own eagerness to please to her father or her tendencies to be overcritical to her mother.

Who we are is a complex blend of intrinsic traits, experience—and an evolving self-concept. Our self-concept is based, among other factors, on what we choose to remember of our experience. Who I think I am influences how I see the world and what I do; in turn, what I do and how it is received determine what I think of myself. This dialogue between self-concept and experience is a lifelong process, continually—and selectively—building on what went before.

A feeling of being loved as a child is remembered "in one's bones" even without specific memories of cuddles and kisses. Having been appreciated encourages a child to approach other people with the expectation of being well received. His openness influences others to respond in kind. If early attempts to reach out for affection were rebuffed, however, one need not recall specific incidents when outstretched arms were met with ridicule or withdrawal to continue to feel discouraged about finding a welcoming embrace. Repeatedly called upon to stop the urge to reach out, the shoulder muscles may be permanently held back, so that extending the arms feels awkward and uncomfortable and evokes sadness. Wilhelm Reich called this accommodation of the body to early experience "character armor." Designed to protect the child from repeated frustrations, these "body memories" prevent the adult he will become from finding satisfactions that may have been unavailable earlier. Even with a child too young to remember, abuse and neglect leave their marks, as do love and protection.

As a therapist I am less interested in excavating the past for buried fragments than in helping the people I work with to rethink their life stories. This does not mean corseting memories to fit the arbitrary shapes of fashion but rather adding new dimensions of meaning. Knowing that memories are distorted and flattened versions of our early experience, we can attempt to round out the fragments of memory to recreate a complexity that is both more charitable and more realistic to who we are today. The child punished for making her parents anxious by her explorations can come to think of herself as a clever adventurer rather than a no-good troublemaker; the child who is pushed to be brave in the face of danger would benefit by relabeling fear as a useful signal of hazard rather than as damning evidence of cowardice.

As adults, we can help our children develop more benevolent memories. Without falsifying and without contradicting a child's feelings about his own experience, we can add a dose of generosity to a memory that might otherwise be a bitter medicine. In choosing to retell anecdotes about the child's early years that present him as lovable, smart, kind, and competent, rather than those that depict him as unworthy, stupid, mean, or clumsy, we are building a store of memories that will help him begin to piece together a past that will enrich his future.

MOOD & MEMORY

GORDON H. BOWER

Gordon H. Bower is chairman of the psychology department at Stanford University. An experimental psychologist, he specializes in human learning and memory, and was coauthor, with Ernest Hilgard, of the textbook *Theories of Learning* (Prentice-Hall), now in its fifth edition. Bower, a member of the National Academy of Sciences, describes his studies of the impact of emotion on learning as a recent sideline. This article is adapted from his Distinguished Scientific Contributions Award address given last year at a meeting of the American Psychological Association. The full address first appeared in the *American Psychologist*.

An American soldier in Vietnam blacked out as he stared at the remains of his Vietnamese girlfriend, killed by Vietcong mortar fire. Vowing revenge, he plunged into the jungle. Five days later an American patrol discovered him wandering aimlessly, dazed, disoriented. His memory of the preceding week was a total blank. He had no idea where he'd been or what he'd been doing for that period. Even after his return to the U.S., he could not recall the blackout period.

Several years later, a psychiatrist treating him for depression put him under hypnosis and encouraged him to reconstruct events from his combat days, both before and during the blackout. He calmly recalled earlier events, but when he neared the traumatic episode, he suddenly became very agitated, and more memories came pouring out. He began to relive the trauma of seeing his girlfriend's body and felt again the revulsion, outrage, and lust for revenge. Then, for the first time, he remembered what had happened after the mortar attack. He had commandeered a jeep, traveled alone for days deep into Vietcong territory, stalked Vietcong in the jungles, and set scores of booby traps with captured weapons before stumbling upon the American patrol. Curiously, after awakening from his hypnotic trance, the patient could remember only a few incidents singled out by the psychiatrist. But further treatments, described in the book *Trance and Treatment* by psychiatrists Herbert and David Spiegel, enabled him to bring more details into consciousness.

This case illustrates an extreme memory dissociation; the blackout events could be recalled in one state (of hypnotic agitation) but not in another (normal consciousness). Hypnosis helped the person return to the psychic state he was in when the blackout started; at that point, the emotional feelings returned, as did memories of the details of the blacked-out events. Psychoanalysts might call this a case of severe repression, which refers to the avoidance of anxiety-provoking memories. I believe such a label equates an observation with an explanation that may or may not be correct. Instead, I believe the soldier's case is an example of state-dependent memory, a more encompassing theory that refers to people's difficulty in recovering during one psychological state any memories acquired in a different state. State-dependency and repression are competing theories of forgetting. Each offers an explanation of why the soldier's blacked-out memories returned as he relived his trauma. But repression could not explain why a happy person can find happy memories easier to recover than sad ones.

The idea of studying the efficiency of memory during different psychological states—for example, while in hypnosis, under the influence of drugs, or after sensory deprivation—has been around for more than 50 years. However, previous investigations have been limited both in method and scope. While many clinical examples of state-dependency occur—for instance, violent "crimes of passion" are often blocked out but hypnotically recoverable by the assailant—such cases are really too rare, inconvenient, and complex for an adequate scientific analysis. In an earlier article in *Psychology Today* ("I Can't Remember What I Said Last Night, But It Must Have Been Good," August 1976), Roland Fischer described several examples and conjectured that memories are bound up with specific levels of physiological arousal. But my research shows that arousal level is not nearly as critical as the type of emotion felt—whether fear, depression, anger, or happiness. The most common laboratory method in previous studies of state-dependency used rats, learning with or without an injection of a drug like Amytal and later tested in either a drugged or nondrugged state.

From *Psychology Today*, June 1981. Originally published in *The American Psychologist*, Vol. 36, No. 2, February 1981. Reprinted by permission.

As an experimentalist, I was challenged to produce state-dependent memory in the laboratory, using normal people and trying to evoke commonly occurring emotions as "states." Two of my students, Steve Gilligan and Ken Monteiro, and I were especially interested in trying to produce such learning using different emotions, such as depression, joy, fear, and anger. This turned into a more ambitious project when we found evidence not only of state-dependent memory but also of related emotional influences on thinking, judging, and perceiving. First, I'll describe our work on state-dependent memory.

The technique we employed for inducing moods used our subjects' imaginations, guided by hypnotic suggestion. College students who were very hypnotizable volunteered for our study. After hypnotizing them, we asked them to get into a happy or sad mood by imagining or remembering a scene in which they had been delightfully happy or grievously sad. Often the happy scene was a moment of personal success or of close intimacy with someone; the sad scenes were often of personal failure or the loss of a loved one. We told them to adjust the intensity of their emotion until it was strong but not unbearable—it was important for them to function well enough to learn. After getting into a mood state, the subjects performed a learning experiment for 20 or 30 minutes, after which they were returned to a pleasantly relaxed state before debriefing. (These procedures are harmless and our subjects have willingly volunteered for further experiments.)

After some pilot work, we found that strong mood state-dependent memory could be produced by teaching people two sets of material (such as word lists)—one while happy, the other while sad—and then asking them to remember one set in a happy or a sad mood. In one study, groups of hypnotized subjects learned List A while happy or sad, then learned List B while happy or sad, and then recalled the List A while happy or sad. The lists were 16 words long; memory was always tested by free recall. The groups can be classified into three conditions. In the first, control subjects learned and recalled both lists in a single mood, happy for half of them and sad for the other half. In the second condition, the subjects learned List A in one mood, learned List B in a different mood, and recalled List A in their original mood; these subjects should have recalled more than the control subjects because their different learning moods helped them to isolate the two lists, thus reducing confusion and interference from List B when they tried to recall List A. The third, interference condition was just the reverse; those students tried to recall List A when they were in their second, List B mood. Their recall of List A should have suffered, because the recall mood evokes memories of the wrong List B rather than the target List A.

When we returned subjects to their original moods, we did so by having them call up scenes different from their original ones. For example, if a woman originally induced happiness by reliving a scene of herself scoring the winning goal in a soccer match, we would instruct her to return to the happy mood by imagining a different scene, such as riding a horse along the beach. We had subjects use a second imagined situation so that any memory advantage obtained for same-mood testing would be due to overlap of moods, not to overlap of imaginary scenes.

A person's retention score was calculated as the percentage of originally learned items that were recalled on the later test. The results are in the chart on page 64; there is an obvious state-dependent effect. People who were sad during recall remembered about 80 percent of the material they had learned when they were sad, compared with 45 percent recall of the material they had learned when they were happy. Conversely, happy recallers remembered 78 percent of their happy list, versus 46 percent of their sad list. The state-dependent memory effect shows up in the crossover of these lines on the chart. A good metaphor for this is to suppose that you have one bulletin board for happy moods and another for sad moods. On each board you post the messages you learn while in that mood. You will be able to read off your messages from the happy bulletin board best if you first get into a happy mood, and the messages on the sad bulletin board best when you get into a sad mood.

Aside from the state-dependent effect, I am often asked whether people learn better when they are happy or when they are sad. Others have found that clinically depressed patients are often poor learners. However, in all of our experiments with word lists, we nev-

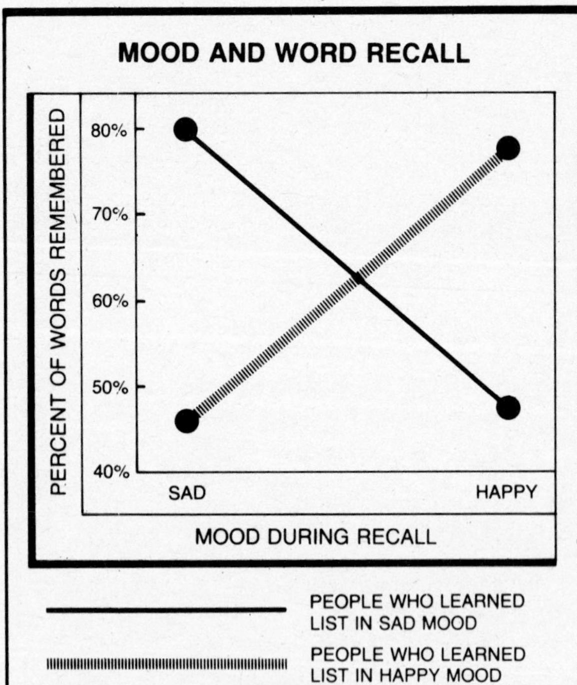

Results of an experiment in which groups of students learned a list of words while in one mood and later tried to recall as many as they could while in the same mood or a different mood. They were able to remember a much larger percentage when their learning mood matched their recall mood. This "state-dependency" effect is seen in the big difference between scores in the two recall situations, dramatized by the steep incline of the two lines connecting them. (The black dots show average percentages for both groups.)

er have found a difference in overall learning rate or later retention that was due to the subject's mood. I suspect this reflects our control over the hypnotic subjects' motivation to do as well as possible in the learning task despite their happy or sad feelings.

We next addressed the issue of whether state-dependency would occur for recall of actual events drawn from a person's emotional life. We enlisted some volunteers who agreed to record such emotional events in a daily diary for a week. We gave these subjects a booklet for recording emotional incidents and discussed what we meant by an emotional incident. Examples would be the joy they experienced at a friend's wedding or the anger they experienced in an argument at work. For each incident they were to record the time, place, participants, and gist of what happened and to rate the incident as pleasant or unpleasant on a 10-point intensity scale.

Conscientious diary-keeping is demanding, and we dropped nearly half of our subjects because they failed to record enough incidents in the proper manner consistently over the week. We collected usable diaries from 14 subjects and scheduled them to return a week later. At that one-week interval they were hypnotized; half were put into a pleasant mood and the other half into an unpleasant mood, and all were asked to recall every incident they could remember of those recorded in their diaries the week before.

The percentages of recall showed the expected results: people in a happy mood recalled a greater percentage of their recorded pleasant experiences than of their unpleasant experiences; people in a sad mood recalled a greater percentage of their unpleasant experiences than of their pleasant experiences.

Remember that when subjects originally recorded their experiences, they also rated the emotional intensity of each experience. These intensity ratings were somewhat predictive: recall of more intense experiences averaged 37 percent, and of less intense experiences 25 percent. The intensity effect is important, and I will return to it later.

After subjects had finished recalling, we asked them to rate the current emotional intensity of the incidents they recalled. We found that they simply shifted their rating scale toward their current mood: if they were feeling pleasant, the recalled incidents were judged as more pleasant (or less unpleasant); if they were feeling unpleasant, the incidents were judged more unpleasant (or less pleasant) than originally. That should be familiar—here are the rose-colored glasses of the optimist and the somber, gray outlook of the pessimist.

Is it possible that recording incidents in a diary and rating them as pleasant or unpleasant encourages subjects to label their experiences in this manner and in some way gives us the results we want? Perhaps. To avoid such contaminants, in our next experiment we simply asked people to recall childhood incidents. We induced a happy or sad mood in our subjects and asked them to write brief descriptions of many unrelated incidents of any kind from their pre-high school days. Subjects were asked to "hop around" through their memories for 10 minutes, describing an incident in just a sentence or two before moving on to some unrelated incident.

The next day, we had the subjects categorize their incidents as pleasant, unpleasant, or neutral while unhypnotized and in a normal mood (so that their mood would not influence how pleasant or unpleasant they rated an event). The few neutral incidents recalled were discarded, and the chart below shows the main results. Happy subjects retrieved many more pleasant than unpleasant memories (a 92 percent bias); sad subjects retrieved slightly more unpleasant than pleasant memories (a 55 percent bias in the reverse direction).

What the subjects reported was enormously dependent on their mood when recalling. That is state-dependent memory: the subjects presumably felt pleasant or unpleasant at the time the incidents were stored, and their current mood selectively retrieves the pleasant or the unpleasant memories.

What kind of theory can explain these mood-state dependent effects? A simple explanation can be cast within the old theory that memory depends upon associations between ideas. All we need to assume is that an emotion has the same effect as an "active idea unit" in the memory system. Each distinct emotion is presumed to have a distinct unit in memory that can be hooked up into the memory networks. The critical assumption is that an active emotion unit can enter into association with ideas we think about, or events that happened, at the time we are feeling that emotion. For instance, as the ideas recording the facts of a parent's funeral are stored in memory, a powerful association forms between these facts and the sadness one felt at the time.

Retrieval of some contents from memory depends upon activating other units or ideas that are associated with those contents. Thus, returning to the scene of a funeral, the associations activated by that place may cause one to reexperience the sadness felt earlier at the funeral. Conversely, if a person feels sad for some reason, activation of that emotion will bring into consciousness remembrances of associated ideas—most likely other sad events.

This theory easily explains state-dependent retrieval. In the first experiment, for example, the words of List A became associated both with the List A label and with the mood experienced at that time. Later, the words from List A can be retrieved best by reinstating the earlier List A mood, since that mood is a strongly associated cue for activating their memory. On the contrary, if a person had to recall List A while feeling in a different (List B) mood, that different mood would arouse associations that competed with recall of the correct items, thus reducing the memory scores. The same reasoning explains how one's current mood selectively retrieves personal episodes associated originally with pleasant or unpleasant emotions.

Beyond state-dependent memory, the network theory also helps to explain a number of influences of emotion on selective perception, learning, judgment, and thinking. When aroused, an emotion activates relevant concepts, thoughts, and frameworks for categorizing the social world. We have confirmed, for example, that people who are happy, sad, or angry produce free associations that are predominantly happy, sad, or angry, respectively. Similarly, when asked to fantasize or make up an imaginative story to pictures of the Thematic Apperception Test (TAT), they produce happy, sad, or hostile fantasies, depending on their emotional state. If asked for top-of-the-head opinions about their acquaintances, or the performance of their car or TV, they give highly flattering or negative evaluations, according to their mood. Also, their mood causes them to be optimistic or pessimistic in prognosticating future events about themselves and the nation. These influences can be seen as veiled forms of state-dependent retrieval of either the positive or negative memories about the person, event, or object.

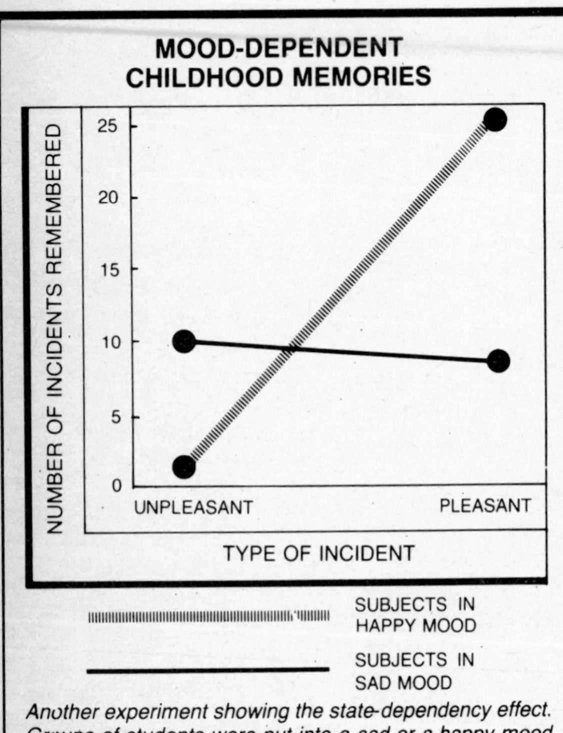

Another experiment showing the state-dependency effect. Groups of students were put into a sad or a happy mood and then asked to remember incidents from childhood. Later, they labeled the incidents as either pleasant or unpleasant. Happy subjects recalled far more pleasant than unpleasant incidents. Sad subjects retrieved slightly more unpleasant memories. (The black dots show averages for both groups.)

Mood affects the way we "see" other people. Social interactions are often ambiguous, and we have to read the intentions hidden behind people's words and actions. Is that person being steadfast in arguing his position or is he being pigheaded and obstructive? Was his action courageous or reckless? Was that remark assertive or aggressive? In reading others' intentions the emotional premise from which we begin strongly influences what we conclude. Thus the happy person seems ready to give a charitable, benevolent interpretation of social events, whereas the grouch seems determined to find fault, to take offense, or to take the uncharitable view. We find that these effects appear just as strongly when people are judging themselves on competence or attractiveness as well as when they're judging others. For example, when our subjects were in a depressed mood, they tended to judge their actions moment-by-moment in a videotaped interview as inept, unsociable, and awkward; but if they were in a happy mood, they judged their behaviors as confident, competent, and warmly sociable. Thus, social "reality" is constructed in the eye of the beholder, and that eye is connected to the emotions.

The network theory further predicts that an emotion should act as a selective filter in perception, letting in signals of a certain emotional wavelength and filtering out others. The emotional state adjusts the filter so that the person will attend more to stimulus material that agrees with or supports the current emotion. An analogy is that our feelings are like a magnet that selects iron filings from a heap of dust, attracting to itself whatever incoming material it can use.

Emotional effects can de demonstrated in attention and perception as well as learning. Thus, a sad person will look at pictures of sad faces more than happy faces; a happy person will dwell longer on happy faces. People who are happy from having just succeeded at an intelligence task have lower thresholds for seeing "success" words; subjects who've failed have lower thresholds for "failure" words.

The main work we've done on this salience effect concerns selective learning. In one of our experiments, subjects were made happy or sad by a posthypnotic suggestion as they read a brief story about two college men getting together and playing a friendly game of tennis. André is happy—everything is going well for him; Jack is sad—nothing is going well for him. The events of the two men's lives and their emotional reactions are vividly described in the story, which is a balanced, third-person account. When our subjects finished reading the story, we asked them to tell us who they thought the central character was and who they identified with. We found that readers who were happy identified with the happy character, thought the story was about him, and thought the story contained more statements about him; readers who were sad identified with the sad character and thought there were more statements about him.

Our subjects tried to recall the text the next day while in a neutral mood. Eighty percent of the facts remembered by the sad readers were about the sad character; 55 percent of the facts remembered by the happy readers were about the happy character. This is a mood-congruity effect; readers attend more to the character whose mood matches their own. Since all recallers were in a neutral mood, their differing recall results from their selective learning; it is not a state-dependent effect, since that requires varying subjects' mood during recall as well as during learning.

How is the mood-congruity effect explained? Why is mood-congruent material more salient and better learned? Two explanations seem worth considering.

The first hypothesis is that when one is sad, a sad incident in a story is more likely than a happy incident to remind one of a similar incident in one's life; vice versa, when one is happy. (Note that this is simply the state-dependent retrieval hypothesis.) An additional assumption is that the reminding is itself an event that enhances memory of the prompting event. This may occur because the old memory allows one to elaborate on the prompting event or to infuse it with greater emotion. In other studies, we have found that people remember descriptions of events that remind them of a specific incident in their lives far better than they recall descriptions that don't cause such reminiscence. To summarize, this hypothesis states that the mood-congruity effect is produced by selective reminding.

The second hypothesis, which complements the first, is that the mood-congruity effect comes from the influence of emotional intensity on memory. We demonstrated this idea in a study in which subjects were put in a sad or happy mood during hypnosis and then asked to read a story that went from a happy incident to a sad incident to a happy incident, and so on. Although our hypnotized subjects in several experiments tried to maintain steady moods, they reported that a mood's intensity would wane when they read material of the opposite quality. Thus happy subjects would come down from their euphoria when they read about a funeral or about unjust suffering; those topics intensified the sad subjects' feelings.

But why are intense emotional experiences better remembered? At present, there are many explanations. One is that events that evoke strong emotional reactions in real life are typically events involving personally significant goals, such as attaining life ambitions, elevating self-esteem, reducing suffering, receiving love and respect, or avoiding harm to oneself or loved ones. Because of their central importance, those goal-satisfying events are thought about frequently and become connected to other personal plans and to one's self-concept.

Intense experiences may also be remembered better because they tend to be rare. Because they are distinctive, they are not easily confused with more numerous, ordinary experiences; they tend to be insulated from interference.

The explanation of the mood-congruity effect that fits our lab results best is that mood-congruous experiences may be rehearsed more often and elaborated or thought about more deeply than experiences that do not match our mood. Thus sad people may be quickly able to embroider and elaborate upon a sad incident, whereas they don't elaborate on happy incidents. Because their sad incidents are elaborated and processed more deeply, sad people learn their sad incidents better than their happy ones. The same principle explains why happy people learn happy incidents better.

Having reviewed some evidence for mood-congruity and mood-dependency effects, let me speculate a bit about the possible implications for other psychological phenomena.

One obvious phenomenon explained by mood dependency is mood perpetuation—the tendency for a dominant emotion to persist. A person in a depressed mood will tend to recall only unpleasant events and to project a bleak interpretation onto the common events of life. Depressing memories and interpretations feed back to intensify and prolong the depressed mood, encouraging the vicious circle of depression. One class of therapies for depression aims at breaking the circle by restructuring the way depressed people evaluate personal events. Thus patients are taught to attend to and rehearse the positive, competent aspects of their lives and to change their negative evaluations.

State-dependent memory helps us to interpret several other puzzling phenomena. One is the impoverished quality of dream recall shown by most people. Most people forget their dreams, which is surprising considering that such bizarre, emotionally arousing events would be very memorable had they been witnessed in the waking state. But the sleep state (even the REM state of dreaming) seems psychologically distinct from the waking state, and dream memories may thus not be easily transferred from one state to the other.

State-dependent retention may also explain the fact that people have very few memories from the first year or two of their lives. In this view, as infants mature, their brains gradually change state, so that early memories become inaccessible in the more mature state. The problem with this hypothesis is that it leads to no novel predictions to distinguish it from the plethora of competing explanations of infantile amnesia, which generally range from Freud's repression theory to the theory that the infant's and adult's "languages of thought" mismatch so badly that adults can't "translate" records of infant memories.

State-dependent memory has been demonstrated previously with psychoactive drugs like marijuana, alcohol, amphetamines, and barbiturates. For example, after taking amphetamines, subjects remember material they have learned while high on the drug in the past better than when they are not high on it. Since such substances are also mood-altering drugs, a plausible hypothesis is that they achieve their state-dependent effect by virtue of their impact on mood.

To summarize, we have now found powerful influences of emotional states upon selective perception, learning, retrieval, judgments, thought, and imagination. The emotions studied have been quite strong, and their temporary psychological effects have been striking. What is surprising to me is that the emotional effects on thinking uncovered so far seem understandable in terms of relatively simple ideas—the notion that an aroused emotion can be viewed as an active unit in an associative memory and that it stimulates memories, thoughts, perceptual categories, and actions. Perhaps this is as it should be—that theories developed in one field (memory) aid our understanding of phenomena in another field (for example, emotional fantasies in the psychiatric clinic). Certainly that is the goal of all basic science.

Our Insatiable Brain

Joann Ellison Rodgers

Joann Ellison Rodgers, an award-winning health and science writer, is a frequent contributor to PRIME TIME.

ALMOST EVERYONE HAS a relative or two who can't recall having had breakfast an hour before or hasn't mastered a new idea or skill since turning forty. Others look with pride on their middle-aged and older family members who strut into their forties, fifties, and sixties in the tradition of Picasso, Pauling, former First Mother Lillian Carter, and the indomitable Charlie Chaplin, creating, matriculating, ever-learning, and clearly in charge of their minds and the monthly math puzzles in *Scientific American*.

Which is the norm? Does older mean wiser? Or is it all downhill after twenty? Can most of us realistically expect to hang on to our youthful mental powers as we enter our fifth or sixth or seventh decades? Or are the Picassos and Paulings oddities of nature?

In some cases, of course, brain structures do deteriorate over time. Blood vessels clog, swell, or burst. Cells die. Neurons misfire and neurochemicals pollute the fragile gray environment in our skulls. But what about brain *function*? Is there an intellectual, as well as physical peak that passes with, say, the thirtieth birthday? Does the ability to adapt, remember, process new information, and combine ideas in fresh forms inevitably dwindle?

Not too long ago, most neurologists, psychologists, and gerontologists would have quickly answered yes. But in the last few years their thinking has begun to change. Researchers, impelled by the specter of epidemic senility in a nation growing proportionately older each year, have challenged traditional views with tough new studies. The research is far from complete. Yet if what they are now reporting continues to be confirmed, this much is for sure: there's a lot of untapped middle-aged brain power out there and a lot less for all of us to be anxious about as we grow older.

One good way to get a handle on the matter is to look at learning abilities of people beyond middle age. It stands to reason that if sixty-, seventy-, and eighty-year-olds can take classes and learn new skills, if *they* can maintain their ability to learn as well as they did decades earlier, then their adult children certainly can.

If the adage "you can't teach an old dog new tricks" was not dead and buried before, notes Dr. David Arenberg of the National Institute on Aging (NIA) in Bethesda, Maryland, the research reported since 1960 "should complete the interment."

Dr. Arenberg and his co-workers *do* acknowledge differences between old and young learners. Younger animals, human and otherwise, do glide more easily through new tasks. What is novel is the discovery of factors that impair or improve learning performance in older persons that have nothing to do with basic intellectual ability.

For example, subtle and previously unrecognized declines in motor skills, vital to rapid processing of information, may sabotage a mature person's performance in IQ and memory tests. Mild arthritic pain may distract a fifty-year-old housewife just enough to wreck mental concentration. IQ and memory tests given to those over forty-five or fifty to evaluate intellectual capacity may also be biased, failing to take into account experience or habitual ways of organizing information.

In short, there's no reason to think adults will have special difficulties learning new skills. Says Dr. Arenberg, "It may take longer, more effort, and more motivation, but a persevering person should not have any special problems."

Dr. Arenberg is a principal member of the Geriatric Research Center's Baltimore Longitudinal Study, one of the best studies of human aging in the world in which subjects are repeatedly tested. "In our twenty-year studies of more than eight hundred men and women," he says, "we don't see substantial changes in memory or learning abilities until you get well into the seventies, and even then there are those who don't decline. Contrary to traditional views, intellectual and physical vigor can be retained well into old age to a startling degree."

"The essential message," says Dr. Robert Butler, the NIA director, "is that normal aging does not include gross intellectual impairment, confusion, depression, hallucinations, or delusions. We will shout, as loudly as

Reprinted from *Prime Time*, Winter 1981. Reprinted by permission.

we can, that fears of becoming 'senile' in old age are based largely on myths."

The reality is that the kind of memory and learning decline we associate with maturity is in fact a "social" disease. We impose on those over forty-five or fifty attitudes that force them to accept the mantle of increasing uselessness and social extinction. Acute depression is a natural result of that attitude.

"It's commonly known that severe depression can disturb what we call cognitive function, or the ability to think logically, to remember familiar things, to find our way around, and to solve problems," says Dr. Paul McHugh, chief of psychiatry at Johns Hopkins Hospital in Baltimore.

"Many patients, young and not so young, report loss of memory after recovery from a serious depression. Our experience at Hopkins is that some patients with senile dementia, an organic form of senility, are really suffering from an extreme form of depression that can be treated and reversed."

A "Mini-Mental State (M-MS)" test, devised by Dr. Marshall Folstein, director of a Hopkins psychology clinic, has been used to support Dr. McHugh's point.

Normal individuals average twenty-four to thirty points on the test of ability to calculate, recall, read, write, solve puzzles, and communicate. Those patients with senile dementia usually score below twenty.

But with electro-convulsive treatment and drugs widely used to treat severe depression, M-MS scores of senile dementia patients soar to normal and stay there in many cases. One seventy-eight-year-old demented woman with an M-MS score of nineteen, earned twenty-five points after only three electro-convulsive sessions. Again, the point is this: if those with demonstrated brain damage in their seventies and eighties can improve their ability to learn and think, which is what the M-MS test demonstrates, then surely taking college courses or embarking on a new career can't be far out of reach for those in their middle years.

Support for the view that learning problems have both social and environmental causes comes from research on both healthy humans and animals.

Some of the best work is being done by Dr. Richard Sprott, a behavioral scientist who works at the internationally acclaimed Jackson Laboratories for genetic research in Bar Harbor, Maine.

Dr. Sprott has spent a career searching for our mental and behavioral roots by looking at mammals that are somewhat easier to study than humans—mice. A mouse is not a human, of course, but both animals share enough basic biology and learning habits to give his research relevance.

For the past six years, Dr. Sprott has given thousands of mature and older mice the rodent equivalent of the good life—good diets, lots of exercise, friends, topnotch health care, fun, and, most of all, challenging occupations. These mice don't get bored or retire or stop meeting new challenges.

He has also given more thousands the same treatment Americans too often give their over-forty citizens: less responsibility at work, isolation from family and friends, boredom, and disrespect.

"No," says Dr. Sprott, "I don't really have a bunch of cute little rodents with bifocals sitting on park benches reading the newspaper after a fabulous day on Wall Street. But I do know a lot of very mature mice who have maintained their mental agility, their IQ, their learning ability, and their desire to learn because their society—my lab—has given them a chance to do that."

Dr. Sprott discovered early in his work that learning capacities are highly individual and have a genetic component—hardly news to any first-grade teacher.

But Dr. Sprott also discovered that the genetic effects on learning are *not* constant throughout the life of mice, but can be overwhelmed and dramatically altered by these environmental influences.

"Simply, biology tells us there's no way an eighty-year-old can drive a car as efficiently as a twenty-year-old. In the same way, an older mouse can't see or hear or jump as far or fast as a younger one.

"But our studies, which are careful to avoid taxing physical skills, have shown us that too often we have confused functional loss with mental loss. Over a long period, poor health may reduce performance, but not necessarily learning ability."

Between 1974 and 1979, Dr. Sprott conducted tests in a variety of environmental settings. Some mice got all the food they wanted but no exercise. Others were kept isolated. Some mice weren't given learning tests and others were tested daily, but periodically starved. The results showed that fully 90 percent of animals in one group and 80 percent in another learned as well in old age as when they were young. Those who had no exercise and got fat, or were isolated, had the shortest periods of stable maturity and learning ability in adulthood. And the daily testing of learning skills—"brain practice"—extended life.

"Lifestyle counts," Dr. Sprott concludes, "in mice and men." His studies prove that healthy adults who keep themselves mentally alert stay that way well into their fifties and sixties. The message is clear: get out there and learn if you wish to retain the ability to do so.

"Most of us have grown up with the idea that we lose 100,000 brain cells a year and that after adolescence it's all downhill, so why keep trying," says Dr. Sprott, who considers the notion a hoax. "The weight of evidence today is that most of the brain can continue to function in a stable, even way as we age. Brain cell loss does occur, but not enough to explain the memory and learning problems that plague us as we grow older. If what I'm seeing with my research holds true, there should be, for most of us, no loss in learning ability until shortly before death."

Mnemonics—mental tricks that help people organize and remember new information—can greatly increase learning ability in older adults. One study put subjects on a mental tour of sixteen places in their own homes, then had them learn a list of random words, associating each one with a trip stop. All subjects remembered more words with the use of mnemonics. The lesson: if schools taught people how to *organize* their thinking, instead of just how to memorize facts, people would have the tools they need throughout life to continue learning.

Today's tests of the impact of age on learning fail to take into account the changes in education. A twenty-year-old person today will no doubt get a better education than his predecessor did who is now seventy-five. Straight comparisons of the current mental abilities of old and young age groups (typical in learning-aging studies) are like measuring apples and oranges, not real deterioration of brain ability. Better tests would demonstrate the differences in their true perspective.

The brain is capable of recovering function after damage and there is now evidence that some brain cells regenerate. If the brain, says the NIA's Dr. Butler, can compensate for loss after a major stroke, it can certainly build new circuitry for learning if it's healthy.

The bottom line in all this seems to be that intelligence—learning ability—does not decline with age, although that statement does require a few qualifications. One of them is that IQ differs from generation to generation, or at least our definition of it does.

Says Detroit psychologist Gisela Labouvie-Vief, "Tomorrow's older people will enjoy greater health and vigor, and will be better educated than today's." Thus, decline in intelligence—if any—should be less than that of earlier generations.

The relationship between learning and aging needs more investigation: But with what is already known, it's a good bet that today's forty-, fifty-, and sixty-year-olds will have as much to learn in the future as they have to teach.

THE MIND OF THE PUZZLER

ROBERT J. STERNBERG AND JANET E. DAVIDSON

Robert J. Sternberg, associate professor of psychology at Yale, was cited last year by the American Psychological Association for his "major theoretical contributions to our understanding of human intelligence and mental abilities." He is the editor of *The Handbook of Human Intelligence*, to be published soon by Cambridge University Press.

Janet E. Davidson is a research associate in the Psychology Department at Yale. She specializes in intelligence and problem-solving.

Before departing from San Francisco on a flight to New York recently, a colleague of ours picked out some reading to test his wits. A professor of some accomplishment, he expected to make short work of the problems in *Games for the Superintelligent*, *More Games for the Superintelligent*, and *The Mensa Genius Quiz Book*. By the time he crossed the Rocky Mountains, however, he had realized that he was neither a genius nor, as *The Genius Quiz Book* puts it, "a secret superbrain who doesn't even know it." By the time he crossed the Mississippi River, he knew that he wasn't "superintelligent," either.

More often than not, the puzzles stumped him. How could two men play five games of checkers and each win the same number of games without any ties? He couldn't figure it out. How could you plant a total of 10 trees in five rows of four trees each? He drew several diagrams, and none of them worked. But he couldn't put the books down.

Our colleague wasn't alone in his frustration. Mental puzzles, whose appeal must be limited to the relatively intelligent, have nevertheless been a staple of the publishing industry for years. Martin Gardner's mathematical puzzles, from the monthly column he used to write for *Scientific American*, have been collected in 10 different books, with total sales of more than half a million copies. *Solve It*, *Games for the Superintelligent*, and *More Games for the Superintelligent*, all by James Fixx, have together sold nearly one million copies.

Puzzles can certainly be fun, and great ego boosters for those who eventually get the right answers. According to James Fixx, many people use mental puzzles to "strengthen their thought processes" and to "tune up their minds." Others use them to test or measure their own intelligence. In fact, *More Games* and *The Mensa Genius Quiz Book* actually contain what are supposed to be short IQ tests.

Many of the problems in these books require flashes of insight or "leaps of logic" on the part of the solver, rather than prior knowledge or laborious computation. We wondered just how people approach such puzzles—which are commonly called insight problems—and whether they provide a valid measure of a person's intelligence. To answer these questions, we examined the literature on problem-solving, and then conducted a mini-experiment to measure the relationship between performance on insight problems and scores on standard intelligence tests.

On the basis of our research, we identified three types of intellectual processes that, separately or together, seem to be required in solving most insight problems: the ability to select and "encode" information—that is, to understand what information is relevant to solving the problem, and how it is relevant; the ability to combine different and seemingly unrelated bits of useful information; and the ability to compare the problem under consideration with problems previously encountered. For example, in solving the problem of the checker players, faulty encoding would lead one to assume that the two men were playing each other. Correctly combining the facts that there were no ties and that each player won the same number of games should lead one to conclude that they couldn't be playing each other.

Similarly, to plant 10 trees in five rows of four trees each, one must get away from the idea of making the five rows parallel. People who are accustomed to thinking in geometric terms will usually imagine several other kinds of patterns, until they hit on the correct one:

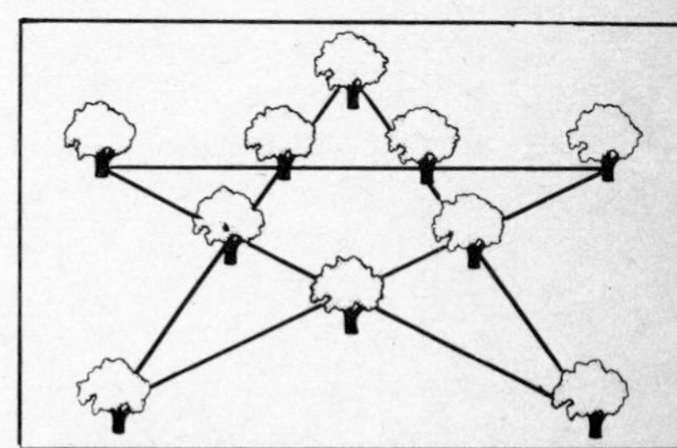

The literature on how people solve insight problems is meager, and includes almost no reports on research relating solution of these problems to intelligence. One of the few studies of this sort was done in 1965 by Norman Maier and Ronald Burke at the University of Michigan. Maier and Burke compared people's scores on a variety of aptitude tests with their skill at solving the "hat-rack problem." The problem calls on them to build a structure, sufficiently stable to support a man's overcoat, using only two long sticks and a C-clamp. The opening of the clamp is wide enough so that the two sticks can be inserted and held together securely when the clamp is tightened. Participants are placed in a small room and are asked to build a hat rack in the center of the room. The solution is shown below:

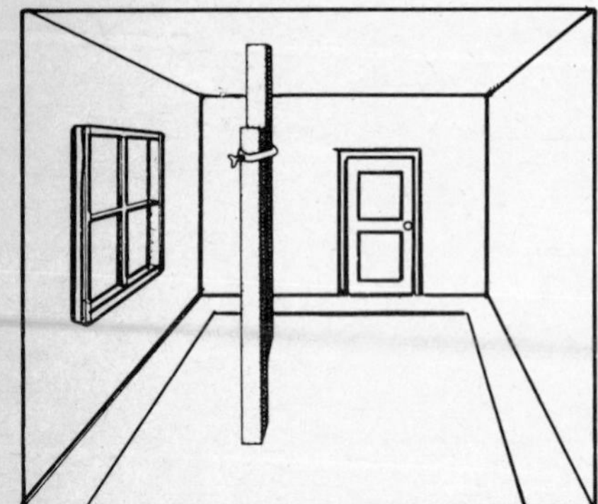

When the researchers compared people's ability to solve the hat-rack problem with their scores on the Scholastic Aptitude Test, the correlations were all trivial. In other words, whatever insight people needed to build the hat rack seemed to be unrelated to their scores on standardized intelligence tests. Burke and Maier concluded that the abilities needed to solve insight problems may be different from those required to solve problems of the kinds found on such tests. Their study is of limited value, however: They used only one problem, and scored the responses only in terms of "right" or "wrong."

We did find in the literature some theoretical basis for the lack of relationship between intelligence and performance on the hat-rack problem. Kjell Raaheim, a psychologist at the University of Bergen, in Norway, wrote in *Problem Solving and Intelligence* that "it is unreasonable to expect intelligence to be an important factor of success in solving tasks which are totally unfamiliar to the individual facing them." According to Raaheim, problems will best measure intelligence if they present a situation that is *intermediate* in its degree of familiarity to a problem-solver. Problems presenting situations that are either too familar or too unfamiliar will provide poorer measures of a person's intelligence.

In an ingenious set of experiments, Robert Weisberg and Joseph Alba, of Temple University, asked people to solve a set of insight problems. One was the familiar nine-dot problem, in which they were shown a three-by-three array of nine equally spaced dots and asked to connect the nine dots using four straight lines without lifting pencil from paper. The solution requires an approach similar to that used to plant the five rows of trees.

What is unique about Weisberg and Alba's study is that participants were actually given the insight they needed to solve the problem: They were told that it could be solved only by drawing the lines beyond the boundaries formed by the dots. Still, even after they were given the relevant insights, people in this study had considerable difficulty in solving the problem. Weisberg and Alba interpreted the results as suggesting that such problems may not really measure insight, but rather problem-specific prior knowledge. Our interpretation is a bit different. As we see it, subjects not only needed to know that they could draw the lines outside the boundaries; they also had to know how to combine what went outside the dots with what went inside. Performance on these insight problems therefore might not correlate with performance on intelligence-test problems.

Even though classic insight problems may not truly measure insight alone, we believed that problems could be found that do provide fairly accurate measures of insight, and that performance on such problems would be correlated with intelligence as it is typically measured by standardized tests.

To test this view, we compiled a set of 12 insight problems from a number of popular books. The problems vary in difficulty, in trickiness, and in the number of possible approaches that can be taken to reach a solution.

We recruited 30 people from the New Haven area by means of a newspaper advertisement that invited them to take part in a problem-solving experiment at Yale. Though not selected by scientific criteria, our small sample—19 men and 11 women—represented a fairly typical cross-section of urban residents, with a wide range of ages, occupations, and educational backgrounds. None were connected with Yale.

First, we gave them a standard IQ test (the Henmon-Nelson Test of Mental Ability), including questions of vocabulary, math, and reasoning. None of the problems were quite like our insight problems. A typical reasoning problem, for example, might require the person to solve an analogy such as: CAR is to GASOLINE as HUMAN is to (a. OIL b. ENERGY c. FOOD d. FUEL); or a number series such as: 3, 7, 12, 18, ___? (a. 24 b. 25 c. 26 d. 27). The IQ test problems were multiple-choice, whereas the insight problems we used required people to generate their own answers.

The average IQ score of our sample on this test was 112, 12 points above the national average. (Elevated average IQs are typical in such experiments, since those who volunteer for studies on problem-solving are likely to be of above-average intelligence. People with very low IQs may not read newspapers, and probably wouldn't volunteer for experiments on problem-solving even if they do.)

Second, we gave our subjects a deductive-reasoning test on nonsense syllogisms, such as "All trees are fish. All fish are horses. Therefore, all trees are horses. Please indicate whether the conclusion is logically valid or not." (This one is.) Third, in a test of inductive reasoning, we presented our subjects with five sets of letters (for example, NOPQ, DEFL, ABCD, HIJK, UVWX) and asked them to choose the set that was based on a rule different from the rule used as a basis for the other four sets.

We included these two specific tests, as well as the more general IQ test, to judge the accuracy of a prediction we had made: If our problems genuinely measured insight, they should be more highly correlated with the inductive test, which requires one to go beyond the information given, than with the deductive test, which merely requires one to analyze the given information and draw the proper conclusion. Normal arithmetic or logic problems, for example, require primarily deductive rather than inductive reasoning skills.

Our subjects found the insight problems fun but sometimes frustrating, since the items varied considerably in difficulty. The easiest item, answered correctly by 73 percent of our sample, was this:

"Next week I am going to have

lunch with my friend, visit the new art gallery, go to the Social Security office, and have my teeth checked at the dentist's. My friend cannot meet me on Wednesday; the Social Security office is closed weekends; the art gallery is closed Tuesday, Thursday, and weekends; and the dentist has office hours only on Tuesday, Friday, and Saturday. What day can I do everything I have planned?" Reaching the answer (Friday) is easy because one can simply check off which days don't work.

The hardest item, answered correctly by only 7 percent of our subjects, was:

"A bottle of wine cost $10. The wine was worth $9 more than the bottle. How much was the bottle worth?" People probably had a hard time coming up with the answer (50 cents) because they misunderstood the word 'more.'

The average score on our insight problem test was 4.4 correct out of 12, or roughly 37 percent. The individual scores ranged from a low of one to a high of 10, with no difference between the average scores of the men and the women. The times people spent solving the problems ranged from 11 minutes to 47 minutes, with an average of 28 minutes.

When we examined the relationship between scores on the set of 12 insight problems and scores on the mental-ability tests, we found relatively high correlations between the insight-problem scores and the scores on the tests of IQ (.66 on a scale from zero to one, on which a correlation of zero means no relationship, and a correlation of one means a perfect relationship) and inductive reasoning (.63), and only a moderate correlation with the scores on the test of deductive reasoning (.34). (All of the correlations were statistically significant.) These correlations suggest that performance on insight problems does provide a good index of intelligence, and that such performance may be more closely related to inductive than to deductive reasoning.

We then looked at the relationship between the test scores and time spent on the insight problems, and found that people who spent the most time working on the problems tended to have a higher number of correct solutions, and higher IQ scores. (The correlation between time spent and number of insight problems correctly solved was .62. The correlation between time spent and IQ was .75, which is remarkably high.) Why did smart people take longer on this task? Although we can only speculate, we suspect it is because they became more absorbed in the problems and more motivated to solve them. Our observations suggested that the less bright people either were too quick to choose the seemingly obvious but wrong answers on trick questions, or simply didn't know how to get started on the tougher problems and gave up more quickly.

When we looked at the correlations between the test scores on the insight problems and the scores on the standardized intelligence test, we found that the problems varied considerably in their validity as indicators of IQ. The problem of which day to schedule a lunch date with a friend had almost no correlation with IQ; the problem that proved to be the best predictor of IQ score was the following:

"Water lilies double in area every 24 hours. At the beginning of the summer there is one water lily on a lake. It takes 60 days for the lake to become covered with water lilies. On what day is the lake half covered?" To find the answer, people must realize that since the water lilies double in area every 24 hours, the lake will be half covered on the 59th day in order to be completely covered on the 60th.

What made some items better measures of IQ than others? We discovered two patterns among the "good" and "bad" indicators of IQ that we thought were striking, at least as preliminary hypotheses.

The best indicators of IQ seemed to be those problems that presented both relevant and irrelevant information: The key to success was the ability to distinguish necessary information from unnecessary. For example, people with high IQs tended to realize that "water lilies double in area every 24 hours" was an important clue to solving this problem. People with low IQs frequently ignored this information and tried to solve the problem by dividing the 60 days by two.

Our interpretation of performance on the problems supports the theory that the ability to detect and use clues embedded in the context of what one reads plays an important role in solving verbal problems. When reading a text—whether it is a newspaper, a science book, or a verbal or arithmetic problem—much of the information may be irrelevant to one's needs; often the hard part is figuring out what is relevant, and how it is relevant.

The problems that proved to be poor indicators of IQ were the "trick" problems in which errors were due primarily to misreading the problem situation—fixing on the apparent question rather than on the actual question. Take the following problem: "A farmer has 17 sheep. All but nine break through a hole in the fence and wander away. How many are left?" People making errors generally failed to comprehend exactly what "all but nine" meant; many assumed that the nine had escaped and thus subtracted that number from 17 to get the number of sheep that remained behind.

If, as we have shown, insight problems do provide a good measure of intellectual ability—at least when they require one to make inductive leaps beyond the given data and when they require one to sift out relevant from irrelevant information—we must ask: Just what is insight? The reason that others have not found any common element in the various insights they have studied is that no one model works for all cases. We have identified three basic kinds of cognitive processes or insightful performance, one or more of which may be required to solve a given problem:

Selective Encoding, or processing of information. This kind of insight occurs when one perceives in a problem one or more facts that are not immediately obvious. Earlier, we referred to the importance of being able to sort out relevant from irrelevant information. This skill can provide the solver with a basis for selective encoding.

Consider the following problem: "If you have black socks and brown socks in your drawer, mixed in the ratio of 4 to 5, how many socks will you have to take out to make sure of having a pair the same color?" Subjects who failed to realize that "mixed in the ratio of 4 to 5" was irrelevant information consistently came up with the wrong solution. (The correct answer: three.) In the hat-rack problem, noticing the relevance of the floor and ceiling as elements in the problem is also an example of selective encoding.

Selective Combination. This type of insight takes place when one sees a way of combining unrelated (or at least not obviously related) elements, as one must do in the following problem: "With a seven-minute hourglass and an 11-minute hourglass, what is the simplest way to time the boiling of an egg for 15 minutes?" Our subjects had all of the necessary facts, but they had to figure out how to combine the two timers to measure 15 minutes. In the hat-rack problem, figuring out how to combine the use of the floor, ceiling, C-clamp, and two sticks constitutes a similar insight of selective combination.

Selective Comparison. This kind of insight occurs when one discovers a nonobvious relationship between new and old information. It is here that analogy, metaphor, and models come into play. In the hat-rack problem, for example, one might think of how a pole lamp can be stabilized by wedging it between the floor and ceiling of a room, and how the same principle could be used in the construction of a hat rack.

Consider another type of selective comparison: If someone doesn't know a word on a vocabulary test, he can often figure out its definition by thinking of words he does know that have the same word stems. For example, if he doesn't know the word 'exsect,' he might be able to guess its meaning by thinking of a word that has the same prefix (such as 'extract,' where *ex* means out) and a word that has the same root (such as 'dissect,' where *sect* means cut). This information might help him realize that 'exsect' means 'to cut out.'

We emphasize the critical role of selection in each kind of information-processing. In Selective Encoding, one must choose elements to encode from the often numerous and irrelevant bits of information presented by the problem; the trick is to select the right elements. In Selective Combination, there may be many possible ways for the encoded elements to be combined or otherwise integrated; the trick is to select the right way of combining them. In Selective Comparison, new information must be related to one or more of many possible old pieces of information. There are any number of analogies or relations that might be drawn; the trick is to make the right comparison or comparisons. Thus, to the extent that there is a communality in the three kinds of insight, it appears to be in the importance of selection to each kind.

We believe that much of the confusion in the past and present literature on problem-solving stems from a failure to recognize the existence of and differences among these three kinds of insight, which together seem to account for the mental processes that have been labeled as insight, and which are involved in everything from solving problems in puzzle books to making major scientific breakthroughs.

Although we have focused on the importance of insight in problem-solving—and also in intelligence—insight alone is not enough to solve problems. Certain other essential ingredients exist, including:

Prior Knowledge. Even apparently simple problems often require a store of prior knowledge for their solution; complex problems can require a vast store of such knowledge. Consider the problem of the seven-minute and 11-minute hourglasses, and how to time a 15-minute egg. If people have used hourglass timers before, and can remember that they can turn them over at any point, the knowledge will certainly help.

Executive Processes. These are the processes used to plan, monitor, and evaluate one's performance in problem-solving. To start with, one must first study the problem carefully, in order to figure out exactly what question is being asked.

Another executive process involves monitoring one's solution process (keeping track of what one has done, is doing, and still needs to do) and then switching strategies if one isn't making progress. Sometimes it helps to try a new approach if an old one doesn't work.

Motivation. Really challenging problems often require a great deal of motivation on the part of the solver. Successful problem-solvers are often those who simply are willing to put in the necessary effort. Indeed, in our mini-study we found that the better problem-solvers were more persevering than the poorer ones.

Style. People approach problems with different cognitive styles. In particular, some tend to be more impulsive and others more reflective. It seems to us—although we have no hard experimental evidence to support our view—that the most successful problem-solvers are those who manage to combine both impulsive and reflective styles. We do not believe that most people follow just one style or the other. Rather, at certain points in the problem-solving process, people act on impulse; at other times, they act only after great reflection. The hard part is knowing which style will pay off at which point in solving problems.

Successful problem-solving involves a number of different abilities. For many problems, one kind of insight may provide a key to a quick solution. But we believe that most problems are like the apartment doors one finds in some of our larger cities: They have multiple locks requiring multiple keys. Without combining different kinds of insights, as well as prior knowledge, executive processes, motivation, and style, the problems remain locked doors, waiting for the clever solver to find the right set of keys.

LEARNING THE MOTHER TONGUE

Acquiring language appears to be either inexplicable or miraculous, but close observation indicates that baby and mother work together and the role of the mother is crucial.

JEROME S. BRUNER

Jerome S. Bruner *is Watts Professor of Psychology at Oxford University and an advisory editor to* Human Nature. *He is also chairman of the Scientific Advisory Committee at the Max Planck Institute of Psycholinguistics in Nijmegen, Holland. Bruner, whose Ph.D. in psychology is from Harvard University, taught at Harvard from 1945 until 1971.*

While he was there, he helped found the Center for Cognitive Studies and was its director until he resigned to go to Oxford. Among his books are The Relevance of Education, Beyond the Information Given, The Process of Education, *and* On Knowing: Essays for the Left Hand. *With Michael Cole and Barbara Lloyd, he is editing* The Developing Child, *a series of books published by Harvard University Press that present research in child development to a general audience.*

Learning a native language is an accomplishment within the grasp of any toddler, yet discovering how children do it has eluded generations of philosophers. St. Augustine believed it was simple. Recollecting his own childhood, he said, "When they named any thing, and as they spoke turned towards it, I saw and remembered that they called what they would point out by the name they uttered. . . . And thus by constantly hearing words, as they occurred in various sentences, I collected gradually for what they stood; and having broken in my mouth to these signs, I thereby gave utterance to my will." But a look at children as they actually acquire language shows that St. Augustine was wrong and that other attempts to explain the feat err as badly in the opposite direction. What is more, as we try to understand how children learn their own language, we get an inkling of why it is so difficult for adults to learn a second language.

Thirty years ago, psychologies of learning held sway; language acquisition was explained using principles and methods that had little to do with language. Most started with nonsense syllables or random materials that were as far as researchers could get from the structure of language that permits the generation of rich and limitless statements, speculations, and poetry. Like G. K. Chesterton's drunk, they looked for the lost coin where the light was. And in the light of early learning theories, children appeared to acquire language by associating words with agents and objects and actions, by imitating their elders, and by a mysterious force called reinforcement. It was the old and tired Augustinian story dressed up in the language of behaviorism.

Learning theory led to a readiness, even a recklessness, to be rid of an inadequate account, one that could explain the growth of vocabulary but not how a four-year-old abstracts basic language rules and effortlessly combines old words to make an infinite string of new sentences. The stage was set for linguist Noam Chomsky's theory of LAD, the Language Acquisition Device, and for the Chomskyan revolution.

According to this view, language was not learned; it was recognized by virtue of an innate recognition routine through which children, when exposed to their local language, could abstract or extract its universal grammatical principles. Whatever the input of that local language, however degenerate, the output of LAD was the grammar of the language, a competence to generate all possible grammatical sentences and none (or very few) that were not. It was an extreme view, so extreme that it did not even consider meaning. In a stroke it freed a generation of psycholinguists from the dogma of association, imitation, and reinforcement and turned their attention to the problem of rule learning. By declaring learning theory dead, it opened the way for a new account. George Miller of The Rockefeller University put it well: We had two theories of language learning—one of them, empiricist associationism, is impossible; the other, nativism, is miraculous. The void between the impossible and the miraculous remained to be filled.

Both explanations begin too late—when children say their first words. Long before children acquire language, they know something about their world. Before they can make verbal distinctions in speech, they have sorted the conceptual universe into useful categories and classes and can make distinctions about actions and agents and objects. As Roger Brown of Harvard University has written, "The concept . . . is there beforehand, waiting for the word to come along that names it." But the mystery of how children penetrate the communication system and learn to represent in language what they already know about the real world has not been solved. Although there is a well-packaged semantic content waiting, what children learn about language is not the same as what they know about the world. Yet the void begins to fill as soon as we recognize that children are not flying blind, that semantically speaking they have some target toward which language-learning efforts are directed: saying something or understanding something about events in a world that is already known.

If a child is in fact communicating, he has some end in mind—requesting something or indicating something or establishing some sort of personal relationship. The function of a communication has to be considered. As philosopher John Austin argued, an utterance cannot be analyzed out of its context of use, and its use must include the intention of the speaker and its interpretation in the light of conventional standards by the person addressed. A speaker may make a request in several ways: by using the conventional question form, by making a declarative statement, or by issuing a command.

Roger Brown observed young Adam from age two until he was four and found that his middle-class mother made requests using a question form: "Why don't you play with your ball now?" Once Adam came to appreciate what I shall call genuine *why* questions (i.e., "Why are you playing with your ball?"), he typically answered these—and these only—with the well-known "Because." There is no instance, either before or after he began to comprehend the genuine causal question, of his ever confusing a sham and a real *why* question.

Not only does conceptual knowledge precede true language, but so too does function. Children know, albeit in limited form, what they are trying to accomplish by communicating before they begin to use language to implement their efforts. Their initial gestures and vocalizations become increasingly stylized and conventional.

It has become plain in the last several years that Chomsky's original bold claim that any sample of language encountered by an infant was enough for the LAD to dig down to the grammatical rules simply is false. Language is not encountered willy-nilly by the child; it is instead encountered in a highly orderly interaction with the mother, who takes a crucial role in arranging the linguistic encounters of the child. What has emerged is a theory of mother-infant interaction in language acquisition—called the fine-tuning theory—that sees language mastery as involving the mother as much as it does the child. According to this theory, if the LAD exists, it hovers somewhere in the air between mother and child.

So today we have a new perspective that begins to grant a place to knowledge of the world, to knowledge of the function of communication, and to the hearer's interpretation of the speaker's intent. The new picture of language learning recognizes that the process depends on highly constrained and one-sided transactions between the child and the adult teacher. Language acquisition requires joint problem solving by mother and infant, and her response to her child's language is close tuned in a way that can be specified.

The child's entry into language is an entry into dialogue, and the dialogue is at first necessarily nonverbal and requires both members of the pair to interpret the communication and its intent. Their relationship is in the form of roles, and each "speech" is determined by a move of either partner. Initial control of the dialogue depends on the mother's interpretation, which is guided by a continually updated understanding of her child's competence.

Consider an infant learning to label objects. Anat Ninio and I observed Richard in his home every two weeks from his eighth month until he was two years old, video-taping his actions so that we could study them later. In this instance he and his mother are "reading" the pictures in a book. Before this kind of learning begins, certain things already have been established. Richard has learned about pointing as a pure indicating act, marking unusual or unexpected objects rather than things wanted immediately. He has also learned to understand that sounds refer in some singular way to objects or events. Richard and his mother, moreover, have long since established well-regulated turn-taking routines, which probably were developing as early as his third or fourth month. And finally, Richard has learned that books are to be looked at, not eaten or torn; that objects depicted are to be responded to in a particular way and with sounds in a pattern of dialogue.

For the mother's part, she (like all mothers we have observed) drastically limits her speech and maintains a steady regularity. In her dialogues with Richard she uses four types of speech in a strikingly fixed order. First, to get his attention, she says "Look." Second, with a distinctly rising inflection, she asks "What's that?" Third, she gives the picture a label, "It's an X." And finally, in response to his actions, she says "That's right."

In each case, a single verbal token accounts for from nearly half to more than 90 percent of the instances. The way Richard's mother uses the four speech constituents is closely linked to what her son says or does. When she varies her response, it is with good reason. If Richard responds, his mother replies, and if he initiates a cycle by pointing and vocalizing, then she responds even more often.

Her fine tuning is fine indeed. For example, if after her query Richard labels the picture, she will virtually always skip the label and jump to the response, "Yes." Like the other mothers we have studied, she is following ordinary polite rules for adult dialogue.

As Roger Brown has described the baby talk of adults, it appears to be an imitative version of how babies talk. Brown says, "Babies already talk like babies, so what is the earthly use of parents doing the same? Surely it is a parent's job to teach the adult language." He resolves the dilemma by noting, "What I think adults are chiefly trying to do, when they use [baby talk] with children, is to communicate, to understand and to be understood, to keep two minds focussed on the same topic." Although I agree with Brown, I would like to point out that the content and intonation of the talk is baby talk, but the dialogue pattern is adult.

To ensure that two minds are indeed focused on a common topic, the mother develops a technique for showing her baby what feature a label refers to by making 90 percent of her labels refer to whole objects. Since half of the remainder of her speech is made up of proper names that also stand for the whole, she seems to create few difficulties, supposing that the child also responds to whole objects and not to their features.

The mother's (often quite unconscious) approach is exquisitely tuned. When the child responds to her "Look!" by looking, she follows immediately with a query. When the child responds to the query with a gesture or a smile, she supplies a label. But as soon as the child shows the ability to vocalize in a way that might indicate a label, she raises the ante.

She withholds the label and repeats the query until the child vocalizes, then she gives the label.

Later, when the child has learned to respond with shorter vocalizations that correspond to words, she no longer accepts an indifferent vocalization. When the child begins producing a recognizable, constant label for an object, she holds out for it. Finally, the child produces appropriate words at the appropriate place in the dialogue. Even then the mother remains tuned to the developing pattern, helping her child recognize labels and make them increasingly accurate. For example, she develops two ways of asking "What's that?" One, with a falling intonation, inquires about those words for which she believes her child already knows the label; the other, with a rising intonation, marks words that are new.

Even in the simple labeling game, mother and child are well into making the distinction between the given and the new. It is of more than passing interest that the old or established labels are the ones around which the mother will shortly be elaborating comments and questions for new information:

Mother (with falling intonation): What's that?

Child: Fishy.

Mother: Yes, and see him swimming?

After the mother assumes her child has acquired a particular label, she generally drops the attention-getting "Look!" when they turn to the routine. In these petty particulars of language, the mother gives useful cues about the structure of their native tongue. She provides cues based not simply on her knowledge of the language but also on her continually changing knowledge of the child's ability to grasp particular distinctions, forms, or rules. The child is sensitized to certain constraints in the structure of their dialogue and does not seem to be directly imitating her. I say this because there is not much difference in the likelihood of a child's repeating a label after hearing it, whether the mother has imitated the child's label, simply said "Yes," or only laughed approvingly. In each case the child repeats the label about half the time, about the same rate as with *no* reply from the mother. Moreover, the child is eight times more likely to produce a label in response to "What's that?" than to the mother's uttering the label.

I do not mean to claim that children cannot or do not use imitation in acquiring language. Language must be partly based on imitation, but though the child may be imitating another, language learning involves solving problems by communicating in a dialogue. The child seems to be trying to get through to the mother just as hard as she is trying to reach her child.

Dialogue occurs in a context. When children first learn to communicate, it is always in highly concrete situations, as when mother or child calls attention to an object, asking for the aid or participation of the other. Formally conceived, the format of communication involves an intention, a set of procedures, and a goal. It presupposes shared knowledge of the world and a shared script by which mother and child can carry out reciprocal activity in that world. Formats obviously have utility for the child. They provide a simple, predictable bit of the world in which and about which to communicate. But they also have an important function for the mother in the mutual task of speech acquisition.

When a mother uses baby talk, her intonation broadens, her speech slows, and her grammar becomes less complex. In addition, baby talk virtually always starts with the here and now, with the format in which the two are operating. It permits the mother to tune her talk to the child's capabilities. She need not infer the child's general competence for language, but instead judges the child's performance on a specific task at a specific time.

A second major function of speech is requesting something of another person. Carolyn Roy and I have been studying its development during the first two years of life. Requesting requires an indication that you want *something* and *what* it is you want. In the earliest procedures used by children it is difficult to separate the two. First the child vocalizes with a characteristic intonation pattern while reaching eagerly for the desired nearby object—which is most often held by the mother. As in virtually all early exchanges, it is the mother's task to interpret, and she works at it in a surprisingly subtle way. During our analyses of Richard when he was from 10 to 24 months old and Jonathan when he was 11 to 18 months old, we noticed that their mothers frequently seemed to be teasing them or withholding obviously desired objects. Closer inspection indicated that it was not teasing at all. They were trying to establish whether the infants really wanted what they were reaching for, urging them to make their intentions clearer.

When the two children requested nearby objects, the mothers were more likely to ask "Do you really want it?" than "Do you want the X?" The mother's first step is pragmatic, to establish the sincerity of the child's request.

Children make three types of requests, reflecting increasing sophistication in matters that have nothing to do with language. The first kind that emerges is directed at obtaining nearby, visible objects; this later expands to include distant or absent objects where the contextual understanding of words like "you, me," "this, that," and "here, there" is crucial. The second kind of request is directed at obtaining support for an action that is already in progress, and the third kind is used to persuade the mother to share some activity or experience.

When children first begin to request objects, they typically direct their attention and their reach, opening and closing their fists, accompanied by a characteristic intonation pattern. As this request expands, between 10 and 15 months, an observer immediately notes two changes. In reaching for distant objects, a child no longer looks solely at the desired object, but shifts his glance back and forth between the object and his mother. His call pattern also changes. It becomes more prolonged, or its rise and fall is repeated, and it is more insistent. Almost all of Richard's and Jonathan's requests for absent objects were for food, drink, or a book to be read, each having its habitual place. Each request involved the child's gesturing toward the place.

When consistent word forms appeared, they were initially idiosyncratic labels for objects, gradually becoming standard nouns that indicated the desired objects. The children also began initiating and ending their requests with smiles. The development of this pattern is paced by the child's knowledge, which is shared with the mother, of where things are located and of her willingness to fetch them if properly asked. Once the child begins requesting distant and absent objects, the mother has an opportunity to require that the desired object be specified. Sincerity ceases to be at issue, though two other conditions are imposed: control of agency (who is actually to obtain the requested object, with emphasis on the child's increasing independence) and control of "share" (whether the child has had enough).

Requests for joint activity contrast with object requests. I think they can be called precursors to invitation. They amount to the child asking the adult to share in an activity or an experience—to look out of the window into the garden together, to play Ride-a-cockhorse, to read together. They are the most playlike form of request, and in consequence they generate a considerable amount of language of considerable complexity. It is in this format that the issues of agency and share (or turn) emerge and produce important linguistic changes.

Joint activity requires what I call joint role enactment, and it takes three forms: one in which the adult is agent and the child recipient or experiencer (as in early book reading); another in which there is turn taking with the possibility of exchanging roles (as in peekaboo); and a third in which roles run parallel (as in looking around the garden together). Most of what falls into these categories is quite ritualized and predictable. There tend to be rounds and turns, and no specific outcome is required. The activity itself is rewarding. In this setting the child first deals with share and turn by adopting such forms of linguistic marking as *more* and *again*. These appear during joint role enactment and migrate rapidly into formats involving requests for distant objects.

It is also in joint role enactment that the baby's first consistent words appear and, beginning at 18 months, word combinations begin to explode. *More X* (with a noun) appears, and also combinations like *down slide, brrm brrm boo knee, Mummy ride*, and *Mummy read*. Indeed it is in these settings that full-blown ingratiatives appear in appropriate positions, such as prefacing a request with *nice Mummy*.

Mothers' questions when children request nearby objects

Type of question	Age in months 10-12	13-14	More than 15
About intention ("Do you want it?")	93%	90%	42%
About referent ("Do you want the x?")	7%	10%	58%
Number of questions	**27**	**29**	**12**

Forms of early requests

Request for:	Age in months 10-12	13-14	15-16	17-18	20-24
Near and visible object	100%	74%	43%	22%	11%
Distant or invisible object	0	16%	24%	8%	24%
Shared activity	0	10%	14%	23%	36%
Supportive action	0	0	19%	47%	29%
Minutes of recording	**150**	**120**	**120**	**120**	**150**
Number of requests/10 minutes	**1.5**	**1.6**	**1.8**	**4.3**	**2.3**

Adult responses to children's requests

Type of response	Age in months 10-12	13-14	15-16	17-18	20-24
Pronominal question					
Open question (who, what, which)	78%	55%	36%	8%	1%
Closed question (yes, no)	3%	10%	18%	30%	22%
Comment/Question (yes, no)	6%	27%	36%	25%	36%
Comment/Question on agency	8%	2%	0	20%	28%
"Language lesson"	6%	6%	9%	14%	4%
Request for reason	0	0	0	3%	5%
Other	0	0	1%	0	4%
Number of utterances	**36**	**51**	**22**	**116**	**100**

As children's requests change with increasing sophistication (center), their mothers switch from establishing the sincerity of a request to identifying the object wanted (top). The sharp increase in replies having to do with who will get or control an action ("agency") reflects a demand for sharing and a difference in wishes (bottom).

Characteristically, less than 5 percent of the mother's responses to a child's requests before he is 17 months old have to do with agency (or who is going to do, get, or control something). After 17 months, that figure rises to over 25 percent. At that juncture the mothers we studied began to demand that their children adhere more strictly to turn taking and role respecting. The demand can be made most easily when they are doing something together, for that is where the conditions for sharing are most clearly defined and least likely, since playful, to overstrain the child's capacity to wait for a turn. But the sharp increase in agency as a topic in their dialogue reflects as well the emergence of a difference in their wishes.

The mother may want the child to execute the act requested of her, and the child may have views contrary to his mother's about agency. In some instances this leads to little battles of will. In addition, the child's requests for support more often lead to negotiation between the pair than is the case when the clarity of the roles in their joint activity makes acceptance and refusal easier. A recurrent trend in development during the child's first year is the shifting of agency in all manner of exchanges from mother to infant. Even at nine to 12 months, Richard gradually began taking the lead in give-and-take games.

The same pattern holds in book reading, where Richard's transition was again quite rapid. Role shifting is very much part of the child's sense of script, and I believe it is typical of the kind of "real world" experience that makes it so astonishingly easy for children to master soon afterwards the deictic shifts, those contextual changes in the meaning of words that are essential to understanding the language. At about this time the child learns that I am *I* when I speak, but *you* when referred to by another, and so too with *you;* and eventually the child comes to understand the associated spatial words, *here* and *there, this* and *that, come* and *go.*

The prelinguistic communicative framework established in their dialogue by mother and child provides the setting for the child's acquisition of this language function. His problem solving in acquiring the deictic function is a *social* task: to find the procedure that will produce results, just as his prelinguistic communicative effort produced results, and the results needed can be interpreted in relation to role interactions.

For a number of years an emphasis on egocentrism in the young child has tended to blunt our awareness of the sensitivity of children to roles, of their capacity to manage role shift and role transformation. Although there is little doubt that it is more difficult for a young child to take the view of others than it will be for him later, this aspect of development has been greatly exaggerated. In familiar and sufficiently simple situations the child is quite capable of taking another's view. In 1975 Michael Scaife and I discovered that babies in their first year shifted their glance to follow an adult's line of regard, and in 1976 Andrew Meltzoff found in our laboratory that babies only a few weeks old appeared to have a built-in mechanism for mimicking an adult's expression, since they obviously could not see their own faces. More recently, Marilyn Shatz has shown that quite young children are indeed able to "take another's position" when giving instructions, provided the task is simple enough.

According to Katherine Nelson and Janice Gruendel at Yale University, what seems to be egocentrism is often a matter of the child not being able to coordinate his own scripts with those of the questioner, although he is scrupulously following turn taking (which is definitely not egocentric). They found that when "egocentric" four-year-olds do manage to find a joint script, they produce dialogues like the following. Two children are sitting next to each other talking into toy telephones:

Gay: Hi.

Dan: Hi.

Gay: How are you?

Dan: Fine.

Gay: Who am I speaking to?

Dan: Daniel. This is your Daddy. I need to speak to you.

Gay: All right.

Dan: When I come home tonight we're gonna have . . . peanut butter and jelly sandwich . . . uh . . . at dinner time.

Gay: Uhmmm. Where're we going at dinner time?

Dan: Nowhere, but we're just gonna have dinner at 11 o'clock.

Gay: Well, I made a plan of going out tonight.

Dan: Well, that's what we're gonna do.

Gay: We're going out.

Dan: The plan, it's gonna be, that's gonna be, we're going to McDonald's.

Gay: Yeah, we're going to McDonald's. And ah, ah, ah, what they have for dinner tonight is hamburger.

Dan: Hamburger is coming. O.K., well, goodbye.

Gay: Bye.

The child takes into account his or her partner's point of view, phrases his turns properly, and says things that are relevant to the script they are working on jointly. That is surely not egocentrism. But even managing the deictic function of language provides evidence that children realize there are viewpoints other than their own.

The last type of request, the request for supportive action, has a very special property. It is tightly bound to the nature of the action in which the child is involved. To ask others for help in support of their own actions, children need at least two forms of knowledge. One of them represents the course of action and involves a goal and a set of means for getting to it. The second requirement is some grasp of what has been called the

Toward the end of the first year the child gradually begins taking the lead in give-and-take games. Through such joint activity a child learns about sharing and taking turns.

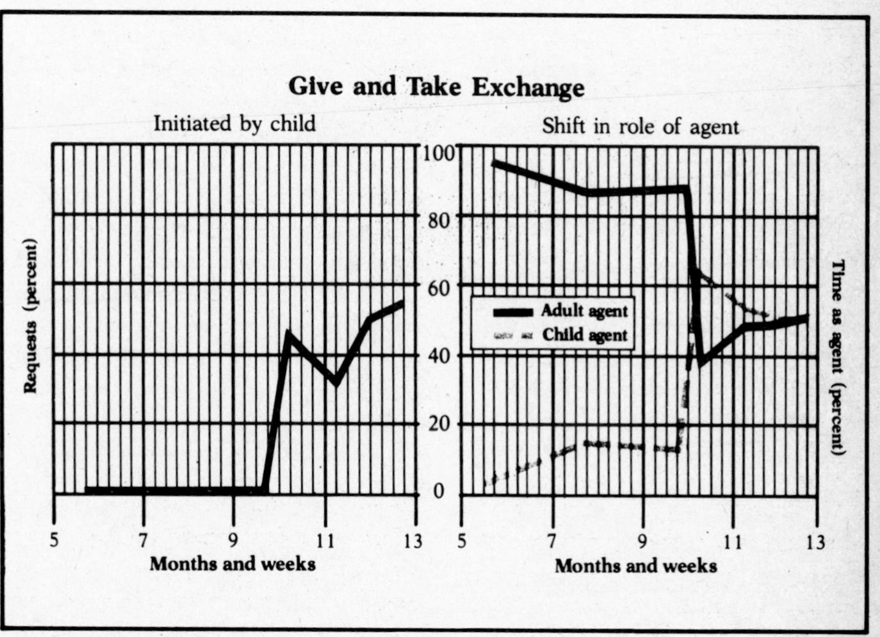

arguments of action: who does it, with what instrument, at what place, to whom, on what object, etc. Once children have mastered these, they have a rudimentary understanding of the concepts that will later be encountered in case grammar.

The degree to which a child comes to understand the structure of tasks is the degree to which his requests for support in carrying them out become more differentiated. These requests do not appear with any marked frequency until he is 17 or 18 months old and consist of bringing the "work" or the "action" or the entire task to an adult: A music box needs rewinding, or two objects have to be put together. In time a child is able to do better than that. He may bring a tool to an adult or direct the adult's hand or pat the goal (the chair on which he wants up). He is selecting and highlighting relevant features of the action, though not in a fashion that depends on what the adult is doing. Finally, at about the age of two, with the development of adequate words to refer to particular aspects of the action, the child enters a new phase: He requests action by guiding it successively. The pacemaker of the verbal output is progress in the task itself.

Let me give an instance of this successive guidance system. Richard, it transpires, wishes to persuade his mother to get a toy telephone from the cupboard; she is seated (and very pregnant). Successively, he voices the following requests:

Mummy, Mummy; Mummy come.... Up, up.... Cupboard.... Up cupboard, up cupboard; up cupboard.... Get up, get up.... Cupboard, cupboard.... Cupboard-up; cupboard-up, cupboard-up. ... Telephone.... Mummy.... Mummy get out telephone.

His mother objects and asks him what it is he wants after each of the first two requests. She is trying to get him to set forth his request in some "readable" order before she starts to respond—to give a reason in terms of the goal of the action. Richard, meanwhile, achieves something approaching a request in sentence form by organizing his successive utterances in a fashion that seems to be guided by his conception of the needed steps in the action. The initial grammar of the long string of task-related requests is, then, a kind of temporal grammar based on an understanding not only of the actions required, but also of the order in which these actions must be executed. This bit of child language is an interpersonal script based on a young child's knowledge of what is needed to reach the goal in the real world; it is the matrix in which language develops.

In looking closely at two of the four major communicative functions (indicating and requesting), we discovered a great deal of negotiating by the mother about pragmatic aspects of communication: not about truth-falsity and not about well-formedness, but about whether requests were sincere, whose turn it was, whether it should be done independently or not, whether reasons were clear or justified.

There is, of course, more to communication than indicating and requesting. Another major function of speech is affiliation, the forming of a basis for social exchange. This involves matters as diverse as learning to acknowledge presence, to take turns, and to enter what has been called the "cooperative principle" underlying all speech acts.

The final function is the use of communication for generating possible worlds, and it has little to do with asking for help or indicating things in the real world or, indeed, with maintaining social connection. The early utterances of the children we have studied show one clear-cut characteristic: Most of the talking by mother and by child is *not* about hard-nosed reality. It is about games, about imaginary things, about seemingly useless make-believe. What is involved in the generation of possible worlds is quite useful for both conceptual and communicative development—role playing, referring to nonpresent events, combining elements to exploit their variability, etc.

Had we gone on to look at the other two functions, affiliative activity during which mother and child learn the rules for interacting and the sort of play in which possible worlds are created, the case for mother-infant interaction would have been as strong. There is an enormous amount of teaching involved in transmitting the language, though very little of it has to do with language lessons proper. It has to do with making intentions clear, as speaker and as actor, and with overcoming difficulties in getting done in the real world what we want done by the mediation of communicating. And this is why learning a second language is so difficult. The moment we teach language as an explicit set of rules for generating well-formed strings out of context, the enterprise seems to go badly wrong. The rule in natural language learning is that language is learned in order to interact with someone about something the two of you share.

Where does that leave the problem of language acquisition? Well, to my way of thinking it brings it back into the sphere of problem solving—the problem being how to make our intentions known to others, how to communicate what we have in consciousness, what we want done in our behalf, how we wish to relate to others, and what in this or other worlds is possible.

Children still have to learn to use their native lexicons and to do so grammatically. They learn this in use, in order to get things done with words, and not as if they were ferreting out the disembodied rules of grammar. I think we have learned to look at language acquisition not as a solo flight by the child in search of rules, but as a transaction involving an active language learner and an equally active language teacher. That new insight will go a long way toward filling the gap between the impossible and the miraculous.

For further information:

Clark, Herbert, and Eve Clark. *Psychology and Language: An Introduction to Psycholinguistics.* Harcourt Brace Jovanovich, 1977.

De Villiers, Jill G., and Peter A. de Villiers. *Language Acquisition.* Harvard University Press, 1978.

Miller, George A. *Spontaneous Apprentices: Children and Language.* The Seabury Press, 1977.

Snow, Catherine E., and Charles A. Ferguson, eds. *Talking to Children.* Cambridge University Press, 1977.

THE LOSS OF LANGUAGE

By destroying their ability to produce or to comprehend language, brain injuries thrust people into a perplexing and frustrating world.

HOWARD GARDNER

Howard Gardner *is a research psychologist who works as a clinical investigator at the Veterans Administration Hospital in Boston. His research there centers on the breakdown of symbol-using abilities in patients with brain damage. In* The Shattered Mind *he explains aphasia and other kinds of brain damage in nontechnical terms.*

Gardner is also codirector of Harvard University's Project Zero, a research group that studies the development of symbol-using capacities in children. His interest in mental processes led Gardner to structuralism, and his book, The Quest for Mind, *discusses the intellectual movement whose best-known adherents are Claude Lévi-Strauss, and Jean Piaget, the Swiss psychologist.*

Skill in language develops so quickly and operates so smoothly that we take our linguistic capacities largely for granted. Most three-year-olds can speak simple grammatical sentences and execute simple commands. Nearly every 10-year-old in our society can read and write at the primer level and most adults can read a novel in an afternoon or write several letters in an evening.

Our linguistic potentials are even more impressive. Placed in a foreign culture, particularly as children, we readily learn the basic phrases of another language; and all of us, bilingual or not, have mastered various language-related codes—the number system (Arabic or Roman), musical notation, Morse code, or the familiar trademarks for commercial products.

The loss of various language abilities in the otherwise normal adult is tragic, and the consequences are as devastating as those of blindness, deafness, or paralysis (which often accompanies it). Deprived of the power to communicate through language and language-like channels, the individual is cut off from the world of meaning. The painting on the opposite page, by a physician stricken with aphasia, projects the frustration people feel when language is no longer at their command. Though loss of language is relatively rare among young persons, it becomes increasingly common with age—about one quarter of a million individuals suffer linguistic impairment each year. The extent and duration of language disability vary greatly, but a significant proportion of the afflicted individuals are left with a permanent impairment. Those who suffer language loss as a consequence of damage to their brains are victims of the strange condition called aphasia.

Aphasic individuals are not always immediately recognizable. One patient whom I recently interviewed appeared to be normal when he entered the room: a nice-looking, well-groomed 62-year-old retired bookkeeper. He answered my first questions appropriately and with a speed that suggested nothing was amiss. Asked his name, the gentleman responded, "Oh, my name, that's easy, it is Tuh, Tom Johnson and I. . . ." It was only when I gave Mr. Johnson a chance to speak a bit more that the extent and nature of his aphasia became clear:

"What kind of work have you done, Mr. Johnson?" I asked.

"We, the kids, all of us, and I, we were working for a long time in the . . . you know . . . it's the kind of space, I mean place rear to the spedwan. . . ."

At this point I interjected, "Excuse me, but I wanted to know what work you have been doing."

"If you had said that, we had said that, poomer, near the fortunate, forpunate, tamppoo, all around the fourth of martz. Oh, I get all confused," he replied, looking somewhat puzzled that the stream of language did not appear to satisfy me.

Mr. Johnson was suffering from a relatively common language disorder called Wernicke's aphasia. Patients with this disorder have no trouble producing

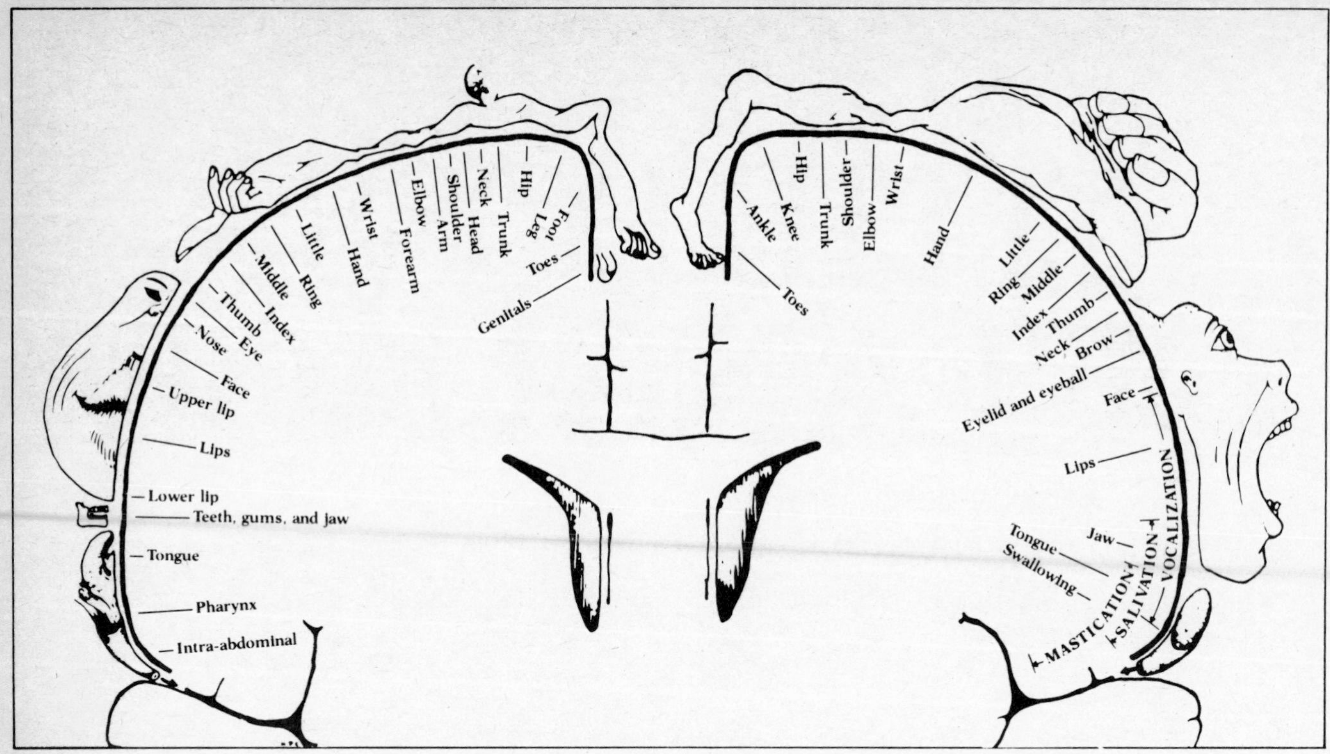

language—if anything, the words flow out too freely and it sometimes proves difficult to silence them. Nor do Wernicke's aphasics have any trouble producing the words that structure and modulate speech—"if," "and," "of," and the like. But when they try to come up with specific substantives—nouns, verbs, and adjectives that specify persons, objects, events, and properties—these patients have great difficulty. As Mr. Johnson exhibited several times, aphasics frequently cannot issue the precise words they want to say, and they frequently wander from the stated topic to another, the meaning of which remains obscure to the listener.

From my description of the interview, it may seem that Mr. Johnson understood what I was saying but was simply encountering trouble in responding appropriately. This supposition was quickly and dramatically dispelled when I took a key and a pencil from my pocket and asked him to point in turn to each one. These two simple words, known to any child, eluded him. When asked to point to other objects and to body parts, he also fared poorly, as he had when trying to name certain objects. He could not read words aloud correctly, nor could he understand most written commands, though he did read letters and numbers aloud. Any bystander would have inferred that Mr. Johnson's understanding was very limited (as indeed it was).

One fascinating island of preserved comprehension remained, however. Toward the close of the interview I said, almost out of the blue, "Oh, Mr. Johnson, would you please stand up and turn around twice?" Suddenly, as if his comprehension had been magically restored, Mr. Johnson stood up and proceeded to rotate in just the way I requested. He was also able to carry out several commands that involved his whole body (like "Lean forward" or "Stand at ease"). However, this preserved comprehension could not be elicited in any other manner.

Mr. Johnson, a Wernicke's aphasic, can be instructively contrasted with another patient whom I recently met. Mr. Cooper, a 47-year-old former Army officer, was seated in a wheelchair, obviously paralyzed on the entire right side of his body. A slight droop on the right side of his face became more noticeable when he opened his mouth or smiled. When I asked what was wrong with him, Mr. Cooper immediately pointed to his arm, his leg, and his mouth. He appeared reluctant to speak at all. Only when I pressed him did he point again to his

Once Paul Broca and Carl Wernicke had linked two varieties of aphasia to specific areas in the brain, neurologists began trying to locate all intellectual functions. Although they failed, they did succeed in identifying the areas connected with most motor and sensory functions. This homunculus locates the relative amount of brain space devoted to various functions. On the right are the areas that control motor functions; the fine muscles that control the lips and hands take up the most space. On the left are the areas that receive sensory input from skin receptors.

mouth and with obvious effort blurt out the sound "Peech."

I posed Mr. Cooper a number of questions that could be answered by "yes" or "no," and in each case he nodded appropriately. I then said that it was important that he try to speak. Noting his wedding ring, I asked, "How many children do you have?" Mr. Cooper looked blank for a time. Then he peered at his fingers and began to raise them, accompanying the motion with low and strained sounds: "one, two, tree, pour, no, pive . . . yes pive," he said triumphantly.

Next, I asked him to tell me about the kind of work he had been doing.

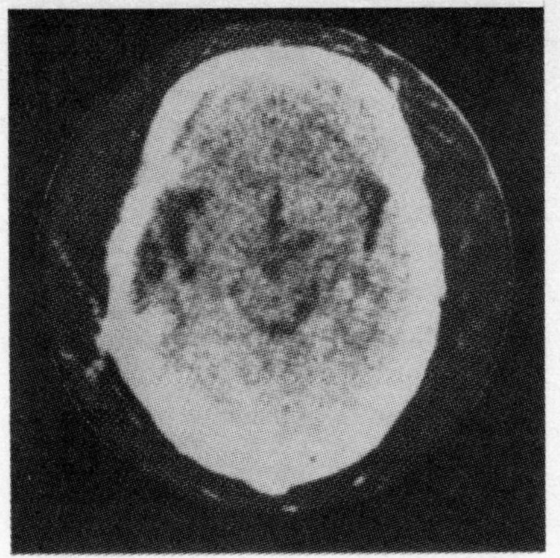

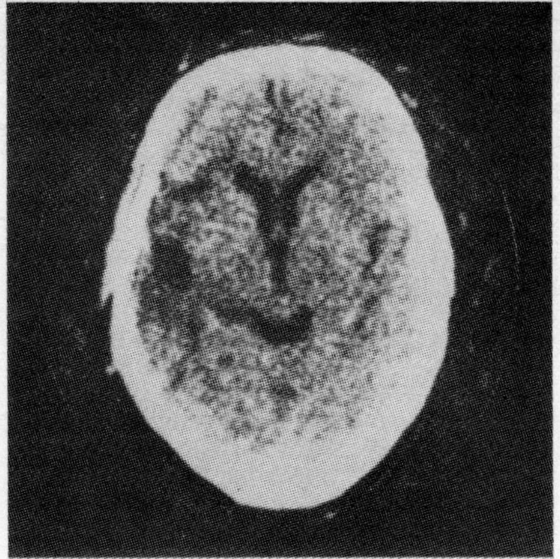

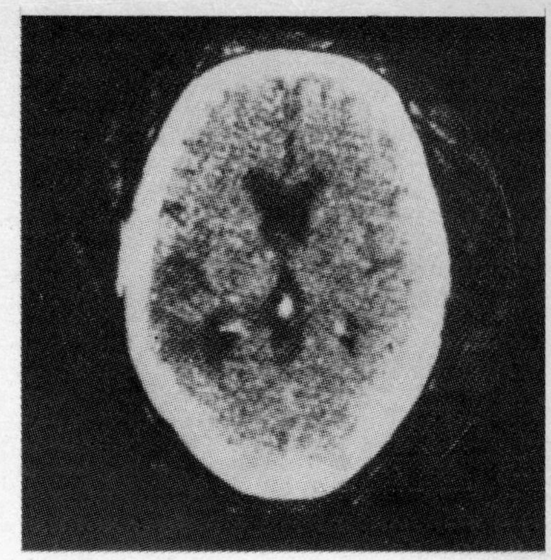

"Me . . . build—ing . . . chairs, no, no cab—in—nets." The words came out slowly, taking him 40 seconds to finish.

"One more question," I said. "Can you tell me how you would go about building a cabinet?"

Mr. Cooper threw up his left hand in frustration, and after I gently insisted that he attempt a verbal explanation, he said, "One, saw . . . then, cutting wood . . . working. . . ." All of this was said with great effort and poor articulation, which left me (and Mr. Cooper) unprepared for a sudden oath, "Jesus Christ, oh boy." This was uttered effortlessly, as if another language mechanism—an island of preserved production—had temporarily been stimulated.

During the rest of our examination, Mr. Cooper performed well on tasks that required little language production. On request he pointed easily to objects around the room and even to a series of objects placed in front of him. He read simple commands silently and carried them out clumsily but properly. He could name some familiar objects and read aloud some names of objects, though he failed at reading aloud letters of the alphabet and small grammatical words such as articles and prepositions. He could read aloud the word "bee," but not "be," though the latter occurs more frequently in spoken and written language. He could carry a melody and sing lyrics to familiar songs more readily than he could recite those same lyrics.

But Mr. Cooper had definite difficulties in understanding. Although he could designate a series of two objects, he sometimes failed at three and he never succeeded at four—the level of success achieved by most normal adults. He caught the drift of nearly all questions in casual conversation, and could almost always produce at least a minimally appropriate response, but he experienced significant problems with questions that involved careful attention to word order and inflection. I could stump him with sentences like "Do you put on your shoes before you put on socks?" or "The lion was killed by the tiger: Which animal is dead?" or "With the pen touch the pencil." Just as Mr. Cooper's spontaneous speech was limited largely to nouns and verbs and virtually devoid of words that modulate meaning, so too he often failed on questions and commands that required him to note the order of words and the meanings of prefixes, suffixes, and other grammatical fixtures.

Mr. Johnson and Mr. Cooper illustrate two of the most common forms of aphasia. In six years of work with aphasic patients, I have seen dozens of patients whose symptoms closely resemble those of one or the other man. Mr. Johnson is a victim of Wernicke's aphasia; as a result of damage to the left temporal lobe of his brain his auditory comprehension has become severely impaired, but he remains able to produce long, often obscure, strings of speech. Mr. Cooper has Broca's aphasia, a condition caused by damage to the left frontal lobe. He understands language, although not perfectly; his chief difficulty is in producing words, specifically those that modify nouns and verbs. The language of the

Tissue damage in a patient with Wernicke's aphasia. Each picture shows a cross section of the brain at a different depth. The black area corresponds to the brain lesion (bone appears as white, healthy brain tissue as gray).

Broca's aphasic is called agrammatic (or telegrammatic), and such a patient's understanding suffers from some of the same limits that affect his spontaneous speech.

These and other aphasic syndromes are the regular and nearly inevitable consequences of significant damage to the left hemisphere of the brain in normal right-handed individuals. As a result of a stroke, head injury, or brain tumor, cortical (or surface) tissue is destroyed in this half of the brain. Such lesions impair linguistic functions and frequently cause paralysis and loss of sensation in the opposite (right) side of the body. (The situation is somewhat different, and much more complex, in left-handers.)

The precise location and extent of the brain damage determines the nature of the linguistic disorder. There are forms of aphasia (called alexia) in which an individual's ability to read is most severely impaired; agraphia, in which disorders of writing are most pronounced; anomia, in which most language functions are preserved but there is magnified difficulty in naming objects; conduction aphasia, in which speech and understanding are relatively intact but the patient experiences enormous difficulty in repetition; and a bizarre complementary condition called mixed

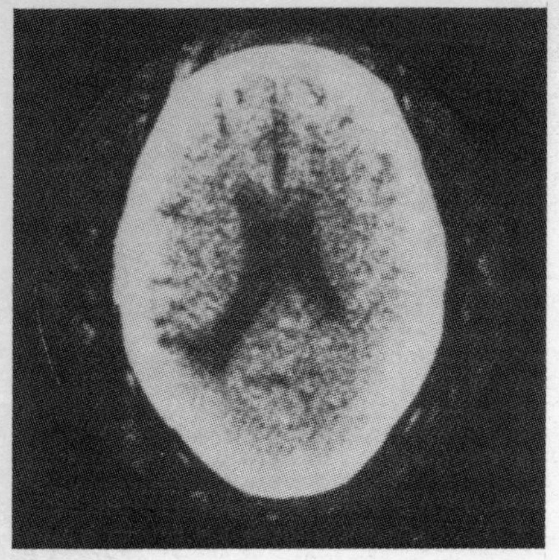

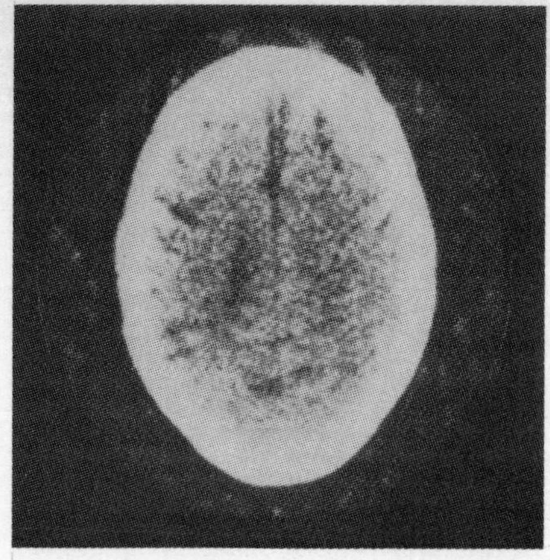

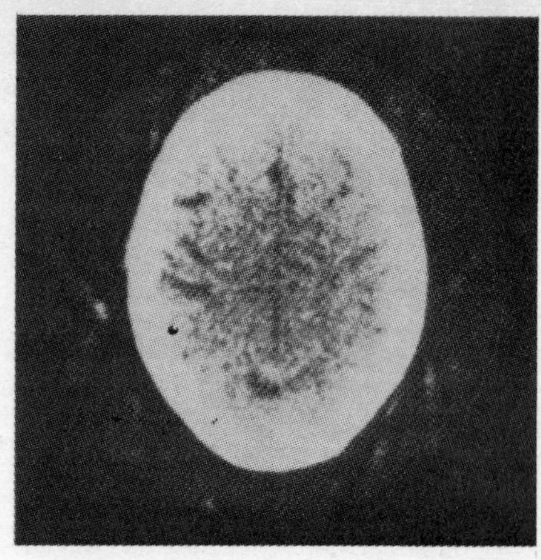

transcortical aphasia, in which both conversational speech and comprehension are almost entirely destroyed, yet the patient retains the capacity to repeat, and even to echo, long strings of meaningful or meaningless words (it makes little difference which). The striking predictability of these syndromes reflects the uniformity with which language functions are organized in normal right-handed individuals.

Each of these conditions cries out for explanation. There are alexics who can read numbers, including Roman numerals, but not words or letters; transcortical aphasics who understand nothing but who will, in their repetitions, spontaneously correct ungrammatical phrases; anomic aphasics who cannot produce a familiar word (e.g., nose) but will readily produce a highly improbable substitute (proboscis). To be sure, not all aphasics show such clear syndromes; the syndromes are most likely to occur in individuals of middle age or older, who are fully right-handed, and who have suffered a stroke. Yet nearly every aphasic patient exhibits some bizarre combination of symptoms, and many exemplify the textbook descriptions in the preceding paragraph.

A first meeting with aphasic patients is often dramatic; their symptoms are frequently fantastic and disturbing. A person's first impulse is to aid these victims of brain disease in any way possible. But the study of their condition has an importance that goes beyond helping victims of aphasia; it holds the promise of clarifying a host of philosophical and psychological issues about the nature of language and the mind.

Reports of aphasia can be found in many classical writings and even in the Bible. Yet the serious scientific study of aphasia began just over a century ago when Pierre Paul Broca, a French anatomist, described two cases whose symptoms resembled Mr. Cooper's. Broca's cases were important not because of the way he described their behavior patterns but because he made an analytic leap. Noting that both of these cases had brain damage in the anterior portion of the left hemisphere, Broca proposed that this part of the brain played a special role in language. Besides immortalizing his name (Broca's aphasia, Broca's area), this discovery laid the groundwork for all aphasia research.

The reason for this breakthrough was simple but instructive. Until Broca's time, nearly all scientists assumed that the two halves of the brain, which on casual inspection look alike, carried out the same functions. It had often been observed that aphasia accompanied strokes and paralysis, but Broca was the first to argue publicly that language disorders are linked to the left portion of the brain. Though his announcement provoked controversy, supporting cases were quickly reported. Thirteen years later Carl Wernicke, a German neuropsychiatrist, described another set of symptoms, this time primarily affecting comprehension. He linked them to the left posterior (particularly temporal) lobe of the brain, thereby contributing his name to another brain area and another type of aphasia. Even more than Broca's discoveries, Wernicke's work stimulated scientists to construct models of language based on the behavior of brain-injured patients.

Broca and Wernicke gave impetus to a group of neurologists who have been called localizers. Adherents of this approach carefully investigated the anatomy of the human brain, the structure of the cortical tissue, and the connections between the different parts of the nervous system. Building on this refined knowledge of human neuroanatomy, they sought to discover the functions that were governed by each part of the brain. Their first step was to locate the motor functions (or voluntary actions), which are associated with sites in the frontal lobe, and the sensory functions, associated with sites in the parietal, temporal, and occipital lobes. But the localizers went beyond these relatively elementary processes and tried to apportion even the highest intellectual and emotional functions to specific regions of the brain.

Findings about language function spurred them on. Researchers had discovered an indisputable "high" human function—one denied all other animals—occupying specific regions in the brain. The type of aphasia discovered by Broca and the startlingly different one described by Wernicke were but the first manifestations of this line of analysis. Within 20 years, a gaggle of aphasias had been described, each traced to a specific area in the brain, each exhibiting its own enigmatic symptoms.

Researchers transcended these correlations between brain and behavior to propose models of language function. In one popular version the language signal entered Wernicke's area, where it was

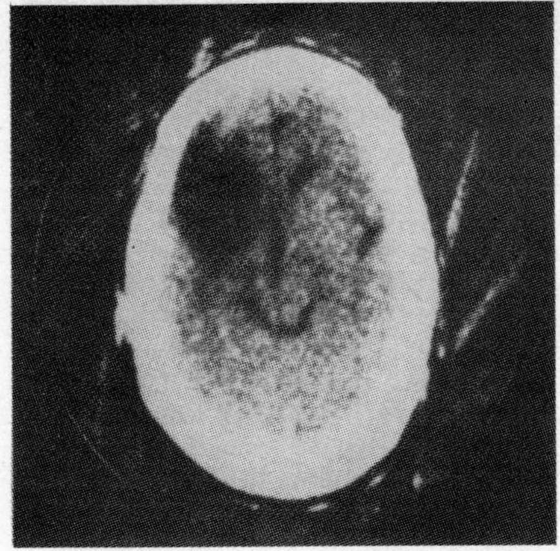
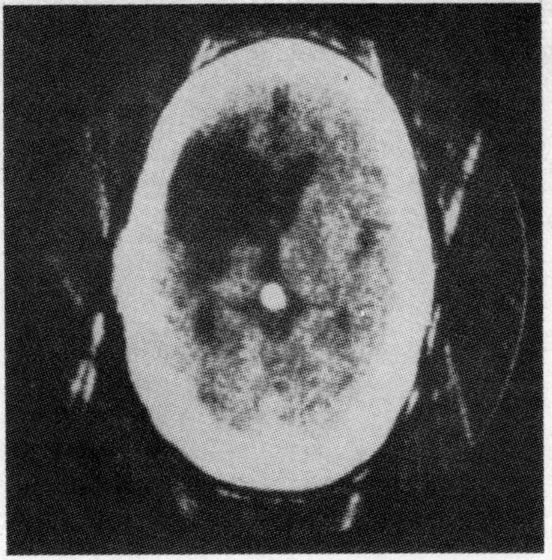
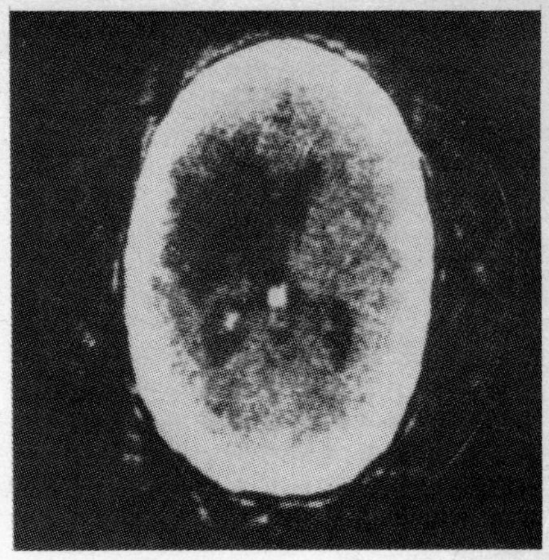

Tissue damage in a patient with Broca's aphasia. The black area shows the extent of the lesion. These pictures, like those on the preceding two pages, were produced by a Syntex System 60 scanner, which translates x-ray absorption into a mathematical model of the head.

comprehended; then a return message was fired forward to Broca's area, where it was fitted out with grammatical trimmings and ultimately spewed forth to the world. It naturally followed that a lesion confined to Broca's area allowed comprehension at the cost of grammatical speech, whereas destruction of Wernicke's area impaired comprehension but allowed a stream of grammatically rich, but often meaningless, speech.

The localizers probably went too far in their approach. In the early part of this century, a rival school reanalyzed Broca's original cases and announced that there was but one type of aphasia, the form stemming from lesions in and around Wernicke's area. Broca's aphasics, they said, were linguistically intact individuals who suffered only from problems in articulating their speech. Followers of this theory pointed out that not even textbook cases of Broca's aphasia showed all the observed symptoms and that some displayed additional symptoms. In their view, lesions anywhere in the left hemisphere could produce aphasia, and its severity reflected primarily the size of the lesion rather than its site. These partisans went on to argue that every aphasic exhibits difficulties in all language functions. Differences among the so-called syndromes, they said, are differences in degree (a little more reading difficulty in one case, a little more repetition difficulty in another) rather than in kind.

Today, after a century of research, there is little sympathy for either of the conflicting theories. Due in large measure to the efforts of Norman Geschwind, professor of neurology at the Harvard Medical School, the genuine contributions of the localizers are again appreciated. At the same time, a range of factors that modulate the classic syndromes—such as the nature of the brain disease, the age of the patient, or the situation of testing—are also recognized. The classic syndromes are seen as useful signposts for describing patients rather than as fixed descriptions of what a patient with a given lesion can and cannot do.

Progress has been stimulated by a number of factors. In the wake of this century's wars, researchers have seen hundreds of patients with aphasia. The publication of numerous cases and countercases has clarified our knowledge of the incidence of full-blown examples of the classic syndromes and produced precise descriptions of the symptoms of aphasia.

But perhaps the biggest contribution has come from interactions among specialists from diverse disciplines, each of whom had approached aphasia from a different perspective. In my own view, the most important infusions have come from linguists, who have brought to the study of aphasia logical and well-conceived categories for the analysis of language, and from psychologists, whose accurate experimental techniques have supplemented the important but necessarily superficial methods of bedside examination evolved by attending physicians.

Issues raised by routine bedside testing often stimulate research by interdisciplinary teams. Consider, for instance, Mr. Cooper's apparent success at understanding spontaneous conversation. Such observations have led many neurologists to conclude that a patient with Broca's aphasia has no difficulties in comprehending language. Teams of linguists and psychologists noted, however, that when such patients were tested, they received multiple cues from the context in which a question was posed and from redundancies within the message. Accordingly, they devised questions that could be understood only if one were processing grammatical inflections and exploiting cues of word order. Deprived of the redundancy of ordinary conversational speech, individuals with Broca's aphasia showed only meager comprehension.

Turning to issues raised by Mr. Johnson, experimenters have also clarified the nature of the comprehension defect in Wernicke's aphasia. Because these patients have difficulty understanding auditory messages and decoding single isolated words, some aphasiologists concluded that the primary impediment for the Wernicke's aphasic lay in his inability to decipher individual phonemes—the smallest discrete sounds of language, such as "th," "p," and "b." Careful experimental studies have documented, however, that Wernicke's aphasics can readily discriminate between individual pho-

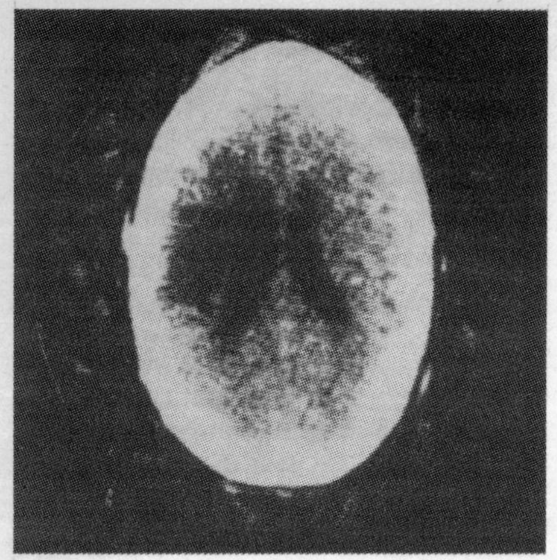

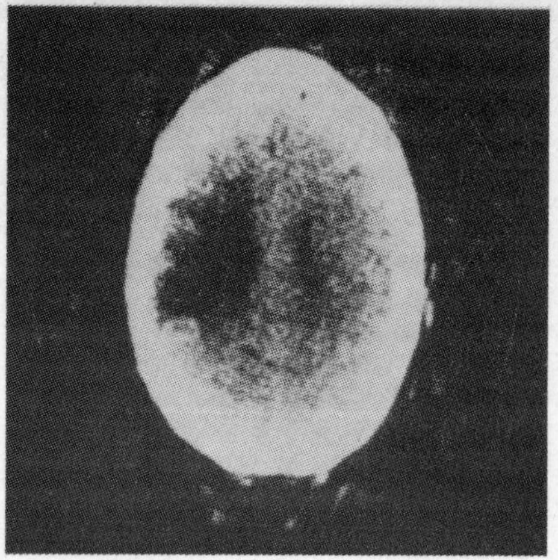

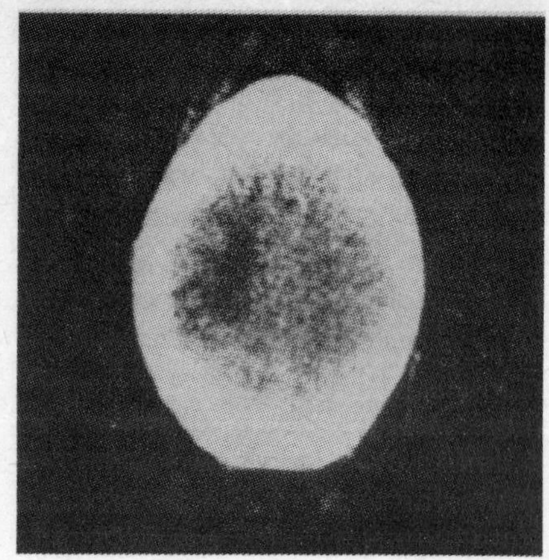

nemes; they may surpass Broca's aphasics at this task. Their difficulty in understanding occurs at a higher level of semantic interpretation.

Not all the contributions have come from research scientists. Demonstrations by clinicians sometimes challenge—and even undermine—the workaday categories embraced by researchers. None of the categorical distinctions honored by psychologists or linguists can explain Mr. Johnson's curious ability to carry out commands that use the whole body. If, however, one takes into account certain anatomical considerations, this behavior becomes clarified. Unlike commands using the face or individual limbs, which are carried out by the major pyramidal motor pathways running from the cortex to the spinal cord, these commands are executed by the alternative nonpyramidal tracts of the nervous system. A lesion in Wernicke's area usually spares these tracts. Here is a case where an anatomical point of view advances the explanation of aphasic behavior.

Constant interplay between bedside testing and experimental work proves crucial, since experimenters tend to devise careful but artificial test situations. When a patient fails on such a test, it becomes difficult to determine whether the patient lacks the ability in question or is simply confused by the instructions or by the task itself. Sometimes a patient fails on an experimenter's test only to demonstrate the skill in question when a natural situation arises in his life. A patient may fail to repeat an arbitrary set of phrases spoken by an experimenter and yet produce just these phrases in situations where they are warranted. Thus, in a curiously productive way, clinicians and experimenters keep one another honest.

It is impossible to understand the mind without considering its linguistic capacities. Yet both linguists and psychologists face a fundamental problem: the categories, distinctions, terminology, and levels of linguistic competence are based on the study of individuals in whom all linguistic capacities are operating efficiently. These individuals can produce the proper sounds, combine words according to the structure of a language, understand the meaning of the words they use, and use language appropriately in natural situations. Scholars have divided the study of language in the same way, analyzing it in terms of its phonological, syntactic, semantic, and pragmatic levels. No independent means exists for examining the validity of these categories, for determining whether another means of slicing the linguistic pie might not prove more comprehensive and accurate.

Here is where aphasia can make a unique contribution. Were it the case, as some researchers once implied, that all language skills break down simultaneously in aphasia, this pathological condition would hold little scientific interest. But aphasia proves remarkably selective in its damage. A patient may have an impaired ability to read while still being able to write, fail to comprehend and yet speak, fail to understand and yet repeat accurately. These and numerous other dissociations can demonstrate the validity of certain categories of analysis. For example, both Broca's aphasia and transcortical aphasia provide evidence for a separate level of syntactic analysis in the brain.

At other times the dissociations call into question some of the distinctions made by linguists. Aphasia gives little support for the linguist's distinction between competence and performance. Symptoms that violate our expectations can suggest new distinctions and categorization that linguists have ignored, as in the case of the dichotomy in the brain's response to "whole-body" and other kinds of commands. Aphasia provides a testing laboratory for the distinctions made by those who study human languages—the primary window to the mind.

The study of aphasia may help to clarify several longstanding philosophical questions. Is language the ultimate symbol system on which all other modes of symbolization are parasitic? Or do other symbol systems exist that are relatively autonomous of language? Results from the study of aphasia indicate that language is but one of man's symbolic competences. Once a person's language ability is impaired, he ordinarily shows a lessened capacity to "read" other symbols. Yet this is not always the case. Many severely aphasic patients can carry out calculations, gesture meaningfully, or read musical notation.

Research on aphasia also pertains to another philosophical chestnut: the extent to which thought depends upon language. Aphasia exacts tolls on performance in various concept-formation tasks, as do all forms of brain damage. Yet it is by no means uncommon to encounter a severely aphasic individual who can solve a difficult maze or puzzle, play a game of chess or bridge, or score above normal on the nonverbal section of the Wechsler Adult Intelligence Scale. Other aphasic individuals have continued to paint, compose, or conduct music at a professionally competent level.

Mental functioning in aphasia is relevant to an issue of great current interest: the functions of the left and right hemispheres of the brain. In nearly all right-handers, the left hemisphere of the brain is specialized for language; lesions there will result in significant impairment of language. Such an injury spares right-hemisphere functioning and the aphasic patient remains relatively skilled in those functions for which the right hemisphere is superior—visual-spatial orientation, musical understanding, recognition of faces, and emotional balance.

In working with hundreds of aphasic patients I have been struck by the extent to which they seem to be well oriented, generally aware of what is going on around them, and appropriately attuned to emotional situations. And I have been struck, in contrast, by the frequently inappropriate and disoriented behavior of patients with right-hemisphere lesions, individuals whose language remains essentially intact but whose intuitive understanding of the world seems to have gone awry. In these areas, which have remained recalcitrant to formal testing, one may secure the best evidence that common sense does not depend on competence in language.

Anyone who has spent time with aphasic individuals will recognize the need to help these victims; their personal frustration is so glaring. In the wake of experiments by aphasiologists, speech pathologists have been able to begin rehabilitation with a greater understanding of the processes (and limitations) of language function, and with a heightened ability to exploit those mental powers ordinarily spared in aphasia. To be sure, no rehabilitation can fully compensate for destroyed brain tissue; the best healers are still time, youth, and—at least in matters of language—the degree of left-handedness in one's family.

Research on brain function has led to certain significant breakthroughs in aphasia therapy. Speech pathologists at the Boston Veterans Administration Hospital have devised a training program that significantly boosts language output. Their work is based on the clinical observation that Broca's aphasics can often sing well, and on experimental findings that musical and intonational patterns are mediated by structures in the right hemisphere. During the first phase of this rehabilitation program, called Melodic Intonation Therapy, patients sing simple phrases; in ensuing phases, they learn to delete the melody, leaving only the words. Mr. Cooper, who could sing lyrics to songs but had difficulty reciting them, would seem a likely candidate for this therapy. If he succeeds as well as other patients, in about three months he should be able to produce short but grammatical and appropriate sentences.

The study of aphasia is still in its infancy, but interest in this field has grown so rapidly that advances in understanding and rehabilitation are likely. Few areas of study feature as close a linkage between the medical and the scientific, the clinical and the experimental, the concerns of the theorist and the practitioner. And the mysteries to be solved are inextricably linked with the vast enigmas of language, brain, and mind. It is paradoxical—yet in a strange way heartening—that those who can say little may help us answer questions that have until now eluded even the most eloquent philosophers.

For further information:

Gardner, Howard. *The Shattered Mind.* Alfred A. Knopf, 1975.

Goldstein, Kurt. *Language and Language Disturbances.* Grune and Stratton, 1948.

Goodglass, Harold, and Norman Geschwind. "Language Disorders, Aphasia." *Handbook of Perception,* Vol. 7, ed. Edward Carterette and Morton Friedman. Academic Press, 1976.

Goodglass, Harold, and Edith Kaplan. *The Assessment of Aphasia and Related Disorders.* Lea and Febiger, 1972.

Luria, A. R. *Traumatic Aphasia: Its Syndromes, Psychology, and Treatment.* Humanities Press, 1970.

Development

4

Human development proceeds through a remarkable set of transformations that shape each individual's personality. From newborn to infant, to toddler, to child, to adolescent, to adult, to old age, we are continually facing new cognitive, social, emotional, and psychosexual challenges. Meeting or failing to meet these challenges is the stuff of growing up. The articles in this section deal with the dynamics of human development.

When thinking about development, many people think first of infancy and childhood. Therefore, the first two articles in this section focus on changes during those two periods of life. "Newborn Knowledge" considers infancy, describing the rather surprising intellect, curiosity, and social competence of the newborn baby, who was once regarded as almost completely undeveloped and helpless. "Childhood," written especially for *Annual Editions,* summarizes current knowledge about development during the formative years from infancy to adolescence in several major areas: physical and motor skills, language, thought, emotion, and social competence.

Psychosocial development depends critically on the social environment in which it takes place. Probably the most important environmental factor in early personal development is the home—or, more specifically, the care one receives there. "Your Child's Self-Esteem" argues that early experiences of love and the ability to control the environment determine later self-esteem and intellectual performance. "Learning Right from Wrong" chronicles moral development and the acquisition of standards of moral conduct. Finally, it is important to realize that the stages of psychosocial development relate more to periods in the unfolding of a life-style than to age per se. "Coping with the Seasons of Life" reinforces this fact by reporting the results of interviews with people at various stages of life in England. In conclusion, "In Search of Youth" discusses biological processes that help to determine the end of life, and some work now being done to slow these processes down.

A review of this section will acquaint you with ongoing research into the roles of genetic, cognitive, and environmental factors in shaping individual development from conception to death. These articles provide an overview of the established theories about human development as well as some of the more controversial theories that we have recently begun to consider.

Looking Ahead: Challenge Questions

What are some of the qualities of effective parenting?

What impact would a national day care system have on our society?

What aspects of development generally hold true for every culture and society? What aspects change from culture to culture?

How important is school to development? What major developmental tasks or accomplishments are made before school starts? Which remain to be achieved after schooling is done and people are on their own?

NEWBORN KNOWLEDGE

Richard M. Restak

Richard M. Restak is a Washington, D.C., neurologist whose book, The Self Seekers, *was published in June 1982.*

Infant researcher Louis W. Sander has a favorite home movie. It depicts a young married couple standing on the lawn outside their home. The woman is holding their eight-day-old baby who, as the film opens, turns fussy and restless. She hands the baby to her husband, who casually takes the child and places it in the crook of his arm while continuing an animated conversation with the cameraman. As the film unfolds, the father appears to ignore his newborn baby. The baby too seems to be unaware of the father. Nevertheless, after just a few seconds the infant stops crying, grows quiet, and finally, drops off to sleep.

A slow motion, frame-by-frame analysis of the movie reveals a different story. The father looks down several times at his baby, who returns the gaze. Infant and father begin to reach for each other. The baby clasps the little finger of the father's hand and, at that moment, falls asleep.

What delights Sander is the sensibility of the infant, a quality not generally associated with newborns. In light of a host of similar observations, partly made possible by innovative use of videotape, scientists are revising a long-held belief that newborns are passive creatures waiting for the world to imprint its wisdom on them. From at least the moment of birth, infants are enormously responsive.

This new knowledge is bringing about a quiet revolution that will affect everything from when and how a baby is delivered to the kind of advice obstetricians and pediatricians offer to new parents.

According to T. Berry Brazelton, Chief of the Child Development Unit of the Children's Hospital Medical Center in Boston, only moments out of the womb, infants are capable of a wide variety of behavior. Eyes alert, they turn their heads in the direction of a voice (they prefer a female pitch), inquisitively searching for the source of the sound that attracted them. Sander, professor of psychiatry at the University of Colorado Medical Center, and William Condon, a professor of psychiatry at Boston University Medical Center, have observed that the infant moves its arms and legs in synchrony to the rhythms of human speech. Disconnected vowel sounds, random noise, or tapping do not suffice; only the natural rhythms of speech will do. And it does not matter what language the infant initially hears: Infants in Sander and Condon's study responded to Chinese in the same way they responded to English. Such behavior provides support for theorists such as Massachusetts Institute of Technology linguist Noam Chomsky, who believes the human capacity for language is inborn and requires only appropriate exposure for normal speech development.

Newborns are particularly attracted to faces. A baby will turn its head and eyes while following a moving drawing of a face, but if pieces of the drawing are scrambled, it loses interest. Soon after birth it recognizes its parents and begins to fasten a special kind of attention on them.

At the Children's Hospital Medical Center in Boston, films of four-week-old infants demonstrate that babies behave differently with their parents than they do with other people and, not surprisingly, with objects. When a bright toy is brought within reach, the infant's attention is hooked, and its fingers and toes point toward the toy with gleeful expectation, but the baby quickly loses interest and gazes elsewhere. A few seconds later a second round of attention begins. The pattern of attention and loss of interest is jagged and irregular. With the mother, in contrast, the baby's movements are smooth and cyclic, and its attention pattern is more sustained.

Babies pay special attention to their fathers as well. "Amazingly enough," says Brazelton, "when several weeks old, an infant displays an entirely different attitude —more wide-eyed, playful, and bright-faced—towards its father than towards its mother." Brazelton describes these cycles with the father as "higher, deeper, and more jagged," corresponding to the father's "more playful, jazzed-up approach." One explanation for the infant's behavior, Brazelton says, is that fathers, on the whole, behave as if they expect more heightened, playful responses from their babies.

Researchers also are beginning to recognize something most relaxed parents have always known:

Playing with one's infant is a very important element in its normal, healthy development. This marks a refreshing change from the rather grim, tight-lipped preoccupation with feeding and elimination that has been fashionable in some circles in recent years.

"I think there are several assumptions about infants that we now have to question very seriously," says Daniel Stern, author of *The First Relationship: Infant and Mother.* In his laboratory at New York Hospital's Payne Whitney Clinic, Stern has captured on film delicate and evanescent exchanges between mother and infant. Often their responses occur within microseconds, suggesting, according to Stern, an inborn mutual readiness of both mother and infant to respond to each other.

Infant researcher Charles A. Ferguson, a linguist at Stanford University, agrees. In a whimsically entitled study, "Baby Talk in Six Languages," he finds that mothers of six different nationalities speaking their native languages all use a special version of baby talk with their infants. Sometimes the baby elicits from its mother behavior she has never practiced nor seen. Her speech is marked by short sentences, simplified syntax, and nonsense sounds, transforming phrases such as "pretty rabbit" into "pwitty wabbit." **When talking to their babies, mothers invariably raise the pitch of their voices, with long stretches of speech in the falsetto range. They prolong eye contact with the infant well beyond what is normal between adults. Two grown-ups will stare at each other with the same intensity only when they are extremely aroused emotionally—enraptured lovers or fierce enemies.**

There are other ways in which infants and parents establish their special relationships. Through trial and error, they establish routines that are mutually gratifying. For example, most parents do not enjoy waking at 3:00 A.M. to feed their babies, so they attempt to persuade the infants to sleep through the night. When the baby learns this routine, a sense of harmony is created not only between infant and parents but with the rest of the household as well. At this point the baby has finally become an authentic family member.

Gradually and painstakingly, parent and infant establish other routines: mealtime, playtime, even time when it's all right to be cranky. As each mutual adjustment is negotiated, the bond between the two is strengthened. But when these routines are interrupted or, worse, never established, family life can become an unpleasant series of interrupted meals, hurt feelings, and short tempers. Anyone who has ever experienced jet lag knows what it's like to be out of phase with other people's biological rhythms—nodding asleep in a chair, for example, while others are ready for dinner. So, too, parents and baby all want to have something to say about when food is served, diapers changed, and games played.

Early on the infant learns a wide variety of useful skills; for instance, it combines sight, sound, and touch into meaningful patterns. A three-week-old, blindfolded and allowed to rub its tongue along a toy block, will later gaze at a picture of a block in preference to other objects, a neat demonstration that the infant already integrates sight and touch.

A three-month-old shown two cartoons simultaneously, with the sound track of one played in the background, will stare selectively at the movie that corresponds to the sound track. The infant's skill at matching sound with picture can be carried even further by superimposing the two movies on top of one another and then slowly separating them. The infant's attention turns to the film that matches the sound track.

In dealing with people the infant exhibits even more astonishing acumen. By one week of age a baby can pick out its mother's voice from a group of female voices and at two weeks can recognize that the mother's voice and face are part of a unit. British researcher Genevieve Carpenter tested two-week-old babies by exposing them to four different situations: 1) the mother speaking to her infant in her own voice, 2) a strange woman speaking to the infant in her own voice, 3) the mother speaking in the female stranger's voice, and 4) the stranger speaking in mother's voice. The babies responded most favorably to the first situation, illustrating that as young as two weeks a baby can tell mother from stranger. More interesting, however, were the infants' responses to the third and fourth situations. They cried and turned away from this bizarre and frightening combination of the familiar and the strange.

Another fascinating study showed that infants and mothers respond to each other when the mother appears on closed-circuit TV screens nearly as effectively as when they are together. But if a baby watches a videotaped recording of its mother, it quickly loses interest, its eyes begin to wander, and it begins to fret. Infants evidently recognize that they get no personal response from their videotaped mothers, while in the live exchanges on closed-circuit TV, baby and mother can make eye contact.

One area of research that is particularly intriguing—and controversial—is whether it is essential for mothers and newborns to spend time together immediately after birth. Marshall Klaus and John Kennell of Case Western Reserve School of Medicine in Cleveland have demonstrated that mothers who are allowed an hour with their infants immediately following birth in addition to five hours in the next three days behave differently from other mothers denied the same amount of time with their newborns. During their first hour, infants may spend an astonishing 85 percent of the time in an alert, wakeful state, eyes wide open and inquisitive, a situation that may promote a bond between mother and child. When filmed during the infant's first exam at one month, for example, the mothers who were allowed more time with their infants (so-called extended contact mothers) were more reluctant to leave their babies with strangers and preferred to stay and watch the exam. When the babies were fussy, these mothers were more soothing. Feeding, too, was different: The extended contact mothers all held their babies so that they could look at them face to face.

When filmed during the infants' first-year checkups, the extended contact mothers continued to demonstrate active interest and participation, often helping the pediatrician if their babies were fearful or restless. At two years, these mothers tended to ask questions of their children rather than issue commands. The vocabulary the mothers used was richer and more stimulating, which according to some studies may result in higher infant IQs.

Intrigued with Klaus and Kennell's findings, other researchers extended their studies and found that increased contact between a mother and her healthy, full-term infant in the first few days and weeks after birth is associated with fewer instances of later child abuse. Increased contact also correlates with less infant crying, more rapid infant growth, increased affection, and more self-confidence on the part of the mother.

In fact, many infant researchers now believe that increased contact between mother and infant in the first few days of life affects maternal behavior and infant development for periods of from one month to five years. Some believe the beneficial effects that stem from increased alertness and responsiveness last a lifetime. No one knows for sure. "We strongly believe that there is a sensitive period in the first few minutes and hours after the infant's birth which is optimal for infant-parent attachment," says Klaus.

Critics of the Klaus-Kennell theory feel there are other factors that contribute to optimal bonding. They argue that adopted children, premature babies, and infants born to mothers too sick to respond to them in their first few days still develop normal, affectionate relationships with their mothers. Nonetheless, even critics agree that allowing mother and infant to be together during the first few hours is humane and natural. As a result, even though all the evidence is not in, hospitals throughout the world are beginning to allow mother and baby time together in the first hours after birth.

Doctors and hospital administrators are also beginning to realize that intensive care units and rigid hospital routines are potential disrupters of the natural interaction between mother and child. Robert N. Emde, professor of psychiatry at the University of Colorado Medical School, believes it is extremely important for parents and children to be together as much as possible. "For years, theories described how mothers shaped babies, but we are now beginning to appreciate how much babies shape mothers"—and fathers as well.

"No longer can we look upon a newborn as a lump of clay ready to be molded by the environment," says Brazelton. "We've come a long way in our understanding of just how marvelous a creature a human infant really is."

Childhood

Catherine T. Best and Lauren Julius Harris

Catherine T. Best is Assistant Professor of Psychology at Teachers College, Columbia University. Lauren Julius Harris is Professor of Psychology at Michigan State University.

The period conventionally called "childhood" begins at the end of infancy as the child starts to talk and ends with the onset of *puberty* that marks the start of the period known as *adolescence.* Like adolescence, the childhood period is a time of great psychological and physical change. These changes, however, are not simply quantitative, for a child is not merely a small, "unfinished" adult, who over the years grows taller, heavier, and more intelligent in a simple quantitative sense. A child instead is a qualitatively different sort of person from an adult or an adolescent, or even from another child several years older or younger.

This article presents highlights of important areas of physical and psychological change from about 2 years to puberty—change in physical and motor skills, language, understanding and the ability to reason, emotion, and social relationships, including learning about social roles.

Physical Development

In physical characteristics and skills, toddlers of 18 months to 3 years already are significantly different from infants. For one thing, their new ability to voluntarily control their bowel and bladder sphincter muscles makes 18 to 24-month-olds better candidates for toilet-training. Bowel training usually is first achieved by 18 months, followed, at around 2 years, by bladder control when children are awake and, still later, when asleep. Boys are typically a bit later than girls at each stage. Also during toddlerhood, the rapid rate of body growth of infancy has begun to slow down. Some body parts, such as the brain and head, show slower growth than the legs, torso, arms, and to a lesser extent, facial features. Some of the fat layers under the skin also stop growing. These changes make toddlers look different from infants: their faces now are not quite so marked by large cheeks and forehead, their heads are not quite so large in proportion to the rest of the body, their bigger torsos leave more room for internal organs so that their abdomens don't bulge so much, and their slightly longer arms and legs are less chubby. The faster growth of legs and arms and facial features relative to head and brain size, and of muscles and bones relative to fat layers, continues through the preschool years (3 to 5) and middle childhood (6 to 12), so that a 12-year-old's body proportions and face are very similar to, though not yet the same as, an adult's. In general, though, the rate of body growth slows down more and more during these successive childhood periods until the adolescent growth spurt occurs.

The overall pattern of physical growth and the simultaneous maturation of different brain areas, affects children's motor skills as do the increasing amounts and types of practice children experience in various activities. The slightly longer legs of toddlers give them better balance than infants, leading to faster 'toddling'. Instead of having to hold their arms out for balance or instead of having to cling to furniture like infants, toddlers are free to carry or pull toys. As legs and practice grow still more, the toddler—now a preschooler—achieves better balance, permitting faster movement and the ability to turn corners without falling and without running into walls. Walking becomes less 'toddly' and more adultlike. Unlike young toddlers who take stairs one at a time, first crawling up and then bumping down, and who push forward on both tricycle pedals at once, preschoolers can alternate their legs to pedal or to climb stairs. Through the school years children adopt physical games that are more and more complicated and require increasing motor skill.

Hand skills likewise grow more refined and complex. Sometime during early toddlerhood, normal children can hold large crayons in their fists and scribble with them. Later, they grasp them awkwardly in their fingers and start drawing roughly circular outlines, including the first "people"—large circles with seemingly random marks. During the preschool period children add shaky lines, crosses, and squares to their repertoire of drawings. Their "people" develop properly placed eyes, mouths, and ears, then arms with blob-hands or sunburst fingers, then feet, and finally stick-legs and stick-bodies. Finger dexterity and accuracy in reaching both increase, so that preschoolers can build block castles and can string beads, although toddlers are limited to activities like banging pans or picking up beads and dropping (or throwing) them. Through the school years children continue to polish their fine-grain motor skills through writing, drawing, and other types of manual activities.

Cognitive Development

Language skills also grow rapidly from toddlerhood to puberty. The young toddler characteristically speaks

An original article written for ANNUAL EDITIONS: PSYCHOLOGY 81/82. The Dushkin Publishing Group, Inc., Guilford, CT., 1980.

in single words, but these usually are not just names for people and objects. Instead they seem to serve as sentences referring to frequently-performed activities or things the child has noticed. For example, "Daddy" may mean, "Daddy, come play with me" or "Look at Daddy coming into the room," depending on the situation. As toddlers add more words to their vocabulary, they begin to utter two-word phrases involving an action or other dynamic change, and an actor ("Birdie fly") or something acted upon ("All gone milk," "Throw ball"). This is usually the start of the "what dat?" labeling stage. Somewhat later toddlers add more words to their telegram-like sentences—"Go bye-bye car see grandma." By the preschool years, the words once left out begin to be included (words like "the," "in," "to," and so on), vocabulary grows larger, and sentences are longer and more complex. During this period and the early school years, children show an ability to recognize language rules from what they hear, but the rules often are applied too broadly. For example, the ed/rule for making a verb past-tense. Preschoolers' vocabulary typically is about literal properties, e.g., red, friendly, rather than abstract, figurative properties. Preschoolers therefore may laugh or be puzzled when hearing about a "sweet old lady" (Is she like sugar?) or that "the cat has my tongue" (How did she get it, and why, and can you get it back?). Children between about 5 and 10 can understand some double-function words like *sweet* or some ideomatic expressions from the way they are used, but can't explain them in other words. Further refinements of language after age 10 include the abstract terms, longer and more complex sentences, and the ability to talk about language rules.

While the general language changes are occurring, language is also gaining in its ability to guide the child's thought and behavior. Toddlers often find it difficult to follow an adult's instructions, and get caught up instead in the situation or in their initial intentions. Thus they may go on banging pots and pans when told to stop unless the objects are removed from reach. Or when an adult impulsively yells, "Take that out of there!" as a child puts a pussy willow into his nostril, the child may excitedly push it in all the faster. These reactions show that children of this age are poor at inhibiting their behavior. Later, however, children stop in response to a command if they are paying attention and decide to do so. They also begin to use their own speech to guide their actions, and tell themselves such things as "No, don't put that there, put it here, and then that goes there" while they build castles and models. Still later, during the early school years, children begin to speak to themselves privately instead of out loud unless the task is very hard. Children around 7 years also begin to use *inner speech* consisting of rehearsal and verbal organization to help them reason and to remember information.

Perceptual and Attentional Development

The way children pick up information through their five senses and the way they reason about things also show interesting changes from infancy to adolescence. Basic perceptual abilities such as sharpness of vision, or hearing pitch differences, increase during the school years. But children over 5 to 7 years also are much better than the preschooler at paying attention only to the important qualities of things they are seeing, hearing, or touching, and at ignoring the unimportant qualities. For instance, younger children often confuse *p* and *q* because they look at the whole letter instead of noticing which parts of the letters are different, whereas older children are better able to pay attention to the different curved parts so they can see and remember the difference. Older children are also better at detecting finer and finer differences between sights, sounds, and textures or shapes. They are more skilled at focusing their attention, at maintaining the focus for a longer time, and at voluntarily shifting focus. Part of their increased perceptual efficiency may be tied to their better ability to integrate information from several senses at once—younger children confuse themselves by paying brief attention to only one of many perceptual characteristics (how an object feels, or its color, or the sound it makes).

Some of the perceptual changes appear to be related to general developmental changes in quality of thinking, or cognitive abilities. Although IQ tests may imply that intelligence is basically the same at all ages, and that the older child simply has learned more than the younger one, research shows that reasoning also changes in quality. Jean Piaget, a Swiss psychologist who has made major contributions to what is known about developmental changes in reasoning or cognition, believed that the toddler thinks in different ways from the infant and preschooler. Whereas infants think only in terms of actions going on in the present, toddlers can form mental symbols for actions, objects, or people without their actual presence. This give toddlers the ability to play make-believe and to ask you to "blow" the candle at their pointed fingers. Toddlers also use their new mental representation ability to imitate somebody's behavior some time later, for instance, throwing their first tantrum shortly after first seeing another child throw one. Unlike older children and adults, though, toddlers tend to focus on only one aspect of a situation or object, and make idiosyncratic comparisons among things and events based on that very limited information. At the same time, toddlers may shift their attention quickly to something new, often unaware of the change. This leads to the idiosyncratic reasoning that adults find puzzling and even amusing. A toddler, seated on a tricycle, may burst into tears as an unknown child rides by on a similar tricycle because the tricycles look the same to the toddler and he may think his was taken because he forgot he was sitting on it. Toddlers may call a butterfly a bird because it flies. When asked to put all the toys that go together in a pile, toddlers may put the truck with the car because they both have wheels, and the blue marble with the vehicles because the car is blue, and the red rubber ball with all of these because it is round like the marble, and so on.

Preschool and early elementary school children are a bit more consistent and don't seem to shift focus so often, but they still focus on only limited information and can't voluntarily shift their attention to see things in a different way. Preschool children think intuitively rather than logically, which *may* lead them to the correct answer by an illogical route, but more often to the wrong answer (by adult standards). Young children can't seem to keep track of major categories and subcategories at the same time. They may say that there are six roses and two daisies in a bunch, and that roses and daisies are flowers, but then will insist that there are more roses than there are flowers. When seated in front of a toy village and asked to show how it looks to a doll on the other side of the table, they often will choose the picture that shows the scene as they see it. A girl with one sister may agree that she has a sister, but be certain that her sister does *not:* her sister is the one that is the sister, in absolute terms, and she herself is not the sister. Further, preschool children often think that everything occurs for a reason directly related to themselves. Thus they may whine, "why is it raining?" not because they want to know the physical causes for rain, but because they think the answer is "the sky wants to keep you from playing outside." In fact, preschoolers' intuitive thinking and egocentrism often prevent them from understanding a simple factual explanation. Even preschoolers who have been told, simply and accurately, where babies come from retell the story in nearly unrecognizable form, along the lines of "someone opens the lady's tummy and puts the baby seed in there, then they close her tummy until the baby is done, and the doctor opens her tummy to get the baby out." Some things may *not* be explainable to children until the school years.

Beginning around 7 years, children start to reason logically, based on their increased ability to focus their attention, voluntarily shift the focus, and integrate several pieces of information. They begin to realize that the quantitative aspects of physical things are conserved, even if their appearance is somehow transformed, unless something is added or taken away from them. A series of "conservation" experiments have shown these changes in many domains. For example, the school-age child knows that if you pour water from a short, wide container into a tall, thin container, there is still the same amount of water. In other words, the school-age child can pay attention to both height and width at once, and can mentally "undo" or reverse the change—"It is the same amount because you could pour it back and it would come to the same level"—or note that you have not added or taken from the quantity of water you started with. The preschooler, though, will say there is more water in the second container because it is "bigger." This suggests that preschoolers focus only on height, do not notice the width difference between the containers, and do not—or can not—mentally reverse the action. During the school years children apply their new logical abilities to solve problems based on physical, or concrete, properties of objects, situations, and social relations. In addition to conservation abilities, they can serially order objects, remember sub-categories, categories, and super-order categories at the same time ("This is a rose, which is a flower, which is a plant, which is a living thing"), know that other people may see things differently or think differently from themselves, and understand relative terms like "brother" and "on the left of this but on the right of that." But because they think mostly in concrete terms, school-age children still lack the abstract logical skills of adults and adolescents which underlie the capacity to make scientific or formal logical deductions.

Social Development

Toddlers usually play alone (solitary play) or alongside but not really with another child (parallel play). Whether alone or with another, their play is characterized predominantly by the use of imagination and make-believe or the practicing of sensorimotor skills, both motor (e.g., bed-jumping) and vocal (e.g., repeating "Upupupupupup!", babble-talking alone in the bedroom before going to sleep or after awakening). More truly 'social' play starts in the preschool years. Early preschool children continue parallel play, but also begin associative play, now playing the same game alongside other children though still without much direct interaction. An example of associative play is the seemingly 'contagious' play of nursery school children. Although they aren't really co-operating, when one child 'dresses up,' soon nearly all the other children are dressed up, apparently on their own. Nursery-schoolers also carry out collective monologues, alternating comments but about totally unrelated topics. Later in the preschool years children begin to play cooperatively, planning mutual activities and setting up rules. Cooperative play continues through life, becoming more and more complex and polished with the years. For preschoolers and school children, it is often dramatic play, an extension of imaginative play in which they practice both their physical and mental skills as well as various social roles. These social roles include the sex roles that define different appropriate behaviors for males and females. Role-practicing reflects their identification with their parents, and their visions of being other admired characters. (For some children this may include imitating aggressive characters on television.) Dramatic play helps children develop a sense of who they are and who they might be as adults. It also provides an opportunity for learning how to change in order to get along with others. For many children, it is only around 8 to 10 years that they first truly realize that others have different thoughts and feelings, and when this happens, the first true friendships develop. At all ages, but especially around 8-10 years, boys show strong tendencies toward playing with all-boy gangs whereas girls tend to play with one or a few other girls.

Emotional Development

Emotional development is closely related to social development, for it is largely based on interactions with others. Erik Erikson is well-known among psychologists for his ideas on stages in emotional and personality development. Erikson believes that toddlers must resolve a conflict between their impulse to feel autonomous in doing things for themselves ("No! *Me* tie shoe!"), and their feelings of shame and doubt about their attempts to be independent. The way parents and other people respond to both the toddler's autonomy and self-doubts influences whether the child ends up being more autonomous or more self-doubting. The preschooler must resolve a conflict beween taking the initiative in trying new things, and feeling guilt over still being a 'baby' who wets the bed or thumb-sucks. The emotional stages of the toddler and preschooler thus focus on two levels of the pull between dependence and independence, which may be one reason children of these ages are so susceptible to sibling jealousies over a new baby. The conflict the school child faces is between industry, or working hard at a task in order to do it well, and feelings of inferiority or incompetence. It is usually at this stage that children become more interested in hearing whether they have done something correctly than in being praised or given some other reward.

Different styles of childrearing may affect emotional development. Permissive childrearing involves little or no discipline, and boys from such homes tend to be less competent than other boys, whereas the girls are more resistant to authority. "Authoritarian" methods involve strict power-based discipline with close regulation of the children, and are associated with high dependence in girls and low social responsiveness in boys. "Authoritative" parents, in contrast, allow independence and often allow some democratic family decisions, but still have clear standards which they enforce consistently through reasoning and other non-physical techniques. Children from such homes tend to be independent, social leaders, well-liked, and socially responsive. They also tend to have high self-esteem. This picture is complicated, however, by findings that children have different basic temperaments from at least 3 months, and for that reason respond differently to various childrearing techniques. Some children are easy, and adapt to most new situations without fuss and often with positive feelings. Others are slower to warm up, and require patience and many repeated exposures to new situations and people before they get used to them. Still other children react strongly and negatively to new situations and things they don't like. They also need much patience and firmness, but may become even more difficult in the face of negative physical and emotional discipline.

Your Child's Self-Esteem

Paul Chance

Paul Chance, Ph.D., is a free-lance writer who specializes in psychology.

Consider Alice, age five. Alice attends kindergarten, where she is making excellent progress. Her teacher thinks she is one of the brightest children in the class, though in fact she has no more natural ability than most. She is often the first to raise her hand when the teacher asks a question, waving it eagerly and sometimes calling out, "I know! I know!" If called on when she does not know an answer, she does not hesitate to make a guess. Sometimes these answers sound foolish to her classmates, but their laughter doesn't bother Alice—she justs laughs right along with them. Alice tackles almost every assignment with enthusiasm. If one approach fails, she tries another. If her persistence does not pay off, she asks the teacher for help. Alice is as comfortable with other children as she is with her schoolwork. She is a popular child, and in group activities she often takes the lead. At home, Alice is eager to do things for herself. She is proud, for instance, that she can already dress herself completely, buttons, shoelaces, and all, without help.

Now consider Zelda, age six. Zelda is in the first grade. She did not do very well in kindergarten, and her progress continues to be slow. Her teacher believes that she is one of the least intelligent children in the class, though in fact she has as much ability as most. She never volunteers, and if called on she usually refuses to say more than "I don't know." Zelda works on most assignments in a lackluster, mechanical manner and often abandons them at the first sign of difficulty. When her teacher asks if she needs help, she says merely, "I can't do it." Zelda is no more adept socially than she is academically. She has few friends, and in group activities she is usually the quiet one on the sidelines. At home, Zelda is more at ease and more loquacious, but not more self-reliant. She waits for others to do things for her because she "can't" do them for herself. Her mother still checks her each morning to be sure that she has dressed herself properly.

Competence has little to do with natural ability.

Alice and Zelda are as far apart as the letters *a* and *z*. The differences that separate them are not, however, due to differences in native ability. The differences are emotional and motivational. Alice is obviously self-assured and self-reliant. She likes herself and her world. Although she could not put her philosophy into words, she is an optimist. She believes that she has some degree of control over her destiny, that success and happiness are goals an individual can achieve through effort. Zelda, on the other hand, is as filled with self-doubt as Alice is with self-confidence. Her self-esteem is low and she thinks the world a harsh, unfriendly place. A philosopher would describe her as a fatalist, a person who believes that what happens is largely a matter of fate or chance. Zelda believes that she can do little to shape her future, that success and happiness are things that "just happen" to people who get lucky. Although Alice and Zelda have about the same amount of intelligence, it is clear that Alice is making far better use of her abilities. The result is that Alice is a highly competent child, while Zelda is best described as helpless.

Why do some children become Alices, while others become Zeldas? This question has received intensive study over the past decade. Most researchers seem convinced that experiences in infancy and early childhood play an especially important role in the development of competence, so their research efforts have focused on experiences in the first three years of life. This is not to say, of course, that whether a person becomes highly competent or utterly helpless is unalterably fixed by age three. People can change at any age. Nevertheless, the evidence suggests that the kinds of experiences that are important to the development of competence typically *begin* in early childhood. What are those experiences? The research on this subject is complex and not easily reduced to a few simple, clear-cut statements. But over and over again, the studies reveal four elements common to the backgrounds of the most competent children but conspicuously missing from the backgrounds of the least competent.

The importance of a strong parent-child bond.

It may come as no surprise to most parents that one common element in the backgrounds of very competent children is a strong bond between the child and the primary care-giver—usually, but not necessarily, the mother. Dr. Alan Sroufe, professor of child development, and his co-workers at the University of Minnesota, Twin Cities, have found, for instance, that infants judged "securely attached" at eighteen months of age were more successful at solving problems, such as getting an object out of a tube, at age two. They were also better able to elicit the help of their mothers to solve problems that were too difficult for them. They were, in other words, already more competent than children who lacked a strong bond with their mothers.

The signs of a secure child.

Dr. Sroufe notes that it is possible to predict which children will be successful preschoolers by studying the relationship a child has with his caretaker at twelve to eighteen months of age. "Even by two years," he says, "secure children will be more enthusiastic, persistent, and cooperative in solving problems than insecure children will be." Children with a good, secure relationship with an adult can function well in a nursery school at a younger age than can children without such a relationship. "Apparently," Dr. Sroufe concludes, "secure children have learned early how to explore and master their environment and function within clear, firm limits."

Perhaps the most extensive work on the relationship between a close attachment and child development is that of Dr. Burton White, former director of the Preschool Project at Harvard University, and his colleagues. Their research followed the progress of 40 children, beginning at age one or two. The researchers went into the homes of these children every other week, 26 times a year, for one or two years, and then retested the children again at the ages of three and five. The researchers concentrated on the interactions of the infants with their mothers and others in the home. They concluded that a close social relationship "was a conspicuous feature in the lives of children who developed best."

Another way to study the benefits of a love bond, as it might be called, is by looking at the development of children for whom such a bond is notably lacking. One sometimes finds such children in poorly staffed institutions. Dr. Sally Provence, professor of pediatrics at Yale University's Child Study Center, who has made a special study of such children, observes that they often become "subdued and apathetic." Given a little tender loving care, however, these children often liven up dramatically.

Providing a stimulating environment.

Another common element in the backgrounds of competent children is a stimulating environment. Dr. K. Alison Clarke-Stewart, associate professor of education and human development at the University of Chicago, studied the interactions of mothers with their firstborn infants, ages nine to thirteen months. She found, among other things, that mothers of competent children talked to or made other sounds when interacting with their babies more often than did the mothers of less competent infants. Dr. White and his co-workers were so impressed by the role of verbal stimulation in the development of competence that they wrote that "live language directed to the child is the most consistently favorable kind of educational experience an infant can have during the eleven- to sixteen-month period." They go on to point out that language from a television or radio or speech directed elsewhere that the child overhears has little if any beneficial effect.

Freedom to explore can make even an ordinary environment more stimulating than it is from afar. An environment that is full of interesting objects a child cannot get to is less stimulating than one with fewer objects that are within reach. Dr. White and his collaborators found, in fact, that freedom of movement was characteristic of the homes of competent children. The more freedom to explore about the house (within the limits prescribed by safety, of course), the more competent a child was likely to be.

The evidence for the benefits of a stimulating environment suggests that a dull, monotonous environment is a prescription for helplessness. This theory seems to be borne out by the classic research of renowned psychiatrist René Spitz, who studied the development of children living in the thoroughly monotonous world of a badly understaffed foundling home. These children had little to do all day but sleep or stare at the blank walls about them. Needless to say, such children do not develop normally, but the degree to which their development is retarded is striking. Dr. Spitz offers this description of the typical child reared in such an impoverished environment: "These children would lie or sit with wide-open, expressionless eyes, frozen immobile face, and a faraway expression as if in a daze, apparently not perceiving what went on in their environment."

Fortunately for such children, a little bit of stimulation can have substantial benefits. For instance, psychologists Wayne Dennis and Yvonne Sayegh gave institutionalized infants in an otherwise impoverished environment items such as flowers, bits of colored sponge, and a chain of colored plastic discs to play with for as little as an hour each day. It is hard to believe that so little improvement in their thoroughly monotonous environment would make a great difference, yet their developmental ages jumped dramatically.

Interactions—with parents . . .

It is, of course, possible to get too much of a good thing. Dr. White believes that too much stimulation, too many things going on around the child, may merely confuse him. This idea is supported by a study conducted by Dr. Jerome Kagan, professor of human development at Harvard University, who watched mothers as they interacted with their four-month-old infants. He noted when the mothers spoke to or cooed to their babies and what else they were doing at the time. He found that upper-middle-income mothers usually spoke to their children while facing them but did *not* simultaneously tickle them or provide other stimulation. Low-income mothers, on the other hand, were likely to talk to their infants while diapering, feeding, or burping them. It is probably not a coincidence, Dr. Kagan observes, that the children of upper-middle-income mothers typically show more precocious language development than do the children of low-income mothers.

Most researchers seem to agree that a varied environment is important to the development of competence, but the quality of the stimulation is more important than the amount.

A third characteristic of the backgrounds of competent children is frequent social interaction. Dr. White has found, for instance, that highly competent children have at least twice as many social experiences as their less competent peers. He says that "providing a rich social life for a twelve- to fifteen-month-old child is the best thing you can do to guarantee a good mind." He also notes that firstborn children have far more opportunities to interact with their parents than do later-born children. The rich social life of firstborns may have something to do with the fact that they are usually (though not always, of course) more competent than their siblings are. They are, for instance, more likely to obtain positions of leadership as adults than are later-born children.

. . . and with others.

Psychologist Michael Lewis, director of the Institute for the Study of Exceptional Children at the Educational Testing Service in Princeton, New Jersey, believes that the child's interactions with other people are more important than his interactions with any other part of the environment. "We learn about others through our interaction with them," he writes, "and at the same time we define ourselves." How does a child learn whether he is a boy or a girl, tall or short, strong or weak? Through his interactions with others who treat him as a boy rather than a girl, and who are taller or shorter, stronger or weaker, than he is. How does he learn whether he is competent or helpless? Partly, argues Dr. Lewis, through his interactions with the people around him.

Studies of social isolation have shown that even when other forms of stimulation are available, a dearth of social experiences can have devastating effects. Dr. Harry Harlow and his colleagues at the University of Wisconsin at Madison found that monkeys reared alone grew up to be timid, wholly inadequate individuals. Monkeys reared by their mothers but separated from other youngsters of their kind fared better, but still developed abnormally. Thus it appears likely that the more opportunities for social encounters a child has, the better. It is even possible to see social competence emerge as a result of such experience. When, for example, California psychologist Jacqueline Becker gave pairs of nine-month-old babies the opportunity to play with one another, she found that they interacted more and more with each succeeding session. When these youngsters were introduced to a new baby, they were much more likely to approach him than were infants who had had less social experience.

A world that responds.

Probably the most important element in the environments of highly competent children is something that researchers call *responsivity*. A responsive environment is one that *responds to* the behavior of the child. There is, in other words, some correspondence between what the child does and what happens to him. Under ordinary circumstances there is at least a minimal amount of responsivity in the life of every child. Take, for example, the baby nursing at his mother's breast. As Dr. Martin Seligman, professor of psychology at the University of Pennsylvania, writes: "He sucks, the world responds with warm milk. He pats the breast, his mother tenderly squeezes him back. He takes a break and coos, his mother coos back. . . . Each step he takes is synchronized with a response from the world." When a child's behavior has clear, unequivocal consequences, he not only learns about those consequences but "over and above this," writes Dr. Seligman, "he learns that responding works, that in general there is *synchrony* between responses and outcomes." This means, in turn, that the child exerts some control over his environment, and many researchers agree with Dr. Seligman that "how readily a person believes in his own helplessness or mastery is shaped by his experience with controllable and uncontrollable events."

A responsive environment, then, inclines a child toward competence, while an unresponsive environment inclines a child toward helplessness. Dr. Lewis illustrates the difference by describing the experiences of two infants, Sharon and Toby. One morning Sharon wakes up wet, hungry, or perhaps just lonely, and cries. Nothing happens. She cries again. Still no response. She continues crying for several minutes, but no one comes. Finally she falls asleep, exhausted. On the same morning another infant, Toby, awakes. She, too, is wet, hungry, or lonely, and cries. Within seconds she has the attention of a warm hand, a smiling face, and the food or dry diaper she needs. Sharon's world is unresponsive; her behavior has no effect. Toby's world is highly responsive; her behavior gets results almost immediately. Now, what is the lesson each child is taught by her respective experience? Sharon learns that making an effort to affect one's condition is useless. Things happen or they don't; what she does is unimportant. Toby learns that her efforts are worthwhile. What happens depends, in part, upon what she does.

Some readers may think at this point that responsivity is just another name for permissiveness. Give the child what he wants, pander to his every whim, deny him nothing. In other words, spoil him. Not so. A responsive environment is not one that gives a child everything and anything he wants. Responsivity means merely that an act produces clear, consistent consequences. Sometimes those consequences will be negative. For example, a four-year-old child who insists upon having cookies for breakfast may send his bowl of cereal flying. A parent might respond to this behavior by saying, "Since you've thrown away your breakfast, you'll have to go without." Another parent might insist that the child clean up the mess he has made. In each case the child's behavior has some effect, but the effect does not necessarily include getting a plate of cookies.

Handling a baby's cry.

But what about Toby's crying? Sure, Toby learns that she can master her environment, but doesn't she inevitably become a crybaby in the process? Doesn't she learn that the way to get what you want is by making a fuss? Interestingly enough, the answer is no. Psychologists Silvia Bell and Mary Ainsworth conducted a study of the effects of responsiveness on crying. They observed the interactions of mothers and their infants during the first year of the child's life. There were wide variations among the mothers in how often and how quickly they responded to their baby's cries. The most responsive mother, for instance, responded 96 percent of the time, while the least responsive mother answered only 3 percent of her baby's cries. Many parents would predict that the first infant would cry constantly. What actually happened, though, was that the children who could control their environment by crying soon learned to use more subtle tactics to exert control, and they also learned to do things for themselves. The researchers conclude that "an infant whose mother's responsiveness helps him to achieve his ends develops confidence in his own ability to control what happens to him." This means that he comes to do more things for himself, which means there are fewer occasions for calling upon Mom.

Other research supports the notion that a responsive environment leads to competence. In one study, for example, Dr. Lewis and psychologist Susan Goldberg watched mothers interact with their three-month-old infants. They noticed that the behavior of some mothers was likely to be a reaction to what the baby did, while the behavior of other mothers tended to be independent of the baby's activity. The researchers found that the first infants, those whose mothers were responsive, were more interested in the world around them and were more attentive.

Toys that foster competence.

Dr. John S. Watson of the University of California at Berkeley demonstrated that the responsiveness of the physical world also is beneficial. Dr. Watson designed a mobile that would rotate whenever a baby exerted pressure on a pillow. When an infant turned his head this way or that, the mobile would spin. Dr. Watson found that with just ten minutes of practice a day, the infants learned to control the mobile within a few days. They also smiled and cooed as the mobile spun to and fro, apparently enjoying the control they exerted over the object. Other babies who saw the mobile spin but had no control over its movement did not show the same reaction.

Providing a child with responsive toys does not necessarily require anything so elaborate as Watson's motorized mobile. Psychologist Robert McCall notes that a mobile can be made responsive simply by tying a piece of soft cotton yarn loosely around a baby's wrist and tying the other end to the mobile. When the baby moves his hand, the mobile moves. Another inexpensive but highly responsive baby toy is the rattle, since it makes a noise only when and if the baby shakes it. Yet another example is a mirror, perhaps made of shiny metal so that there is no danger of broken glass. The child looks in the mirror and sees someone looking back. The person looking back does all sorts of things—smiling, laughing, frowning—but only if the child looking into the mirror does them first. As the child gets a bit older, a spoon and a pie pan provide responsive, if noisy, diversion. It may well be the case that the more responsive toys tend to be the least expensive. Toys that "do it all" rarely require much activity from the child. Thus, the *least* responsive toy available is probably the $500 color television set, while one of the most responsive toys around is the $1 rubber ball.

There is evidence that if a child's environment is thoroughly *un*responsive, he is almost certain to become helpless rather than competent. Dr. Seligman and his colleagues have conducted a number of studies that demonstrate just how devastating the lack of control over events can be. They have found that when a laboratory animal is unable to escape an unpleasant situation, it eventually quits trying. More important, when the animal is later put into another situation from which it could readily escape, it does not do so. In fact, it makes no effort to escape. Psychologist Donald Hiroto got similar results when he studied the effects of uncontrollable unpleasant events on college students. Some students heard an unpleasantly loud noise, which they could do nothing about. Other students heard the same noise but learned to control it by pushing a button. Afterward, the students were put into another situation in which they could turn off a noise simply by moving their hand from one part of a box to another. Those who had learned to control the noise in the first situation did so in the second, but most of those who could do nothing about the first noise made no attempt to escape the second. They simply sat there and did nothing. They had been made helpless, at least momentarily.

Helping a child master his world.

Researchers have not, of course, deliberately set out to make children helpless by exposing them to unpleasant situations from which they cannot escape. They have, however, noted that children reared in unresponsive environments are not likely to become highly competent. Dr. Seligman points out that a lack of control was characteristic of the environment of Dr. Spitz's institutionalized children and may have been more important to their helplessness than the lack of stimulation they received.

All children are subjected to some unpleasant events that they cannot control. An infant's diaper rash is beyond his control, as is the misery of most childhood illnesses. And even the brightest child must eventually experience failure. But if the child is usually able to exert some control over the events in his life, this may give him some immunity against the adverse effects of unpleasant events he is powerless to control.

It appears, then, that the kind of experiences a child has in the first few years of life plays an important role in his development. The child who has a close, warm relationship with an adult; who lives in interesting surroundings; who has ample opportunity to interact with other people; and, most important, who lives in an environment that is responsive, has an excellent chance of becoming competent. The earlier these experiences begin, the better. "I believe," Dr. Seligman told me, "that motivation and emotion are more plastic than intelligence. I am no longer convinced that special kinds of experiences will raise a child's IQ by twenty points or induce him to write piano concertos at age five, as Mozart did. But I am convinced that certain kinds of experiences during childhood will produce a child who is helpless, while other experiences will produce a child who is competent."

There is in every child an Alice and a Zelda. The question is, which is to prevail?

Learning Right From Wrong

Ellen Sherberg

Ellen Sherberg is a free-lance writer and a reporter for KMOX (CBS radio in St. Louis).

Ten-year-old Eddie was feeling pretty lucky. It was the last day of school, and a special lunch—hamburgers and ice cream—was on the cafeteria menu. Since he had gym class before lunch period, and the gym was right next to the cafeteria, he could rush to be among the first in the lunch line. His friend Tom, however, had to walk much farther to the cafeteria, and found more than 60 students waiting by the time he got there.

"Can I cut in front of you?" Tom asked Eddie. "I'll give you my ice cream."

Should Eddie let Tom cut in line? Would Tom still be Eddie's friend if he said no? What about the other kids who had been waiting? What about that extra ice cream? What if Tom told Eddie he'd miss an important ride to a doctor's appointment if he didn't cut in line? Should that matter?

Ethical dilemmas.

"Cutting in line" is one of many minor discipline problems that crop up during the average school day. But it is not only a discipline problem; for the child, it is also an ethical problem.

"Commonplace situations are often moral dilemmas," explains Peter Scharf, co-author of *Growing Up Moral* (Winston Press, Inc.). "And it's critical that children learn to confront these dilemmas if they're going to grow into morally responsible adults."

Discussions about morality used to be reserved for parents and the pulpit, but today's schools are playing a larger and larger role in children's moral education.

Two approaches to teaching about values.

Of course, questions of moral behavior are not new to the classroom setting. Sensitive teachers have always been aware of the moral issues raised by their curricula, current events, and children's personal experiences.

But today's educators rely on two specific approaches to moral education. The more widely used approach is based on the ideas of educator Louis Raths, who built upon the thinking of John Dewey to formulate his system of *values clarification*. The other approach, based on the theories of Harvard educator/psychologist Lawrence Kohlberg, is known as *cognitive moral development*.

Values clarification: the process is the key.

The values-clarification approach developed by Raths focuses on the *process* people use to develop their beliefs and behavior. Through a variety of analytical techniques applied to classroom discussion, teachers point out to their students the three major aspects of decision-making, all of which are part of what Raths calls "the process of valuing."

First, students are made aware of their own values (for example, "It is wrong to cooperate with the enemy because it is disloyal to your own country"); then they're asked to identify their priorities ("Saving people's lives, especially your parents', is more important than being loyal to your country"); finally, they are brought to recognize the relation of their individual beliefs to the values held by the culture in which they live ("After the war, members of your family may consider you a hero, but others may call you 'traitor' ").

Looking at old lessons a new way.

With the values-clarification techniques, even material that appears to be universally accepted can be used to stir classroom controversy. For example, a history lesson about the Pilgrims at Plymouth Colony could lead a teacher to ask, "Is there anything you value so strongly that you would leave this town or country if it were taken away?"

If a student says yes, it doesn't matter if he prizes his dog, his family, or his freedom. What is important is how he arrived at that decision and how consistent it is with his other beliefs and actions. It's also important for him to understand how other people perceive his decision.

Other students might snicker if a ten-year-old says his dog is as important to him as his friends are. But if the student goes on to explain how the dog's presence keeps him from being scared at night, his decision takes on new merit in the class. Others begin to see that his preference for his dog is consistent with his values and with qualities that most people consider important, such as loyalty, companionship, and protectiveness.

According to the values-clarification system, it doesn't really matter if Eddie—the little boy in the cafeteria line—decides to let his friend "cut in" or not. If, during his decision-making process, he said loyalty is more important to him than anything and for that reason he is willing to let his friend in line despite the glares of other students, his decision would be acceptable. If, on the other hand, Eddie said that ice cream is more important to him than anything and his friend has promised him extra ice cream—and he doesn't care if his actions make other kids angry—his decision would be just as acceptable because, again, it would be consistent with his values.

While the process of decision-making is the key to the values-clarification approach, the *decision itself* is what counts in Kohlberg's philosophy. In a classroom where cognitive moral development is taught, Eddie's decision to let his buddy in line might not be acceptable.

Cognitive moral development: an offshoot of Piaget's work.

Kohlberg's theory is based directly on the philosophy of Jean Piaget, who was the first modern psychologist to observe that a child's conception of social rules evolves in stages.

Piaget's research consisted of watching children of different ages playing, and then questioning them about the rules of their games. He found that toddlers, who tend to play by themselves, have no sense of rules as social obligations. As children begin to play together, around the time they enter school, they play games according to rules that must be strictly obeyed. They consider these rules to have emanated from adults and, as such, to be unchangeable. Piaget noticed that preadolescents also play according to a defined set of rules. But these rules are viewed as being based on the mutual consent of the group of players, and must be followed if one wants to be loyal; one can change the rules, however, if the majority of the group agrees to the change.

Kohlberg takes Piaget's observation that a child's view of rules evolves as he grows older and extends it to the concept that a child's moral consciousness develops through stages. According to this theory, if Eddie were six or seven years old, he might not let his friend cut in line because he would be afraid his teacher would yell at him. At this point, Eddie would be at the first stage of moral development.

At stage two, when Eddie is slightly older, he begins to understand sharing in a very pragmatic ("you scratch my back, I'll scratch yours") sense; at this stage he might let his friend in line in exchange for the ice cream.

Stage-three development has a connotation of peer approval. "Right" is defined by what others expect, and behavior is often judged by intentions. At this stage, Eddie might reason that it's okay to let his friend cut in because all the other children in line would expect him to let their friends cut in.

Stage four is known as "the law-and-order orientation"; now judgments of right and wrong are based on rules and on respect for formal authority. Because cutting in line is against the rules, Eddie at this stage might turn his buddy down.

Following Kohlberg's Piaget-based system, as Eddie grows older and becomes a teenager he should begin making his own moral decisions. He might, for example, decide to let his friend in line, not because of the ice cream, but because he knows his pal has to eat in a hurry or miss his ride.

At this point Eddie is measuring the needs of the individual against the rules of the school. He considers issues of fairness and justice and makes a decision he thinks he can live with. Consequently, he considers how fair it would be to those who have been waiting in line if his buddy cut in. If his friend is actually going to miss a ride that will take him to the doctor or to a job where he makes money to support his family, Eddie might decide to allow him to cut in line; if the ride is to a movie, Eddie might decide to favor the feelings of the other students waiting in line.

That most teenagers would consider all these factors may sound a bit farfetched. Most adolescents—and adults as well—would simply say to a pal, "It's okay, stand in front of me."

That's why Kohlberg's theory is far more than a description of moral development. It's based on a strong belief that discussions of moral dilemmas led by a well-trained teacher can bring students to a higher level of moral reasoning, where they will consider—and act on—the issues of fairness applied to society as a whole.

While recognizing that students must progress naturally through the various stages of moral development, Kohlberg also believes that constructive discussions can sometimes hasten progress by increasing moral consciousness.

This facet of the Kohlberg philosophy was tested by one of his graduate students, who tried to raise the level of reasoning in his Sunday-school class through debate of dilemmas such as Eddie's. At the end of the year, the graduate student reported that his pupils had advanced by an average of one-third of a stage.

Moral education is making a difference.

In a much less structured environment, Sarah Wallace, former chairman of the values committee at John Burroughs School, a private coeducational school in St. Louis, Missouri, says she's seen definite changes in her teenage children and their friends since the moral-education program was instituted three years ago.

"The kids are learning a bit more maturity," Mrs. Wallace says. "They're more understanding of why somebody acts a certain way."

Moral growth can also be encouraged in younger children. Bill McCoy, who co-authored *Growing Up Moral*, uses film, written material, and discussions to explore moral dilemmas with his fourth, fifth, and sixth graders at Top of the World Elementary School in Laguna Beach, California.

"Students who at one time could only talk about stage-two, or person-to-person, relationships on an 'I'll do this for you if you'll do this for me' basis start to consider other people. They suddenly begin to ask, 'What's expected of us?' " he reports.

In McCoy's homeroom, fifth graders arrange their chairs in a circle and spend 20 to 40 minutes discussing problems such as cutting in the lunch line.

In his social-studies classes, McCoy uses California history to illustrate moral dilemmas. For example, the Chinese migration in the 1860s, when the expanding railroads inspired a wave of settlement, presents an opportunity to discuss racial issues.

Even more dramatic discussions take place about the Donner Party, a legendary group of California settlers who resorted to cannibalism to survive a harsh winter. Among the questions posed: "Was it right or wrong for the survivors to eat the bodies of the people who died?" "Why?" "Would it ever be right to kill a person for food in order for a larger group to survive?"

Teachers following Kohlberg's moral-development approach will lead the discussion toward questions affecting the good of the entire group; their goal is to create a consciousness that will lead to a more caring, just society.

What the critics say.

But that's a tall order, and although a 1975 Gallup poll showed that more than 75 percent of the parents queried favored school instruction in moral behavior, there have also been critics of moral education. They include some religious organizations that question what morals are being taught in today's secular classrooms.

But even supporters of moral education acknowledge that teachers must be wary of some of its pitfalls. Because the theory deals with the cognitive domain—or how a child thinks—sometimes teachers forget that how a child feels is equally important. For example, little Eddie in the cafeteria line might decide it's not right to let his friend cut in line, but burst into tears because he's afraid of hurting his buddy's feelings. Or maybe he will cry because he isn't sure if he made the right decision. His fears and self-doubts must be reckoned with as well as his decision-making process.

According to Dr. Ann DiStefano, assistant professor of education at Washington University in St. Louis, another drawback to both the values-clarification approach and Kohlberg's theories (indeed, to much of today's education) is the possibility of creating a classroom situation that "rewards kids who are especially adept at debating and can think clearly on their feet." A teacher's ability to direct a discussion is crucial to avoid the creation of a verbal elite among students, she feels. When the emphasis is on how well a decision is articulated, it may not be on how well it is carried out. The teacher must also remind his or her students that morality is more than just saying what's "right" and espousing democratic values; it's acting in a concerned and consistent manner.

One of the strongest criticisms of moral education is that parents aren't part of the process. Some schools are trying to correct that. When moral education was introduced in the Brookline, Massachusetts, public schools, for instance, great care was taken to include presentations to parents' groups and to explain the philosophy during parent-teacher meetings. The adult evening school offered a course on moral education, but parents were slow to develop interest.

At Crossroads School, a private junior high school in St. Louis, Missouri, parents and children go to school together for an evening. They're divided into groups of about ten persons (with no parent in the same group as his or her child), and discussions center on curfews, reporting to parents, drugs, and relationships. As with discussions among students in the classroom, the purpose of this is not to change minds or to decide who is right. Instead, the evening gives parents and children an opportunity to examine one another's thinking. It's been so popular that what started out as an interesting experiment has become a tradition at Crossroads.

But Crossroads is the exception, not the rule. For the most part, schools—especially public schools—only have time to deal with their students. That means problems can arise when parents want only one moral position presented, and the teacher is presenting alternatives.

Parental disapproval.

If a parent believes a child should always agree with the President, for example, conflicts can erupt if classroom conversation dwells on how to disagree in a democracy and students explore the possibility of differing with government policy. Supporters of moral education in the schools say the same parent who objects to this would also object to a traditional history lesson if it concerned the Bay of Pigs fiasco and focused on President John Kennedy's misjudgments.

According to those who support moral education, it is intended to help young people think clearly, know what they believe, and understand how their beliefs fit into or affect the society as a whole. Supporters of moral education emphasize that it does not aim to promote values that are in opposition to those a child learns from his family. However, it does aim to provoke discussion; and, at the very least, the kinds of stimulating conversation it can inspire in a home where open communication is encouraged will provide a thought-provoking and beneficial alternative to watching television.

Coping with the Seasons of Life

John Nicholson

John Nicholson is the author of "Seven Ages" (Fontana Paperbacks). This article is excerpted from the social science weekly "New Society" of London.

There are two very different views about the importance age plays in people's lives. There is the Shakespearean tradition, encapsulated in the "Seven Ages of Man" speech in *As You Like It*, which suggests that our lives fall into distinct phases and that people change as they get older, generally for the worse. Other writers take the view that we are "as old as we feel." André Gide remarked at the age of seventy-three, "If I did not keep telling myself my age over and over again, I am sure I should hardly be aware of it." Which view is right? In an attempt to answer this question, some 600 men, women, and children between the ages of five and eighty were interviewed last winter in the Colchester Study of Aging. The aim of this survey was to build up by objective means a subjective picture of the human lifecycle.

A few years ago you got the "key to the door" at twenty-one. But only one in eight of the adults we interviewed gave twenty-one as the age at which they considered they became adult. Most men judged that they became adult sometime between eighteen and twenty-one, while women gave more varied answers, with a significant proportion of them designating the mid-to-late-twenties.

What are young adults like? Though some functions—notably the performance of our hearts and circulatory systems—reach a peak slightly earlier, the years between twenty and twenty-five represent the pinnacle of our biological development. Physically and intellectually, we have never before been so good and never will be again.

On the negative side we found young adults to be self-centered and still naïve in their views on what life is all about. In psychological terms many of them were still in the throes of the identity crisis that had begun to disturb them in adolescence. Particularly among the unmarried, there seemed to be an internal conflict between wanting to establish a position which commands respect and not wanting to get into a rut. They were afraid of slipping into the habits of their boss, for example, by taking a briefcase home in the evening. And yet many were anxious to carve out a niche for themselves and enjoy the status and economic advantages of their jobs.

On the positive side they enjoyed the feeling of "no longer being a kid." Some—particularly the married—expressed pleasure in mapping out the future. Others complained that they were required to make once-and-for-all decisions, that their options were closing, and that they were anxious about their ability to cope with the future.

For some young adults the feeling of emotional insecurity far outweighs the self-confidence which comes from standing on their own two feet. Psychiatrists consider that many early marriages are "take-care-of-me contracts," entered into in a spirit of panic rather than out of conviction that one has found the ideal partner for life.

This is only one of the dangers presented by the freedom of young adulthood. For some people freedom becomes an obsession, to be guarded at all costs. As one example of this, many young adults we spoke to in Colchester were strongly opposed to the idea of having children, mainly because of the restrictions they felt it would impose on their sense of freedom.

People tend to look back on their early twenties with pleasure. When we asked our sample what age they would most like to be if they had the choice, the twenties proved to be a popular decade. Those who favored it did so because that was when life had been most enjoyable.

Perhaps the most striking feature of young adulthood is its exclusiveness with regard to age. At no other period of life do we spend less time in the company of people older or younger than ourselves; and it may well be that never again are we so sensitive to the difference of even a year.

People who reach young adulthood without having had any sexual experience are now in a minority (though barely). Since most adolescents say that they are opposed to casual sex, and seem to feel quite strongly that sex ought to occur only in the context of an established loving relationship, it may well be that many of today's teenagers have at least one such relationship before young adulthood.

In some respects, the intimate relationships young adults try to form are similar to earlier relationships with their parents and friends. They may well have loved their parents and felt deeply committed to best friends. The new dimension is being in love, and the problem which has taxed young adults since time began is how to distinguish between being in love and liking, depending on, or being infatuated.

"One of the pleasures of middle age is to find out that one was right, and that one was much righter than one knew at, say, seventeen or twenty-three." Or so said the poet Ezra Pound.

People in their forties are sandwiched between two demanding and often—in their eyes — unreasonable generations, both of which rely on them for psychological and practical support. At no other stage in their lives do so many people depend on them, and that realization causes people in their forties to brood darkly on the cyclical nature of life and the passing of time. They also ask themselves more mundane questions like: Should a woman/man of my age really be wearing slit-skirts/jeans? So although the forties may not precisely be middle age, they are an age-conscious decade.

Our appearance does begin to change in the forties. The full effects of these changes are not yet apparent, but we are beginning to look different. The balance between physical improvement and physical degeneration wavers during the thirties, then tips toward degeneration.

During our survey in Colchester we asked people in their forties what was the worst thing about life now compared with ten years ago. Their main complaints were the feeling of being so much older and worries about their appearance and health. But they were not aware of any significant change in their sex life. Most of those we interviewed disagreed strongly with the suggestion that sexual relationships are more important to young people.

The people we talked to seemed to be more concerned about physical than mental decline, and they were right, because in this period of our lives there is little cause for alarm. Any fears about declining mental faculties are more likely to be imaginary than real.

Our survey asked if any age since adolescence had seemed particularly dif-

"Coping with the Seasons of Life," John Nicholson, *World Press Review*, November 1980. Reprinted by permission of Jonathan Clowes Limited, London, England.

ficult, and we were astonished to find that none of the people in the forty-to-forty-five age group described their present age in these terms. Our results clearly support those who deny existence of a midlife crisis, and we must conclude that if there is such a thing as the male menopause, it affects only a small group.

Unless we decide to tear up our roots and start again, we have to alter the emphasis in our personal relationships from sexuality to sociability, particularly in marriage. It is in the forties that husbands and wives start sizing each other up and wondering how they will adjust to living as a couple again without the shared responsibility of parenthood to bind them. Most couples of this age realize that an enormous emotional vacuum is about to open up, and it is interesting to see how they prepare to deal with it. In Colchester, we found that more women had jobs in the thirty-five-to-forty-nine age bracket than in any other.

The importance of women's jobs rose steadily from one age group to the next. It overtook money as a priority at forty, and by the end of the fifties ranked almost equal with friends. The fact that this was the only change in life-priorities shown by either sex between twenty-nine and fifty-nine clearly establishes this as one of the most significant changes in the forties.

How do men prepare themselves for the future? Although we didn't find that the majority of men in their forties in Colchester were becoming more interested in hobbies, some clearly were prepared to run the gamut of their wives' and children's sneers and were developing new interests to take their minds off worries and prepare for retirement.

Psychologists describe the qualities we need to develop in the forties as mental flexibility and the ability to broaden our emotional investment to include new people, activities, and roles. One person in ten of those in their early forties in Colchester said they found it more difficult than ten years ago to adapt to change or to accept new ideas, whereas three times this number said they found it less difficult.

When the Colchester survey asked its participants to list the things they worried about, we found that concern about children among people of thirty-six to forty-five was the largest single worry of either sex at any age. Nine out of ten of the women we interviewed, whose eldest child was between sixteen and nineteen, said they were worried about their child's future. The men in our survey were much less likely than their wives to worry about their children. Their most frequent worry was money.

People in their forties wonder whether permissiveness hasn't gone too far, and increasingly find themselves identifying with their own parents and defending their values rather than rebelling against them. So as middle age approaches, there seems to be a clear shift in our loyalties and attitudes, which is part of a growing awareness that we are about to join the older generation.

Perhaps the most uncertain feature of life is its length. The uncertainty makes it inevitable that thoughts about death should color the final stage of our lives. But the prospect of dying does not seem to destroy our ability to make the best of whatever age we happen to be. An old woman in Colchester said, "Some people thought I was doing too much and I ought to slow down a bit. I said, 'I've retired from work, I didn't retire from life'."

Researchers have constructed a table of events old people find most stressful. The death of a spouse comes at the top of this list, followed by being put into an institution, the death of a close relative, major personal injury or disease, losing a job, and divorce. Being widowed seems to affect men more severely than women. A recent British study found that the death rate among men and women during the year after they are widowed is ten times higher than among people of the same age who are still married.

As we approach the end of our lives we become less interested in the outside world and more concerned with ourselves. The psychological task that becomes increasingly important is to come to terms with ourselves, to find some justification for our lives, and to reconcile ourselves to the fact that it is going to end. Paradoxically, the person who believes that his or her life has been most worthwhile seems to have the fewest qualms about the prospect of its coming to an end.

What is the recipe for a successful old age? Some people say that unless old people keep themselves active and engaged, they will become a misery to themselves and a burden on others. Others take the view that an old person who continues to devote his energy to worldly matters cannot possibly have time to solve the psychological problems of old age. We now know that there is no single pattern which can be recommended as the recipe for a successful old age.

Perhaps the most useful characteristics we can possess at this stage of our lives are flexibility and acceptance. Changes need to be made, and the unpalatable fact of our own mortality has to be accepted. There is some evidence that we can predict in advance how easily an individual will come to terms with the final realities on the basis of how well he or she has made adjustments earlier in life. For example, people who had problems resolving the intimacy-versus-isolation crisis in their twenties, and who found it difficult to maintain an intimate relationship at age thirty, seem to have difficulty coping with the psychosocial crisis that comes with old age.

Younger people often complain about the way the old ramble on about the past. But research shows that the tendency some old people have to review the events of their lives can actually be therapeutic. It increases their chances of facing death with equanimity.

Some of the strongest fears of death expressed in our interviews came from people in their teens and twenties. Among the old, advancing age seems to produce a greater interest in death, but certainly no greater fear. One old woman said, "I feel that from the day you're born your life is mapped out for you. As for death, well, whatever way that comes, I can't stop it, so it doesn't worry me." An eighty-year-old said, "Dying doesn't worry me. The only thing I do worry about is if I go unexpectedly and leave a muddle for everyone to clear up."

Two major conclusions can be drawn from our Colchester Study of Aging. First: We ought to bury the notion of universal, age-related life crises. Many people never experience any discernible psychological crisis. And when crises do occur they tend to be caused by events which just happen to fall at roughly the same point in most people's lives, rather than because a person has reached a certain age.

Second: Age has remarkably little effect at any stage in life on how we think of ourselves or on how we view the world. As as eighty-year-old Colchester woman said, "I don't put things into blocks. If you just think, 'Well, I'm only one day older than I was,' you don't really feel very much different."

In Search of Youth

Albert Rosenfeld

Albert Rosenfeld is a frequent contributor to GEO and the author of a book on aging, Pro-Longevity.

In the past, a special brand of pity was reserved for any benighted soul impertinent enough to seek a Fountain of Youth. But look at what's been happening lately in gerontology, the scientific study of the aging process. Listen to the theorists discuss the possibility that there exists within each of us a "clock of aging" that we can hope to locate and adjust to our liking. Observe the experimenters in their laboratories extending the life-spans of cells in tissue culture; keeping skin and blood cells going by transplanting them from older to younger animals; combating the ravages of aging in animals, extending their life-spans and restoring youthful functions that would once have been lost. Observe the explosive advances throughout the biomedical sciences—advances that suggest we have scarcely begun to touch the power we will have to transform our lives.

Sociologists and demographers go on making projections oblivious to these developments, expressing alarm sometimes bordering on panic at the prospect of a population made up of an ever larger percentage of doddering old folks. But all our perceptions may soon be radically revised in light of scientific advances. A significant number of researchers have come to believe that aging as we have always known it may not be our inevitable lot after all. The elderly of the future may well turn out to be healthy, self-sufficient and productive, requiring less medical care. We may even see the nursing home follow the once flourishing TB sanatorium into obsolescence. It is not at all preposterous to imagine that in the not-too-distant future, most Americans will be able to live out their full natural lifespans—say, 110 years—in the best of health.

Many gerontologists here and abroad are focusing on the mechanism of the aging process itself. There are, of course, "early-onset" forms of nearly all major diseases, some of them occurring in earliest childhood. These are increasingly believed to be specifically genetic or familial in origin and quite distinct from later forms of the same disease. Moreover, aging itself is beginning to be thought of as a genetically programmed phenomenon—not merely the accumulated effects of wear and tear on the organism over the years but rather a built-in time clock guaranteeing that life will run down approximately on schedule.

A handful of vigorous gerontologists are trying to track down this genetic clock of aging; many more are content to spend their energies studying the individual ravages of senescence to see what might be done to alleviate its symptoms, to minimize the degenerative changes and retard the loss of function. Both groups have a common goal—to add high-quality years to our lives—and we will need the insights and contributions of both to achieve it. But the news is that the achievement has now become a realistic prospect in our time.

Among those inclined toward the concept of programmed aging, the principal controversy revolves around the question, If there is a clock of aging, where is it? There are two main schools of thought. One says that the clock is in the brain, specifically in the hypothalamus and pituitary regions, which exercise control over the body's hormonal systems. The other holds that the clock is in each individual cell, most probably in the nucleus, where DNA, the genetic material, is in control. Either or both may, of course, be wrong. Either or both may be right.

I happen to think that both schools are right. Each is supported by feasible theoretical arguments as well as by experimental data, and in my view they are in no way incompatible. When space engineers design vehicles for interplanetary missions, they almost always include built-in backup systems to enhance the odds that all will go as scheduled. Why would God and nature possess less wit and foresight than our space-hardware designers?

A hormonal clock of aging would be a naturally attractive idea. We know that hormones regulate nearly all of the body's cellular processes as well as its overall physiological functioning. We know, too, that all of the activities of our hormones and the endocrine glands that secrete them are regulated by the "master gland"—the pea-size pituitary, which sits at the base of the brain. We have also learned that the master has a master of its own, the hypothalamus, located just above the pituitary. Before the pituitary can release a hormone, it must get a green light from the hypothalamus in the form of a chemical messenger, actually a much smaller hormone called a releasing factor, or RF. There seems to be a specific RF for virtually every hormone, and perhaps an inhibitor for each as well, though they are not yet all known to us.

The notion that the aging process is somehow intimately involved with the hypothalamus and the pituitary—perhaps acting at given times in response to feedback signals provided by the levels of hormones circulating in the body—has a number of adherents. In this country, the man who has kept closest track of the relationship between hormones and aging is Caleb Finch of the University of Southern California. He and his associates at USC have studied changes in the reproductive cycles of aging rodents—with fascinating results. In mice, for example, the regular cycle of ovulation stops at the age of about 12 months (the equivalent of about 30 years in human terms). But if the apparently worn-out ovary of an old female mouse is transferred to a young female, the organ begins its cycles again, demonstrating that it wasn't used up after all. On the other hand, if the ovary of a young mouse is implanted in an old mouse, the organ functions as though it were as old as its host—that is, until the scenario is varied a bit. When the ovary of a young mouse is removed, the mouse has no experience of ovulation by the time it ages. If a new ovary is then implanted in that aging mouse, the ovary will begin its cycles. What happens, according to Finch, is that the brain area around the hypothalamus responds to the female hormone estradiol, and when the mouse has gone through its allotted number of cycles, that brain area is programmed to turn off—or it has been damaged or depleted by the wear and tear of all that ovulation activity.

The most daring of the seekers of the hormonal brain clock is endocrinologist W. Donner Denckla of the George Washington University School of Medicine in Washington, D.C. His experiments have convinced him that the pituitary *induces* our bodies to age by means of a mystery substance that has been called the aging or death hormone—but not by Denckla, who prefers the neutral term DECO, an acronym for "decreasing consumption of oxygen." DECO achieves this effect, Denckla believes, primarily by blocking the thyroid hormone—which affects virtually all of the body's major systems, including the immune and the cardiovascular systems.

Does he have the hormone in hand? Not yet. Not in purified form, at least. But even with the impure extract, he has been able to bring on signs of premature aging in rats. And what of the opposite effect—that is, reversing the signs of aging? So far, the only way of withholding DECO that Denckla knows of is to remove the pituitary altogether, a delicate piece of surgery. He has done this with several thousand rats, under varying circumstances, over the years. By excising the pituitary and then providing these handicapped rats with shots of thyroid and other hormones, Denckla has been able to "restore juvenile competence," as he puts it, in a number of important systems ranging from vital lung capacity to fur growth, from immune and cardiovascular functions to the rate at which cells can replace their genetic material.

Denckla's hope is that after purifying and synthesizing DECO, he can find a natural substance that will inhibit its release. Such natural hormone inhibitors do exist in the body; in fact, current birth-control pills work in just that way. If Denckla succeeds in blocking DECO, most if not all of the programmed ravages of aging might be vanquished, leaving only actual wear and tear to deal with.

Cell biologist Leonard Hayflick, now director of the Center for Gerontological Studies at the University of Florida, is the man who proved that normal human embryo cells in tissue culture will divide about 50 times and then stop (the older the cell, the fewer times it will divide). Now, if cells isolated in laboratory vessels—outside of any living organism and far from the direct influence of the brain or of any hormone—can age and die, apparently on a regularly programmed schedule of their own, then how can it be said that the clock of aging is hormonal and located in the brain? In a series of ingenious experiments in which old nuclei were implanted in young cells and vice versa, Hayflick and other researchers neatly demonstrated that the true "age" of a cell is governed by DNA. Vastly oversimplified, the experiment went as follows: Suppose you take two cells programmed for roughly 50 divisions. Cell A has undergone only 10 doublings, with 40 still to go, while cell B has already divided 40 times and has only 10 divisions left. Transplant A's nucleus into B and vice versa—and suddenly A, now prematurely aged, can only divide 10 more times, while B, rejuvenated, can go on for another 40 doublings!

Any number of scientists have held that genetic material is the key to aging. Biochemist F. Marott Sinex of Boston University is among those who believe that changes, mutations or damage to DNA, or loss of DNA's own repair capacities, could be critical to the process of senescence. It was Dr. Ron Hart of the Food and Drug Administration (formerly of Ohio State University) and Dr. Richard B. Setlow of the Brookhaven National Laboratory who first showed, in the early 1970s, that DNA repair is related to longevity. In a whole spectrum of mammalian species, those that lived longest were those that had the best repair capability. A few years later, zoologist Joan Smith-Sonneborn of the University of Wyoming conducted a startling experiment that underlined the findings of Hart and Setlow. First, she deliberately damaged the DNA of protozoans (single-celled animals) by exposing them to ultraviolet radiation. She then activated their DNA-repair mechanism (a known enzyme) merely by shining black light on them—and discovered that after repeated treatments of damage and repair, these organisms lived a third longer than protozoans that had never been damaged at all. She assumed that increased repair capacity could be used for other kinds of damages—including those associated with aging. It is as if the carburetor in a car had conked out, and the mechanic, while repairing it, had also done a lot of additional tuning and tightening up. The car might now be in better shape and last longer than a similar car in which the carburetor had gone on working and thus never received the mechanic's attention.

Geneticist Philip Lipetz, who worked with Hart at Ohio State and is now collaborating with Smith-Sonneborn, specializes in the very complex ways in which DNA coils itself into tightly wound "superhelixes" that may represent whole clusters of genetic instructions controlling diverse cellular (and therefore bodily) functions. Lipetz believes that these supercoils, as they tighten or loosen or become somewhat disorganized, may interfere with the carrying out of genetic instructions. This would make them responsible for much of the deterioration we recognize as aging.

For a long time, gerontologist Richard Cutler of the National Institute on Aging in Baltimore has argued that because a single, critically placed gene can control whole clusters of other genes, the entire aging process could feasibly be carried out under the influence of a very few genes—perhaps contained in one of those tightly coiled superhelixes. If there does exist a genetic clock of aging, then where might it be? Pathologist Roy Walford of UCLA, one of the most imaginative and productive investigators of aging, believes that evidence increasingly points to a particular supergene on chromosome number 6 (we each have 46 chromosomes) called the major histocompatibility complex, or MHC, which appears to govern nearly all of the body's major immune functions. Walford's name is the one most often associated with the immune theory of aging—the theory that aging is largely due to the running down of the immune defenses that protect us against invading microorganisms and reject foreign grafts. With aging, Walford speculates, the immune cells are somehow damaged so that their recognition capabilities are lost or impaired; hence they might fail to recognize foreign invaders or, perhaps worse still, mistake the body's own cells as foreign and attack them, resulting in autoimmune diseases such as rheumatoid arthritis. Since the MHC is intimately involved in all of these processes, it is Walford's prime suspect for the role of aging supergene—especially since it has now been shown to be related to many other aspects of the cell that affect aging, including DNA repair.

There is no reason why there could not be two (or even more) clocks of aging. There does seem to be a separate "genetic metabolic rate" built into nuclear DNA that is quite apart from the body's overall metabolic rate, and this rate could be controlled by Denckla's DECO through its influence on the thyroid. Such a genetic cellular clock could still play itself out in tissue culture, away from the influence of the brain's hormonal clock—much as a violinist could still play through his part in a symphony even if isolated from orchestra and conductor. Since hormones are known to be able to turn genes on and off, it is even quite possible that DECO could work by influencing the MHC in individual cells—or conversely, that the MHC in the genes of particular brain cells could control the release of DECO. So the two clocks, if they exist, could interact; it would perhaps be surprising if they did not.

The failing immune system may or may not be the major cause of aging and may or may not be the result of genetic programming. But the body's defenses do undeniably decline with age, rendering us more vulnerable to infection and every variety of stress. We may be able to do something about this without waiting for the knowhow required to modify genes or aging clocks. David Harrison of the Jackson Laboratory in Bar Harbor, Maine, has shown that the "stem cells" (precursors of all immune cells) produced by bone marrow can be transplanted and retransplanted from aging animals to younger animals, where they continue to function. Because young marrow that is transplanted to old mice seems to boost faltering immune systems under certain circumstances, Harrison speculates that young stem cells that are transplanted to aging human bodies might well produce similar results.

Boosting the immune system, however, may come about more easily through the administration of chemical immune boosters, such as the hormone called thymosin. The thymus gland, which shrivels early in life, controls the development of whole families of immune cells. As these cells run out late in life, our bodies can no longer make new ones. Biochemist Allan Goldstein of George Washington University School of Medicine, codiscoverer and principal developer of thymosin, is convinced that thymosin will not only be effective against immune-deficiency diseases, cancer and other serious maladies but will also considerably improve the quality of our later years by shoring up the body's defenses against infection and stress.

All of these procedures are directed toward minimizing the effects of wear and tear due to our mere exposure to the world over the years. Much of this wear, if it is the result of genetically programmed aging, will be diminished or abolished once we can do something about the clock of aging. Even then, however, there will be leftover damage to contend with. And meanwhile, we have *all* the wear and tear to manage. A failing immune system is only one aspect of the problem.

As the years go by, for instance, our cells—particularly heart and nerve cells—build up quantities of a fatty pigment called lipofuscin, generally assumed to be undisposed-of waste material. The accumulation of lipofuscin can seriously interfere with cell functions. Among chemicals now being tested are lipofuscin inhibitors that may be able to dissolve it or prevent its accumulation. We also suffer from the effects of "cross-linkage" (the irreversible linking together of large molecules that should be free to do their own work), which causes the stiffening of connective tissue, among other deleterious effects. Chemist Johan Bjorksten, who runs his own research foundation in Madison, Wisconsin, has for many years held that cross-linkage is the principal cause of all aging. He is currently at work testing some cross-link inhibitors that could be beneficial to all of us regardless of what the cause—if there is a single cause—of aging turns out to be.

Cross-linkage—extensive and ubiquitous though it be—may primarily be the result of "free-radical" damage. The free-radical theory of aging has in fact gained ground since it was first put forth in the 1950s by biochemist Denham Harman of the University of Nebraska College of Medicine in Omaha. Harman holds that free radicals, the short-lived but highly destructive by-products of the body's normal oxidation reactions, cause most of the degenerative changes of aging—including not only cross-linkage and lipofuscin buildup but also the decline of immune systems. Again, whether or not free radicals represent the principal mechanism of aging, they surely contribute to it by inflicting various kinds of damage on neighboring molecules. One means of combating the steady assault of free agents is through the use of "antioxidants" that mop them up before they can do much harm, or prevent them from being produced in harmful quantities.

Antioxidants added to the human diet show great promise in being able to slow down the effects of free-radical damage. Pathologist Harry Demopoulos of New York University Medical Center is among those who have done a great deal of high-technology research in this area over the past few years. Demopoulos employs such "micronutrients" as vitamin C, vitamin E, beta-carotene and the mineral selenium in careful dosages and a high purity as yet unobtainable in health-food products. His preliminary results suggest that antioxidant micronutrients will be an important element in our anti-aging arsenal.

There may well be other purely dietary approaches to delaying senescence. It now seems likely, for example, that the slippage of memory that often accompanies aging may be due largely to the shortage of a single brain chemical that can be boosted by eating a diet rich in the natural substance lecithin. It is too early in the experimental work to report any sure results.

The most straightforward technique—for the highly disciplined, at least—may prove to be simply eating less while maintaining adequate nutrition. Most long-lived people seem to eat frugally—and there is a scientific basis for this impression. In a classic series of experiments begun more than 50 years ago at Cornell University, biochemist Clive M. McCay was able to extend the lives of rats considerably by severely restricting their caloric intake—while seeing to it that their limited food contained a proper mix of nutrients. This life-extension technique only worked, however, if the semistarvation began early in the animal's life, well before puberty. The result was a decelerated growth and maturation, as if the development-and-aging process had been run in slow motion. At the University of California at Berkeley, Dr. Paola Timiras and Paul Segall were able to achieve virtually the same results merely by restricting the intake of a single vital protein ingredient, an amino acid called tryptophan. Only last year, Segall was able to demonstrate the efficacy of this dietary regime when a few of his female rats, long past the age when procreation would normally have been possible, gave birth to healthy offspring.

Since dietary restriction had to begin before puberty and continue over a lifetime in order to extend life, there seemed to be no way of trying it on human subjects. But in the past few years, breakthroughs have occurred. Charles Barrows of the National Institute on Aging and UCLA's Walford have each learned how to extend the life-spans of experimental animals by starting dietary restriction in adulthood. Again, the indefatigable Walford has carried this the furthest, experimenting on himself as well as on his subjects; and he has been gradually putting together what may turn out to be the first workable anti-aging diet for humans.

All this only begins to suggest the riches and diversity of what is going on in aging research today. But it is already feasible to speculate that before too long, we may know for sure whether or not there is a genetic aging program, and if there is, how to control it for our own benefit. Even sooner, we will probably have at our disposal an array of easily available substances—immune boosters, antioxidants, memory improvers, cross-link inhibitors and lipofuscin scavengers, among many others. These—combined with health measures such as getting enough rest and exercise, eating properly and resisting the urge to smoke—should substantially improve the quality of our later years and even abolish many of the symptoms we have come to identify as "old age." If we also learn to cultivate attitudes that enhance the spirit, equipping us to deal successfully with the stresses of a changing world, our chances for healthy longevity are even better.

Individual Differences 5

What accounts for the diversity in the ways that people think, feel, and act? Psychologists have long been interested in both measuring and explaining individual differences. Through the years, a classic debate has taken shape about what accounts for individual differences: heredity (nature) or environment (nurture). Of course, both factors are important, and this section deals with the ways in which they interact to shape the individual. The articles focus on two issues of current sociopolitical as well as theoretical importance: the nature of intelligence and the differences between males and females.

"Attitudes, Interests, and IQ" reports on several studies to determine the influence of heredity on intelligence and behavior. Among other things, the authors present evidence that genetic factors may exert a strong influence on IQ, vocational interests, and even attitudes like prejudice. If we are to discuss these issues meaningfully, though, we need to agree on just what we mean by "intelligence". In "Who's Intelligent?" Robert Sternberg reports on the similarities and differences between what lay people regard as intelligent behavior and what psychologists include in their theories. Once a definition of intelligence is adopted, one can return to the evidence that heredity plays a critical role in determining it. In "The Remedial Thinker," Paul Chance argues that intelligence is in fact a very plastic and modifiable human characteristic. Reuven Feuerstein, who developed the idea of "The Remedial Thinker," has enjoyed remarkable success at teaching people diagnosed as mentally retarded to be successful thinkers and problem-solvers.

Sex roles and sexuality are important aspects of the individual's social and psychological adjustment. The next two articles—"Males and Females and What You May Not Know About Them" and "Girls versus Boys—How Different Are They?"—review extensive data compiled to determine sex differences in areas of neurophysiology, physical ability, motivation, social behavior, and intellectual ability. Some sex stereotypes are upheld or qualified, others are dismissed altogether. Lastly, "Prisoners of Manliness" takes up an issue that is argued hotly with respect to women, but more often is ignored with respect to men—the influence of sex-role stereotypes on self-concept and life opportunities.

A review of this section will contribute to your understanding of the links between genetics and environment and how these factors affect and distinguish each individual.

Looking Ahead: Challenge Questions

What are some of the practical applications of our growing understanding of the factors affecting individual differences?

Given Feuerstein's results, how should we interpret the findings of Scarr and Weinberg? What differences between males and females do you think are important ones? Why?

ATTITUDES, INTERESTS, AND IQ

When the environment is good, heredity exerts a strong influence on IQ. Heredity also affects a person's interests and attitudes toward authority.

SANDRA SCARR
AND
RICHARD A. WEINBERG

Sandra Scarr, *who received her Ph.D. from Harvard, is professor of psychology at Yale University. She was formerly on the faculty of the Institute of Child Development, University of Minnesota, and in 1976-1977 she was a fellow at the Center for Advanced Study in the Behavioral Sciences in Stanford, California. Scarr is a fellow of the American Association for the Advancement of Science and of the American Psychological Association, associate editor of the* American Psychologist, *and has finished a term on the APA's Board of Scientific Affairs. She is the author of many articles in the areas of human development and the genetics of behavior.*

Richard Weinberg *received his Ph.D. from the University of Minnesota, where he is professor of educational psychology and on the graduate faculties in psychology and child development. He is coordinator of the Psychology in the Schools Training Programs, associate director of the Center for Early Education and Development, and coauthor of* The Classroom Observer: A Guide for Developing Observation Skills. *Scarr and Weinberg have collaborated on their research since 1973, and are writing a child-development text, to be published by Harcourt Brace Jovanovich.*

The studies reported in their article were supported by the Grant Foundation, the National Institute of Child Health and Human Development, the graduate school of the University of Minnesota, and done in collaboration with the Minnesota State Department of Public Welfare, Adoption Unit.

Each generation of scientists rediscovers the nature-nurture problem. In our day we were taught an environmentalism gone amok. Given the "right" experiences, we learned, any infant can become if not an Einstein at least a competent nuclear physicist.

Most parents (and many psychologists) probably had reservations about this view—in private—but the public stance dominated the Western philosophy of child rearing and social policy for many years. It was inevitable that the pendulum would swing far back toward biology, and now a spate of books has appeared arguing that genes, not cultures, control our fate and account for most of our social customs.

To write about the influence of heredity on intelligence and behavior is to court controversy, if not outrage. We are about to court both. Our data show the importance of experience on the development of human behavior, and dispel racist notions of genetic differences in the abilities of blacks and whites. But our studies also demonstrate the unmistakable contribution of genetic factors to individual differences in intellectual ability, interests, and even prejudices.

Let us get two facts straight. First, of course the environment has a strong effect on a person's development. We do not need sophisticated studies to prove that a child raised in a neglectful or abusive family will generally not turn out as well as a child raised in a warm, supportive one. Yet changes in environment cause changes in behavior, a process called malleability. Improvements in the former improve the latter.

Second, it is also true that human beings are not infinitely adjustable. Malleability does not mean that given the same environment all individuals will end up alike. Common sense and a sheaf of studies indicate that people bring idiosyncratic responses to the same situations. Even in a perfect world, some people will be unhappier, more hyperactive, or less capable than others. The reason for these individual differences has much to do with genetic make-up.

Too many people believe the myth that if a characteristic is genetic, it cannot be changed. This is nonsense. Human behavior is much more complicated than a particular physical trait, such as blue eyes. Although genes may dictate the color of eyes or hair, they do not specify that Sally will have an IQ of 139 rather than 125 or 150. Genes do not fix behavior; rather, they establish a range of possible reactions to the range of possible experiences that the environment provides.

How people behave or what their measured IQs turn out to be depends on the quality of their environments and on the genetic endowments they have at birth. Some elements of the environment, such as having nurturing parents, are better for everyone, but some individuals respond better to one environment and others respond better to another. What occurs is an interaction between genes and environment, as the disease phenylketonuria (PKU) illustrates. Normal children need the amino acid phenylalanine in their diets to be healthy; children with PKU are literally poisoned by it. The nutritional environment that allows normal children to flourish is deadly to children with this genetic deficiency. Similarly, many children thrive in a world that is rich and varied, whereas others react badly to overstimulation.

In these examples, a person's genetic make-up affects, or limits, the kind of environment he or she can tolerate. In other cases, genes and environment have reciprocal effects. Children who are skillful at sports spend more time on them than awkward children; adults who cannot carry a tune are embarrassed if they try out for a glee club; aggressive boys in elementary school are punished more often than docile ones. These predispositions affect what people do and do not enjoy and therefore the activities they continue to seek or avoid.

A child's particular genetic combination may cause him or her to develop in certain ways and to seek out some aspects of the environment but not others. The extreme examples are people—like Paul Gauguin, a financier who ran off to paint, and Elizabeth Blackwell, the first woman physician in America—who doggedly find ways to express their talents in spite of such huge environmental obstacles as parents who want them to run the family business or to produce babies, not to deliver them.

For too long we have assumed that people are passive lumps, to be molded into models of good or evil by surrounding influences. Some behavior is shaped by rewards and punishments, but just as often people actively select the environments that suit them and reject the aspects of those environments they dislike. Their choices are likely to be influenced by their genetic talents and interests. Some parents expect that their children can be molded into little replicas of themselves. They may be totally surprised when their children turn up with attitudes and ambitions that seem to spring from thin air: "No one in *our* family plays the piccolo" (or excels in geometry or runs the four-minute mile). Such is the nature of genetic sculpturing when parents and children share only half their genes. But our work shows that members of biological families do resemble one another more than adoptive, genetically unrelated family members.

In 1973 we launched two large-scale studies of adoption in Minnesota, one of white adolescents, the other of black and interracial children adopted into white homes. The first study was designed to measure the cumulative impact of family environment (in contrast to biological heritage) at what should be its most discernible time, after some 15 to 20 years of living at home. The second study was expressly designed to see whether life in middle- and upper-middle-class families would significantly improve the IQ scores and school performance of black children.

We interviewed hundreds of children and their parents; we gave comparable tests for intelligence, interests, and attitudes to both generations; and our interviews and tests covered a great deal of information other than IQ. Most important, we were able to assess the relative effects of heredity and environment because we could compare biological and adopted children within the same family, compare adopted children with their biological and their adoptive parents, and explore the origins of differences between children who grow up in similar environments.

Some of our findings were expected. Others surprised us. In general, we found no evidence of genetic differences in IQ between blacks and whites; strong evidence of genetic origins of intellectual differences between individuals within each race; strong evidence of a genetic component in individual differences in some attitudes having to do with prejudice and authoritarianism; and good evidence of a genetic component in some vocational and personal interests.

Because these findings are, we have since discovered, controversial, we are presenting them here with considerable detail to support our conclusions.

For the white adoption study, we selected two groups of families that had at least two children in late adolescence: 122 "biological" families that had had children of their own and 115 "adoptive" families that had adopted children as infants. The children in both sets of households were close in age, the average being 18½.

We found the adoptive families through the Minnesota Department of Public Welfare, which sent letters on our behalf to families who had adopted children between 1953 and 1959 (and who were thus at the ages we wanted for our study). To make sure our final sample of volunteers was representative of adoptive parents, we compared the participants with nonparticipants on critical characteristics. We found no differences between them in age, income, education, or occupational status at the time of adoption. Next we recruited a comparable sample of biological families through newspaper articles and advertisements, by word of mouth, and from the adoptive families themselves. The 122 families we eventually chose did indeed match the adoptive families in income (both groups averaged about $25,000 a year), education (generally at least two years of college for mothers and fathers), occupation (typically teacher and social worker), and IQ (an average of 117 for fathers and 113 for mothers). In short, both the biological and adoptive families were well above the national American average in socioeconomic status and intellectual ability. It is also significant that some families had incomes of $11,000; that some mothers and fathers were secretaries and electricians; that some parents had gone to work right after high school; and that some parents had IQs in the 90s—in other words, the sample was varied.

In contrast, the biological parents of the adopted children were of average intelligence, as we inferred from their educational levels. (In a large study we did recently, we found that education is an indirect but accurate index of intellectual ability.) Further, a survey of 3,600 unmarried mothers in Minnesota between 1948 and 1952, when IQ tests were required for all women who gave up children for adoption, found that their average IQ was right on the national mean: 100. Although our group of mothers had had their children between 1953 and 1959, there is no reason to think that they would differ from the in-

In biological families, IQ scores are significantly correlated between mother and child, father and child, and siblings. In adoptive families, adoptive children show a similarity to their parents and siblings only in vocabulary. (A correlation runs from 0 to 1 and is considered strong at about 0.3.)

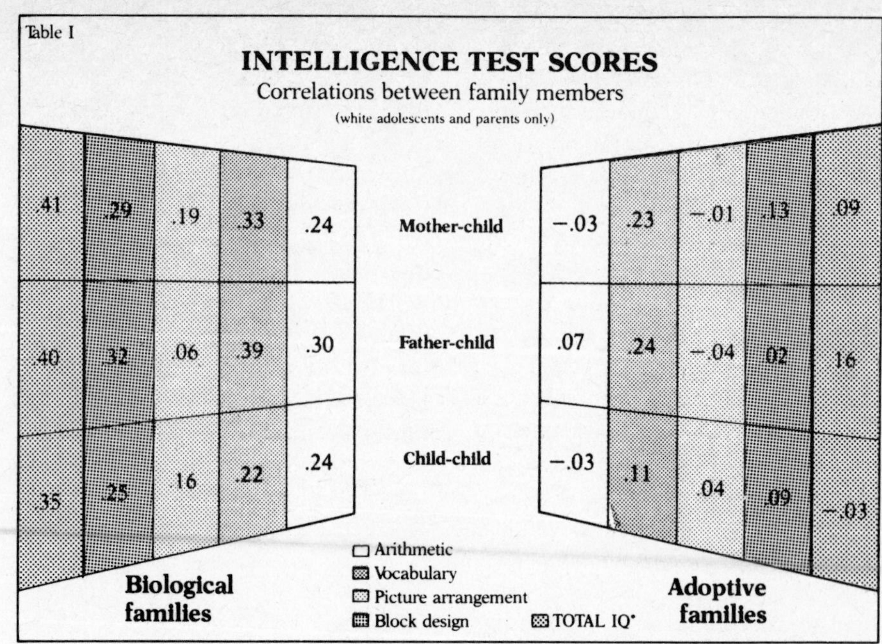

Table I
INTELLIGENCE TEST SCORES
Correlations between family members
(white adolescents and parents only)
.41 .29 .19 .33 .24
Mother-child
−.03 .23 −.01 .13 .09
.40 .32 .06 .39 .30
Father-child
.07 .24 −.04 .02 .16
.35 .25 .16 .22 .24
Child-child
−.03 .11 .04 .09 −.03
Biological families
Arithmetic
Vocabulary
Picture arrangement
Block design
TOTAL IQ*
Adoptive families

*On Wechsler Adult Intelligence Scale

tellectually average generation that preceded them.

For the black adoption study, we recruited 101 families consisting of 176 adopted black children who had one or two black parents and 145 biological white children. Like our other sample of adoptive parents, these families were above average in income and education, stability and mental health, and interest in children. The biological parents of these adoptees were about average intellectually and educationally, as we determined from the adoption records.

The biological children in our two studies had the benefits of both genes and environment; the adopted children were born to intellectually average parents but raised in intellectually enriched homes. To make environmental conditions as similar as possible, we most often limited our analyses to the children who had been adopted in the first year of life—most during the first three months.

The benefit children derive from living in intellectually rich homes is astoundingly apparent. The IQs of the black adopted children averaged 110, which represents at least a 15-point jump over the scores of American black children reared by their own parents. The scores of the adoptees were higher than those estimated for their own biological parents, but not as high as those of their adoptive parents (about 119) or those of the biological children of the adoptive parents (116.7).

Next we looked at school achievement records—vocabulary, reading, mathematics, and overall aptitude (an IQ measure). The school tests are important because they come from many school districts and are unblemished by any biases that may have occurred in the testing situation in the children's homes. They are even more important as a measure of the children's daily intellectual performance on a range of tasks.

Again we found that the black children scored above the national norms on the standard achievement tests, as their above-average IQ levels would predict. Regardless of their age at adoption, the children averaged in the 55th percentile in reading and math, for example, whereas the average black child in Minneapolis scored in the 15th to 20th percentile. The biological children from these enriched homes, however, performed better than their adoptive siblings on the achievement tests (in the 70th percentile), also as their IQ scores would predict.

This pattern of results is exactly what we found in the study of adopted white adolescents. The IQs of the adopted children averaged 6½ points lower than those of the biological children but 6½ points higher than those of their own parents, whose scores were estimated to be average for the population.

Because the scores of the black children are exactly comparable to those of the white adopted children raised in similarly advantaged homes, it is unlikely that the heralded differences between blacks and whites are genetically based. Black children from families that teach them the culture, vocabulary, and skills that IQ and achievement tests reward perform well above the average.

Some people who believe in genetic differences between blacks and whites think that there is an easy way to prove their point: Blacks who have more European and less African ancestry should have higher IQs than blacks with less European and more African ancestry. Working with Andrew Pakstis, Solomon Katz, and William Barker, we tested this notion by giving several tests of intellectual skill to a sample of 350 blacks in the Philadelphia area. Instead of asking the participants directly what their heritage was, we could estimate each person's degree of African and European ancestry from blood samples, because Africans and Europeans differ in the average frequencies of certain types of blood groups and serum protein. If a person had a particular blood group or serum protein gene, the researchers could assign a probability that he got it from a European or African ancestor. The estimates were based on 12 genes. Though some error undoubtedly crept into the estimates, they were accurate enough, because they matched up with skin color and were similar for siblings.

The results were unequivocal. Blacks who had a large number of European ancestors did no better or worse on the tests than blacks of almost total African ancestry. These studies dispute the hypothesis that IQ differences between blacks and whites are in large part the result of genetic differences.

But this is not the same thing as saying that heredity is totally unrelated to an individual's performance. The origins of differences between groups are not necessarily the origins of differences between individuals. The question that remains is: Given similar home environments, why does one child turn out to be brighter than another, and why is one determined by the age of four to become a musician while another sets his or her young sights on science? We know that improving the intellectual environment of children raises their average IQs; this happened to the adopted children in both the black and white studies. But what accounts for the persistent differences between siblings, adopted or not?

Our two studies show that in advantaged environments, differences between children are largely due to differences in genetic programming. We reached this conclusion by using two statistical methods. First we put all the factors that might have something to do with intelligence (such as qualities of the parents and the children's home life) into a long equation that told us the relative importance of each factor in predicting a child's IQ.

In the first set of equations, we tried father's education and occupation, mother's education, and family income as predictors of the differences in the children's IQs. These factors had a mild impact on differences in the biological children's scores, but hardly any impact on the adoptees' scores. When we added parental IQ, however, we got an enormous effect in predicting the biological children's scores—but parents' IQs had virtually no effect on the scores of the adoptees. The power of adding parental IQ to the equation must reflect the genetic contribution of the biological parents to their children's intelligence.

In contrast, the best predictor of IQ differences in adopted children was the education of their biological mothers (and, when we had the information, of their biological fathers). The education of the biological mothers was more closely related to IQ differences in their children than the same information about the adoptive parents—the adults with whom these children grew up. In both groups of adoptees, the black children and the white adolescents, the biological parents best accounted for the children's differences in IQ.

AUTHORITARIAN ATTITUDES

Correlations between.	Biological families	Adoptive families
Father-daughter	.34	.31
Father-son	.44	−.05
Mother-daughter	.40	.06
Mother-son	.41	−.06
Son-son	.46	*
Daughter-daughter	.36	*
Son-daughter	.41	.04
Mother-father	.43	.34

*Too few cases

Attitudes toward authority appear to have a genetic component. In biological families, parents and children predictably shared the same level of authoritarianism. But adopted children were no more likely to share their parents' views than strangers,' with the exception of fathers and daughters.

Our second method was to study the correlations of scores between related and unrelated family members. A correlation indicates the extent to which two items, such as events or attitudes or scores, are linked in predictable ways. A positive correlation may run from 0 (no relationship at all) to 1 (a perfect relationship, in which a high score on test X always means a high score on test Y). A negative correlation runs from 0 to −1 (a perfectly inverted relationship, in which a high score on test X means a low score on test Y). A correlation of about 0.3 is, in the case of our samples, unlikely to have occurred by chance.

More evidence of genetic effects came from the white study,when we correlated IQs for all pairs of adoptive and natural relatives. Whether we used the overall IQs or the scores on the four subtests of the IQ tests (e.g., vocabulary, arithmetic), the correlations between biological family members were high and statistically significant, whereas the correlations between adopted children and their unrelated parents and siblings were weak or negligible. The only scores that were significant between adoptees and other family members were in vocabulary. This is not surprising, since people who live together tend to talk together. Vocabulary abilities are the most amenable to the influence of environment. But the lack of correlations between adopted children and their parents—with whom they have lived, remember, since infancy—must point to the influence of genetic factors on intellectual abilities. (See Table I.)

In our studies we expected that genetic background would be important in accounting for intelligence scores but that it would have nothing to do with political or social attitudes. To demonstrate our point, we included in the test battery a 20-item version of the California F-Scale, a set of 20 questions that measure a person's degree of authoritarianism, rigidity of belief, and prejudice. People taking the test indicate on a scale of 1 to 7 how much they agree or disagree with such statements as, "What youth needs most is strict discipline, rugged determination, and the will to work and fight for family and country," and "One of the most important things children should learn is when to disobey authorities."

Confident that our F-Scale would measure the effects of environment, we were utterly astonished by our findings. The attitudes captured by the authoritarianism test appear to be transmitted genetically from parents to children, just as verbal ability and intelligence are.

We make this remarkable statement because we found no correlation between the authoritarian attitudes of the adopted children and those of their parents or siblings, even though the adoptees had been exposed to their parents' attitudes since infancy. The parents' attitudes and those of the adopted children, in other words, were as different as if the adults and teenagers had been randomly paired on a street corner. But we found a highly significant correlation between the authoritarian attitudes of biological children and parents. Whether both were highly authoritarian or both were anti-authoritarian, their attitudes tended to be very similar.

All the strong correlations of attitudes toward authority occurred between biological relatives—fathers and children, mothers and children, brothers and sisters. Among adoptive relatives, the only significant correlation, the only predictably shared attitude, occurred between fathers and daughters. The reason for this exception we do not know.

One possible explanation for the similarities between biological relatives and the differences between adoptive relatives was that mothers and fathers of adopted children disagreed on their attitudes toward authority, whereas the parents of biological children shared similar attitudes. In that case, adopted children would have a choice of two opinions and values, one set being less authoritarian than the other. Not so. As the chart indicates, husbands and wives in both kinds of families tended to share their political and social attitudes.

We then looked at the comparable table of correlations of IQ scores. The patterns were amazingly similar to those for authoritarianism, including that baffling father-daughter resemblance in the adoptive families—which we are beginning facetiously to call the Electra phenomenon.

Another possibility for these results was that adoptive parents, knowing that their children were not "their own," somehow treated them differently from the way parents treat natural-born children. But if this were so, we would still expect to find the correlations between adoptive siblings to be similar to the correlations between biological siblings. They are not.

Perhaps, we thought, the finding reflected an artificial problem in the samples. For instance, more adoptive families than biological families came from small towns and rural areas. But then we would have been hard-pressed to explain why the authoritarianism patterns consistently distinguished adopted children from biological ones, and other personality traits did not. On tests of introversion, neuroticism, and some forms of anxiety, parent-child correlations within adoptive and biological families were similar. Something unique about authoritarianism and IQ was afoot.

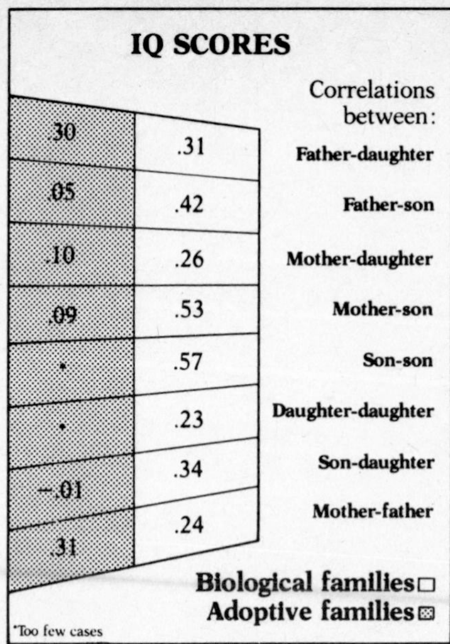

IQ SCORES
Correlations between:
.30
.31
Father-daughter
.05
.42
Father-son
.10
.26
Mother-daughter
.09
.53
Mother-son
*
.57
Son-son
*
.23
Daughter-daughter
−.01
.34
Son-daughter
.31
.24
Mother-father
Biological families
Adoptive families
*Too few cases

Biologically related parents and children were as similar in IQ as in authoritarianism, but among adoptive families, only fathers and daughters showed a similarity in IQ—as they had in authoritarianism (F-scale). The F-Scale apparently tests intellectual skills that are partly heritable.

To track it down, we took a closer look at the relationship of intelligence to the F-Scale. One measure we used was the vocabulary subtest of the Wechsler Adult Intelligence Scale; the other was the Raven Standard Progressive Matrices, a nonverbal measure of intellectual ability. At this point the pieces of the puzzle began to fit.

Scores for authoritarianism turned out to be negatively correlated with verbal ability—the higher one's score on the WAIS vocabulary subtest, the lower the F-Scale score (the correlation for all participants in the study was −0.42, which is strong). In other words, the most articulate, verbal family members were the least authoritarian, and vice versa. But the relationship between the nonverbal IQ measure and authoritarianism was much weaker.

These results suggest to us that F-Scale scores are similar in biological but not in adoptive families because the F-Scale measures intellectual skills that are partly heritable. Many of those skills have to do with thinking and reasoning ability. The similarity of scores in biological families was remarkable and largely a result of the intellectual similarity of genetic relatives. Adopted children barely resembled their adoptive parents in F-Scale scores, and what little similarity there was could be ascribed to their similar vocabulary scores.

Previous studies had also found that authoritarianism was more characteristic of lower-class than of middle-class people, but psychologists assumed that this reflected the powerlessness and poorer circumstances of the working class. Our results require another interpretation. Differences in social class of the adoptive families were not related to the expected differences in authoritarianism and IQ: Although the adoptive parents varied in intelligence, education, occupation, and income (to be sure, none was truly poor), their adopted children were no more or less authoritarian because of their class backgrounds.

In our view, the only adequate explanation of the link between low IQ and high authoritarianism begins with a person's mental abilities. Scores on the F-Scale are the results of moral-reasoning ability that reflects the general level of verbal intelligence. We believe that moral decisions and authoritarian views are not learned by rote or by imitation of one's parents, teachers, and friends; instead, they represent conclusions that a person reaches by applying mental skills to social and political experiences, and through schooling that teaches abstract concepts that broaden perspective.

The F-Scale is a set of complex intellectual judgments about the world, examples of opinions that people have accepted or rejected about politics and values. IQ tests also contain items that tap everyday, commonsense judgments about social problems precisely to see how people use intellectual abilities to solve daily dilemmas. Consequently, in a way it is not surprising that the F-Scale should correlate with some of the broad

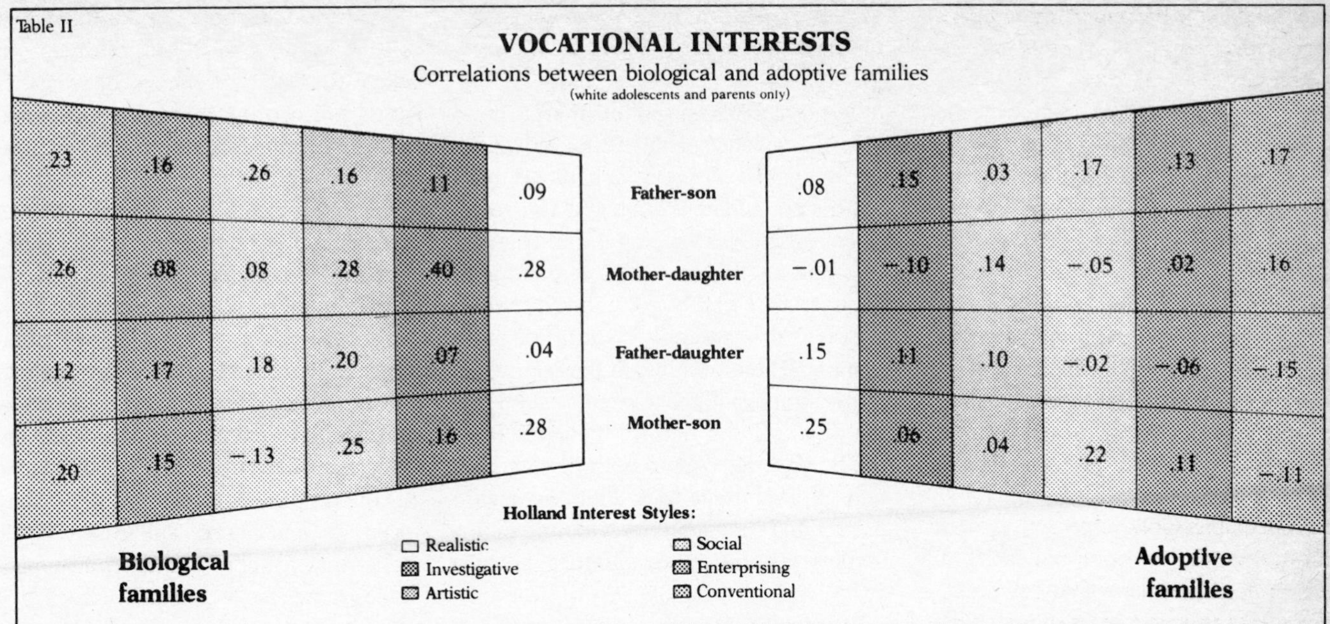

Table II

VOCATIONAL INTERESTS

Correlations between biological and adoptive families

(white adolescents and parents only)

Biological families	Realistic	Investigative	Artistic	Social	Enterprising	Conventional
Father-son	.09	.11	.16	.26	.16	.23
Mother-daughter	.28	.40	.28	.08	.08	.26
Father-daughter	.04	.07	.20	.18	.17	.12
Mother-son	.28	.16	.25	−.13	.15	.20

Adoptive families	Realistic	Investigative	Artistic	Social	Enterprising	Conventional
Father-son	.08	.15	.03	.17	.13	.17
Mother-daughter	−.01	−.10	.14	−.05	.02	.16
Father-daughter	.15	.11	.10	−.02	−.06	−.15
Mother-son	.25	.06	.04	.22	.11	−.11

Holland Interest Styles: Realistic; Investigative; Artistic; Social; Enterprising; Conventional

measures of intellectual functioning that IQ tests represent.

Many developmental psychologists and parents believe that children acquire ambitions and interests by modeling themselves after their parents. Typically, boys model themselves after their fathers, girls after their mothers; some children, for unknown reasons, imitate their parents of the opposite sex. If the modeling theory were true, adoptive and biological children would be equally likely to resemble their parents.

But there is evidence for a genetic contribution to vocational interests. In 1934, for example, H. D. Carter reported a case study of a pair of identical twins who, having grown up together, had been separated for 20 years in adulthood. When they took a test of personal preferences and interests, their scores were so similar that it was as if, Carter observed, the same person had taken the test twice.

In association with Harold Grotevant, we gave our white adolescents and parents a reliable test on this question, the Strong-Campbell Interest Inventory. This inventory includes John L. Holland's model of vocational interests, which classifies people according to their scores on six "styles": (1) realistic (practical, aggressive persons who enjoy working outdoors and with their hands); (2) investigative (scientifically oriented persons); (3) artistic (self-expressive and creative persons); (4) social (humanistic or religious persons who wish to help others); (5) enterprising (persons who like to sell, dominate, lead); and (6) conventional (persons who prefer highly ordered verbal or numerical work). People are scored on this test not only according to the style they most prefer but also according to how they score on each of the six types. The result is a profile of interests for each individual.

On six measures of personal interests, biologically related family members resembled each other more closely than adopted children resembled their siblings or parents. In the biological family pairs, 15 correlations out of 24 were significant; only two such correlations held up in adoptive pairs.

Once again our expectation, that children would model themselves after their parents, was not fulfilled. On the average, adoptive family members no more resembled one another in interests than parents and children paired randomly from the outside world. For all their similarity to their adoptive parents, the adopted children of teachers and engineers could have grown up with cattle ranchers or plumbers. (See Table II.)

We looked at the interest profiles of each family member in comparison with every other family member—mothers with sons and daughters, fathers with sons and daughters, siblings with one another. Of the 24 possible correlations (each of the six interest scales by mother, father, daughter, son), only two were significant for the adoptive family pairs, and one of those would have been expected just by chance. In the biological family pairs, fully 15 correlations were significant. For example, biological fathers and sons resembled one another most on social interests; mothers and daughters, on investigative interests; fathers and daughters, on artistic interests; and mothers and sons, on realistic interests. Further, scores of biological siblings were strongly correlated on five of the six scales, but scores of adoptive siblings were correlated on only one scale.

The fact that biological parents and children shared the same specific interests and disinterests, whereas their adoptive counterparts did not, suggests that there is a small but reliable hereditary influence in people's professional ambitions. In most families, the interests of the parents were not alike, even after 20 years of marriage; but the biological siblings were the most alike—as a genetic explanation would predict. Also, siblings resembled one another more than they resembled their parents, because the children were raised in the same place and time. When Mozart composed his first minuets at the age of five, his precocious talent reflected his father's teaching, his opportunities to get to a harpsichord—and a little help from his genes.

Our review of family studies convinces us that the evidence for some genetic influence on intelligence, attitudes, and interests is simply overwhelming. How large is the component? It is impossible to put a precise number on the exact proportion of our behavior that is inherited, although many scientists are fighting over just this issue. One reason is that at different stages of a person's development, environment may play a greater or lesser role. Another is the problem of tests themselves. Different studies of different age groups using different tests—some of which are more culturally biased than others—produce inconsistent results. Some studies find a greater genetic role in certain behavior than do other studies; but no studies find that environment is everything.

Remember too that we are talking about genetic variability within a range of reasonably good environments. Few studies have dealt with children from abusive, hostile families. If one could include research on such children, environmental differences would undoubtedly show a greater impact on behavior and intelligence. When a child's environment is basically humane, we find that genetic background plays a larger part in accounting for individual differences.

We do not think that this conclusion is pessimistic in the slightest. Many people think that genetic studies automatically suggest conservative social policy; if everyone is born smart or stupid, there is no reason to change the educational system. If artists and scientists are born, not made, there is no reason to improve the schools.

It is true that some politicians and laymen use evidence of heritability to justify the status quo. It is no longer God, but "instincts" or "genes" that glue us to our roles and make sweeping social change impossible—human beings cannot fight the fact that they are "naturally" aggressive, or "naturally" stratified into dominance hierarchies. At the other extreme, some political systems (such as the Soviet Union and the People's Republic of China) deny genetic heritability altogether, maintaining that the state creates and changes human nature. Economics giveth, and economics taketh away.

We think that both of these extreme political interpretations of scientific research on heritability miss the point. Social policy should be determined by political and ethical values. Justice has nothing to do with genetics, and the latter cannot be summoned to excuse fascism or to deny a group fair play.

Once social policy has been determined, however, research can be useful. Governments can do a better job of designing effective intervention programs if people know which variations in the environment make a difference and which do not. The average level of a culture's environment determines the average level of individual achievement. By providing good schools, nutrition, health care, and psychological services a society can raise the overall level of health and attainment for the whole population. Resources spent in these areas should eliminate conditions that have definite deleterious effects on individual development.

But governments will never turn their entire populations into geniuses, or altruists, or entrepreneurs, or whatever their philosophy inspires. Biological diversity is a fact of life, and respect for individual differences derives from the genetic perspective. This research can spare us all a homogeneity of customs imposed on society by an omniscient professional or political class.

Three decades of naive environmentalism have locked most Westerners into wrong-headed assumptions about the limitless malleability of mankind, and programs based on this premise can lead a country into a thicket of unrealistic promises and hopes. The fallacy is the belief that equality of opportunity produces sameness of outcome. Equality of opportunity is a laudable goal for any society. Sameness of outcome is a biological impossibility.

For further information:

Grotevant, Harold, Sandra Scarr, and Richard Weinberg. "Patterns of Interest Similarity in Adoptive and Biological Families." *Journal of Personality and Social Psychology*, Vol. 35, 1977, pp. 667-676.

Jencks, Christopher. *Inequality: A Reassessment of the Effects of Family and Schooling in America*. Basic Books, 1972.

Loehlin, J., G. Lindzey, and J. N. Spuhler. *Race Differences in Intelligence*. W. H. Freeman, 1975.

Scarr, Sandra. "Genetics and the Development of Intelligence." *Review of Child Development Research*, Vol. 4, ed. by F. D. Horowitz. University of Chicago Press, 1975.

Scarr, Sandra, and Richard Weinberg. "IQ Test Performance of Black Children Adopted by White Families." *American Psychologist*, Vol. 31, 1976, pp. 726-739.

Scarr, Sandra, and Richard Weinberg. "Intellectual Similarities within Families of Both Adopted and Biological Children." *Intelligence*, Vol. 1, 1977, pp. 170-191.

WHO'S INTELLIGENT?

ROBERT J. STERNBERG

Robert J. Sternberg is associate professor of psychology at Yale. He received his Ph.D. in psychology in 1975 from Stanford, where he won the Sidney Siegel Memorial Award for his dissertation on human intelligence. In 1981, he received an American Psychological Association Distinguished Scientific Award for an Early Career Contribution to Psychology. The citation recognized his "major theoretical contributions to our understanding of human intelligence and mental abilities."

When experts try to define intelligence, they generally consult one another or their own intuition. But to the layman, the definitions they come up with often seem to be rarefied abstractions, unconnected with real people or real life. And formal IQ tests frequently seem unfair or beside the point.

Almost everyone likes to think that he or she pretty much knows what intelligence is and how to judge who has it and who doesn't. Indeed, people make informal judgments about others' intelligence all the time, and don't seem to need intelligence tests to do so. One could argue that the bulk of intelligence testing is not the kind that takes place in schoolrooms and psychologists' consulting rooms, but the kind that goes on in face-to-face encounters between people: in job and admission interviews, in classrooms, in meetings, at cocktail parties, during coffee breaks, and in initial encounters with strangers. As Ulric Neisser of Cornell has pointed out, psychologists have done many studies of intelligence as measured by IQ tests, but they have done practically none of intelligence as judged by people in everyday encounters.

Some research that my colleagues and I have recently done was designed to find out what laymen mean when they speak of intelligence. Our main conclusion is a simple one: Ordinary people have very definite ideas about what intelligence is, and their ideas are not too different from those of the experts. Moreover, the conception of intelligence held by scientists and nonscientists alike is not abstruse or theoretical but is firmly and clearly anchored in the real world.

Laymen Know What Intelligence Is

We drew several other conclusions from our research. First, despite the general agreement of experts and laymen, intelligence does not mean precisely the same thing to everyone; there are some differences between the views of laymen and those of experts, and among different groups of laymen. Second, the confidence of nonscientists in their ability to judge intelligence seems justified. Third, it is possible to predict people's IQ scores from the kinds of intelligent or unintelligent behavior that they list as characteristic of themselves. This last finding leads to the provocative idea that a simple behavioral checklist might some day be used as a formal device for estimating intelligence. Such a checklist could perhaps supplement traditional IQ tests in situations where cultural differences and test anxiety obscure real abilities.

The best-known example of the experts-only approach to defining intelligence is a symposium published in the *Journal of Educational Psychology* in 1921. That year, 14 psychologists and educators gave their views on the nature of intelligence. Lewis M. Terman said that intelligence is "the ability to carry on abstract thinking." Herbert Woodrow called it "the capacity to acquire capacity." S. S. Colvin said that a person "possesses intelligence insofar as he has learned, or can learn, to adjust himself to his environment."

Three years later, in a *Psychological Review* article that is still frequently quoted, Edward L. Thorndike offered yet another definition. "Let intellect," he wrote, "be defined as that quality of mind (or brain, or behavior if one prefers) in respect to which Aristotle, Plato, Thucydides, and the like, differed most from Athenian idiots of their day, or in respect to which the lawyers, physicians, scientists, scholars, and editors of reputed greatest ability at constant age differ most from idiots of that age in asylums."

In 1978, Barbara Conway, Jerry Ketron, Morty Bernstein, and I began asking laymen for *their* views on intelligence. In a series of experiments carried out over a year, we personally interviewed or questioned by mail 476 men and women, including students, commuters, supermarket shoppers, and people who answered newspaper advertisements or whose names we selected at random from the phone book. To compare the ideas of our lay subjects with those of experts, we also sent questionnaires to 140 research psychologists specializing in intelligence.

We did not think it would be useful to ask laymen directly for their definitions of intelligence. Such a request seemed less likely to elicit genuine convictions than to produce platitudes: stale ideas dredged up, perhaps, from memories of old courses taken in school or college, or from articles read long ago. We decided instead on an indirect approach. In our first experiment, for instance, we gave people a blank sheet of paper and asked them to list behaviors that they considered to be characteristic of "intelligence," "academic intelligence," "everyday intelligence," or "unintelligence."

We found our subjects in natural

COMPARING IDEAS ABOUT INTELLIGENCE

Intelligence researchers and laymen who participated in the final phase of the author's study agreed on many characteristics of intelligent behavior, but gave them somewhat different emphases. The columns below reflect the two groups' ratings. They are based on a statistical analysis of expert and lay responses to a list of characteristics mentioned by a group of laymen in the study's initial phase.

LAYMEN

I. Practical problem-solving ability

Reasons logically and well.
Identifies connections among ideas.
Sees all aspects of a problem.
Keeps an open mind.
Responds thoughtfully to others' ideas.
Sizes up situations well.
Gets to the heart of problems.
Interprets information accurately.
Makes good decisions.
Goes to original sources for basic information.
Poses problems in an optimal way.
Is a good source of ideas.
Perceives implied assumptions and conclusions.
Listens to all sides of an argument.
Deals with problems resourcefully.

II. Verbal ability

Speaks clearly and articulately.
Is verbally fluent.
Converses well.
Is knowledgeable about a particular field.
Studies hard.
Reads with high comprehension.
Reads widely.
Deals effectively with people.
Writes without difficulty.
Sets aside time for reading.
Displays a good vocabulary.
Accepts social norms.
Tries new things.

III. Social competence

Accepts others for what they are.
Admits mistakes.
Displays interest in the world at large.
Is on time for appointments.
Has social conscience.
Thinks before speaking and doing.
Displays curiosity.
Does not make snap judgments.
Makes fair judgments.
Assesses well the relevance of information to a problem at hand.
Is sensitive to other people's needs and desires.
Is frank and honest with self and others.
Displays interest in the immediate environment.

EXPERTS

I. Verbal intelligence

Displays a good vocabulary.
Reads with high comprehension.
Displays curiosity.
Is intellectually curious.
Sees all aspects of a problem.
Learns rapidly.
Appreciates knowledge for its own sake.
Is verbally fluent.
Listens to all sides of an argument before deciding.
Displays alertness.
Thinks deeply.
Shows creativity.
Converses easily on a variety of subjects.
Reads widely.
Likes to read.
Identifies connections among ideas.

II. Problem-solving ability

Is able to apply knowledge to problems at hand.
Makes good decisions.
Poses problems in an optimal way.
Displays common sense.
Displays objectivity.
Solves problems well.
Plans ahead.
Has good intuition.
Gets to the heart of problems.
Appreciates truth.
Considers the result of actions.
Approaches problems thoughtfully.

III. Practical intelligence

Sizes up situations well.
Determines how to achieve goals.
Displays awareness to world around him or her.
Displays interest in the world at large.

ttings. Sixty-three of them were mmuters about to board trains at e New Haven station; 62 were usewives and others about to enter New Haven supermarket; and 61 re students studying in a Yale li- ary. Almost no one had trouble with r request; people were apparently nvinced that certain kinds of behav- r indicated certain kinds of intelli- nce—or the lack of it.

From people's responses we com- led a master list of 250 behaviors, 0 that had been named as character- ic of intelligence and 80 that had en called signs of unintelligence. me of the behaviors most frequent- listed as intelligent were "reasons gically and well," "reads widely," isplays common sense," "keeps an en mind," and "reads with high mprehension." For unintelligence, e most commonly listed behaviors cluded "does not tolerate diversity views," "does not display curios- y," and "behaves with insufficient nsideration of others." The great di- rsity of the behaviors cited showed at our subjects held eclectic views intelligent and unintelligent behav- r, and suggested that people prob- ly do not consider any one-dimen- onal scale adequate for measuring telligence.

A study of this kind runs the risk of ding some idiosyncratic responses at reflect just one or two people's culiar notions. For example, one rson listed "bores people" as char- teristic of an intelligent person, hereas another person listed "is fun be with"—almost the opposite. In der to deal with this problem, we d 28 people from the New Haven ea—nonstudents answering a news- per advertisement—rate on a scale 1 (low) to 9 (high) how characteris- they thought each of the 250 be- viors on the master list was of an eally intelligent person, an ideally ademically intelligent person, and ideally everyday-intelligent per- n. We then applied a statistical tech- que called "factor analysis," which alyzes people's tendencies to view rtain subsets of behaviors as related. he method grouped together all the haviors that people viewed as simi- r and grouped separately all those at they viewed as dissimilar, and al- wed us to determine the few basic ctors underlying people's diverse and, in a few instances, highly unusual responses. The result was to give us, in effect, a simple characterization of intelligence as viewed by our subjects.

It turned out that people conceived of intelligence as having three facets, which we labeled *practical problem-solving ability, verbal ability,* and *social competence.* Practical problem-solving ability included such behaviors as "reasons logically and well," "identifies connections among ideas," "sees all aspects of a problem," and "keeps an open mind." Under the heading of verbal ability came such behaviors as "speaks clearly and articulately," "is verbally fluent," "converses well," and "reads with high comprehension." Social competence was marked by such behaviors as "accepts others for what they are," "admits mistakes," "displays interest in the world at large," and "thinks before speaking and doing."

Since we had asked people not only about intelligence in general but also about academic intelligence and everyday intelligence, we also factor-analyzed the behaviors that had been cited as evidence for these two additional qualities. Our subjects, we learned, conceived of academic intelligence as composed of *verbal ability, problem-solving ability,* and *social competence.* These factors sound almost identical to the ones that emerged for intelligence in general; they were, in fact, quite similar, but the specific behaviors that had been listed reflected greater emphasis on academic skills, such as studying hard. The factors that emerged for everyday intelligence we called *practical problem-solving ability, social competence, character,* and *interest in learning and culture.* These, too, overlapped with those for intelligence in general, but less so, and had more of an everyday slant.

The Experts Emphasize Motivation

The resemblance between the views of scientists and nonscientists is surprisingly clear. On the whole, the informal theories of intelligence that laymen carry around in their heads—without even realizing that their ideas constitute theories—conform fairly closely to the most widely accepted formal theories of intelligence that scientists have constructed. That is, what psychologists study as intelligence seems to correspond, in general, to what people untrained in psychology mean by intelligence. On the other hand, what psychologists study corresponds to only *part* of what people mean by intelligence in our society, which includes a lot more than IQ tests measure.

The data on which these conclusions are based come from two questionnaires that we sent to a group of laymen and to a group of recognized authorities in the field of intelligence. The latter hold doctorates in psychology and teach in major American universities; each has published several major books or articles about intelligence. The two questionnaires named the 250 behaviors on our master list. One questionnaire asked respondents to rate how characteristic each behavior was of an ideally intelligent, ideally academically intelligent, and ideally everyday-intelligent person. The other asked respondents to rate how important each behavior was to defining the respondents' conceptions of each of these three kinds of people.

Taking into account both the characteristicness and the importance ratings for the three kinds of intelligence (academic, everyday, and general), the median correlation between the response patterns of experts and those of laymen was .82 (on a scale where 0 indicates no relationship and 1 indicates a perfect correspondence).

There were two main differences between the groups. One was that the experts considered motivation to be an important ingredient in academic intelligence—an ingredient that did not emerge when we factor-analyzed the responses of the laymen. Behaviors central to this motivational factor included "displays dedication and motivation in chosen pursuits," "gets involved in what he or she is doing," "studies hard," and "is persistent."

The second difference was that laymen seemed to place somewhat greater emphasis on the social-cultural aspects of intelligence than did the experts. Behaviors such as "sensitivity to other people's needs and desires" and "is frank and honest with self and others" showed up in the "social competence" factor for laymen but not in the analogous "practical intelligence" factor for experts.

In order to get a better sense of just how experts and laymen differ in their views of intelligence, I went back to the original ratings of the importance of the various behaviors to people's conceptions of intelligence. I was particularly interested in those kinds of behaviors that received higher ratings from laymen than from experts, and in those that received higher ratings from experts than from laymen. The pattern was clear. Consider first some of the behaviors that laymen emphasized more than experts did in defining intelligence: "acts politely," "displays patience with self and others," "gets along well with others," "is frank and honest with self and others," and "emotions are appropriate to situations." These behaviors, which are typical of those rated higher by laymen, clearly show an emphasis on *inter*personal competence in a *social* context. Consider next some of the behaviors that experts typically emphasized more than laymen did in defining intelligence: "reads with high comprehension," "shows flexibility in thought and action," "reasons logically and well," "displays curiosity," "learns rapidly," "thinks deeply," and "solves problems well." These behaviors clearly show an emphasis on *intra*personal competence in an *individual* context. To the extent that there is a difference, therefore, it is clearly in the greater emphasis among laymen on intelligence as an interpersonal and social construct.

Another way of comparing the views of experts with those of laymen is to ask in what specific ways laymen's informal conceptions of intelligence resemble formal scientific theories. Some theorists, like most laymen, consider social competence an element of intelligence. In addition, many theorists have proposed a fundamental distinction between problem-solving abilities on the one hand (also called, in the psychological literature, "fluid" abilities) and verbal abilities on the other (also called "crystallized" abilities). This distinction is basic to the conception of intelligence held by our lay subjects.

Why, if we know people's informal theories of intelligence, do we need formal scientific theories at all? A careful examination of the kinds of behaviors people have listed will show why we do. Consider some examples of such behaviors: "reasons logically and well," "makes good decisions," "is verbally fluent," and "reads with high comprehension." One might well ask just what it means to do any of these things. These descriptions label behaviors without really explaining them or even defining what goes into them. What does it mean, psychologically, to reason logically and well, or to read with high comprehension? What makes some people reason or read better than others? These are the kinds of questions psychologists must address in their scientific theories. Thus, the informal theories of laymen can be seen as setting up a framework within which scientists can work; the detailed contents falling within that framework can be filled in only by scientific research.

Yet another comparison can be made by considering the content of IQ tests. In particular, how do people's conceptions of intelligence correspond to what IQ tests measure? The correspondence is striking indeed. Behaviors such as "reads with high comprehension" are measured by tests that ask people to remember facts and make inferences from short reading passages. "Is verbally fluent" is measured by word-fluency tests, such as those that ask people to think of as many words as they can beginning with the letter *r* in a brief time period. "Displays a good vocabulary" is directly measured by vocabulary tests. "Displays a good memory" is measured by memory tests, like those that ask a person to remember a string of digits such as 3-5-1-8-6-2. "Is knowledgeable about a broad range of things" is measured by tests of world knowledge. "Works puzzles well" is measured by tests such as anagrams, which present scrambled words (r-t-d-o-o-c) to be unscrambled (doctor). "Solves problems well" is measured by tests such as arithmetic word problems, which require people to solve real-world types of problems by using numerical calculations.

What's Smart for the Baganda Is Dumb for the Batoro

A fine-grained analysis of our data reveals not only differences between experts and laymen, but also distinguishable subpopulations among laymen. Students, we found, gave greater weight to academic ability as a component of general intelligence than commuters did. Commuters, on the other hand, considered everyday intelligence—the ability to function well in daily life—more important.

The differences in conceptions of intelligence become much greater if one goes outside our own culture. Mallory Wober, an African psychologist, investigated conceptions of intelligence among members of different tribes in Uganda and found considerable variation. The Baganda, for example, tended to associate intelligence with mental order, whereas the Batoro associated it with some degree of mental turmoil. When Wober asked his subjects to associate descriptive words with intelligence, he found that members of the Baganda tribe thought of intelligence as persistent, hard, and obdurate, whereas the Batoro thought of it as soft, obedient, and yielding.

Cross-cultural differences in conceptions of intelligence can have practical as well as theoretical implications, as I have discovered from my own experience. I recently attended a meeting on intelligence in Venezuela, where the government has established a Ministry for the Development of Intelligence to raise the intellectual level of the Venezuelan population. The meeting consisted of morning, afternoon, and evening sessions, with speakers and listeners representing a wide range of cultural backgrounds. In the early days of the meeting, my North American colleagues and I consistently arrived promptly at the time that a given session was scheduled to begin. We were acting in a way that is adaptive in meetings we have attended in the United States: If one wishes to hear a whole session, one arrives on time. Indeed, a behavior that was rated as very highly characteristic of intelligence by people in our experiments was being on time for appointments. But we quickly learned that what was adaptive and intelligent in the United States was quite maladaptive and unintelligent in Venezuela. Meetings simply never started on time, and delays of an hour or two were quite common. Someone who arrived on time for every session (or any session!) would waste countless hours waiting for meetings to begin—hours that could be better spent doing any of a number of other things.

That kind of difference has practical implications for me because I have been asked to conduct a trainin course in intellectual skills for Venezuelan schoolchildren. Obviously I will have to study Venezuelan ideas of intelligence before instituting the training; wholesale importation of North American conceptions of intelligence into the Venezuelan culture would make no sense at all.

We Use Our Theories of Intelligence

Just as psychologists administering IQ tests can measure intelligence on the basis of some (at least allegedly) scientific theory of what intelligence is, so ordinary people should be able to assess intelligence—their own and others'—on the basis of their own theories of what intelligence is. Indeed, we found that laymen not only *have* internalized conceptions of intelligence, but that they make good use of them in evaluating intelligence.

To find out whether or not what people say they think about intelligence is actually reflected in their judgments of intelligence, we sent lay subjects a series of character sketches of fictitious people, employing behaviors taken from our master list. Here are two typical sketches:

Susan:

She keeps an open mind.
She is knowledgeable about a particular field.
She converses well.
She shows a lack of independence.
She is on time for appointments.

Adam:

He deals effectively with people.
He thinks he knows everything.
He shows a lack of independence.
He lacks interest in solving problems.
He speaks clearly and articulately.
He fails to ask questions.
He is on time for appointments.

The respondent's task was to rate the intelligence of each person on a scale of 1 to 9. Our task was to find out whether or not the respondent's ratings were consistent with laymen's theoretical conceptions of intelligence as revealed in one of our earlier studies—the one described on page 33, in which we asked subjects to rate the degree to which each of the 250 master behaviors is characteristic of intelligent or unintelligent people. "Keeps an open mind," for example, had been rated 7.7, while "shows a lack of independence" was worth 2.7. Averaging the ratings for each fictitious person, we came up with a score of 6 for Susan and of 4.3 for Adam. By comparison, our respondents rated Susan's intelligence at 5.8 (above average) and Adam's at 4.3 (below average). Overall, when we calculated the correlation between the two sets of ratings, it was an extremely high .96 (on a scale where 1 would mean a perfect relationship). In other words, laymen's ratings of people's intelligence are firmly grounded in their theories about intelligence.

In the course of doing this part of our study, we found that unfavorable characterizations of people—"fears the unfamiliar," "likes to argue but not to think about arguments," "is slow to learn," "acts indecisively," and "succumbs to propaganda"—carry more weight in reducing an evaluation of someone's intelligence than do favorable characterizations in increasing an evaluation of the person's intelligence. That is, ordinary people can be very harsh in their judgments of unintelligent behavior; when people do something stupid, they may find that others brand them as stupid without giving them full credit for the intelligent things they do.

As for people's ability to assess their own intelligence, we found a correlation of .23 between self-ratings on general intelligence and actual IQ. That correlation is not impressive; it is higher than chance, but it shows that most people have only a very modest ability to assess their own intelligence.

However, we found that people's self-*descriptions* can tell us much more about their intelligence than their self-*ratings*. Specifically, we discovered that if we presented people with our master list of 250 intelligent and unintelligent behaviors and asked them to rate how characteristic each behavior is of themselves, we could then estimate, from their responses, not only their overall IQ, but their subscores on such aspects of intelligence as problem-solving ability, verbal ability, and social competence. The correlation between overall scores on the checklist for intelligence and IQ was .52, more than twice as high as the correlation of self-rating with IQ. Moreover, this correlation compares favorably with correlations obtained by psychologists in the laboratory using "cognitive measures," such as the time it takes to complete intellectual tasks: for example, analogies and anagrams. In other words, we seem to have found a potential measure of intelligence that could supplement, though not replace, conventional IQ tests. This, we think, is the major value of our research.

The estimates of intelligence that we can calculate from the master list of behaviors are only fairly accurate, not absolutely so. For that reason, I would not go so far as to suggest that the checklist replace IQ tests. But the checklist does have several desirable features as a supplementary measure of intelligence. First, its questions deal with *typical performance*, rather than with the *maximal performance* required by IQ test questions. There are few situations in one's life that require quite the expenditure of mental effort that is involved in taking an IQ test. Second, the checklist is not stressful, or at least it is much less stressful than an IQ test, making it especially appropriate for people who for one reason or another do not show their true abilities in an IQ testing situation. Third, the items on the checklist deal with real-world behaviors rather than with the highly artificial behaviors required by IQ tests.

Fourth, the checklist is more wide-ranging in the kinds of behaviors it inquires about than are IQ tests. For example, the checklist includes items assessing the kinds of social competence all but ignored by IQ tests. Moreover, the checklist can be tailored to different cultural groups by constructing and scoring it on the basis of behaviors that members of a given group consider to be important ingredients of intelligence. Both the content and the scoring are thereby made culturally relevant for the particular person whose intelligence is being assessed. Finally, the circumstances of administering the checklist would not have the inherent biases found in IQ testing situations, which place a premium on rapid solution of test items little resembling the tasks in ordinary people's lives.

One might attempt to dismiss the behavioral checklist by arguing that people would simply rate themselves as showing a maximum of desirable behaviors and a minimum of undesirable ones. But such a dismissal would be ill-advised. The scoring system we have developed calls for figuring out how much resemblance there is between a person's self-description and other people's descriptions of the ideally intelligent person; the greater the resemblance, the higher the real person's IQ. Thus, what matters is not the *level* of people's responses (on the 1 to 9 scale), but the *pattern* of responses; the correlational resemblance is indifferent to the magnitude of the ratings. Moreover, we know that subjects do not, in fact, simply check off for themselves the "ideal" pattern. No subjects came anywhere near depicting themselves as ideal.

On a theoretical level, our research can help enrich scientifically based theories of intelligence with intuitively based ones. The two kinds of research are complementary. Conducted in tandem, with each informing the other, they can provide greater understanding of the nature of intelligence than can either kind pursued alone. At the very least, the research we have done on people's conceptions of intelligence has taught us that what psychologists study as intelligence does have some connection with what people mean by intelligence in everyday life.

For further information read:

Neisser, Ulric, "The Concept of Intelligence," in *Human Intelligence Perspectives on Its Theory and Measurement.* Robert J. Sternberg and Douglas K. Detterman, eds., Ablex, 1979, $16.50.

Sternberg, Robert J., "The Nature of Intelligence," *New York University Education Quarterly*, Vol. 12, No. 3, pp. 10-17, 1981.

Sternberg, Robert J., "Testing and Cognitive Psychology," *American Psychologist*, 36 (1981), 1181-1189.

Sternberg, Robert J., et al., "People's Conceptions of Intelligence," *Journal of Personality and Social Psychology*, 41(1981), 37-55.

Wober, Mallory, "Towards an Understanding of the Kiganda Concept of Intelligence," in *Culture and Cognition: Readings in Cross-Cultural Psychology.* J.W. Berry and P.R. Dasen, eds., Methuen, 1974, paper. $10.95.

Yussen, Steven R., and Patrick Kane, "Children's Conceptions of Intelligence," in *The Development of Insight in Children*, Academic Press, in press.

THE REMEDIAL THINKER

'AUL CHANCE

aul Chance is a psychologist and former ssistant managing editor of *Psychology Toay*. He received his doctorate in experiiental psychology from Utah State Universi-, completing a thesis on learning and probm solving. He is the author of *Learning hrough Play* (Gardner Press, 1979) and *earning and Behavior* (Wadsworth, 1979), nd is currently writing a book on thinkingkills instruction.

She was six, maybe seven years old, with maple skin and mahogany eyes. Mary was part of the control group for an experiment, and I was giving her an in-:elligence test. She seemed bright enough, but she was not doing well at all. In fact, she would receive an IQ of about 80, one short step above mental retardation. I remember thinking that I must have been fooled by those dark, thoughtful eyes. Yet somehow I could not shake the belief that Mary had far more ability than the test revealed. . . .

That was 15 years ago, before an Israeli clinical psychologist aroused considerable attention in this country and abroad by providing new evidence that children like Mary may be bright after all. Today, Reuven Feuerstein's ideas about the nature of intelligence and the awakening of dormant mental powers are being adopted in many classrooms around the world. In Israel, where his techniques for improving thinking skills have been used systematically in schools for more than a dozen years, 1,300 classes receive his training program. In Venezuela, all college students preparing to be teachers are now required to study his theories and methods. In the United States, where educators have become concerned that traditional "basics" are not teaching children how to think, his methods are already being used in 300 school systems.

The source of all the interest is a professor of psychology at Bar Ilan University and the Director of Psychological Services at Youth Aliyah, an organization for wayward, orphaned, or abandoned children. I first met Feuerstein (*foý-er-schtyne*) a year ago at a conference. Sixtyish, portly, with a full white beard and a large, dark beret, Feuerstein looked as if he had just stepped out of a Tolkien novel.

This overgrown Hobbit stood before the assembled researchers and told them in an eclectic European accent that intelligence was not carved in cerebral marble but was, rather, a soft plastic that could be shaped almost at will. Feuerstein did not deny that there is such a thing as natural endowment, but he maintained that except in the most severe cases, subnormal intelligence can be improved; that many people with IQs of 80, 60, or even 40 can, with appropriate training, perform at near-normal or even above-average levels.

In a way, it is odd that Feuerstein should think so. He is a former pupil of the late Swiss psychologist Jean Piaget, who held that the development of intelligence is essentially a maturational process, an unfolding of innate biological talents. Feuerstein's very different views may have begun to evolve during his childhood in Romania. He learned to read at age three and by eight was teaching Hebrew to the slower Jewish children in the community, whose numbers included some who would today be called learning disabled or mentally retarded.

In 1938 the Germans gained control over Romania. Two years later, Feuerstein, then living in Bucharest, was sent to a labor camp. After nine months in the camp, Feuerstein was permitted to return to Bucharest. There he embarked on the first part of an erratic education that later included his studies with Piaget in Geneva and culminated in 1970 with a Ph.D. in psychology from the Sorbonne.

In Bucharest, Feuerstein worked at a school for children whose parents had been sent to labor camps. "I was fortunate because the government needed teachers for dealing with the children. The Romanians still had some reservations about the final solution." Feuerstein again turned his attention to working with slow learners. When he made aesthetic experiences available to them, especially the opportunity to hear and play music, he encountered opposition from teachers who believed that such students were suited only for menial tasks. One complained that they "should listen to only one music, the music of the hammer."

While Feuerstein hammered away at his students and the teachers who opposed him, he also was active in underground Zionist activities. He was arrested in 1944 but released ("miraculously redeemed") after a few hours. Three days later, he found himself on the first ship bound for what would become the new state of Israel. In his new homeland, Feuerstein worked for Youth Aliyah, organized to cope with the influx of displaced Jewish children who had survived the Holocaust.

Measuring Learning Directly

To determine how they might best be helped, the youngsters were given a battery of psychological tests, including standardized intelligence tests. It soon became clear, however, that the tests were of little value in determining the children's intellectual strengths and weaknesses. Traditional intelligence tests assume that intelligence is an immutable quality that sets limits on how much a person will learn: given approximately equal opportunities for learning, individual differences in performance should reflect differences in intelligence. But Feuerstein could not assume that the Youth Aliyah children had had opportunities for learning equal to those of normal children when they had spent much of their lives sleeping in doorways and fighting for survival in concentration camps. Many of them performed at the retarded level, yet their IQs did not reveal whether their retardation was due to a lack of learning ability or to a lack of opportunity for learning. Perhaps, reasoned Feuerstein, instead of measuring past learning and inferring ability, one ought to measure learning ability directly.

With that goal in mind, Feuerstein and his colleagues gradually developed the Learning Potential Assessment Device (LPAD), a clinical tool that bears only the vaguest resemblance to other measures of intelligence. Most traditional tests include many items that depend on previous knowledge—arithmetic problems and questions based on general information, for example. For the most part, the LPAD avoids such familiar content. In one part of the test, for example, the task is to identify geometric forms embedded among configurations of dots. (See illustration, right.) In another, four square plates are arranged in tiers. Each plate contains nine buttons, one of which is glued down. The task is to find out which buttons are fixed and remember where they are located. On such items, past learning of facts and skills (how to divide 27 by 4 or how to mail a letter) should be of little help. Thus, everyone who takes the test starts off more or less equally ignorant.

In a traditional IQ test, the examiner offers no help, no hints, no explanations, no feedback of any kind. The purpose of the test is to find out what a child already knows. Feuerstein's purpose is to find out what a child can learn, and his methods are drastically different. The testing session is in fact a tutorial that lasts four to five hours or more. Students and teachers often get so involved that they complete the entire session without a break. The examiner/teacher presents a task and sees how far the pupil can go with it if taught. The session proceeds in a test-teach-test fashion through more and more complex levels of each task. Along the way, Feuerstein writes, the examiner "constantly intervenes, makes remarks, requires and gives explanations whenever and wherever they are necessary, asks for repetition, sums up experiences, anticipates difficulties and warns the child about them, and creates reflective, insightful thinking." The examiner also notes what the child does and does not grasp.

I saw the kind of intervention Feuerstein practices in testing sessions when I watched him work with Ruth, an American black girl of about 13. At one point Feuerstein tested her understanding of right and left. Asked to hold up her right hand, Ruth did so; but asked to tap Feuerstein's right hand (he was seated across from her), she touched his left. "Show me your right hand," Feuerstein then asked. The girl complied. "Now show me my right hand." She touched his left hand. Feuerstein turned around and, with his back to the girl, put his hands out behind him. This time she touched Feuerstein's right hand, the one nearest her own right hand. Slowly, he turned to her, holding his arms out to accentuate their position. Again, he asked: "Which is my right hand?" True to form, Ruth touched Feuerstein's left. Feuerstein turned around again, as before, but this time he marked an "X" on the back of his right hand with a felt-tipped pen, and asked Ruth to touch his right hand. She did so, and Feuerstein turned around to face her, so that the marked hand was clearly visible. Ruth still did not get it, but Feuerstein got a far better idea of the extent of her learning disability than he might have had he stopped after her first mistake.

Thinking Problems

As Feuerstein developed the LPAD, he found that his new test told a very different story about the intellectual potential of his charges than the traditional measures had. Youngsters who had initially shown a remarkable ignorance of facts in the test proved that they could acquire them; those who showed no grasp of the most basic concepts, such as right and left, came to master them; those who demonstrated no evidence of abstract reasoning reasoned abstractly. This evidence convinced Feuerstein that retarded performance on traditional tests revealed little about capacity, and that many "retarded performers," as he came to call them, were far more capable than their IQs suggested.

Over years, working with children

SPOTTING POTENTIAL

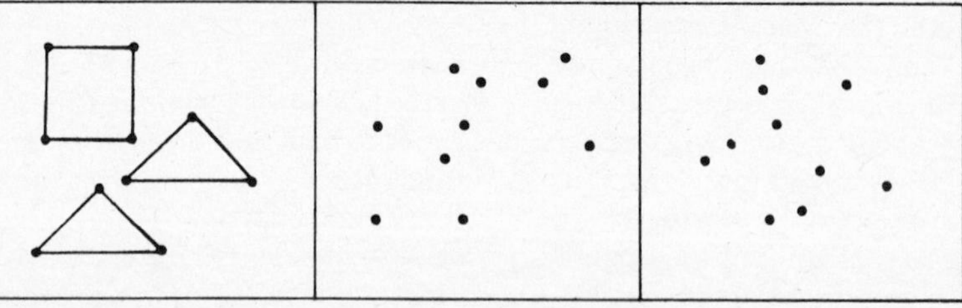

In the Learning Potential Assessment Device, the object is not to find out what a student knows but what he can learn with instruction. He is tested on a task, then trained, then retested. The result reveals not only his learning potential but the flawed thinking skills that hold him back. In the sample item above, the object is to find the square and two triangles embedded in each set of dots. Each dot is used just once, but the figures may overlap. The forms in the second and third boxes are exactly the same shape and size as those in the first. *See page 200 for solution.*

immigrating to Israel from Europe, Asia, and Africa, and later working with displaced children from within Israel, Feuerstein began to see why so many of them were functioning below their potential. Over and over again the test results revealed serious flaws, some of them overlapping, in the way the youngsters thought:

☐ *Impulsivity.* Children with low IQ scores tend to approach tasks in an unsystematic, trial-and-error fashion. For instance, when asked to identify geometric shapes solely by touch, many youngsters palmed the objects instead of taking time to finger them carefully. On multiple-choice items, they often began looking for the answer before they understood the question. While impulsivity is sometimes due to organic impairment, it more often represents a failure to learn that deliberate behavior that follows a plan is useful.

☐ *Failure to recognize problems.* Many intellectual problems involve inconsistencies. Feuerstein cites the case of Moses and the burning bush: Moses was able to recognize a discrepancy between his everyday experience with fire and the bush that burned but was not consumed. The retarded performer does not always recognize such inconsistencies. One reason for that failure may be impulsivity, but another can be a failure to learn that discrepancies are important.

☐ *Episodic grasp of reality.* Retarded performers view events and objects in isolation: they do not try to make connections, to see relationships, to put things in context. They often have no sense, for example, that the events of today are integrally related to the events of yesterday and the events of tomorrow. A teenager who has an episodic view is apt to say he or she plans to become a doctor or lawyer and then, in the next breath, that he can hardly wait to be old enough to quit school. What such people have not learned is that episodes in life are connected.

☐ *Failure to make comparisons.* When shown two geometric figures and asked to describe what they see, low-IQ children typically describe only one figure or else describe first one and then the other. They seldom use the words *like, similar, different* or *resembles*. Yet their failure to make comparisons routinely does not necessarily reflect an inability to compare. Given a choice between two pieces of cake, a retarded child typically picks the larger one.

☐ *Inadequate spatial orientation.* Many retarded performers have considerable difficulty learning the positions of squares in a grid or locations on a map. The reason is that they do not orient themselves to the materials by using terms such as upper-left or lower-right. They may know what the terms mean: if they are asked to point to the upper-left corner of the square, they often do so. Yet they have not become used to using such concepts to solve spatial problems.

This list is merely a sampling of the kinds of flaws in basic thinking skills that Feuerstein has found in slow-learning children. In one of his books he describes 21 such "cognitive deficiencies," admitting considerable overlap among them. Underlying all, he finds, is a passive approach to the environment. He notes that retarded performers fail to recognize that their own intellectual efforts may contribute to the solution of a problem. He cites the student who answers immediately, when asked to recall a fact: "I don't know." It does not occur to the student that he or she might be able to come up with the answer by working on it a bit. Retarded performers see themselves at best as passive receptacles of information, Feuerstein says, not as generators of information.

What causes this passive approach and the various cognitive deficiencies that manifest it? Feuerstein speculates that the answer lies in the kinds of experiences that are available—or

INSTRUMENTAL ENRICHMENT

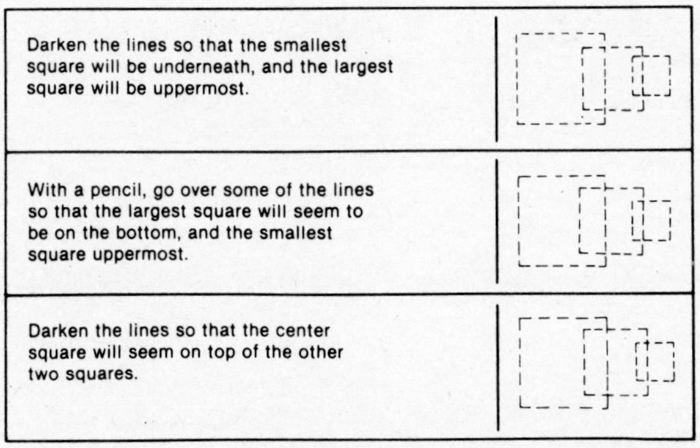

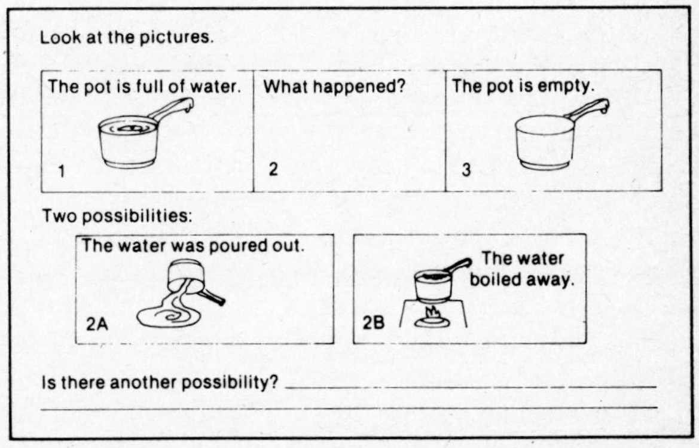

The object of these instructional exercises is to help students overcome various "cognitive deficiencies." Throughout, the teacher models, criticizes, praises, prompts, prods, and wheedles as necessary to help overcome flaws in the students' basic thinking skills. In Exercise 1, the task is to trace broken lines so that some squares appear to be above others. Students who jump into the task too quickly are apt to make mistakes; with help, they learn the value of controlling impulsivity. Exercise 2, explaining how the full pot of water became empty, is designed to help students overcome the tendency to see related objects and events in isolation. The goal of the exercises is not to learn solutions to the problems but to master the thinking skills that can lead to solutions.

not available—to these youngsters. He postulates that while children can learn a great deal from ordinary interaction with the environment, such experiences are of limited value in the acquisition of mental skills. Feuerstein has come to believe that many cognitive deficiencies are not due to a lack of interaction with the environment but due to a lack of instruction about those interactions. From the standpoint of intellectual development, what counts is not direct experience but mediated experience.

In a mediated experience, a more knowledgeable person, usually an adult, intervenes between the person and the environment. The mediator "transforms, reorders, organizes, groups, and frames the stimuli in the direction of some specifically intended goal and purpose." Virtually any experience is mediated when someone intervenes to order and clarify it. The everyday experience of stopping at a traffic light serves as a simple example. To make it a mediated experience, an adult might point out to a child that the red light means stop and the green light go, and that the apparently arbitrary relationship has a rational justification: the need to control traffic. Adult and child might then go on to discuss other instances in which it is necessary to control behavior through conventions.

Even simple commands can become mediated experiences. By way of example, Feuerstein points to the difference between saying to a child "Go to the store and buy three bottles of milk" and "Go to the store and buy three bottles of milk so we'll have enough left over tomorrow when the shops are closed." In the first case only the command exists; in the second, the child is made privy to the reasoning behind the command. The specific content of an experience, according to Feuerstein, is unimportant: what matters is the extent to which the experience provides insight into the thinking process.

According to Feuerstein's theory, then, too few mediated experiences result in poor thinking skills, which in turn reduce the individual's ability to learn from further direct experiences. The retarded performer's low IQ is therefore an accurate reflection of a current level of functioning, although not necessarily of capacity. It follows from this theory that remedial efforts aimed at providing a stimulating environment ("filling the rooms with posters, toys and colorful mobiles," as Feuerstein puts it) are not apt to be effective. Nor will intensive educational programs bear much fruit if the emphasis is on traditional academics such as spelling or the multiplication table. Neither stimulation nor the acquisition of facts will, in themselves, improve retarded performers' thinking skills, which are what Feuerstein believes must change.

Feuerstein's efforts to make changes resulted in Instrumental Enrichment, or IE, a program that has been more than 25 years in the making and is still being refined. IE consists of 15 "instruments," so called because the sequence of paper and pencil exercises in each is said to be instrumental in overcoming one or more cognitive deficiencies. The materials comprise over 500 pages of exercises that teachers administer individually or in groups in hourly sessions three to five times a week over a period of two to three years. The materials are intended for use with students between the ages of 10 and 18. The goal of the IE exercises is not to arrive at solutions but to understand how solutions are arrived at; not to acquire facts but to learn how facts are acquired.

The same test-teach-test method used in the LPAD is used in Instrumental Enrichment. The teacher instructs, models, asks for explanations, praises, prompts, prods, and wheedles as necessary to help a youngster overcome cognitive deficiencies. For instance, one exercise requires the pupil to trace the outlines of a number of overlapping figures drawn in dotted outlines so that some will appear to have been placed above others. (See illustration on page 67.) The impulsive child is apt to jump into the task without thinking through what it requires or how the end result can best be accomplished. If that happens, the instructor stops the overeager pupil and asks for a detailed explanation of what he must do. In this way the two of them analyze the task and work out a plan of attack; the process, Feuerstein believes, gives the student an idea of the value of a systematic, thoughtful approach.

The chief function of the "Numerical Progressions" instrument is to help the student overcome an episodic grasp of reality. The exercises involve finding relationships among disparate objects and events, including not only progressions of numbers but relationships among figures and common cause-and-effect connections. For instance, in one item the student is asked to account for the fact that a full pot of water becomes empty. (See illustration on page 67.) He is helped to see that the full pot and the empty pot are connected by an intervening event, such as evaporation or pouring, and that more than one event may have accounted for the change.

Assessing the Gains

The IE program was developed to help slow-learning children improve cognitive skills, but it also is a test of Feuerstein's theory of intelligence: good results will support his idea that retarded performance is largely due to the cognitive deficiencies he has identified and, further, that those deficiencies are due to a lack of mediated experiences. The question is, *do* students benefit from IE?

Feuerstein says that many students with low IQs who have gone through the IE program have gone on to become teachers, school principals, professors, executives, government officials. The stories are intriguing, even inspiring, but not entirely convincing. After all, tens of thousands of Israeli students have received IE training. Any training program involving so many people is bound to include among its graduates some spectacular success stories. But carefully controlled research is needed in order to demonstrate that the successes are due to IE.

Fewer studies have been done than one might expect, considering how long Feuerstein and his colleagues have been at work. Perhaps the most extensive to date was conducted just a few years ago by Feuerstein and Ya'acov Rand, one of his colleagues at Bar Ilan University. The study involved 218 adolescents, most of them male, with an average IQ of 80 on the Primary Mental Abilities test (a conventional instrument widely used in schools). Most of the youngsters came from low-income blue-collar families. Many had records of poor school attendance and discipline problems;

some had been in trouble with the police. Many were reading far below age level; some were almost illiterate. The experimental group received about 300 hours of IE for a two-year period; the control group spent the same time receiving intensive supplementary academic instruction.

At the end of the training period, all students took a battery of tests, including a retest on the Primary Mental Abilities scale. They also took three standard nonverbal tests of intelligence requiring them to do such things as match analogous figures, and four tests measuring more specific cognitive abilities. The researchers compared the scores of 57 youths from each group matched for IQ, age, sex, and ethnic background. The results favored the IE group; the control group did not do better on a single measure of intellectual skill.

The results of a follow-up study are even more encouraging. Two years after their training, 164 of the students were tested by the army when they were drafted. The Israeli Army uses an intelligence test called the Dapar, which includes both verbal and nonverbal items and yields a single score ranging from a low of 1 to a high of 9 (5 is average). The researchers found that students who had had two years of IE obtained an average Dapar score of 5.38, equivalent to an IQ of about 103. The students who had received two years of supplementary instruction obtained an average of 4.64, equivalent to an IQ of about 97. It is difficult to compare these results with the pretraining IQ of 80 for the entire study group, but it does at least appear that students in the IE group made substantial gains when compared to the control group and maintained their lead even after two years.

The focus of IE research in this country is the John F. Kennedy Center for Research on Education and Human Development at George Peabody College, Vanderbilt University. Carl Haywood, the psychologist who is director of the center, and his associate Ruth Arbitman-Smith conducted a study in which some slow-learning adolescents took time away from their ordinary classwork for an average of 59 hours of IE over a five-month period, while a control group of similar students spent the same time pursuing the standard curriculum. At the end of the study, the IE students showed greater gains on a nonverbal test of intelligence.

In a second study, funded by the U.S. Office of Special Education, secondary students in the public schools of Nashville, Louisville, and Phoenix received IE for two years. The first year of training (about 93 hours of IE) produced little benefit. The results of the second year may tell a different story.

The data are just now emerging from the computer, but the researchers believe the final analysis will reveal substantial gains by the IE students on a variety of measures of intellectual skill. The fact that not much happened after only one year of training is taken to mean that real changes in cognitive skills take time to develop. Says Arbitman-Smith: "I see great changes in kids, but I also see that it's a slow process. You don't see major results in a few months."

Another ongoing project at Vanderbilt under the direction of Haywood, Arbitman-Smith, and John Bransford includes academically successful students as well as academically unsuccessful ones. The poor students have an average IQ of about 90 and are up to three years behind in academic achievement; the good ones have an average IQ of about 110 and are at or above grade level in achievement. In a preliminary report to the National Institute of Education (which is sponsoring the work), the researchers note that good students did twice as well as the slow ones on the "Organization of Dots" instrument before training, but after training, the slow students nearly matched their faster peers, even though the faster students also had benefited from training. In a later stage of the study, slow learners tackled a problem new to them. Those who had received IE did nearly twice as well on the novel task as poor students who had not received IE training.

Of course, the real test of IE and of Feuerstein's theory of intelligence will be what happens in the regular classroom. If the training improves learning ability and not just IQ scores, IE students should begin to get more out of the standard curriculum. Eventually that should result in higher scores on conventional achievement tests. Feuerstein and Rand found in their study that after two years of training, IE students showed a slight advantage over controls, even though the latter had received more course work. Data on the scholastic achievement of children with IE training are just now being collected at Vanderbilt, Columbia, and Yale universities. They also look promising.

Even if the first results are good, success may have more to do with the excitement that a new program generates than with the program itself. Still, some usually tight-lipped psychologists are beginning to mutter favorably about it. J. McVicker Hunt, professor of psychology emeritus at the University of Illinois who has visited Feuerstein in Israel and met some of his students, admits that he is much impressed. And Bransford, who struck me as rather skeptical when I met him at the conference where Feuerstein spoke, now says of IE: "I wouldn't say it's the answer—nor would Feuerstein—but I am convinced that it does something pretty dramatic in some students."

The "some" is important. None of the researchers I talked to, least of all Feuerstein, claim that IE will produce uniformly good results in all students. The program derives from a theory of intelligence that proposes that cognitive skills are acquired primarily through mediated experiences. It follows that IE is likely to be beneficial to the extent that mediated experiences have been inadequate.

Teacher training for IE has to be fairly elaborate. Even those who sing the praises of IE warn that it is not a snap to use. Hunt is a strong supporter of IE, but when I talked to him he said, "That IE is a very, very hard thing to do. It takes brains, by God. You've got to work at it and you've got to think it through."

Even so, if providing mediated experiences does have dramatic effects on some students, the implications are awesome. It means that Feuerstein may be right about the plasticity of intelligence. It means that thinking skills can, indeed must, be taught. And it means that many people who are a drain on society might be self-supporting, contributing members of their communities, that many people may needlessly spend their entire lives in institutions or drifting aimlessly along the edges of society. Above all it means that there may be thousands of people in this country, to say nothing of the rest of the world, who are functioning well below capacity—a waste of human talent.

It was that thought that troubled me as Feuerstein and I neared the end of a long late-night talk. He sighed in agreement. "This," he said, "is one of the tragic things making me restless: the waste." I thought about Mary, who had seemed so much more capable than her 80 IQ. Yes, Reuven, the waste.

Solutions to problems on p. 196:

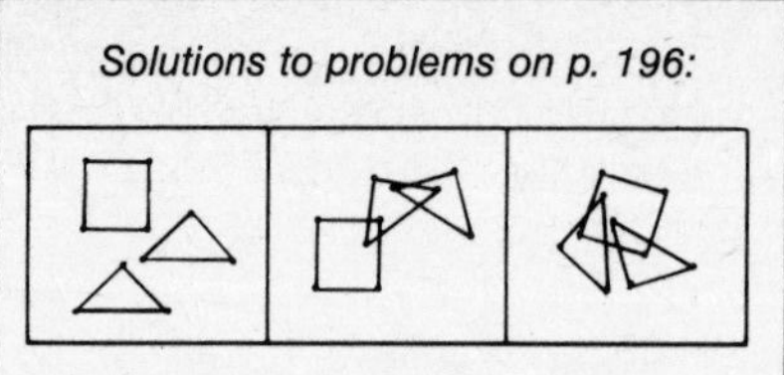

For further information, read:

Feuerstein, Reuven, in collaboration with Ya'acov Rand and Mildred B. Hoffman. *The Dynamic Assessment of Retarded Performers*, University Park Press, 233 East Redwood St., Baltimore, Md. 21202, 1979, $24.50.

Feuerstein, Reuven, in collaboration with Ya'acov Rand, Mildred B. Hoffman, and Ronald Miller. *Instrumental Enrichment*, University Park Press, 1980. $24.95.

Feuerstein, Reuven, and Mogens Riemer Jensen. "Instrumental Enrichment: Theoretical Basis, Goals, and Instruments," *The Educational Forum*, May 1980.

Instrumental Enrichment materials are published by University Park Press but are available only to those trained in their use. For information write Dr. Frances Link, Curriculum Development Associates Inc., Suite 414, 1211 Connecticut Avenue N.W., Washington, D.C., 20036.

Males and females and what you may not know about them

THE POTENTIAL DIFFERENCE between men and women begins with the assembly of a new set of chromosomes at conception, when one pair is coded either XX for females or XY for males. The difference a Y chromosome makes becomes physiologically explicit about six to seven weeks later. What else chromosome and hormone patterns do to set males and females apart—in behavior as well as body—is more problematic.

Most scientists believe both nature and nurture are responsible for sex differences. Some stress the striking degree of similarity between the sexes and the way this resemblance has grown through the ages.

Yet men and women *are* different, and these differences emerge in the realms of education, child rearing, sports, the military, the marketplace and the workplace, triggering some of the hottest social controversies of our day.

How, exactly, are they unalike? Here's what scientists know—and would like to know—about this engrossing topic.

Bigger boys, more mature girls

At birth, boys are on average half an inch longer and five ounces or so heavier than girls. They remain slightly larger throughout most of childhood. Newborn girls are about four to six weeks more advanced than boys in skeletal development, according to a leading expert on growth, Dr. J.M. Tanner of the University of London. Certain other organ systems are also more mature in female infants. Girls continue to mature more rapidly; according to some researchers they generally walk, talk and become toilet trained sooner than boys. Girls get their permanent teeth earlier and reach puberty about two years before boys do. They also have their adolescent growth spurt earlier, making them temporarily taller than boys.

But men end up longer-legged and about five inches taller. The average American woman between age 35 and 44 is 5 feet 4 inches tall and weighs 152 pounds; the average man in the same age group is 5 feet 9 inches and weighs 179.

After puberty, males and females differ significantly in heart, lungs, blood, bone, muscle and fat. Boys develop larger hearts and lungs, more red blood cells and more hemoglobin. Their skeletons broaden at the shoulders; they put on muscle and develop a greater capacity than females for neutralizing the chemical by-products of muscular exercises.

The female skeleton at puberty broadens at the hips, and the female body builds up an energy reserve of fat—both changes in preparation for possible childbearing. Young adult males average about 50% muscle and 16% fat, females about 40% muscle and 25% fat.

More muscle is one reason why men tend to be better adapted for heavy physical work than women. Male and female muscle fibers are not very different in strength; however, men have more of them relative to their size.

The other key to physical performance is aerobic power, the maximum amount of oxygen an individual can get into the body and to the cells. Boys and girls start out about equal in this respect, but a Swedish study showed that after puberty women's aerobic maximums averaged about 80% to 85% of men's on the basis of weight. Under conditioning programs, however, women can narrow the gap in aerobic power and muscular strength. For example, sedentary college men in one study had 22% more aerobic power than sedentary college women before both went through an eight-week training program; men had only 8% more after.

Men and women differ most in muscular strength of the upper body, and they are most nearly equal in strength of legs and abdominal muscles. After seven weeks of Army basic training, women demonstrated, pound for pound, 84% as much strength as men in the abdominal muscles and 79% in the legs but only 70% in the upper body. Army physical training standards reflect the recognition of sex differences in strength. Young women must do at least 16 push-ups, for instance, but young men must do at least 40.

Both men and women athletes enjoy advantages related to their gender. Women gain balance and agility from their lower center of gravity. Men, with more muscle mass, more aerobic capacity, greater upper body strength and longer bones, can in general throw harder, jump farther and run faster.

The running and swimming speed gaps, however, have been narrowing in recent decades—men are only about 10% faster in current world records. In long-distance swims a woman's narrower shoulders, lighter body and insulating, buoyant body fat are a plus. The English Channel swimming record is held by a woman.

The vulnerable male

In life as in sports, the physiological advantage of women is most apparent over the long haul. On average, American women live nearly eight years longer than men. Some researchers say that three-quarters of this sex difference can be explained by learned behavior that has been encouraged or condoned more for men than for women, especially smoking and the excessive competitiveness, aggressiveness, hostility and impatience often lumped together as "coronary prone" behavior.

Other investigators emphasize biological and genetic explanations for the male's greater vulnerability, which begins, in fact, at conception. Although at least 120 boys are conceived for every 100 girls, male rates of spontaneous abortions and stillbirths are so much higher that at birth the ratio is 105 to 100.

More male than female babies are born malformed; more die at childbirth, in the first week and year of life, and in every year thereafter. Men suffer from higher rates of chronic conditions that are leading causes of death. By the time the male and female survivors are old enough to have children, their numbers are about equal. By age 65 there are seven surviving men for every ten women.

Why should males be more fragile than females? Physiological maturity may be a factor. Girls, after all, are more mature in the womb and are born with a four- to six-week head start to help them weather the risks of infancy.

The endocrine system may hold a clue, too. Dr. Estelle Ramey and her colleagues at Georgetown University theorize that the male hormone testosterone has a gradually damaging effect on the cardiovascular system.

Another source of vulnerability is the difference in the sex chromosome pattern: XX for females, XY for males. The genes that govern the presence or absence of dozens of genetic diseases and disorders are carried on X chromosomes. Females with a defective gene on one X chromosome are likely to have a protective, healthy, matching gene on the other X. Males don't have a second X, so chances are that with one bad gene they will manifest—not just carry—such X-linked disorders as hemophilia and some kinds of muscular dystrophy.

The genetic shield of women doesn't end there. According to Dr. David T. Purtilo and Dr. John L. Sullivan of the University of Massachusetts Medical School, research indicates women have extra disease-fighting genes, twice as many as men carry on their sex chromosomes. Not surprisingly, the recovery rate of women from most diseases is better than that of men.

The vulnerable female

The immunological advantage of females is a double-edged sword, Purtilo and Sullivan point out. It's good for fighting disease, but it also predisposes women to form antibodies against their own system, as in lupus erythematosus, a connective tissue disorder that strikes nine females for every male.

Women appear to be sick more frequently than men, and no one is certain of all the reasons. Data analyzed by University of Michigan demographer Dr. Lois M. Verbrugge shows women have more episodes of acute respiratory and gastrointestinal problems and higher rates of chronic conditions, such as arthritis, anemia, diabetes, hypertension and some forms of heart disease. They are also more poorly nourished and have poorer vision. On the other hand, females tend to have better teeth and better hearing than men.

In terms of absence from work, the two health profiles almost balance out: an average of 4.9 workdays a year lost by men, 5.7 lost by women.

The way we act

Mental illness strikes the sexes rather evenhandedly, with two exceptions. Men are more subject to personality disorders, including antisocial behavior and drug or alcohol abuse. Women seem more vulnerable to anxiety and depression—not just the everyday blues but also clinical depression, a mood disturbance severe enough to impair functioning.

In the case of depression, researchers are following tangled clues, biological as well as psychological and social. One difference they have uncovered is that marriage protects men from mental illness but increases the risk for women.

Research on sex differences in social behavior, learning, motivation and perception is extensive. Yet after scrutinizing hundreds of studies, Dr. Eleanor Maccoby and Dr. Carol Jacklin, Stanford University psychologists, found the evidence insufficient or too ambiguous to answer a number of key questions. For instance, they couldn't say with confidence whether females are more fearful, timid and anxious than males; whether males are more competitive; whether females are really more disposed to be nurturant or motherly.

What Maccoby and Jacklin could report in 1974 in *The Psychology of Sex Differences* (published by Stanford University Press) was that on most psychological measures males and females are more alike than different. They uncovered no proof that girls are more interested in social, boys in nonsocial stimulation. Studies indicated that the sexes persist on tasks to a similar degree, follow a similar course in the development of moral reasoning, and are about equally helpful and altruistic. Nevertheless, the researchers noted ways in which development varies.

▶ Boys tend to obey their parents less than girls do.

▶ Up to about age 18 months the incidence of angry outbursts triggered by frustration is similar in boys and girls. After that, such outbursts decrease quickly for girls but not for boys. One study found nursery school boys and girls crying with equal frequency but usually for different reasons: the girls because of physical injury, the boys because an object or adult wouldn't do what they wished.

▶ From as early as age 2 to 2½, males are more aggressive—readier to fight and more willing to hurt another person physically or verbally. This difference in aggression is the most solidly established sex difference in social behavior. Maccoby and Jacklin believe that although aggression is learned, there is a biological basis for boys' greater ease, on average, in absorbing the lesson.

▶ Neither sex appears to be more oriented toward people, but girls tend to stick together in pairs or small groups and to like their playmates. Boys congregate in larger groups, and liking or not liking each other seems secondary to the activity at hand.

▶ Maccoby and Jacklin found little reliable evidence that boys are consistently more active than girls, but beginning in the preschool years "boys appear to be especially stimulated to bursts of high activity by the presence of other boys." Boys also make many more attempts to dominate each other than girls do in their groups, possibly because large groups may need a pecking order more than small ones do. Boys tend to overestimate their status in their peer group more often than girls do.

▶ Girls generally get better grades than boys throughout their school years yet tend to underestimate their intellectual abilities more than boys. By the time they reach college, young women have less confidence in their ability to perform assigned tasks well.

Although they found no sex difference in overall intelligence, Maccoby and Jacklin found "fairly well established" evidence of some differences related to learning. On average, girls from age 11 on do better on tests of verbal skills, from spelling to understanding difficult passages and writing creatively. (Recent findings from the National Assessment of Educational Progress confirm this conclusion, with girls scoring three to four percentage points higher than male peers on reading tasks, as much as ten to 20 points higher on writing skills.)

Girls are also less vulnerable to language disturbances: Three to four times more boys than girls stutter; three to ten times more boys suffer reading disabilities.

From adolescence on, males outperform females on visual-spatial tasks—visualizing shapes and mentally moving or rotating them. (However, a number of recent research studies, including two with a national sample, have not found this sex difference.)

Sex and the teaching of math

On the average, the sexes are intellectual specialists. Females tend to outperform men in verbal skills; males in general are better at math.

Lately, the mathematics gap has become a hot topic. According to Dr. Elizabeth Fennema of the University of Wisconsin, it should be. Lack of verbal skills doesn't seem to stand in the way of men's success, she says, but lack of math skills keeps women from doing a number of things, particularly from qualifying for well-paid jobs in science, engineering and technology.

Actually, the lack of language skills undoubtedly does hold some men back. But serious language deficiencies show up early in the school years, and the need to do something about them has been well accepted. As measured by the Scholastic Aptitude Test (SAT) verbal scores of high school seniors, college-bound boys eventually catch up to the girls. Since 1972 boys have even outperformed girls slightly.

The math disparity, on the other hand, doesn't show up until adolescence and has no similar tradition of remediation. Recent research has defined the discrepancy more precisely. In a national sample of 13-year-olds and of 12th-graders the younger girls did as well as their male counterparts on algebra and word problems and did better by five percentage points on computation. By senior year, boys and girls who had taken the same math courses achieved about the same in algebra and computation, but the boys outperformed the girls by six to 12 percentage points on word problems.

On the math section of the SAT, young men averaged 491 out of 800 possible points in 1980; young women averaged 443. Women are not absent from the higher-scoring SAT takers, just outnumbered—10% of the females and 20% of the males score 600 or above.

Could there be some innate factor that primes men for superior math performance? If so, its identity is still unknown. Some researchers, thinking spatial visualization might be the key, have been searching for evidence of inborn spatial superiority. But that theory seems less convincing than it once did. In any event, no sex difference has been found in some recent tests of spatial visualization.

Another group of researchers used to believe that girls scored lower simply because they took fewer math courses. That argument, too, seems less persuasive these days. Fennema believes a more promising clue lies in the specific kind of math problem that tends to trouble girls more than boys. This stumbling block is the nonroutine problem that calls for putting math knowledge together on your own in a fresh way.

Why the difference? "Somewhere along the way we are not allowing girls to develop independence of thought in learning," Fennema warns. Yet the difference isn't inevitable. Some junior high classes do a good job of developing mathematical skills among both sexes. The University of Wisconsin researcher is trying to find out why.

Dr. Patricia Casserly of the Educational Testing Service has also been looking closely at individual math classrooms to see what elicits high performance. Out of about 100 high school advanced calculus classes in which boys and girls performed equally well and both achieved above the national average on standardized tests, she chose 20 classes with varied and modest family backgrounds. The key to the students' success turned out to be good instruction from teachers who had a degree in mathematics, science or engineering rather than in education. These teachers treated both boys and girls as "partners in a quest." They got across the idea that "all mathematicians have problems if they go far enough; it's O.K. to struggle," a particularly encouraging message for bright girls who are used to doing everything easily and well and face their first real challenge in math class.

EQUALS, a University of California project to promote women's participation in mathematics, has published an informative handbook containing a how-to section on the teaching of problem solving and a collection of engrossing problem-solving activities. For a copy of the 134-page handbook, write to Lawrence Hall of Science, University of California, Berkeley, Cal. 94720, Attn.: EQUALS. Enclose a $5 check or money order payable to Regents, University of California.

▶ On average, boys do better than girls in math beginning about age 12 or 13 (see the box at left).

Are brains alike?

Now an intriguing new question arouses controversy. Do men and women act differently because their brains are different?

Primarily on the basis of work with lower animals, some respected researchers speculate that prenatal sex hormones program pathways in the brain and central nervous system, laying down predispositions for certain kinds of behavior.

As Dr. John Money, director of the Psychohormonal Research Unit at the Johns Hopkins Medical Institutions, explains it, "... the irreducible difference between the sexes is that men impregnate, and women menstruate, gestate and lactate." Other than these biological functions, the sexes share all behaviors; only the prevalence of the behavior "or the ease with which it is elicited can be labeled masculine or feminine," Money writes. Parental care is a case in point: "... regardless of species, males or females can be parental, but the threshold for the release of parental care when the helpless young demand it is different, the mother being more immediately responsive."

Can you solve this problem?

When the National Assessment of Educational Progress gave the following problem to a sample of 2,200 17-year-olds, 46% of the boys but only 39% of the girls were able to answer correctly in the 88 seconds allotted. Problems of this sort require not only basic computation but also use of various reasoning skills; some researchers attribute the different success rates to failure of the schools to encourage such skills in girls to the extent that they are encouraged in boys.

Juan's mother has three five-dollar rolls of dimes and two ten-dollar rolls of quarters to use for Juan's school lunch.

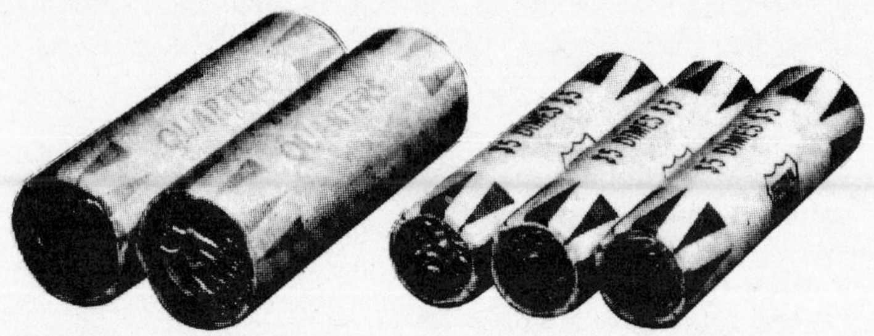

If Juan takes exactly 45 cents to school every day for his lunch, which of the following statements is true?

A. *He uses all of the quarters before all of the dimes.*
B. *He uses all of the dimes before all of the quarters.*
C. *He spends all of both coins at the same time.*
D. *I don't know.*

ANSWER: B

A number of investigators are trying to relate left and right hemisphere brain organization to female verbal ability and male math and spatial ability. This research builds on the assumption that in most right-handed individuals, the left brain dominates verbal and sequential thought, and the right brain is more critical for the performance of spatial and other nonverbal tasks. Some studies suggest that women are more likely to use both sides of the brain for language, whereas men have a tendency to process it exclusively on the left, theoretically leaving the right hemisphere unimpeded for solving spatial problems.

However, Stanford psychologist Dr. Diane McGuinness and neuroscientist Dr. Karl Pribram point out a flaw in the theory: Some right hemisphere specialties, such as recognizing faces, are tasks in which women excel. They theorize that priming by prenatal hormones produces greater visual acuity in males and greater sensitivity to loudness and speech sounds in females. They also think it's possible that the difference in muscular competence (men do better with their large muscles and women excel in fine muscle and finger dexterity) reinforces the difference in sensory biases and leads to major differences in behavior and personality. McGuinness and Pribram point to the "manipulative" male who enjoys "the challenge of coming to grips with the physical environment" and the "communicative" female with "a strong interest in people and social situations."

Biology and culture

Even the most biologically oriented researchers warn that the human product is unpredictable because human beings, individually and in groups, are more susceptible than any other animal to learning and to being influenced by the impact of the social environment. Male and female Eskimos score the same on spatial tests. British boys often score better than girls on verbal tests. Is it their cultures that make the difference?

Then, too, a culture may assign roles with or without regard for innate qualifications. Although men in general are clearly better adapted than women for strenuous physical labor, there are societies in which women carry all the heavy burdens.

What is the most useful knowledge to be gleaned from all the research thus far? It may be this: As individuals, we are not predestined, bound or limited by the fact of gender. The only inevitable differences between the sexes are the few irreducible distinctions—the ones you knew about all along.

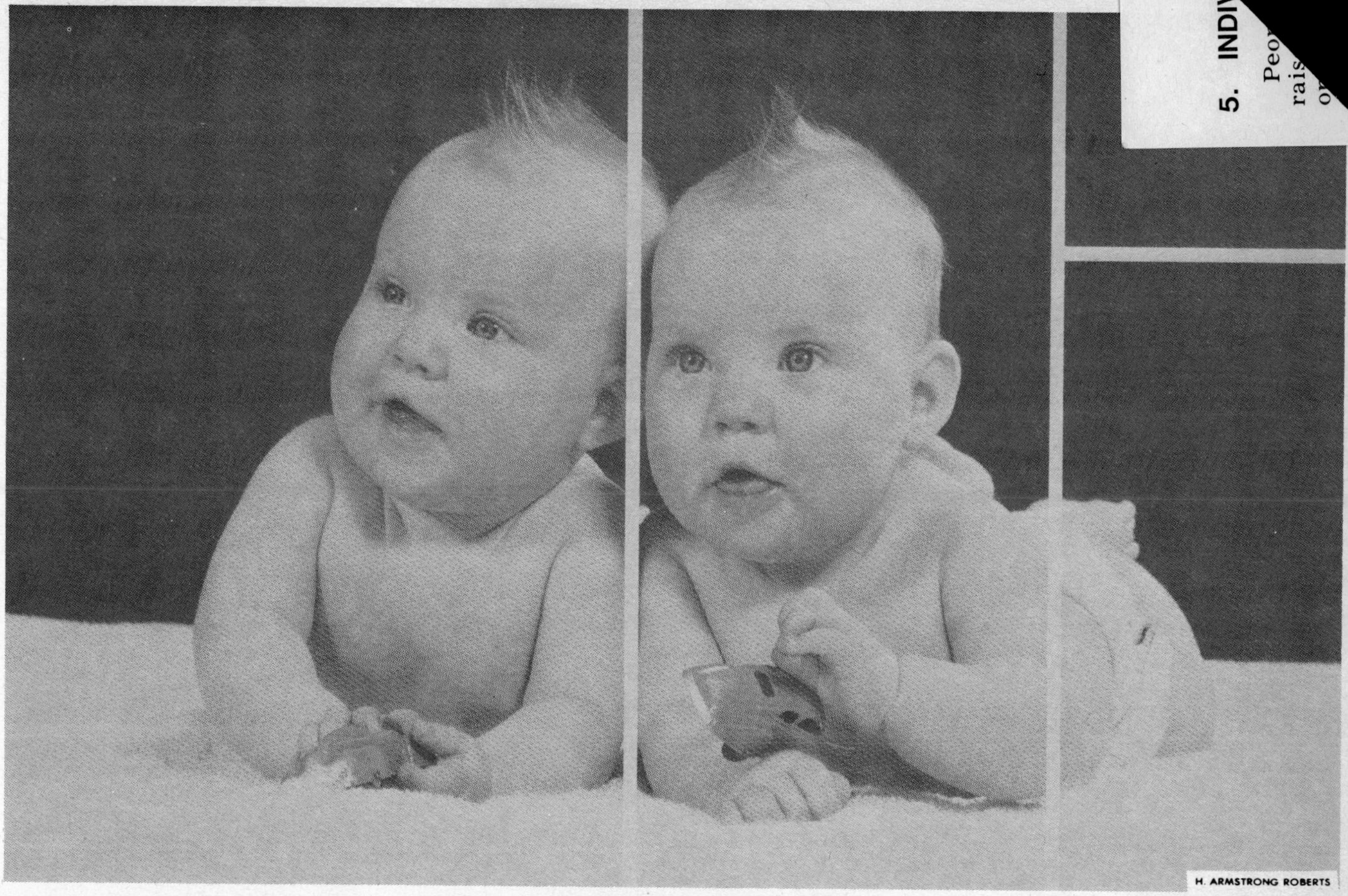

H. ARMSTRONG ROBERTS

GIRLS VERSUS BOYS—HOW DIFFERENT ARE THEY?

Lynne Martin

Lynne Martin is a free-lance writer who lives in Roslyn Heights, New York. She is the author of several nature-science junior books published by William Morrow, and has had nature-science articles published in *Science Digest*, *International Wildlife*, and *Americas* magazines.

With their diapers on, it is almost impossible to tell male and female infants apart. But try waving Christmas-tree lights over the crib. It will be the girl who breaks into a smile, her eyes eagerly following the glittering colors.

From earliest infancy, the female human has far better color sense than the male. (A flower isn't just red, but a sort of strawberry pink; the new dress is definitely green, but not too green, and of course not that awful sickening green!) Color means more to a girl and gives her greater pleasure because she actually *sees* more color. Color deficiencies, moreover, are ten times more common in men than in women. Red-green deficiency affects some 7 percent of men, but is rare in women.[1]

And what about the following beliefs—are they sex-based, or sex-biased? *Do* girls wiggle their hips when they walk? *Are* women more emotional than men? *Do* they talk more? And *are* men really stronger? Answers: Yes. Yes. Yes. And Yes.

Observations such as these are unpopular, for it is fashionable nowadays to erase the differences between the sexes and to blame such "stereotyping" on social conditioning. Up until recently psychologists thought that girls were feminine and boys masculine because of training. Little girls played with dolls, they said, because they were encouraged to imitate their mothers. They were better behaved than their brothers because they were taught to be gentle and ladylike, whereas boys were permitted and even prompted to develop into little ruffians because it was manly.

...ple assumed that a girl ...ed like a boy would act like ...e, but when experiments were tried, she fooled them. Girls treated like boys from birth still reacted to most psychological tests as girls.

Within the past decade, mounting biological evidence has revived the ancient idea that the minds of boys and girls are not the same but are specialized to perform in somewhat different ways.

Biologically speaking, the basic difference between a girl and a boy is that *she* started out with two X chromosomes and *he* started out with an X chromosome and a Y chromosome. Sex is set at the moment of conception and is determined by the father.[2] By pure chance, he supplies either the X (female) or Y (male) sex chromosome that pairs with the X chromosome from the mother. Chromosomes, with their genes, contain a "blueprint" of information, and everything else follows from this sexual inheritance.

So, quite apart from their sex organs, infant girls and infant boys do not arrive in the world the same. Even before birth, their experiences have been different—although until the sixth week male and female fetuses look alike. The male develops faster at first, revealing his sex about four weeks earlier than the female does; after that, the male slows down.[3]

Differences in newborns

By the time they are born—and boys more often than girls arrive ahead of their predicted birthdays—boy babies are larger but girl babies are more mature. Boys' hearts and lungs are already slightly bigger (though their livers are lighter).[4] A girl's heart beats faster, though, making about six to eight more beats a minute than a boy's.[5] Occasionally, doctors use this fact in an attempt to forecast the sex of a child before birth. The boy's brain is larger, too. The newborn girl's nervous system, however, is physically more highly developed.[6]

Male-female differences show up early. According to observations made by Corinne Hutt, a psychologist at the Human Development Research Unit at Park Children's Hospital, Oxford, England, female infants tend to be more attentive to sounds and colors, while male infants are more attracted by visual patterns. Girls engage in rhythmic mouthing, smiling, and sucking, while the boys' motions consist mainly of startles.[7]

On the whole, girl babies begin to pronounce words earlier than boys and soon move on to fairly complex sentences. At the age of 2 years the average girl can use twice as many words as the average boy.[8]

It has been known for some time that the two hemispheres of the human brain do not perform the same functions. Not only does your stubbed right toe report "Ouch!" to the left side of your brain, but that side is also specialized for speech performance. The right hemisphere, on the other hand, normally serves the left side of the body and is also dominant in the processing of spatial information and other material that is hard to put into words.[9]

Left/right brain specialization has been studied in both verbal and spatial performance and seems to develop differently in boys than in girls. Girls may get a boost from their mothers after all—Harvard University psychologist Jerome Kagan reports that mothers tend to talk to and touch their infant daughters more than they do their sons.[10] However, Doreen Kimura, an experimental psychologist at the University of Southern Ontario, suggests that dominance for speech perception proceeds more rapidly in the young female brain than in the young male brain. In a separate Ontario study, boys as early as age 6 excelled in visual/spatial and mathematical ability, a right-hemisphere talent.[11]

Scientific studies, incidentally, turn up data that *do not* support what some people think: boys are not more intelligent, do not have higher self-esteem, and are not more analytical or less sociable than girls. Girls do seem to be more persevering in their thinking. And boys were found to be more aggressive.[12]

Physiological differences

Then, too, there's one of the most noticeable differences between the sexes: his physique versus her figure. Although only about one fifth smaller than men (6 percent shorter, and 20 percent lighter in weight), women have little more than half the muscular strength. Testosterone is a hormone not only of male sex drive and aggression but also of protein synthesis—which gives males their greater upper-body strength. Nearly half a man's weight is muscle, mainly distributed in the trunk and neck; 14 percent is fat.[13]

People constantly waging war against fat forget that fat represents stored energy. Females have 10 percent more fat than males, much of it layered beneath the skin. Moreover, the female sex hormones that influence fat accumulation and the distribution that adds up to a woman's curves may enable women to utilize fats more easily. This would explain the stamina of women during long-haul events such as pregnancy and lactation.[14]

Boys *and* girls, by the way, have both male and female sex hormones; the difference is one of proportion. Compulsive gamblers (three out of four are male) thrive on action and may have extra-high levels of a male hormone.[15] Evidence of male aggressiveness—found in other animals as well as in humans—may be a natural trait of maleness. Experiments prove that increased male hormones result in increased aggressiveness.[16]

It's a fact, too, that women walk with a wiggle. A girl's pelvis grows wider than a boy's, and her thighs are hooked onto her trunk at a different angle. Since her thighs are further apart and her legs shorter, many a girl naturally swings her hips as she walks.

Males and females also differ in the angle at which the forearm attaches to the arm. This leads to an entirely different throwing action between the sexes and affects the ways boys and girls carry things.

Does a woman's rhythmicity make her moody? Unpredictable? Mysterious? Again and again, men in polls speak vaguely of these traits—about women's emotions in short. It may, indeed, be part of a girl's nature to express herself freely, including how she feels. And it may be, so, that she's seldom iscouraged from leaping with .ee, moaning in despair, xploding with anger.

Men will tell you that because ey have learned to control their notions—perhaps from iildhood's earliest no-no: "Don't e a crybaby"—does not mean at they don't have sensitive elings. They do. To them, aying on top of their elings—no sudden rages, no npromptu hugs—means not ndermining everything from a b to a friendship. Control quals maturity to them.

We all know that changes in xual attitudes and roles are ing on: that decidedly boyish ales give spontaneous hugs, are cuberant talkers, nurture their iildren—and write poetry; that osolutely girlish females build ee houses, climb telephone oles professionally—and win obel Prizes in science.

Still, if the masculine and feminine approaches to life are basically different, the human race may be grateful, since both have value and make day-to-day living richer and more fun.

REFERENCES

[1] Ernest R. Hilgard, Richard C. Atkinson, and Rita L. Atkinson, *Introduction to Psychology,* sixth ed. (New York: Harcourt Brace, Javanovich Inc., 1975), p. 115.

[2] Susan Michelmore, *Sexual Reproduction* (Garden City, New York: Natural History Press, 1964), p. 121.

[3] John Money and Anke A. Ehrhardt, *Man and Woman, Boy and Girl* (Baltimore and London: The Johns Hopkins University Press, 1972), p. 36.

[4] *Man's Body: An Owner's Manual,* by the Diagram Group, David Heidenstam, ed. (New York: Paddington Press, Ltd., 1976), p. A05.

[5] *Ibid.*, p. B15.

[6] Corinne Hutt, "Sex Differences in Human Development," *Human Development,* (1972).

[7] *Ibid.*

[8] ———, "Sex, What's the Difference?" *New Scientist,* May 16, 1974.

[9] Hilgard, Atkinson, and Atkinson, *op. cit.*, pp. 45, 50.

[10] Jerome Kagan and M. Lewis, "Studies in Attention in the Human Infant," *Merrill-Palmer Quarterly* 11:95-127.

[11] Doreen Kimura, "The Asymmetry of the Human Brain," *Scientific American,* vol. 228, No. 3, March, 1973.

[12] Eleanor E. Maccoby and Carol N. Jacklin, *The Psychology of Sex Differences* (Stanford, California: Stanford University Press, 1974).

[13] *Man's Body: An Owner's Manual,* p. A21.

[14] *Women. A Book for Men,* produced by James Wagenvoord and Peyton Bailey (New York: Avon Books, 1979), p. 222.

[15] "Compulsive Gambler Diagnosed: A Success Type With a 'Disease,'" *The New York Times,* Dec. 10, 1978, p. 103.

[16] Richard M. Restak, "Birth Defects and Behavior: A New Study Suggests a Link," *The New York Times,* Jan. 21, 1979.

PRISONERS OF MANLINESS

JOSEPH H. PLECK

Joseph H. Pleck is program director for the Family, Employment, and Male Role Programs at the Wellesley College Center for Research on Women. A clinical psychologist trained at Harvard, he edited, with Jack Sawyer, *Men and Masculinity* (Prentice Hall). With his wife, Elizabeth H. Pleck, he edited *The American Man* (Prentice Hall). His *The Myth of Masculinity* (MIT), on which this article is based, will be published in the fall.

True or false:

☐ Boys need a father figure when they are growing up in order to become secure men.

☐ Boys are harmed academically and psychologically because so many teachers in the early grades are women.

☐ Male homosexuality reflects a man's confusion over his masculine role.

☐ Men who have not developed a secure masculine identity are more likely than other men to be violent, hostile to women, and irrationally afraid of homosexuality.

☐ Black men are especially vulnerable to problems with masculinity.

The macho image of the male may have softened recently; many men now realize that they can express tender feelings without jeopardizing their performance in business or in bed. However, the belief that it is essential for men to acquire a "sex-role identity"—expressed by masculine traits, attitudes, and interests—remains firmly entrenched. So does the belief that it is hard for men to develop this secure sense of masculinity, especially now that women are becoming more assertive.

If you answered true to all or most of the above statements, the chances are that you are still hold to the belief that a strong sex-role identity is crucial to male psychological health. The notion is not just a popular prejudice. It is the creation of decades of research in psychology, including the work of some of the most prominent investigators—among them Alfred Adler, Lewis Terman, Talcott Parsons, Jerome Kagan, and E. Mavis Hetherington. It has been disseminated by other writers, notably by Benjamin Spock and by the psychologist Fitzhugh Dodson, who advised fathers in his 1974 book, *How to Father:* "Your preschool boy needs contact with you so that he can imitate you and stabilize his gender identity as a male."

Psychologists have been preoccupied with masculinity over the past several decades. Research on sex roles actually has focused primarily on men and has been dominated by two insistent questions: what makes males less masculine than they should be and what can we do about it? The answers given, both by psychologists and by other social scientists, are based on the theory of male sex-role identity, whose key assertions are summarized in the true/false statements that appear above.

My own examination of the evidence suggests that the theory is unsubstantiated and has damaging consequences for men, women, and society as a whole. The conventional expectations of what it means to be a man are difficult to live up to for all but a lucky few and lead to unnecessary self-deprecation in the rest when they do not measure up. Even for those who do, there is a price: they may be forced, for example, to inhibit the expression of many emotions.

The emergence of male-identity theory since the 1930s can best be interpreted as a response to the gradual breakdown of social and institutional structures that supported traditional sex roles—for example, the decline of the large family, which kept a woman home having babies. With industrialization and urbanization, these structures waned, leaving doubts about just what it meant to be female or male. The vacuum was neatly filled by the "discovery" that masculinity and femininity had deep psychological bases. It is no accident that the work that founded male-identity theory, *Sex and Personality,* by the Stanford psychologists Lewis Terman and Catherine Miles, was published in 1936, at the depths of the Depression, which posed the single greatest threat to the male role in U.S. history by taking away men's ability to support their families, traditionally their most important responsibility. If holding a job could no longer be counted on to define manhood, perhaps a masculinity/femininity test could.

To understand how poorly substantiated the theory of male sex-role identity is, it is important to examine the psychological research underlying each of the five basic assertions above.

☐ *Boys need a father figure when they are growing up in order to become secure men.*

At issue here is not *whether* it is good for a boy to have

positive relationships with his father or other adult males, but *why*. This notion implies that the most important result of a boy's contact with his father is the boy's sex-role identity—and that view raises several problems.

The research that people most often think demonstrates the point above has examined the effects on boys of having fathers who were not present. Between 1945 and 1975, this topic was more popular than almost any other in sex-role research. Many studies found no differences. Others produced conflicting results. In one experiment, E. Mavis Hetherington of the University of Virginia compared boys with fathers and boys without them by giving them a test in which children guessed the preferences for toys of an imaginary child named "It" (represented by a stick figure), who was supposed to be sexually neutral. Hetherington found that boys whose fathers were absent beginning in the first four years of life made fewer "masculine" choices, saying that "It" liked to play with a necklace rather than a dump truck, for example. She interpreted this as a sign that they were having difficulty in thinking of themselves as male. Another study, by psychologists David Lynn and William Sawrey, found that the sons of Norwegian sailors who were away at least nine months a year were *more* masculine than average. The investigators interpreted the boys' behavior as indication that they were overcompensating—trying to make up for inner sexual insecurities.

These findings may indicate that father absence causes identity problems, but they may also indicate that researchers stack the deck in favor of the hypothesis: they interpret both low *and* high masculinity as signs of sexual insecurity. Proponents of the boys-need-male-models hypothesis explain these inconsistent results by claiming that father absence can make boys either more or less masculine depending on their personalities and circumstances.

In my view, these arguments are feeble attempts to make recalcitrant data fit the theory.

In their 1971 report, *Boys in Fatherless Families*, Elizabeth Herzog and Cecilia Sudia of the federal Office of Child Development concluded that the evidence "offers no firm basis for assuming that boys who grow up in fatherless homes are more likely, as men, to suffer from inadequate masculine identity as a result of lacking a resident male model." In school performance, Herzog and Sudia also found that if factors like class and education were equal, boys with absent fathers appeared to turn out as well as boys whose fathers were present. They did show slightly more delinquent behavior.

Other research on fathers and sons concerns the impact on a son's masculinity of variations in the father's characteristics, especially his power, his warmth, and his own degree of masculinity. Some important studies, such as the 1965 work *Identification and Child Rearing* by Stanford psychologists Robert Sears, Lucy Rau, and Richard Alpert, have found that almost no relationship exists. Other research, such as the studies conducted by Paul Mussen in the Berkeley psychology department in the 1950s and 1960s, for example, has found some relationship. However, Mussen's studies require a greater degree of faith in his measures than is usually the case in psychological research. His oft-cited findings of relationships between fathers' warmth and sons' masculinity assume, for example, that a father is friendly if a boy depicts a male character in a doll-play game as friendly and that a boy is masculine if he declares that the stick figure named "It" likes to play with a dump truck rather than a necklace. (Those who cite Mussen's studies also usually fail to report his further finding that males who were ranked high on masculinity scales as youths displayed considerable maladjustment in adulthood.)

Today, a new generation of research is focusing on a broader range of questions: when a father is close to his children, how does his presence affect his children's thinking; how does childrearing affect his feelings about himself? As part of the contemporary reappraisal, many people now believe that if fathers are more involved in raising children than they were, children, and sons in particular, will learn that men can be warm and supportive of others as well as be high achievers. Thus, fathers' involvement may be beneficial not because it will help *support* traditional male roles, but because it will help break them down.

☐ *Boys are harmed academically and psychologically because so many teachers in the early grades are women.*

Most current attention to sex-role issues in education concerns the disadvantages that girls seem to face in schools. But an older elaboration of the boys-need-male-models hypothesis is still around: the theory that boys are damaged by the predominance of women in the educational system.

In her 1969 study, *The Feminized Male*, New York University sociologist Patricia C. Sexton argued: "Though run at the top by men, schools are essentially feminine institutions, from nursery school through graduate school. In the school, women set the standards for adult behavior, and many favor students, male and female, who most conform to their own behavior norms—polite, clean, obedient, neat,and nice." Sexton concluded, then, that "if the boy absorbs school values, he may become feminized himself."

The "feminization" argument involves three hypotheses: (1) boys do better with male teachers, (2) teachers "reinforce" (respond to and/or encourage) femininity in boys, and (3) boys perceive school as feminine. The evidence for all three is weak.

Studies of academic performance do not show that boys with male teachers do any better academically than boys with female teachers. On measures of social adjustment, many studies find no differences and others find only weak or inconsistent ones. For example, Dorothy J. Sciarra, now a professor of child development at the University of Cincinnati, hypothesized that male models in the early years of school would enhance boys' self-esteem, thereby decreasing both their aggression and their susceptibility to peer-group influence. When she compared boys with adult males in the classrooms and boys without, however, she found a tendency for boys with male models to be *more* susceptible to peer-group influences, although statistical tests showed that the result could have been due to chance.

Sciarra handily transformed the trend disconfirming the feminization thesis into one confirming it by redefining, after the fact, the meaning of what she measured: she argued that susceptibility to peer-group pressure (a negative characteristic) was actually peer-group *cooperation* (a desirable one) and thus showed the positive effect that male models had on boys.

Reviewing the research on boys with male teachers, psychologists Dolores Gold of Concordia University and Myrna Reis of the Jewish Vocational Service of Montreal concluded that "increasing the number of male teachers in the early school grades is a proposed panacea to alleviate boys' school difficulties which . . . appeals to common sense as well as to widespread bias. However, it is an alternative which likely will not be effective."

The evidence that teachers encourage femininity in boys is also weak. Researchers often cite a 1969 study by Beverly Fagot and Gerald Patterson, psychologists at the University of Oregon, showing that teachers reinforce feminine behaviors in boys more often than masculine ones. Detailed examination of this study—which includes only two nursery school classes and four teachers—reveals, however, that the major "feminine" behaviors being reinforced were art activities and listening to stories. Perhaps more interesting than the finding that teachers reinforced those behaviors is the psychologists' interpretation of art and listening to stories as feminine.

A study that may be closer to the truth is a 1973 survey of preschool through second-grade teachers by developmental psychologist Patrick Lee and Annie Wolinsky at Columbia Teachers College. They classified only 14 percent of the activities that female teachers reinforced as female-typed; 17 percent were male-typed, and the vast majority were neutral.

Another study that is widely cited as showing teachers' alleged reinforcement of femininity was done in 1972 by psychologists Teresa Levitin and David Chananie at the University of Michigan. It found that teachers approved more of obedient and dependent fifth-grade boys than of disobedient and aggressive ones (though they reported liking the disobedient boys no less). But there too, the cards were stacked by selecting male traits that are socially undesirable and female ones that are desirable. Given such a bias, it comes as no surprise that teachers disapproved of the undesirable ones—but they disapproved of them regardless of the child's sex and because they are socially undesirable, not because they are masculine.

The idea that boys perceive school as feminine originated in an ingenious study done in the 1960s by developmental psychologist Jerome Kagan at Harvard. Kagan's second and third graders were taught to pair sexually neutral nonsense syllables with objects pertaining to men and women—"DEP" with men's trousers and a baseball bat, "ROV" with a women's shoe and lipstick. After learning the associations, the children were then asked to guess the category, whether DEP or ROV, of each of a new set of objects, including eight related to schools; for example, a pencil, a school building, a blackboard, a page of arithmetic.

It is by no means clear from the results of Kagan's study that boys perceive school as feminine. Of the eight school-related objects, the second-grade boys rated only two (blackboard, page of arithmetic) as feminine significantly more often than masculine, but they saw two others (map, book) as masculine more often than feminine—and more strongly so. In the third grade, the boys perceived the arithmetic page as masculine, the blackboard as neutral. Thus, far from demonstrating that boys see school as feminine, Kagan's study actually found that second-grade boys perceived a minority of school objects as feminine, but they viewed an equal minority of other objects as even more strongly masculine, and that only one grade later they had discarded or even reversed their perceptions of the feminine school objects.

☐ *Male homosexuality reflects a man's confusion over his masculine role.*

As psychologist Donald Brown of the U.S. Air Force Academy put it in 1957, "The male invert psychologically perceives himself as a female, and accordingly looks to the 'opposite' sex for sexual gratification. . . . Inversion has its roots in the earliest years of life when the child forms, at first involuntarily and later consciously, an identification-attachment to the parent of the opposite sex and thereby internalizes the sex role of the opposite sex."

Homosexuality has always been a central preoccupation of those concerned about male identity. A major portion of Terman and Miles's *Sex and Personality* is devoted to studies of homosexuals—primarily male homosexuals. When people say they are concerned about how "male identity" is affected by whatever it is they see it threatened by (single-parent families, a mother's employment, girls in school sports, and so forth), very often what they have in mind is an increased rate of male homosexuality. Homosexuality, especially in men, is thus viewed as the quintessential failure in development of normal sex-role identity.

One kind of evidence that might support this interpretation is data showing that male homosexuals emerge as more feminine than heterosexuals on tests of masculinity and femininity. The tests place people on a scale ranging from masculine to feminine according to their answers to such questions as "I prefer a shower to a bath" (Yes = masculine); "I would like to be a singer" (Yes = feminine); and "I like artichokes" (Yes = feminine). These items have distinguished men from women in at least some samples.

Data showing male homosexuals as more feminine than heterosexuals on these tests exist, but whatever they mean, much of the research is based on prisoners, who are hardly typical of all heterosexuals and homosexuals. One study actually used heterosexual rapists as the control group against whose masculinity the masculinity of homosexuals was compared!

A second problem with interpreting homosexuality as a failure to develop a masculine identity is that many studies completely fail to find significant differences in masculinity between male homosexuals and male heterosexuals. Three recent studies, with samples of college students and improved measures that assess masculinity and femininity as separate dimensions that can coexist in anyone, yield completely inconsistent results.

In response to the empirical failings, male-identity theorists like Donald Brown and British psychiatrist D. J. West now argue that there are actually two kinds of male homosexuals: "passive" ones, who are psychologically feminine and therefore fit the original theory, and "active" ones, who are not and therefore don't. This interpretation assumes a distinction that most authorities now reject. It also has the interesting implication, quite troubling for a larger theory of male identity, that there are no differences in sex-role identity between heterosexual males and "active" homosexual males. Such intellectual surgery may reconcile the theory with the data, but it amputates a vital spot in the patient. In short, whatever does cause homosexuality, there is little evidence to show that the factors involve an inadequate sense of a masculine identity.

☐ *Men who have not developed a secure masculine identity are more likely than other men to be violent, hostile to women, and irrationally afraid of homosexuality.*

Weakness in sex-role identity may be reflected in too much masculinity as well as too little. The notion is that male crime, misogyny, and homophobia represent overcompensations for underlying male insecurity. To describe that phenomenon, Alfred Adler in 1927 coined the term "masculine protest." Harvard sociologist Talcott Parsons proposed in 1947 that the Western pattern of close mother-child relationships causes boys to have an unresolved feminine identification against which they psychologically defend themselves through aggression and delinquency. The idea has been further developed by numerous theorists and researchers.

In the 1950 study *The Authoritarian Personality*, Theodor Adorno and other psychologists at Berkeley suggested that this character type was, in part, the result of male insecurity. The researchers interpreted authoritarianism, which included rigidity, contempt for weakness, and intolerance of deviance—especially sexual deviance—as the underlying psychological basis of World War II fascism. (Adorno and one of his co-investigators, Else Frenkel-Brunswick, had earlier fled from Hitler.) Nevitt Sanford, another of the investigators, wrote later that the researchers "became convinced that one of the main sources of this personality syndrome was ego-alien femininity—that is to say, underlying femininity that had to be countered by whatever defenses the subject had at his disposal." In effect, they linked men's insecure sex-role identities to the rise of Hitler and to the Holocaust.

Researchers have applied the "hypermasculinity" hypothesis most often to the relationship between delinquency and father absence, especially in black males. There, too, the evidence is thin. Herzog and Sudia concluded that in studies in which social class is controlled (a relative rarity), father absence may have a weak effect on delinquency, but that the effect is too small to have any practical significance. For example, in a 1969 study, Lawrence Rosen, a sociologist at Temple University, surveyed a probability sample of 1,098 black male youths in a 10-square-mile area of Philadelphia and found that having an absent father was connected to only 1.2 percent of the variation in the amount of delinquency among the youths. More intensive studies examining variations among delinquents, such as those conducted in 1970 by Charles Harrington at Columbia Teachers College and in 1974 by Ohio State University sociologists Ira Silverman and Simon Dinitz, find few differences among subgroups of delinquents and other institutionalized males, with or without fathers, in hypermasculinity and sex-role identity. Harrington concludes that his study "throws into some question the view of aggression as 'protest masculinity.' "

The idea that many men fear women, a fear rooted in insecure masculinity, has attracted a number of feminist scholars. Nancy Chodorow, a psychoanalytic sociologist at the University of California, Santa Cruz, argued in 1974 that "in his attempt to gain an elusive masculine identification . . . the boy tries to reject his mother and deny his attachment to her and . . . tries to deny the deep personal identification with her that has developed during his early years. He does this by repressing whatever he takes to be feminine inside himself, and, importantly, by denigrating whatever he considers to be feminine in the outside world (that is, women)."

It is unclear what kind of data might provide a definitive test of this theory. Some studies find that men who say they have the closest relationships with their mothers report the most favorable attitude toward women—not the least favorable, as the theory predicts. Or do those data actually *support* the theory, because the men's profemale attitudes prove how much they are identified with their mothers? The theory's protean ability to interpret both profeminist and antifeminist attitudes as signs that a man is identified with his mother makes it possible to interpret any data as supporting the hypothesis.

There are, no doubt, some men who hate and fear women because of complex psychological dynamics deriving from their relationship with their mothers. But it is questionable whether those dynamics in the few should be invoked as the basis of the far more common, garden-variety male sexism so evident in our culture. Simpler theories can account for much, if not most, male antipathy to women: for example, negative male attitudes toward women may justify male social privilege.

Male dispositions to crime and violence, fear of women, and extreme fear of homosexuality are profoundly undesirable and cause serious social problems. Many men do indeed try to act "masculine." The question is how best to interpret their behavior. The hypermasculinity approach assumes that men have a natural inner urge to learn the male role, that many fail to attain it and therefore overcompensate, and that they—and their mothers—are ultimately at fault.

An alternative view is that people are not born with an inner psychological need to take on roles or traits different from those of the other sex, but that their culture strongly inculcates this need. If they do not spontaneously fit the cultural mold, they may try to force themselves into it. Thus, exaggerated masculinity, rather than being a reaction to inner insecurities, may reflect an overlearning of the externally prescribed role or an overconformity to it. The alternative interpretation, part of the emerging new theory of sex-role strain, puts the burden of responsibility for destructive, extreme male behavior on society's unrealistic male-role expectations—where it belongs—and not on the failings of individual men and their mothers.

Hypermasculinity arguments narrowmindedly ignore the direct role psychology has played in fostering hypermasculinity. After decades of psychological pronouncements about the deficiencies of women and the psychopathology of homosexuals, it seems a self-serving evasion of moral responsibility for psychologists to claim that the real reason that men dislike women and homosexuals is because of a sex-role identity problem caused by identifying too closely with their mothers.

☐ *Black men are especially vulnerable to problems with masculinity.*

According to this idea, acquiring a secure sense of masculinity is more difficult for blacks than for whites because black fathers are absent more often and because many of them, even when present, are poor role models for their children.

Identity problems are then supposedly compounded in adulthood by higher rates of unemployment and overrepresentation in low-paying, low-prestige jobs among black men, especially such "feminine" service jobs as waiting on tables. As Harvard's social psychologist and race-relations expert Thomas F. Pettigrew expressed it in 1964, among black males "the sex-identity problems created by the fatherless home are perpetuated in adulthood." In their 1968 best-seller, *Black Rage*, psychiatrists William Grier and Price Cobbs asserted that "whereas the white man regards his manhood as an ordained right, the black man is engaged in a never-ending struggle for its possession."

Pettigrew based his conclusions about blacks' greater sex-role identity problems (as shown by masculinity/femininity measures) on only two studies—one involving a sample of Alabama convicts, the other a sample of tubercular working-class veterans in Wisconsin—hardly a broad base of evidence. More recent studies, with both more representative samples and better sex-role measures, have not found the same differences between blacks and whites.

The "black emasculation" hypothesis was in vogue in the late 1960s and early 1970s. Its appeal to liberals arguing for equal rights is obvious: it holds that the racial oppression of blacks, in addition to producing the obvious consequences of poverty, shorter life expectancy, and so forth, has an even more insidious and subtle effect—the destruction of black men's masculinity. That apparently radical critique of racism conceals a patronizing view of blacks as psychological cripples and masks as well a deeply conservative notion of what proper sex roles ought to be.

Nowhere is that more evident than in Daniel Patrick Moynihan's 1967 work, *The Negro Family: The Case for National Action*, the famous "Moynihan Report." Moynihan argued for the worthy objective of a federal policy to promote full employment targeted especially at black males. But his justification for it hinged on the hypothetically devastating consequences of unemployment on black males' sex-role identities. In Moynihan's view, "the very essence of the male animal, from the bantam rooster to the four-star general, is to strut." Writing as America mobilized for a war in Vietnam, he praised military service as an almost ideal solution to black men's frustrated masculinity: "Given the strains of the disorganized and matrifocal family life in which so many Negro youth come of age, the Armed Forces are a dramatic and desperately needed change: a world away from women, a world run by strong men of unquestioned authority."

Another example of the patronization inherent in the black-emasculation hypothesis occurred in a popular book on fatherhood, *Father Power*, published in 1965 by University of Rhode Island psychologist Henry Biller and journalist Dennis Meredith. Material on black fathers appears in a chapter titled "Fathers with Special Problems." The only other example given there is the physically handicapped father.

Like the hypermasculinity hypothesis, the black-emasculation hypothesis ultimately blames the victim of a social problem for having it. Many critics have responded to this idea in narrow terms, arguing that black men have other role models, that their sexual identities are not impaired, or even that they actually are more masculine than white men. Few critics, unfortunately, have questioned the concept of sex-role identity itself. Few have asked just how much the notion of sex-role identity really does add to our understanding of the more basic issues—issues involving the negative impact of poverty, unemployment, or unsatisfying jobs on black (or any other) men.

On the basis of the evidence, we cannot go so far as to say that these five assertions have been proven false; in research, negative findings can never conclusively prove that a relationship does not exist, but can only show that a relationship has not been confirmed. We can say, however, that many popular ideas about masculinity that are widely thought to be backed up by the decades of research have not been substantiated.

Unsubstantiated theories of masculinity have negative consequences for both sexes. In making women responsible for male insecurity and hostility, traditional male sex-role identity theory has made women both villains and victims in a male struggle for masculinity. The theory also holds that sex roles cannot change substantially because male identity is so fragile, a belief that leads to policies and strategies for imprisoning men in traditional roles, just as exaggerated ideas of women's fragility support restrictions on them. When a school district in West Virginia introduced a home economics curriculum that included homemaking skills for boys, members of the community opposed it on the grounds that it would turn their sons into homosexuals. The argument, typical of many, implies that the only way to make a man secure in his sex-role identity is to lock him up within it.

At last, a new approach to understanding masculinity and femininity is emerging, based on quite different assumptions—the theory of sex-role strain. In this view, there is no special need to encourage men and women to take different roles. If women and men do differ biologically in ways that cause different psychological traits (researchers are still debating, this approach says these differences will express themselves without help from parents and psychologists anxious about their children's sex-role identity. The point is not that we have to make men and women the same, but rather, that we do not have to strive so hard to make them different.

Researchers taking the new approach are investigating how traditional cultural standards for men and women create feelings of inadequacy if those standards are not achieved and other problems if they are. For example, what are the consequences of raising women to inhibit their achievement and men to inhibit their emotions? How does perceiving a difference between oneself and a cultural ideal for one's sex impair well-being? In the new view, the problem of sex roles is not how to learn a predetermined sex-role identity but rather how to avoid the strain built into traditional roles.

The feminist journalist Letty Cottin Pogrebin recently noted that feminist parents often find it easier to understand what nonsexist childrearing means for their daughters than for their sons. They support nontraditional activities and interests for daughters, but are often concerned if their sons are not aggressive and competitive or are sensitive or artistic ("They eventually have to face the real world, don't they?"). The journalists Lindsy Van Gelder and Carrie Carmichael reported in *Ms.* magazine in 1975 that when they asked a sample of feminist parents what they were doing to make their sons less like typical males, parents either had no response or expressed fears that any changes in traditional childrearing would make their sons homosexual. Van Gelder and Carmichael suggest that unless something is done to support change in men's roles, when today's daughters "reach womanhood in the 1990s, they will be confronted with a new generation of perfectly preserved 1960s males." So, indeed, they will—unless we demystify psychological myths of masculinity.

For further information, read:

Gold, Dolores, and Myrna Reis. *Do Male Teachers in the Early School Years Make a Difference?* ERIC Clearinghouse, 1978, $3.65.

Herzog, Elizabeth and Cecilia Sudia. "Children in Fatherless Families," in *Review of Child Development Research, Vol. 3.* Bettye Caldwell and Henry N. Ricciuti, eds., University of Chicago Press, 1973, $20.

Pogrebin, Letty Cottin. *Growing Up Free.* McGraw-Hill, 1980, $14.95.

Personality and Social Processes

Lifelong processes of development working in concert with the factors that produce individual differences result in a relatively unique personality for each of us: no two people are exactly identical in their psychological makeup. But just what is "personality" and how does it get firmly established—or *does* it get firmly established? "The Many Me's of the Self-Monitor" meets these two questions head on, asking whether personality consists of an enduring "real me" or a varied collection of me's, one for every occasion. Whatever the answer to the "real me" question, we can be quite certain that personality consists of more than meets the eye. For example, everyone feels internal pressures, stresses, and anxieties, and there seem to be ways of dealing with them positively. Two complementary views on healthy and unhealthy ways to deal with life are taken up in the next three articles. "Psycho-Immunity" and "Stress Can Be Good for You" are about the complex relationships among stress, mental attitude, and bodily health. Carl Rogers, the leader of the person-centered approach within humanistic psychology, summarizes the theory of self-actualization in "The Foundations of the Person-Centered Approach." These articles emphasize that people can control their own destinies and states of being. However, each article takes a rather different view on what that means.

External as well as internal forces shape our personalities and our behavior. A well-known psychologist once asked what would have happened if B.F. Skinner had put two pigeons in the Skinner box instead of one. The result would have been the social psychology of pigeons—how pigeons behave in the presence of other pigeons rather than by themselves. The remaining articles in this section sketch several important themes that run through current social psychology, which is concerned with what happens during interactions between people.

"The Friendship Bond" describes the results of a poll designed to discover patterns of friendship among individuals, and the roles that friends play in one another's lives. This article paints a detailed picture of how important friends are and how much they are valued in today's society. Given that concerns over racial and ethnic prejudice are once again rising as economic problems put pressure on our society, the next article may carry an especially important message. "Self-Fulfilling Stereotypes" discusses how interactions between people can often work to confirm rather than disconfirm the mistaken stereotypes that people hold about one another.

A review of this section will give you a feeling for the range of questions about personality for which we have answers and the range for which we don't. It will also acquaint you with some current views on the healthiest and unhealthiest ways to deal with life's difficulties and to go about developing and expressing your own personal uniqueness. Finally, it will familiarize you with some of the manifestations of social behavior, some of the factors that affect it, and some of the ways that psychologists study it.

Looking Ahead: Challenge Questions

If there is no such thing as "the real me," how is it possible to deal with one another in open, honest, and trusting ways?

Under what circumstances is civil disobedience and resistance to institutional rules a positive social phenomenon?

What means are available to help the individual resist unwanted social pressures?

THE MANY ME'S OF THE SELF-MONITOR

Is there a "true self" apart from the social roles we play? Perhaps not for people identified in studies as high self-monitors, who are keenly aware of the impression they are making and constantly fine-tuning their performance.

MARK SNYDER

Mark Snyder is professor of psychology at the University of Minnesota in Minneapolis, where he teaches a graduate-level course called "The Self." In addition to his research on self-monitoring, he is studying stereotypes and the effect of stereotypes on social relationships.

"The image of myself which I try to create in my own mind in order that I may love myself is very different from the image which I try to create in the minds of others in order that they may love me."

—W. H. Auden

The concept of the self is one of the oldest and most enduring in psychological considerations of human nature. We generally assume that people are fairly consistent and stable beings: that a person who is generous in one situation is also likely to be generous in other situations, that one who is honest is honest most of the time, that a person who takes a liberal stance today will favor the liberal viewpoint tomorrow.

It's not always so: each of us, it appears, may have not one but many selves. Moreover, much as we might like to believe that the self is an integral feature of personal identity, it appears that, to a greater extent, the self is a product of the individual's relationships with other people. Conventional wisdom to the contrary, there may be striking gaps and contradictions—as Auden suggests—between the public appearances and private realities of the self.

Psychologists refer to the strategies and techniques that people use to control the impressions they convey to others as "impression management." One of my own research interests has been to understand why some individuals are better at impression management than others. For it is clear that some people are particularly sensitive to the ways they express and present themselves in social situations—at parties, job interviews, professional meetings, in confrontations of all kinds where one might choose to create and maintain an appearance, with or without a specific purpose in mind. Indeed, I have found that such people have developed the ability to carefully monitor their own performances and to skillfully adjust their performances when signals from others tell them that they are not having the desired effect. I call such persons "high self-monitoring individuals," and I have developed a 25-item measure—the Self-Monitoring Scale—that has proved its ability to distinguish high self-monitoring individuals from low self-monitoring individuals. (See box on page 34.) Unlike the high self-monitoring individuals, low self-monitoring individuals are not so concerned about taking in such information; instead, they tend to express what they feel, rather than mold and tailor their behavior to fit the situation.

My work on self-monitoring and impression management grew out of a long-standing fascination with explorations of reality and illusion in literature and in the theater. I was struck by the contrast between the way things often appear to be and the reality that lurks beneath the surface—on the stage, in novels, and in people's actual lives. I wanted to know how this world of appearances in social relationships was built and maintained, as well as what its effects were on the individual personality. But I was also interested in exploring the older, more philosophical question of whether, beneath the various images of self that people project to others, there is a "real me." If we are all actors in many social situations, do we then retain in any sense an essential self, or are we really a variety of selves?

Skilled Impression Managers

There are striking and important differences in the extent to which people can and do control their self-presentation in social situations: some people engage in impression management more often—and with greater skill—than others. Professional actors, as well as many trial lawyers, are among the best at it. So are successful salespeople, confidence artists, and politicians. The onetime mayor of New York, Fiorello LaGuardia, was particularly skilled at adopting the expressive mannerisms of a variety of ethnic groups. In fact, he was so good at it that in watching silent films of his campaign speeches, it is easy to guess whose vote he was soliciting.

Of course, such highly skilled performances are the exception rather than the rule. And people differ in the extent to which they can and do exercise control over their self-presentations. It is the high self-monitoring individuals among us who are particularly talented in this regard. When asked to describe high self-monitoring individuals, their friends say that they are good at learning which behavior is

"The Many Me's of the Self-Monitor," by Mark Snyder, *Psychology Today*, March 1980. Reprinted with the permission of the author.

appropriate in social situations, have good self-control of their emotional expression, and can effectively use this ability to create the impression they want. They are particularly skilled at intentionally expressing and accurately communicating a wide variety of emotions both vocally and facially. As studies by Richard Lippa of California State University at Fullerton have shown, they are usually such polished actors that they can effectively adopt the mannerisms of a reserved, withdrawn, and introverted individual and then do an abrupt about-face and portray, just as convincingly, a friendly, outgoing, and extraverted personality.

High self-monitoring individuals are also quite likely to seek out information about appropriate patterns of self-presentation. They invest considerable effort in attempting to "read" and understand others. In an experiment I conducted with Tom Monson (then one of my graduate students), various cues were given to students involved in group discussions as to what was socially appropriate behavior in the situation. For example, some of them thought that their taped discussions would be played back to fellow students; in those circumstances, I assumed they would want their opinions to appear as autonomous as possible. Others believed that their discussions were completely private; there, I assumed they would be most concerned with maintaining harmony and agreement in the group. High self-monitoring individuals were keenly attentive to these differences; they conformed with the group when conformity was the most appropriate behavior and did not conform when they knew that the norms of the larger student audience would favor autonomy in the face of social pressure. Low self-monitoring individuals were virtually unaffected by the differences in social setting: presumably, their self-presentations were more accurate reflections

MONITOR YOUR SELF

On the scale I have developed to measure self-monitoring, actors are usually high scorers, as are many obese people, who tend to be very sensitive about the way they appear to others. For much the same reason, politicians and trial lawyers would almost certainly be high scorers. Recent immigrants eager to assimilate, black freshmen in a predominantly white college, and military personnel stationed abroad are also likely to score high on the scale.

The Self-Monitoring Scale measures how concerned people are with the impression they are making on others, as well as their ability to control and modify their behavior to fit the situation. I believe that it defines a distinct domain of personality that is quite different from the traits probed by other standard scales.

Several studies show that skill at self-monitoring is not associated with exceptional intelligence or with a particular social class. Nor is it related, among other things, to being highly anxious or extremely self-conscious, to being an extravert, or to having a strong need for approval. They may be somewhat power-oriented or Machiavellian, but high self-monitoring individuals do not necessarily have high scores on the "Mach" scale, a measure of Machiavellianism developed by Richard Christie of Columbia University. (Two items from the scale: "The best way to handle people is to tell them what they want" and "Anyone who completely trusts anyone else is asking for trouble.") The steely-eyed Machiavellians are more manipulative, detached, and amoral than high self-monitoring individuals.

The Self-Monitoring Scale describes a unique trait and has proved to be both statistically valid and reliable, in tests on various samples.

At left is a 10-item abbreviated version of the Self-Monitoring Scale that will give readers some idea of whether they are low or high self-monitoring individuals. If you would like to test your self-monitoring tendencies, follow the instructions and then consult the scoring key. —M.S.

These statements concern personal reactions to a number of different situations. No two statements are exactly alike, so consider each statement carefully before answering. If a statement is true, or mostly true, as applied to you, circle the T. If a statement is false, or not usually true, as applied to you, circle the F.

1. I find it hard to imitate the behavior of other people. T F
2. I guess I put on a show to impress or entertain people. T F
3. I would probably make a good actor. T F
4. I sometimes appear to others to be experiencing deeper emotions than I actually am. T F
5. In a group of people I am rarely the center of attention. T F
6. In different situations and with different people, I often act like very different persons. T F
7. I can only argue for ideas I already believe. T F
8. In order to get along and be liked, I tend to be what people expect me to be rather than anything else. T F
9. I may deceive people by being friendly when I really dislike them. T F
10. I'm not always the person I appear to be. T F

SCORING: Give yourself one point for each of questions 1, 5 and 7 that you answered F. Give yourself one point for each of the remaining questions that you answered T. Add up your points. If you are a good judge of yourself and scored 7 or above, you are probably a high self-monitoring individual; 3 or below, you are probably a low self-monitoring individual.

of their personal attitudes and dispositions. Thus, as we might have guessed, people who are most skilled in the arts of impression management are also most likely to practice it.

Although high self-monitoring individuals are well skilled in the arts of impression management, we should not automatically assume that they necessarily use these skills for deceptive or manipulative purposes. Indeed, in their relationships with friends and acquaintances, high self-monitoring individuals are eager to use their self-monitoring abilities to promote smooth social interactions.

We can find some clues to this motive in the way high self-monitoring individuals tend to react to, and cope with, unfamiliar and unstructured social settings. In a study done at the University of Wisconsin, psychologists William Ickes and Richard Barnes arranged for pairs of strangers to spend time together in a waiting room, ostensibly to wait for an experiment to begin. The researchers then recorded the verbal and nonverbal behavior of each pair over a five-minute period, using video and audio tapes. All possible pairings of same-sex undergraduates at high, moderate, and low levels of self-monitoring were represented. Researchers scrutinized the tapes for evidence of the impact of self-monitoring on spontaneous encounters between strangers.

In these meetings, as in so many other aspects of their lives, high self-monitoring individuals suffered little or no shyness. Soon after meeting the other person, they took an active and controlling role in the conversation. They were inclined to talk first and to initiate subsequent conversational sequences. They also felt, and were seen by their partners to have, a greater need to talk. Their partners also viewed them as having been the more directive member of the pair. It was as if high self-monitoring individuals were particularly concerned about managing their behavior in order to create, encourage, and maintain a smooth flow of conversation. Perhaps this quality may help self-monitoring people to emerge as leaders in groups, organizations, and institutions.

Detecting Impression Management In Others

High self-monitoring individuals are also adept at detecting impression management in others. To demonstrate this finely tuned ability, three communications researchers at the University of Minnesota made use of videotaped excerpts from the television program "To Tell the Truth." On this program, one of the three guest contestants (all male in the excerpts chosen for the study) is the "real Mr. X." The other two who claim to be the real Mr. X are, of course, lying. Participants in the study watched each excerpt and then tried to identify the real Mr. X. High self-monitoring individuals were much more accurate than their low self-monitoring counterparts in correctly identifying the real Mr. X. and in seeing through the deception of the other two contestants.

Not only are high self-monitoring individuals able to see beyond the masks of deception successfully but they are also keenly attentive to the actions of other people as clues to their underlying intentions. E. E. Jones and Roy Baumeister of Princeton University had college students watch a videotaped discussion between two men who either agreed or disagreed with each other. The observers were aware that one man (the target person) had been instructed either to gain the affection or to win the respect of the other. Low self-monitoring observers tended to accept behavior at face value. They found themselves attracted to the agreeable person, whether or not he was attempting to ingratiate himself with his discussion partner. In contrast, high self-monitoring observers were acutely sensitive to the motivational context within which the target person operated. They liked the target better if he was disagreeable when trying to ingratiate himself. But when he sought respect, they were more attracted to him if he chose to be agreeable. Jones and Baumeister suggest that high self-monitoring observers regarded agreeableness as too blatant a ploy in gaining affection and autonomy as an equally obvious route to respect. Perhaps the high self-monitoring individuals felt that they themselves would have acted with greater subtlety and finesse.

Even more intriguing is Jones's and Baumeister's speculation—and I share their view—that high self-monitoring individuals prefer to live in a stable, predictable social environment populated by people whose actions consistently and accurately reflect their true attitudes and feelings. In such a world, the consistency and predictability of the actions of others would be of great benefit to those who tailor and manage their own self-presentation in social situations. From this perspective, it becomes quite understandable that high self-monitoring individuals may be especially fond of those who avoid strategic posturing. Furthermore, they actually may prefer as friends those comparatively low in self-monitoring.

How can we know when strangers and casual acquaintances are engaged in self-monitoring? Are there some channels of expression and communication that are more revealing than others about a person's true, inner "self," even when he or she is practicing impression management?

Both scientific and everyday observers of human behavior have suggested that nonverbal behavior—facial expressions, tone of voice, and body movements—reveals meaningful information about a person's attitudes, feelings, and motives. Often, people who engage in self-monitoring for deceptive purposes are less skilled at controlling their body's expressive movements. Accordingly, the body may be a more revealing source of information than the face for detecting those who engage in self-monitoring and impression management.

More than one experiment shows how nonverbal behavior can betray the true attitude of those attempting impression management. Shirley Weitz of the New School for Social Research reasoned that on college campuses where there are strong normative pressures supporting a tolerant and liberal value system, all students would avoid saying anything that would indicate racial prejudice—whether or not their private attitudes supported such behavior. In fact, she found that among "liberal" white males at Harvard University, the most prejudiced students (as determined by behavioral measures of actual attempts to avoid interaction with blacks) bent over backwards to *verbally* express liking and friendship for a black in a simulated interracial encounter. However, their *nonverbal* behaviors gave them away. Although the prejudiced students made every effort to say kind and favorable things, they continued to do so in a cool and distant tone of voice. It was as if they knew the words but not the music: they knew *what* to say, but not *how* to say it.

Another way that prejudice can be revealed is in the physical distance people maintain between themselves and the target of their prejudice. To demonstrate this phenomenon, psychologist Stephen Morin arranged for college students to be interviewed about their attitudes toward homosexuality. Half the interviewers wore "Gay and Proud" buttons and mentioned their association with the Association of Gay Psychologists. The rest wore no buttons and simply mentioned that they were graduate students working on theses. Without the students' knowledge, the distance they placed their chairs from the interviewer was measured while the interviews were going on. The measure of social distance proved to be highly revealing. When the student and the interviewer were of the same sex, students tended to establish almost a foot more distance between themselves and the apparently gay interviewers. They placed their chairs an average of 32 inches away from apparently gay interviewers, but only 22 inches away from apparently nongay interviewers. Interestingly, most of the students expressed tolerant, and at times favorable, attitudes toward gay people in general. However, the distances they chose to put between themselves and the interviewers they thought gay betrayed underlying negative attitudes.

Impression Managers' Dilemmas

The well-developed skills of high self-monitoring individuals ought to give them the flexibility to cope quickly and effectively with a diversity of social roles. They can choose with skill and grace the self-presentation appropriate to each of a wide variety of social situations. But what happens when the impression manager must effectively present a true and honest image to other people?

Consider the case of a woman on trial for a crime that she did not commit. Her task on the witness stand is to carefully present herself so that everything she does and says communicates to the jurors clearly and unambiguously her true innocence, so that they will vote for her acquittal. Chances are good, however, that members of the jury are somewhat skeptical of the defendant's claims of innocence. After all, they might reason to themselves, the district attorney would not have brought this case to trial were the state's case against her not a convincing one.

The defendant must carefully manage her verbal and nonverbal behaviors so as to ensure that even a skeptical jury forms a true impression of her innocence. In particular, she must avoid the pitfalls of an image that suggests that "she doth protest her innocence too much and therefore must be guilty." To the extent that our defendant skillfully practices the art of impression management, she will succeed in presenting herself to the jurors as the honest person that she truly is.

It often can take as much work to present a truthful image as to present a deceptive one. In fact, in this case, just being honest may not be enough when facing skeptical jurors who may bend over backwards to interpret any and all of the defendant's behavior—nervousness, for example—as a sign of guilt.

The message from research on impression management is a clear one. Some people are quite flexible in their self-presentation. What effects do these shifts in public appearance have on the more private realities of self-concept? In some circumstances, we are persuaded by our own appearances: we become the persons we appear to be. This phenomenon is particularly likely to occur when the image we present wins the approval and favor of those around us.

In an experiment conducted at Duke University by psychologists E. E. Jones, Kenneth Gergen, and Keith Davis, participants who had been instructed to win the approval of an interviewer presented very flattering images of themselves. Half the participants (chosen at random) then received favorable reactions from their interviewers; the rest did not. All the participants later were asked to estimate how accurately and honestly their self-descriptions had mirrored their true personalities.

Those who had won the favor of

WILLIAM JAMES ON THE ROLES WE PLAY

A man has as many social selves as there are individuals who recognize him and carry an image of him in their mind . . . . But as the individuals who carry the images form naturally into classes, we may practically say that he has as many different social selves as there are distinct *groups* of persons about whose opinions he cares. He generally shows a different side of himself to each of these different groups. Many a youth who is demure enough before his parents and teachers swears and swaggers like a pirate among his 'tough' young friends. We do not show ourselves to our children as to our club companions, to our masters and employers as to our intimate friends. From this there results what practically is a division of the man into several selves; and this may be a discordant splitting, as where one is afraid to let one set of his acquaintances know him as he is elsewhere; or it may be a perfectly harmonious division of labor, as where one tender to his children is stern to the soldiers or prisoners under his command."

—William James
***The Principles of Psychology*, 1890**

their interviewers considered their self-presentations to have been the most honest of all. One interpretation of this finding is that those people were operating with rather pragmatic definitions of self-concept: that which produced the most positive results was considered to be an accurate reflection of the inner self.

The reactions of other people can make it all the more likely that we become what we claim to be. Other people may accept our self-presentations at face value; they may then treat us as if we really were the way we pretend to be. For example, if I act as if I like Chris, chances are Chris will like me. Chris will probably treat me in a variety of friendly ways. As a result of Chris's friendliness, I may come to like Chris, even though I did not in the first place. The result, in this case, may be beneficial to both parties. In other circumstances, however, the skilled impression manager may pay an emotional price.

High self-monitoring orientation may be purchased at the cost of having one's actions reflect and communicate very little about one's private attitudes, feelings, and dispositions. In fact, as I have seen time and again in my research with my former graduate students Beth Tanke and Bill Swann, correspondence between private attitudes and public behavior is often minimal for high self-monitoring individuals. Evidently, the words and deeds of high self-monitoring individuals may reveal precious little information about their true inner feelings and attitudes.

Yet, it is almost a canon of modern psychology that a person's ability to reveal a "true self" to intimates is essential to emotional health. Sidney Jourard, one of the first psychologists to hold that view, believed that only through self-disclosure could we achieve self-discovery and self-knowledge: "Through my self-disclosure, I let others know my soul. They can know it, really know it, only as I make it known. In fact, I am beginning to suspect that I can't even know *my own soul* except as I disclose it. I suspect that I will know myself "for real" at the exact moment that I have succeeded in making it known through my disclosure to another person."

Only low self-monitoring individuals may be willing or able to live their lives according to Jourard's prescriptions. By contrast, high self-monitoring individuals seem to embody Erving Goffman's view of human nature. For him, the world of appearances appears to be all, and the "soul" is illusory. Goffman defines social interactions as a theatrical performance in which each individual acts out a "line." A line is a set of carefully chosen verbal and nonverbal acts that express one's self. Each of us, in Goffman's view, seems to be merely the sum of our various performances.

What does this imply for the sense of self and identity associated with low and high self-monitoring individuals?

I believe that high self-monitoring individuals and low self-monitoring individuals have very different ideas about what constitutes a self and that their notions are quite well-suited to how they live. High self-monitoring individuals regard themselves as rather flexible and adaptive people who tailor their social behavior shrewdly and pragmatically to fit appropriate conditions. They believe that a person is whoever he appears to be in any particular situation: "I am me, the me I am right now." This self-image fits well with the way high self-monitoring individuals present themselves to the world. It allows them to act in ways that are consistent with how they believe they should act.

By contrast, low self-monitoring individuals have a firmer, more single-minded idea of what a self should be. They value and strive for congruence between "who they are" and "what they do" and regard their actions as faithful reflections of how they feel and think. For them, a self is a single identity that must not be compromised for other people or in certain situations. Indeed, this view of the self parallels the low self-monitoring individual's consistent and stable self-presentation.

What is important in understanding oneself and others, then, is not the elusive question of whether there is a quintessential self, but rather, understanding how different people define those attributes of their behavior and experience that they regard as "me." Theory and research on self-monitoring have attempted to chart the processes by which beliefs about the self are actively translated into patterns of social behavior that reflect self-conceptions. From this perspective, the processes of self-monitoring are the processes of self—a system of operating rules that translate self-knowledge into social behavior.

For further information, read:

Gergen, Kenneth. *The Concept of Self*, Holt, Rinehart & Winston, 1971, paper, $4.50.

Goffman, Erving. *The Presentation of Self in Everyday Life*, Doubleday (reprint of 1959 edition), paper, $2.50.

Snyder, Mark. "Self-Monitoring Processes," in *Advances in Experimental Social Psychology, Vol. 12*, Leonard Berkowitz, ed., Academic Press, 1979, $24.

Snyder, Mark. "Cognitive, Behavioral, and Interpersonal Consequences of Self-Monitoring," in *Advances in the Study of Communication and Affect, Vol. 5: Perception of Emotion in Self and Others*, Plenum, 1979, $24.50.

Snyder, Mark. "Self-Monitoring of Expressive Behavior," *Journal of Personality and Social Psychology*, 30(1974): 526-537.

PSYCHO-IMMUNITY

DIANNE HALES

Dianne Hales, the former editor of the New Physician, *writes for the* New York Times *and is a contributing editor of* Science Year.

Dr. George Engel's longtime interest in sudden death took on a personal urgency in 1964. One day short of eleven months after the death of his twin brother, also a distinguished physician, he suffered a heart attack. "It was the last day of mourning in the Jewish faith, and I had been anticipating the anniversary of my brother's death with considerable anxiety. He had died as a result of a heart attack. I knew this was more than coincidence."

Engel, who is professor of psychiatry and medicine at the University of Rochester, has since scoured the press for reports of deaths that occurred within minutes or hours of a major life event. He has found victims of both sexes and all ages, from children to octogenarians. There were more men than women, and the men died at an earlier age. Most of the victims were not obviously ill at the time of their collapse; those who had been sick were not in imminent danger of dying.

Of all the circumstances linked with sudden death, Engel has found none that can match what he calls "the killing potential of grief." Men and women in prime health drop dead at the loss of a cherished mate, parent or child. The vigorous 27-year-old Army captain in charge of the ceremonial troops at President John F. Kennedy's funeral died 10 days after the President's burial. The wife of the owner of the motel where Martin Luther King was shot died the next day. Others, like Engel himself, have been struck down on the anniversary of a loss. One 17-year-old boy collapsed and died at 6:00 A.M. on June 4; his 14-year-old brother, injured in a car accident, had died at 5:12 A.M. on June 4 of the previous year. Louis Armstrong's widow suffered a fatal heart attack at a memorial concert as she played a Satchmo favorite, "St. Louis Blues."

There are also poignant tales of those who seem to die of broken hearts and dashed dreams. For example, one college president, who had prided himself on his support of black students, died when a group of black students occupied the college's administration building.

There have been "happy" endings too. A 63-year-old opera singer collapsed while acknowledging an ovation. A prisoner died on his way home after a 15-year sentence. Some victims have died in the midst of good luck, one while holding a royal flush in a poker game.

Whatever the setting or circumstance, each event was so abrupt, dramatic, intense or persistent that it cannot be ignored. Engel postulates that a traumatic incident triggers—almost simultaneously—the body's two emergency mechanisms: the fight-or-flight response and the withdrawal-conservation response. The former mobilizes our internal forces for quick action, enabling us to leap out of the path of a speeding car without pausing to think. The latter turns down the body's energy when no action is the wisest strategy of all; this response is what saves defenseless animals from predators by allowing them to "play dead." Engel believes that the rapid firing of these contradictory mechanisms, especially in the presence of preexisting heart damage, may send the heart into a state of confusion so profound that it produces dangerously deranged rhythms.

SHOCKING REACTIONS

Such reactions aren't unique to humans. As trappers and zoo keepers have long realized, animals can die of shock or fear when they're captured, transported or immobilized. Yet in monkeys and mice, and in humans as well, some survive while others succumb. Why?

The answer to that question may lie in the mind rather than the body. In a now classic experiment, Curt Richter, a psychobiologist at Johns Hopkins, restrained wild rats in a black canvas bag so they couldn't escape, clipped their whiskers to disorient them and dropped them into a tank of water. After just a few minutes, the rats gave up trying to swim. Autopsies showed that their lungs contained no fluid; they died not from drowning but from cardiac arrest. But if a rat were rescued shortly after its plunge and then dropped into the water a second time, it could swim longer than the others—as though it had learned its situation might not be so hopeless after all.

Vulnerability may depend on the powers of mind as well as the strength of body—in both animals and people. But sudden death, the ultimate in vulnerability, may not be triggered as precipitously as it might seem. Medical reports on premature deaths indicate that the fatal attack is often the last link in a chain of stressful events. In interviews, close relatives have reported that the victims displayed signs of mounting tension, dejection, depression and disappointment in the months before death. A study on stress and the heart revealed that of a group of 54 men who died suddenly, 41 had been depressed for weeks or months, usually because of an estrangement, separation or disappointment involving a family member, usually a son or daughter. Shortly before death, half the men had sunk deeper into depression; the others had become angry, anxious or physically overactive. There was another common denominator in the victims' final months: a high number of life changes in areas such as employment or place of residence—for better or for worse.

The link between change and vulnerability, particularly to infectious disease, is well established. The microbiologist René Dubos illustrated this relationship by charting the incidence of tuberculosis in the early 1900s, before the advent of antibiotics and vaccines. In times of war or woe, the numbers climbed; in peace and prosperity, they fell. "As long as there is change," Dubos asserts, "there will be disease."

Yet it is not change per se that makes us vulnerable but the way we react to and cope with change. Dr. Hans Selye, who has pioneered the study of stress and the body's struggle to adapt to an ever-changing world, distinguished between positive challenge and stimulation, which he calls "*eu*stress," and the *dis*tress of too many or too sudden changes. Even when the stimulus is identical, the stress response is individual. One person's eustress can be another's distress.

Drs. Thomas Holmes, of the University of Washington, and Richard Rahe, of the

"Psycho-Immunity," Dianne Hales, *SCIENCE DIGEST,* November 1981. Reprinted by permission.

U.S. Navy Medical Corps, developed a Social Readjustment Rating Scale to assess life changes in terms of the degree of adaptation each requires. At the head of their index of 43 significant life events is the death of a spouse, which registers 100 points. This was also the trauma most often implicated in sudden deaths. The runner-up is divorce (73 points); marriage (50 points) is not too far behind. Almost any ripple in the status quo, from losing a job to getting a better one, has an effect on body and mind, and the cumulative impact can hit like a tidal wave. In one study using the Holmes-Rahe scale, 80 percent of those whose life-change units totaled more than 300 in a 12-month period became ill in the following months. Aboard a Navy ship on a six-month cruise, the sailors most likely to report to sick bay were those who had experienced the most life changes prior to leaving port.

DAMPENING EFFECT

How is it that the strain of coping with change makes the body more vulnerable? Medical scientists have correlated stress with a dampening or suppression of the immune system—the network of organs, circulating white blood cells and the proteins they produce that defend against disease. In the 1970s an Australian study found that sorrow diminished the fighting ability of bereaved spouses' immune systems. Only as the mourners adjusted to their loss did their natural protectors return to full strength.

Immune-deficient states can make the body vulnerable to a range of diseases, including infectious ailments (from the common cold to tuberculosis) and disorders of the immune system itself (such as autoimmune illness, in which antibodies turn against themselves).

Researchers have found intriguing clues to the roles that stress, personality, coping styles and the immune system play in the onset and course of ailments such as rheumatoid arthritis, a disorder of the joints that afflicts an estimated 1 million Americans. Rheumatoid arthritis often strikes when particular psychological defenses and coping mechanisms are overwhelmed or when they are ineffective because of life circumstances. Its onset has been traced to times of loss or separation and to occasions, such as retirement, that invalidate the use of habitual coping behavior. The course of the disease parallels the patient's psychological state, easing when he's coping well and flaring up during periods of crisis or conflict.

Personality also affects vulnerability to the disease. Researchers have put together a portrait of a rheumatoid arthritic as a person who is shy, inhibited, self-sacrificing, perfectionist, incapable of expressing anger and hostility, often troubled by unresolved tensions regarding a parent or by sexual difficulties—and three times more likely to be female than male. Dr. Harold Levitan, of McGill University in Montreal, found characteristic unconscious recurring patterns in the dreams of rheumatoid arthritis patients: acts of extreme cruelty to others, incidents in which they are the victims of brutality, acts of incest and situations in which others express their own repressed feelings.

The connection between psychological well-being and physical vulnerability may also apply to other diseases and even to general health. More than 40 years ago researchers at Harvard University decided to follow a group of 185 undergraduates through the decades of adulthood.

Looking back on the professional and personal lives of these men, Harvard psychiatrist George Vaillant has charted the course of this admittedly elite group. As Harvard students, the men started out well; they generally did even better in their professional life. But some of the best and the brightest turned out to be healthier and happier than the others. Of the 59 men judged to be in this category, only two developed chronic illnesses or died by age 53. Of the 48 whose mental health was poorest, 18—more than a third—were chronically ill or dead by age 53. The critical difference lay in how they dealt with change and challenge. Not even the quality of childhood had as much impact on adult well-being as did good mental health and coping ability. In some men, early deprivation had acted like the grain of sand that stimulates an oyster to create a pearl, observes Vaillant. "It is not stress that kills us," he concludes. "It is effective adaptation to stress that permits us to live."

Before medical science can make real progress toward developing preventive therapies for mental as well as physical health, it has to map the pathways of vulnerability, the mechanisms by which distress and poor mental health suppress the responses of the immune system.

Scientists realize that they have just begun to unravel the intricacies of the immune system's relation to emotion and stress. Sickness, some say, may itself be a means of coping with problems—or of avoiding them—and even fatal illness, like successful suicide, may be no more than a cry for help.

This viewpoint is a controversial one, but a growing number of physicians are realizing that there is more to illness than physical signs and symptoms. One doctor involved in a study of heart disease reported that his most striking observation was of "the high level of misery among the middle-aged male participants."

Yet the new insights into human vulnerability may even have more impact on patients than on doctors. Just as the negative emotions—anger, fear, sorrow, frustration—wear away our resistance to illness, the positive emotions—joy, love, affection—may preserve and restore our health. Centuries ago King Solomon observed, "A merry heart doeth good like a medicine: but a broken spirit drieth the bones." That message was repeated much more recently by Norman Cousins, who described his reliance on regular doses of zestful laughter to recover from a serious disorder of the connective tissue.

The concept that love and laughter are indeed the best of medicines is more than a cliché. Vaillant found that the healthiest of the Harvard men relied on humor and stable relationships to tide them over crises. Dr. George Solomon and his coworkers at the University of California, San Francisco, found that baby rats fondled during their first three weeks of life had a more vigorous immunological response (that is, they made more antibodies) as adults than their uncuddled cohorts. Throughout life, social supports, as scientists refer to friends and family, provide strong preventive and therapeutic aids. A recent Johns Hopkins study found that widowed men who remarried lived longer than those who did not. In a study of pregnant women undergoing numerous life stresses, 90 percent of those who faced these changes alone developed complications before or during delivery, as compared with 33 percent of those who had "good social support."

BALANCING FORCES

All these insights into a field that has been dubbed psychoimmunology are creating a new image of what it means to be human—and vulnerable. The causes of our vulnerability may lie, not in our stars or in twists of fate or in roving pathogens, but in ourselves. We are not simply creatures composed of mind and body. As we learn more about the regions of self where mind and body act as one, indivisible and interdependent, we may also understand more about the internal dynamics that can make us ill and the balancing forces that may keep us well.

Stress Can Be Good For You

Susan Seliger

Every weeknight in New York, thousands of people remain hunched over their desks until well past the dinner hour. They leave the office with stuffed briefcases, unwind with a couple of drinks and a late meal, and finish their day's labors with a few hours of reading in bed. In the morning, they crowd into buses, trains, and cars and inch their way back to the office. Noontime finds them waiting on line to get into overpriced, understaffed restaurants. And when the sun sets on the city, once again those thousands of desk lamps will shine on in almost empty offices.

Stress? Of course.

A sure prescription for an early grave? Nonsense.

It's not that stress can't be harmful. It's been linked to every disease from asthma to heart disease to ulcers. But a number of recent studies have turned upside down the prevailing wisdom about who is most at risk. More important, these studies have found that stress is not always harmful, that it is in fact a crucial, often productive part of life—in short, that stress can actually be good for you. A person who feels in control of his life can channel the stressful energy that accompanies both the drive to achieve and city living and can make himself healthier than those who avoid cities, conflict, and competition altogether. And this new research raises serious questions about the multi-million-dollar anti-stress industry, with its 72-million annual tranquilizer prescriptions and its hundreds of stress clinics and counseling businesses—most often aimed at exactly the wrong people.

According to the latest research, the ability to control stress is within each person's power. It is the perception of and attitude about both self and environment that most influence whether a person will be hurt by stress. What researchers are finding is that bad stress is triggered not by the pressures of decision-making but rather by the feeling that one's decisions are useless, that life is overwhelming and beyond personal control.

Those people making the decisions, the high-powered, high-pressure executives that many have believed are most vulnerable, turn out, therefore, not to be. And it is not that they are genetically more fit to cope that accounts for their rise to the top. It is their attitude. Yet, the notion that they are at risk has been perpetuated by those selling stress services to employers who are all too willing to spend money for stress counseling for their top people. Unfortunately, it's the underlings these managers supervise who are at far greater risk, people the employers pay little attention to.

"An executive who makes a lot of decisions is better off than his secretary," says Dr. Kenneth Greenspan, director of the Center for Stress Related Disorders, at Columbia-Presbyterian Medical Center. "Secretaries—along with assembly-line workers—are at a great deal of risk from stress because all their decisions are predetermined: when they start work, when they stop, what they do. They fear that they can be easily replaced; they see themselves as victims. And that produces bad stress."

When she came to New York from the Midwest to be a nurse, Joanna Sedgwick* never imagined she would experience stress. She thought stress only affected higher-level people, like doctors. Sedgwick moved into an apartment on the Upper West Side and soon found a job. She also found bedpans, bureaucracy, and belittling treatment by doctors. By the end of a workday, she invariably had a migraine.

Seeking relief, Sedgwick went to the Center for Stress Related Disorders. The biofeedback treatment she was given eased her pain, but it didn't stop the migraines from coming on. With encouragement from Dr. Greenspan, she came to realize that what was wrong with her were her feelings about her work.

"I got no respect; I couldn't make any decisions. Doctors looked down their noses at me and the other nurses," Sedgwick recalls. She ended up returning to school and became a research nurse. One year later, she was appointed head administrative nurse. She gets respect; her headaches are gone.

"I'm under a lot more stress now than I was as an ordinary nurse, and I work harder, But it's different," Sedgwick says. "I decide about treatment; I supervise other nurses. I no longer feel as if everyone is running my life. And I don't get those migraines anymore."

Nor does Joe Carter get his workday headaches anymore, or the dizziness and anxiety he felt as he headed home at night. Joe works for a utility company, managing about 60 people and answering to several bosses. Unlike most of the middle

* *The patients' names have been changed.*

managers around him, he has no college education, and that disparity worried him. Whenever some minor thing went wrong at work—and there were often emergencies that made him work more than 24 hours straight—he used to worry that he'd lose his job. His supervisors were much quicker to point out his mistakes than to pat him on the back.

And no relaxation awaited him when he got home at night. His wife always seemed to have some chore for him to do, and he found himself constantly worrying about earning enough money to put his teenage children through college.

Finally, Carter decided to undergo biofeedback and relaxation training at the Center for Stress Related Disorders, and that led to a more important decision: to talk to his bosses about their assessment of his work. He found that they regarded him as a more valuable employee than he had thought. His symptoms began to fade. Soon he found his confidence had increased enough to allow him to feel comfortable telling his wife he wanted to spend time at home just relaxing with her. If not as dramatic as Joanna Sedgwick's, Carter's recovery proved the same point: An increase in his self-confidence led to an increase in his sense of control over his life and eliminated the chronic stress he was undergoing.

Dr. Greenspan himself could be considered a stress case. Having squeezed three interviews into the morning, he rushes to the deli around the corner and wolfs down a sandwich so that he can race back to the center, see more patients, and then buzz over to another wing of the hospital to check on his latest research project. He talks fast; he walks fast. By most objective standards, he is under a great deal of stress. "But it isn't *bad* stress," insists Greenspan. "I love what I'm doing, and I know how and when to ease up. That makes all the difference."

SO DOES SUCCESS. IN 1974, THE METROPOLITAN LIFE Insurance Company examined 1,078 men who held one of the three top executive positions in Fortune 500 companies and found that their mortality rate was 37 percent lower than that of other white males of a comparable age.

The explanation may come in a study of 259 executives at Illinois Bell conducted by Suzanne Kobasa, Ph.D., a psychologist at the University of Chicago. She found that certain people seemed to be particularly able to handle stress—their health was not affected no matter how intense their job pressures or how ominous their family medical history. Based on her research, Kobasa concluded that if people felt a sense of purpose, viewed change as a challenge and not a threat, and believed that they were in control of their lives, they were not adversely affected by stress.

Executive women—presumably under a great deal of stress to make it in the corporate world—must feel some of this sense of control. Recent studies show no signs that their push into the upper ranks is causing them bad health. Metropolitan Life's 1979 study of 2,352 women listed in *Who's Who* showed their annual death rate to be 29 percent lower than that of their contemporaries. Indeed, the groups of women who have the highest rates of heart disease are secretaries and saleswomen—"women in jobs with little security, status, or control," explains Suzanne Haynes, Ph.D.

Another myth is that city life is bad for mental health. Back in 1954, Dr. Leo Srole, now professor emeritus of social sciences at Columbia University's Center for Gerontology, did a study of Manhattan residents that seemed to confirm that "stressful" living conditions in the city were driving people crazy. Dr. Srole reported that 23.4 percent of his white midtown Manhattan sample were suffering some kind of "emotional impairment" that interfered with their daily lives. That percentage seemed high until 1975, when Dr. Srole matched it with the findings of a similar Cornell University sample of a rural county in Nova Scotia. His conclusion was startling: New Yorkers had a "significantly lower" incidence of mental impairment than did the rural folk. According to Dr. Srole, one reason may be that "cities have resources for satisfaction that rural communities don't have."

These findings are reinforced by a 1978 report by the President's Commission on Mental Health that found that "rural communities tend to be characterized by a higher-than-average rate of psychiatric disorder, particularly depression . . . by restricted opportunities for developing adequate coping mechanisms for facing stress . . . by an acceptance of conditions as being beyond individual control."

RESEARCHERS HAVE COME TO BELIEVE THAT THERE are actually three kinds of stress: normal stress; distress, or bad stress, which is normal stress that has become chronic; and eustress, or good stress.

Each of these kinds of stress is basically a three-stage series of reactions within the body that enable it to adapt to change. Since life is constant change, such reactions are obviously important; without them the body cannot survive. These reactions are most extreme (and thus easiest to monitor) under acute stress, a form of normal stress that one feels when threatened—a car swerving toward you; a child about to put his hand into a fire; the sound of footsteps behind you on a dark, lonely street.

The first stage of any stress reaction is alarm. The endocrine glands release hormones, including adrenaline; the heartbeat speeds up, as does breathing; oxygen-rich blood is directed away from the skin to the brain and the skeletal muscles for fast action. Pupils dilate to take in more information; hormones enter the blood to increase its coagulating ability in case of injury; and digestion slows so that more of the body's energy can be devoted to fighting or fleeing. The surge of energy, concentration, and power that comes with the stress alarm enables people to perform in a crisis—sometimes beyond their normal physical capacities.

Once the alarm stage of stress has passed, the body enters the second stage, one of recuperation in which it repairs any damage caused by the demands of the fight-or-flight response. This is the stage where one can say "Whew!" The third stage is a return to the body's normal state of relaxed alertness.

A diagram of this process would look something like this:

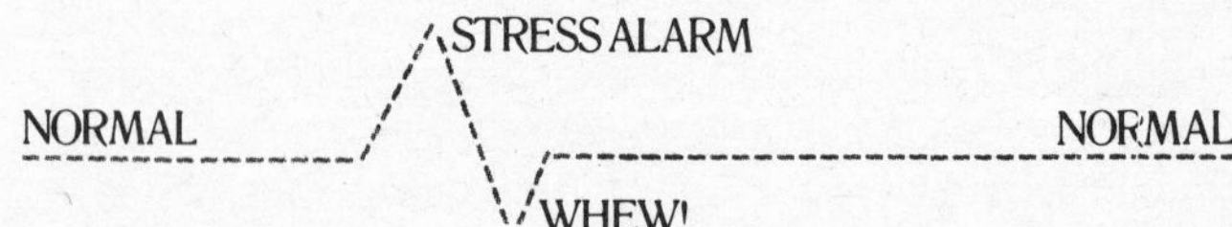

These large sawtooth jags of acute (or normal) short-term stress are part of regular living and are necessary for it. "A certain amount of stress is needed to tune you up for action and keep you on your toes," writes Dr. Hans Selye, the granddaddy of stress research.

Bad stress is normal or acute stress that becomes chronic, continuing for weeks and months so that the body never gets much time to say "Whew!" and recuperate. This kind of stress means trouble.

A normal, healthy life pattern might look like this on the stress diagram:

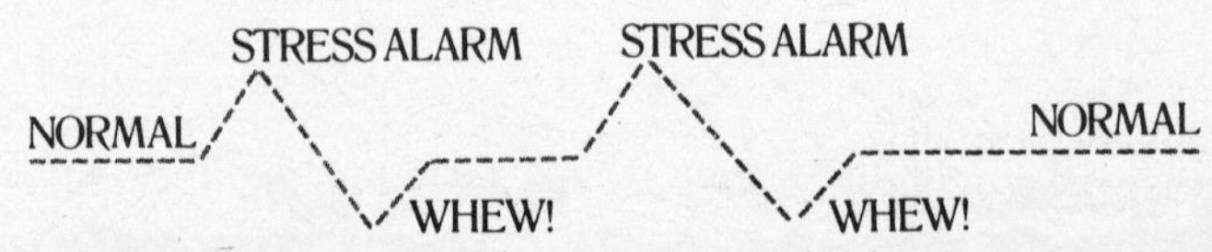

On the other hand, chronic stress might look like this:

One person who found herself in a chronic-stress cycle was Leslie Friedman, who ran a personnel department in a bank, overseeing the careers of about twenty employees. Friedman worked more than 50 hours a week, and when she went home at night, she had a second job: helping her husband with his business. Friedman didn't think her bosses appreciated her efforts, and by noon each day she'd have a splitting headache and a backache too. But at the end of the evening, although she was dead tired, she couldn't fall asleep. In the morning, she would drag herself out of bed and begin the punishing cycle all over again.

Friedman was able to break out. She discovered that her boss didn't expect her to do all that she was doing and that that was the reason she didn't get the appreciation she thought she deserved. So she quit and found another job, where her skills at managing people were put to good use. She also convinced her husband that he had to hire an assistant. Going home doesn't mean going on to a second job anymore, and, although Friedman still works very long hours, she says that the challenge of the new job seems to be energizing rather than enervating her.

Chronic stress can inflict real bodily harm. First, it can lower resistance to disease. According to Dr. Paul J. Rosch, an internist and president of the American Institute of Stress, in Yonkers, "interferon, a non-specific polypeptide which is one of the basic defenses against virus infections and is now being investigated in the treatment of cancer, is also suppressed under some conditions of emotional stress." If acute stress is occasional, the body's immune system can bounce back. If it is prolonged, the immune system is thrown out of whack.

Second, repeated and unremitting episodes of acute stress mean repeated release of adrenaline. If the problem prompts no physical exertion to use up the adrenaline—and most stresses in modern life are of a mental rather than a physical nature—then excess adrenaline will remain in the system and can play a part in the buildup of cholesterol in the arteries that can lead to heart disease.

There are early, recognizable signs that can allow a person to avoid entering a cycle of long-term, chronic stress. In addition, people can actually increase their capacity to cope with potentially stressful events.

"Knowing the danger signals can help you operate successfully at much higher levels of stress," says Dr. Sidney Lecker, director of Corporate Stress Control Services, in Manhattan. Once you become aware of the symptoms, there are definite steps you can take (see box on page 24) so that, as Dr. Lecker puts it, "you can go back into the thick of things and operate on the ragged edge of disaster—safely."

THE FLIP SIDE OF THE STRESS COIN IS EUSTRESS. IT comes from successfully rising to a challenge, feeling confidence and a sense of control over one's destiny. Dr. Rosch believes that people who thrive on stress might die without it. "I take care of patients who are recuperating from heart attacks," he says. "Now, the ideal prescription for one guy is to lie on a beach in the Bahamas, but for another kind of patient that same prescription would be lethal.

"I'm convinced that good stress is healthy," continues Rosch, who began his stress research three decades ago with Selye. "Look at symphony conductors. They undergo physical exertion, deadlines, traveling, dealing with prima donnas in the orchestra. But, on the other hand, they have pride of accomplishment, the approbation of their peers, the plaudits of the audience.

"Look at the life and health records of conductors and you'll see it's outstanding. They live forever. Look at them." Waving his arms enthusiastically, he checks off their names: "Stokowski, Fiedler, Toscanini." He pauses. "The real secret to a long and healthy life is to enjoy what you're doing and be good at it. It's not to avoid stress."

One of the leading popular advocates of the theory that good stress may have the power to heal is Norman Cousins, the former editor of *Saturday Review*. Cousins says that laughter is one of those forms of good stress—and, as he wrote in *The New England Journal of Medicine* and in his book *Anatomy of an Illness*, he's convinced it saved his life.

Laughter? Yes, laughter. It might seem to be just another form of physical exertion, making the body respond much as it does under any kind of acute stress: The oxygen supply to the brain increases; the heartbeat speeds up, rushing oxygen-rich blood to the muscles; the pupils dilate; and so on. But recent brain research indicates that something far more powerful is at work on a biochemical level: Endorphins, the body's natural painkillers, are also being released. What the researchers do not yet know is whether endorphins, which may actually reverse some of the damage of the distress reaction, are secreted in equal amounts under all kinds of stress or in greater quantities during eustress.

"We're just on the frontier of discovering the nature of the biochemical reactions of stress, such as the release of endorphins," says Dr. Lorenz Ng, former chief of the Pain Studies Program at the National Institute on Drug Abuse, in Bethesda, Maryland, and medical director of the Washington Pain Center. "It's the newest thing in stress research, and it may lead us to understand the differences between good and bad stress," says Ng.

Dr. Rosch believes that the biochemical effects of eustress may actually reverse the course of various diseases, including cancer. He's written on this subject in a chapter of *Cancer, Stress and Death* for the "Sloan-Kettering Institute Cancer Series." "Cancer and other diseases set in when the immune system weakens," Rosch says. "There is evidence that on the cell walls of lymphocytes responsible for mediating the immune response there are receptor sites for ACTH, which is the prime hormone released under stress, endorphins, met-enkephalin, and other brain hormones. This implies that the brain can talk directly to the immune system and that the immune system talks back. The intriguing possibility is that people may be able to tune in to that conversation—and even influence it, just as they can be trained to influence other systems, like pulse rate and skin temperature, through biofeedback. People may have the ability to cure themselves."

ACTUALLY, THE IDEA OF STRESS'S BEING HEALTHY HAS been around for a long time. In *Stress Without Distress*, published in 1974, Selye explained that this was possible, but no one in the stress field paid much attention. They were too busy making a living convincing people that stress was affecting their health. They wanted people to continue popping down their daily anti-stress pill and to spend $1,500 per week at anti-stress clinics. "Stress has become so popular that a variety of entrepreneurs and charlatans have capitalized on it," says Rosch.

The medical profession is also campaigning against stress, acknowledges Rosch. For example, Dr. Theodore Cooper, while dean of the Cornell University Medical College, headed a three-year program called "The Consequences of Stress: The Medical and Social Implications of Prescribing Tranquilizers." The program's message went by closed-circuit television lectures to nearly 20,000 physicians in 26 cities and to 100,000 more physicians through similar tape recordings. The financier for all this was Hoffmann-LaRoche, Inc., makers of Valium, which is the biggest-selling tranquilizer in the world.

Yet, there is still great dispute in the medical community over the usefulness of tranquilizers for dealing with stress. Many doctors are convinced that they can do more harm than good. "Avoidance of stress has led to abuse of tranquilizers," says Dr. Nelson Hendler, the head of Mensana, a pain clinic in Baltimore, and a psychiatric consultant at Johns Hopkins Hospital's Pain Treatment Center. Valium doesn't help stress, insists Hendler. It inhibits the release of serotonin, which stimulates sleep naturally. And it may interfere with stage-three sleep—perhaps the most restful stage in the sleep cycle, in which REM (rapid eye movement) sleep occurs—and stage-four sleep, which is the deepest.

"One in three people who goes to a doctor about stress gets a prescription for a tranquilizer," Hendler says. "Most people should not fill it."

The anti-stress brigade has also been joined by hundreds of companies that provide counseling on stress, alcoholism, and other problems. Millions of workers are now eligible for such benefits. For instance, Isidore Lefkowitz Elgort, an advertising agency in New York, pays for employees to attend T.M. sessions to help them handle stress.

Many of these efforts may indeed be useful. However, a good number are misguided—aimed at the people under the least stress, the executives, instead of at their underlings. Other anti-stress efforts seem to cause more problems than they cure.

"Most organizations buy one-shot educational packages—a lecture on stress," says James Manuso, Ph.D., creator of the in-house biofeedback stress-counseling center at Equitable Life in New York. "Someone goes in there and tells the employees how much stress they're under, scares the hell out of them, and then leaves. That just *adds* to the stress."

Even Dr. Roy Menninger, president of the Menninger Foundation, in Topeka, Kansas, which charges New York corporation executives up to $2,300 each to learn, among other things, how to handle stress, believes the view that "stress is bad" has gone too far. Dr. Lecker is more emphatic: "Stress is essential for meeting challenges. If you didn't have stress, you'd be dead."

How to Convert Bad Stress Into Good

THERE ARE CERTAIN PHYSICAL signals that provide a warning that the body's habitual response to stress is becoming destructive. People can learn to recognize these signals and to change their characteristic responses to daily tensions. They thus can endure higher levels of stress and perhaps even profit from them.

The telltale signals:

☐ Cold hands, especially if one is colder than the other.

☐ Indigestion, diarrhea, too frequent urination.

☐ Being susceptible to every cold or virus that goes around (which could mean that the physical strains of distress are weakening the immune system).

☐ Muscle spasms or a soreness and tightness in the jaw, back of the neck, shoulders, or lower back.

☐ Shortness of breath.

☐ Headaches, tiredness, sleeping too much or too little.

☐ Becoming suddenly accident-prone.

When someone recognizes any of these signals, he should stop what he is doing—if only for two or three minutes—take several deep breaths, and try to relax. If the tension also shows itself through tapping toes or drumming fingers, he should stand up and do a few jumping jacks or take a brisk walk around the office or the block, trying to look at everything as if for the first time.

The most important key to defusing distress is to become conscious of that inner voice each person has. Human beings are constantly assessing themselves and their environment and reporting silently to themselves: "This looks threatening; I don't think I can handle it. I certainly can't handle it without a cigarette. . . ."

Many people are not conscious of this internal commentator, but if a person learns to listen to the way he talks to himself, he may find that he is usually not being as encouraging as he could be—that he is actually making matters worse for himself.

Instead of standing on the line at the bank checking his watch and listening to his inner voice computing how long it has taken "those incompetent tellers" to handle each transaction, worrying about how late he will be to his appointment, and wondering why he didn't get cash for the weekend yesterday, he should make his inner voice be soothing: "I don't like waiting on this line, but there is nothing I can do about it now, so I might as well relax. Look how tense everyone else is getting. It's actually kind of funny."

Another trick is to stop thinking about the time. It may be slipping by, but counting the seconds only fritters away energy and activates the stress response. Dr. Meyer Friedman and Dr. Ray H. Rosenman, the authors of *Type A Behavior and Your Heart,* found that time consciousness, or "hurry sickness," was a key personality trait of the heart-attack-prone Type A personality. One stress researcher says she found that simply removing her wristwatch for several weeks greatly reduced the time pressures she felt.

To convert bad stress to good, remember the following:

Before an event expected to be stressful, visualize what may take place. Such a rehearsal will make the actual event seem familiar, helping one to relax and handle the situation with confidence.

During a tense situation, such as taking a test or meeting a tight deadline, talk nicely to oneself, don't harp on poor preparation or performance. Instead, one should make one's inner voice offer praise for what one did accomplish, and reassurance that the situation isn't so bad after all.

Afterward, luxuriate in the relief of the burden's being lifted. Even if things didn't go so well, avoid puritanical self-criticism. This refreshing interlude can help strengthen the system to better resist the wear and tear of future distress.

"Any bad stress can be turned around," insists Dr. Kenneth Greenspan, "if you take steps that make you feel that you are controlling your life and it isn't controlling you." **—S.S.**

The Foundations of the Person-Centered Approach

Carl R. Rogers

Resident Fellow
Center for Studies of the Person,
La Jolla, California 90237

I wish to point to two related tendencies which have acquired more and more importance in my thinking as the years have gone by. One of these is an actualizing tendency, a characteristic of organic life. One is a formative tendency in the universe as a whole. Taken together they are, I believe, the foundation blocks of the person-centered approach.

Its Characteristics

But what do I mean by a person-centered approach? For me it expresses the primary theme of my whole professional life, as that theme has become clarified through experience, interaction with others, and research. I smile as I think of the various labels I have given to this theme during the course of my career—nondirective counseling, client-centered therapy, student-centered teaching, group-centered leadership. As the fields of application have grown in number and variety, the label "person-centered approach" seems the most descriptive.

The central hypothesis of this approach can be briefly stated. (See Rogers, 1959, for a complete statement.) It is that the individual has within him or herself vast resources for self-understanding, for altering the self-concept, basic attitudes, and his or her self-directed behavior—and that these resources can be tapped if only a definable climate of facilitative psychological attitudes can be provided.

There are three conditions which constitute this growth-promoting climate, whether we are speaking of the relationship between therapist and client, parent and child, leader and group, teacher and student, or administrator and staff. The conditions apply, in fact, in any situation in which the development of the person is a goal. I have described these conditions in previous writings; I present here a brief summary from the point of view of psycho therapy, but the description applies to all of the foregoing relationships.

The first element has to do with genuineness, realness, or congruence. The more the therapist is himself or herself in the relationship, putting up no professional front or personal facade, the greater is the likelihood that the client will change and grow in a constructive manner. It means that the therapist is openly being the feelings and attitudes that are flowing within at the moment. The term transparent catches the flavor of this condition—the therapist makes himself or herself transparent to the client; the client can see right through what the therapist is in the relationship; the client experiences no holding back on the part of the therapist. As for the therapist, what he or she is experiencing is available to awareness, can be lived in the relationship, and can be communicated if appropriate. Thus there is a close matching, or congruence, between what is being experienced at the gut level, what is present in awareness, and what is expressed to the client.

The second attitude of importance in creating a climate for change is acceptance, or caring or prizing—unconditional positive regard. It means that when the therapist is experiencing a positive, acceptant attitude toward whatever the client *is* at that moment, therapeutic movement or change is more likely. It involves the therapist's willingness for the client to be whatever immediate feeling is going on—confusion, resentment, fear, anger, courage, love, or pride. It is a nonpossessive caring. The therapist prizes the client in a total rather than a conditional way.

"The Foundations of the Person-Centered Approach," by Carl R. Rogers, *Education,* Vol. 100, No. 2, Winter 1979, pp. 98-107. Reprinted by permission.

The third facilitative aspect of the relationship is empathic understanding. This means that the therapist senses accurately the feelings and personal meanings that are being experienced by the client and communicates this understanding to the client. When functioning best the therapist is so much inside the private world of the other that he or she can clarify not only the meanings of which the client is aware but even those just below the level of awareness. This kind of sensitive, active listening is exceedingly rare in our lives. We think we listen, but very rarely do we listen with real understanding, true empathy. Yet listening, of this very special kind, is one of the most potent forces for change that I know.

How does this climate which I have just described bring about change? Briefly, as the person is accepted and prized, he or she tends to develop a more caring attitude toward him or herself. As the person is empathically heard, it becomes possible for him or her to listen more accurately to the flow of inner experiencings. But as the person understands and prizes self, there is a development of a self more congruent with the experiencings. He or she is thus becoming more real, more genuine. These tendencies, the reciprocal of the therapist attitudes, mean that the person is a more effective growth-enhancer for him or herself. There is a greater freedom to be the whole person that he or she inwardly is. (Rogert, 1962)

The Evidence

There is a body of steadily mounting research evidence which by and large supports the view that when these facilitative conditions are present, changes in personality and behavior do indeed occur. Such research has been carried on from 1949 to the present. Studies have been made of psychotherapy with troubled persons; with schizophrenics; of the facilitation of learning in the schools; of other interpersonal relationships. Some excellent and little known recent research has been done by Aspy, Roebuck and others in education (1972, 1976) and by Tausch and colleagues in Germany in many different fields (summary, 1978).

A Directional Process

Practice, theory and research make it clear that the whole person-centered approach rests on a basic trust in the organism. There is evidence from many disciplines to support an even broader statement. We can say that there is in every organism, at whatever level, an underlying flow of movement toward constructive fulfillment of its inherent possibilities. In man, too, there is a natural tendency toward a more complex and complete development. The term that has most often been used for this is the actualizing tendency, and it is present in all living organisms.

Whether we are speaking of a flower or an oak tree, of an earthworm or a beautiful bird, of an ape or a man, we will do well, I believe, to recognize that life is an active process, not a passive one. Whether the stimulus arises from within or without, whether the environment is favorable or unfavorable, the behaviors of an organism can be counted on to be in the direction of maintaining, enhancing, and reproducing itself. This is the very nature of the process we call life. This tendency is operative at all times. Indeed it is only the presence or absence of this total directional process which enables us to tell whether a given organism is alive or dead.

The actualizing tendency can of course be thwarted or warped, but it cannot be destroyed without destroying the organism. I remember that in my boyhood the potato bin in which we stored our winter supply of potatoes was in the basement, several feet below a small basement window. The conditions were unfavorable, but the potatoes would begin to sprout—pale white sprouts, so unlike the healthy green shoots they sent up when planted in the soil in the spring. But these sad, spindly sprouts would grow two or three feet in length as they reached toward the distant light of the window. They were in their bizarre, futile growth, a sort of desperate expression of the directional tendency I have been describing. They would never become a plant, never mature, never fulfill their real potentiality. But under the most adverse circumstances they were striving to become. Life would not give up, even if it could not flourish. In dealing with clients whose lives have been terribly warped, in working with men and women on the back wards of state hospitals, I often think of those potato sprouts. So unfavorable have been the conditions in which these people have developed that their lives often seem abnormal, twisted, scarcely human. Yet the directional tendency in them is to be trusted. The clue to understanding their behavior is that they are striving, in the only ways they perceive as available to them, to move toward growth, toward becoming. To us the results may seem bizarre and futile, but they are life's desperate attempt to become itself. It is this potent constructive tendency which is an underlying basis of the person-centered approach.

Some Confirming Examples

I am not alone in seeing such an actualizing tendency as the fundamental answer to the question of what makes an organism "tick." Goldstein (1947), Maslow (1954), Angyal (1941, 1965), Szent-Gyoergyi (1974), and others have held similar views and have influenced my own thinking. I have pointed out that this tendency involves a development toward the differentiation of organs and functions; it involves enhancement through reproduction. Szent-Gyoergyi says that he cannot explain the mysteries of biological development "without supposing an innate 'drive' in living matter to perfect itself" (*op. cit.*, p. 17)

The organism, in its normal state, moves toward its own fulfillment and toward self-regulation and an independence from external control.

But is this view confirmed by other evidence? Let me point to some of the work in biology which supports the concept of the actualizing tendency. One example, replicated with different species, is the work of Driesch with sea urchins many years ago. Driesch learned how to tease apart the two cells which are formed after the first division of the fertilized egg. Had they been left to develop normally it is clear that each of these two cells would have grown into a portion of a sea urchin larva, the contributions of both being needed to form a whole creature. So it seems equally obvious that when the two cells are skilfully separated, each, if it grows, will simply develop into some portion of a sea urchin. But this is overlooking the directional and actualizing tendency characteristic of all organic growth. It is found that each cell, if it can be kept alive, now develops into a whole sea urchin larva—a bit smaller than usual, but normal and complete.

I am sure that I choose this example because it seems so closely analogous to my experience in dealing with individuals in a therapeutic relationship, my experience in facilitating intensive groups, my experience of providing "freedom to learn" for students in classes. In these situations the most impressive fact about the individual human being seems to be his directional tendency toward wholeness, toward actualization of his potentialities. I have not found psychotherapy or group experience effective when I have tried to create in another individual something which is not there, but I have found that if I can provide the conditions which make for growth, then this positive directional tendency brings about constructive results. The scientist with the divided sea urchin egg is in the same situation. He cannot cause the cell to develop in one way or another, but if he focuses his skill on providing the conditions which permit the cell to survive and grow, then the tendency for growth and the direction of growth will be evident, and will come from within the organism. I cannot think of a better analogy for therapy or the group experience, where, if I can supply a psychological amniotic fluid, forward movement of a constructive sort will occur.

I would like to add one comment which may be clarifying. Sometimes this growth tendency is spoken of as if it involved the development of all the potentialities of the organism. This is clearly not true. The organism does not, as someone has pointed out, tend toward developing its capacity for nausea, nor does it actualize its potentiality for self-destruction, nor its ability to bear pain. Only under unusual or perverse circumstances do these potentialities become actualized. It is clear that the actualizing tendency is selective and directional, a constructive tendency if you will.

Support from Modern Theory and Experience

Pentony (unpublished paper, 1978) points out forcefully that those who favor this view of an actualizing tendency "do not need to be inhibited by the belief that it is in conflict with modern science or theories of knowledge (p. 20). He describes the differing recent epistemologies, particularly that of Murayama (1977). It is now theorized that the "genetic code" does not contain all the information necessary to specify the mature organism. Instead, it contains a *set of rules* determining the interaction of the dividing cells. Much less information is needed to codify the rules, than to guide every aspect of maturing development. "Thus information can be generated within the organism system—information can *grow*" (p. 9, italics mine). Hence Driesch's see urchin cells are doubtless following the coded *rules,* and consequently are able to develop in original, not previously or rigidly specified ways.

All this goes deeply against the current (and possibly outdated) epistemology of the social sciences, which holds that a "cause" is followed in a one-way direction by an "effect." Murayama and others see it quite differently—that there are *mutual* cause-effect interactions which amplify deviations and permit new information and new forms to develop. This "morphogenetic epistemology" appears to be basic to an understanding of all living systems, including all such growth processes as the growth of an organism. Murayama states that an understanding of biology "lies in the recognition that the biological processes are reciprocal causal processes, not random processes" (1977, p. 130). On the other hand, as he points out elsewhere, an understanding of biology does *not* emerge from an epistemology based on one-way cause-effect systems. Thus there is great need to rethink the stimulus-response, cause-effect basis on which most social science rests.

The work in the field of sensory deprivation shows how strong is the organismic tendency to amplify diversities and create new information and new forms. Certainly tension reduction or the absence of stimulation is a far cry from being the desired state of the organism. Freud could not have been more wrong in his postulate that "The nervous system is . . . an apparatus which would even, if this were feasible, maintain itself in an altogether unstimulated condition" (1953, p. 63). On the contrary, when deprived of external stimuli, the human organism produces a flood of internal stimuli sometimes of the most bizarre sort. John Lilly (1972) was one of the first to tell of his experiences when suspended weightless in a soundproof tank of water. He speaks of the trance-like states, the mystical experiences, the sense of being tuned in on communication networks not available to ordinary consciousness, of experiences which can only be called hallucinatory. It is very clear that when he is receiving an absolute minimum of any external stimuli, the person opens himself to a flood of experiencing which goes far beyond that of everyday living. The individual most certainly does not lapse into homeostasis, into a passive equilibrium. This only occurs in diseased organisms.

A Trustworthy Base

Thus, to me it is meaningful to say that the substratum of all motivation is the organismic tendency toward fulfillment. This tendency may express itself in the widest range of behaviors, and in response to a very wide variety of needs. To be sure, certain wants of a basic sort must be at least partially met before other needs become urgent. Consequently the tendency of the organism to actualize itself may at one moment lead to the seeking of food or sexual satisfaction, and yet unless these needs are overpoweringly great, even these satisfactions will be sought in ways which enhance rather than diminish self-esteem. And other fulfillments will also be sought in the transactions with the environment—the need for exploration, for producing change in the environment, for play, for self-exploration when that is perceived as an avenue to enhancement—all of these and many other behaviors are basically an expression of the actualizing tendency.

We are, in short, dealing with an organism which is always seeking, always initiating, always "up to something." There is one central source of energy in the human organism. It is a trustworthy function of the whole system rather than of some portion of it. It is perhaps most simply conceptualized as a tendency toward fulfillment, toward actualization, involving not only the maintenance but also the enhancement of the organism.

A Broader View: The Formative Tendency

But there are many who are critical of this point of view. They regard it as too optimistic, not dealing adequately with the negative element, the evil in persons, the dark side of human beings.

Consequently, I would like to put this directional tendency in a broader context. In doing so I shall draw heavily on the work and thinking of others, from disciplines other than my own. I have learned from many scientists, but I wish to mention a special indebtedness to the works of Albert Szent-Gyoergyi (1974), a Nobel Prize biologist, and Lancelot Whyte (1974), a historian of ideas.

My main thesis is this. There appears to be a formative tendency at work in the universe which can be observed at every level. This tendency has received much less attention than it deserves.

Physical scientists up to now have focused primarily on entropy, the tendency toward deterioration. They know a great deal about this tendency toward disorder. Studying closed systems they can give this tendency a clear mathematical description. They know that order or organization tends to deteriorate into randomness, each stage less organized than the last.

We are also very familiar with deterioration in organic life. The system—whether plant, animal, or human—eventually deteriorates into a lower degree of functioning organization, into a lesser and lesser degree of order, until decay reaches a stasis. In one sense this is what a part of medicine is all about—a concern with the malfunctioning or the deterioration of an organ, or the organism as a whole. The complex process of the death of the physical organism is increasingly well understood.

So a great deal is known of the universal tendency of systems at all levels to deteriorate in the direction of less and less orderliness, more and more randomness. When it operates, it is a one-way street. The world seems to be a great machine, running down and wearing out.

But there is far less recognition of, or emphasis on, the even more important formative tendency which can be equally well observed at every level of the universe. After all, every form which we see or know emerged from a simpler, less complex form. This is a phenomenon which stands as being at least as significant as entropy. Examples could be given from every form of inorganic or organic life. Let me illustrate with just a few.

It appears that every galaxy, every star, every planet, including our own, was formed from a less organized whirling storm of particles. Many of these stellar objects are themselves formative. In the atmosphere of our sun hydrogen nuclei collide to form molecules of helium, more complex in nature. It is hypothesized that in other stars even heavier molecules are formed by such interactions.

I understand that when the simple materials of the earth's atmosphere which were present before life began—hydrogen, oxygen and nitrogen, in the form of water and ammonia—are infused by electric charges or by radiation, heavier molecules first begin to form, then amino acids. We seem only a step away from the formation of viruses and more complex living organisms. It is a creative, not a disintegrative process at work.

Another fascinating example is the formation of crystals. In every case, from less ordered and less symmetrical fluid matter, there emerges the startingly unique, ordered symmetrical and often beautiful crystalline form. All of us have marvelled at the perfection and complexity of the snowflake. Yet it emerged from formless vapor.

When we consider the single living cell, we discover that it often forms more complex colonies, as in the coral reef. Even more order enters the picture as the cell emerges into an organism of many cells with specialized functions.

I do not need to picture the whole gradual process of organic evolution. We are familiar with the steadily increasing complexity of organisms. They are not always successful in their ability to cope with the changing environment, but the trend toward complexity is always evident.

Perhaps for most of us the process of organic evolution is best recognized as we consider the development of the single fertilized human ovum through the simplest stages of cell division, then the aquatic gill stage, and on to the vastly complex, highly organized human infant. As Jonas Salk has said, there is a manifest and increasing order in evolution.

Thus, without ignoring the tendency toward deterioration, we need to recognize fully what Szent-Gyoergyi terms "syntropy" and what Whyte calls the "morphic tendency," the ever-operating trend toward increased order and interrelated complexity evident at both the inorganic and the organic level. The universe is always building and creating as well as deteriorating. This process is evident in the human being too.

The Function of Consciousness

What part does our awareness have in this formative function? I believe that consciousness has a small but very important part. The ability to focus conscious attention seems to be one of the latest evolutionary developments in our species. It is a tiny peak of awareness, of symbolizing capacity, topping a vast pyramid of nonconscious organismic functioning. Perhaps a better analogy, more indicative of the continual change going on, is to think of the individual's functioning as a large pyramidal fountain. The very tip of the fountain is intermittently illuminated with the flickering light of consciousness, but the constant flow of life goes on in the darkness as well, in nonconscious as well as conscious ways. It seems that the human organism has been moving toward the more complete development of awareness. It is at this level that new forms are invented, perhaps even new directions for the human species. It is here that the reciprocal relationship between cause and effect is most demonstrably evident. It is here that choices are made, spontaneous forms created. We see here perhaps the highest of the human functions.

Some of my colleagues have said that organismic choice—the nonverbal, subconscious choice of being—is guided by the evolutionary flow. I would agree and go one step further. I would point out that in psychotherapy we have learned something about the psychological conditions which are most conductive to increasing this highly important self-awareness. With greater self-awareness a more informed choice is possible, a choice more free from introjects, a *conscious* choice which is even more in tune with the evolutionary flow. Such a person is more potentially aware, not only of the stimuli from outside, but of ideas and dreams, and of the ongoing flow of feelings and emotions and physiological reactions which he senses in himself. The greater this awareness, the more surely he/she will float in a direction consonant with the directional evolutionary flow.

When a person is functioning in this way, it does not mean that there is a self-conscious awareness of all that is going on within, like the centipede whose movements were paralyzed by becoming aware of each of his legs. On the contrary such a person is free to live a feeling subjectively, as well as be aware of it. She/he might experience love, or pain, or fear, and live in these experiences subjectively. Or she/he might abstract self from this subjectivity and realize in awareness, "I am in pain;" "I am afraid," "I do love." The crucial point is that there would be no barriers, no inhibitions, which would prevent the full experiencing of whatever was organismically present. This person would be moving in the direction of wholeness, integration, a unified life. Consciousness would be participating in this larger, creative, formative tendency.

Altered States

But some would take us further. Researchers like the Grofs (1977) and John Lilly (1973) would take us beyond the ordinary level of consciousness. Their studies appear to reveal that in altered states of consciousness persons feel they are in touch with, and grasp the meaning of, this evolutionary flow. They experience it as tending toward a transcending experience of unity. They picture the individual self as being dissolved in a whole area of higher values, especially beauty, harmony and love. The person feels at one with the cosmos. Hard-headed research seems to be confirming the mystic's experience of union with the universal.

For me this point of view is confirmed by my more recent experience in working with clients, and especially in working with groups. I described earlier those characteristics of a growth-promoting relationship which have been investigated and supported by research. But recently my view has broadened into a new area which cannot as yet be studied empirically.

When I am at my best, as a group facilitator or a therapist, I discover another characteristic. I find that when I am closest to my inner, intuitive self, when I am somehow in touch with the unknown in me, when perhaps I am in a slightly altered state of consciousness, then whatever I do seems to be full of healing. Then simply my *presence* is releasing and helpful. There is nothing I can do to force this experience but when I can relax and be close to the transcendental core of me, then I may behave in strange and impulsive ways in the relationship, ways which I cannot justify rationally, which have nothing to do with my thought processes. But these strange behaviors turn out to be *right,* in some odd way. At those moments it seems that my inner spirit has reached out and touched the inner spirit of the other. Our relationship transcends itself, and has become a part of something larger. Profound growth and healing and energy are present.

This kind of transcendent phenomenon is certainly experienced at times in groups in which I have worked, changing the lives of some of those involved. One participant in a workshop put it eloquently. "I found it to be a profound spiritual experience. I felt the oneness of spirit in the community. We breathed together, felt together, even spoke for one another. I felt the power of the 'life force' that infuses each of us—whatever that is. I felt its presence without the usual barricades of 'me-ness' or 'you-ness'—it was like a meditative experience when I feel myself as a center of consciousness, very much a part of the broader, universal consciousness. And yet with that extraordinary sense of oneness, the separateness of each person present has never been more clearly preserved."

Again, as in the description of altered states of consciousness, this account partakes of the mystical. Our experiences, it is clear, involve the transcendent, the indescribable, the spiritual. I am compelled to believe that I, like many others, have underestimated the importance of this mystical, spiritual dimension.

Science and the Mystical

Here many readers, I am sure, will part company with me. What, they will wish to know, has become of logic, of science, of hard-headedness? But before they leave me entirely, I would like to adduce some surprising support for such views, from the most unexpected quarters.

Fritjof Capra (1975), a well known theoretical physicist, has shown how present-day physics has almost completely abolished any solid concepts of our world except energy. In a summarizing statement he says:

"In modern physics the universe is thus experienced as a dynamic, inseparable whole which always includes the observer in an essential way. In this experience the traditional concepts of space and time, of isolated objects, and of cause and effect, lose their meaning. Such an experience, however, is very similar to that of the Eastern mystics" (*op. cit.*, p. 81). He then goes on to point out the astonishing parallels of Zen, Taoism, Buddhism, and other Oriental views. His own conviction is that physics and Eastern mysticism are separate but complementary roads to the same knowledge, supplementing one another in providing a fuller understanding of our universe.

Recently the work of Ilya Prigogine (Ferguson, 1979), Nobel prize-winning chemist, offers a different perspective which also throws new light on what has been presented.

In trying to answer the basic question of how order and complexity emerge from the process of entropy, he has originated a whole new theoretical system. He has developed mathematical formulas and proof which demonstrate that the world of living nature is probabilistic, rather than solely deterministic. His views apply to all open systems in which energy is exchanged with the environment. This obviously includes the human organism.

Briefly, the more complex the structure—whether a chemical or a human—the more energy it expends to maintain that complexity. For example, the human brain, with only two percent of body weight, uses 20 percent of the available oxygen! Such a system is unstable, has fluctuations or "perturbations," as he calls them. As these fluctuations increase, they are amplified by the system's many connections, (and thus drive it—whether chemical compound or human individual—into a new, altered, state, *more* ordered and coherent than before. This new state has still greater complexity, and hence even more potential for creating change.

The transformation of one state to another is a sudden shift, a non-linear event, in which many factors act on each other at once. It is especially interesting to me that this has already been demonstrated in investigating Gendlin's concept of "experiencing" in psychotherapy (Gendlin, 1978). When a hitherto repressed feeling is fully and acceptantly experienced in awareness in the relationship, there is not only a definitely felt psychological shift, but a concomitant physiological change, as a new state of insight is achieved (Don, 1977-78).

Prigogine's theory appears to shed light on meditation, relaxation techniques, and altered states of consciousness, in which fluctuations are augmented by various means. It gives support to the value of fully recognizing and expressing one's feelings—positive or negative—thus permitting the full perturbation of the system.

He recognizes the strong resemblance between his "science of complexity" and the views of Eastern sages and mystics, as well as the philosophies of Whitehead and Bergson. His view points, he says, toward "a deep collective vision." Rather amazingly, the title of his forthcoming book is "From Being to Becoming," a strange label for a volume by a chemist-philosopher (Prigogine, 1979, in press).

His conclusion can be stated very briefly. "The more complex a system, the greater its potential for self-transcendance: its parts cooperate to reorganize it" (Ferguson, 1979).

Thus from theoretical physics and chemistry comes some confirmation of experiences which are transcendent, indescribable, unexpected, transformational—the sort of phenomena which we have observed and felt as concomitants of the person-centered approach.

A Hypothesis for the Future

As I try to take into account the scope of the various themes I have presented, and some of the available evidence which appears to support them, I am led to formulate a broad hypothesis. In my mind it is very tentative in nature, but for the sake of clarity I will state it in definite terms.

It is hypothesized that there is a formative directional tendency in the universe, which can be traced and observed in stellar space, in crystals, in micro-organisms, in organic life, in human beings. This is an evolutionary tendency toward greater order, greater complexity, greater interrelatedness. In humankind it develops from a single cell origin to complex organic functioning, to knowing and sensing below the level of consciousness, to a conscious awareness of the organism and the external world, to a transcendent awareness of the harmony and unity of the cosmic system including humankind.

It seems to me just possible that this hypothesis could be a base upon which we could begin to build a theory for humanistic psychology. It definitely forms a base for the person-centered approach.

Concluding Summary

What I have been saying is that in our work we have discovered the attitudinal qualities which are demonstrably effective in releasing constructive and growthful changes in the personality and behavior of individuals. Persons in an environment infused with these attitudes, develop more self-understanding, more self-confidence, more ability to choose their behaviors. They learn more significantly, they have more freedom to be and become.

The individual in this nurturing climate is free to choose *any* direction, but actually selects positive and constructive ways. The actualizing tendency is seen as operative in the human being.

It is still further confirming to find that this is not simply a tendency in living systems, but is part of a strong formative tendency in our universe, which is evident at all levels.

Thus when we provide a psychological climate which permits persons to *be*—whether clients, students, workers, or persons in a group—we are not involved in a chance event. We are tapping into a tendency which permeates all of organic life—a tendency to become all the complexity of which the organism is capable. And on an even larger scale, I believe we are tuning into a potent creative tendency which has formed our universe, from the smallest snowflake to the largest galaxy, from the lowly amoeba to the most sensitive and gifted of persons. And perhaps we are touching the cutting edge of our ability to transcend ourselves, to create new and more spiritual directions in human evolution.

It is this kind of formulation which, for me, forms a philosophical base for a person-centered approach. It justifies me in engaging in a life-affirming way of being.

References

Angyal, A. *Foundations for a Science of Personality.* New York: Commonwealth Fund, 1941.

________. *Neurosis and Treatment.* New York: John Wiley & Sons, 1965.

Aspy, D. *Toward a Technology for Humanizing Education.* Champaign, Illinois: Research Press, 1972.

________, and Roebuck, F.M. *A Lever Long Enough.* Washington, D.C.: National Consortium for Humanizing Education, 1976.

Capra, F. *The Tao of Physics.* Boulder, Colorado: Shambala, 1975.

Don, N.S. The transformation of conscious experience and its EEG correlates. *Journal Altered States of Consciousness,* c, 1977-78, p. 147.

Ferguson, M. Special issue: Prigogine's science of becoming. *Brain/Mind Bulletin,* 4, No. 13, May 21, 1979.

Freud, S. Instincts and their vicissitudes. *Collected Papers, Vol. 4.* London: Hogarth Press and Inst. of Psychoanalysis, 1953, 60-83.

Gendlin, E.T. *Focusing.* New York: Everest House, 1978.

Goldstein, K. *Human Nature in the Light of Psychopathology.* Cambridge: Harvard University Press, 1947.

Grof, S., and Grof, J.H. *The Human Encounter with Death.* New York: E.P. Dutton Co., 1977.

Lilly, J.C. *The Center of the Cyclone.* New York: Bantam Books, 1973. (Originally Julian Press, 1972.)

Maslow, A.H. *Motivation and Personality.* New York: Harper and Brothers, 1954.

Murayama, M. Hetereogenetics: an epistemological restructuring of biological and social sciences. *Acta Boiotheretica,* 26: 120-137, 1977.

Pentony, P. Rogers' formative tendency: an epistemological perspective. University of Canberra, Australia. Unpublished mss., 1978.

Prigogine, I. *From Being to Becoming.* San Francisco: W.H. Freeman, 1979 (in press).

Rogers, C.R. A theory of therapy, personality, and interpersonal relationships. In S. Koch (ed.), *Psychology: A Study of a Science, Vol. III.* New York: McGraw-Hill, 1959, 184-256.

________. Toward becoming a fully functioning person. *Perceiving, Behaving, Becoming,* 1962 Yearbook, Assoc. for Supervision and Curriculum Dev. Washington, D.C.: National Education Association, 1962, 21-23.

________. The actualizing tendency in relation to "motives" and to consciousness. In Marshall Jones (ed.), *Nebraska Symposium on Motivation,* University of Nebraska Press, 1963, 1-24.

________. The formative tendency. *J. Humanistic Psychol.,* 18, No. 1, 1978, 23-26.

Szent-Gyoergi, A. Drive in living matter to perfect itself. *Synthesis,* Spring, 1974, 12-24.

Tausch, R. Facilitative dimensions in interpersonal relations: verifying the theoretical assumptions of Carl Rogers. *College Student Journal,* 12, No. 1, 1978. 2-11.

Whyte, L. *The Universe of Experience.* New York: Harper and Row, 1974.

PT's Survey Report on Friendship in America

THE FRIENDSHIP BOND

More than 40,000 readers told us what they looked for in close friendships, what they expected of friends, what they were willing to give in return, and how satisfied they were with the quality of their friendships. The results give cold comfort to social critics.

MARY BROWN PARLEE AND THE EDITORS OF *PSYCHOLOGY TODAY*

Mary Brown Parlee, a psychologist, is director of the Center for the Study of Women and Sex Roles at the Graduate Center of the City University of New York.

☐ Loyalty, warmth, and the ability to keep confidences are the qualities most valued in a friend; age, income, and occupation are less important.

☐ People who have frequently moved have fewer casual friends than people who have stayed put.

☐ Feeling betrayed by a friend is one of the most important reasons for ending a friendship.

☐ In a crisis, 51 percent of our sample say they would turn first to friends, not family.

☐ Thirty percent of women and 32 percent of men say they had sexual intercourse with a friend in the past month.

☐ Twenty-nine percent say they have a close friendship with someone who is a homosexual.

☐ Thirty-eight percent say they have close friends of a different racial group.

☐ Only 26 percent think career success interferes with friendship opportunities.

☐ Seventy-three percent agree that friendships with the opposite sex are different from those with the same sex.

☐ Thirteen percent would lie for a friend in a divorce proceeding.

Friendship appears to be a unique form of human bonding. Unlike marriage or the ties that bind parents and children, it is not defined or regulated by law. Unlike other social roles that we are expected to play—as citizens, employees, members of professional societies and other organizations—it has its own subjective rationale, which is to enhance feelings of warmth, trust, love, and affection between two people.

Feelings of friendship can develop within other roles, of course, as when coworkers begin to feel and act like friends, but such relationships grow more out of free choice than necessity. Because friendship lies outside—or transcends—the structured roles and institutions of society, it is a topic that allows an exploration of the ways that people relate to others at the times when they are most free.

The questionnaire on friendship that appeared in the March issue of *Psychology Today* presented such an opportunity. As far as we know, the survey is the first large-scale descriptive study of friendship completed in the 1970s; indeed, relatively few studies of friendship were done before then. The response was enthusiastic. We received more than 40,000 questionnaires from readers, one of the largest returns of all *Psychology Today* surveys. With the questionnaire forms, many readers offered comments on friendship, poems, and (at our invitation) descriptions of a single cherished friendship.

The findings—highlighted above—confirm that issues of trust and betrayal are central to friendship. They also suggest that our readers do not look for friends only among those who are most like them, but find many who differ in race, sexual preference, religion, and ethnic background. Arguably the most important conclusion that emerges from the data, however, is not something that we found—but what we did not find.

In books such as Vance Packard's *A Nation of Strangers*, social critics have pointed to the dislocation and isolation that they think grows out of the high mobility rate among Americans and a loss of community supports. Ever since the work of sociologist Émile Durkheim, they have described the impersonality and anomie of life in modern cities, where increasing numbers of people choose to live alone. They have written a good deal about a trend toward self-indulgence and lack of commitment in our society, which could very well lead to tensions in friendships just as it may be contributing to the divorce rate among married couples.

In the questionnaire responses, we looked for signs of dissatisfaction with the quality of people's friendships, but we found few. Do people confide in their friends these days? Do they tend to turn to them in times of emotional crises? Do friends become more important as one gets older? Turned around, all of these questions provide clues as to whether people today find deficits in their friendships. Most of the responses to our survey strongly

FRIENDS IN OUR SURVEY

The number of people answering the *PT* friendship questionnaire was too large for us to analyze every reply. We chose a random subsample by withdrawing every 10th response, in the order received. Here is a breakdown of that sample:

WOMEN	72%
MEN	28%

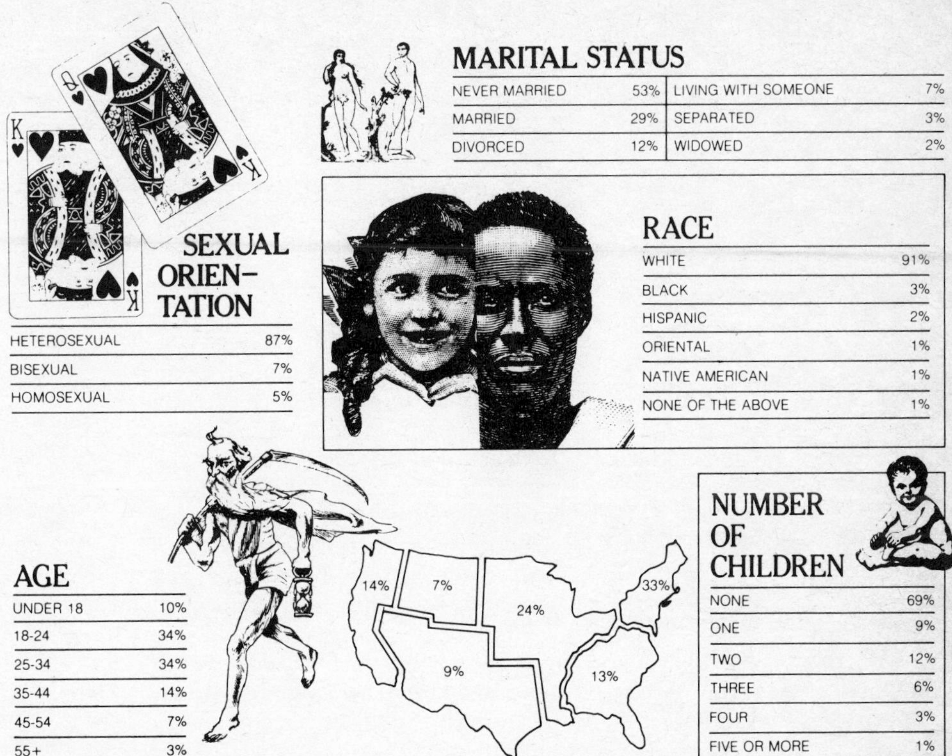

SEXUAL ORIENTATION

HETEROSEXUAL	87%
BISEXUAL	7%
HOMOSEXUAL	5%

MARITAL STATUS

NEVER MARRIED	53%	LIVING WITH SOMEONE	7%
MARRIED	29%	SEPARATED	3%
DIVORCED	12%	WIDOWED	2%

RACE

WHITE	91%
BLACK	3%
HISPANIC	2%
ORIENTAL	1%
NATIVE AMERICAN	1%
NONE OF THE ABOVE	1%

AGE

UNDER 18	10%
18-24	34%
25-34	34%
35-44	14%
45-54	7%
55+	3%

NUMBER OF CHILDREN

NONE	69%
ONE	9%
TWO	12%
THREE	6%
FOUR	3%
FIVE OR MORE	1%

EDUCATION

SOME HIGH SCHOOL	8%
HIGH SCHOOL DIPLOMA OR HIGH SCHOOL-EQUIVALENCY DIPLOMA	14%
SOME COLLEGE	31%
COLLEGE DEGREE	19%
SOME GRADUATE OR PROFESSIONAL SCHOOL	11%
GRADUATE OR PROFESSIONAL DEGREE	18%

POLITICAL VIEWS

	FOR	AGAINST
CAPITAL PUNISHMENT	53%	47%
ABORTION	70%	30%
THE EQUAL RIGHTS AMENDMENT	82%	18%
LEGALIZATION OF MARIJUANA	67%	33%
AFFIRMATIVE-ACTION PROGRAMS FOR MINORITIES AND WOMEN	82%	18%
PROPOSITION 13	59%	41%
NATIONAL HEALTH INSURANCE	72%	28%
GAY RIGHTS	71%	29%

OCCUPATION

PROFESSIONAL	31%
STUDENT	25%
CLERICAL WORKER	9%
EXECUTIVE OR MANAGER	8%
HOUSEWIFE	7%
FOREMAN OR SKILLED WORKER	4%
SALESPERSON	4%
SEMISKILLED OR UNSKILLED WORKER	3%
OTHER	9%

ATTITUDE TOWARD THE WOMEN'S LIBERATION MOVEMENT

VERY POSITIVE	31%
SOMEWHAT POSITIVE	40%
NEITHER POSITIVE NOR NEGATIVE	17%
SOMEWHAT NEGATIVE	10%
VERY NEGATIVE	3%

INCOME

LESS THAN $5,000	14%	$20,000-$29,999	18%
$5,000-$9,999	13%	$30,000-$49,999	15%
$10,000-$14,999	18%	$50,000-$99,999	6%
$15,000-$19,999	16%	$100,000+	1%

(Because the percentages are rounded off, they do not always add up to 100 percent.)

suggest they do not. When asked, for example, whether they felt that many of their friendships are not completely reciprocal, almost 60 percent answered no. At least among our readers and others like them, friendship in America appears to be in sound health.

In general, those who responded to the survey (for a breakdown of the survey sample, see box page 235) are representative of *Psychology Today* readers on every dimension but sex: women made up approximately 70 percent of the survey sample, while the sex ratio of our readers is closer to 50:50. Unfortunately, we cannot tell from survey data alone why proportionately more women responded; it is possible that either women are more likely in general to answer questionnaires, or there is something about the topic of friendship that is of greater interest to women than to men.

The respondents represent a range of educational, occupational, and income levels; they hold fairly liberal views on political issues. The majority (68 percent) are between the ages of 18 and 34, and over half are unmarried and as yet have no children.

The difficulty of capturing the essence of friendship in a survey was of particular concern to several readers. One wrote: "I don't think it can be taken apart, labeled, studied, and stuffed back together." Undoubtedly, there is something inexpressible about the feelings on which friendships are often based.

Art and poetry surely convey some of these feelings much more adequately than does scientific research. What science—and science alone—can do is allow us to find out in a systematic way what people expect from a friend, how they behave with friends, and what they think about friendship.

Qualities of Friends

The diversity among friends is revealed in the letters people wrote describing a close friendship. A partial list of people whom readers described as their best friends includes: a cousin, sister, fiancé, wife, husband, mother, boyfriend, college roommate, 83-year-old godmother, husband's grandmother, "a gay guy," "a person I took a total dislike to at first," and "a reflection of myself."

In the survey, people said they find it easy to distinguish between close and casual friends, and reported they have more close friends than casual ones. The majority of the respondents (68 percent) have between one and five close friends: those with more than 15 casual or work friends form a slightly smaller group, although still a majority (55 percent). Those with larger numbers of close friends than average also have larger numbers of casual friends, and were less likely to say they feel lonely.

A full 92 percent believe friendship is a form of love, and 77 percent say they would tell a friend that they love him or her. (Would the percentage have been that high if we had asked how many had actually received declarations of love from a friend?) Comparing friendship with love, slightly more respondents agree you can form friendships at first sight than say you can fall in love at first sight (52 percent compared with 39 percent), but the majority of the respondents (62 percent) believe that friendships end more gradually than love affairs.

Similarity—at least on the outside—is not what attracts friends to each other and keeps them together. About 38 percent of our sample report having close friends of a different racial group, while about 47 percent have close friends from a different ethnic or religious background. A slight majority of 55 percent say most of their close friends are of the same sex. Overall, the questionnaire responses are consistent with the letters describing actual friends, letters that indicate the ease and frequency with which friendships cut across social categories and boundaries.

Judging by the survey replies, readers believe that possible candidates for friendship are virtually limitless. Almost everyone seems to think it is possible to be friends with one's parents, children, bosses, or employees, someone one is romantically involved with, and (though there is less agreement here) former spouses or lovers. Many readers may know from their own experience that such friendships are not only possible but very satisfying as well.

Other people may think that such friendships ought to be possible, even if they don't know it from their own experience. One of the limitations of all questionnaire data, of course, is that there is no way of knowing whether people's responses reflect their true opinions, or are to some extent influenced by what they believe is socially desirable.

In their letters, readers were divided on the importance of similarity in friendship. Some said they think opposites attract, others said that at least some similarities of experience are important (going through the same life crises, for example). For one reader, the issue of similarity and friendship was a major concern: "My greatest disappointment in seeking friends . . . is that the groups I have been exposed to are made up of carbon-copy people. They don't share [just] one or two common interests, but *all* the same interests. Acceptance into a group depends on similarity in schedules, sports, crafts, home decor, children, religion, etc. I enjoy doing different things with different people . . . . I like to become more involved with a person than the social habits they identify with. I like to know how they feel about a lot of things."

When we asked our readers to tell us what qualities they believe to be important in a friend, they valued, above all, loyalty and the ability to keep confidences. Warmth, affection, and supportiveness were also high on the list, while external characteristics, such as age, income, and occupation, were not (see box page 237). Again, in the letters commenting on friendship in general, similar themes recurred: typical words and phrases were "trust," "honesty," "accepts me even when he doesn't totally approve," "supportive," and "understanding."

When we designed the survey, we decided to compare the qualities people thought important in a friend with their own estimate of how much they had those same qualities. We wanted to see whether people who regard themselves as independent, for example, value independence (or perhaps dependence) in their friends. People's descriptions of themselves, though, were uniformly positive.

For positive qualities, the majority of respondents rated themselves as "two's" on a scale of one (very) to five (not at all). Because of the impressive two-ness of our readership (or perhaps the very human tendency to put one's best foot forward even on an anonymous questionnaire), we could not reach conclusions about the relationship between the respondents' personalities and the qualities they value in their friends.

Some insight into what holds friendships together can be gained from looking at what drives them apart. When asked about reasons for a friendship's cooling off or ending, readers gave as the two most important reasons (aside from "One of us moved") feeling betrayed by a friend, and discovering that a friend had very different views on issues the respondent felt were important (see box page 238). The questionnaire answers thus confirm what many readers said explicitly in their comments: in a satisfying friendship, trust and feeling accepted are two of the most essential components.

Activities of Friendship

Given the importance of trust, it is not surprising that "Had an intimate talk" is the activity most or second-most frequently mentioned by both men and women as something they have done with friends in the past month. Two other items high on the list of activities also presuppose a certain amount of trust and involvement: helping out a friend and turning to a friend for help.

Social psychologists have proposed a link between trust and liking that seems to fit these friendship data. The theory suggests that trust encourages

INGREDIENTS OF FRIENDSHIP

"How important to you is each of these qualities in a friend?"

Numbers represent percentage of respondents who said a quality was "important" or "very important."

KEEPS CONFIDENCES	89%
LOYALTY	88%
WARMTH, AFFECTION	82%
SUPPORTIVENESS	76%
FRANKNESS	75%

SENSE OF HUMOR	74%
WILLINGNESS TO MAKE TIME FOR ME	62%
INDEPENDENCE	61%
GOOD CONVERSATIONALIST	59%
INTELLIGENCE	57%
SOCIAL CONSCIENCE	49%

SHARES LEISURE (NONCULTURAL) INTERESTS	48%
SHARES CULTURAL INTERESTS	30%
SIMILAR EDUCATIONAL BACKGROUND	17%

ABOUT MY AGE	10%
PHYSICAL ATTRACTIVENESS	9%
SIMILAR POLITICAL VIEWS	8%

PROFESSIONAL ACCOMPLISHMENT	8%
ABILITIES AND BACKGROUND DIFFERENT FROM MINE	8%
ABILITY TO HELP ME PROFESSIONALLY	7%
SIMILAR INCOME	4%
SIMILAR OCCUPATION	3%

self-disclosure (revealing aspects of yourself that are both precious and vulnerable). If self-disclosure meets with continued acceptance (not necessarily the same as approval of the feelings or actions), liking and affection deepen—as well as trust. In this theory, self-disclosure and trust must be reciprocated in order for the relationship to deepen.

Two letters from readers illustrate different facets of this trust/self-disclosure/liking cycle. One noted: "The definite and observable switch from a casual to a close friendship came about when my friend told me something about herself she felt I would disapprove of. After leaving the safe ground of constant agreement, our true feelings and thoughts flowed without the normal hesitancy one has with a casual friend or acquaintance." Another reported: "My closest friend asked for advice, which I gave and which turned out to be good. However, the friendship is not the same, because it bothers her that I know about the problem and its resolution. . . . The problem was due to a course of action she took that I can understand and sympathize with but cannot condone. It bothers me that she took that course . . . and the bother always nags at the back of my mind when I think of her or when I see her. [Now] I think less of her."

One might expect that men engage in quite different activities with friends than women do; for example, men might fit the stereotype of drinking buddies. Likewise, women might fit the cliché of indulging in gossip. Judging from our readers' answers, however, sex-role stereotypes are not a good way to predict men's and women's behavior with friends. With the notable exception of "Gone shopping with a friend" (which women say they do more than men), men's and women's reports of what they did with friends in the past month are surprisingly similar—both in actual percentages, and when the activities are ranked by the percentages of men or of women who say they engaged in them (see box, page 239).

For all that, 73 percent agree that friendships with someone of the opposite sex are different from same-sex friendships. A major reason given for the difference is that sexual tensions complicate the relationship; other reasons included having less in common with the opposite sex and the fact that society does not encourage such friendships. Almost half the respondents (49 percent) have had a friendship turn into a sexual relationship, and nearly a third (31 percent) reported having had sexual intercourse with a friend in the past month.

WHEN FRIENDSHIP COOLS
"Which, if any, of the following has led to a friendship's cooling off or ending?" The most frequently checked reasons, in order, were:
ONE OF US MOVED.
I FELT THAT MY FRIEND BETRAYED ME.
WE DISCOVERED THAT WE HAD VERY DIFFERENT VIEWS ON ISSUES THAT ARE IMPORTANT TO ME.
ONE OF US GOT MARRIED.
MY FRIEND BECAME INVOLVED WITH (OR MARRIED) SOMEONE I DIDN'T LIKE.
A FRIEND BORROWED MONEY FROM ME.
WE TOOK A VACATION TOGETHER.
ONE OF US HAD A CHILD.
ONE OF US BECAME MARKEDLY MORE SUCCESSFUL AT WORK.
I GOT DIVORCED.
MY FRIEND GOT DIVORCED.
ONE OF US BECAME MUCH RICHER.
I BORROWED MONEY FROM A FRIEND.

Rules of Friendship

In addition to inquiring about actual activities, we asked some specific questions about what people would or would not do with friends, both in general and in certain hypothetical situations. (For some respondents, of course, the "hypothetical" may actually have occurred.) We wanted our survey to give us an idea of some of the "rules" that govern, or perhaps define, behavior between friends.

As both theory and the data suggest, one rule of friendship is that friends confide in each other, sharing intimate aspects of their personal lives and feelings. Perhaps most significantly, bad as well as good news can be shared. Even though in our society, one's success is often equated with success at work, 89 percent of our sample said they would tell a close friend about a failure at work. Furthermore, over two-thirds (68 percent) said that if they had a terminal illness, they would tell a friend. Eighty-seven percent of the respondents say they talk with friends about sexual activities (60 percent discussing activities in general, 27 percent in detail). Completely inexplicably, respondents from Jewish backgrounds were more likely to talk about sexual activities in detail (35 percent) than were respondents from Catholic or Protestant backgrounds (25 and 26 percent).

According to the rules of friendship, friends confide more than facts about their personal lives. They also share their intimate feelings about each other. For example, 54 percent say they sometimes talk with friends about the quality of the friendship. Another 19 percent say they do so often, compared with 44 percent who reported they have such discussions with spouses and lovers often. It is impossible to tell from these responses whether the difference means that relations with a spouse or lover are more important than relations between friends—or that they are more problematic.

Our respondents clearly indicated that in some situations, the rules of friendship involve the right to ask for help (presumably the obligation to help a friend is also implicitly acknowledged). When asked who they would turn to first in a crisis, over half (51 percent) said they would turn to friends before family. This was true for all subgroups, even though older people in the sample said they tend to rely more on family and professional counselors in a crisis than do the younger age groups, and a higher proportion of men than women said they go it alone.

Yet friendship has limits. Only 10 percent of the sample said they thought a friend should help another commit suicide if the friend wanted to but was too feeble to do it alone (41 percent said no and 36 percent were opposed to suicide).

In short, there are no striking contradictions between people's descriptions of actual friendships, their beliefs about friendship in general, and their perception of the rules that apply to these relationships. This consistency, and the glowing descriptions of friends and friendship we received, suggest that our readers are satisfied with their friendships, even though 67 percent of the respondents also acknowledge feeling lonely "sometimes" or "often" (see box page 240).

Lasting Friendships

Asked how and when they had met most of their close friends, readers reported most frequently that such friendships began in childhood. Next in order of frequency were close friendships that originated in college, and through friends of friends.

Only slightly more than one-fourth of our sample (26 percent) agree that professional success reduces the opportunities for friendship. Life at the top (at least as it is measured by income) seems to promote an even more optimistic view of friendship opportunities: people with incomes of over $100,000 generally disagree more than others that it's lonely at the top.

Friendships do not end because one friend becomes more successful at

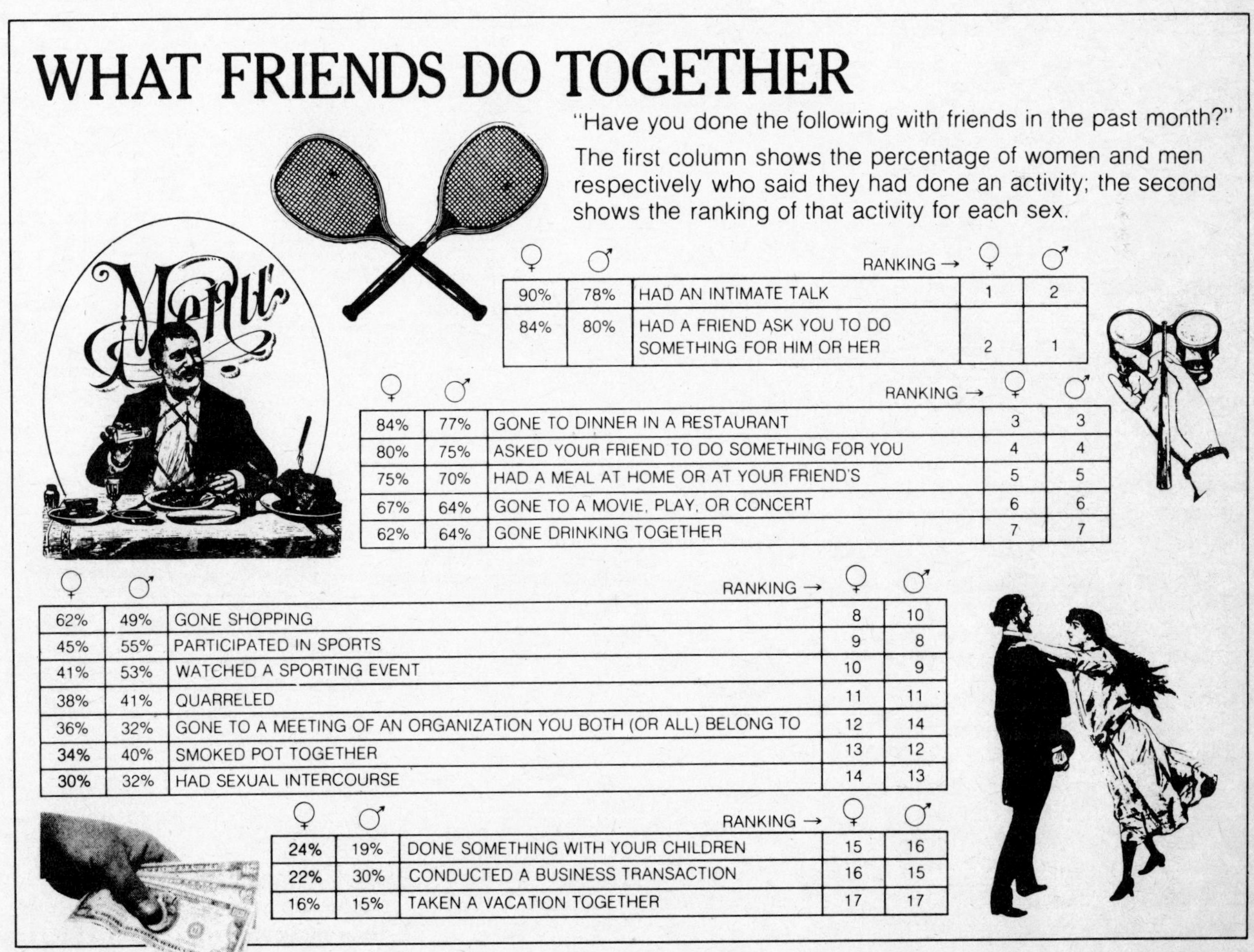

WHAT FRIENDS DO TOGETHER

"Have you done the following with friends in the past month?"

The first column shows the percentage of women and men respectively who said they had done an activity; the second shows the ranking of that activity for each sex.

♀	♂		RANKING → ♀	♂
90%	78%	HAD AN INTIMATE TALK	1	2
84%	80%	HAD A FRIEND ASK YOU TO DO SOMETHING FOR HIM OR HER	2	1
84%	77%	GONE TO DINNER IN A RESTAURANT	3	3
80%	75%	ASKED YOUR FRIEND TO DO SOMETHING FOR YOU	4	4
75%	70%	HAD A MEAL AT HOME OR AT YOUR FRIEND'S	5	5
67%	64%	GONE TO A MOVIE, PLAY, OR CONCERT	6	6
62%	64%	GONE DRINKING TOGETHER	7	7
62%	49%	GONE SHOPPING	8	10
45%	55%	PARTICIPATED IN SPORTS	9	8
41%	53%	WATCHED A SPORTING EVENT	10	9
38%	41%	QUARRELED	11	11
36%	32%	GONE TO A MEETING OF AN ORGANIZATION YOU BOTH (OR ALL) BELONG TO	12	14
34%	40%	SMOKED POT TOGETHER	13	12
30%	32%	HAD SEXUAL INTERCOURSE	14	13
24%	19%	DONE SOMETHING WITH YOUR CHILDREN	15	16
22%	30%	CONDUCTED A BUSINESS TRANSACTION	16	15
16%	15%	TAKEN A VACATION TOGETHER	17	17

work, say 90 percent of the sample. We might speculate that time at work interferes with time for friends ("Willingness to make time for me" is considered an important quality in a friend), but otherwise work and friendship do not seem to conflict. The fact that "Ability to help me professionally" is not believed to be an important quality in a friend suggests that any positive connection between work and friends is not simply a matter of mutual back-scratching.

The stability of childhood friendships seems somewhat surprising, given the geographic mobility of the respondents. Forty-six percent of them have moved two or more times in the past five years, and 48 percent of them moved at least that often before they were 16 years old.

Other data support the suggestion that networks of friends develop from psychological rather than physical closeness, a suggestion that is getting increasing confirmation in the research of sociologist Claude Fischer. Although in TV-land, the neighborhood has traditionally been portrayed as a source of close friends, in real life our readers ranked the neighborhood fifth in importance as a place where friendships start. Fewer than half as many people cite neighborhood than cite childhood as a source.

Close friendships can transcend geographic distance and persist over time with impressive robustness. A full 97 percent of our respondents say they have friends they don't see often. Seventy-two percent of them keep in touch by phone and 33 percent by means of regular reunions once or twice a year. (Many respondents indicated they keep in touch by more than one means, so these percentages do not add up to 100.) Future historians will be pleased to note that the epistolary tradition is far from dead: 70 percent of our sample say they keep in touch with absent friends by letter.

Although people take active steps to stay in touch with their friends, friendship is clearly a relationship that is valued for its special quality rather than frequency or mode of contact. A full third of the sample have friends they don't keep in touch with at all. One unusually optimistic reader put it this way: "When we meet again 100 years from now, we are certain to feel close and be able to pick up where we left off as though no separation had occurred."

The majority of our respondents (82 percent) report that their oldest close friendship is one they've had for more than six years, with a hefty 22 percent reporting close friendships of longer

WHO FEELS LONELY

Percentage of respondents who said they feel lonely "sometimes" or "often."

WOMEN 67%
MEN 67%

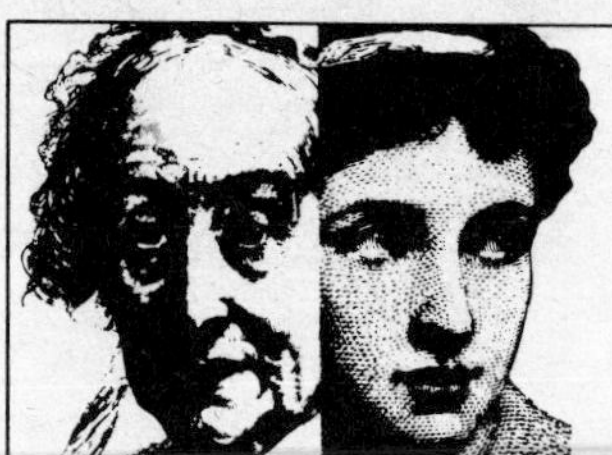

AGE

UNDER 18	79%	35-44	60%
18-24	71%	45-54	53%
25-34	69%	55+	37%

SEXUAL ORIENTATION

HETEROSEXUAL	66%
BISEXUAL	73%
HOMOSEXUAL	72%

INCOME

LESS THAN $5,000	70%	$20,000-$29,999	60%
$5,000-$9,999	73%	$30,000-$49,999	57%
$10,000-$14,999	74%	$50,000-$99,999	54%
$15,000-$19,999	69%	$100,000+	55%

MARITAL STATUS

NEVER MARRIED	72%	LIVING WITH SOMEONE	62%
SEPARATED	70%	WIDOWED	59%
DIVORCED	68%	MARRIED	56%

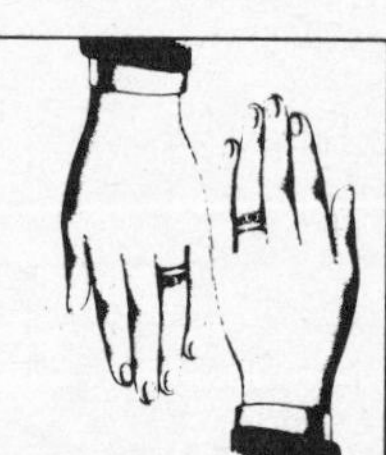

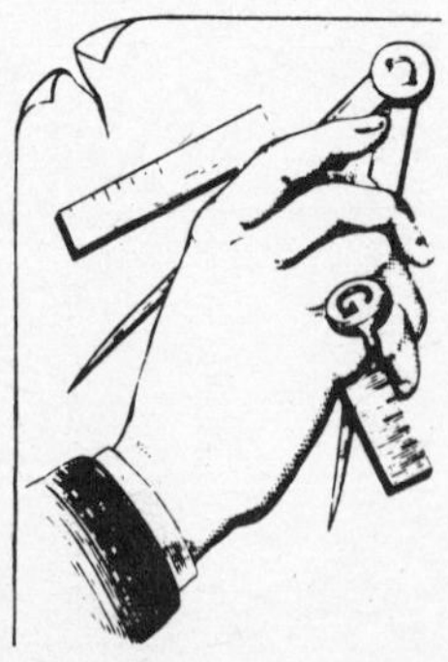

OCCUPATION

SEMISKILLED OR UNSKILLED WORKER	80%
STUDENT	69%
CLERICAL WORKER	69%
SALESPERSON	67%
HOUSEWIFE	65%
PROFESSIONAL	64%
FOREMAN OR SKILLED WORKER	62%
EXECUTIVE OR MANAGER	61%
OTHER	70%

than 20 years. About 66 percent of our sample say that friendship has become more important to them as they grow older, but this sentiment is less common among people with incomes over $100,000 and among those with high educational levels.

Cutting Across Cultures

The picture of friendship that emerges from our survey is surprisingly consistent, holding true almost regardless of the respondents' sex, race, or geographic location. A very different finding might have been predicted. Sociologists and historians, not to mention common sense and everyday observation, tell us that the experiences a person has are in many ways determined by that person's sex, race, religion, and the region of the country where he or she lives. Such differences could very well lead to differences in the way people think about all of the important aspects of living, including friendship.

In our survey, however, friendship—what it is like, the rules governing behavior among friends, and beliefs about it—seems to be a common denominator of experience that cuts across major social categories. This consistency could, of course, mean that we simply didn't ask the "right" questions—assuming there are questions that would have been answered differently by different groups. We think, however, that the questions were varied enough so that major differences would have been found if they exist. Although psychologists are generally reluctant to conclude that no differences exist (since real ones may not have been tapped by the questions), readers' responses to our survey do suggest that in many ways, friendship is not only a deeply satisfying experience, but a universal one as well.

For further information, read:

Brain, Robert. *Friends and Lovers*, Basic Books, 1976, $10.95.

Brenton, Myron. *Friendship*, Stein & Day, 1974, $6.95; paper, $2.45.

Fischer, Claude, et al. *Networks and Places: Social Relations in the Urban Setting*, The Free Press, 1977, $14.95.

Kahn, Robert L. and Toni Antonucci. "Convoys Over the Life Course: Attachment, Roles and Social Support," Institute for Social Research, University of Michigan, Ann Arbor, Mich.

ALONE
Yearning for Companionship in America

Louise Bernikow

Louise Bernikow, the author of "Among Women," frequently writes and lectures on human behavior.

Jasper Evian is the pen name of a New York author, divorced 10 years ago. His daughter moved with his former wife to California, and Jasper's longing for his child is constant and dull, like a toothache. In spite of a web of connections to friends, business associates and transient lovers, Jasper suddenly has begun waking up at 4 in the morning consumed by loneliness. "My ambition," he says, "is wholly personal now. I can't understand people pursuing worldly success. All I want to do is fall in love."

Linda, a Dallas bank executive, is driving home on the freeway. She had had a busy day at the office, handled a tricky negotiation, lunched with a colleague, dined with clients. It took years to achieve her current position as the highest-placed woman in the bank. She plans to work at home on Sunday, but she still thinks of Sundays as family days and being alone then is like being a dateless teen-ager on Saturday night. "I've become a workaholic because I'm so lonely," she admits privately.

For several years, drugs were Antonio Rico Harris's best friends. He started smoking marijuana and snorting cocaine, moved on to smoking cocaine and taking angel dust. At Tuum Est, a drug-rehabilitation center on the beach in Venice, Calif., Antonio, 20, puts his hands through his groomed Afro and stretches a basketball-player body on a couch. He has been without drugs for seven months. "People look at me and say, 'What's wrong? You look mad.' I'm not. It just feels like I'm the only person in the world."

□

As early as the 1830's, Alexis de Tocqueville wrote about the loneliness of Americans, describing the citizens of this country as "locked in the solitude of their own hearts." The dictionary defines loneliness as "an absence of companionship or society," but anyone who has ever been lonely—and that's just about everyone—knows that it is not quite so simple. People can be lonely in isolation or lonely in a crowd; lonely because they have no one to be with or lonely because they are with someone they can no longer reach.

Yet Americans are also more than a little ambivalent about loneliness. We view it as something to admire as much as avoid. You can hardly say "cowboy," that venerated American archetype, without adding "lonesome." The private eye, another idealized American hero, is almost always a loner. School-children are taught to respect Thoreau for going without "companionship or society" at Walden Pond. "The courage to stand alone" is a long-standing American virtue. Self-made men who battle to victory in business without aid or comfort are pointed out for emulation. (Women are not as often praised, in our history, for going it alone.)

A growing number of social scientists and mental-health professionals are now studying contemporary American loneliness. Some say that we are more lonely than in the past; others argue that we just think we are. More persuasive is the evidence that the physical and emotional consequences of loneliness pose greater dangers than anyone thought. Dr. Stephen E. Goldston, director of the Office of Prevention at the National Institute of Mental Health in Washington, an organization not known for its interest in subjects of merely philosophical value, believes that "persistent and severe" loneliness can lead to alcoholism, drug abuse and suicide. Recently, his office convened a conference to raise the question of whether such loneliness can be prevented or cured.

And loneliness may have a larger impact on society than we have realized. "We must do something about any circumstances in which a person can say, 'No one knows who I am or cares to know,' " says Dr. Philip G. Zimbardo, a psychologist at Stanford University. "For anyone in such a predicament can turn into a vandal, an assassin or a terrorist." The most recent example that comes to mind is that of John W. Hinckley Jr., the wandering loner who pined for the love of a movie star and shot a President just to get her attention.

Current research reveals that the people who are loneliest don't necessarily fit the popular stereotypes. Adolescents appear to be more plagued by loneliness than anyone else; older people, surprisingly, may be less so. Homosexuals may be no more prone to loneliness than heterosexuals. Success seems to offer scant protection against loneliness—especially for women. Geography has little to do with it either. Social psychologists Carin Rubenstein and Philip Shaver surveyed several rural communities and large metropolises and found no less loneliness in the small friendly towns than in the big, unfriendly cities.

It is not that people have become more isolated in any tangible way. On the contrary, electronic communications and jet-age transportation have made it possible to stay in closer contact than ever before. Rather, there is a sense that our connections are somehow inadequate. The cause of this dissatisfaction is elusive. To some extent, experts say, it has to do with the ascendance of a culture that places so much emphasis on acquiring possessions and status that most people devote little time or energy to forming and maintaining relationships. Exaggerated expectations created by the idealized versions of life on television, in films and in the scores of "self-help" books on the best-seller lists may also play a role. And because of increasing freedom and mobility, ties to spouses, family, church and community unravel more easily.

□

The America de Tocqueville traveled through was a rural country in which the ties holding people together were essentially those of family and community. Some of the current alarm stems from looking at the 1980 census and seeing how complete the progressive dissolution of those ties now seems to be. More people live alone today than ever before: almost one fourth of the population. Within this group are a large number of people under 40 who, for a variety of reasons, have chosen not to marry. The women in this group are often the first women in their families to live alone. A generation earlier, they would have become housewives; now they are working or going to school instead. Pursuing a career undoubtedly brings many women new fulfillment. But it may also take a toll that, until recently, has gone largely unexamined.

Many of those who live alone are divorced, separated or widowed, and the rising number of people in this category is also a cause for concern. America's divorce rate is not only the highest in the world, it is also the highest it has ever been: One out of every two marriages now fails. One out of five children lives with only one parent. One out of eight children in a two-parent family lives with one natural parent and one stepparent.

Because life expectancy is increasing, there are more people over 65 than ever before. Currently, they make up 11.3 percent of the population. More than a third of this group are widows, many living alone on limited incomes. In the past, people over 65 with children and grandchildren lived with them or near them. Today, that is uncommon.

Economic conditions have made matters even worse. However alienated people may feel from their work, those who don't have it are likely to be much more lonely than those who do. When mental-health experts point to the stress that unemployment puts on individuals and families, they talk about depression and self-blame, which often accompany feelings of loneliness. In Cleveland, for example, the population has declined 23.6 percent in the past 10 years because of dwindling economic opportunity. Joe Stevens, driving his cab between the airport and a major downtown hotel, says Cleveland has become an especially lonely place for him. One son moved to Houston two years ago and another is planning to go soon. Neither wanted to leave, but neither could find work at home.

Ordinary people cope with loneliness in ordinary ways. They keep the radio or the television on for company. They smile back at the anchorman on the evening news when he says, "See you tomorrow." For companionship and society, they turn to soap operas that offer the illusion of involvement in other people's daily lives. People take tranquilizers and go to bed, read or go to a movie, join churches, evangelical movements or even cults, buy things they don't really want, go to doctors more often than necessary and dial the weather report just to hear a friendly voice. They think loneliness is to be lived with, like the weather. They don't think they are in danger.

Dr. James J. Lynch, a specialist in psychosomatic disease at the University of Maryland School of Medicine, thinks they are wrong. Loneliness is dangerous, he believes especially to the heart. A broken heart, Dr. Lynch argues, is not a metaphor. His 1977 book, "The Broken Heart: The Medical Consequences of Loneliness," made frightening connections between lack of human companionship and heart disease. A nurse's hand can slow a patient's pounding pulse; the simple routine of pulse-taking often clams arrhythmic heartbeats. People often develop heart ailments when they lose love or companionship. "The rise of human loneliness," he concludes, "may be one of the most serious sources of disease in the 20th century."

Since then, Dr. Lynch has been studying other "loneliness diseases," especially hypertension and migraine headaches. In each case, he has found connections between loneliness and illness. His hypertensive patients experienced a steep rise in blood pressure whenever they spoke to anyone. "These people are out of contact with what is going on. It's like a baby crying inside an adult. Where there is real communication," he adds, "there is no physiological disruption."

"Pain turned inward," is Dr. Lynch's medical definition of loneliness, and "ruptured patterns of discourse." We are experiencing an epidemic of this, he says, and you see it "especially in self-destructive diseases like cigarette smoking and drinking."

Dr. Robert N. Bellah, a Berkeley sociologist, sees the epidemic as a continuation of national tradition, intensified by recent history. A team of interviewers under his direction has been asking people what they believe in and finding that we still hold certain truths to be self-evident.

"Personal freedom, autonomy and independence are the highest values for Americans," Dr. Bellah says.

"You're responsible for yourself. We place a high value on being left alone, on not being interfered with. The most important thing is to be able to take care of yourself. As soon as possible, we believe, a child should take care of itself. It's illegitimate to depend on another human being." People no longer have communities to which they are irrevocably tied, Dr. Bellah adds. "Communities are chosen, not given. They're brittle, fragile, with a tremendous turnover." And few people are happy with this situation. In fact, Americans are awash in nostalgia for old-fashioned families and small, tightknit communities. Individualism is "a terrifying demand," Dr. Bellah says. Throughout the country, he finds, "there is an element of loneliness not far below the surface."

□

There are profits to be made from all this loneliness. The promise of companionship and society sells everything from banking services ("You have a friend at Chase Manhattan") to real estate (a road sign outside Houston advertising a condominium promises, "You won't be a stranger for long"). The telephone company's advertising aims directly at the lonely. If you want to "reach out and touch someone," you'll have to pay for a long-distance telephone call.

A large and growing industry promises romantic companionship for a price. Increasing numbers of single people are willing to pay $400 or more to subscribe to video dating services. Intro, the first national singles magazine, claims an initial circulation of 100,000. To serve an obviously growing market, a black magazine, Chocolate Singles, has recently been launched as well. In New York, Dr. Martin V. Gallatin, a sociologist, teaches an adult-education course on "Lover Shopping at Bloomingdale's" and is organizing a lecture called "Be Your Own Matchmaker."

Such high-priced courses and the video dating operations are popular largely because they promise efficiency. Why waste time wading through the unsuitables life turns up when for a few dollars more you can preselect your potential partners? This logic appeals to Frank Matticola, who came to Two's Company, a Houston video dating service, because, he says, he had his "priorities." Two's Company recently opened its doors in a complex not far from the fashionable Galleria area. It's in a one-story row of new buildings and looks as fresh and spare as a dentist's office. Frank is 36, twice divorced, a bit overweight, with a receding hairline and an open face. In his three months in Houston, where he moved from New Jersey, he has taken care of two priorities. First, he got a job as a production superintendent in the oil industry. Second, he found an apartment at Tennis World, a singles complex right near the Two's Company office. This is his first day off in 10 weeks and he has come to take care of his third priority.

He wants "someone to share my free time with, which is very little." As Frank talks, his face softens, the coldness in his language gives way. Frank doesn't want anyone to know it, but he is lonely. Sheepishly, he makes what he thinks is an unfashionable confession: "I miss being married. You get home early and you'd like to have someone there. It's harder after you have been married."

JoAnn is filling out her application in another room. She is 33, has springy blonde curls and half-giggles whenever she speaks. This subject makes her nervous. She has just moved to Houston from Oklahoma, where she was a sales representative. "I didn't know one person," she says, "and I traveled the whole state. I'd come back into Oklahoma City on Friday night and I'd be in my apartment, throwing myself on the floor sobbing, until Monday morning, when I left to go back out on the road." She asked for a transfer. Now, she says, "all the guys I work with are old and married. I just want somebody else to be part of my life. I've thought of adopting as a single parent. I do want more than I have now, whether it be a child or a husband."

She thinks she knows what kind of man would make her feel less alone: "A nice guy with a sense of humor, someone sensitive." Other women enrolled in the service have filled out questionnaires in which they, too, talk about "sensitivity," "being able to express his feelings" and "warmth" as important qualities in a man.

"But JoAnn," her friend Barbara, who has also come to enroll, interrupts, "you would never date a man who makes less than you, would you?"

"No."

Therein lies a cross fire between the sexes, a stalemate in expectations that explains, in part, why so many men and women who say they are lonely and looking for companionship never seem to find it. JoAnn wants a "New Man," a sensitive, nurturing fellow, and an "Old Man," a powerful breadwinner, at the same time. Frank wants a woman who will be there when he gets home, but most of the women he will meet through Two's Company are professional and ambitious and likely to be working late at their own offices. The manager of Two's Company says that most of the men who go there prefer "independent women—no "born-again housewives." But further probing reveals that while they may not want to pay all the bills, they are still uncomfortable with many of the consequences of female independence.

Dr. Sol Landau sees the same stalemate at his Mid-Life Services Foundation, an organization he has just set up in an office building near Dadeland, in South Miami. A hearty, expansive man, Dr. Landau had been a practicing rabbi for 17 years. Now, he mostly counsels people in "midlife" and finds the lack of companionship between husbands and wives a direct consequence of the women's movement and the inability of men to change. "Men need to be mentors," he says, "and they're married to women who now need to throw off their mentors. The men I see are threatened by their wives working or going to school. They can still only function from the throne."

Unable to attach themselves seriously to someone else, often because men and women don't know what to expect of each other anymore, a lot of people immerse themselves in their work. The most acute loneliness Dr. Landau sees is in "the most successful men, workaholics, men unconnected to their personal lives." But an increasing number of women now fall into this category as well.

In Houston, Dr. Dale Hill's therapy practice is made up almost exclusively of professional women who see loneliness as their greatest problem. In rural Massachusetts, Dr. Frances Lippman, a clinical psychologist, says the same: "The women I see still feel that deep loneliness about meeting somebody, no matter how successful they are."

□

When researchers note that women say they are lonely far more often than men do, they interpret this, in part, as a greater willingness on the part of women to talk about feelings, but it also suggests different expectations of companionship and intimacy. In a recent survey of adolescents prepared for the National Institute of Mental Health, 61.3 percent of the girls, as opposed to 46.5 percent of the boys, said they were lonely.

When the Berkeley sociologist Claude Fischer asked adults whom they talked with about personal matters and whose opinion they considered in making important decisions, he found that women, married or not, were likely to have several confidants. Many unmarried men said the same, but a substantial number indicated that they had no one in whom they could confide. The most significant difference, however, was that married men usually named only their wives as confidants. And the older a man was, the less likely he was to have a friend or relative in whom to confide.

Adolescents, more than others, complain that they feel as if the world were away for the weekend and never coming back. No one to talk to. No one who cares. Dr. Harvey Greenberg, a specialist in adolescent psychiatry and a professor at the Albert Einstein College of Medicine in New York, believes loneliness in adolescents stems from "a breakdown of family, the fact that there are now lots of only children, lots of older parents and working mothers." Some girls are getting pregnant to "have a baby to take care of as protection against loneliness."

Although a large measure of loneliness is normal in adolescence—"the specific psychological task of adolescence is mourning the loss of the omnipotent parent"—Dr. Greenberg finds today's teen-agers "encouraged by a garbage culture with no values, nothing to latch onto; they're preoccupied with themselves. Kids need a mentor or patron. Teachers used to do this, but they do it less now because they're worn down, angry, bitter and paranoid." Dr. Greenberg adds that loneliness in adolescents is an important factor in the increase in teen-age suicide, which has risen 300 percent over the last 25 years.

The elderly, on the other hand, may not be as badly off as we expect. A Harris poll conducted last year showed that 65 percent of nonelderly persons considered loneliness "a serious problem" for the aged. But only 13 percent of people over 65 agreed. This may have something to do with lessening expectations in old age. But it may also show, according to Dr. Anne Peplau, a psychologist at the University of California at Los Angeles, that "older adults value privacy and independence. They view living alone as an achievement rather than a sign of rejection by others." Friends, she says, are more important to older people, in terms of companionship, than children or relatives. Indeed, several studies have found greater loneliness among single elderly people living with relatives than among those who live alone or with friends.

Dr. Peplau, who has been studying loneliness and aging, finds gender differences significant in terms of how people handle loneliness. "Men rely on wives and girlfriends for social relationships, for intimacy. If their wives die before they do, men are in trouble. Women usually have both a heterosexual relationship and a reliance on friends. They seem to keep making friends throughout the life cycle. If friends die or move away, women replace them. Men don't as often."

Dr. Peplau thinks women have greater social skills and are better able than men to adjust to widowhood and old age. Four women at Wynmoor Village, a retirement community in Cocoanut Creek, Fla.—all widowed and in their 60's—don't necessarily agree. It's small comfort to them to know that men in their circumstances stand a greater chance of becoming ill or dying.

"I walk into the apartment, close the door and something happens to me," Honey Albert says. "I feel nauseous. It's not because I don't have friends. I can be with you all day," she tells Gloria Winetsky, "and I'm still lonely."

Gloria Winetsky shifts on the couch. Her experience is different. She is not lonely and she thinks that a large part of the reason is that she was less dependent on her husband when he was alive than her friends were on theirs. She arrived in Florida thinking, "Here is where you pick up your life," and she has done it. She is self-reliant and generally pleased with the quality of her friendships.

Shirley Moses, an energetic, dark-haired woman, is pouring coffee. "Your children don't take away your loneliness," she says, "only your contemporaries." But her contemporaries don't seem able to do it, in fact. "I play cards with eight people and none of them gives a damn about me," she admits. "You can't ever find a place for yourself on Sunday." The others agree.

"The worst loneliness is going out with couples,"

Shirley Moses says, "You feel part of you is missing." As a result, these women stay away from the organized activities at Wynmoor Village that attract couples. Married women, they say, don't want them around. They're guarding their husbands.

When Honey Albert moved to Florida, she said to herself: "I'm not going to spend the rest of my life alone in an apartment." She went to the swimming pool and introduced herself to everyone. One of the women laughs as Honey Albert tells of dashed expectations and failed resolve. Didn't she put up signs, too, inviting people to coffee? Honey denies it.

Listening to the widows argue, it is clear how easily discouraged anyone can be when attempts to break out of loneliness find no support; how much simpler it might seem to resign yourself to a life alone in your apartment.

□

Our increasing loneliness is not only a yearning for companionship. People feel alone when they don't belong to something larger, when they don't feel connected to a "family" or a "community."

"A lot of men not raising their kids," says Dr. Paul Lippmann, a New England psychoanalyst, "are so lonely for those kids, but they have all kinds of tricks not to think about it." Although people often marry or have children to avoid loneliness, family therapists are concerned about the widespread inability of parents to be intimate with either each other or their children. Guy Berley, a family therapist at the Johnson County Mental Health Facility outside Kansas City, Kan., calls it "distancing behavior"—children putting themselves at a remove from their parents, and parents from their children. Working mothers, however, don't seem to him to cause or experience increased loneliness in their families. "It can be a good thing," he says. "The women are making a needed economic contribution to the family and they feel better about themselves."

Working has traditionally offered opportunities for companionship and society, but increasing numbers of people work alone and some suffer immensely because of it. This was made clear one recent sunny Sunday morning in Houston. Volunteers were answering the crisis-line telephone in a small, partitioned office. Most of the volunteers had come to work at the crisis line because they were new to town and this was their way of being around other people.

A man called, weeping. He didn't give his name. His wife, he said, had left him because "I blew up and hit her." The volunteer on the telephone suggested he find someone to talk to, perhaps a friend at work. He was silent. Then he said, "I can't. Where I work I stare at dials all day. There's no one around."

Gilley's bar is just outside Houston, in Pasadena. In the movie "Urban Cowboy," John Travolta enjoyed a lot of companionship and society at Gilley's, competitive though it was. Now someone at the door takes a few dollars from you and you bump almost immediately into a row of video games. You can't buddy up to the bar—there is no space around it—but you can hide out alone with Pac-Man. Or you can hover around the edges of the dance floor while the band plays "Cotton-Eyed Joe"—which is what Bob White is doing.

Trim, wearing high-heeled boots, tight shirt and jeans, White looks like a lonesome cowboy but is, in fact, an enterprising furniture trucker out of North Carolina. He has a wife back home and he sees her about every two week. Nights on the road, he goes stir-crazy with loneliness. "I lay up in the Days Inn Motel with the TV on and I can't stop thinking about my first wife leaving me and maybe this one's going to leave and I've got to get out and be around where there's people." Why, then, stay on the road? "Because I wouldn't make even $5 an hour back in North Carolina."

Thomas J. Peters is wearing running shoes and swiveling back and forth in his chair. He has a small office on the third floor of the Stanford Business School, where he lectures, and he knows a lot about loneliness in American business. The "unbelievable and deep-felt need to be part of something is rarely met in the working world," he says. The few corporations that do meet this need are the best-run companies in America. The "magic," he says, "at I.B.M., Hewlett-Packard or Procter & Gamble comes from creating a sense of community or family."

Peters thinks the Japanese do much better at making workers feel part of the community at work. As a result, "you've got Honda workers racing around straightening out windshield wipers in their free time while General Motors workers sit silently watching a piece of junk go by and don't do anything about it because they know they won't be listened to."

"Look at middle management in the auto industry," Peters says. "There are five layers between the first line worker and the chairman at Toyota, and there are 17 at Ford. Middle management has no job. You're sitting there manipulating numbers, going bug-eyed looking at the computer display, worrying about abstractions like profits and writing reports to ace out the people next to you. It's bound to be a god-awful lonely existence."

Companies create a sense of family, Peters says, "with hokey stuff, Mickey Mouse things like company picnics." Like Tupperware holding a weekly ceremony in which almost all its saleswomen win awards. Or the I.B.M. sales branch that staged an event at the Meadowlands in New Jersey, the sales force running through the players' entrance, their names in lights on the big board. "I.B.M.," Peters says, "probably gives its employees more community within the corporate environment than most of us have outside where we work. You move from I.B.M., San Jose, to I.B.M., Armonk, N.J., and you probably don't know you've moved, except for the temperature difference."

□

People concerned about loneliness talk in terms of

disease. They speak of a nationwide "epidemic." They search for a cure. But the desert seems a more appropriate metaphor. And out there in the desert of eroding families and unfulfilled hunger to connect with other people, oases are being discovered or built.

Crystal Lugo found one. She lived in a section of East Los Angeles that, she says, "was all retired people. There was no one to talk to." She watched soap operas and talked on the telephone. Then her marriage broke up and she was left with a 4-month-old daughter. A social worker told her about the community's Displaced Homemaker's Program. Now, she is learning office skills, but she is also learning how to be with people. "The people in the program are all used to staying home. We're scared. We don't have any confidence." This is a precarious solution because the program, federally funded, is in danger of being cut next year.

Alan Leavitt, program chief of mental-health services for the city of San Francisco, says his city is "the last refuge of the lonely" and points out that San Francisco has the highest mortality rate from cirrhosis of the liver in the country. If alcoholism and drug abuse are good indicators of loneliness, he is right. But Toby Marotta finds an oasis in San Francisco.

In little more than a decade, Marotta says, the city has gone from being one of the country's loneliest places to being "a community replacing the family for gay men. A dozen years ago, there were few social institutions apart from sex-oriented ones, the bars and bathhouses, almost all private businesses, illicit." A homosexual man arriving in San Francisco would go to the Tenderloin, which is like Times Square. "He'd feel despicable," Marotta says, "he'd be surrounded by ugliness. Today, he would go to the Castro."

Marotta, a trim, earnest, light-haired man, speaks as though he were lecturing at Harvard, from which he did, in fact, receive a doctoral degree in government and education. He is the author of several books relating to homosexuality. The Castro (the neighborhood around Castro Street), he explains, is a real community. The bars are bright and airy, with plate-glass windows. Although they used to be "places where you went to score, like singles bars," now they exude almost a family atmosphere. Patrons know the bartenders. The crowd is the same every week. They offer low-priced meals.

In the community around the bars, Marotta says, "connections are no longer solely sexual." He cites a long list of institutions, beginning with musical choruses and ending with an array of self-help groups. The Castro is thriving in difficult economic times, partly because of the high proportion of men who, Marotta says, "have money, mobility and no dependents."

Because they tend to be more sexually active than heterosexuals, fewer homosexual men suffer the loneliness that comes from never being physically intimate with another person, according to Marotta. "Gay culture facilitates sexual connections," he says, although he admits that homosexual life can leave another kind of emptiness, "the loneliness that comes from not being known, from being unable to sustain emotional relationships."

Mildred Murray has found yet another kind of oasis. A bustling 68-year-old woman, she has been divorced three times and is not interested in another marriage. A year ago, she was living in a trailer on property owned by one of her three sons. "I thought I had it licked by the tail," she says, "but I started feeling very lonely. All my friends died off or I just lost touch with them." She heard about a new program in southern California matching senior citizens with each other as housemates. Gene was a widower living in his own home in Van Nuys. Neither of them had ever thought about such an unconventional arrangement, but they decided to try it. Mildred Murray asked permission of each of her three sons.

The night she moved in, she lay staring at the bedroom door. "I knew he was clean, but I didn't know if he was a moral person." A year later, she can't imagine living any other way. Sometimes, she makes Gene's bed and cooks his meals. She likes visiting her children or taking a trip and "not having to report to him." She is not lonely, but many of her friends are. "One of them's so lonely, she's at the senior citizens' center all day long. I," Mildred Murray boasts, "am always just in and out of there."

The people creating such oases have several things in common. They don't deny their loneliness, they don't castigate themselves for being alone, and they recognize the need to build bridges to others, rather than waiting for their loneliness simply to go away. Too many of us, however, are ambivalent about the spaces between us. We want independence and a faithful lover, we want the support of a family but not its demands, we want a community but we don't want to conform to its codes.

Historically, too, we swing from one extreme to the other. The reigning ideal of the 1950's was the family as a self-contained society. In the 60's, it was a group culture. In the 70's, beating a retreat from so much togetherness, the cultural ideal became the solitary individual pursuing his or her own best career and being his or her own best friend. The pendulum is swinging again. The language of the 80's tends to be a rather cold language of connection. We speak of "networking" and "interfacing," but underneath that we're really looking for people we can depend on, people who will laugh at our jokes and listen to our nightmares. We don't really want to interface with our networks. We want to cuddle our grandmothers and take walks with our lovers. Above all, we want someone to talk to.

SELF-FULFILLING STEREOTYPES

MARK SNYDER

Mark Snyder is professor of psychology at the University of Minnesota and spent the 1980-81 academic year as a fellow at the Center for Advanced Study in the Behavioral Sciences at Stanford University. Besides investigating stereotypes, he is currently studying the nature of the self.

Gordon Allport, the Harvard psychologist who wrote a classic work on the nature of prejudice, told a story about a child who had come to believe that people who lived in Minneapolis were called monopolists. From his father, moreover, he had learned that monopolists were evil folk. It wasn't until many years later, when he discovered his confusion, that his dislike of residents of Minneapolis vanished.

Allport knew, of course, that it was not so easy to wipe out prejudice and erroneous stereotypes. Real prejudice, psychologists like Allport argued, was buried deep in human character, and only a restructuring of education could begin to root it out. Yet many people whom I meet while lecturing seem to believe that stereotypes are simply beliefs or attitudes that change easily with experience. Why do some people express the view that Italians are passionate, blacks are lazy, Jews materialistic, or lesbians mannish in their demeanor? In the popular view, it is because they have not learned enough about the diversity among these groups and have not had enough contact with members of the groups for their stereotypes to be challenged by reality. With more experience, it is presumed, most people of good will are likely to revise their stereotypes.

My research over the past decade convinces me that there is little justification for such optimism—and not only for the reasons given by Allport. While it is true that deep prejudice is often based on the needs of pathological character structure, stereotypes are obviously quite common even among fairly normal individuals. When people first meet others, they cannot help noticing certain highly visible and distinctive characteristics: sex, race, physical appearance, and the like. Despite people's best intentions, their initial impressions of others are shaped by their assumptions about such characteristics.

What is critical, however, is that these assumptions are not merely beliefs or attitudes that exist in a vacuum; they are reinforced by the behavior of both prejudiced people and the targets of their prejudice. In recent years, psychologists have collected considerable laboratory evidence about the processes that strengthen stereotypes and put them beyond the reach of reason and good will.

My own studies initially focused on first encounters between strangers. It did not take long to discover, for example, that people have very different ways of treating those whom they regard as physically attractive and those whom they consider physically unattractive, and that these differences tend to bring out precisely those kinds of behavior that fit with stereotypes about attractiveness.

In an experiment that I conducted with my colleagues Elizabeth Decker Tanke and Ellen Berscheid, pairs of college-age men and women met and became acquainted in telephone conversations. Before the conversations began, each man received a Polaroid snapshot, presumably taken just moments before, of the woman he would soon meet. The photograph, which had actually been prepared before the experiment began, showed either a physically attractive woman or a physically unattractive one. By randomly choosing which picture to use for each conversation, we insured that there was no consistent relationship between the attractiveness of the woman in the picture and the attractiveness of the woman in the conversation.

By questioning the men, we learned that even before the conversations began, stereotypes about physical attractiveness came into play. Men who looked forward to talking with physically attractive women said that they expected to meet decidedly sociable, poised, humorous, and socially adept people, while men who thought that they were about to get acquainted with unattractive women fashioned images of rather unsociable, awkward, serious, and socially inept creatures. Moreover, the men proved to have very different styles of getting acquainted with women whom they thought to be attractive and those whom they believed to be unattractive. Shown a photograph of an attractive woman, they behaved with warmth, friendliness, humor, and animation. However, when the woman in the picture was unattractive, the men were cold, uninteresting, and reserved.

These differences in the men's behavior elicited behavior in the women that was consistent with the men's stereotyped assumptions. Women who were believed (unbeknown to them) to be physically attractive behaved in a friendly, likeable, and sociable manner. In sharp contrast, women who were perceived as physically unattractive adopted a cool, aloof, and distant manner. So striking were the differences in the women's behavior that they could be discerned simply by listening to tape recordings of the women's side of the conversations. Clearly, by acting upon their stereotyped beliefs about the women whom they would be meeting, the men had initiated a chain of events that produced *behavioral confirmation* for their beliefs.

Similarly, Susan Andersen and Sandra Bem have shown in an experiment at Stanford University that when the tables are turned—when it is women who have pictures of men they are to meet on the telephone—many women treat the men according to their presumed physical attractiveness, and by so doing encourage the men to confirm their stereotypes. Little wonder, then, that so many people remain convinced that good looks and appealing personalities go hand in hand.

Sex and Race

It is experiments such as these that point to a frequently unnoticed power of stereotypes: the power to influence social relationships in ways that create the illusion of reality. In one study, Berna Skrypnek and I arranged for pairs of previously unacquainted students to interact in a situation that permitted us to control the information that each one received about the apparent sex of the other. The two people were seated in separate rooms so that they could neither see nor hear each other. Using a system of signal lights that they operated with switches, they negotiated a division of labor, deciding which member of the pair would perform each of several tasks that differed in sex-role connotations. The tasks varied along the dimensions of masculinity and femininity: sharpen a hunting knife (masculine), polish a pair of shoes (neutral), iron a shirt (feminine).

One member of the team was led to believe that the other was, in one condition of the experiment, male; in the other, female. As we had predicted, the first member's belief about the sex of the partner influenced the outcome of the pair's negotiations. Women whose partners believed them to be men generally chose stereotypically masculine tasks; in contrast, women whose partners believed that they were women usually chose stereotypically feminine tasks. The experiment thus suggests that much sex-role behavior may be the product of other people's stereotyped and often erroneous beliefs.

In a related study at the University of Waterloo, Carl von Baeyer, Debbie Sherk, and Mark Zanna have shown how stereotypes about sex roles operate in job interviews. The researchers arranged to have men conduct simulated job interviews with women supposedly seeking positions as research assistants. The investigators informed half of the women that the men who would interview them held traditional views about the ideal woman, believing her to be very emotional, deferential to her husband, home-oriented, and passive. The rest of the women were told that their interviewer saw the ideal woman as independent, competitive, ambitious, and dominant. When the women arrived for their interviews, the researchers noticed that most of them had dressed to meet the stereotyped expectations of their prospective interviewers. Women who expected to see a traditional interviewer had chosen very feminine-looking makeup, clothes, and accessories. During the interviews (videotaped through a one-way mirror) these women behaved in traditionally feminine ways and gave traditional feminine answers to questions such as "Do you have plans to include children and marriage with your career plans?"

Once more, then, we see the self-fulfilling nature of stereotypes. Many sex differences, it appears, may result from the images that people create in their attempts to act out accepted sex roles. The implication is that if stereotyped expectations about sex roles shift, behavior may change, too. In fact, statements by people who have undergone sex-change operations have highlighted the power of such expectations in easing adjustment to a new life. As the writer Jan Morris said in recounting the story of her transition from James to Jan: "The more I was treated as a woman, the more woman I became."

The power of stereotypes to cause people to confirm stereotyped expectations can also be seen in interracial relationships. In the first of two investigations done at Princeton University by Carl Word, Mark Zanna, and Joel Cooper, white undergraduates interviewed both white and black job applicants. The applicants were actually confederates of the experimenters, trained to behave consistently from interview to interview, no matter how the interviewers acted toward them.

To find out whether or not the white interviewers would behave differently toward white and black job applicants, the researchers secretly videotaped each interview and then studied the tapes. From these, it was apparent that there were substantial differences in the treatment accorded blacks and whites. For one thing, the interviewers' speech deteriorated when they talked to blacks, displaying more errors in grammar and pronunciation. For another, the interviewers spent less time with blacks than with whites and showed less "immediacy," as the researchers called it, in their manner. That is, they were less friendly, less outgoing, and more reserved with blacks.

In the second investigation, white confederates were trained to approximate either the immediate or the nonimmediate interview styles that had been observed in the first investigation as they interviewed white job applicants. A panel of judges who evaluated the tapes agreed that applicants subjected to the nonimmediate styles performed less adequately and were more nervous than job applicants treated in the immediate style. Apparently, then, the blacks in the first study did not have a chance to display their qualifications to the best advantage. Considered together, the two investigations suggest that in interracial encounters, racial stereotypes may constrain behavior in ways that cause both blacks and whites to behave in accordance with those stereotypes.

Rewriting Biography

Having adopted stereotyped ways of thinking about another person, people tend to notice and remember the ways in which that person seems to fit the stereotype, while resisting evidence that contradicts the stereotype. In one investigation that I conducted with Seymour Uranowitz, student subjects read a biography of a fictitious woman named Betty K. We constructed the story of her life so that it would fit the stereotyped images of both lesbians and heterosexuals. Betty, we wrote, never had a steady boyfriend in high school, but did go out on dates. And although we gave her a steady boyfriend in college, we specified that he was more of a close friend than anything else. A week after we had distributed this biography, we gave our subjects some new information about Betty. We told some students that she was now living with another woman in a lesbian relationship; we told others that she was living with her husband.

To see what impact stereotypes about sexuality would have on how people remembered the facts of Betty's life, we asked each student to answer a series of questions about her life history. When we examined their answers, we found that the students had reconstructed the events of Betty's past in ways that supported their own stereotyped beliefs about her sexual orientation. Those who believed that Betty was a lesbian remembered that Betty had never had a steady boyfriend in high school, but tended to neglect the fact that she had gone out on many dates in college. Those who believed that Betty was now a heterosexual tended to remember that she had formed a steady relationship with a man in college, but tended to ignore the fact that this relationship was more of a friendship than a romance.

The students showed not only selective memories but also a striking facility for interpreting what they remembered in ways that added fresh support for their stereotypes. One student who accurately remembered that a supposedly lesbian Betty never had a steady boyfriend in high school confidently pointed to that fact as an early sign of her lack of romantic or sexual interest in men. A student who correctly remembered that a purportedly lesbian Betty often went out on dates in college was sure that these dates were signs of Betty's early attempts to mask her lesbian interests.

Clearly, the students had allowed their preconceptions about lesbians and heterosexuals to dictate the way in which they interpreted and reinterpreted the facts of Betty's life. As long as stereotypes make it easy to bring to mind evidence that supports them and difficult to bring to mind evidence that undermines them, people will cling to erroneous beliefs.

Stereotypes in the Classroom and Work Place

The power of one person's beliefs to make other people conform to them has been well demonstrated in real life. Back in the 1960s, as most people well remember, Harvard psychologist Robert Rosenthal and his colleague Lenore Jacobson entered elementary-school classrooms and identified one out of every five pupils in each room as a child who could be expected to show dramatic improvement in intellectual achievement during the school year. What the teachers did not know was that the children had been chosen on a random basis. Nevertheless, something happened in the relationships between teachers and their supposedly gifted pupils that led the children to make clear gains in test performance.

It can also do so on the job. Albert King, now a professor of management at Northern Illinois University, told a welding instructor in a vocational training center that five men in his training program had unusually high aptitude. Although these five had been chosen at random and knew nothing of their designation as high-aptitude workers, they showed substantial changes in performance. They were absent less often than were other workers, learned the basics of the welder's trade in about half the usual time, and scored a full 10 points higher than other trainees on a welding test. Their gains were noticed not only by the researcher and by the welding instructor, but also by other trainees, who singled out the five as their preferred co-workers.

Might not other expectations influence the relationships between supervisors and workers? For example, supervisors who believe that men are better suited to some jobs and women to others may treat their workers (wittingly or unwittingly) in ways that encourage them to perform their jobs in accordance with stereotypes about differences between men and women. These same stereotypes may determine who gets which job in the first place. Perhaps some personnel managers allow stereotypes to influence, subtly or not so subtly, the way in which they interview job candidates, making it likely that candidates who fit the stereotypes show up better than job-seekers who do not fit them.

Unfortunately, problems of this kind are compounded by the fact that members of stigmatized groups often subscribe to stereotypes about themselves. That is what Amerigo Farina and his colleagues at the University of Connecticut found when they measured the impact upon mental patients of believing that others knew their psychiatric history. In Farina's study, each mental patient cooperated with another person in a game requiring teamwork. Half of the patients believed that their partners knew they were patients; the other half believed that their partners thought they were nonpatients. In reality, the nonpatients never knew a thing about anyone's psychiatric history. Nevertheless, simply believing that others were aware of their history led the patients to feel less appreciated, to find the task more difficult, and to perform poorly. In addition, objective observers saw them as more tense, more anxious, and more poorly adjusted than patients who believed that their status was not known. Seemingly, the belief that others perceived them as stigmatized caused them to play the role of stigmatized patients.

Consequences for Society

Apparently, good will and education are not sufficient to subvert the power of stereotypes. If people treat others in such a way as to bring out behavior that supports stereotypes, they may never have an opportunity to discover which of their stereotypes are wrong.

I suspect that even if people were to develop doubts about the accuracy of their stereotypes, chances are they would proceed to test them by gathering precisely the evidence that would appear to confirm them.

The experiments I have described help to explain the persistence of stereotypes. But, as is so often the case, solving one puzzle only creates another. If by acting as if false stereotypes were true, people lead others, too, to act as if they were true, why do the stereotypes not come to *be* true? Why, for example, have researchers found so little evidence that attractive people are generally friendly, sociable, and outgoing and that unattractive people are generally shy and aloof?

I think that the explanation goes something like this: Very few among us have the kind of looks that virtually everyone considers either very attractive or very unattractive. Our looks make us rather attractive to some people but somewhat less attractive to other people. When we spend time with those who find us attractive, they will tend to bring out our more sociable sides, but when we are with those who find us less attractive, they will bring out our less sociable sides. Although our actual physical appearance does not change, we present ourselves quite differently to our admirers and to our detractors. For our admirers we become attractive people, and for our detractors we become unattractive. This mixed pattern of behavior will prevent the development of any consistent relationship between physical attractiveness and personality.

Now that I understand some of the powerful forces that work to perpetuate social stereotypes, I can see a new mission for my research. I hope, on the one hand, to find out how to help people see the flaws in their stereotypes. On the other hand, I would like to help the victims of false stereotypes find ways of liberating themselves from the constraints imposed on them by other members of society.

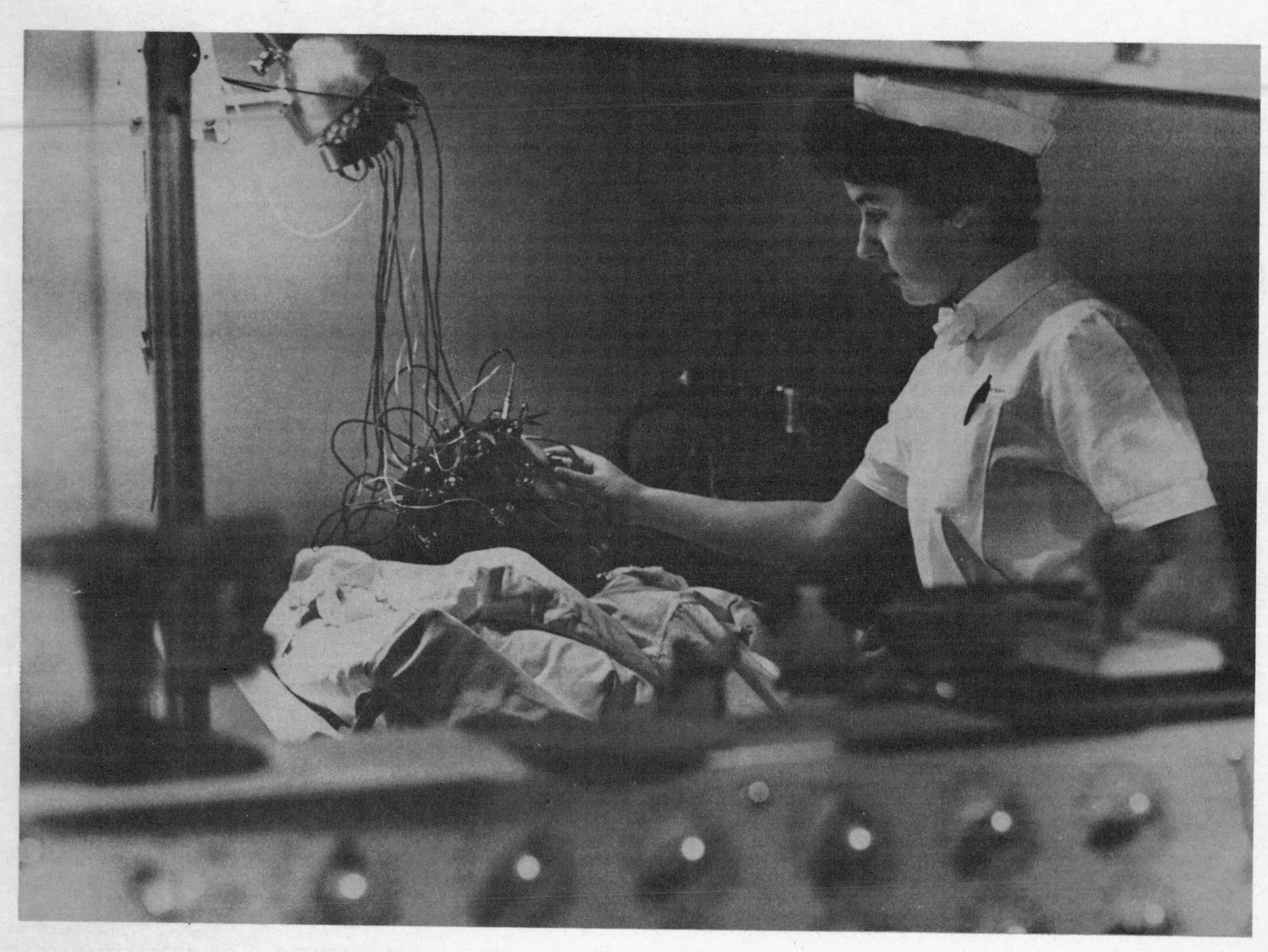

Disorders and Therapeutic Processes

The diagnosis and treatment of psychological disorders is a widely recognized aspect of psychology. A major issue within the field of clinical psychology today is whether or not psychological disorders should be thought of in terms of "mental illness." Many people take for granted the historical change from regarding the disordered as possessed by demons to regarding them as suffering from a sickness comparable to a physical illness. In recent years, however, a number of psychologists have begun to contest the "illness" point of view. As a result, a large number of different kinds of psychotherapies, chemical therapies, and behavioral approaches are now used in treating mental disorders. "Finding the Hidden Freud" puts a new light on psychoanalysis—the once-dominant tradition in clinical psychology—and discusses some of the changes in the psychoanalytic view that are currently being adopted.

Another approach to mental illness—using pharmacological treatments to change abnormal biochemical processes—is covered in "The Healing Brain." The psychological nature rather than the biochemical origins of mental illness are examined in "Roots of Madness." Yet a different view of psychological disorder and therapy comes from behavior theory, and the behavioral approach is described in "Fight Fat with Behavior Control."

A review of this section will provide some insight into the central issues of mental disorder. The most common forms of mental and behavioral disorders—schizophrenia, depression, phobia, and dysfunctional habit—are discussed, as well as the variety of forms of therapy currently available.

Looking Ahead: Challenge Questions

How can psychiatric diagnosis serve to perpetuate mental disorder?

What are some potential roles of nonprofessionals in the field of psychotherapy?

Could some kind of therapy help you with a problem? Or have psychologists ignored or missed the boat on many important difficulties that face people in their everyday lives?

Finding the Hidden Freud

Sigmund Freud might have appreciated the irony. Four decades after his death, more than 80 years after his own epic self-analysis struck the mother lode of insights into human behavior, scholars are putting *him* on the couch. They are examining family relationships, reinterpreting his dreams and poring over his vast correspondence—in effect asking, like the two psychiatrists after greeting each other in the old joke, "I wonder what he meant by that?" Freud emerges from the scrutiny with his genius undimmed, but his portrait darkened: envious, often malicious, sometimes a pilferer of colleagues' ideas, a man who may have seduced his sister-in-law under his own roof.

Freud's monument seems secure. In "The Interpretation of Dreams," published in 1900, he charted the dark underside of civilized consciousness, a hellish "unconscious" where even the most upright citizen harbors forbidden lusts and aggressions. In that and subsequent works he traced the sinuous routes by which these repressed feelings produced neurotic symptoms. But the founder of psychoanalysis gave the world more than a theory and a therapy. He provided a world view. His ideas about dreams, religion, creativity and the unconscious motivations underlying all human behavior are so pervasive that it would be difficult to imagine twentieth-century thought without them. Few would quarrel with poet W. H. Auden's assessment of Freud's impact on Western culture: "To us he is no more a person/Now but a whole climate of opinion."

That climate has always been stormy. Freud offered an essentially bleak view of individual destiny. In his own day he was reviled as a purveyor of "filth" for his notions about the Oedipal lusts and aggressions that molded character. Later analysts founded revisionist schools that gave more weight to "interpersonal" influences on personality development, and changes in the Freudian canon have continued to the present (following story).

But in the past few years the attack has shifted to the founder himself, in books that call Freud's own character into question. The figure that steps from recent biographies is no longer the majestic prophet of the legend, but more like one of the neurotic egoists who might have frequented his own couch. One massively researched tome, science historian Frank Sulloway's "Freud: Biologist of the Mind," contends that Freud's devoted followers carefully nurtured the image of his pioneering originality to establish a cultlike orthodoxy around his theories. Moreover, according to Sulloway, Freud got more than an inkling of some of those theories from his cherished friend and confidant, Wilhelm Fliess, a Berlin nose and throat specialist with some far-ranging ideas of his own about human sexuality.

Freud's letters to Fliess, written during his most troubled and creative period (1887 to 1902), have been a major source for scholarly sleuths interested in both his professional progress and his personal quirks. In them, he first outlined the early themes of psychoanalysis—and acknowledged his debt to Fliess. But there is also an ardent, almost lovesick tone to the writing. Freud himself ultimately guessed that "some piece of unruly homosexual feeling" lay at the root of his relationship to Fliess, who had become a kind of father figure to him during his self-analysis. No doubt significantly, the friendship ended in a violent quarrel in 1900.

Researchers would love to know more. But only a portion of Freud's half of the correspondence—discreetly edited and against his wishes—was published. (Freud claimed to have lost or destroyed Fliess's replies, and they have never been found.) Freud's daughter, Anna, at 85 the gray eminence of psychoanalysis, insisted that she and analyst Ernst Kris, who edited the correspondence, had included mainly those letters and passages that were of scientific interest. Scholarly intrigue was stirred afresh recently by the decision of Freud's heirs to permit publication of all 284 letters Freud wrote to his beloved friend, as well as thousands of other communiqués to colleagues and relatives.

Seduction: The new Fliess material is to be published about two years hence, but it has already rekindled an old controversy centered on Freud's abandonment of the seduction theory—his belief that neurotics were the victims of childhood sexual abuse, usually by their fathers. Sociologists and revisionist analysts have argued that psychoanalysis took a fateful turn away from the "real world" when Freud shifted the blame for neurosis to the innate eroticism of children. Some researchers say the real reason for Freud's change of mind was his suspicion that his own father might be implicated in the seduction thesis. Last summer Jeffrey Masson, the impetuous young analyst-scholar assigned to edit the new volume of Fliess letters, stirred the argument again when he cited fragments of the unpublished letters as proof that Freud recognized the reality of childhood seductions even after he renounced the thesis. By turning his back on the truth, said Masson in a talk at Yale, Freud himself set psychoanalysis on a course that led to its "present-day sterility."

For that heretical assertion—and for his unscholarly conduct in quoting the still-unpublished letters—Masson was fired earlier this month from his post as projects director of the Sigmund Freud Archives. But not without a parting shot from Masson: if actual sexual abuse—not fantasies—was after all the real source of neurosis, Masson suggested cheekily, analysts "would have to recall every patient since 1901. It would be like the Pinto."

It was a piece of hyperbole, uttered in anger after Masson had been virtually disenfranchised by the Freudian establishment (though under a separate agreement with Harvard University Press, he is still editor of the Fliess volume). But it is typical of the passions that Freud scholarship can still arouse, and the new materials are apt to fan the flames. In fact, psychoanalysts regard Freud's abandonment of the seduction thesis as a milestone. In the traditional account, this shift of emphasis from literal experience to the truths of symbol and fantasy paved the way for Freud's perception of infantile sexuality and Oedipal conflicts as the true source of neurosis. But to revisionists it merely bears out their own pet thesis: that the man who claimed to have discovered the sources of neurosis was himself a neurotic who projected his own character kinks as universal afflictions.

In the extreme view, that character could be kinky indeed. Last week a young Welsh-born scholar named Peter Swales gave a paper before the psychology faculty at New York University. He claimed to have documented that Freud seduced his wife's sister, Minna Bernays, while she was living in his home, then arranged an abortion for her—an allegation that has been dismissed as spurious by Freudians. Swales, who is working on a biography of Fliess, also believes there was some basis in fact for Fliess's supposedly "paranoid" belief that Freud wanted to kill him and thus retain sole possession of the precepts of psychoanalysis. Freud, says Swales, "was playing out his own Oedipal fantasy, with Minna as the desired mother figure and Fliess as the feared father."

Perspective: Swales does not argue that his findings invalidate Freud's theories. But he says they put Freud's work in a different perspective: "There's a major subjective component in it, and it's only by properly evaluating that component that one can know what to subtract."

Freudians say the news that the master was not the most stable of heroes is no news. It was by plumbing the murkiest depths of his own psyche, after all, that Freud achieved his breath-taking perceptions about human frailty. "Of course he was a little cracked," says Dr. Mark Kanzer, a member of the prestigious New York Psychoanalytic Society. "How else do you understand all these things except by working them through yourself?" In any case, adds Dr. Robert Michels, director of New York's Payne Whitney Psychiatric Clinic, such biographical issues are "just gossip. The important issue is what do we now know and where is it taking us?" The investigators insist that they are addressing precisely those questions. By penetrating the mind of the founder of psychoanalysis, they believe they can shed light on the story of how and why Freud made his revolution in the way human beings perceive themselves.

Few features of that story have prompted more fanatical research recently than Freud's seduction theory and its abandonment. A virtual network of scholars has crossed continents and oceans to examine Freud's most marginal scribblings in the search for answers. Significantly, many of these scholars are sociologists, perhaps spurred on by the continuing, major problem of real-life incest (page 68). As they reconstruct the tale, it is as full of intriguing clues and red herrings as a good detective novel—or one of Freud's own psychoanalytic case studies.

'Adventurer': At the beginning of the 1890s, Freud had already achieved an admirable reputation as a neurologist. But he was enormously ambitious. He had been his mother's favorite—"my golden Sigi," as she called him. He identified at times with Hannibal and Napoleon, describing himself half seriously once as "not really a man of science . . . but by temperament a *conquistador,* an adventurer—with the curiosity, the boldness and the tenacity that belong to that type of being." Psychology became the "tyrant" he needed to spur him on to greatness. He hoped to use it, he told Fliess, not merely to understand mental disturbance but to penetrate the secret of "all mental activity."

Freud first picked up hints of the importance of sexual trauma when he studied under the French neurologist, Jean Martin Charcot. From another mentor, the Viennese physician Josef Breuer, he had heard about the case of "Anna O.," whose hysterical symptoms seemed to vanish when hypnosis helped her recall buried memories of distressing events. In his own practice, Freud began to hear tales of childhood sexual abuse from his patients, most of them young Viennese women suffering from hysterical paralyses or obsessions. Most often the culprit seemed to be the father, he told Fliess. Drawing on the Anna O. episode and other cases of hysteria he had explored with Breuer, Freud reasoned that the seduction tales concealed even earlier childhood experiences of sexual abuse. Repressed by the patient, they provoked anxieties that resulted in neurosis.

Freud triumphantly announced this thesis at an 1896 meeting of the Vienna Psychiatric and Neurological Society, declaring it to be a *caput Nili*—a "source of the Nile"—for neurosis. He had reason to be excited. Prevailing psychiatric opinion, under the leadership of the eminent Richard von Krafft-Ebing, held that most neurotic disturbances were the result of hereditary factors which disposed young people toward such debilitating practices as masturbation. Freud, with characteristic audacity, had flouted that wisdom by proposing that hysteria originated in events, not in genes. His listeners were not impressed. "It sounds," Krafft-Ebing dourly observed, "like a scientific fairy tale." Another critic later called it "horrible old wives' psychiatry."

Freud, yearning for greatness, was bitterly disappointed. He complained to Fliess of his "icy reception from the asses," adding (in an unpublished aside), "They can all go to hell." Yet a little over a year later he appeared to renounce his source of the Nile. "Let me tell you straight away the great secret which has been slowly dawning on me in recent months," he wrote to the ever-attentive Fliess. "I no longer believe in my neurotica [the seduction theory]." Freud cited four reasons for changing his mind, principal among them "the astonishing thing that in every case . . . blame was laid on perverse acts by the father . . . though it was hardly credible that perverted acts against children were so general."

Suspicion: What had happened to shake Freud's faith in a theory he held so dear only a year earlier? Scholars suggest an interesting explanation. Clearly Freud was engaged in a psychic struggle of his own at the time. At the root of it was his suspicion, confided in at least one unpublished letter to Fliess, that because he detected hysterical symptoms in his brother and sisters, his own theory meant even *his* father was implicated as a sexual abuser of his children. Researchers have noted a significant omission in the first published versions of the letter renouncing the seduction theory. After the words "in every case blame was laid on perverse acts by the father," Freud had written, "not excluding my own." But that crucial phrase did not come to light until it was restored in a later German edition of the letters.

Florence Rush, a psychiatric social worker who researched the subject for her recent book on child abuse, "The Best Kept Secret," notes that Freud seemed unable to point the finger in public at his or any male parent. When he presented the seduction theory to the Vienna society, she says, he cited "nurses, maids, governesses, teachers and near relations"—but not fathers. And years later Freud admitted to having concealed the guilt of fathers in at least two case studies of childhood seduction.

European scholars have added another wrinkle to the mystery. According to official biographies, Freud's father, Jakob, had been married twice, first to a woman named Sally Kanner, then to Sigmund's mother, Amalie, twenty years his junior. But in 1968 author Josef Sajner found evidence that between those two wives, there was a third, Rebekka. Her name appears in the town registry of Freud's native Freiberg, Moravia, then mysteriously vanishes two years later. Nothing further is known about Rebekka. But in the letter in which he gives up his caput Nili, Freud ruefully observes that he has surrendered his ticket to greatness, and then remembers a line from a Jewish joke: "Rebekka, you can take off your wedding gown, you're not a bride any longer!"

Freud later wrote a treatise on "Jokes and Their Relation to the Unconscious." But it fell to others to speculate on the significance of the Rebekka joke. For though it was meant as a comment on his dashed hopes, it may also have been an unwitting allusion to the fate of Rebekka. Did Freud know of her existence? Was his father's original sin the seduction and abandonment of a young girl? Several writers have conjectured that this was yet another reason for his problem with paternal guilt.

The turning point may have come just after Jakob died. In a letter dated Feb. 11, 1896, Freud tells Fliess how "deeply" his father's death has affected him, then notes the scornful criticism directed at his seduction theory. Next, he reports a dream he had on the night after his father's funeral, in which he pays his daily visit to the barbershop and sees a sign reading: "You are requested to close the eyes." The master of dreams offered a pedestrian interpretation: his family was displeased with the simple funeral arrangements he had made, and the sign expressed his wish to be forgiven his failure, "as though I had not done my duty." But to later analysts the dream duty, clearly, was to overlook his *father's* failure.

Memories: Abandoning the seduction theory seemed to have a salubrious effect on Freud. Within weeks his temporarily stalled self-analysis resumed at full tilt, producing a remarkable spurt of memories and perceptions. He was certain now, he told Fliess, that his father "played no active role" in his neurosis. He remembered a train trip with his mother that probably provided his first glimpse of her in the nude, arousing "libido towards matrem." And three weeks after renouncing the seduction idea, he arrived at his first clear expression of the Oedipus theory. "I have found love of the mother and jealousy of the father in my own case too, and now believe it to be a general phenomenon of early childhood," he wrote to Fliess. "... If that is the case, the gripping power of *Oedipus Rex*... becomes intelligible... Every member of the audience was once a budding Oedipus in phantasy..."

The son had thus taken the guilt of the father upon himself, says Marianne Krüll, a West German sociologist whose book, "Freud and His Father," is to be published in English next year. It was a creative compromise of the kind sometimes used by children with parental conflicts. But instead of seeking the real source of hostility toward his father, Freud hit upon the Oedipus myth and made it a parable of all human motivation—ultimately, one of the most pervasive parables of modern intellectual life.

Even so, Freud may have stood Oedipus on his ear. Krüll and others argue strenuously that a "Laius complex" would have been more to the point. It was Laius, the father, who—because of a prophecy that he would one day be murdered by his son—left the infant Oedipus on a mountaintop to die. Freud chose to believe that the "gripping power" of Sophocles's drama lay in the tragic destiny of the son who, not knowing his real parentage, unwittingly murders his father and marries his mother. Krüll says it was only Freud's bias that prevented him from recognizing the primal guilt of Laius.

Indictment: Two Manhattan-based psychoanalysts, Milton Klein and David Tribich, contend that Freud extended this bias to his treatment of patients. In a 1979 paper, "On Freud's 'Blindness'," they reviewed five of Freud's major case studies, among them the "Dora" case, which was a prime exhibit in the feminist indictment of Freud in the 1970s. Brought to Freud by her father as a depressed, suicidal 18-year-old, Dora was a pawn in an unlikely triangle. Her father had struck up an affair with the wife of a friend, "Herr K." In return, he tacitly submitted Dora as a sex offering to the friend. She had threatened suicide as a result.

Freud recognized the vileness of the arrangement, but seemed interested only in Dora's hysterical reaction. Questioning her with unusual ruthlessness (one writer suggests Freud was fighting his own attraction to Dora), Freud determined that Dora was actually excited by Herr K.'s advances while furiously rejecting them, and was sexually attracted to Frau K. as well. He traced these feelings to her Oedipal love-hate for her own parents, whom she had once heard in the act of making love. Klein says this was typical of Freud's mind-set: "He simply did not see the role of parents as causal factors, but placed the burden on the child."

Freudians insist that Dora's real-world predicament by itself might not account for her hysterical symptoms, and that she couldn't be cured before she realized the underlying Oedipal truth. But Klein and Tribich argue that it was the palpable reality of an unloving mother and a treacherous father that caused Dora's hysteria. Says Klein: "Freud's instinctual drives give a very narrow role to the real world. Many of us want to bring back the emphasis on the need for love, acceptance, security. We're not urging a literal return to seduction theory, but in its broadest sense, it does contain the potential for encompassing parent-child or interpersonal relationships, the idea of what has *happened* to the child."

Brutality: As it turned out, Freud never completely dismissed the reality of seduction. In unpublished passages of the Fliess letters cited by Masson, he continued to describe cases of sexual brutality by fathers. He had also long suspected that many of these stories were "phantasies," arising "from an unconscious combination of things experienced..." But whether real or imaginary, the result was the same. It was the neurotic "consequences" that mattered.

That, finally, was the point for Freud—what happened to the child in the arena of the psyche. It was this "finer structure of a neurosis" that absorbed all his brilliant energies, and the ways in which repressed memories or fantasies made people ill became the substance of psychoanalysis.

Freud's strange relationship with Fliess may also have played a part in the direction his theories took. The two first met in 1887, when Fliess attended one of Freud's lectures and began corresponding with him. The friendship lasted until 1900. But between those years, it was almost a romance. Fliess, a short but handsome man, quickly graduated in the letters from "My Dear Dr. Fliess" to "Dear one" and "My supreme arbiter." As Freud expounded his developing ideas, Fliess's praise became "nectar and ambrosia" to him. He "panted" for their frequent "congresses" together.

Fliess, meanwhile, was working on his own startling ideas. As a nose and throat specialist, he believed he had found a connection between disturbances in the mucous membranes of the nose, the female menstrual cycle and genital arousal. From this he constructed a bold, ultimately unfathomable, thesis about laws of "periodicity"—23- and 28-day cycles that governed not only the stages of sexual development, but the dates of birth and death and the onset of illnesses. He was the first to advance the idea of bisexuality in humans and all organisms. And from observations of his own son, he had hit upon the idea of infantile sexuality.

Noses: Freud appeared totally taken with Fliess's ideas. He became obsessed with the notion that he would die at 51—the sum of 28 and 23—and the two men were preoccupied with the state of each other's nose. Fliess repeatedly operated on Freud's nose to relieve neurotically based sinus pains, and even on a patient of Freud's (who nearly died because Fliess accidentally left a strip of gauze in the incision area).

These were also Freud's most troubled years, a period when he experienced heart arrhythmia, sharp mood swings and migraine headaches—and commenced his lonely journey of self-analysis. Biographers have concluded that, in effect, he made Fliess his own analyst-father figure, confessing all to him, investing him with ideal qualities and overlooking his excesses. Like an analytic patient's regression to childhood, Freud's dependence on Fliess had "almost the appearance of a delayed adolescence," wrote Ernest Jones, whose 1953 biography was long considered the definitive study of Freud. But as Freud worked through his self-analysis and his conflicts about his real father, he seemed to grow less dependent. The correspondence thinned out and the friendship ended, for most purposes, in a violent quarrel at their last congress, when Freud introduced the bisexuality thesis as his own.

Just how important Fliess's contribution was has been difficult to say in the absence of his letters. Frank Sulloway makes a persuasive case that Freud got his initial clues to the anal-oral-phallic stages of development from Fliess. He argues, moreover, that after Freud abandoned the seduction theory, he lost faith in psychoanalysis, then rescued it by seizing upon Fliess's theories of innate infantile sexuality. There Freudians dispute him, noting that most of Freud's formulations on sexuality and psychic conflict were by then already visible.

The current attacks on the Freudian legacy reflect almost every wave of revisionism that has been directed against his theories, from the early neo-Freudian emphasis on the importance of personal relationships up through the feminists of the 1970s, who took arms against Freud's Victorian condescension toward women. The seduction-theory advocates seem to be in the tradition of those revisionists who have sought to turn psychoanalysis into a kind of social work, more optimistic about human destiny, more humanitarian in its concerns.

Revisions: Freud himself conceded he had little interest in helping "suffering humanity," only in understanding it. From the outset he believed his therapy could promise little more than the prospect of converting "hysterical misery into common unhappiness"—scarcely an inspiration for today's tireless seekers of self-improvement. But by now psychoanalytic training encompasses most of the revisions of early Freudian dogma, including attention to the interaction between a patient and the important figures in his everyday life.

Yet Freud's long shadow still falls over the profession. In the years since his death, there has been no fresh synthesis, no major theoretical advance comparable to his own. Conventional psychotherapy remains a protracted, expensive process of uncertain out-

An Epidemic of Incest

Freud recoiled when his probing of human souls touched on incest, and his conclusion that child seduction was mainly fantasy may have helped keep society's secret for a few additional decades. But in the past year or two, therapists and sociologists have concluded that incest verges on an epidemic. Scholars project that one of every 100 adult women in the United States was sexually molested as a child by her father—an astonishing figure in itself, and one that many experts think is far too low. "We're talking about a major public-health problem on the same scale as diabetes," says Judith Lewis Herman, a Massachusetts psychiatrist.

As with other epidemics, social or economic class offers no protection. Indeed, the alarming statistics come from studies of middle-class white women. "There's more of it going on in good substantial houses than we ever dreamed of," says Robert Wallerstein, a professor of psychiatry at the University of California at San Francisco. "There's a significant amount in the 'normal society'."

Incest is primarily a male problem that young girls are forced to bear. Research is still scanty, but some common patterns of the incestuous family have begun to emerge. The mean age for the first assault is about 8, but sometimes the victims are still in diapers. A weak or absent mother, unable to protect or teach her child, is the most typical sign of trouble. Abusive fathers—or stepfathers—tend to be strong authoritarian figures who are desperately insecure about their sexuality. Says sociologist Joyce Spencer, who has studied incest victims, "Frequently the incestuous father can't sustain a relationship with a mature woman, so he turns to a child who cannot judge him like a man." Sibling incest, if it occurs between brothers and sisters of similar ages, is a less serious problem (sexual contact between siblings is often simply experimental). And mother-son affairs are so rare as to be regarded as a novelty.

Illicit: The incest can continue for many years, until the child is old enough to complain or move away. Sometimes a father's jealousy over his daughter's teen-age dating can force the disclosure of an illicit relationship. Whenever it stops, the psychological effects continue. "I'll never forgive him," says a San Jose, Calif., woman, now 19, whose stepfather slept with her for six years. "He was supposed to love me like my dad."

An Atlanta woman who discusses incest under the pseudonym Mary Raeburn suffered from a textbook case. Her mother is a nurse who worked away from home most of the day. From the time she was 8, Mary became a surrogate mother for her three younger brothers. She also aided her parents. She opened a bank account for her mother and listened to her father's business problems. As she grew older, Mary watched her mother turn to tranquilizers, and saw her father turn to her. When she was 11, Mary's father first had intercourse with her. "His word was law to me," she says now. Their sexual relationship lasted for eight years until Mary came apart emotionally during a college psychology course. Eventually she and her mother left home.

With the recognition that the ancient taboo is routinely breached, it is a bit easier for victims to come forward. Courts, prosecutors and counselors are trying to deal with the issue more sensitively. Still, it's difficult for young girls to escape from the mazes their abusers have erected. A child who speaks up not only must describe intensely embarrassing events, but risks destroying the family—and the love—she has been trying to keep intact. Sociologist Spencer says that while a young girl may sense that something is wrong, she is obeying her father—and her mother often is condoning the arrangement or at least preferring not to know. In the end, the victims may blame themselves. "They have it bad either way," says David Finkelhor, director of the University of New Hampshire's Family Violence Research Center. "They get a terrible sense of isolation by keeping quiet, or stigma and harassment if they talk." Most victims still choose silence.

Confession: Some help is available. The incest program that gets the most attention, Parents United, is run by an eleven-year-old group in San Jose that has worked with 3,500 families. Incestuous families usually referred to Parents United by the courts and police are treated as units; the aim is to bring them back together under one roof—and the program claims a 75 percent success rate. About 70 other communities have copied the idea, which borrows heavily from Alcoholics Anonymous for its public-confession techniques. However, PU has been criticized for its emphasis on restoring the family. Some critics say that the important relationship to be restored is between the mother and daughter; the abusive father can—and perhaps should—be sent packing.

However effective therapy may be, prevention is a better route. The most notable efforts have been built around small theatrical productions which bring schoolchildren skits about abuse and neglect. After the shows, children in the audience talk about the problems and sometimes, in the process, disclose real-life crises. These programs carefully distinguish between loving hugs and abusive gropes. Psychiatrist William Walter Menninger says that often kids can readily recognize the differences between touches. "One little boy told me that with affection there is a feeling that you are being given something," Menninger says. "But with incest he felt a sense that something was being taken away."

come and mostly unprovable benefits. Even traditional analysts, while revering the Freudian legacy, chafe at their inability to rejuvenate it. Observes Robert Wallerstein, a past president of the American Psychoanalytic Association: "Psychoanalysis hasn't yet come to terms with Freud's death. Too many people have taken what Freud said as a kind of gospel beyond which we don't need to know anything."

Changing that attitude may be one positive outcome of the relentless review of the Freudian record—and some Freudians accordingly welcome the debunking effort. "There is some productive effect in all that," says Kurt Eissler, who serves as secretary and effective head of the Freud Archives. "In order to open the way for the new, you have to destroy the old."

At bottom, however, the analytic community remains cautious and closeminded, tolerating no dissent from upstarts like Jeffrey Masson. As such, it is much like its founder. Freud branded the rebellious disciples of his own day as Oedipal ingrates, determined to overthrow the fathers. He was ever watchful. "We must make a dogma of it, an unshakable bulwark," he wrote his anointed "crown prince" and heir, Carl Jung. When Jung left to practice his own revisionist therapy (he maintained that hunger was a more basic drive than sex), Freud was biting. "The truth is," he wrote, "that these people have picked out a few cultural overtones from the symphony of life and have once more failed to hear the mighty and primordial melody of the instincts."

Gifts: Freud had reason to worry about how an iconoclastic posterity would view him. But in the end he came to terms with it. In a speech accepting the Goethe Prize for Literature in 1930—an occasion that provided an example of the literary gifts for which he was being hailed and the theoretical conviction to which they gave such magisterial authority—he told his audience: "It is unavoidable that if we learn more about a great man's life we shall also hear of occasions on which he has in fact done no better than we, has in fact come near to us as a human being. Nevertheless, I think we may declare the efforts of biography to be legitimate. Our attitude to fathers and teachers is, after all, an ambivalent one since our reverence for them regularly conceals a component of hostile rebellion. That is a psychological fatality; it cannot be altered without forcible suppression of truth and is bound to extend to our relations with the great men whose life histories we wish to investigate."

By then Freud was already dying of the cancer that had been eating away his jaw since 1923. He had only nine years left to live. Oedipus was still king, though his empire was coming under siege in every province. It is a measure of his size that he has not even now been toppled.

DAVID GELMAN

Psychotherapy in the '80s

If Freudian theory were revised to satisfy its critics, how would it change psychoanalysis? To a great extent, that evolution has already happened. Classic "couch" analysis has been in decline for years. It has been supplanted largely by briefer, less doctrinaire varieties of psychotherapy that downplay the inner drama of psychic conflict and focus more on the vicissitudes of daily life. Analysis is no longer as preoccupied with the implications of Oedipus as it once was. It is apt to bear more on such worldly matters as work, intimacy and success. In effect, the therapist is less likely to ask about last night's dreams than to say, "What's new at the office?" And in place of the classic neutrality, he is likely to offer some considered advice on how to handle the boss or the boyfriend.

There has been a strong push toward "short-term dynamic therapy"—led by such prominent analysts as Judd Marmor—which sets firm deadlines and specific goals to spur the patient's will to be well. Some of today's therapists have all but abandoned the quest for insight in favor of aggressive "behavior modification" techniques, literally conditioning their patients to change habitual patterns of response. Others use "cognitive therapy," pioneered by Aaron Beck, which relies primarily on rational persuasion within a time limit to change a patient's distorted perception of himself and his basic worth. Group therapy reinforces the analyst's insights with the reassurance and fellow pressure of patients, and family therapy sees neurosis as part of a system of intense, interacting family relationships. Most psychotherapists use a combination of approaches, including some form of analytic "talk" therapy. "The buzzword in our profession these days is 'pragmatic eclecticism'," says Donald C. Greaves, head of psychiatry at Evanston Hospital in Illinois. "What we have done, really, is pull Freud together with what we know about biology, society and behavior."

The range of treatment is impressive. Troubled patients are seeking out not only M.D. psychiatrists and Ph.D. psychologists, but therapists with master's degrees in social work—whose services are cheaper—and a growing throng of self-styled lay analysts, many of whom offer quackish quick fixes on the order of assertiveness training or sensory deprivation. Some officials of psychiatric associations are concerned about the erosion of their claim on the mental-health field. Psychiatry is no longer the glamour specialty that it once was; the number of medical-school graduates deciding to take the psychiatric course has dropped from 12 percent to 2 percent over a fifteen-year period.

Framework: Despite the eclecticism, mainstream therapies actually are less divergent than they seem. Most continue to operate in a Freudian framework. Almost every conventional approach draws on Freud's concepts of "resistance" and "transference"—the uncanny processes by which a patient first struggles against confronting conflicts and then plays them out on the figure of the therapist. In every human being, Freud believed, a kind of intrapsychic warfare is waged among a demanding "id" (the lustful, belligerent infant self), a mediating "ego" and a punishing "super-ego," or conscience. Eventually he came to stress the importance of the defense mechanisms by which the ego protects itself.

Analysts now have a different way of assessing patients because they know more about the whole process of development. Besides sexual and aggressive instincts, for example, they recognize the importance of the crucial period when an infant begins to develop a sense of "self" that is independent of a nourishing, approving mother. Damage occurring during that stage often produces "narcissistic" personalities—a disorder that seems as characteristic of modern patients as hysteria was in Freud's day.

Therapists have also moved away, for the most part, from the much caricatured image of the inscrutable sage nodding off over the mumblings of a supine patient. They are more apt to see people face to face, sitting up and once a week rather than the traditional five times. They provide more direct feedback and guidance—"Sounds like a bad move" instead of, "What comes to mind about that?" Where Freud fastened on dreams as "the royal road" to the unconscious, his successors find other roads just as useful—character quirks, for instance, or hostile attitudes. Few hesitate to use mood-altering drugs like Elavil to rally the patient's spirits for the therapeutic crunch. But they still aim at the essential "working through" process that Freud outlined. "The idea is not only to have them vent their hostility on the analyst," explains one practitioner, "but to get them to understand it, modulate it and sublimate it in less self-destructive ways."

'Superficial': Aside from revisions of theory, the rising demand for therapy—and the charge that it isn't accessible to the poor—have helped bring about some of the changes in style. The demand appears to be higher than ever. Millions of Americans opt each year for anything from a single session with a Valium prescription to the long, costly course of traditional analysis. Most, however, are in the market for fast relief. "People don't have the time or the money to go for the big thing," says one West Coast psychiatrist. "Psychotherapies are trying to get inside people's minds much quicker. Most of them are concerned with alleviating symptoms." Traditional analysts express misgivings about such "superficial" treatment. They warn that it can lead to the recurrence of the same symptoms or substitute symptoms. "The profession . . . has become something like a medical specialty, emphasizing the therapeutic goals over Freud's primary aim of understanding man's inner life," wrote analysts John Gedo and George Pollock.

Paradoxically, the nature of patients' complaints these days suggests anything but a quick-cure approach. A few decades ago, therapists say, they were encountering more "structured" symptoms—hand-washing compulsions and phobias about crossing bridges or odd-numbered streets. Now patients more commonly bring in what therapists call "life situation" problems—chronic dissatisfaction and vague feelings of "emptiness" in their lives that are typical of narcissistic disorders. To Jerome Frank, emeritus professor of psychiatry at Johns Hopkins University, the malaise is symptomatic of a "psychological society," in which more and more people are seeking help "for things that are part of the human condition. There's an unwillingness to tolerate distress." For many patients, Frank believes, psychotherapy has become a substitute for religion.

The proliferation of patients—and the resulting clamor for health-insurance reimbursement—has put pressure on the profession to prove not only that therapy effectively cures neurosis, but to say which therapies work best for which symptoms. A review by the National Institute of Mental Health in 1978 concluded that psychotherapy does improve the sense of well-being in as many as 90 percent of patients. But there is little hard evidence that a year of deep analysis is any more salving to the psyche than a week of deep body massage. An NIMH plan to test the relative effectiveness of two different psychotherapies and drug therapy in the treatment of major depression is already under way, with pilot studies scheduled to begin next February. Some analysts resist the pressure to demonstrate specific results, because of the difficulty of measuring so subjective a process. Says one analyst: "You can tell if someone no longer has a phobia. But how can you prove he is happier or has a better sense of himself?" But the paucity of "outcome" data leaves the profession vulnerable to the familiar charge that it is not a science at all, but rather a "belief system" that depends on an act of faith between the troubled patient and a supportive therapist.

Credentials: That relationship, indeed, seems the one essential ingredient for all the cures of neurosis. And at least one study has shown that it can be provided even by friendly college professors, with no credentials at all as therapists. Freud himself was troubled from the beginning by the lack of concreteness in his psychoanalytic concepts. In his "Project for a Scientific Psychology," begun and supposedly abandoned in 1895, he attempted to define a scientifically based "mental apparatus." Eventually he came to feel that analytic success depended, in large measure, on the intuitive gifts of the analyst. His own were supreme—but without a matrix of science, he wasn't sure how well his theories would weather the years. He looked to some sophisticated biochemistry of the future to find the final answers. "So long as the organic factors remain inaccessible," he wrote, "analysis leaves much to be desired."

The current decline of orthodox analysis seems to prove him right on one count. New advances in brain research—pointing toward the neurological roots of pain, drug addiction and depression—may prove him right on the other. Many analysts think that the future of therapy will belong mainly to the neurochemists, who may yet complete Freud's unfinished "mental apparatus." Even so, they think there will always be a need for the talking cure he developed over 80 years ago—what one unreconstructed Freudian fondly calls "the slow, patient construction of a psychic narrative." But these days, attention spans are shorter—and so is the narrative.

DAVID GELMAN with MARY HAGER in Washington and bureau reports

The Healing Brain

Douglas Garr

It is another hectic morning in a cramped neurophysiology laboratory. Hunched over his microscope, a researcher focuses on a nerve cell taken from the spinal cord of a mouse. He will hook up an amplifier to measure the neuron's activity, then punch the results into a computer.

Yesterday's figures light up the video display, and Dr. Jeffrey Barker, casually dressed in a blue turtleneck, checks them and nods. Dr. Barker and his assistant break into an arcane language fraught with references to synapses, dendrites, and axons. Brainspeak. If not for the Haydn on the stereo, a couple of stray fish tanks, and his daughter's playful crayon drawings, Barker's lab might belong to the ill-fated Dr. Jekyll.

But Barker's work at the National Institute of Neurological and Communicative Disorders and Stroke, in Bethesda, Maryland, is decidedly beneficial. "We're trying to find out how nerve cells communicate," he says. "We're taking the central nervous system apart. Right now all we have is unidentified flying neurons."

Thirty miles to the northeast, at Johns Hopkins Medical School, in Baltimore, Dr. Caroline Bedell Thomas is doing some very different sleuthing. Dr. Thomas has no fancy scientific hardware. Instead, she relies on questionnaires and the U.S. Postal Service.

In one of the longest-running studies ever conducted, Thomas asked 1,337 Johns Hopkins medical students who graduated between 1948 and 1964 to undergo a battery of psychological and biological tests—while they were students. She's been checking their health ever since. The experiment, known as the Precursors Study, was designed to uncover the medical effects of dozens of mental and physical factors from alcohol consumption and cigarette smoking to anxiety and depression.

As the first students reach middle age—some have already died—Thomas is beginning to draw some preliminary conclusions. Those students whose personalities she calls "irregular-uneven"—brilliant, moody, over- or under-demanding, and over- or undercautious—developed cancer, hypertension, or coronary occlusions much more often than the "slow-solid" or "rapid-facile" types. The "irregular-unevens" are considerably more likely to die younger than the other groups.

Though Barker's and Thomas's studies appear to have little in common, they—and many related projects—are contributing to a fundamental change in clinical medicine. From two distinct vantage points—Barker probing inside and Thomas peeking in from the outside—they are discovering that the brain exerts far more control over our bodies than we ever imagined possible.

Doctors once saw the brain as little more than a sophisticated computer nearly independent of the body, which carried it almost as a parasite. That view started to change with the "chemical revolution" in the Seventies. First came the discovery that the brain manufactures endorphins and enkephalins, opiatelike substances that relieve pain and stress. More recently researchers have noticed that the brain is responsible for a variety of hormonal and chemical activities that affect our appetite, our blood pressure, and even our sex drive.

"It is quite clear that the brain is connected to everything else in a way that's beyond our understanding," says Dr. Robert Orenstein, of the Institute for the Study of Human Knowledge. "We've had to step back enormously in awe, as ordinary people, and in less awe, as scientists."

We've known for some time that anxiety and depression can worsen such illnesses as diabetes, asthma, headaches, peptic ulcers, and cardiovascular disorders. For more than two decades Dr. Hans Selye, a Nobel laureate and founder of the International Institute for Stress, in Montreal, has been publicizing the psychic battleground and its physical implications.

The author of 38 books on stress and health, Dr. Selye believes that peaceful thoughts release beneficial hormones while fearful ones let out harmful hormones. Cortisone, in Selye's words, is "a tissue tranquilizer," and adrenalin causes us to be aggressive. But Selye is careful to note that stress is a normal part of life. "You can't make many generalizations, because some people take stress very well and others don't," he says.

René Dubos, the Pulitzer Prize-winning author and renowned microbiologist at Rockefeller University, offers a case in point. Now eighty, Dr. Dubos recalls his first wife's death nearly four decades ago with startling clarity. In 1942 she contracted tuberculosis, and Dubos says he was able to trace the origins of her illness to her childhood. Her father was a painter of china, and she was exposed to silica, a compound that might have promoted the development of TB. With standard medical treatment, she was partially cured and led a fairly normal life.

After two years, however, the diseas reappeared. Dubos remembers attendin a concert at New York's Carnegie Ha some time later. While walking along Fifty seventh Street, his wife, a former pianis became sullen when she realized sh could no longer play. "Two weeks later sh was dead," Dubos says. Though h doesn't claim that she died because sh was upset, he realized that her depressio might have exacerbated her illness. "Th evidence of the psychological componer in disease is overwhelming," Dubos no concludes.

Backed by a torrent of scientific papers such incidents have caught the attention c doctors across the country. When authc Norman Cousins contracted a rare an painful connective-tissue disease, physi cians gave him a 1-in-500 chance of recov ering fully. But Cousins took an active, ag gressive role in his fight, often ignoring th dictates of conventional medicine. He le the hospital earlier than he was suppose to, took charge of his own therapy, an watched Marx Brothers movies, hopin that humor would ease his pain. After h recovered, Cousins wondered, "Does th mean that laughter stimulated productic of the endorphins?"

Science hasn't yet answered his ques tion. The same question has occurred t many physicians. When Cousins wrot about his illness in the *New England Jou nal of Medicine*, 3,000 doctors responde with letters.

Stress effects can be subtle, accordin to Dr. Barney Dlin, a psychiatrist at Templ University, in Philadelphia, who has found correlation between emotion and coronar disease. "For example, in our study w worked with a patient who had a heart a tack when his child was four years old. W learned in our interview that his father ha suffered a heart attack when the patier was four years old," Dr. Dlin noted in the jou nal *Psychosomatics*. "Consciously or ur consciously, a patient may forecast hi own sickness or death."

And at the University of Maryland Medi cal School, psychologist James Lynch has conducted numerous clinical studies o emotion and its relation to blood pressure and heart disease. Though he commands a laboratory full of impressive monitoring equipment, Dr. Lynch is often more fasci nated by the intangible factors that influ ence human health.

He likes to point to a 1965 study of hear disease in the United States: Nevada hac ne of the highest rates; neighboring Utah, ne lowest. What caused such a disparity? bviously, it wasn't a simple answer like ne quality of water or air or the medium-come level. They were nearly identical in ne two states. But the people of Utah gen-rally are very religious; the state has a able population and an unusually low di-orce rate. Nevada's principal industry is ambling. The state's inhabitants are often ansient; and Nevada's divorce rate is tri-e Utah's.

Perhaps the explanation lay somewhere the patient's mind, Lynch speculated. ould it be that loneliness had something do with heart disease? In those days that as a brash proposal.

Lynch found the mortality statistics for eart disease in the United States are two five times higher among unmarried eople than among marrieds. Obviously, ynch admits, being single doesn't mean ou're automatically destined to suffer a eart attack. But he thinks it would pay edical science to study the problem fur-er. Lynch isn't optimistic that the research ill take place, however. "Can you imagine riting a grant proposal for a project on ve?" he asks rhetorically.

How is it that the brain affects our ability resist illness? One likely route is through e immune system. In one study, the ypothalamus, a section of the brain that gulates the pituitary hormones, has been nked with the body's ability to form anti-odies to fight off infection. And recent re-earch on one kind of infection-fighting hite blood cell, the T lymphocyte, reveals e presence of brain hormones on the ell's outer membrane.

It is far from certain just how important is link between the brain and the immune ystem will prove. But scientists have eculated that a few of our healthy cells ay turn malignant each day. The white ood cells, they suspect, recognize this ansformation and destroy the cells before e cancer spreads. So if someone does ontract an infection or develop cancer, his ody's immune system may have broken own. Then the connection could be very portant indeed.

One of the more striking examples oc-urred two years ago in Fort Lupton, Col-ado. Jim Kunzman, a farmer, suddenly ad to contend with the loss of his two oung children, who were killed in an au-mobile accident. Kunzman, whose story as documented on film, found that he had st interest in his work and in his life. hough never sick in the past, he began to el ill, slept long hours, and lost his appe-e. Eighteen months after his children had ed, doctors found he had multiple my-oma, a bone cancer. Kunzman under-ent chemotherapy, but its side effects nly made him feel worse. Then, early in 980, he began seeing a psychologist and talking about his feelings. Remarkably his cancer regressed. Today he's actively tilling his farmland.

"My immune system was at a very low ebb," Kunzman now says evenly. "I think that subconsciously I wanted to punish myself in some way, and my body simply obliged me."

Oncologists are very careful to note that Kunzman's cancer might have disappeared for any number of reasons. But no one discounts the possibility that his sickness and subsequent good health had a psychological basis.

In fact, physicians at the Cancer Counseling Research Center, in Fort Worth, Texas, have turned this idea into a practical—and highly successful—cancer treatment. Developed by Stephanie Matthews-Simonton, a psychologist, and Dr. Carl Simonton, a radiation oncologist, the center's treatment program focuses on the psychology factor in cancer. The Simontons combine conventional psychotherapy with such standard medical techniques as radiation and chemotherapy.

Though the Simontons are careful not to make any miracle claims for their success stories, the results have been encouraging. In the past five years their 200 patients have survived an average of twice as long as cancer victims who received only medical treatment. Some of the patients at the research center have had their cancer disappear completely.

The Simontons' technique grew out of experiments with biofeedback, which enjoyed its greatest popularity in the late Sixties and early Seventies. During the biofeedback studies, Mrs. Simonton says, she and her husband began to ask themselves, "If a person could be taught to influence heart rate, blood flow, and blood pressure, all physiological systems under the autonomic nervous system, could people be taught to put energy into building their immune system?"

The first patient they experimented on was a sixty-one-year-old man with an advanced, probably fatal, throat cancer. (The Simontons publish scientific papers only on patients who are diagnosed as having 12 to 18 months to live.) In addition to radiation treatment, the Simontons asked the man to relax and visualize a pleasant setting for a few minutes, three times a day: a quiet mountain scene or an idyllic setting by a stream. Later the patient began to visualize his tumor. Then he was told to think about his body's white blood cells invading the tumor in his throat and eventually destroying it.

In two months his throat cancer went into remission. "What was astonishing," Mrs. Simonton says, "was not so much that his tumor shrank—which you would expect during radiation treatment—but that he experienced nothing in the way of side effects." The man got stronger, gained weight, and became cheerful. "When arthritis began to bother him, he turned his white blood cells on that, and it cleared up," she adds.

Soon the Simontons began to notice distinct emotional similarities among their cancer patients. "Typically what we saw was a high-stress pattern six to eighteen months before the diagnosis of cancer," Mrs. Simonton reports. "Frequently there will be a real or imagined loss of some kind—death of a spouse, a child leaving home—leading to a profound despair. This is something that the cancer-prone personality has a lot of difficulty dealing with, the mind-body connection."

The idea that cancer patients share a broad psychological profile is new and controversial. There are, after all, thousands of carcinogens to which many of us are exposed every day; any of them can surely cause death after 15 to 20 years of exposure.

In the late Fifties Lawrence LeShan, a clinical psychologist who practices on Manhattan's Upper West Side, developed the notion that people who got cancer had certain psychological traits in common. This idea was scoffed at. Today LeShan smiles wryly when he recalls the resistance that greeted his wish to conduct a study to confirm his idea. Thinking he was a charlatan, the administrators of hospitals and cancer clinics refused to let him interview terminal patients.

Finally, though, LeShan was allowed to talk with cancer patients at a program run by the Institute for Applied Biology. Two patterns began to emerge. First, he found cancer patients lacked a strong will to live. Second, the patients found it difficult to express their anger or resentment.

In one experiment, considering psychological factors alone, LeShan was able to predict correctly who had cancer in 24 of 28 cases. Of 22 "terminal" cancer patients whom he began treating a decade ago, 12 are still alive.

Since then, two Rochester, New York, doctors have tried to guess—again basing their guess on personality traits—which of the women who entered the hospital for cervical biopsies actually had cancer. They were right 72 percent of the time.

Though we have grown to accept the theory of the cancer-prone personality, LeShan hints that American clinics may be lagging behind those in the rest of the world. During a trip abroad he was startled to find great interest in the psychological treatment of cancer. "In West Germany," he learned, "if you want to set up a cancer clinic, you can't get federal funding unless you agree to set up a psychological rehabilitation ward."

All this raises some questions: How do the patients who survive cancer react to their illness? Do they take an active role, as author Norman Cousins did? Or do they remain passive?

"What we're seeing," Mrs. Simonton finds, "is that the ornery, scrappy, cantankerous patient does better than the passive, compliant, sweet, denying patient who bottles everything inside."

LeShan adds, "Bad patients do better than good patients. The oncologists know this, but they haven't really come to grips with it."

One of the mind's most puzzling influences on the body appears in cases of chronic pain. Pain is subjective; it is the brain that feels it and decides how severe it is. We've known for years that soldiers wounded in battle often don't feel pain until hours later. And in dozens of studies doctors have reported that ordinary sugar pills or salt pills relieve pain in up to half of the patients who take them. Recently researchers have suggested that the placebo, though it has no direct effect, eases pain by triggering the release of enkephalins in the brain. Anthropologists have even seen primitive cultures in which the husband feels pains during his wife's labor and the woman seems comfortable.

It seems that our culture has a great influence on how we feel pain. Dr. Richard Black, codirector of the Pain Treatment Center at Johns Hopkins, believes that he has seen the proof among his own patients. "We have found some interesting sociological problems with our own chronic-pain patients," he says. "Some have what I guardedly call inadequate personalities. They have never been able to hold down a job; when they do, they get injured frequently. They're always running for the pill or the bottle. A high percentage tend to be child abusers and were abused as children themselves. So you are dealing with a deep-seated problem that goes on from generation to generation."

Dr. Black says that pain patients are often misdiagnosed, frequently because of psychology. He recalls the case of one patient, a fifty-two-year-old woman who'd had a mastectomy seven years earlier. She was technically cured, and although her arm was swollen and her chest was scarred, she experienced only mild pain.

"Then her next-door neighbor got a fulminating carcinoma of the breast and died within six months," Black reports. "This was a neighbor our patient hardly knew, but she had an intense grief reaction nevertheless." Soon afterward the woman sought out another doctor and complained to him of severe pain.

"He diagnosed her as hurting rather than having an anxiety attack," Black continues. "He gave her a painkiller and a tranquilizer to help her sleep. Both drugs, because of their chemical effect on the central nervous system, made the woman feel depressed. When you're depressed, everything's worse and you hurt more. Meanwhile the doctor had done nothing to ease her anxiety. In fact, by doing nothing, he had made it worse."

One of Black's colleagues at Johns Hopkins, Dr. Nelson Hendler, saw so many patients with back pain that he devised a ten-minute psychological test to sift out people who lack an apparent "organic" basis for their pain. Dr. Hendler says the "objective" pain patient has "a history of stability, a sense of independence, and a resentment of incapacitation."

Hendler is also director of the Mensana Clinic, a pain center in Stevenson, Maryland. At Mensana, treatment concentrates on the behavioral aspects of pain. The patients take responsibility for their own medication. There are no nurses to coddle them. "In group therapy, patients are encouraged to talk about their pain, sort of like Pain Anonymous," Hendler says.

As clinical medicine is adjusting to our new understanding of the brain's role in health, neuroscience is ferreting out still newer insights. For example, Dr. Quentin Pittman, assistant professor of pharmacology at the University of Calgary, in Alberta, Canada, and his colleague, Dr. Warren Veale, have discovered that the brain may control fever. During their experiments, Drs. Pittman and Veale noticed that newborn lambs never developed a fever; so the pharmacologists began to search for natural substances that might repress fever.

What they found was vasopressin, a hormone first discovered in the Fifties. Acting on the kidneys, vasopressin controls the body's water content and helps regulate blood pressure. And, according to Pittman and Veale, the higher the level of vasopressin in a test subject's bloodstream, the lower the fever.

"As a result, we have come to suspect that the brain has its own type of aspirin," Pittman says, much as it has its own morphinelike substances. "The next question is obvious: Is there some way we can stimulate the body to produce its own aspirin?" If so, he hopes, we may soon be able to eliminate a headache at will.

And brain research is just beginning to help us understand our sex drive. In 1971 scientists first isolated a substance know as LH-RH (for luteinizing hormone-releas ing hormone) in the pituitary gland. Short thereafter Dr. Robert Moss, of the Dallas Southwestern Medical School's depar ment of physiology, found that LH-RH i duced sexual activity in female rats, eve after the animals' adrenal and pituita glands had been removed. "The only plac LH-RH could have acted was in the brain Dr. Moss concluded.

Moss repeated the tests on other ar mals, both male and female, with simil results. In humans, however, LH-RH se dom worked, except when it was given people with sexual dysfunctions. "Stil Moss reflects, "the idea of chemical rea tions affecting neural activity . . . we've ju scratched the surface."

The work continues. Dr. Barker, Bethesda, is struggling to find out ho brain cells talk to one another. Someday h may identify some of his flying neurons. D Thomas, at John Hopkins, continues to co lect data on her surviving medical st dents, helping to unravel the physical ar psychological bases of cancer, heart di ease, and even suicide. She has publish 80 papers so far, and another researcl will probably pick up where she leaves o

Scientists are beginning to look at me ory as a physiological problem. Is senil simply an inevitable part of old age, or i an ailment that can be evaded or cure Dr. Dubos likens the brain to a muscle. If n exercised, it atrophies in every way.

At the neurological-research arm of t National Institutes of Health, there is ready talk of neural prostheses for pa lyzed limbs: Why can't a microcomput activated by brain waves and embeddec that limb, be programmed to control ba motor functions? It may soon happen.

Meanwhile the mold of Western me cine is slowly wearing away and being cut. "I've seen a swami take random spo on his hand and raise the temperature one and lower it on the other," LeShan m vels. "But what does this do? We can get alpha wave and control our electroencep alogram, but why? What's the value?

"Everyone expects the easy route health, but it cannot be done in two wee ends. People think that if they jog and if th take ten extra milligrams of vitamin C a d zinc, and so on, they'll be sexually attra tive and will live forever. But it doesn't wo that way."

How it does work, we're not exactly su Today's studies of the brain will eventua show us the path.

Roots of Madness

Joann Ellison Rodgers

Franz, 23, says he is a riddle of bones. He hears buzzing noises, penetrating squeals, and voices with messages he sometimes understands but cannot remember. He sees flashes of light and shadow in the middle of the room. Strangers, he says, can send their shadows to visit him in bed. He tastes soap in his mouth and absorbs poison from the bedpost. He chews his tie, hoards garbage, sits in a stupor for weeks, and hits his nurses. Occasionally he clowns and walks on his hands.

Franz is a textbook case of schizophrenia, one of three million in the United States, 45 million worldwide, who share the most devastating of the mental illnesses. He experiences all the symptoms we associate with madness: hallucinations, delusions, paranoia, disembodied voices.

Schizophrenics fill more hospital beds than all other mental patients combined. A third of them—including some like Franz—can achieve a functional life for limited periods of time with the assistance of hospital care, forms of psychotherapy such as group counseling, traditional therapy, and art therapy, and the so-called neuroleptic drugs like Thorazine.

But most will never recover. At least no one ever has since the disease was described in great detail, in 1906, by a Swiss doctor named Eugen Blueler. Blueler coined the word *schizophrenia* from the Greek, meaning split mind, to suggest the breakup of the mind's unity. He recognized that the minds of schizophrenics operate not as integrated systems but in bits and pieces that distort reality, muddy perceptions, and loosen the links between thoughts. As time goes on, the afflicted confuse fantasy with reality for longer and longer periods. They make peculiar movements. Some giggle at tragedy, others go for decades without speaking.

The disease generally strikes in adolescence or young adulthood and lasts a lifetime. "The natural history of the disease is deterioration," says Joseph Coyle, a Johns Hopkins University psychiatrist and chief of its outpatient schizophrenia clinic. "That has been the case in every schizophrenic I have ever seen."

Early in their illnesses, some have grandiose illusions: "Nijinsky has faults, but Nijinsky must be listened to because he speaks the words of God," wrote the famed ballet dancer during one of his worst schizophrenic episodes. "I am God, Nijinsky is God . . . I hope that my teachings will be understood. All that I write is necessary to mankind." Nijinsky's symptoms, typical of paranoid schizophrenia, which is marked by delusions of grandeur or persecution, were diagnosed in 1919, when he was 29, by Blueler himself. The star never danced again.

Generally such delusions of grandeur taper off after a few years, and emotions become blunt and flat. Personality seems to wear away, giving lie to the popular notion that schizophrenics are often like the creative heroes portrayed in such literary successes as Hannah Green's *I Never Promised You a Rose Garden* or Mark Vonnegut's autobiographical *Eden Express*. "Anyone who has worked with schizophrenics for even a few weeks knows that neither Vonnegut nor Deborah in *Rose Garden* was schizophrenic. There is nothing joyous, positive, romantic, or productively creative about this disease," says Solomon Snyder, award-winning professor of psychiatry at Johns Hopkins and authority on the brain chemistry of schizophrenia. "It destroys lives. It represents a fundamental abnormality in how the brain works."

But if schizophrenics are not creative romantics, neither are they particularly dangerous or violent. Nor is there even the slightest evidence to support the popular myth that the affliction is brought on by passive fathers and domineering mothers.

The roots of madness are still buried. "What we have learned about schizophrenia," says Sam Keith, chief of the schizophrenia study center of the National Institute of Mental Health in Bethesda, Maryland, "is like watching a baseball game from an orbiting satellite. You might, on a clear day, see the stadium. But you can't see what player is up, or the score, and certainly not the catcher's signals. Our overall outcome in terms of getting patients functioning again hasn't really changed in 100 years."

Part of the reason is that there

are many crucial statistics that researchers don't have on the disease—whether males or females are more at risk, for example, or whether the disease is more likely to occur in urban or rural settings. Most epidemiological studies estimate that one percent of the world population has the disease, but different cultures define schizophrenia differently, so even these statistics are uncertain. A recent study sponsored by the National Institute of Mental Health reports, for example, that in the highly developed West, schizophrenics withdraw slowly from the real world and never recover fully. Among more primitive peoples, by contrast, schizophrenics seem to act "crazier." Some anthropologists feel such people are more likely to get well, partly because they act out their psychoses but partly because bizarre behavior is better tolerated in such societies. There is some evidence that the rates of schizophrenia rise when new beliefs and environments replace the old. This evidence seems to suggest that stress may be a factor in initiating some schizophrenic attacks. But no one really knows.

Because of the uncertainties that come with efforts to interpret human emotions, most scientists now look more to biology than to the environment for clues to schizophrenia's causes. They are getting closer to identifying the roots of schizophrenia and to pinpointing its biochemical markers. "There is no question," says Snyder, "that schizophrenia is genetic, at least in the sense that the genes, which code for proteins that regulate brain function, are involved." Evidence is growing that a number of other biological factors—brain chemicals, hormones, perhaps even viruses—are implicated in schizophrenia. When causes have finally been pinpointed, of course, it will be a great deal easier to control the disease with whatever it requires: specially tailored drugs, vaccines, perhaps even diet.

Right now, though, conventional tranquilizers and psychotherapy are the only effective treatments. The drugs help control symptoms, and psychotherapy helps some patients sort out social problems that arise from their illness. Patients can, for instance, learn to recognize such early signs of a psychotic relapse as increased restlessness and heightened anxiety and try to avoid social stresses—confrontation with family members, for example—that precipitate the relapses.

At the National Institute of Mental Health, Keith has treated hundreds of schizophrenic patients with the limited success that marks such attempts. "A typical rewarding case," he says, "is someone who passes through the public school system by being quiet but who has massive delusional symptoms and hallucinations. You work with him and he begins to develop a few skills, perhaps first relating to a pet where before he related to nothing and no one. And then perhaps he begins to do small things independently, like take on a paper route at the age of 19 or 20 while others are applying to college or working full-time. Then maybe he achieves real independence getting a job cleaning out stables.

"You and I might not want our 20-year-olds to clean stables. But a 20-year-old schizophrenic who does that has made fantastic progress. If you're willing to establish therapeutic and career goals that are meaningful to your patients instead of to you, it can be rewarding."

But understanding madness is taxing, even for psychiatrists. Some doctors deliberately avoid schizophrenic patients. "We all, no matter how many degrees we have," says Keith, "carry within us a fear of irrationality. Our own irrationalities are things we don't like to come face-to-face with. The more you deal with schizophrenia, however, the less frightening it becomes. You accept the idea that there is a rationality even to irrationality. Many of my colleagues still believe Freud's dictum that schizophrenia defies psychological understanding. I don't think that is so. You can relate to schizophrenics if you agree to meet them wherever they happen to be. They are very interesting people if you are willing to change your idea of what a relationship is."

"Well, when he was first bit on the slit on the rit and the man on the ran or the pan on the band and the sand on the man and the pan on the ban on the can on the man on the fan on the pan . . . that's to keep the boogers from eating the woogers. Well it was a jigger and a figger and a figger and a bigger and me, and I'll swamp you for a got you and a fair-haired far for a bar and jar for tar and rang dang ting tang with a bee shag, he shag . . . "

"The lion will have to change from dogs into cats until I can meet my father and mother and we dispart some rats. I live on the front of Whitton's head. You have to work hard if you don't get into bed . . . It's all over for a squab true tray and there ain't no squabs, there ain't no men, there ain't no music, there ain't no nothing besides my mother and my father who stand alone upon the Island of Capri where is no ice. Well it's my suitcase sir."

"He's a tie-father. Besides generation ties and generation hangages, he gave love a lot. I was raised in packs . . . since I was in littlehood."

Just as schizophrenia breaks up the mind's unity, so it distorts speech patterns, resulting in what psychiatrists call clang associations, word salads, and neologisms. In order to track down the causes of the mental jumble such odd speech patterns represent, scientists are using a variety of new technologies, including one that allows them to get inside a living schizophrenic brain and have a look around.

PET, or positron emission tomography, represents the most daring attempt to beat schizophrenia on its own cerebral turf since ancient Peruvians bored holes through the skulls of madmen thousands of years ago hoping to release the victim's evil humors. PET works by sugar coating radioactive tracers with a synthetic form of glucose, the brain's main fuel. The more active the brain is, the more glucose it uses. As brain cells use glucose, the radioactive material decays and registers on detectors surrounding the patient's head.

The resulting computer-generated pictures in the past year

have revealed unique patterns of activity in schizophrenic brains. During hallucinations, the speech and hearing centers of the brain burn sugar more rapidly than do those of normal people. But in the frontal lobes, where scientists speculate that action is planned and organized, there is evidence of reduced activity. Another new technique called xenon inhalation tomography gives corresponding results: Cerebral blood flow in the frontal lobes of schizophrenics is lower than normal, also suggesting that less work is being performed. There may be structural differences too. Computerized tomography (CT) scanners show that some schizophrenics, including those experiencing a first attack, have enlarged brain ventricles—evidence that surrounding brain tissue has died or been damaged.

Despite such technological advances, researchers are still pursuing certain key leads, which need further research. They want to know more, for example, about dopamine, a chemical brain messenger, or neurotransmitter, so long associated with schizophrenia that it has become its chemical stigmata. Discovered in 1958, dopamine, which enables nerves to communicate with each other, accounts for only a tiny portion of the brain's chemical output, but it seems to play a major role in areas of the brain concerned with emotion, behavior, and movement. All of the common drugs that stop hallucinations and other psychotic symptoms of schizophrenia work by blocking the receptor sites where dopamine is normally received. Recent studies show that schizophrenics have more dopamine in some areas of the brain during onset than during remission.

Another brain chemical under investigation is the enzyme called platelet monoamine oxidase (MAO), which breaks down neurotransmitters. A few researchers have found a tie-in between paranoid symptoms and a low level of the enzyme, and in fact some scientists suspect that variation in enzyme levels may be involved in susceptibility to a whole range of mental disorders. Others, however, think different amounts of the enzyme are caused by drugs used in treatment.

Ken Davis, chief of psychiatry at the Bronx Veterans Administration Hospital in New York, is among many who believe that schizophrenia, like cancer, is not a single disease but a group of disorders, and he is trying to distinguish as well as identify them biochemically. Using patients as their own controls (comparing each one to himself or herself at various times during illness and treatment), Davis has conducted batteries of tests, measuring such body chemicals as histamines, prostaglandins, neurotransmitters, and enzymes.

Davis gave 10 schizophrenics in remission L-dopa, a form of dopamine used in treatment of Parkinson's disease, a shaking palsy. By following their progress, he could predict those who would eventually relapse quickly: They suffer severe symptoms after one week on the drug, while those likely to have a long term remission are unaffected by the L-dopa.

With Alexander Mathe, Davis has also discovered that schizophrenics have a 250 percent elevation in a natural hormonelike substance called prostaglandin E, which in nonschizophrenics has already been linked to excessive muscle activity and inflammation. Herbert Meltzer at the University of Chicago has made detailed microscopic studies of muscles and the nerves that serve them and demonstrated a large number of abnormalities in schizophrenics consistent with those found in people with nerve diseases like Parkinson's.

He has biopsied small pieces of thigh muscles in schizophrenics in remission, comparing their muscles with those of a control group. In normal people, there is just one nerve ending per muscle fiber. If the nerve is damaged, other adjacent nerves sprout, and the muscle gets two or three per fiber. In the paranoid schizophrenic and his close relatives, the count is also two or three, even when there is no evidence that the muscle is impaired.

Extending that work, two of Meltzer's students, John Metz and John Crayton, studied a knee-jerk reflex tied closely to dopamine production in the body. Many schizophrenic patients have hyperactivity in this reflex. Further, Metz found that by giving patients destyrosine gamma endorphin, a brain peptide already known to suppress psychosis in some schizophrenics, the muscles calmed down in seven of eight people tested.

E. Fuller Torrey at St. Elizabeths Hospital in Washington is exploring yet another avenue for causes of schizophrenia. He has reported an increased level of antibodies to a type of herpes virus in the spinal fluid of schizophrenic patients as well as in some patients with chronic neurological diseases such as multiple sclerosis. This could mean that certain nerve cells are targets of viral attacks that slowly, over a lifetime, can produce the symptoms we call schizophrenia.

For at least as long as chemicals have been prime suspects, scientists have also believed that schizophrenia, or at least the tendency to get it, is inherited. In some families, such as the Genain quadruplets, who are all schizophrenics, there is little doubt. "But it is very difficult in the midst of all this flux about what schizophrenia is to make a hard statement about its genetics," says Kenneth Kidd, a Yale University geneticist. "Past studies suggested that 10 percent of the brothers and sisters of schizophrenics had schizophrenia." Kidd, however, is now using mathematical formulas to compare the prevalence of schizophrenia in certain families with known patterns of inheritance for other diseases. He has, for example, already identified a possible single gene for certain manic-depressive disorders and believes that in time, genes will be located for schizophrenia.

"If we find them, I see a tremendous gain," he says, "but it is clear that whatever genetic element is involved, it is not the whole story by a long shot." He cites as evidence the fact that if an identical twin has schizophrenia, there is only a 40 to 50 percent chance that the other twin will also become affected. "That observation alone is proof that genes are not sufficient for the development of schizophrenia," says Kidd. "Nongenetic factors—

All in the family

The birth of the Genain quadruplets in 1930 caused something of a stir. Curiosity seekers paid a quarter to see the identical baby girls, and Mr. Genain ran a successful campaign for constable using their pictures. But by the time they reached high school, Nora, Iris, Myra, and Hester were labeled "different" for other reasons. It began with Hester. In her junior year she broke light bulbs and tore buttons off her clothes. She never finished school. Nora was 20 when she became obviously confused, moaning at meals and complaining that the bones in her neck were slipping out of place. When she went to bed, she would stand on her knees and elbows until her elbows bled. Iris quit her job two years later, saying "I am pinned down. Someone wants to fight, and I don't want to." Myra fared better but panicked easily and couldn't be reassured.

The Genains have been in and out of hospitals all their lives. The diagnosis for all four: schizophrenia. The chances of it happening are one in two billion.

Because the quadruplets are genetically identical, they provide a unique opportunity for studying schizophrenia: The variation in the degree of illness each one suffers must have nongenetic roots. Researchers at the National Institute of Mental Health in Bethesda, Maryland have been following the Genains for more than 20 years to determine whether their differences were brought on by family pressures or by biological abnormalities. In 1958, when the only tools available to doctors were case histories, observations, and some physiological tests, psychologist David Rosenthal concluded that although the quads probably inherited the disease, relationships among family members influenced how sick each daughter was. Myra, the least ill, was her mother's favorite. Hester, the most severely afflicted, was "bad" according to her family.

While Rosenthal's hypothesis is still viable, sophisticated new instruments now can measure any differences quantitatively. Last year a team led by neuropsychologist Allan F. Mirsky found biological differences that accorded with the psychological ones found earlier.

Nora and Hester are the sickest. They are also the most abnormal according to tests that measure brain activity. Positron emission tomography scanners that map how much glucose the brain uses indicate that Nora's and Hester's frontal lobes burn less energy than their sisters'. Because the frontal lobes act as a coordinating center where incoming information is organized, this lessened activity may explain why they have trouble anticipating events and responding flexibly to them. Moreover, EEGs that measure the brain's electrical activity reveal that Nora and Hester have few of the fast brain waves associated with thinking. Instead, some tests show their brains produce more of the type of slow waves seen in epileptics or people who are sleeping. Nor do the two sisters respond normally to noises. A new type of EEG that assesses the brainstem, the structure responsible for setting activity levels in the rest of the brain, indicates that the pair react slowly and weakly to a series of clicking sounds.

Iris and Myra both have the same symptoms as Nora and Hester but to a lesser extent. What this new evidence suggests to Mirsky is that the quads suffered varying degrees of brain damage according to the order of their birth—Nora, Iris, Myra, and Hester (fictionalized names corresponding to the initials of the National Institute of Mental Health). Nora may have suffered trauma because she was the first to push her way down the birth canal; since Hester was the last she could have been deprived of oxygen. Mirsky thinks the damage occurred deep within the quads' brainstems since computerized tomography scanners reveal no abnormalities in the outer structures of their brains.

After spending three months last spring at the National Institute of Mental Health, the Genains went home. Nora, Hester, and Iris still live with their 82-year-old mother. Without the neuroleptic drugs they take daily, they would be hospitalized. Their father, who doctors think was also schizophrenic, is dead. Only Myra seems to lead a normal existence. She lives nearby with her husband and no longer has schizophrenic attacks. But her two teenage sons often get into trouble, and doctors fear they may be showing the first signs of the disease. —*Blythe Hamer* viruses, prenatal health, all sorts of things—affect the way the brain operates."

The goal of all this research is to link behavior and biology, to discover easy-to-manage, predictable, and consistent biological markers that will permit earlier diagnosis, more selective treatment, and accurate prediction of the outcome of treatment. It is a Herculean task, says Keith. "There is absolutely nothing that is a 100 percent specific biological or behavioral marker for schizophrenia the way high blood sugar is a tip-off to diabetes." No single symptom, from buzzing in the ears to high amounts of certain enzymes, can ever be found in more than 20 to 60 percent of patients. The job of untangling the many clues to cause and treatment will be painfully slow and expensive.

The schizophrenia outpatient clinic at Johns Hopkins Hospital in Baltimore operates in a subterranean area full of signs displaying information about fees and appointment schedules. The patients shuffle in. Few of them smile. A woman in a purple dress and sneakers paces back and forth, constantly flicking cigarette ashes into ashtrays she has strategically placed around the room. An old man murmurs "oh boy oh boy oh boy" as he walks the corridors. A young woman complains loudly about a fouled-up laboratory procedure.

In a small interview room with shabby curtains at the window, three wooden chairs, a metal desk, and a box of tissues, psychiatrist Joseph Coyle, head of the clinic, sees his patients.

Tommy, in his early 20s, has a long history of violent outbursts. He is calm, dressed neatly in T-shirt and jeans. He speaks and answers questions in one word monotones. He is tense and doesn't look Coyle in the eye. He needs more medicine. No, he hasn't been in any trouble lately. He likes to listen to disco music at his sister's. He wants a job, there isn't one.

"These patients, in a time of economic troubles, are at the absolute bottom of the job market," says Coyle. "We've tried to help. They need work, like anyone else, to feel useful and a part of the world."

Janet is elderly; she has suffered from schizophrenia for 30 years and has advanced tardive dyskinesia, a palsy that results from the drugs she takes. Her tongue pokes in and out of her mouth every few seconds. She says she has to keep rocking her body and kicking her legs as she sits because it makes her feel better. Yes, her daughter and son-in-law holler at her when she fails to do the housework on time. No, she doesn't hear voices now. She is agitated because her medicine has run out early. "Thank you," she says, when she is complimented on her new dress. "I bought it myself on the avenue."

Myrna, middle-aged, is in remission but on the possible edge of a relapse. She works as a domestic. She explains that her father, a preacher, was replaced by a new minister and that she was the new minister's lover. The minister's wife was trying to kill her, so she left the church. "That sounds like a good idea," Coyle tells her. She thought so too. "Voices tell me I do bad things, very bad things," she says. "They sometimes talk about me and sometimes to me." None of her story about the minister is true.

Like patients in the Hopkins clinic, schizophrenia remains a jumble of individual symptoms and anguish. Its victims display different levels of competence, intelligence, family support, and access to care. There is no magic cure for them, just a few new strategies that must await more research to offer certain relief. Their physicians and caretakers know it. They know it too. "They are," says Joe Coyle, "among the most courageous people I have ever met."

"I am," writes one schizophrenic, "a unique and interesting person. I don't always quite fit the world, but I think I add something to it."

FIGHT FAT
With Behavior Control

Fad diets fail because they focus on food, not the eating that makes us fat. Here are seven steps, the SCIENCE method, to use behavior mod to keep out calories.

Michael J. Mahoney
and Kathryn Mahoney

Michael J. Mahoney is professor of psychology at Pennsylvania State University, at University Park. He received his Ph.D. from Stanford, where he specialized in the study of experimental psychopathology. His interests include the psychologies of science and sport, as well as the psychology of fat. To help keep himself fit, Mahoney lifts weights Olympic-style; this 5'4", 123-pounder can lift more than 200 pounds and holds six Penn State U. records.

Kathryn Mahoney has a masters degree from the University of Illinois. She worked as a social worker before turning to the Clinical Psychology Program at Penn State. Kathryn works out regularly to help keep her 5'2" frame under 100 pounds. She doesn't lift weights competitively, but she can leg press 270 pounds.

AMERICANS HUNGER FOR DIETS. The average person goes on—and off—1.4 diets per year. In the search for slimness, dieters drink gallons of water, diet colas and grapefruit juice; munch on rice, carrots and celery; and satiate themselves with yogurt and cottage cheese. The rush to slimness often has physical costs. Diets can cause headaches, dizziness, diarrhea, fatigue, indigestion, skin disorders, and constipation. And there are psychological costs: dieters often suffer from irritability and depression. They sacrifice, agonize, and lose sleep, but they seldom stay thin. The problem is that permanent weight control requires focusing more on behavior and less on food.

For everyone, including those who say, "I was meant to be fat," "Obesity runs in my family," or "I have a hormone problem," being overweight means consuming more calories than the body uses. Adults require a minimum of about 1,200 calories a day for good health; those who get less risk serious health problems. How many calories a person needs above the 1,200-calorie level depends upon his metabolic rate, how active he is and his present weight.

Vicious Spiral. Calories that are not needed to maintain body processes or to move us about are converted into fat. The fat-conversion formula varies from person to person, but the average is one pound of fat stored for every 3,500 excess calories. A little over 100 extra calories a day—a handful of peanuts or a glass of beer—and in one month the eater is one pound heavier. Eating both peanuts and beer means two extra pounds. In a year, it's possible to go from thin to plump without ever being gluttonous.

Occasional binges add up the same way. A person may eat sensibly all week, but if he helps himself to extra servings of cake on the weekends, extra pounds will slowly appear. Most people become less active as they grow older, and this has the same result as eating more. With additional pounds to carry around, people become still less active, add more fat, and so on in a vicious spiral interrupted only by periodic stints of dieting. Maintaining a sensible weight does not mean a lifetime of carrots and celery, nor does it require hours of painful calisthenics, but it does mean keeping calorie consumption and activity in harmony. It's like balancing a checkbook, and the human body is a fierce accountant.

Most diets are lists of do's and don'ts, but they usually tell us nothing about *how* to do the do's and avoid the don'ts. The implication is that the answer is will power; it's the dieter against the chocolate-cream pie. Trouble is, as many dieters have discovered, the pie seems to get stronger as they get weaker. All too often, dieters resist temptation long enough to shed the unwanted pounds, and then go back to the old habits that put on those flabby ripples in the first place.

Permanent weight control requires an entirely different focus: you must concentrate on behavior, not will power or a magic list of permissible foods. It is your daily eating and exercise habits, the input and output of energy, that must be changed.

Changing your behavior does not require that you endure hunger pangs or the nausea, headaches, and other side effects of many diets. But it does require effort and a long-term commitment. Realistic changes in behavior will result in slower weight loss, and if you do establish new behavior patterns, you will keep the pounds from coming back.

We have worked with hundreds of overweight people over the past five years. Out of that work we have developed the SCIENCE program for permanent weight control. Since we know that behavior is the villain that keeps people fat, many of our techniques are those of the behavior therapist. In fact, we ask our overweight clients to study their own eating and exercising habits the same way a behavior therapist might study the tics of a neurotic patient. The SCIENCE approach consists of seven simple steps:

1 specify the problem,
2 collect data,
3 identify patterns,

4 examine possible solutions,
5 narrow options and experiment,
6 compare current and past data, and
7 extend, revise, or replace solutions.

Specify the Problem. If you are overweight, you are doing something wrong. The goal is to find out what. You may be eating too much, eating the wrong kinds of foods, or exercising too little. The more overweight you are, the more likely it is that you are doing all three.

Collect Data. You need to have an objective measure of what you actually do. Many overweight people complain about the unjustness of their condition and back it up with "facts": "I had only *one* egg for breakfast," or "I starve myself and still gain weight." Such statements may get you sympathy, but they won't get you thin. While it may be true that you had only one egg for breakfast, it is also true that you had two chocolate eclairs as a midnight snack. The point is, you will have to keep an honest record of your eating habits in order to know the changes that are necessary.

Dieters are used to counting calories, and that information is helpful. But other facts are equally important. Keep a record for one week of when and where you eat, as well as what and how much. Also keep track of your exercise habits—the amount of time spent walking, jogging, doing calisthenics, playing tennis, etc. Remember that the purpose of data collecting is to get an objective measure of what you ordinarily do, so make no special effort to exercise more or eat less during this period.

Identify Patterns. After a week of data collecting, you are ready to search for the source of your energy imbalance. You might begin by computing the average number of calories you eat in a day, and checking that number against the number you need for your desired weight (see box, page 270). If the numbers agree, your problem may be more a matter of inactivity than of overeating.

Most overweight people will find they consume too many calories. The problem is to find out where those calories come from. For example, the hypothetical record shown in the box is like many of the diaries we get from our obese clients. While it shows sensible eating at meals, it also reveals a tendency toward recreational eating. Many people take a morning break and have coffee and doughnuts with their friends. In the afternoon they have candy or pie during breaks from studying or other monotonous work. In the evening they munch on potato chips and cookies while watching TV or reading. These are the people who often complain at meals, "See, I eat no more than Mary, but she stays thin and I get fat; all I have to do is look at a piece of cheesecake and I gain weight." The hard data of a diary will often convince the weight watcher that he is doing more than just looking.

In our society, food is often connected with recreation. We go out for coffee, invite friends over for drinks, celebrate special occasions with cakes or big meals. We can't think of baseball without thinking of hot dogs and beer, and eating is so often an accompaniment to watching TV that we talk of TV snacks and TV dinners. Just as Pavlov's dogs learned to salivate at the sound of a bell, the activities we associate with food can become signals to eat. Watching TV becomes a signal for potato chips; talking with friends becomes a signal for coffee and doughnuts; nodding over a book tells us it's time for pie and milk.

SAMPLE DIETER'S DIARY

Monday Oct. 1

8:30 2 pieces buttered toast, 1 bowl cornflakes with milk (light sugar), 2 cups black coffee

10:30 4 peanut-butter cookies, cup black coffee

12:45 tuna-fish sandwich on whole-wheat toast, dill pickle, glass of milk (10 oz.)

2:15 cup of coffee, half piece of toast with peanut butter

4:30 2 peanut-butter cookies

6:00 1 serving corn, 2 servings fish, 1 small boiled potato, 2 cups coffee

9:20 1 Coke (16 oz.) and about 25 potato chips

10:30 1 cup chocolate ice-cream

Tuesday Oct. 2

8:30 1 bowl corn flakes with milk (light sugar), 2 cups black coffee

10:00 Coke and doughnut

12:15 (restaurant) BLT sandwich, small serving coleslaw, cup of coffee

3:00 4 peanut-butter cookies, 1 Coke (16 oz.)

6:00 2 servings rice casserole, small salad with dressing, 1 slice buttered bread, 1 cup coffee

9:00 1 Coke (16 oz.) and 6 vanilla wafers

10:00 1 glass milk, 2 pretzel sticks

Examine Possible Solutions. The next step is to decide which inappropriate behaviors are easiest to change. For the hypothetical case shown above, the following solutions seem reasonable:

1 reduce the number of snacks,
2 when at home, snack only in the kitchen,
3 exercise at times when snacking might occur,
4 snack on low-calorie desserts, and
5 join an exercise class.

After listing possible solutions, the next step is to select those that seem most likely to succeed. It is tempting to make a list of perfectionistic rules, especially if you aren't hungry at the moment. This should be avoided. Remember that if you were perfect, you wouldn't be fat. Rigid rules, such as no snacks, no high-calorie desserts, are bound to be broken eventually, and that leads to a sense of failure. Stick with rules you think you can follow.

For example, some people cannot stand diet desserts; it makes little sense for them to try substituting diet colas and diet cookies for tastier snacks. Similarly, a thin roommate is apt to show little enthusiasm for the idea of having only diet desserts in the house. On the other hand, a roommate might be induced to buy snacks that are the weight watcher's least favorite foods. And while a person who hates exercise is not likely to suddenly become a jogging enthusiast, he might succeed in substituting short walks for pies and candy as afternoon breaks. Since moderate exercise tends to lessen appetite, the walks might also mean eating less at meals.

Compare Current and Past Data. It is not enough to come up with possible solutions; you must see if the solutions work. Continue to keep track of your habits for at least three weeks; by then you should be able to tell whether your plan is working. Do not search for immediate results in the mirror or on the bathroom scale. Most bathroom scales are too inaccurate to measure subtle weight changes, and your daily weight fluctuates slightly anyway. We recommend that you check the scale no more than twice a month. The goal is to change your behavior, and if you do that, the pounds will take care of themselves. It is often helpful to convert your data from the diary to charts, such as the one shown here for snacking (see the chart on page 271).

After three or four weeks you should have enough data to see trends. If your plan shows signs of working, then you should continue the program or extend it to include other solutions. If your plan is not working out, you will have to

How Much Should You Weigh?

Many people try to determine how much they should weigh by reading height-weight tables, but since these tables often indicate average weights rather than optimum weights, the figures tend to be too high. There is, however, a formula for estimating your healthiest weight.

Adult women of average build can compute their ideal weight by multiplying their height in inches by 3.5 and then subtracting 110 from the product. Thus, a woman who is five feet tall should weigh about 100 pounds (60 X 3.5 - 110 = 100). For men of average build the formula is height in inches times four, minus 130. A six-foot man should weigh about 158.

It is reasonable to make allowances for bone structure and muscularity: even if Woody Allen and Rosie Grier were the same height, they should not weigh the same amount. But be careful that in making these allowances, you don't mistake fat for muscle. And remember that if you are 30 pounds overweight, it is unlikely that the difference is all in your bones.

The amount of food you need to maintain your ideal weight depends upon how active you are. Begin by rating yourself on the scale below:

13	very inactive
14	slightly inactive
15	moderately active
16	relatively active
17	frequently, strenuously active

If you are a sedentary office worker or a housewife you should probably rate yourself a 13. If your physical excercise consists of occasional games of golf or an afternoon walk, you're a 14. A score of 15 means that you frequently engage in moderate exertion—jogging, calisthenics, tennis. A 16 requires that you are almost always on the go, seldom sitting down or standing still for long. Don't give yourself a 17 unless you are a construction worker or engage in other strenuous activity frequently. Most adult Americans should rate themselves 13 or 14.

To calculate the number of calories you need to maintain your ideal weight, multiply your activity rating by your ideal weight. A 200-pound office worker, for example, needs 2,600 calories a day; a 200-pound athlete needs 3,400 calories.

To estimate how many calories you are getting now, multiply your current weight times your activity level. If your weight is constant at 140 pounds and you are inactive, you are consuming about 1,820 calories a day (13 times 140). Subtract the number of calories you need for your ideal weight from the number of calories you are consuming, and you will know the size of your energy imbalance.

To reach your ideal weight, we recommend that you correct your calorie imbalance slowly. It's a good idea to lose no more than one percent of your current weight a week. Cut your daily caloric consumption by two times your current weight and you should achieve that goal. Regardless of your weight, you should not get less than 1,200 calories a day. Reducing by much more than one percent of your body weight a week could mean destruction of muscles and organs as well as fat. The same is true of diets that prohibit all fats and carbohydrates.

—Michael and Kathryn Mahoney

reexamine your data and look for other solutions. You should also check your record to see if you have developed any bad habits while working on adopting good ones: e.g., you may find that while you were able to cut down on snacks, you began eating more at meals.

When you apply the SCIENCE method to your own eating and exercise habits, you may find that your problems are much different from those discussed above. You may find that you are a social eater and eat whenever you are with friends. Or you may find that you can't resist the sight or fragrance of food, so that you eat whenever food is available.

Many obese people find themselves obsessed by thoughts of food. Thinking about food makes them hungry, which, in turn, makes it difficult to stop thinking of food. The SCIENCE method can be applied to changing thinking habits as well as overt behavior. Keeping a record of your thoughts about food will tell you when, where, and under what circumstances your thoughts turn to food.

Housewives, for example, often find that they think about food primarily when working in the kitchen. One obvious strategy for them might be to avoid the kitchen whenever possible. Maybe someone else in the family can wash dishes or fix meals once in awhile. Or they might prepare simple meals that can be put together in minutes. Other people find that they think of food primarily when talking to weight-conscious friends. They talk about their latest diets, how much weight they have lost or gained, or the new diet dish they've discovered. A solution might be to ask their friends to help by not discussing food; if that doesn't work, they might try changing the subject whenever the conversation shifts to food.

Eating by the Clock. Another common problem of obese people is the inability to listen to their bodies. They eat because food is available or because it is time to eat. For example, Richard Nisbett, at the University of Michigan, found that when he offered food to thin people, they ate as much as they wanted and then stopped, but obese people were influenced by how much food was put in front of them: if they were given one sandwich, they were satisfied with that, but if they were given three sandwiches, they ate them. Many of us learn as children that we must clean our plate; children are starving in India, and somehow we are made to feel that any wasted food will contribute to their misery.

Clocks can also push people to eat. At Columbia, Stanley Schachter and Larry Gross rigged two clocks so that one ran fast and the other ran slow. They began the experiment at 5 p.m. By 5:30, the slow clock registered 5:20 and the fast clock showed 6:05. When overweight people were given a chance to snack, they ate an average of twice as much when the clock told them it was after six than when they thought it was 5:20.

If your own data tell you that you are easily influenced by such external cues, you can set up a plan to avoid them. For example, try taking smaller portions of food at meals. If you are still hungry, you can make the effort of going back for seconds, but you will be eating because you want the food, not just because it is on your plate. You can also make it a practice to put foods out of sight; don't leave candies, nuts, or crackers around the house. If you find that you listen to the clock rather than your stomach, you might try going without a watch or rearranging your

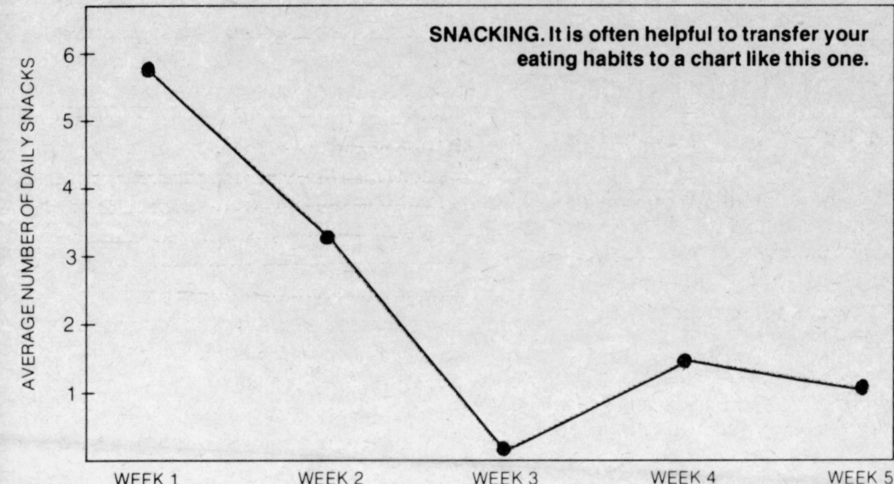

SNACKING. It is often helpful to transfer your eating habits to a chart like this one.

schedule so that when it is time to eat you are busy with something.

How you eat can also influence how much you eat. If, after studying your own eating habits, you find that you are one of the faster forks around, you might take steps to slow down: Put your fork down between bites, chew each mouthful thoroughly. One reason that eating fast is bad is that it doesn't give your body a chance to react to the food you've eaten. By the time the body is able to say, "that's enough," you've already had too much. A simple solution that works for many is to eat what seems a reasonable amount and then leave the table for 30 minutes. If you are still hungry after half an hour, go back to the table and resume your meal. You may find that you no longer feel hungry.

No Magic Involved. Exercise is often a neglected factor in weight control. In a study of obese adolescent girls, Jean Mayer found that the girls actually ate less than their thin classmates, but they were also far less active. The fact is that exercise is almost 50 percent of the weight-control formula: taking off excess weight means eating less or exercising more. In most cases it is advisable to do both. Staying active does not necessarily mean spending hours on the tennis court. If your personal data convince you that you are not active enough, try working more exercise into your day: walk instead of ride, take the stairs instead of the elevator, go to the bowling alley instead of a movie, play golf on Saturday afternoon instead of watching others play it on TV.

There is no magic to the SCIENCE method. It is a program that is based on well-grounded behavior-modification principles and it can mean the end of dieting, but it demands concentration and serious effort over a long period.

It means making permanent changes in your lifestyle, and some of those changes may be hard to take. But the reward, in many cases, is better than a sequence of slothful plumpness and desperate diets. You have a strong chance of joining the world of the permanently thin.

Mahoney, Michael J. and Kathryn Mahoney. *Permanent Weight Control: A Total Solution to the Dieter's Dilemma*, Norton, 1976, $7.95.

Mahoney, Michael J. and Carl E. Thoresen. *Self-Control: Power to the Person*, Brooks/Cole, 1974, paper, $5.95.

Thoresen, C.E. and Michael J. Mahoney. *Behavioral Self-Control*, Holt, 1974, paper, $3.95.

Some Important Contributors To This Edition

Bernikow, Louise is the author of "Among Women" and frequently writes and lectures on human behavior.

Bernstein, Anne is a family therapist and author of "The Flight of the Stork," a book about how to discuss sex and birth with children.

Best, Catherine T. is an assistant professor of psychology at Teachers College, Columbia University.

Bower, Gordon H. is an experimental psychologist at Stanford University who specializes in human learning and memory.

Bruner, Jerome S. is a cognitive and child psychologist who developed ideas on child development and thinking that have influenced educational, as well as experimental, psychologists all over the world. He is presently a professor at Oxford University.

Chance, Paul is a psychologist and former assistant managing editor of *Psychology Today.*

Garcia, John is professor of psychology and psychiatry at UCLA. His past research includes work on the behavioral effects of x-rays, toxins and vitamins.

Gardner, Howard is codirector of Harvard University's Project Zero, a research project in the field of the arts and human cognition. His area of specialization is cognitive psychology and the role of the arts in human development.

Gould, Carol Grant is a writer and researcher in Princeton University's biology department.

Gould, James L. is professor of biology at Princeton University.

Greenberg, Joel is a reporter who won an award from the American Psychological Association in 1976 for outstanding reporting.

Gustavson, Carl R. is known for his research on the application of psychological techniques to wildlife management.

Hales, Dianne is the former editor of the *New Physician* and now writes for *The New York Times* and is a contributing editor of *Science Year.*

Harris, Lauren Julius is professor of psychology at Michigan State University.

Heeb, Donald O. is widely known for contributions to the fields of learning, perception, and neuropsychology. He has recently retired from the faculty of McGill University in Montreal.

Lazarus, Richard S. is a professor of psychology at the University of California, Berkeley, and has made major contributions to an understanding of stress, health and the coping process.

Mahoney, Kathryn is involved with the Clinical Psychology Program at Pennsylvania State University.

Mahoney, Michael J. is professor of psychology at Pennsylvania State University. His fields of research include the psychologies of science and sport as well as the psychology of fat.

May, Rollo is the father of existential psychotherapy in the U.S. and has edited the major work in the field, "Existence: A New Dimension in Psychiatry and Psychology." He currently teaches, writes, and practices psychotherapy in California.

McClelland, David C. is professor of psychology at Harvard and is a leading investigator of psychological motives, maturity, and occupational competence.

Milgram, Stanley is best known for his research in obedience, conformity, and crowd behavior. His series of investigations on obedience to authority, done at Yale in 1960-1963, caused controversy on the social implications and ethics of conducting such a study.

Miller, Neal E. is professor emeritus and head of a laboratory of physiological psychology at Rockefeller University in New York City. He is known for his research leading to the development of biofeedback techniques.

Neisser, Ulric is a professor of psychology at Cornell and is known for his books, "Cognitive Psychology" (1967) and "Cognition and Reality" (1976) as well as for his experimental studies of visual search and selective attention.

Neugarten, Bernice L. is a professor of human development at the University of Chicago and has done much research in the field of Gerontology.

Parlee, Mary Brown is a psychologist and the director of the Center for the Study of Women and Sex Roles at the City University of New York.

Pleck, Joseph H. is a clinical psychologist and program director for the Family, Employment, and Male Role Programs at the Wellesley College Center for Research on Women.

Rensberger, Boyce is a senior editor of *Science 81.*

Restak, Richard is a neurologist and an author of numerous articles and books dealing with human psychology.

Richards, Guy is an associate professor of sociology at the University of Saskatchewan and has taught and written about medical sociology, demography, and sociobiology.

Richardson, James is a professor of sociology at the University of Nevada at Reno. He has written a number of books and articles on recruitment and resocialization in the new religions, including an analysis of the People's Temple mass suicide in Guyana.

Rodgers, Joann Ellison is an award-winning health and science writer.

Rogers, Carl R. is known as the founder of the client-centered approach to personality and psychotherapy, which focuses on the current feelings and attitudes of the client and does not concern itself with early childhood experiences and unconscious conflicts. He is presently a resident fellow at the Center for Studies of the Person in La Jolla, California.

Rubin, Jeffrey Z. is professor of psychology at Tufts University, where he directs the Center for the Study of Decision Making.

Scarr, Sandra is professor of psychology at Yale University and has authored many articles in the areas of human development and the genetics of behavior.

Skinner, B.F. (Burrhus Frederic) is a professor emeritus of psychology at Harvard University. He developed methods for studying behavior within the framework of operant conditioning.

Snyder, Mark is professor of psychology at the University of Minnesota and does his research in self-monitoring and the effects of stereotypes on social relationships.

Sommer, Robert is a professor of psychology and environmental studies at the University of California at Davis.

Sternberg, Robert J. is an associate professor of psychology at Yale and has made major theoretical contributions to the understanding of human intelligence and mental abilities.

Tavris, Carol is a social psychologist who writes about adult development and social change.

Weinberg, Richard is professor of educational psychology at the University of Minnesota where he is the coordinator of the Psychology in the Schools Training Programs and associate director of the Center for Early Education and Development.

Zimbardo, Philip G. is a professor of psychology at Stanford and has done much research in the area of social roles and imprisonment.

INDEX

Credits/Acknowledgments

Cover design by Charles Vitelli

1. The Science of Psychology
Facing overview—Dover *Pictorial Archives* Series, Dover Publications.
2. Biological Bases of Behavior
Facing overview—WHO/photo. 44—M.E. Challinor. 58—Courtesy of Dr. Thomas Bouchard, University of Minnesota. 69—Alan E. Cober. 93—Diagram by Judy Glick.
3. Psychological Bases of Behavior
Facing overview—WHO photo by Pierre Pittet. 148 & 149—From *Human Nature,* September 1978. Copyright ©1978 by Human Nature, Inc. Reprinted by permission of the publisher. 152—Chart by Cambridge University Press. 153-156—Robert W. Hayward, M.D.
4. Development
Facing overview—United Nations/photo by John Isaac.
5. Individual Differences
Facing overview—Dover *Pictorial Archives* Series, Dover Publications. 184-187—From Human Nature, April 1978. Copyright ©1978 by Human Nature, Inc. Reprinted by permission of the publisher.
6. Personality and Social Processes
Facing overview—WHO photo by J. Mohr.
7. Disorders and Therapeutic Processes
Facing overview—WHO photo by Zoltan Zzabo.

WE WANT YOUR ADVICE

ANNUAL EDITIONS: PSYCHOLOGY 83/84

Article Rating Form

Here is an opportunity for you to have direct input into the next revision of this reader. We would like you to rate each of the 55 articles listed below, using the following scale:

1. **Excellent: should definitely be retained**
2. **Above average: should probably be retained**
3. **Below average: should probably be deleted**
4. **Poor: should definitely be deleted**

Your ratings will play a vital part in the next revision. So please mail this prepaid form to us just as soon as you complete it.
Thanks for your help!

Rating	Article
	1. Understanding Psychological Man: A State of the Science Report
	2. The Freedom to Change
	3. Why Aren't We Using Science to Change Behavior?
	4. Shaping Behavior Contest for Minds
	5. Toward a Psychology of Natural Behavior
	6. Genetics: The Edge of Creation
	7. The Clock Within
	8. Do Diets Really Work?
	9. The Three Brains of Paul MacLean
	10. Twins
	11. Tinkering with Life
	12. The Violent Brain
	13. The Origins of Violence
	14. Searching for Depression Genes
	15. Chemical Feelings
	16. Images of the Night
	17. Going Beyond Pain
	18. Biofeedback Seeks New Medical Uses for Concept of Yoga
	19. Brain Flash: The Physiology of Inspiration
	20. The Way of the Journal
	21. The Instinct to Learn
	22. Sociobiology Stirs a Controversy Over the Limits of Science
	23. Sociobiology Redefended
	24. Pulling a Gag on the Wily Coyote
	25. Caught by Choice
	26. Conversion, Brainwashing, and Depro-gramming
	27. My Memory/Myself
	28. Mood and Memory
	29. Our Insatiable Brain
	30. The Mind of the Puzzler
	31. Learning the Mother Tongue
	32. The Loss of Language
	33. Newborn Knowledge
	34. Childhood
	35. Your Child's Self-Esteem
	36. Learning Right from Wrong
	37. Coping with the Seasons of Life
	38. In Search of Youth
	39. Attitudes, Interests, and IQ
	40. Who's Intelligent?
	41. The Remedial Thinker
	42. Males and Females and What You May Not Know About Them
	43. Girls versus Boys—How Different Are They?
	44. Prisoners of Manliness
	45. The Many Me's of the Self-Monitor
	46. Psycho-Immunity
	47. Stress Can Be Good for You
	48. The Foundations of the Person-Centered Approach
	49. The Friendship Bond
	50. Alone
	51. Self-Fulfilling Stereotypes
	52. Finding the Hidden Freud
	53. The Healing Brain
	54. Roots of Madness
	55. Fight Fat with Behavior Control

(continued on back)

About you

Name ____________________ Date ____________________

Address ____

City ____________________ State ____________________

Zip ____________________ Telephone ____________________

1. What do you think of the Annual Editions concept?

2. Have you read any articles lately that you think should be included in the next edition?

3. Which articles do you feel should be replaced in the next edition? Why?

4. In what other areas would you like to see an Annual Edition? Why?

PSYCHOLOGY 83/84

NO POSTAGE NECESSARY IF MAILED IN THE UNITED STATES

BUSINESS REPLY MAIL

First Class Permit No. 84 Guilford, Ct.

Postage Will Be Paid by Addressee

Attention: Annual Editions Service
The Dushkin Publishing Group, Inc.
Sluice Dock
Guilford, Connecticut 06437-0389